Communications
in Computer and Information Science 1172

Commenced Publication in 2007
Founding and Former Series Editors:
Phoebe Chen, Alfredo Cuzzocrea, Xiaoyong Du, Orhun Kara, Ting Liu,
Krishna M. Sivalingam, Dominik Ślęzak, Takashi Washio, Xiaokang Yang,
and Junsong Yuan

More information about this series at http://www.springer.com/series/7899

Ernesto Damiani · George Spanoudakis ·
Leszek A. Maciaszek (Eds.)

Evaluation of Novel Approaches to Software Engineering

14th International Conference, ENASE 2019
Heraklion, Crete, Greece, May 4–5, 2019
Revised Selected Papers

 Springer

Editors
Ernesto Damiani
Department of Electrical
and Computer Engineering
Khalifa University of Science
and Technology
Abu Dhabi, United Arab Emirates

George Spanoudakis
Department of Computer Science
City University of London
London, UK

Leszek A. Maciaszek
Wroclaw University of Economics
Wroclaw, Poland

Macquarie University
Sydney, Australia

ISSN 1865-0929   ISSN 1865-0937   (electronic)
Communications in Computer and Information Science
ISBN 978-3-030-40222-8   ISBN 978-3-030-40223-5   (eBook)
https://doi.org/10.1007/978-3-030-40223-5

This Springer imprint is published by the registered company Springer Nature Switzerland AG
The registered company address is: Gewerbestrasse 11, 6330 Cham, Switzerland

Preface

The present book includes extended and revised versions of a set of selected papers from the 14th International Conference on Evaluation of Novel Approaches to Software Engineering (ENASE 2019), held in Heraklion - Crete, Greece, during May 4–5, 2019.

ENASE 2019 received 102 paper submissions from 40 countries, of which 19% were included in this book. The papers were selected by the event chairs and their selection was based on a number of criteria that included the classifications and comments provided by the Program Committee members, the session chairs' assessment, and also the program chairs' global view of all papers included in the technical program. The authors of selected papers were then invited to submit a revised and extended version of their papers having at least 30% innovative material.

The mission of ENASE is to be a prime international forum to discuss and publish research findings and IT industry experiences with relation to novel approaches to software engineering. The conference acknowledges evolution in systems and software thinking due to contemporary shifts of computing paradigm to e-services, cloud computing, mobile connectivity, business processes, and societal participation. By publishing the latest research on novel approaches to software engineering and by evaluating them against systems and software quality criteria, ENASE conferences advance knowledge and research in software engineering, including and emphasizing service-oriented, business-process driven, and ubiquitous mobile computing. ENASE aims to identify the most hopeful trends and proposes new directions for consideration by researchers and practitioners involved in large-scale systems and software development, integration, deployment, delivery, maintenance, and evolution.

The papers included in this book contribute to the understanding of relevant trends of current research on novel approaches to software engineering for the development and maintenance of systems and applications, specifically in relation to: model-driven software engineering, requirements engineering, empirical software engineering, service-oriented software engineering, business process management and engineering, knowledge management and engineering, reverse software engineering, software process improvement, software change and configuration management, software metrics, software patterns and refactoring, application integration, software architecture, cloud computing, and formal methods.

We would like to thank all the authors for their contributions and the reviewers for ensuring the quality of this publication.

May 2019

Ernesto Damiani
George Spanoudakis
Leszek Maciaszek

Organization

Conference Chair

Leszek Maciaszek — Wroclaw University of Economics, Poland, and Macquarie University, Australia

Program Co-chairs

Ernesto Damiani — EBTIC-KUSTAR, UAE
George Spanoudakis — City University London, UK

Program Committee

Muhammad Ovais Ahmad — Karlstad University, Sweden
Marco Aiello — University of Stuttgart, Germany
Apostolos Ampatzoglou — University of Groningen, The Netherlands
Claudio Ardagna — Universita degli Studi di Milano, Italy
Mourad Badri — University of Quebec at Trois-Rivières, Canada
Paul Bailes — The University of Queensland, Australia
Richard Banach — The University of Manchester, UK
Jan Blech — RMIT University, Australia
Glauco Carneiro — Universidade Salvador (UNIFACS), Brazil
Tomas Cerny — Baylor University, USA
William Chu — Tunghai University, Taiwan, China
Rem Collier — University College Dublin, Ireland
Rebeca Cortazar — University of Deusto, Spain
Bernard Coulette — Université Toulouse Jean Jaurès, France
Guglielmo De Angelis — CNR-IASI, Italy
Fatma Dhaou — Faculty of Sciences of Tunis, Tunisia
Sophie Ebersold — IRIT, France
Mahmoud El Hamlaoui — ENSIAS Mohammed V University in Rabat, Morocco
Vladimir Estivill-Castro — Griffith University, Australia
Anna Fasolino — Università degli Studi di Napoli Federico II, Italy
Maria Ferreira — Universidade Portucalense, Portugal
Tarik Fissaa — ENSIAS Mohammed V University Rabat, Morocco
Stéphane Galland — Université de Technologie de Belfort Montbéliard, France
Juan Garbajosa — Technical University of Madrid (UPM), Spain
Atef Gharbi — INSAT, Tunisia
Claude Godart — Henri Poincaré University, France
José-María Gutiérrez-Martínez — Universidad de Alcalá, Spain

Hatim Hafiddi	INPT, Morocco
Peter Herrmann	NTNU, Norway
Lom Hillah	LIP6, CNRS, Sorbonne Université, France
Benjamin Hirsch	Degussa Bank, Germany
Hoda Hosny	The American University in Cairo, Egypt
Mirjana Ivanovic	University of Novi Sad, Serbia
Stefan Jablonski	University of Bayreuth, Germany
Ozgur Kafali	University of Kent, UK
Georgia Kapitsaki	University of Cyprus, Cyprus
Somnuk Keretho	Kasetsart University Bangkok, Thailand
Siau-cheng Khoo	National University of Singapore, Singapore
Diana Kirk	The University of Auckland, New Zealand
Piotr Kosiuczenko	WAT, Poland
Robert Laramee	Swansea University, UK
Bixin Li	Southeast University, China
Jorge López	SAMOVAR, CNRS, Télécom SudParis, Université Paris-Saclay, France
Ivan Lukovic	University of Novi Sad, Serbia
Lech Madeyski	Wroclaw University of Science and Technology, Poland
Nazim Madhavji	University of Western Ontario, Canada
Johnny Marques	Instituto Tecnológico de Aeronáutica, Brazil
Patricia Martin-Rodilla	University of A Coruña, Spain
Raul Mazo	Université Paris 1 Panthéon-Sorbonne, France
Francesco Mercaldo	Institute of Informatics and Telematics of Pisa, CNR, Italy
Breno Miranda	Federal University of Pernambuco, Brazil
Arthur-Jozsef Molnar	University of Babes-Bolyai, Romania
Inès Mouakher	Faculty of Sciences of Tunis, University of Tunis El Manar, Tunisia
Sascha Mueller-Feuerstein	Ansbach University of Applied Sciences, Germany
Malcolm Munro	Durham University, UK
Andrzej Niesler	Wroclaw University of Economics, Poland
Janis Osis	Riga Technical University, Latvia
Meriem Ouederni	IRIT/INPT, France
Mourad Oussalah	Laboratoire Lina, CNRS, University of Nantes, France
Claus Pahl	Free University of Bozen-Bolzano, Italy
Dana Petcu	West University of Timisoara, Romania
Marcelo Pimenta	UFRGS, Brazil
Deepika Prakash	NIIT University, India
Naveen Prakash	IIITD, India
Adam Przybylek	Gdansk University of Technology, Poland
Elke Pulvermueller	University of Osnabrueck, Germany
Lukasz Radlinski	West Pomeranian University of Technology, Poland
José Redondo López	University of Oviedo, Spain
Philippe Roose	LIUPPA, IUT de Bayonne, UPPA, France

Francisco Ruiz	Universidad de Castilla-La Mancha, Spain
Stefano Russo	Universita degli Studi di Napoli Federico II, Italy
Antonella Santone	University of Molise, Italy
Markus Schatten	University of Zagreb, Croatia
Rainer Schmidt	Munich University of Applied Sciences, Germany
Richa Sharma	BML Munjal University, India
Josep Silva	Universitat Politècnica de València, Spain
Ouali Sonya	University of Sfax-Tunisia, Tunisia
Ioana Sora	Politehnica University of Timisoara, Romania
Andreas Speck	University of Kiel, Germany
Maria Spichkova	RMIT University, Australia
Witold Staniszkis	Rodan Development, Poland
Miroslaw Staron	University of Gothenburg, Sweden
Ulrike Steffens	HAW, Hamburg University of Applied Sciences, Germany
Chang-ai Sun	University of Science and Technology Beijing, China
Jakub Swacha	University of Szczecin, Poland
Stephanie Teufel	University of Fribourg, Switzerland
Feng-Jian Wang	National Chiao Tung University, Taiwan, China
Bernhard Westfechtel	University of Bayreuth, Germany
Danny Weyns	KU Leuven, Belgium
Martin Wirsing	Ludwig-Maximilians-Universität München, Germany
Igor Wojnicki	AGH University of Science and Technology, Poland
Alfred Zimmermann	Reutlingen University, Germany

Additional Reviewers

Saloua Bennani	ENSIAS Mohammed V University in Rabat, Morocco
Natalia Kushik	Télécom SudParis, France
David Lo	Singapore Management University, Singapore
Juan Ochoa-Zambrano	Universidad Politécnica de Madrid, Spain
Abdelfetah Saadi	Houari Boumediene University of Science and Technology, Algeria
Fadel Touré	University of Quebec at Trois-Rivières, Canada
Sihan Xu	China

Invited Speakers

Sotiris Ioannidis	Foundation for Research and Technology Hellas, Greece
Danny Menasce	George Mason University, USA
Mike Papazoglou	Tilburg University, The Netherlands

Contents

Using Stanford CoreNLP Capabilities
for Semantic Information Extraction
from Textual Descriptions

Erika Nazaruka$^{(\boxtimes)}$ ⓘ, Jānis Osis ⓘ, and Viktorija Griberman ⓘ

Riga Technical University, 1 Setas Str., Riga, Latvia
{erika.nazaruka,janis.osis,
viktorija.gribermane}@rtu.lv

Abstract. Automated extraction of semantic information from textual descriptions can be implemented by processing results of application of Stanford CoreNLP tools. This paper presents a sequence of processing steps and initial results of their application for two examples of a description of system's functionality. The processing steps allow identifying main functional characteristics of the system and its operational domain. Results obtained as a result of application of the steps are compared with data obtained as a result of analysis by a developer. Application of Stanford CoreNLP parsers in certain cases can produce errors and can influence results of further processing. The comparison of the two results sets showed that variability of language constructs in descriptions affects an amount of implicitly expressed knowledge. Nevertheless, results of this research can be used as a start point of automated text processing for creation of analysis models.

Keywords: Knowledge acquisition · Topological functioning model · Computation independent model

1 Introduction

Models as a means for analysis and design of a system and as a base for source code acquisition are suggested in the Object Management Group's Model Driven Architecture [1]. MDA helps in considering a system from three main viewpoints, namely, a computation independent viewpoint, a platform independent viewpoint and a platform specific viewpoint. Each viewpoint is represented by its corresponding model. The development process starts from the computation independent model (CIM). Then, the CIM is transformed to the platform independent model (PIM) and, finally, to the platform specific model and corresponding code.

Transformations between models can be manual and automated. The automated approach is more preferable. The MDA suggests automated transformations from the PIM, since the CIM consists of either textual descriptions (software requirements, use cases, user stories, etc.) or schemes with textual explanations, where text is written in a natural language. However, it is necessary to note that the OMG suggests a standard entitled "Semantics of Business Vocabulary and Rules" (SBVR) [2]. SBVR is dedicated for business domain analysis. It allows creating a formal vocabulary of a business

© Springer Nature Switzerland AG 2020
E. Damiani et al. (Eds.): ENASE 2019, CCIS 1172, pp. 1–21, 2020.
https://doi.org/10.1007/978-3-030-40223-5_1

domain and specifying business rules in a formal manner but using a natural language as a concrete syntax. However, a use of SBVR is perspective only if analysis and transformation of SBVR documents to design models is automated and the models are used for generation of code. Otherwise, a natural language is a good choice, because it does not require additional effort for study and use [3].

The modern state of computer linguistics in general, and natural language processing (NLP) in particular, gave an impetus for research on text analysis by using NLP where the aim is automated creation of analysis, design and testing models. This paper focuses on automated creation of analysis models and extends information presented in [4] with a discussion on key feature of existing CoreNLP tools for textual specification analysis and refined steps for knowledge extraction demonstrated on two textual examples.

Our vision of principles of intelligent software development presented in the paper is related to use of a knowledge model based on the Topological Functioning Model (TFM) as the CIM to generate code via an intermediary model – Topological UML model [5]. The TFM elaborated by Janis Osis at Riga Technical University [6] specifies a functioning system from three viewpoints – functional, behavioural and structural. This model can serve as a core model for further system and software domain analysis and transformations to design models and code [7].

Extraction of TFM elements requires textual description of functionality of the system. At the present, we have manual processing of the unstructured, but processed text, and automated processing of use case specifications in the form of semi-structured text [8, 9]. In the latter, results are kept in XMI (XML Metadata Interchange) files using XML (eXtensible Markup Language) structures. In its turn, the new approach supposes using a Natural Language Processing (NLP) pipeline for text processing [10] and a knowledge base [11, 12] for keeping and managing results of the processing. We assume that joint use of NLP and an inferring mechanism and flexibility of the knowledge base can give such additional advantages as discovering conflicts in knowledge, managing synonyms, and inferring new knowledge from the existing one.

The goal of this research is to clarify what key features of the assisting tool are necessary and to outline steps for processing Stanford CoreNLP outcomes in order to achieve automated knowledge acquisition of the core elements of the TFM functional characteristics.

The paper is organized as follows. Section 2 describes the core elements of the TFM functional characteristics as well as how Stanford CoreNLP is used now. Section 3 presents initial guideline for processing CoreNLP outcomes, demonstrates them using two examples as well as illustrates main results and limitations of text parsing and outcomes processing. Section 4 gives an overview of the related research. Section 5 concludes the paper.

2   Core Elements of the Topological Functioning Model

2.1   TFM Functional Characteristics

The TFM is a formal model for representing and analysis of functionality of the system of any kind, e.g., business, software, biological, mechanical, etc. [7]. The TFM may represent functionality as a directed graph (X, Θ), where X is a closed set of inner functional characteristics (hereinafter called functional features) of the system, and Θ is a topology set on them in the form of a set of cause-and-effect relations. TFM models can be compared for similarities and differences using the continuous mapping mechanism of topological spaces [13]. The continuous mapping mechanism is used also for keeping information during transformations, i.e., simplification and refinement.

The TFM is characterized by its topological and functioning properties [14]. The topological properties origins are in algebraic topology, they are connectedness, neighborhood, closure and continuous mapping. The functioning properties come from the system theory, they are cause-and-effect relations, cycle structure, inputs and outputs [6].

Determination of a set domain functional characteristics (e.g., a business process, a task, an action, or an activity) [15] includes determination of domain objects, external systems, subsystems, actors, and actions. This information allows determining a set of functional characteristics (features). A functional feature can be specified by a unique tuple (1). The tuple can be extended and shortened if needed, but the core elements are an object O, an action A, a result R, a set of preconditions and a set of executors.

$$FF = \langle A, R, O, PrCond, PostCond, Pr, Ex, S \rangle \tag{1}$$

Where:

- A is object's action,
- **R** is a set of results of the object's action (it is an optional element),
- O is an object set which contains domain objects that is used or get the result of the action; for atomic functional feature the size of the set is equal to 1,
- **PrCond** is a set of preconditions or atomic business rules,
- **PostCond** is a set of post-conditions or atomic business rules,
- **Pr** is a set of providers of the feature, i.e. entities (systems or sub-systems) which provide or suggest action A with a set **O** of certain objects,
- **Ex** is a set of executors (direct performers) of the functional feature, i.e. a set of entities (systems or sub-systems) that enact action A.
- S is a variable *Subordination* that holds changeable value of belonging of the functional feature either to the system or to the external environment according to the value of **Pr**.

Comparing to the original tuple (1), we have added element D for the better understanding of meaning of the feature. D is a description of a functional feature, that can be used for human-understandable representation of the characteristic.

2.2 Natural Language Processing in the IDM Toolset

The starting point of applying NLP of the textual description of system functioning for acquiring knowledge for the TFM is implementation in the IDM (Integrated Domain Modelling) toolset, where processing of use case scenario text is performed using the Stanford Parser Java Library for identifying the executors (**Ex**) and the description of the functional feature D that is the *verb phrase* from the text of a step in a use case scenario [8, 9].

The prerequisite for parsing is that sentences of use case steps must be in the simple form to answer the question "Who does what?", e.g., "Librarian checks out the book".

Parsing is done according to these steps:

- Identify *coordinating conjunctions* to split a sentence into several clauses, and, thus, several functional features.
- Identify the *verb phrase* (VP tag) that is considered as a union of action A, object O and result R (if it is indicated) and forms the so-called *description* of the functional feature.
- Identify the *noun phrase* (NP tag) that is marked as executor Ex if it meets the same noun in the list of actors for the use case.
- Preconditions and postconditions are taken directly from the corresponding preceding step in the use case (if they are specified).

As a result, the following elements of the tuple (1) are obtained: (1) A, **R, O** implicitly in the description of functional feature, (2) **Ex** (single element), (3) **PrCond** and **PostCond** if they are specified for the use case. The existing process is limited to use case specification that is manually proceeded and structured text.

3 Processing Stanford CoreNLP Outcomes for Semantic Information Extraction

3.1 Task of Semantic Information Extraction

The evolution of the topological functioning modelling leads us to the solution, where knowledge extracted from text must be kept in the knowledge-frame base. A piece of knowledge can be generated from the manually entered facts [11]. According to an initial scheme of the knowledge frame system, the current research puts the focus on knowledge that is to be entered manually [10]: domain objects, properties of the domain objects, and TFM functional features.

In case of unstructured text in formal style (hereinafter, *formal text*) we can process results of the following NLP tasks: tokenization, part-of-speech (POS) tagging, chunking, and Name Entity Recognition (NER)/Classification as well as semantic analysis of noun and verb phrases [10]. In step of NER/Classification noun and verb ontology banks must be used.

Therefore, the existing processing must be improved to proceed formal text and to achieve:

- Clear identification of action A, set of results **R** and a set of domain objects, namely, objects **O** with their properties.
- Identification of the **Pr** and **Ex** directly or from the context, if it is not stated explicitly.

- Identification of **PrCond**, **PostCond** from the text according to the context and logical operators (OR, AND, XOR).
- Initialization of the default value of Subordination as "not defined", since the actual value depends on the values of **Pr** and a system (sub-system) under analysis.

Since, the last two points require discourse analysis in text, it will be omitted in this research. Here, the focus is on the sentence and word level analysis.

The Stanford CoreNLP toolkit [16] contains components that deal with tokenization, sentence splitting, POS tagging, morphological analysis (identification of base forms), NER, syntactical parsing, coreference resolution and other annotations such as gender and sentiment analysis. Phrases can be parsed using both constituent and dependency representations based on a probabilistic parser that is more accurate according to the parsers that relate to some predefined structures. Discovering basic dependencies can help in identification of actions and corresponding objects, results, modes (that can serve for identification of causal dependencies), executors and providers. Besides that, the Stanford CoreNLP implements mention detection and pronominal and nominal coreference resolution that can help in dealing with pronouns and noun phrases that denote concrete phenomena.

3.2 Guidelines for Processing Outcomes

For the given research we use Stanford CoreNLP version 3.9.2 that for POS tagging uses tags listed in Penn Treebank II [17]. In this research the following tags are mentioned: S – simple declarative clause, NN – noun, single, NNS – noun, plural, NP – noun phrase, PRP – personal pronoun, VBZ – verb, 3rd person singular present, VBP – verb, non-3rd person singular present, VBD – verb, past tense, VBG – verb, gerund or present participle, VBN – verb, past participle, VB – base form, VP – verb phrase, IN – preposition or subordinating conjunction, RP – particle.

Preparational Step "Coreference resolution". When a personal pronoun (PRP tag) takes part in the relation, it must be substituted with the corresponding noun (tagged NN or NNS) using results of coreference resolution. A personal pronoun and the corresponding noun are linked using the edge *coref.* For example, in the sentence "When the reader completes the request for a book, he gives it to the librarian" (Fig. 1), the pronoun "he" relates to "the reader" and "it" to "the request for a book".

Step 1. Identification of action A. First, verb phrases VPs must be identified in the sentence. We are interested only in verbs as such, not their modality. Therefore, in the found VPs, verbs tagged as VBZ, VBP, VBD, VBN, VBG, or VB must be determined. The verb word we need to extract must be linked with a noun (tag NN, NNS, or PRP) by using *nsubj, dobj,* or *nsubjpass* edges. The value of action A is the infinitive form of the verb that can be found using lemmas analysis, as for example for verb in VBZ "creates" it will be "create". If the verb has link *compound:prt* to the particle tagged RP, then it must be extracted together with it, e.g., "check out".

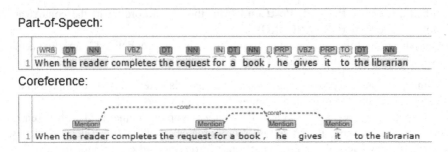

Fig. 1. Results of POS identification and coreference resolution [4].

Step 2. Identification of elements of set Ex. An element of **Ex** is such a noun phrase NP where a noun (tag NN, NNS, or PRP) is linked with the found verb in step 2 (tag VBZ, VBP, or VBD) by using: (a) edge *nsubj* for active voice, or (b) edge *nmod:agent* for passive voice. If *basic dependencies* are used, then *nmod:agent* (used in *enhanced++ dependencies*) is replaced by *nmod* to the noun, and the noun is linked with the preposition "by" (tag IN) using edge *case*. This is illustrated by the results of analysis of two sample sentences: "The authorized librarian creates a new reader account" (Figs. 2 and 3) and "The new reader card is created by the authorized librarian" (Fig. 4). The value of Ex_i is equal to the whole NP that contains the mentioned noun. In the sample sentence, it is NP "the authorized librarian". The NER task can be applied to check extracted nouns whether they are tagged as "TITLE". However, NER tagging works only for NN; moreover, NNS are skipped.

```
1    (ROOT (S
2      (NP
3        (DT The) (VBN authorized)
4        (NN librarian)
5      )
6      (VP
7        (VBZ creates)
8        (NP
9          (DT a) (JJ new)
10         (NN reader) (NN account)
11       )
12     )
13     (. .)
14   ))
```

Fig. 2. The result of constituency parsing of the sentence in the active voice (at the sentence and phrase levels) [4].

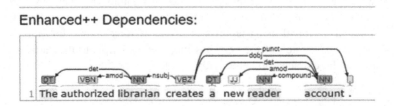

Fig. 3. Dependency analysis results of the sentence in the active voice (the word level) [4].

Basic Dependencies:

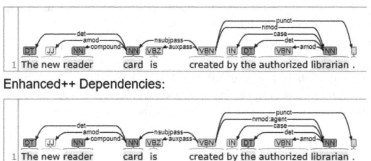

Enhanced++ Dependencies:

Fig. 4. Dependency analysis results of the sentence in the passive voice (at the word level) [4].

Step 3. Identification of object O_i and result R_i should be done in one and the same step. Object O_i (with or without the compound result R_i) is a direct object of the verb found in step 1 [15].

    Step 3.1. Identification of the direct object of the verb – action A. If a sentence contains a verb (action A) in the active voice, then the VP structure includes substructure NP, where the direct object is located, i.e. word n_1 tagged as NN, NNS, or PRP and linked by using edge dobj.

In case of the passive voice, the VP structure contains sub-structure NP, where the subject is located. Thus, we need to extract word n_1 tagged as NN, NNS, or PRP that is linked with the verb by using edge *nsubjpass*.

    Step 3.2. Determination of the object and result of the functional feature.

If the VP of the verb – action A is **not** linked by using any edge *nmod* but *nmod: agent* with another word n_2 tagged as NN, NNS, or PRP, then the following is true:

- If noun n_1 **is not** linked with another noun n_2 in *the same structure NP* by using either edge *compound* or *in the same structure VP* by using one of edges *nmod:-poss, nmod:of, nmod:to, nmod:into, nmod:from, nmod:for, nmod:in* (in enhanced++ dependencies; otherwise, *nmod* to word n_2 tagged as NN, NNS or PRP and *case* to the preposition "of", "to", "into", "from", "for", or "in" tagged as IN), then the value of O_i is equal to n_1. Otherwise, if such links do exist, the value of O_i is equal to *linked NP that contains noun n_2*.
- In case if noun n_1 **is** linked with n_2 by using edge *compound*, then leaves of the whole structure NP that contains n_1 are extracted and the preposition "of" is added to the end of the extracted string. The obtained string is the value of element R_i.
- In case if noun n_1 is linked with n_2 by using edge *nmod* (and its variations), then leaves of the whole structure NP that contains n_1 are extracted and the preposition tagged IN linked with n_2 by using edge *case* is added to the end of the extracted string. The obtained string is the value of element R_i.
- Otherwise, the value of R_i is left empty.

Otherwise, if the VP of the verb – action A **is** linked with another word n_2 (not a direct object or nominal passive subject) tagged as NN, NNS, or PRP using edge *nmod* but *nmod:agent*, too, then the following is true:

- Word n_2 located in the corresponding NP in the prepositional phase PP is a value of the element O_i.
- Leaves of the whole structure NP that has direct child n_1 are extracted. The preposition tagged IN in the sibling prepositional phrase PP is added to the end of the extracted string. The result string is the value of element R_i.

Basic Dependencies:

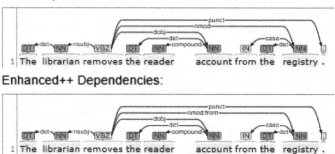

Enhanced++ Dependencies:

Fig. 5. The results of dependency parsing for the sentence with more complex NP [4].

```
11  (ROOT (S
12    (NP (DT The) (NN librarian))
13    (VP
14      (VBZ removes)
15      (NP
16        ((NP
17          (DT the)
18          (NN reader)
19          (NN account)
20        )
21        (PP
22          (IN from)
23          (NP (DT the) (NN registry))
24        )
25      )
26    )
27  )
28    (. .)
29  ))
```

Fig. 6. The results of the constituency parsing for the sentence with more complex NP [4].

Let us consider the sentence "The librarian removes the reader account from the registry." The verb "removes" is linked with the noun "account" (tag NN) by using edge *dobj* (Fig. 5). Leaves of the corresponding NP are extracted as string "the reader account" and supplemented with the preposition "from" (Fig. 6). The final string "the reader account from" is written as a value of R_1. The noun "registry" (tag NN) is recorded as a value of O_1.

In case of conjunctions of NPs, e.g. "creates an account and a card", the head noun or proposition will be linked with the verb by using edge *dobj*, while other nouns or propositions will be linked with the head noun by using edge *conj*. All the linked words must be found and processed according to the abovementioned principles.

Let us consider the sentence in the active voice: "The authorized librarian creates a new reader account". The VP (Fig. 2) contains the verb creates (tagged VBZ) that is not linked to any noun or proposition by using *nmod* (Fig. 3).

The VP contains structure NP, where the direct object (edge *dobj* in Fig. 3) is the noun "account". Let us denote it as n_1. Within the same NP, n_1 = "account" is linked to noun n_2 = "reader" by the edge *compound*. Thus, $O_1 = n_2$ = "reader". The NP that contains n_1 = "account" is "a new reader account". As n_1 is linked with n_2 by using edge *compound*, then, after adding the proposition "of", R_1 = "a new reader account of".

In case of the passive voice, "The new reader card is created by the authorized librarian" (Fig. 4), edge *nsubjpass* links the verb "created" with noun n_1 = "card". The verb "created" is linked only with NP that contains the agent "librarian" (Fig. 7). Thus, following the rules, $O_1 = n_2$ = "reader", and R_1 = "the new reader card of".

```
25   (ROOT (S
26     (NP (DT The) (JJ new) (NN reader) (NN card))
27     (VP
28       (VBZ is)
29       (VP (VBN created)
30         (PP
31           (IN by)
32           (NP
33             (DT the)
34             (VBN authorized)
35             (NN librarian)
36           )
37         )
38       )
39     )
40     (. .)
41   ))
```

Fig. 7. The result of constituency parsing of the sentence with the verb in the passive voice [4].

Step 4. Identification of description D. The description is a visible part of the functional feature that is needed for its unique identification by a human. The original form is as in expression (2).

$$action\,A - ing\,[[the]\,result\,R]\,[prepos.]\,[a]\,object\,O \qquad (2)$$

For simplicity we have excluded the ending "ing" and articles. The final form is $D = <A>\ [<R_i>]\ <O_i>$. If one of the elements is empty, then it is replaced by the question mark "?".

Step 5. Identification of preconditions. At the beginning, we plan identification of conditions by using several syntactical patterns. According to the previous results [10] and logical speculations, the following initial list of patterns could be applied for text processing:

- "When <clause1>, <clause 2>". Clause 1 is a precondition for clause 2.
- "When <condition>, <clause>". A condition in "when" part is a precondition for a clause in the second part of the sentence.
- "<clause1>. Then/after that <clause 2>". Clause 1 is a precondition for clause 2 that is a sentence that starts from words "then" or "after that". In this case, the algorithm must take the last previously defined functional feature as a precondition.
- A sequence of verb phrases "<verb phrase 1> and <verb phrase 2> and...", where "and" meaning is "if <action 1> is successful, then <action 2>". The previous verb phrase is a condition for the consequent verb phrase. However, not in every case this pattern is valid. Sometimes, consequential verb phrases indicate parallel actions.
- "If <condition>, <clause>". A condition in the IF part is a precondition for the clause from implicit THEN part.
- "If <condition>, "<verb phrase 1> and <verb phrase 2>"". A condition in the IF part is a precondition for the clause from implicit THEN part.
- "If <clause1>, [then] <clause 2>". A clause in the IF part is a precondition for the clause from implicit or explicit THEN part.
- "After <clause1>, <clause 2>". Clause 1 is a precondition for clause 2.
- "Before <clause1>, <clause 2>". Clause 2 is a precondition for clause 1.

In general, precondition will be the corresponding clause or condition, i.e. the complete text fragment as it is given in the description. Since lexical constructs may differ, we need to use results of the constituency parsing:

- Rule 1: If a sentence contains a fragment marked as SBVR, it must be recorder as a value of **PreCond** for all the functional features created from this sentence that are not located in the SBVR part. The pattern is "S (SBAR(text))".
- Rule 2: If a sentence contains a fragment marked as SBVR inside a VP, then the fragment must be recorder as a value of **PreCond** for the functional features created from this VP. The pattern is "S (VP (...SBAR (text)...))".
- Rule 3: If a sentence contains a VP that contains a sequence of VP joined by the conjunction "and" (tag CC), then IF clause 1 is a predecessor to clause 2 THEN $PreCond_i$ = clause 1. The pattern is "S (...VP (VP () CC= 'and' VP())...)".

3.3   Examples and Discussion

Let us analyze two fragments of text. The text is manually composed in a formal style to describe functionality of a system. The results of manual processing of the text according to TFM4MDA approach are done previously and published [18, 19]. Therefore, they can be used to compare them with results obtained using the steps of the guideline.

Example 1 "Library". The description is the following [18]: "*When an unregistered person arrives, the librarian creates a new reader account and a reader card. The librarian gives out the card to the reader. When the reader completes the request for a book, he gives it to the librarian. The librarian checks out the requested book from a book fund to a reader, if the book copy is available in a book fund. When the reader returns the book copy, the librarian takes it back and returns the book to the book fund. He imposes the fine, if the term of the loan is exceeded, the book is lost, or is damaged. When the reader pays the fine, the librarian closes the fine. If the book copy is hardly damaged, the librarian completes the statement of utilization, and sends the book copy to the recycling organization*".

Table 1. Elements of the functional features extracted from text for the example "Library" [4].

Id	Description D	Action A	Result R	Object O	Executors **Ex**
1	Arrive <?> <?>	arrive	?	?	an unregistered person
2	Create a new reader account of reader	create	a new reader account of	reader	the librarian
3	Create a reader card of reader	create	a reader card	reader	the librarian
4	Give out the card to reader	give out	the card to	reader	the librarian
5	Complete the request for book	complete	the request for	book	the reader
6	Give the request for book	give	the request for	book	the reader
7	Check out the requested book from a book fund	check out	the requested book from	book fund	the librarian
8	Return the book copy of book	return	the book copy of	book	the reader
9	Take back the book copy of book	take back	the book copy of	book	the librarian
10	Return the book to book fund	return	the book to	book fund	the librarian
11	Impose <?> fine	impose	?	fine	the librarian
12	Exceed the term of loan	exceed	the term of	loan	?
13	Lose <?> book	lose	?	book	?
14	*Damage <?> book*	*damage*	*?*	*book*	*?*
15	Pay <?> fine	pay	?	fine	the reader
16	Close <?> fine	close	?	fine	the librarian
17	*Damage the book copy of book*	*damage*	*the book copy of*	*book*	*?*
18	Complete the statement of utilization	complete	the statement of	utilization	the librarian
19	Send the book copy to recycling organization	send	the book copy to	recycling organization	the librarian

Going through the steps, from eight full sentences we have obtained 19 functional features (Table 1). Functional feature 1 lacks a direct object. The 6th and 7th sentences have no results (Table 1, features 11, 13–16). Functional features 12–14 and 17 have undefined executors (Table 1), they describe some events that happened beyond the system.

Table 2. Identification of preconditions for the example "Library".

Id	Description D	Precondition	Rule
2	Create a new reader account of reader	When an unregistered person arrived	1
3	Create a reader card of reader	When an unregistered person arrived	1
6	Give the request for book	When the reader completes the request for a book	1
7	Check out the requested book from a book fund	If the book copy is available in a book fund	2
9	Take back the book copy of book	When the reader returns the book copy	1
10	Return the book to book fund	The librarian takes the book copy back	3
11	Impose <?> fine	If the term of the loan is exceeded, the book is lost, or is damaged	2
16	Close <?> fine	When the reader pays the fine	1
18	Complete the statement of utilization	If the book copy is hardly damaged	1
19	Send the book copy to recycling organization	The librarian completes the statement of utilization	3

Looking at functional features 14 and 17 (Table 1), one can found that the 17th is a refinement of the 14th. Indeed, if we look closer to the initial text, the text "If the book copy is hardly damaged..." concretizes the statement "...if the book...is damaged". So, we may say, that this is one and the same "action" happened outside the system.

Going through the steps, from eight full sentences we have obtained 19 functional features (Table 1). Functional feature 1 lacks a direct object. The 6th and 7th sentences have no results (Table 1, features 11, 13–16). Functional features 12–14 and 17 have undefined executors (Table 1), they describe some events that happened beyond the system.

Table 2 contains preconditions identified in Step 5. They are not completely equal to preconditions presented in [18], since the approach of specifying preconditions in the TFM may differ. This means that preconditions that are clauses may be extracted as a separate functional feature (as it is demonstrated also in this example) and assigned to their functional features – effects as a cause feature by using cause-and-effect relations. However, all the mentioned conditions for actions are correctly extracted using the three rules.

Discussion on Example 1. Analysis of the results obtained by two approaches shows main differences of human and step-driven processing of text in the context of understanding explicit and implicit information. Comparison of the 19 functional features with 22 features got after manual text processing is illustrated in Table 3.

First, executors are correctly defined for all extracted features.

Second, identification of verbs phrases allowed extracting "outside actions" from adverbial and conditional clauses (features 12–14, 17 on the left side), while in manual processing the "outside actions" have been transformed into "inner actions" that check results of those "outside actions" (features 14, 15 on the right side). Besides that, the obtained feature list is supplemented with implicit "actions" (features 10, 11, 22 on the right side).

Table 3. Functional features extracted using NLP outcomes and manual processing for the example "Library" [4]. Denotation: UP is an unregistered person, P is a person, L is a librarian, R is a reader, RO is recycling organization.

Functional features extraction (using NLP)			Functional features extraction (manual processing)		
Id	Description $D = <A> <R> <O>$	Ex	Id	Description $<A>$-ing [the $<R>$] [$<PRP>$] [a] $<O>$	Ex
1	Arrive <?> <?>	UP	1	Arriving [of] a person	P
2	Create a new reader account of reader	L	2	Creating a reader account	L
3	Create a reader card of reader	L	3	Creating a reader card	L
4	Give out the card to reader	L	4	Giving out the card to a reader	L
			5	Getting the status of a reader	R
5	Complete the request for book	R	6	Completing a request_for_book	R
6	Give the request for book	R	7	Sending a request_for_book	R
			8	Taking out the book copy from a book fund	L
7	Check out the requested book from a book fund	L	9	Checking out a book copy	L
			10	Giving out a book copy	L
			11	Getting a book copy [by a registered reader]	R
8	Return the book copy of book	R	12	Returning a book copy [by a registered person]	R
9	Take back the book copy of book	L	13	Taking back a book copy	L
10	Return the book to book fund	L	17	Returning the book copy to a book fund	L
11	Impose <?> fine	L	16	Imposing a fine	L
12	Exceed the term of loan	?			
			14	Checking the term of loan of a book copy	L
13	Lose <?> book	?			
14	Damage <?> book	?			
			15	Evaluating the condition of a book copy	L
15	Pay <?> fine	R	18	Paying a fine	R
16	Close <?> fine	L	19	Closing a fine	L
17	Damage the book copy of book	?			
18	Complete the statement of utilization	L	20	Completing a statement_of_utilization	L
19	Send the book copy to recycling organization	L	21	Sending the book copy to a recycling organization	L
			22	Recycling a book copy	RO

Third, identified objects differ, too. For NLP processed text they are "reader" (properties: reader account, reader card/card), "book" (properties: request, book copy), "book fund" (properties: book), "fine", "loan" (properties: term), "utilization" (properties: statement), "recycling organization" (properties: book copy), while in the manual approach they are "person", "reader account", "reader card", "reader" (properties: card, status), "request_for_book", "book fund" (properties: book copy), "book copy" (properties: term_of_loan, condition), "fine", "statement_of_utilization", "recycling organization" (properties: book copy). During manual processing, the expert has used his knowledge to abstract and unify several concepts.

Table 4. Elements of the functional features extracted from text for the example "management of the research group activities".

Id	Description D	Action A	Result R	Object O	Executors **Ex**
1	Investigate issues in the field of interest	Investigate	issues in	the field of interest	the research group
2	Obtain ? some valuable results	Obtain	?	some valuable results	?
3	Prepare a paper as authors	Prepare	a paper	as authors	one or more members
4	Submit the completed paper to the conference	Submit	the completed paper to	the conference	the responsible author
5	Accept ? the paper	Accept	?	the paper	the conference organizers
6	Prepare ? a camera-ready paper	Prepare	?	a camera-ready paper	the authors
7	Submit the camera-ready paper to the conference	Submit	the camera-ready paper to	the conference	the responsible author
8	Present the camera-ready paper at the conference	Present	the camera-ready paper at	the conference	the responsible author
9	Publish ? the paper	Publish	?	the paper	?
10	Record paper's bibliographical description in authors' personal files	Record	paper's bibliographical description in	authors' personal files	the responsible author
11	Record his/her visit to the conference	Record	his/her visit to	the conference	the referent
12	Attend conferences without accepted papers	Attend	conferences without	accepted papers	the group members
13	Record these visits in their personal files	Record	these visits in	their personal files	?
14	Archive ? personal files	Archive	?	personal files	?

Table 5. Identification of preconditions for the example "management of the research group activities".

Id	Description D	Precondition	Rule
3	Prepare a paper as authors	Once some valuable results are obtained	1
6	Prepare ? a camera-ready paper	If the paper is accepted	1
10	Record paper's bibliographical description in authors' personal files	If the paper is published	1

Example 2 "Management of the Research Group Activities". The fragment is as follows [19]: *"The research group investigates issues in the field of interest. Once some valuable results are obtained, one or more members of the group prepare a paper as its authors. The completed paper is submitted to an appropriate conference by the responsible author. If the paper is accepted by the conference organizers, then the authors prepare a camera-ready paper in accordance with the obtained reviews. The responsible author submits the camera-ready paper to the conference and presents it at the conference. If the paper is published, the responsible author records paper's bibliographical description in authors' personal files. The referent records his/her visit to the conference and the title of the paper in his/her personal file. Group members may attend conferences without accepted papers; these visits also are recorded in their personal files. Personal files of former group members are archived."*

Going through the steps, from nine full sentences we have obtained 14 functional features (Table 4). Functional feature 2, 5, 6, 9 don't have a result value (but it is an optional value). Functional features 2, 9, 13, 14 don't have a defined executor.

Functional feature "Attend conferences without accepted papers" is logically correct from the first sight. However, "accepted papers" here plays a role of an object that is responsible for the action "attend" and the result of this action is "conferences". This is the case, when the same lexical pattern gives a false result.

Functional feature "Prepare a paper as authors" also just seems correct. However, it contains the explanation "as authors" that can be considered as an object. That is incorrect, since here "authors" plays a role of a synonym to the executor "member of the research group".

In the sentence *"The referent records his/her visit to the conference and the title of the paper in his/her personal file"*, Stanford CoreNLP could not correctly determine dependencies between "records" and "the title". The sentence has two clauses. The first is recoding a visit to the conference and the second is recording the title of the paper. However, the dependencies analyzer relates the word "title" to the noun "a visit" and not to the verb "record". As a result, the second clause is not determined and recorded as a functional feature (Table 4).

Table 6. Functional features extracted using NLP outcomes and manual processing for the example "Management of the research group activities", where RG is the research group, M is a member of the group, C is a conference, RA is a responsible author, CO is conference organizers, A is authors, R is a referent, EE is the external environment.

Functional features extraction (using NLP)			Functional features extraction (manual processing)		
Id	Description $D = <A> <R> <O>$	Ex	Id	Description $<A>$-ing [the $<R>$] [$<PRP>$] [a] $<O>$	Ex
1	Investigate issues in the field of interest	R G	1	Investigating an issue in the field of interest	M
2	Obtain ? some valuable results	?			
3	Prepare a paper as authors	M	2	Preparing a new paper	M
4	Submit the completed paper to the conference	R A	3	Submitting a new paper	RA
5	Accept ? the paper	C O	4	Notifying the status of a paper	CO
6	Prepare ? a camera-ready paper	A	5	Preparing a camera-ready paper	A
7	Submit the camera-ready paper to the conference	R A	6	Submitting a camera-ready paper	RA
8	Present the camera-ready paper at the conference	R A	7	Presenting a camera-ready paper	R
9	Publish ? the paper	?	8	Publishing a paper	CO
10	Record paper's bibliographical description in authors' personal files	R A	9	Recording the bibliographical description of the paper in a personal file	RA
11	Record his/her visit to the conference	R	10	Recording the visit to the conference in a personal file	R, M
			11	Recording the title of the paper in a personal file	R
14	Archive personal files	?	12	Archiving a personal file	RG
12	Attend conferences without accepted papers	M	13	Visiting a conference	M, R
13	Record these visits in their personal files	?			
			14	Identifying the issues in a paper	A
			15	Ending a membership in the research group	M
			16	Starting a membership in the research group	P
			17	Creating a personal file	M
			18	Renewing a membership in the research group	M
			19	Restoring a personal file	M
			20	Existence of an issue in the field	EE
			21	Appearance of a new member	P
			22	Appearance of a membership finishing reason	M

Table 5 shows identified preconditions for functional features 3, 6, 10 that semantically are the same as at the example in [19]. Preconditions for other functional features initially are found by discourse analysis (at the paragraph level) that is not considered in this paper.

Discussion. Analysis of the results obtained by two approaches shows main differences of human and step-driven processing of text in the context of understanding explicit and implicit information. Comparison of the 14 functional features with 22 features got after human text processing is illustrated in Table 6.

First, executors are correctly defined for most extracted features. However, in step-driven processing they are got as mentioned in the text. At the same time, in human processing they are modified to present information more accurately. For example, an executor of functional feature 1 (Table 6) is the research group (as in the text) and the member of this group. The same for functional feature 8, where a presenter is either a responsible author (as in the text) or a referent.

The second variant is less specific, since not only a responsible author can present a paper at the conference. The same generalization is done in features 10 and 13.

Second, functional features 14–22 obtained as a result of human analysis of the domain give knowledge not presented in the text fragment. They complement the explicit knowledge about the research group work with the implicit knowledge on causes and effects of some actions. In other words, this information is inferred by a human based on their own experience.

Third, identified objects also differ. Thus, the domain objects defined by a human are a research group, an issue, a field of interest, a [valuable] result, a [current, former] member of the group, a [new, completed, accepted, camera-ready, published] paper (properties: title), a [responsible, co-] author, a(n) [appropriate] conference, conference organizers, a(n) [obtained] review, a bibliographical description of the paper, a personal file, a referent, a visit. Step-driven results are not so consistent. They are a field of interest (properties: issues), [some valuable] results, authors (properties: a paper), conference (properties: a [completed, camera-ready] paper, a visit), a [completed, camera-ready, accepted] paper (properties: conference), [authors'] personal files (properties: paper's bibliographical description, visits). This means that the initial text contains incomplete and general information. This requires re-formulating the text or additional processing of the results.

3.4 Parsing Issues

The result of parsing and POS tagging may be affected by errors in lexical analysis. Parser models used by CoreNLP sometimes can provide outputs with incorrect lexical analysis. Until v.3.6.0, the default parser was englishPCFG.ser.gz [20]. Using this parser alone in CoreNLP GUI, the POS stage was performed correctly, i.e., verbs "checks" and "records" were recognized as VBZ. While using the newer one English model in CoreNLP from the command line as well as in online web application *coreNLP.run* they were mistakenly recognized as plural nouns NNS. The cause is that the form of the verb is identical to the form of the plural noun. Thus, the result highly depends on the language model used by the parser. As a result, some actions can be undefined; however, at the same time some additional domain objects O will be defined.

Sometimes dependency parser indicates incorrect links between words. For example, in the sentence *"The referent writes his/her visit to the conference and the title of the paper in his/her personal file."* (Fig. 8) a direct object of the verb "write" is only "a visit". "A title" is related not to the verb but to the noun "a visit" as a modifier (edge *nmod:to*). Such cases lead to the undefined actions.

Enhanced++ Dependencies:

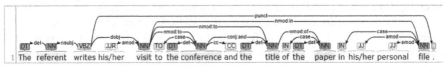

Fig. 8. Incorrect dependency parsing.

Another recommendation is to exclude situations when an adjective or a cardinal number describes the noun. For example, it is better to write rather "Subtract the first digit from the second digit" than "Subtract the first digit from the second" or "… from the second one". Otherwise, the processing will show incorrect results.

4 Related Work

Automated knowledge extraction and model creation can help in reducing time for analysis of large amount of information.

Creation of models and UML diagrams from textual documents is presented in several researches, for example:

- Creation of use case diagrams [21] and UML Activity Diagrams using identification of simple verbal sentences [22] from textual requirements in Arabic.
- Creation of UML class diagrams from textual requirements [23], and from use case descriptions [24] in English.
- Creation of Use Case Path models, the Hybrid Activity Diagrams model and the Domain model from textual user requirements in natural language and requirements engineering diagrams [25].
- Creation of conceptual diagrams from texts in natural language [26] with a participation of a human, because sentence structures may have completely unpredictable forms, syntactical errors, as well as ambiguity in determining attributes as aggregations and in generalization.
- Creation of UML Class diagrams, Object diagrams, Use Case diagrams, and several of them provide composition of Sequence, Collaboration and Activity diagrams from textual documents in different approaches [27].

All the solutions have certain limitations: some require user intervention, some cannot perform analysis of irrelevant classes, some require structuring text in a certain form before processing, and some cannot correctly determine several structural relationships between classes. Some approaches use ontologies predefined by experts in the field and self-developed knowledge acquisition rules in order to extract knowledge on necessary properties or elements and their values from text documents [28, 29]. The only approach that allows complete derivation of the business process model mentioned by the authors in [27] is presented by Friedrich, Mendling and Puhlmann [30].

The presented approach also is dedicated for automated extraction of knowledge and generation of the design models or source code. However, a human participation is necessary to analyse lexical and syntactical constructs that may have one form but different meaning for analysis of a system's functionality.

5 Conclusions

This paper presents the initial sequence of steps for semantic information extraction from textual descriptions of system's functionality. The steps cover such points as pronoun substitution with corresponding noun phrases, identification of actions, their executors, participating objects, expected results and preconditions of the actions using predefined patterns formed from parts-of-speech tags and constituency dependencies.

The steps and patterns are applied to two examples of descriptions. The first example is a description of library's functioning. The second one is a description of "Management of the research group activities". Practical application of steps to the example texts showed that Stanford CoreNLP parsers can produce errors in tagging verbs and indicating dependencies between verbs and direct objects.

Comparison of the result set pairs showed that incompleteness in findings in most cases are caused by implicit knowledge, that a developer can infer based on his experience. Such a capability is not available for automated processing. Besides that, a developer applies additional ad hoc modification of the initial text even loosing direct links with it.

As a result, application of Stanford CoreNLP requires thorough selection of a parsing model. Particularities of the natural language related to incomplete or implicit knowledge can be solved to some degree by using machine learning models. Future research directions are related to finding solutions of these issues.

References

1. Miller, J., Mukerji, J.: Model driven architecture (MDA) (2001)
2. OMG: SBVR (semantics of business vocabulary and rules) (2019). https://www.omg.org/spec/SBVR
3. Elstermann, M., Heuser, T.: Automatic tool support possibilities for the text-based S-BPM process modelling methodology. In: Proceedings of the 8th International Conference on Subject-Oriented Business Process Management, S-BPM 2016, pp. 1–8. ACM Press, New York (2016)

4. Nazaruka, E., Osis, J., Griberman, V.: Extracting core elements of TFM functional characteristics from stanford CoreNLP application outcomes. In: Damian, E., Spanoudakis, G., Maciaszek, L. (eds.) Proceedings of the 14th International Conference on Evaluation of Novel Approaches to Software Engineering - Volume 1: MDI4SE, pp. 591–602. SciTePress (2019)

5. Osis, J., Donins, U.: Topological UML Modeling: An Improved Approach for Domain Modeling and Software Development. Elsevier, Amsterdam (2017)

6. Osis, J.: Topological model of system functioning. Autom. Comput. Sci. J. Acad. Sci. **6**, 44–50 (1969). (in Russian)

7. Osis, J., Asnina, E.: Topological modeling for model-driven domain analysis and software development: functions and architectures. In: Model-Driven Domain Analysis and Software Development: Architectures and Functions, pp. 15–39. IGI Global, Hershey (2011)

8. Osis, J., Slihte, A.: Transforming textual use cases to a computation independent model. In: Osis, J., Nikiforova, O. (eds.) Model-Driven Architecture and Modeling-Driven Software Development: ENASE 2010, 2nd MDA&MTDD Whs, pp. 33–42. SciTePress (2010)

9. Slihte, A., Osis, J., Donins, U.: Knowledge integration for domain modeling. In: Osis, J., Nikiforova, O. (eds.) Model-Driven Architecture and Modeling-Driven Software Development: ENASE 2011, 3rd MDA&MDSD Whs, pp. 46–56. SciTePress (2011)

10. Nazaruka, E., Osis, J.: Determination of natural language processing tasks and tools for topological functioning modelling. In: Proceedings of the 13th International Conference on Evaluation of Novel Approaches to Software Engineering, pp. 501–512. SciTePress – Science and Technology Publications, Lda., Funchal (2018)

11. Nazaruks, V., Osis, J.: Joint usage of frames and the topological functioning model for domain knowledge presentation and analysis. In: Proceedings of the 12th International Conference on Evaluation of Novel Approaches to Software Engineering – Vol. 1: MDI4SE, pp. 379–390. SciTePress - Science and Technology Publications, Porto (2017)

12. Nazaruks, V., Osis, J.: Verification of causality in the frame system based on the topological functioning modelling. In: Proceedings of the 13th International Conference on Evaluation of Novel Approaches to Software Engineering, Portugal, Funchal, Madeira, 23–24 March 2018, pp. 513–521. SciTePress – Science and Technology Publications, Lda. (2018)

13. Asnina, E., Osis, J.: Computation independent models: bridging problem and solution domains. In: Proceedings of the 2nd International Workshop on Model-Driven Architecture and Modeling Theory-Driven Development, pp. 23–32. SciTePress - Science and Technology Publications, Lisbon (2010)

14. Osis, J., Asnina, E.: Is modeling a treatment for the weakness of software engineering? In: Model-Driven Domain Analysis and Software Development, pp. 1–14. IGI Global, Hershey (2011)

15. Asnina, E., Osis, J.: Topological functioning model as a CIM-business model. In: Model-Driven Domain Analysis and Software Development, pp. 40–64. IGI Global, Hershey (2011)

16. Manning, C.D., Surdeanu, M., Bauer, J., Finkel, J., Bethard, S.J., Mcclosky, D.: The Stanford CoreNLP natural language processing toolkit. In: Proceedings of the 52nd Annual Meeting of the Association for Computational Linguistics: System Demonstrations, pp. 55–60 (2014)

17. Bies, A., et al.: Bracketing guidelines for Treebank II style (1995)

18. Osis, J., Asnina, E., Grave, A.: Computation independent modeling within the MDA. In: IEEE International Conference on Software-Science, Technology & Engineering (SwSTE 2007), pp. 22–34. IEEE, Herzlia (2007)

19. Asnina, E., Osis, J., Jansone, A.: System thinking for formal analysis of domain functioning in the computation independent model. In: Proceedings of the 7th International Conference

on Evaluation of Novel Approaches to Software Engineering - ENASE 2012, pp. 232–240. SciTePress, Lisbon (2012)

20. Stanford: CoreNLP version 3.9.2. Understanding memory and time usage (2018). https://stanfordnlp.github.io/CoreNLP/memory-time.html
21. Jabbarin, S., Arman, N.: Constructing use case models from Arabic user requirements in a semi-automated approach. In: 2014 World Congress on Computer Applications and Information Systems, WCCAIS 2014, pp. 1–4. IEEE, Hammamet (2014)
22. Nassar, I.N., Khamayseh, F.T.: Constructing activity diagrams from Arabic user requirements using natural language processing tool. In: 2015 6th International Conference on Information and Communication Systems (ICICS), pp. 50–54. IEEE, Amman (2015)
23. Krishnan, H., Samuel, P.: Relative Extraction Methodology for class diagram generation using dependency graph. In: 2010 International Conference on Communication Control and Computing Technologies, pp. 815–820. IEEE (2010)
24. Elbendak, M., Vickers, P., Rossiter, N.: Parsed use case descriptions as a basis for object-oriented class model generation. J. Syst. Softw. **84**, 1209–1223 (2011). https://doi.org/10.1016/j.jss.2011.02.025
25. Ilieva, M.G., Ormandjieva, O.: Models derived from automatically analyzed textual user requirements. In: Fourth International Conference on Software Engineering Research, Management and Applications (SERA 2006), pp. 13–21. IEEE (2006)
26. Vidya Sagar, V.B.R., Abirami, S.: Conceptual modeling of natural language functional requirements. J. Syst. Softw. **88**, 25–41 (2014). https://doi.org/10.1016/j.jss.2013.08.036
27. Osman, C.-C., Zalhan, P.-G.: From natural language text to visual models: a survey of issues and approaches. Inform. Econ. **20**, 44–61 (2016). https://doi.org/10.12948/issn14531305/20.4.2016.01
28. Amardeilh, F., Laublet, P., Minel, J.-L.: Document annotation and ontology population from linguistic extractions. In: Proceedings of the 3rd International Conference on Knowledge Capture, K-CAP 2005, pp. 161–168. ACM Press, New York (2005)
29. Jones, D.E., Igo, S., Hurdle, J., Facelli, J.C.: Automatic extraction of nanoparticle properties using natural language processing: NanoSifter an application to acquire PAMAM dendrimer properties. PLoS ONE **9**, e83932 (2014). https://doi.org/10.1371/journal.pone.0083932
30. Friedrich, F., Mendling, J., Puhlmann, F.: Process model generation from natural language text. In: Proceedings of the 23rd International Conference on Advanced Information Systems Engineering (CAiSE 2011), pp. 482–496 (2011)

An Overview of Ways of Discovering Cause-Effect Relations in Text by Using Natural Language Processing

Erika Nazaruka[(⊠)] [iD]

Riga Technical University, 1 Setas Str., Riga 1048, Latvia
erika.nazaruka@rtu.lv

Abstract. Understanding of cause-effect relations is vital for constructing a valid model of a system under development. Discovering cause-effect relations in text is one of the difficult tasks in Natural Language Processing (NLP). This paper presents a survey on trends in this field related to understanding how linguistically causal dependencies can be expressed in the text, what patterns and models exist, which of them are more and less successful and why. The results show that causal dependencies in text can be described using plenty lexical expressions as well as linguistic and syntactic patterns. Moreover, the same constructs can be used for non-causal dependencies. Solutions that combine the patterns, ontologies, temporal models and a use of machine learning demonstrate more accurate results in extracting and selecting cause-effect pairs. However, not all lexical expressions are well studied. There are few researches on multi-cause and multi-effect domains. The results of the survey are to be used for construction of a Topological Functioning Model (TFM) of a system, where cause-effect relations are one of key elements. However, they can be used also for construction of other behavioral models.

Keywords: Causality extraction · Natural Language Processing · Topological Functioning Model · System modeling · System analysis

1 Introduction

Models are wide used in software development. They represent a system at different levels of abstraction, using different representation formats, describing a system with different precision and in different scale. Software industry uses mostly graphical models for analytical and design purposes to simplify understanding of key characteristics of the product. Knowledge sources for building models are mostly textual, i.e., requirements specified in a variety of forms, for example, use case scenarios, user stories, descriptions.

A usage of models as a main source for code generation was presented by the Object Management Group in a guide on Model Driven Architecture (MDA) in 2001 [1]. MDA suggests a chain of model transformations, namely, from a computation independent model (CIM, mostly textual) to a platform independent model (PIM, mostly graphical), then to a platform specific model (PSM, graphical) and to source code. The less developed place in this chain is a transformation of the CIM. The CIM

© Springer Nature Switzerland AG 2020
E. Damiani et al. (Eds.): ENASE 2019, CCIS 1172, pp. 22–38, 2020.
https://doi.org/10.1007/978-3-030-40223-5_2

contains software and system requirements, knowledge about the problem and solution domains, a domain vocabulary and so on. Textual descriptions and schemes are manually analyzed to discover explicit and implicit knowledge about system's (software's) functioning, behavior and structure. Domain object analysis and causal reasoning [2] results in identification of structural and cause-effect relations. The latter are those of control flows in the systems and influence also some structural relations [3–10].

Research on the formalization of the CIM leads us to a use of a knowledge model based on the Topological Functioning Model (TFM) [11]. The TFM elaborated by Janis Osis at Riga Technical University [12] specifies a functioning system from three viewpoints – functional, behavioral and structural. Cause-effect relations are one of the key elements in the TFM. The source of information for the TFM is verbal descriptions that could be processed in two ways:

- manually as in the TFM4MDA (Topological Functioning Model for MDA) approach [13, 14] and
- automatedly from steps in use case scenarios as in the IDM (Integrated Domain Modelling) toolset [15, 16].

Preparation of text descriptions as well as manual knowledge acquisition are too resource-consuming [17]. In practice, developers prefer either to skip the step of preparation of complete descriptions and start from modelling results of analysis of the available information, or to automate or semi-automate this process.

The key aspect of successful construction of the domain model is correct and complete identification of causes and effects. The same is in case of the TFM, where identification of cause-effect (topological) relations between functional characteristics of the system is crucial. The goal of the given research is to make a survey on ways and completeness of extracting causal dependencies from text using Natural Language Processing (NLP), Natural Language Understanding (NLU) and linguistics techniques. This research is an extended version of the results published in [18]. This paper supplements them applying the published results to the structured texts used in software development, i.e. to the use case scenarios and user stories, and finding out more and less controlled moments in their processing.

The research questions are the following:

- RQ1: What natural language constructs for expressing cause-effect relations in text are used?
- RQ2: What models, patterns for identification of cause-effect relations in text are used?
- RQ3: What automatic techniques for extracting cause-effect relations from text are used?
- RQ4: Is the preprocessed text (in a form of use case scenarios and user stories) able to eliminate efforts put for identification of cause-effect relations?

The aim is to understand what natural language constructs may be ambiguous for NLP, what pitfalls exist in discovering cause-effect relations in text and what issues have been found in application of extracting tools.

The paper is organized as follows. Section 2 describes the meaning of cause-effect relations in the TFM. Section 3 presents research results on ways of discovering cause-effect relations from text with their pros and cons. Section 4 presents a discussion on application of findings to use case scenarios and user stories. Conclusions contain the findings and enumeration of future research steps.

2   Cause-Effect Relations in the TFM in Brief

Cause-effect relations in the TFM represents structural relationships between domain objects and control flows between functional characteristics of a system. They are allowed having multiple causes and multiple effects joined by logical operators AND, OR and XOR (exclusive OR).

The TFM is a formal mathematical model that represents system's functionality in a holistic manner. It describes functional and structural aspects of the software system in the form of a directed graph (X, θ), where a set of vertices X that are functional characteristics of the system named in human understandable language, while θ is a set of edges representing cause-effect relations (topology) between them. Specification in a form of a digraph is more accurate and explicit then a big amount of verbal descriptions. The TFM can be validated according to its topological and functioning properties [19]. The topological properties are connectedness, neighborhood, closure, and continuous mapping. The functioning properties are cause-effect relations, cycle structure, inputs, and outputs. The composition of the TFM is presented in [14].

Rules of composition and derivation processes within TFM4MDA from verbal descriptions of system's functionality is provided by examples and described in detail in [14, 20–22]. The TFM can also be generated automatically from the business use case scenario specifications, which can be specified in the IDM toolset [23]. It also can be manually created in the TFM Editor from the IDM toolset.

The cause-effect relations in a TFM are those of causal dependencies that exist between functional characteristics of the system and define a cause from which triggering of an effect occurs. Formal definitions of a cause-effect relation and a logical relation among those relations as well as their incoming and outgoing groups are as follows [11, 24].

Formal Definition of a Cause-Effect Relation. A cause-effect relation T_i is a binary relationship that relates exactly two functional features X_c and X_e. Both X_c and X_e may be the same functional feature in case of recursion. The synonym for cause-effect relation is a topological relation. A cause-effect relation is a unique 5-tuple (1) where:

- *ID* is a unique identifier of the relation;
- X_c is a cause functional feature;
- X_e is an effect functional feature;
- N is a Boolean value of the necessity of X_c for generating X_e;
- S is a Boolean value of the sufficiency of X_c for generating X_e.

$$T_i = \langle ID, X_c, X_e, N, S \rangle \tag{1}$$

Formal Definition of a Logical Relation. Alogical relation L_i specifies the logical operator conjunction (AND), disjunction (OR), or exclusive disjunction (XOR) between two or more cause-effect relations T_i. The logical relation denotes system execution behavior, e.g. decision making, parallel or sequential actions. Each logical relation is a unique 3-tuple (2), where:

- ID is a unique identifier of the relation;
- T is a set of cause-effect relations $\{T_i, ..., T_n\}$ that participate in this logical relation;
- R_T is a logical operator AND, OR, or XOR over T; operator OR is a default value.

$$L_i = \langle ID, T, R_T \rangle \tag{2}$$

Formal Definition of Incoming Topological Relations. A set of logical relations that join cause-effect relations, which go into functional feature X_i, is defined as a subset L_{in} of set $L = \{L_i, ..., L_n\}$, where at least one topological relation T_i such that its effect functional feature X_e is equal to X_i is found in the set T of topological relations in each logical relation L_i.

Formal Definition of Outgoing Topological Relations. A set of logical relations that join cause-effect relations, which go out from functional feature X_i, is defined as a subset L_{out} of set $L = \{L_i, ..., L_n\}$, where at least one topological relation T_i such that its cause functional feature X_c is equal to X_i is found in the set T of topological relations in each logical relation L_i.

The connection between a cause and an effect is represented by a certain conditional expression, the causal implication. It is characterized by the nature or business laws (or rules) not just by logic rules. In causal connections "something is allowed to go wrong", whereas logical statements allow no exceptions. Using this property of cause-effect relations, logical sequences wherein execution of a precondition guarantees execution of an action can be prescinded. This means that even if a cause is executed, none corresponding effect can be generated because of a functional damage.

A cause can be characterized by its "causal power", temporal dimension, sufficiency and necessity:

- In order to construct "a theory of the causal mechanism that produced the effect", the human mind applies very sophisticated mechanism as well as empirical information and world knowledge [2]. Trying to discover this "causal mechanism" they analyze "causal power" of events to generate an effect.
- A cause chronologically precedes an effect. This means that the cause-effect conditions contain a time dimension.
- Causes can be sufficient or necessary (or complete or partial, correspondingly) [25]. A sufficient (complete) cause generates its effect ever, or in any conditions. A necessary cause (partial) only promotes its effect generating and is also a condition. The effect occurs only if this partial cause joins other conditions. However, it does not mean that each condition is a cause. Most cause-effect relations involve

multiple factors as in series as in parallel. Thus, a structure of cause-effect relations can form a causal chain. The causal chain begins with the first cause and follows with series of intermediate actions or events to some final effect. Though one link may not be as important or as strong like the other ones, they are all necessary to the chain.

3 Discovering Cause-Effect Relations in Text

This section represents overview of means for explicit and implicit expressing cause-effect relations in natural language, what patterns may indicate cause-effect relations in text at the sentence and discourse levels, as well as overview of research papers on automatic discovering cause-effect relations from text using NLP tools and other techniques.

The general view on the process of discovering cause-effect relations is illustrated in Fig. 1. Parsing text into clauses or phrases allows searching cause-effect pairs within and between them. The process of discovering cause-effect pairs is highly dependent on the quality of linguistic/syntactic and semantic patterns in causal or joint causal and temporal models. The obtained set of cause-effect pairs must be checked manually using knowledge-based inferring performed by an expert.

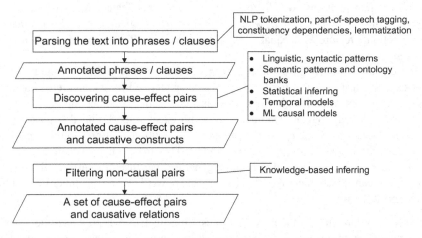

Fig. 1. General view on the process of discovering cause-effect pairs from text.

3.1 Natural Language Constructs for Expressing Cause-Effect Relations

Considering NLP and NLU tasks, researchers noted that causes and effects usually are states or events that can have different duration [2, 26]. Besides that, similar language constructs are used to express both temporal and causal relations [27]. The cause-effect relations in text may be expressed both explicitly and implicitly.

Explicitly Expressed Relations. Several authors mentioned that linguists have identified language elements for explicit expression of causes and effects [2, 26]. They are causal links (used to link two phrases, clauses or sentences) causative verbs, resultative constructions, conditionals (i.e., if...then constructions), causative adverbs, adjectives, and prepositions. One may say that causal links include as causal reasons as temporal reasons [27].

As Khoo et al. [2] stated, Altenberg [28] had classified causal links into four main types:

- the *adverbial* link (e.g., *so, hence, therefore*). It can have a reference to the preceding clause or to the following clause;
- the *prepositional* link (e.g., *because of, on account of*). It connects a cause and an effect in the same clause;
- *subordination*. It can be expressed using *a subordinator* (e.g., *because, as, since*), *a structural link* marked by a non-finite-*ing* clause, and *a correlative comparative construction* (e.g., *so...that*);
- the *clause-integrated* link (e.g. *that's why, the result was*). Here they distinguish *thematic link,* when the linking words serve as a subject of the sentence, and *a rhematic link*, when the linking words serve as the complement of the verb.

A causal link is usually a reference to a clause that plays a role of explanation in a complex sentence or a discourse. A clause is a group of words that includes at least *a subject and a verb*. A clause can be independent and express a complete thought. A dependent clause can act as a noun, an adjective, or an adverb.

Causative verbs are "verbs the meaning of which include a causal element" [2], e.g. "register" that in "X registers Y" means that "X causes Y to be *registered*". One of the working definitions of the causative verbs can be such that "Causative verbs specify the result of the action, whereas other action verbs specify the action but not the result of action" [2]. Besides that, causative verbs can be defined taking into account whether they represents a causal link alone or a causal link with causally related components [29]: simple, resultative and instrumental causatives. The only pure synonyms for the verb *cause* are the simple causatives (e.g., lead to, generate, force etc.). The resultative causatives refer also a part of the resulting situation (e.g., kill, dry, copy, delete, etc.). The last one, instrumental, refer to a part of the causing event and the result (e.g., punch, clean, hang, etc.). Belonging of the verb to a semantic hierarchy (like, for example, the verb *develop* belongs to the hierarchy of the verb *cause to <do something>*) can be determined in the WordNet ontology bank.

A resultative construction [2] is "a sentence in which the object of a verb is followed by a phrase describing the state of the object as a result of the action denoted by the verb", e.g. "A user marked records yellow". A resultative phrase can be an adjective (the most common kind), a noun phrase, a prepositional phrase or a particle.

If-then conditionals often indicate that the antecedent (the *if* part) causes the consequent (the *then* part). However, sometimes they just indicate a sequence of events not their cause-effect relation [2].

Causative adverbs, adjectives and prepositions also can have a causal element in their meaning [2]. Causative adverbs can be different, the most interesting for us are adverbs that involve the notion of a result whose properties are context dependent (e.g.

successfully), adverbs that refer not to causes but to effects (e.g. *consequentially*), and adverbs of means (e.g. *mechanically*). Causative adverbs and adjectives are not well studied [2].

Prepositions also can be used to express causality [2]. They can indicate a cause as proximity, a cause as a source, and a cause as volume.

Implicitly Expressed Relations. Implicit cause-effect relations usually are inferred by the reader using information in text and their background knowledge [2, 26, 27]. Implicit causality can be inferred from experiential and action verbs [30, 31]. These groups of verbs "have "causal valence" – they tend to assign causal status to their subject or object" [2]. Since the experiential verbs usually describes someone's psychological or mental experience, they can be skipped for software development. Action verbs describe events. The subject of the verb can take the semantic role *agent* or *actor*. The object of the verb takes the role of *patient*. Some verbs give greater causal weight to the subject (*actor verbs*), other – to the object (*non-actor verbs*). At the present, causal weight seems not so important for domain analysis in software development. However, the interesting thing is that both verbs groups have derived adjectives referring to the subject or object. This means that some preceding actions can be expressed in text using not verbs, but adjectives. Some implicit causative verbs trigger expectations of explanations to occur in subsequent discourse [26].

3.2   Models and Patterns for Identification of Cause-Effect Relations

Models. Many theories exist for identification, modeling and analysis of cause-effect relations in psycholinguistics, linguistics, psychology and artificial intelligence. Those of theories attempting to reduce causal reasoning to a domain-general theory can be grouped as associative theories, logical theories and probabilistic theories [32].

Associative theories underestimate aspects of causality that are important for causal reasoning. However, in some cases causes and effects can be identified only using associations [32]. Logical theories model causal reasoning as a special case of deductive reasoning. However, *conditionals do not distinguish between causes and effects*, and background knowledge can be necessary to distinguish them as well as some temporal priorities [32]. In their turn, probabilistic theories considers causes as *"difference makers, which raise (generative cause) or reduce (preventive cause) the probability of the effect"* [32]. However, as the authors noted, covariation does not necessarily reflect causation.

All the theories have their limitations in identification of causes and effects. In case of processing verbal (written) information to develop software, causes and effects mostly relate to business, mechanical and physical domains that certainly make a task easier for developers. At the present, logical theories seem to be the most suitable for this task and domains.

Additionally, temporal reasoning and temporal models can help in identifying causal dependencies. Many of NLP research papers focus on the lexical-syntactical patterns (such as causative verb, causal links, discourse relations, etc.) underestimating temporal reasons. However, several works demonstrate that joint consideration of causal models and temporal models is more valuable for identifying and extracting cause-effect relations from text [27, 33–35]. Besides that, joint temporal and causal reasoning correctly identify *counterfactual* clauses [27]. They include such constructs as *might, would, if only*. They indicate possible "state of the world" in case of some "action" that would be done [26]. For example, as in the sentence "If librarian would not have ordered the book, a manager assistant would have".

Patterns. There are several levels where cause-effect relations can be presented. The one is a sentence level, where cause-effect relations are presented between words, phrases or clauses. The another is a discourse, where they exist between clauses or sentences. Patterns are used for initial search of causes-effect pairs in text. The result of this search is then checked and filtered.

Patterns with Events (Within a Sentence). In case of explicit causality, verbs, both causative and action, indicate a cause between two events [26] and it can be identified by using the lexical-syntactical pattern (3) [26] and (4) [36].

$$[[event1]] \ CAUSE \ [[event2]] \tag{3}$$

$$[[event2]] \ is \ the \ result \ of \ [[event1]] \tag{4}$$

In this pattern, [[event1]] is when the subject does something, and [[event2]] is when the object changes its state. Besides that, it is inferred that the object was not in this state before the [[event1]] if otherwise is not mentioned in the text. In many cases, the [[event]] is represented as a noun phrase. Classification of semantic relations between pairs of nominals is discussed based on the results of SemEval-2010 Task 8 [37]. Besides the events, the entities that represent causes or effects can also be conditions, states, phenomena, processes and sometimes facts [29]. The subject of the verb describing the event must be some *agent* or *actor* represented by an object, an abstract property or an event [26]. In case of implicit causality, verbs in most cases express causality between two *animate* objects followed by explanation [26].

CAUSE may be introduced using the preposition "by" [26] together with a passive causative verbs [38], a noun with a preposition (e.g., cause of), simple causative verbs, phrasal verbs, and single prepositions (e.g., form, after). Besides that, in order to extent a number of potential pairs, the ontology bank WordNet can be used [29, 39], where belonging of a verb to a causative verbs group can be identified. A use of openIE [40] to extract multiple relationships from the sentence and check whether they form "a chained reaction" can increase the number of the potential pairs [39].

Patterns with Propositions (a Discourse). The same as within a sentence, in a discourse causal relations may be expressed explicitly using causal links or implicitly using explanations and suggesting inferring by a reader [26].

Some researchers [26, 41] indicate that at this level causal relations differ from those of at the sentence or clause level. Here, they are supplemented with reasons and explanations. The authors assumed that the causal relations exist between entities that are propositional in nature and can be expressed by the lexical-syntactical pattern (5).

$$[[proposition1]] \; CAUSE \; [[proposition2]] \tag{5}$$

Even when explicitly expressed, it is hard to understand are they describe parallel or sequential propositions or explanations, as, for instance, in the sentence "The user access was denied. The hackers taken the control."

In case of implicit causality, verb and discourse domains are mixed, where causal expressions connect causative verbs with reasoning and explanations within the same sentence [26].

Patterns with Conditionals. Conditionals do not express causal relations explicitly, but they involve causal models in their evaluation. Conditionals, i.e. *If...then* constructs (or *When...then*), may form the so called *counterfactual* conditionals that are hard for NLP analysis [26]. Although the counterfactual conditionals may be used in expert systems [42], they are rear in the descriptions of system's functionality.

3.3 Automated Acquisition of Cause-Effect Relations

Causal Model. Using linguistic and lexical-syntactic patterns pairs of causes and effect are identified and then filtered using supplementing rules and regular expressions as well as ontology banks. The patterns, rules and regular expressions are created manually (at least at the beginning). Linguistic and syntactic patterns are based on means for explicit expressing causes and effects, e.g. causal links and causative verbs for linguistic patterns and verb phrases and noun phrases for syntactic patterns [27, 34, 38, 43–45]. Most of the existing techniques consider that an event represented within a sentence is represented by a single word (a nominal noun) skipping other semantically related words [39].

A comprehensive survey of automatic extraction of causal relations is presented by Asghar [33]. The author divided automatic methods into two groups. The first group employ pattern matching, while the second group uses statistical methods and machine learning (ML). According to Asghar survey, historically the first group started from small text fragments prepared manually and evolved till large text corpuses prepared by automatic processing [44]. At the present, this group uses NLP techniques to prepare cause-effect pairs (by using linguistic patterns) and then filtering them to reduce a number of non-causal pairs. Filtering takes into account such features as lexical features, semantics features (hyponyms and synonyms) and dependency features [33, 38, 46]. Evolution of the second group started from the early 2000s, when ML techniques first have been used to gain extracting cause-effect pairs. These techniques do not require a large set of manually predefined linguistic patterns. However, quality of learning depends on corpuses used for learning. In order to exclude non-causal pairs, a Bayesian inference can be applied [38, 46]. The potential of ML application for specialized domains is low due to a lack of sufficient amount of text corpuses for learning and testing a causal model. In such cases in order to exclude non-causal pairs a set of logical rules is used together with filtering.

Joint Temporal Causal Model. Joint usage of both the temporal reason model and the causal model that uses ML helps in dealing with counterfactual conditionals and increases accuracy of discovered cause-effect pairs.

Such models are presented by several authors [27, 34]. The temporal model discovers a temporal relation between two events. The temporal relation can be annotated as *before, after, include, is_included, vague* [27], and *simultaneous, begins/begun_by, ends/ended_by, during/during_inv, identity* [34]. Other authors [35] use another annotations, i.e., *before, meets, overlaps, finishes, starts, contain* and *equals.* Their model distinguishes between *a precondition* and *a cause.* The causal models of all the mentioned authors discover causal relations between events using linguistic patterns. The authors state that analysis of both relation types allows extracting cause-effect relations even if they lack explicit causal reason.

3.4   Pros and Cons

Explicitly Expressed Cause-effect Pairs. Discovering cause-effect pairs using linguistic and lexical-syntactic patterns for text processing has small cost of preparation of patterns and is domain-independent [27, 33, 38, 44, 46]. However, the result of discovering can be ambiguous. The use of patterns limits discovered types of cause-effect relation only to these patterns. In order to increase accuracy, a huge number of potential patterns is required.

Most of overviewed research papers is focused on analysis of explicitly expressed cause-effect relations by using causal links and causative verbs [33–35, 38, 43, 46]. However, few research papers pay their attention also to resultative constructions and causative prepositions [33, 38, 43, 46]. In other words, causal links, causative verbs and prepositions are more valuable for creation of linguistic/syntactic patterns for text processing. Causative adverbs and adjectives up to 2018 are not well studied comparing to the main studies on causative verbs, causal links and temporal aspects of events and propositions.

Although conditionals have the strict syntactical pattern *if-then*, accuracy of results of extracting conditionals is satisfactory only using ML techniques [33].

Extracting multiple causes and effects is a very domain-specific task; Therefore only few researches solve it directly [38, 46, 47].

Implicitly Expressed Cause-Effect Pairs. Discovering implicitly expressed cause-effect pairs requires a use of ontology banks and inferring elaborated using ML techniques. Cause-effect relations implicitly expressed by action verbs are analyzed in the same group of causative verbs. While automated analysis of counterfactual conditionals is a quite hard task and some results are presented just in a few papers [27, 42].

Increase of Accuracy. ML Techniques are used for increasing accuracy of extracting cause-effect pairs, but they are rather expensive. Filtering and statistical inferencing may be considered as a less expensive solution in comparison with ML techniques.

The patterns and propositions are limited to the manually predefined set and does not require large corpuses of text for learning. However, a use of explicit causal indicators in most cases leads to ignoring implicit causalities. Additionally, in case of ambiguous linguistic constructs semantic filtering based on verb's senses depends on a set of linguistical/semantic patterns [33, 38, 46], but statistical inferencing requires large datasets [33]. Ontology banks can also be used, but researchers use the WordNet in general. VerbNet, PropBank and FrameNet are used sparsely [33, 35, 41].

The more successful results are shown by hybrid solutions where patterns, temporal reasons, ML and ontologies are presented [27, 33–35]. The limitation of the hybrid solutions is a lack of enough text corpuses for learning.

4 Implicit and Explicit Cause-Effect Relation in Structured Descriptions for TFM Construction

TFM construction requires processing verbal descriptions of the modelled environment. The descriptions contain information on system functioning within and interacting with its environment. Sources of two types of knowledge can be processed for construction of the TFM. The first one is knowledge about a problem domain or system's processes and data. The second one is knowledge about required processes and data of a corresponding sub-system. Here system and sub-system can be such pairs like, for instance, an organization and its information system or an information system and a software product to be included in it. Requirements to the sub-system's processes and data are presented in a form of structured text such as requirements specifications, use case scenarios, user stories and features. Use case scenarios and user stories has more structured format that a plain text. Therefore, it is interesting to understand what benefits their structure gives since the main part of knowledge still is presented as plain text. Thus, discovering cause-effect relations from use case scenarios and user stories is discussed here.

4.1 Use Case Scenarios

Use case scenarios may have forms with different degrees of structuration. The less structured form is similar to the plain text with the only exception that it describes logical scenario or scenarios in a sequential manner. The more structured is a form with numbered steps. Usually, this form contains slots for a use case name, a purpose or short description, actors, preconditions, event flows, alternative event flows, postconditions and in some forms also a dependency from another use case [48, 49].

There are several mechanisms how cause-effect relations are expressed:

- A numbering (sequence) of steps,
- Keywords and predefined phrases for redirections and iterations,
- Dependency links,
- Discourse in plain text.

A numbering is the simplest way that allows indicating a sequence of events in the flow. Successful termination of each preceding step initiates its direct subsequent step. Thus, if each step represents just one event, then the current step is a cause of its direct followers, i.e. effects.

Redirections can be to the indicated step, to an alternative flow, from an alternative flow and to the subordinated use case. If it is necessary to indicate causal dependency to a numbered step, then some predefined phrases are used, e.g., "the use case continues at <flow> step <number>". However, if an alternative flow can be expressed in several sentences, then it does not contain numbered steps. It is expressed as a plain text within the same step. The only indicator here is a group's precondition. If an alternative flow is not structured, then analysis of sentences or discourse is required. Redirection from an alternative flow is used when a basic flow contains only the "correct" flow of events without any redirections. Then an indicator to the basic flow is in the point, where alternatives start, and is expressed by phrases like "In step <number>, <precondition>, <step/event>". Redirections to the subordinated use case usually make a use of phrases that contains a keyword "include" together with a use case name as a marker. An extending use case is invoked using its name as a marker indicating a precondition before the invocation. In order to indicate iterative sequences constructs *For each <element>... end loop* and *While <action/event>... end loop* or similar are used.

Dependency links are used when there is a need to indicate another independent use case. Here dependencies may be causal and non-causal, what can be inferred only by a developer or an expert.

The main pitfall related to use case scenarios is that a step can be represented as a discourse. Then, the same analysis of clauses and causal links (adverbial, prepositional, subordination and clause integrated) is required. This means that a set of linguistic/syntactic as well as semantic patterns must be predefined. For example, a step may contain such text, "The customer enters a number of the product to make an order". A clause "to make an order" acts as an adverb. But "making an order" is a separate event that must be analyzed whether it is a cause for the "entering" or it is just an explanatory statement. Moreover, accuracy of discovering causes and effect will be the same as in case of ordinary textual descriptions.

The conclusion is that structuration of use case scenarios solves the task just partially, and the completeness and accuracy of discovering cause-effect pairs is highly dependent on the using of short discourses in steps.

4.2 User Stories

User stories are another form of domain knowledge representation widely used in agile software development. They are represented by sentences that expresses what a user needs at the high level of abstraction [50]. There are many forms of a user story description, but the general form is like "As a [role] I want [feature or function] so that [value delivered to the business]" [51]. For instance, "As a Lecturer I want to add a lecture presentation to my course so that my students are able to download it or view online". Branches and sequences of different user stories may be presented in a story map by horizontal and vertical set of activities.

Looking at a user stories structure from the TFM construction perspective, one can identify functional characteristics that are presented by features/functions as well as within the value/benefit to the business. In case if they are single events, the former element is a cause, while the second element is an effect. However, some form for a free form description remains in the last two parts [52].

Researches on transforming user stories to other behavioral diagrams using NLP mostly are related to derivation of use cases. Generation of an UML use case diagram [50, 51] is based on identification of an actor as a nominal noun or a noun phrase, a use case name as a predicates of a verb phrase and a noun that are associated to the actor, and an association relationship derived from the link between the predicate and the actor. The percentage of correctly obtained use cases and their relationships is 85–87%.

Researchers working on transforming user stories to test cases [53] note that a user story can contain information similar to a use case scenario, namely, a story name, a description, an actor, preconditions, postconditions and conditions of satisfaction, i.e. a flow of events that constitute the correct execution of a feature/function. Here events can be processed from the precondition's, conditions' and postcondition's phrases/sentences. Moreover, relations between causes and effects is equal to the logical sequence of conditions. In order to simplify processing of sentences and phrases, several restrictions on language constructs are put on. Thanks to them the precision of NLP is more that 90%.

User story processing for creation of conceptual diagrams [52, 54] increases accuracy of identification of events, i.e. pairs of the main verb and the main object. Nevertheless, cause-effect pairs are not investigated there, causal relations can be potentially obtained from a story map and corresponding sub-stories.

Processing natural language in user stories may help in discovering events. However, cause-effect pairs here match the pattern "what-why". Other pairs may be obtained only by considering the whole story map and processing sequences in it.

4.3 Benefits and Weaknesses

Considering use case scenarios vs user stories as inputs sources for cause-effect pairs identification, it is clear that the both formats lack information for complete discovering of the pairs.

Use case scenarios contain all flows in one specification, explicitly indicating logical sequences and conditions. However, they lack cause-effect relations between independent use cases. Since they are independent as paths with branches but relationships between paths cannot be inferred from the available information.

A user story can be used for identification of a single cause-effect pair. Chains of causes and effects can be inferred only from a story map.

Therefore, from one side a part of cause-effect pairs can be discovered easier than from a plain text. However, both formats allow free text adding. The free text has a range from a phrase to a discourse. And here all the difficulties related to the NLP in text appears, especially in a use case scenario. In this case, the only effective solution is limitation of sentence structures and a size of the text.

5 Conclusions

Discovering and extracting cause-effects pairs is vital for correct identification and specification of system's functional characteristics and causal dependencies between them. Most of research papers investigate cases with one cause and one (or two) sequential effects. The TFM may have relationships between causal relations. Thus, multi causes and multi effects must be identified and extracted. However, there is just a few research papers presenting results on this, since this is a quite hard task.

Starting point for extracting cause-effect pairs is preparation of a corpus of linguistic/syntactic and sematic patterns as well as more thorough analysis of conditionals. However, main issue with a use of the patterns is that it is impossible to identify all patterns for all types of cause-effect relations. The expression means of the natural language differ more than any set of predefined rules, as well as the same pattern may be applied for both causal and non-causal relations. Moreover, pattern that include, for example, causal adverbs and adjectives are not well investigated. Accuracy of identification of the pairs can be increased by using ML techniques for training a causal model. However, a use of temporal models, filtering and ontology banks for creation of a set of the patterns seems more promising for specialized (or narrow) domains than a use of ML techniques.

The more prominent are hybrid solutions that use machine learning, ontology banks and statistics. However, a challenge is their unsuitability for specific domains due to a lack of an enough number of text corpuses for model training.

The two considered trends are controversial, since increasing of the accuracy by ML, ontologies and statistics is expensive, while a use of only the linguistic/syntactic patterns will always be unsatisfactory. The potential solution is limitation of the source documents types to the specifications (requirements, scenario, etc.) having less variability in expressing causality. However, it requires manual effort for text-preprocessing, what is likely to increase the cost of the development.

The future research direction is related to implementation of extracting causes and effects from the description of system functioning and forming a knowledge base of events and cause-effect pairs as well as finding a solution that would show acceptable accuracy of results and will not be expensive for narrow domains.

References

1. Miller, J., Mukerji, J.: Model driven architecture (MDA) (2001)
2. Khoo, C., Chan, S., Niu, Y.: The many facets of the cause-effect relation. In: Green, R., Bean, C.A., Myaeng, S.H. (eds.) The Semantics of Relationships. ISKM, vol. 3, pp. 51–70. Springer, Dordrecht (2002). https://doi.org/10.1007/978-94-017-0073-3_4
3. Nazaruka, E.: Meaning of cause-and-effect relations of the topological functioning model in the UML analysis model. In: Proceedings of the 12th International Conference on Evaluation of Novel Approaches to Software Engineering, pp. 336–345. SciTePress - Science and Technology Publications (2017)
4. Kardoš, M., Drozdová, M.: Analytical method of CIM to PIM transformation in model driven architecture (MDA). J. Inf. Organ. Sci. **34**, 89–99 (2010)

5. Kriouile, A., Gadi, T., Balouki, Y.: CIM to PIM transformation: a criteria based evaluation. Int. J. Comput. Technol. Appl. **4**, 616–625 (2013)
6. Kriouile, A., Addamssiri, N., Gadi, T., Balouki, Y.: Getting the static model of PIM from the CIM. In: 2014 Third IEEE International Colloquium in Information Science and Technology (CIST), pp. 168–173. IEEE, Tetouan (2014)
7. Kriouile, A., Addamssiri, N., Gadi, T.: An MDA method for automatic transformation of models from CIM to PIM. Am. J. Softw. Eng. Appl. **4**, 1–14 (2015). https://doi.org/10.11648/j.ajsea.20150401.11
8. Bousetta, B., El Beggar, O., Gadi, T.: A methodology for CIM modelling and its transformation to PIM. J. Inf. Eng. Appl. **3**, 1–21 (2013)
9. Rhazali, Y., Hadi, Y., Mouloudi, A.: CIM to PIM transformation in MDA: from service-oriented business models to web-based design models. Int. J. Softw. Eng. Appl. **10**, 125–142 (2016). https://doi.org/10.14257/ijseia.2016.10.4.13
10. Essebaa, I., Chantit, S.: Toward an automatic approach to get PIM level from CIM level using QVT rules. In: 2016 11th International Conference on Intelligent Systems: Theories and Applications (SITA), pp. 1–6. IEEE, Mohammedia (2016)
11. Osis, J., Donins, U.: Topological UML Modeling: An Improved Approach for Domain Modeling and Software Development. Elsevier, Amsterdam (2017)
12. Osis, J.: Topological model of system functioning. Autom. Comput. Sci. J. Acad. Sci. **6**, 44–50 (1969). (in Russian)
13. Osis, J., Asnina, E., Grave, A.: Formal computation independent model of the problem domain within the MDA. In: Zendulka, J. (ed.) Proceedings of the 10th International Conference on Information System Implementation and Modeling, Hradec nad Moravicí, Czech Republic, 23–25 April 2007, pp. 47–54. Jan Stefan MARQ (2007)
14. Osis, J., Asnina, E.: Topological modeling for model-driven domain analysis and software development : functions and architectures. In: Model-Driven Domain Analysis and Software Development: Architectures and Functions, pp. 15–39. IGI Global, Hershey (2011)
15. Osis, J., Slihte, A.: Transforming textual use cases to a computation independent model. In: Osis, J., Nikiforova, O. (eds.) Model-Driven Architecture and Modeling-Driven Software Development: ENASE 2010, 2nd MDA&MTDD Whs., pp. 33–42. SciTePress (2010)
16. Slihte, A., Osis, J., Donins, U.: Knowledge integration for domain modeling. In: Osis, J., Nikiforova, O. (eds.) Model-Driven Architecture and Modeling-Driven Software Development: ENASE 2011, 3rd MDA&MDSD Whs., pp. 46–56. SciTePress (2011)
17. Elstermann, M., Heuser, T.: Automatic tool support possibilities for the text-based S-BPM process modelling methodology. In: Proceedings of the 8th International Conference on Subject-Oriented Business Process Management, S-BPM 2016, pp. 1–8. ACM Press, New York (2016)
18. Nazaruka, E.: Identification of causal dependencies by using natural language processing: a survey. In: Damian, E., Spanoudakis, G., Maciaszek, L. (eds.) Proceedings of the 14th International Conference on Evaluation of Novel Approaches to Software Engineering - Volume 1: MDI4SE, pp. 603–613. SciTePress (2019)
19. Osis, J., Asnina, E.: Is modeling a treatment for the weakness of software engineering? In: Model-Driven Domain Analysis and Software Development, pp. 1–14. IGI Global, Hershey (2011)
20. Asnina, E.: The computation independent viewpoint: a formal method of topological functioning model constructing. Appl. Comput. Syst. **26**, 21–32 (2006)
21. Osis, J., Asnina, E., Grave, A.: MDA oriented computation independent modeling of the problem domain. In: Proceedings of the 2nd International Conference on Evaluation of Novel Approaches to Software Engineering, ENASE 2007, pp. 66–71. INSTICC Press, Barcelona (2007)

22. Osis, J., Asnina, E., Grave, A.: Formal problem domain modeling within MDA. In: Filipe, J., Shishkov, B., Helfert, M., Maciaszek, L.A. (eds.) ENASE/ICSOFT -2007. CCIS, vol. 22, pp. 387–398. Springer, Heidelberg (2008). https://doi.org/10.1007/978-3-540-88655-6_29

23. Šlihte, A., Osis, J.: The integrated domain modeling: a case study. In: Proceedings of the 11th International Baltic Conference on Databases and Information Systems (DB&IS 2014), pp, 465–470. Tallinn University of Technology Press, Tallinn (2014)

24. Asnina, E., Ovchinnikova, V.: Specification of decision-making and control flow branching in topological functioning models of systems. In: International Conference on Evaluation of Novel Approaches to Software Engineering (ENASE 2015), pp. 364–373. SciTePress, Barcelona (2015)

25. Khoo, C., Chan, S., Niu, Y., Ang, A.: A method for extracting causal knowledge from textual databases. Singap. J. Libr. & Inf. Manag. **28**, 48–63 (1999)

26. Solstad, T., Bott, O.: Causality and causal reasoning in natural language. In: Waldmann, M. R. (ed.) The Oxford Handbook of Causal Reasoning. Oxford University Press, Oxford (2017)

27. Ning, Q., Feng, Z., Wu, H., Roth, D.: Joint reasoning for temporal and causal relations. In: Proceedings of the 56th Annual Meeting of the Association for Computational Linguistics (Long Papers), pp. 2278–2288. Association for Computational Linguistics, Melbourne (2018)

28. Altenberg, B.: Causal linking in spoken and written English. Stud. Linguist. **38**, 20–69 (1984)

29. Girju, R.: Automatic detection of causal relations for question answering. In: Proceedings of the ACL 2003 Workshop on Multilingual Summarization and Question Answering, pp. 76–83. Association for Computational Linguistics, Morristown (2003)

30. Corrigan, R.: Causal attributions to the states and events encoded by different types of verbs. Br. J. Soc. Psychol. **32**, 335–348 (1993)

31. Corrigan, R., Stevenson, C.: Children's causal attribution to states and events described by different classes of verbs. Cogn. Dev. **9**, 235–256 (1994)

32. Waldmann, M.R., Hagmayer, Y.: Causal reasoning. In: Reisberg, D. (ed.) Oxford Handbook of Cognitive Psychology. Oxford University Press, New York (2013)

33. Asghar, N.: Automatic extraction of causal relations from natural language texts : a comprehensive survey. CoRR abs/1605.0 (2016)

34. Mirza, P.: Extracting temporal and causal relations between events. In: Proceedings of the ACL 2014 Student Research Workshop, pp. 10–17. Association for Computational Linguistics, Baltimore (2014)

35. Mostafazadeh, N., Grealish, A., Chambers, N., Allen, J., Vanderwende, L.: CaTeRS : causal and temporal relation scheme for semantic annotation of event structures. In: Proceedings of the Fourth Workshop on Events, pp. 51–61. Association for Computational Linguistics, San Diego (2016)

36. Khoo, C.S.G., Kornfilt, J., Oddy, R.N., Myaeng, S.H.: Automatic extraction of cause-effect information from newspaper text without knowledge-based inferencing. Lit. Linguist. Comput. **13**, 177–186 (1998)

37. Hendrickx, I., et al.: SemEval-2010 task 8: multi-way classification of semantic relations between pairs of nominals. In: Proceedings of the 5th International Workshop on Semantic Evaluation, ACL 2010, Uppsala, Sweden, 15–16 July 2010, pp. 33–38. Association for Computational Linguistics (2010)

38. Sorgente, A., Vettigli, G., Mele, F.: Automatic extraction of cause-effect relations in natural language text. In: Lai, C., Semeraro, G., Giuliani, A. (eds.) Proceedings of the 7th International Workshop on Information Filtering and Retrieval Co-Located with the 13th

Conference of the Italian Association for Artificial Intelligence (AI*IA 2013), pp. 37–48 (2013)

39. Dasgupta, T., Saha, R., Dey, L., Naskar, A.: Automatic extraction of causal relations from text using linguistically informed deep neural networks. In: Proceedings of the 19th Annual SIGdial Meeting on Discourse and Dialogue, pp. 306–316. Association for Computational Linguistics, Stroudsburg (2018)

40. Mausam, Schmitz, M., Bart, R., Soderland, S., Etzioni, O.: Open language learning for information extraction. In: Proceedings of the 2012 Joint Conference on Empirical Methods in Natural Language Processing and Computational Natural Language Learning, pp. 523–534. Association for Computational Linguistics (2012)

41. Kang, D., Gangal, V., Lu, A., Chen, Z., Hovy, E.: Detecting and explaining causes from text for a time series event. In: Proceedings of the 2017 Conference on Empirical Methods in Natural Language Processing, pp. 2758–2768. The Association for Computational Linguistics (2017)

42. Pearl, J.: The seven tools of causal inference, with reflections on machine learning. Commun. Assoc. Comput. Mach. **62**, 54–60 (2019). https://doi.org/10.1145/3241036

43. Blanco, E., Castell, N., Moldovan, D.: Causal relation extraction. In: Proceedings of the Sixth International Conference on Language Resources and Evaluation (LREC 2008), pp. 28–30. European Language Resources Association (ELRA) (2008)

44. Blass, J.A., Forbus, K.D.: Natural language instruction for analogical reasoning : an initial report. In: Workshops Proceedings for the Twenty-Fourth International Conference on Case-Based Reasoning (ICCBR 2016), pp. 21–30 (2016)

45. Cao, M., Sun, X., Zhuge, H.: The contribution of cause-effect link to representing the core of scientific paper—the role of Semantic Link Network. PLoS ONE **13**, 1–14 (2018). https://doi.org/10.1371/journal.pone.0199303

46. Sorgente, A., Vettigli, G., Mele, F.: A hybrid approach for the automatic extraction of causal relations from text. In: Lai, C., Giuliani, A., Semeraro, G. (eds.) Emerging Ideas on Information Filtering and Retrieval. SCI, vol. 746, pp. 15–29. Springer, Cham (2018). https://doi.org/10.1007/978-3-319-68392-8_2

47. Mueller, R., Hüttemann, S.: Extracting causal claims from information systems papers with natural language processing for theory ontology learning. In: Proceedings of the 51st Hawaii International Conference on System Sciences (HICSS). IEEE Computer Society Press, Hawaii (2018)

48. Schneider, G., Winters, J.P.: Applying Use Cases: A practical Guide, 2nd edn. Pearson Education Inc., London (2001)

49. Leffingwell, D., Widrig, D.: Managing Software Requirements: A Use Case Approach, 2nd edn. Addison-Wesley, Boston (2003)

50. Elallaoui, M., Nafil, K., Touahni, R.: Automatic transformation of user stories into UML use case diagrams using NLP techniques. Procedia Comput. Sci. **130**, 42–49 (2018). https://doi.org/10.1016/j.procs.2018.04.010

51. Azzazi, A.: A framework using NLP to automatically convert user-stories into use cases in software projects. Int. J. Comput. Sci. Netw. Secur. (IJCSNS) **17**, 71–76 (2017)

52. Lucassen, G., Robeer, M., Dalpiaz, F., van der Werf, J.M.E.M., Brinkkemper, S.: Extracting conceptual models from user stories with Visual Narrator. Requir. Eng. **22**, 339–358 (2017). https://doi.org/10.1007/s00766-017-0270-1

53. Masud, M., Iqbal, M., Khan, M.U., Azam, F.: Automated user story driven approach for web-based functional testing. Int. J. Comput. Inf. Eng. **11**, 91–98 (2017)

54. Robeer, M., Lucassen, G., van der Werf, J.M.E.M., Dalpiaz, F., Brinkkemper, S.: Automated extraction of conceptual models from user stories via NLP. In: 2016 IEEE 24th International Requirements Engineering Conference (RE), pp. 196–205. IEEE (2016)

From Requirements to Automated Acceptance Tests with the RSL Language

Ana C. R. Paiva[1,2(✉)], Daniel Maciel[1], and Alberto Rodrigues da Silva[3]

[1] Faculdade de Engenharia da Universidade do Porto,
Rua Dr. Roberto Frias, s/n, 4200-465 Porto, Portugal
apaiva@fe.up.pt
[2] INESC TEC, Rua Dr. Roberto Frias, s/n, 4200-465 Porto, Portugal
daniel.ademar.maciel@gmail.com
[3] INESC-ID, Instituto Superior Técnico, Universidade de Lisboa, Lisbon, Portugal
alberto.silva@tecnico.ulisboa.pt

Abstract. Software testing can promote software quality. However, this activity is often performed at the end of projects where failures are most difficult to correct. Combining requirements specification activities with test design at an early stage of the software development process can be beneficial. One way to do this is to use a more structured requirements specification language. This allow to reduce typical problems such as ambiguity, inconsistency, and incorrectness in requirements and may allow the automatic generation of (parts of) acceptance test cases reducing the test design effort. In this paper we discuss an approach that promotes the practice of requirements specification combined with testing specification. This is a model-based approach that promotes the alignment between requirements and tests, namely, test cases and also low-level automated test scripts. To show the applicability of this approach, we integrate two complementary languages: (i) the ITLingo RSL (Requirements Specification Language) that is specially designed to support both requirements and tests rigorously and consistently specified; and (ii) the Robot language, which is a low-level keyword-based language for specifying test scripts. This approach includes model-to-model transformation processes, namely a transformation process from requirements (defined in RSL) into test cases (defined in RSL), and a second transformation process from test cases (in RSL) into test scripts (defined according the Robot framework). This approach was applied in a fictitious online store that illustrates the various phases of the proposal.

Keywords: Requirements Specification Language (RSL) · Test case specification · Model-based Testing (MBT) · Test case generation · Test case execution

1 Introduction

Software systems are becoming increasingly complex and operating on more critical systems. This reality makes it more urgent to run software tests that promote the quality of these systems. One aspect of software quality is its ability to meet the implicit and

© Springer Nature Switzerland AG 2020
E. Damiani et al. (Eds.): ENASE 2019, CCIS 1172, pp. 39–57, 2020.
https://doi.org/10.1007/978-3-030-40223-5_3

explicit needs of customers. For this, it is important to reach a common understanding between clients and developers about what should be developed.

Requirements Engineering (RE) helps to create the basis of understanding between stakeholders and programmers about the software system to develop. The resulting system requirements specification (SRS) document helps to structure the view on the software system and allows [1–4] to agree between users and developers on the validation and verification support of the scope of the project and support future system maintenance activities. The problem is that the manual effort required to produce requirements specifications is high and suffers from problems such as incorrectness, inconsistency, incompleteness and ambiguity [2, 3, 6].

ITLingo is a long-term initiative aimed at researching, developing and applying rigorous IT specification languages, i.e., Requirements Engineering, Test Engineering and Project Management [22]. ITLingo takes a linguistic approach to improve the accuracy of technical documentation (e.g., SRS, test case specification, project plans) and, as a consequence, promote productivity through reuse and model transformations as well as promote systems quality through semi-automatic validation techniques.

Requirements Specification Language (RSL) is a controlled and integrated natural language with ITLingo that assists in the production of requirements specifications in a systematic, rigorous and consistent manner [5]. RSL includes an advanced set of constructs that are logically organized into views according to specific RE concerns at different levels of abstraction, such as business, applications, software, or even hardware levels.

Software testing can also be useful as a measure for assessing the software development process by measuring the number of tests that pass or fail and conducting regression tests to foster product quality by alerting developers to potential defects as soon as code is changed.

Acceptance tests are those that are most closely related to requirements as they reflect what the end user considers important to test (needs, requirements and business processes) to accept or not the software that is being developed [25].

To reduce the time and resources required, it may be helpful to perform acceptance test design and specification requirements in parallel [11]. Although it is considered a good practice to start testing activities at the beginning of the project when requirements are elicited, this does not always happen because elicitation and requirements testing are separate in traditional development processes. This research paper presents an approach based on the Model-Based Testing (MBT) technique [25] that aims to foster the initiation of testing activities early in line with the requirements specification. MBT is a software testing approach that generates test cases from abstract representations of the system, named models, either graphical (e.g., Workflow models [16], PBGT [19,20]) or textual (e.g., requirements documents in an intermediate format) [24].

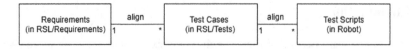

Fig. 1. Key structural concepts [28].

The process (Fig. 1) starts by producing RSL *Requirements* specifications based on the set of constructs provided by the language and according to different perspectives and concerns. From those *Requirements*, it is possible to generate RSL *Test Cases* specifications, and from these, to generate *Test Scripts*. Finally, those test scripts can be automatically executed by the Robot Test Automation Tool[1] in the application under test.

This paper extends [28] in the following aspects:

- It extends Sect. "2.2 – Tests Specification" by detailing the grammar of RSL in what concerns the following constructs: $UseCaseTest$, $TestScenario$, $TestStep$, $TestOperation$ and $TestCheck$.
- It adds new figures: one to illustrate the RSL/Tests Extension and another to illustrate the Mapping process between GUI elements and keywords.
- It restructures Sect. 4 by splitting it into two sections: Sect. 4 to describe the overall approach; Sect. 5 called "5 - Illustrative Example" where it illustrates, in more detail, the applicability of the overall approach over a fictitious online store developed to practice and validate the test automation.
- It extends the state of the art.

This paper is organized in 7 sections. Section 2 overviews the RSL language, showing its architecture, levels of abstraction, concerns and grammar. Section 3 introduces the concepts of the selected test automation tool, the Robot Framework. Section 4 presents the proposal approach with a running and illustrative example. Section 5 presents a case study illustrating the overall approach. Section 6 identifies and analyzes related work. Finally, Sect. 7 presents the conclusion and future work.

2   RSL Language

ITLingo research initiative intends to develop and apply rigorous specification languages for the IT domain, such as requirements engineering and testing engineering, with the RSL (Requirements Specification Language) [7–10,17,18]. RSL provides a vast set of logically organized constructs in views that describe different concerns. These constructs are defined by *linguistic patterns* which are represented textually according to concrete *linguistic styles* [5]. RSL can be used and adapted by different organizations because it is a process and tool independent language [5,22]. The constructs used by RSL can be classified according to two perspectives [22]: concerns and abstraction levels. The concerns are: active structure (subjects), behaviour (actions), passive structure (objects), requirements, tests, other concerns, relations and sets. The abstraction levels are: business, application, software and hardware levels. This paper focuses the discussion on the requirements and tests concerns and, in particular, focuses on the RSL constructs particularly supportive of use case approaches (e.g. actors, use cases, data entities and involved relationships) as it is further discussed in [22].

---

[1] http://robotframework.org/.

2.1   Requirements Specification

Figure 2 shows a part of the RSL metamodel. It defines the hierarchy established among requirement types, namely: goal, functional requirement, constraint, use case, user story and quality requirement. This paper focuses only on the discussion of *UseCase* requirement and test types.

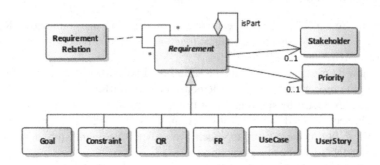

Fig. 2. RSL partial metamodel: the hierarchy of requirements [28].

RSL specifications based on *Use Cases* may involve defining some views with their inherent constructs and relationships, namely:

- *DataEntity view*: defines the structural entities within an information system, commonly associated with data concepts captured and identified from domain analysis. A *Data Entity* denotes an individual structural entity that may include specifying attributes, foreign keys, and other verification data constraints;
- *DataEntityCluster view*: denotes a cluster of various structural entities that have a logical arrangement with each other;
- *Actor view*: defines the participants of *Use Cases* or *user stories*. They represent end users and external systems that interact directly with the system under study and, in some particular situations, may represent timers or events that trigger the start of some *Use Cases*;
- *Use Case view*: defines the *use cases* of a system under study. Traditionally, a *use case* means a sequence of actions that one or more actors perform on a system to achieve a specific outcome [12].

2.2   Tests Specification

RSL supports Test Cases specification and generation directly from the requirements specifications. As shown in Fig. 3, RSL provides an hierarchy of Test constructs that supports specifying the following test case specializations [22]:

- *DataEntityTest* are obtained from equivalence class partitioning and boundary value analysis techniques applied over the domains defined for the *DataEntities* [23] in RSL *DataEntities*;

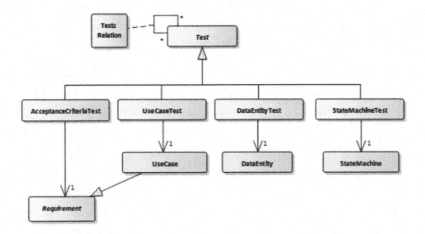

Fig. 3. RSL partial metamodel: the hierarchy of Tests [28].

- *UseCaseTest* explores different sequences of steps defined in RSL *use cases*' scenarios, and associates data values to the involved *DataEntities*;
- *StateMachineTest* applies different algorithms to traverse RSL state machines so that different test cases can be defined that correspond to valid or invalid paths through their state machine;
- *AcceptanceCriteriaTest* defines acceptance criteria based on two distinct approaches: scenario based (i.e., based on the Given-When-Then pattern) or rule based; this test case is applied generically to any type of RSL Requirement.

Regardless of these specializations, a Test shall be set to Valid or Invalid depending on the intended situation. In addition, it is possible to establish relationships with other test cases through *TestsRelation*; these relationships can be classified as *Requires*, *Supports*, *Obstructs*, *Conflicts*, *Identical*, and *Relates*.

With respect to the different RSL Test constructs described, *UseCaseTests* best fit the acceptance test. Figure 4 shows the structure and relationships of *UseCaseTests*. A *UseCaseTest* (Listing 1.1) inherits *UseCase* data associated with it, including *Actors*. Optionally, it is possible to add variables for testing purposes as well.

An *UseCaseTest* may have different *TestScenarios* (Listing 1.2). Each scenario must have, at least, one *TestStep* and, if necessary, values assigned to *DataEntities* and *Variables*. Since *DataEntities* are entities of the Application Under Test, it may be useful to create instances of these entities and assign them values that may be used later in test cases.

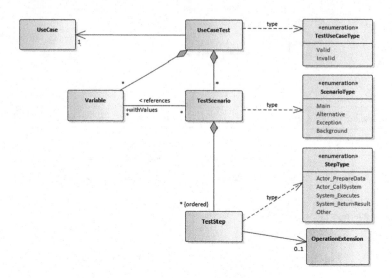

Fig. 4. RSL/tests extension.

Listing 1.1. UseCaseTest RSL grammar [31].

```
UseCaseTest:
'UseCaseTest' name=ID (nameAlias=STRING)? ':' type=TestType ('['
'useCase' useCase=[UseCase | QualifiedName]
('actorInitiates' actorInitiates=[Actor | QualifiedName] )
('actorParticipates' actorParticipates+=RefActor)?
('background' background=[UseCaseTest | QualifiedName] )?
(variables+=TestVariable)*
(scenarios+=TestScenario)*
(tags+=Tag)*
('description' description=STRING)?
']')?;
```

Variables are temporary data that may be exchanged among *TestSteps*, e.g., a variable may be used to save text needed to validate the dynamic content on the GUI.

Listing 1.2. TestScenario RSL grammar [31].

```
TestScenario:
'testScenario' name=ID (nameAlias=STRING)? ':' type=ScenarioType ('['
((isConcrete ?= 'isConcrete') | (isAbstract ?= 'isAbstract'))?
('variable' variable= [TestVariable | QualifiedName] ('withValues' '('
variableTable= DataVariableValues ')'))?
('dataEntity' entity= [DataEntity | QualifiedName] ('withValues' '(' entityTable=
DataAttributeValues ')'))?
('executionMode' mode=('Sequential'|'Parallel'))?
('description' description=STRING)?
testSteps+= TestStep+
']')?;
```

The *TestStep* (Listing 1.3) is classified by a *StepOperationType* and, optionally, by a *StepOperationSubType*. The operation types are used to define the action that are performed in each step.

Listing 1.3. TestStep RSL grammar [31].

```
TestStep:
'step' name=ID ':' type=StepOperationType (':' extension=OperationExtension)? ('['
(simpleTestStep= SimpleTestStep );

OperationExtension:
(subType=StepOperationSubType)
((target=TestOperationTarget)|(check=TestCheck))?;

enum StepOperationType: Actor_PrepareData | Actor_CallSystem | System_Execute | System_ReturnResult | Other |
    None;
enum StepOperationSubType: OpenBrowser | CloseBrowser | Reload | GetData | PostData | Select | Click | Over |
    Check | Other;
```

There are four general types of operations performed in *TestSteps* [30]:

- *Actor_PrepareData*: input data will be entered by the actor, such as text, passwords or even choose a file to upload;
- *Actor_CallSystem*: actions performed by the actor in the application, e.g., click a button, select checkbox;
- *System_ReturnResult*: collect application data to be stored in temporary variables. This is usually helpful to perform some type of verification;
- *System_Execute*: actions executed by the system, e.g., open the browser and validations.

The *StepOperationSubTypes* are an extension of the previous types specifying the operations performed. These sub types are [31]:

- *Open/CloseBrowser*: action to open/close the browser;
- *Reload*: action to reload the browser page;
- *GetData*: action to collect specific data from the AUT;
- *PostData*: action to post specific data to the AUT;
- *Select/Click/Over*: to specify the action to be performed in an AUT element;
- *Check*: action to verify some AUT content or response; Each step operation must have a target (*TestOperationTarget*) or a verification (*TestCheck*) depending on the action associated (Listing 1.4).

If the action is an interaction with a GUI element, the *TestOperationTarget* (Listing 1.4) will specify that element through the *OperationTargetType*. It can be a button, a generic element, a checkbox or a list. Additionally, the *OperationTargetType* may also be used to clarify if such element is used to "write to" or to "read from". Finally, the *TestOperationTarget* can also have a description that is sent as a parameter through a variable value or a string.

Listing 1.4. TestOperation and TestCheck RSL grammar [31].

```
TestOperationTarget:
(type=OperationTargetType)
((variable+=[DataAttribute | QualifiedName] (','variable+=[DataAttribute |
QualifiedName] )*)|
('(' content+=(STRING) (','content+=STRING)* ')'))?;
enum OperationTargetType : button | element | checkbox | listByValue | readFrom |
writeTo;


TestCheck:
(type=CheckType) ('('
(variable=[DataAttribute | QualifiedName] '=' expected=[DataAttribute |
QualifiedName])?
('text' (textVariable=[DataAttribute | QualifiedName]| textString=STRING))?
('timeout' (timeoutVariable=[DataAttribute | QualifiedName]| timeoutINT=
DoubleOrInt) metric=Metric?)?
('limit' (limitVariable=[DataAttribute | QualifiedName]| limitINT=INT))?
('url' (urlVariable=[DataAttribute | QualifiedName]| urlString=STRING))?
('code' (codeVariable=[DataAttribute | QualifiedName]| codeString=STRING))?
')');
enum CheckType: textOnScreen | textOnElement | elementOnScreen | responseTime | variableValue | script | screen |
    Other | None;
```

The *TestCheck* defines the validation to perform in the step where it was specified. There are seven types of validations (*CheckTypes*) and each of them has different parameters. Table 1 shows the set of validations available. Each *TestScenario* must end with a *TestStep* that has a *TestCheck*. If the check succeeds the test passes. If the check does not succeed, the test fails.

Table 1. Test step validations [31].

CheckType	Parameter	Validation
textOnScreen	text	checks if a specific text is presented in the GUI
textOnElement	text	checks if a specific text is presented in a specific element of the GUI
elementOnScreen	limit?	checks if a specific element is presented in the GUI. If a limit is sent as parameter checks if a specific element appears less than the limit established
responseTime	timeout	checks if the response time is less or equal than the given timeout
variableValue	variable	checks if a variable value is equal to the expected value
	expected	
screen	URL	checks if the page represents the given URL
script	Code	uses a custom script to validate an unusual case

3   Robot Framework

Test cases can be run manually by the tester or automatically by a test automation tool. When a test case is run manually, the tester must execute all test cases and have to repeat the same tests several times throughout the product life cycle. On the other hand, when test cases are run automatically, there is the initial effort to develop test scripts, but from there, the execution process will be automatic. Therefore, if a test case is to be run multiple times, the automation effort will be less than the effort of frequent manual execution.

The Robot framework stands out for its powerful keyword-based language, which includes out-of-the-box libraries. The robot does not require any implementation as it is possible to use keywords with implicit implementations (using specific libraries such as Selenium[2]). Robot is open source and related to acceptance test-driven development (ATDD) [27]. It is operating system independent and is implemented natively in Python and Java, and can be run on Jython (JVM) or IronPython (.NET).

The structure of the script is simple and can be divided into four sections. The first section, *Settings*, where the paths to helper files and libraries used are set. The second section, *Variables*, specifies the list of variables used as well as the associated values. The third and most important section is the *Test Cases*, where test cases are defined. Finally, the *Keywords* section defines custom keywords to implement the test cases described in the Test Cases section. Among all four sections, only *Test Cases* is mandatory.

As seen in the example shown in Listing 1.5, the libraries used are initially defined. One of the most widely used is the Selenium library, which introduces keywords related to interactive application testing, such as 'Open Browser' and 'Input text'. The variables section assigns 'Blouse' to the variable 'product' so whenever 'product' is used it has the value 'Blouse'. The Keywords section defines keywords and their parameters. In test cases that use keywords, the values are assigned to the corresponding parameters, placing the values in the same place where the parameters are set.

Listing 1.5. Robot Framework specification example [28].

```
*** Settings ***
Documentation  Web Store Acceptance Test
Library  Selenium2Library

*** Variables ***
${product}  Blouse

*** Test Cases ***
Login
  Open the browser on <www.http://automationpractice.com>
  Input Text id=searchBar ${product}
  ...

*** Keywords ***
Open the browser on <$(url)>
    Open Browser $(url)
```

4 Proposed Approach

Although it is considered a good practice to start testing activities early in the project, this is not frequently the common situation due to the traditional separation between the requirements and testing phases. This research intends to reduce this problem through a

---

[2] www.seleniumhq.org/.

framework that encourages and supports both requirements and tests practices, namely by generating test cases from requirements or, at least, foster the alignment of such test cases with requirements. The proposed approach (defined in Fig. 5) begins with the (1) requirements specification that serves as a basis for the (2) test cases specification, which can be further (3) refined by the tester. Then, (4) tests scripts are generated automatically from the high-level test cases, and (5) associated the Graphical User Interface (GUI) elements. Finally, (6) these test scripts are executed generating a test report.

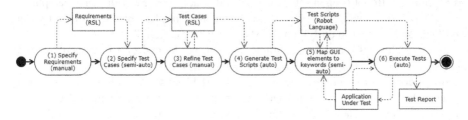

Fig. 5. Proposed approach (UML activity diagram) [31].

This set of tasks covers the process of acceptance tests in interactive applications from the specification of requirements to the execution of tests. Applying the approach will establish an alignment between the specification of requirements and the specification of tests, in addition to increasing the processes automation. Besides the use and extension of the RSL grammar, the approach also uses support tools such as the Robot framework and Web Scrapper.

4.1 Specify Requirements

The first task of this approach is the requirements definition, an activity that usually involves the intervention of requirements engineers, stakeholders and eventually testers. After reaching a consensus, the specification of the requirements in RSL follows, through the constructs provided by the language that most fit the requirements domain. In this approach, the specification focuses on the most relevant RSL constructs at the application and software level, namely: $Actor$, $UseCase$, $DataEntity$ and involved relationships. This task is usually performed by business analysts or by requirement engineers.

4.2 Specify Test Cases

$UseCaseTests$ are derived from the various process flows expressed by a RSL $UseCase$. Each test contains multiple test scenarios which encompasses of a group of test steps. From the requirement specifications, it is possible to specify test cases. $UseCaseTest$ construct begins by defining the test set, including ID, $name$ and the $usecasetype$. Then it encompasses the references keys $[UseCase]$ indicating the Use Case in which the test is proceeding and $[DataEntity]$ referring to a possible data entity that is managed.

In the $UseCaseTest$ specification, the respective $UseCase$ and $DataEntities$ specifications are associated, temporary variables are initialized, the $TestScenarios$

are specified where values are assigned to the variables and *TestSteps* are inserted which contain the necessary information for the test scripts.

4.3 Refine Test Cases

Generated test cases may be refined manually (e.g., assign values to entities and create temporary variables), which results in other test cases.

The information introduced in the requirements specification phase and the RSL constructs allow to simplify the test cases construction.

The *DataEntities* and the temporary *Variables* are fundamental for transmitting data between the *TestSteps* involved in the test and are defined within *TestScenarios*.

The values of *DataEntities* and *Variables* may be defined in table. By using this table structure, when an attribute is associated with N values, the test scenario may be executed N times (one time for each value in the table).

4.4 Generate Test Scripts

Once the specification is complete, the generation of the test scripts for the Robot tool follows. This generation process is based on relations established between the RSL specification and the syntax of the Robot framework. An association of the RSL concepts with the Robot framework syntax and some of the keywords made available by the Selenium library are shown in Table 2.

Table 2. Mapping between test case (RSL) and test scripts (Robot) [28].

Step type	Operation extension type	Operation extension	Keyword generated
Actor_PrepareData	Input	readFrom	INPUT TEXT $locator $variable
Actor_CallSystem	Select	checkbox	SELECT CHECKBOX $locator
		list by value	SELECT FROM LIST BY VALUE $locator $value
	Click	button	CLICK BUTTON $locator
		element	CLICK ELEMENT $locator
	Over	–	MOUSE OVER $locator
System_ReturnResult	GetData	writeTo	$variable GET TEXT $locator
System_Execute	OpenBrowser	–	OPEN BROWSER $url
	CloseBrowser	–	CLOSE BROSER
	PostData	readFrom	INPUT TEXT $locator $variable
	Check	textOnPage	PAGE SHOULD CONTAIN $text
		elementOnPage	PAGE SHOULD CONTAIN ELEMENT $locator $msg? $limit?
		textOnElement	ELEMENT SHOULD CONTAIN $locator $text
		responseTime	WAIT UNTIL PAGE CONTAIN ELEMENT $locator $timeout?
		variableValue	$variable = $expected
		jScript	EXECUTE JAVASCRIPT $code

4.5   Map GUI Elements to Keywords

At this phase of the process, there is the need to complete the test scripts generated previously with the locators [26], i.e. queries that return a single GUI element which are used to locate the target GUI elements (e.g., GUI element identifier, xpath, CSS selector).

This mapping can be established by the user inserting directly the identifiers of the UI elements in the test script, or by using a 'point and click' process (similar to the one presented in [21]). In this last option Table 2, the user accesses the AUT and, with the help of the Web Scrapper, points to the desired elements.

The Web Scrapper saves the locators (unique CSS selector) and exports this information to JSON code. Then, the tester can execute the Mapping script that creates a XML file with the relation between locators found and the ones missing from the Robot test script generated previously. For this process to succeed, it is important to maintain consistency between the descriptions of the elements in both Web Scrapper and test case specification. Finally, the tester may execute the Replacement Script that completes the Robot Script with the locators based on the data provided in the XML file.

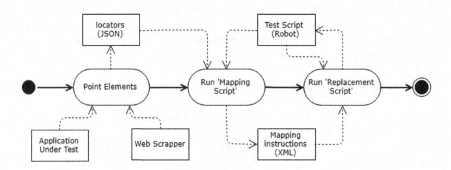

Fig. 6. Map GUI Elements to keywords (UML activity diagram) [31].

4.6   Execute Tests

The generated test script is executed by using the Robot framework. For that, the user should use, at the command prompt, following command:

$robot[script\_name].robot$

During execution, a browser instance will open performing automatically every steps specified in the test script while showing the results of each test case at the command prompt.

5   Illustrative Example

In order to illustrate and discuss the suitability of the proposed approach, we show its application with an interactive web application as the application under test (AUT). We selected the "Web Store"[3] app: This is a popular e-commerce web site developed on purpose to practice test automation. It simulates common online shopping workflows. Figure 7 shows the home page of this online store.

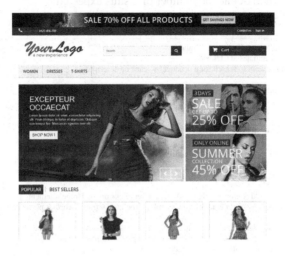

Fig. 7. Web Store application - Search Product [31].

We consider the use case "Search Product" because it is a simple and illustrative example. In this use case, the user searches for a product by its name and the number of items matched must be equal to the expected one defined in the respective test case.

After the requirements specification, that is partially shown in Listing 1.6, it follows the definition of test cases, where the relationships between the (use case) requirement and the (use case) tests are kept. A *UseCaseTest* is generated or manually created based and aligned with the corresponding *UseCase*. After that, the test case can be refined with *TestScenarios*, *TestSteps* and references to involved *DataEntities* and *Variables*.

Listing 1.6. Example of a RSL specification of DataEntity Actor and UseCase [28].

```
DataEntity e_Product "Product" : Master [
    attribute ID "ID" : Integer [isNotNull isUnique]
    attribute title "title" : Text [isNotNull]
    attribute price "Price" : Integer [isNotNull]
    attribute composition "Composition" : Text
    attribute style "Style" : Text
    attribute properties "Properties" : Text
    primaryKey (ID)]

Actor aU_Customer "Customer" : User [
    description "Customer uses the system"]

UseCase uc_Search "Search Products" : EntitiesSearch [
    actorInitiates aU_Customer
    dataEntity e_Product]
...
```

---

[3] http://automationpractice.com.

Listing 1.7 shows a test case specified and refined with the necessary information to define such tests. In this case, two variables were associated. The first one, $v1.search$, is the keyword used to input the name of the search products; the second variable, $v1.expected$, is used to define the number of results expected.

Listing 1.7. Example of 'Search Products' test case RSL specification [28].

```
UseCaseTest t_uc_Search "Search Products" : Valid [
    useCase uc_Search actorInitiates aU_User
    description "As a User I want to search for a product by name or descripton"
    variable v1 [
        attribute search: String
        attribute expectedResults: String
    ]

testScenario Search_Products :Main [
    isConcrete
    variable v1 withValues (
    | v1.search | v1.expectedResults +|
    | "Blouse" | '1'     +|
    | "Summer" | '3'     +|)
    step s1:Actor_CallSystem:Click element('Home')["The User clicks on the Home' element"]
    step s2:Actor_PrepareData:PostData readFrom v1.search ["The User writes a word or phrase in the search text field
        "]
    step s3:Actor_CallSystem:Click button('Search_Product')["The User clicks on the 'Search' button"]
    step s4:System_Execute:Check elementOnScreen(limit v1.expectedResults) ["The
System checks if the number of results is the expected one" ] ]
```

In the $TestScenario$ (Listing 1.7) it is defined the ordered steps that are necessary to perform the actions to get the number of search results and compare it with the expected number.

Once the test case specification is completed, it follows the generation of the equivalent test scripts for the Robot framework: that code generator (integrated in the ITLingo-Studio) generates a set of test scripts (in Robot language), resulting in a script similar to the one shown in Listing 1.8. However, there still miss the elements locators specified in the script, so that the Robot framework could know in which concrete elements of the AUT it shall perform the command specified by the test script.

Listing 1.8. Generated Test Script example (in Robot) [28].

```
*** Variables ***
${search1} Blouse
${search2} Summer
${expectedResults1} 1
${expectedResults2} 4

*** Test Cases ***
Search_Products−Test_1
    [Documentation] As a User I want to search for a product by name or descripton
    Click element [Home]
    Input text [Search_Bar] ${search1}
    Click button [Search_Product]
    Page Should Contain Element [Product_box] limit=${expectedResults1}

Search_Products−Test_2
    [Documentation] As a User I want to search for a product by name or descripton
    Click element [Home]
    Input text [Search_Bar] ${search2}
    Click button [Search_Product]
    Page Should Contain Element [Product_box] limit=${expectedResults2}
```

To provide this missing information, it is necessary to map GUI elements with appropriate keywords as suggested in Fig. 6.

Fig. 8. Web Scrapper [31].

For that purpose the tester shall access the AUT and shall point to the desired elements with the help of the Web Scrapper (Fig. 8). The information of every locators is exported to the JSON file. After executing the Mapping script, the XML file (Fig. 9) is generated with the information about the missing locators of the previous phase. Finally, the replacement scripts fills in the missing information resulting in a concrete script as illustrated in Listing 1.9. In this Listing it is possible to see that $css : img.logo$ is the CSS locator for the element that redirects the user to the "Home Page". Once complete, the test script will be able to be executed.

Listing 1.9. Test Script with GUI elements xpath (in Robot) [31].

```
*** Variables ***
${search1} Blouse
${search2} Summer
${expectedResults1} 1
${expectedResults2} 4


*** Test Cases ***
Search_Product−Test_1
    [Documentation] As a User I want to search for a product by name or descripton
    Click Element css:img.logo
    Input text css:input.search_query ${search1}
    Click button css:div.col−sm−4 button.btn
    Page should contain element css:li.ajax_block_product limit=1

Search_Product−Test_2
    [Documentation] As a User I want to search for a product by name or descripton
    Click Element css:img.logo
    Input text css:input.search_query ${search2}
    Click button css:div.col−sm−4 button.btn
    Page should contain element css:li.ajax_block_product limit=3
```

```
<?xml version="1.0"?>
- <rsl>
    <locator name="[HOME]" locator="img.logo"/>
    <locator name="[Search_Bar]" locator="input.search_query"/>
    <locator name="[Search_Product]" locator="div.col-sm-4 button.btn"/>
    <locator name="[Product_box]" locator="li.ajax_block_product"/>
  </rsl>
```

Fig. 9. XML file – Map between locators and test script [31].

Once the script is completely filled in, these test scripts can be executed and such test results can be obtained, as shown in Fig. 10. Regarding the use case "product search", when searching for products associated to the word *Blouse* (Test_1), the test returned "1" which is the expected result and so, the test succeeded. On the other hand, when searching for products related to the word *Summer* (Test_2), the test returned "4" products which is different from the expected result ("3") and so, the test failed.

```
Search_Product-Test_1 :: As a User I want to search for a product ... | PASS |
Search_Product-Test_2 :: As a User I want to search for a product ... | FAIL |
Page should have contained "3" element(s), but it did contain "4" element(s).
```

Fig. 10. Result of the test case execution [28].

6   Related Work

It is common to derive acceptance test cases for complex IT systems manually from functional requirements described in natural language. This manual process is challenging and time consuming.

One way to diminish this effort is to generate test cases automatically from textual or graphical models. This is not a new idea. In fact, there are some approaches that require graphical models (e.g. workflow models [16], or domain models [13]) or, others, requiring textual models (e.g., use cases [14, 15]) of the system.

The approach followed by [16] uses a workflow notation in which the focus is the casual relationship of the steps without specification of detailed message exchange and data. From these models it is possible to generate end-to-end test cases that are automated using the Junit[4] testing framework. This approach does not align requirements and tests like the one described in this paper.

In [13], the UMTG (Use Case Modeling for System Tests Generation) approach generates automatically system test cases from use case specifications and domain models (class diagram and constraints). This research work does not include any test execution automation tool to run the generated tests.

Hsieh et al. [14] proposed the Test-Duo framework for generating (and executing) acceptance tests from use cases. The testers add specific use cases annotations to clarify the system behaviour. The final test scripts are compatible with Robot framework. However, this approach does not align requirements with tests.

---

[4] https://junit.org/junit5/.

TestMEReq is an automated tool for early validation of requirements [15] described by semi-formalized abstract models called Essential Use Cases. From these abstract models it generates abstract test cases to help validate the requirements. This approach does not include the execution of the generated abstract test cases.

In [29], the authors present the design of a test automation platform, ETAP-Pro, to test end-to-end business processes that aims to overcome some challenges in validating business processes. ETAP-Pro works over BPMN models and is based on a keyword-driven approach. It generates test cases specifications in Gherkin. This approach promotes alignment between test cases and requirements since it maintains traceability information among test cases, requirements and keywords. However, test scripts should be generated manually to be executed afterwords.

In contrast with some tools and approaches mentioned above, our proposal particularly promotes the alignment between high-level requirements and tests specifications, and with low-level test scripts, that is ensured by the adoption of languages like RSL and Robot. In addition, this proposal promotes the quality and productivity of both (Requirements an Testing) tasks by considering model-to-model transformation features (e.g., RSLfrom Requirements into RSL Test Cases, or from RSL Test Cases into Robot Test Scripts), and execution of Robot Test Scripts, with the integration of tools like ITlingo-Studio and Robot framework.

7 Conclusion

This paper describes a model-based testing approach where acceptance test cases are derived from RSL requirements specifications and automatically adapted to the test automation Robot framework to be executed against a web application under test.

This process begins with the requirements elicitation and specification in the RSL. From these requirement specifications (defined in RSL) are created manually or generated test case specifications (also in RSL), which are strongly kept aligned. When these test cases are completely defined, a second model-to-model transformation process is performed, which produces quasi-executable test scripts (in Robot language), which needs to be mapped to concrete GUI elements before be executable by the Robot framework. This generation is based on mappings between the characteristic constructs of RSL and the GUI elements identifiers of the AUT with the syntax of the Robot automation tool. Once test scripts are completed, they are executed and the results presented in a test execution report.

This approach encourages the practice of specifying both requirements and tests during the early stages of the projects, and keeping these specifications aligned with each other. It also promotes the productivity by reducing manual effort, time and resources dedicated to the development of tests, also ensures higher quality of requirements. The adoption of a language like RSL, that supports both requirements and tests specification in a more consistent and systematic way, is therefore less prone to errors and ambiguities.

As future work, we intend to extensively apply this approach in both controlled and real-world scenarios. We also intend to further improve the productivity of the proposed approach by automatically generating RSL test specifications from RSL requirement specifications (e.g., considering other types of test cases and other situations like security or performance) and generating these test specifications into executable test scripts that may be executed by multiple test automation frameworks, such as Gherkin/Cucumber[5].

Acknowledgements. This work was partially supported by national funds under FCT projects UID/CEC/50021/2019 and 02/SAICT/2017/29360.

References

1. Cockburn, A.: Writing Effective Use Cases, 1st edn. Addison-Wesley, Boston (2000)
2. Kovitz, B.L.: Practical Software Requirements: Manual of Content and Style. Manning Publications, Greenwich (1998)
3. Robertson, S., Robertson, J.: Mastering the Requirements Process: Getting Requirements Right, 3rd edn. Addison-Wesley Professional, Boston (2012)
4. Withall, S.: Software Requirements Patterns, 1st edn. Microsoft Press (2007)
5. Silva, A.R.: Linguistic patterns and linguistic styles for requirements specification (i): an application case with the rigorous RSL/business-level language. In: Proceedings of the 22nd European Conference on Pattern Languages of Programs. ACM (2017)
6. Pohl, K.: Requirements Engineering: Fundamentals, Principles, and Techniques, 1st edn. Springer, Heidelberg (2010)
7. Ferreira, D.A., Silva, A.R.: RSLingo: an information extraction approach toward formal requirements specifications. In: 2nd IEEE International Workshop on Model-Driven Requirements Engineering, MoDRE 2012 - Proceedings, pp. 39–48 (2012)
8. Videira, C., Ferreira, D., Silva, A.R.: A linguistic patterns approach for requirements specification. In: Proceeding 32nd Euromicro Conference on Software Engineering and Advanced Applications (Euromicro 2006). IEEE Computer Society (2006)
9. Ferreira, D.A., Silva, A.R.: RSL-PL: a linguistic pattern language for documenting software requirements. In: 3rd International Workshop on Requirements Patterns, RePa 2013 - Proceedings, pp. 17–24 (2013)
10. Ferreira, D.A., Silva, A.R.: RSL-IL: an interlingua for formally documenting requirements. In: 3rd International Workshop on Model-Driven Requirements Engineering, MoDRE 2013 - Proceedings, pp. 40–49 (2013)
11. Silva, A.R., Saraiva, J., Ferreira, D., Silva, A.R., Videira, C.: Integration of RE and MDE paradigms: the ProjectIT approach and tools. IET Softw. **1**, 294–314 (2007)
12. Jacobson, I., et al.: Object Oriented Software Engineering: A Use Case Driven Approach. Addison-Wesley, Boston (2015)
13. Wang, C., Pastore, F., Goknil, A., Briand, L., Iqbal, Z.: Automatic generation of system test cases from use case specifications. In: Proceedings of the 2015 International Symposium on Software Testing and Analysis, pp. 385–396 (2015)
14. Hsieh, C., Tsai, C., Cheng, Y.C.: Test-duo: a framework for generating and executing automated acceptance tests from use cases. In: 8th International Workshop on Automation of Software Test, AST 2013 - Proceedings, pp. 89–92 (2013)
15. Moketar, N.A., Kamalrudin, M., Sidek, S., Robinson, M., Grundy, J.: TestMEReq: generating abstract tests for requirements validation. In: Proceedings - 3rd International Workshop on Software Engineering Research and Industrial Practice, SER and IP 2016, pp. 39–45 (2016)

---

[5] https://cucumber.io/.

16. Boucher, M., Mussbacher, G.: Transforming workflow models into automated end-to-end acceptance test cases. In: Proceedings - 2017 IEEE/ACM 9th International Workshop on Modelling in Software Engineering, MiSE 2017, pp. 68–74 (2017)
17. Silva, A.R., Paiva, A.C.R., Silva, V.: Towards a test specification language for information systems: focus on data entity and state machine tests. In: Proceedings of the 6th International Conference on Model-Driven Engineering and Software Development (MODELSWARD) (2018)
18. Silva, A.R., Paiva, A.C.R., Silva, V.: A test specification language for information systems based on data entities, use cases and state machines. In: Hammoudi, S., Pires, L., Selic, B. (eds.) MODELSWARD 2018. CCIS, vol. 991, pp. 455–474. Springer, Heidelberg (2019). https://doi.org/10.1007/978-3-030-11030-7_20
19. Moreira, R.M.L.M., Paiva, A.C.R., Nabuco, M., Memon, A.: Pattern-based GUI testing: bridging the gap between design and quality assurance. Softw. Test. Verif. Reliab. **27**(3), e1629 (2017)
20. Moreira, R.M.L.M., Paiva, A.C.R.: PBGT tool: an integrated modeling and testing environment for pattern-based GUI testing. In: Proceedings of the 29th ACM/IEEE International Conference on Automated Software Engineering, ASE 2014, pp. 863–866 (2014)
21. Paiva, A.C.R., Faria, J.C.P., Tillmann, N., Vidal, R.A.M.: A model-to-implementation mapping tool for automated model-based GUI testing. In: Lau, K.-K., Banach, R. (eds.) ICFEM 2005. LNCS, vol. 3785, pp. 450–464. Springer, Heidelberg (2005). https://doi.org/10.1007/11576280_31
22. Silva, A.R.: Rigorous specification of use cases with the RSL language. In: Proceedings of International Conference on Information Systems Development 2019. AIS (2019)
23. Bhat, A., Quadri, S.M.K.: Equivalence class partitioning and boundary value analysis - a review. In: 2nd International Conference on Computing for Sustainable Global Development (INDIACom) (2015)
24. Paiva, A.C.R.: Automated specification-based testing of graphical user interfaces. Ph.D. thesis, Faculty of Engineering of the University of Porto, Porto, Portugal (2007)
25. ISTQB, ISTQB & #x00AE; Foundation Level Certified Model-Based Tester Syllabus (2015)
26. Leotta, M., Clerissi, D., Ricca, F., Tonella, P.: Approaches and tools for automated end-to-end web testing. In: Advances in Computers, 1st edn., vol. 101, pp. 193–237. Elsevier Inc. (2016)
27. ISTQB, ISTQB & #x00AE; Foundation Level Extension Syllabus Agile Tester, p. 28 (2014)
28. Maciel, D., Paiva, A.C.R., Silva, A.R.: From requirements to automated acceptance tests of interactive apps: an integrated model-based testing approach. In: 14th International Conference on Evaluation of Novel Approaches to Software Engineering (ENASE) (2019)
29. Paiva, A.C.R., Flores, N.H., Faria, J.C.P., Marques, J.M.G.: End-to-end automatic business process validation. In: the 8th International Symposium on Frontiers in Ambient and Mobile Systems (FAMS) (2018)
30. Silva, A.R., Savic, D., et al.: A pattern language for use cases specification. In: Proceedings of EuroPLOP 2015. ACM (2015)
31. Maciel, D.A.M.: Model based testing - from requirements to tests. MSc thesis, Master in Informatics and Computing Engineering, Faculty of Engineering of the University of Porto, Portugal (2019)

Experimenting with Liveness in Cloud Infrastructure Management

Pedro Lourenço[1,3], João Pedro Dias[1,2,3(✉)], Ademar Aguiar[1,2,3],
Hugo Sereno Ferreira[1,2,3], and André Restivo[1,2,3]

[1] DEI, Faculty of Engineering, University of Porto, Porto, Portugal
{pedro.lourenco,jpmdias,ademar.aguiar,hugosf,arestivo}@fe.up.pt
[2] INESC TEC, Porto, Portugal
[3] LIACC, Porto, Portugal

Abstract. Cloud computing has been playing a significant role in the provisioning of services over the Internet since its birth. However, developers still face several challenges limiting its full potential. The difficulties are mostly due to the large, ever-growing, and ever-changing catalog of services offered by cloud providers. As a consequence, developers must deal with different cloud services in their systems; each managed almost individually and continually growing in complexity. This heterogeneity may limit the view developers have over their system architectures and make the task of managing these resources more complex. This work explores the use of *liveness* as a way to shorten the feedback loop between developers and their systems in an interactive and immersive way, as they develop and integrate cloud-based systems. The designed approach allows real-time visualization of cloud infrastructures using a visual city metaphor. To assert the viability of this approach, the authors conceived a proof-of-concept and carried on experiments with developers to assess its feasibility.

Keywords: Cloud computing · Internet-of-things software
engineering · Live programming

1 Introduction

The concept of cloud computing was predicted back in 1961 by John McCarthy. He stated that "computing may someday be organized as a public utility just as the telephone system is a public utility" [10]. However, it was only in the early 2000's that this prediction became a reality with the introduction of the Elastic Compute Cloud (EC2) developed by Amazon Web Services (AWS)—an Amazon subsidiary [3]—providing computing power in an on-demand self-service way. Currently, AWS offers more than ninety distinct services spread among twenty different categories [39], and more companies are providing this kind of services, *e.g.*, Google and Microsoft.

© Springer Nature Switzerland AG 2020
E. Damiani et al. (Eds.): ENASE 2019, CCIS 1172, pp. 58–82, 2020.
https://doi.org/10.1007/978-3-030-40223-5_4

These services are typically made available to the general public, as what is known as public cloud hosting solution, in a pay-as-you-go fashion by the so-called Cloud Services Providers [7], who monitor, meter, and price the usage of resources, depending on service type and usage.

Different service models are offered by cloud providers, depending on the level of granularity and configuration that the developers require, being the following the most common [25]:

Infrastructure as a Service (IaaS). The cloud provider gives developers access to resources such as storage, networking, and servers in a pay-as-you-go fashion.

Platform as a Service (PaaS). Cloud providers offer developers access to a cloud-based environment on top of which they can build and deliver applications, abstracting the underlying infrastructure.

Software as a Service (SaaS). Service providers deliver software and applications through the Internet and users can subscribe to the software and access it remotely, *e.g.*, via a web portal or vendor APIs.

This paradigm reshaped how companies provide services, by allowing them to abstract, at different levels, from hardware infrastructure management, focusing on the virtual architecture and eradicating any possible concerns dealing with resource maintenance while improving manageability [7].

Alongside the reduced costs of using cloud computing when compared to on-premises solutions (*i.e.*, running on computers on the premises of the person or organization using the software), there is another key advantage: elasticity. The resources needed to meet the expected Quality-of-Service (QoS) can be rapidly provisioned, allowing the quick scale outwards and inwards to compensate for unpredictable business demands. This elasticity gives organizations more flexibility to focus on the core business instead of focusing on maintaining provisioned infrastructure. As a consequence, in most cases, there is no definite sense of location over the provided services beyond the ability, in some cases, to specify multiple higher regions which can be used as a strategy to increase reliability and avoid network outages [36].

As the market evolves, it becomes more demanding in terms of cloud services required, thus new "as-a-service" models start to emerge, leading to what has been called Everything as a Service (XaaS) [16,33] solutions (*e.g.*, Functions as a Service (FaaS), also known as Serverless [16,33,44]). As new paradigms emerge, in terms of connectivity and computation, they directly influence the market landscape with cloud providers offering even more services to fill the market needs. Internet-of-Things (IoT) as one of those paradigm-shifts, has lead diverse cloud providers to offer specialized services that answer the IoT scale, heterogeneity, and data-throughput needs. These services range from device management systems, to handle the ever-growing number of cloud-connected sensors and actuators, to specialized data analytics tools [11,42,44].

It is noticeable that cloud computing has brought several benefits for organizations in terms of interoperability and versatility, easing the process of meeting established QoS levels. However, there is a substantial amount of complexity in building and managing consistent and reliable infrastructures, resulting in the need of expert developers capable of implementing cloud-based systems [9].

In addition to the inherently complex nature of software systems [19,37], there is extra complexity in building systems within a cloud ecosystem. First, there is an ever-growing number of different services offered by cloud providers that make it harder to decide what is the best solution for a given problem [39]. Second, the final cost of a cloud solution can be highly volatile and hard to calculate *a priori* [14]. Third, there is no common taxonomy (or standards) among cloud providers, which leads to confusion and makes comparing solutions harder [14,55]. And last, the different services provided by each cloud vendor can lead to a vendor-lock that impacts an eventual process of migrating a solution, if needed [14,43,55].

As we move towards more complex cloud-based software systems, we will eventually come to an explosion of different services, each one managed individually, possibly leading to serious management challenges. This complexity makes it harder to understand cloud-based systems and the value that they bring to the business [31].

Even further, the 2017 edition of RightScale's State of the Cloud Report [46], an yearly survey on cloud computing trends, inquired 1002 IT professionals, and showed that when comparing the years 2016, 2017 and 2018, the most relevant cloud challenges are the lack of resources/expertise and security in cloud management (Fig. 1). Moreover, even though there is a decline in nearly all challenges compared with the previous year, it is interesting to note that governance/control is the only challenge that has almost stagnated in the three-year comparison.

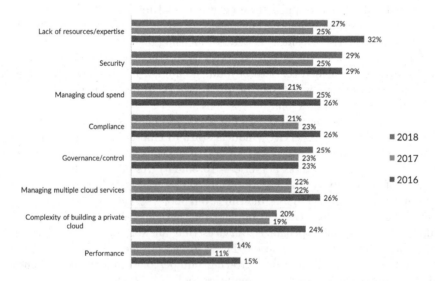

Fig. 1. Cloud challenges comparing the years 2016, 2017 and 2018. Adapted from [46].

Software systems are designed, implemented, tested, debugged, analyzed, and maintained by many different developers. All these tasks can be facilitated by using several different visualization techniques. From a historical perspective, software understanding tasks leveraged the use of models and visual notations. An example is the Unified Modeling Language (UML), which has been widely used not only to represent and visualize software systems' structure, behavior, and evolution [13], but also to simplify the process of understanding large-scale architectures [17], and even develop new cloud-based systems [23].

This work addresses the challenges mentioned above by exploring how cloud management can benefit more from a model-based approach, combined with more liveness, leading to the notion of live models at run-time. On the one hand, models would help to abstract the lower-level details by creating and exploiting domain models, in a similar way to UML [26]. On the other hand, more liveness would shorten the feedback loop between the developers and the system under development [1,53], thus helping to reduce management complexity by making it easier to understand quickly what the system is doing or is supposed to do.

To explore the pros and cons of this combination of concepts, we developed the *CloudCity* prototype [32], a live management environment tailored for cloud infrastructures. *CloudCity* aims to offer developers a way to gather continuous feedback about their cloud systems, allowing quick and interactive management of a running cloud system, and therefore ease the process of fault location (usually carried by log analysis) and evolution.

The work here presented extends previous work from the authors in the *Live Software Development* paradigm [1,2,32], delving further into the catalog of visual metaphors for representing cloud infrastructures. It also presents the carried out experiments that evaluate the *CloudCity* solution both in terms of scalability and feasibility as well as the obtained results.

This paper is structured as follows: Sect. 2 provides an overview of the main background concepts of this work and presents some related work. Section 3 gives an overview of our approach, followed by some implementation details. Section 5 explains the validation process using a controlled experiment, along with the discussion of the obtained results, followed by final remarks in Sect. 6.

2   Background and Related Work

To ease the process of understanding and managing complex software, many researchers have investigated different techniques, from high-level abstractions to tool support aiming at improving the programming experience. In the context of this work, we found of high relevance the state-of-the-art on Software Visualization, Model-Driven Engineering, and Live Programming, especially the work more closely related to Cloud Management. In particular, we searched for similarities with previous research results, key features, and ideas that could influence our research.

2.1 Software Visualization

Software visualization is the depiction of software—its structure, behavior, and evolution—and its development process in a visual fashion, leveraging static, interactive and multi-dimensional visual metaphors [13]. Different visualization techniques have been used to ease the understanding of source code, architectural design, use cases, system modules, and more.

Kapec [24] presented a hypergraph-based software visualization system to create a *visual programming environment for software developers*. In this approach, relations between components can be transposed to source code as function calls or class inheritance with visible links between edges, storing information about developers and tasks. As heterogeneous programming environments (*i.e.*, using diverse languages) are a common practice that contributes to software complexity, their approach combines hypergraphs with visual data mining techniques hiding the actual implementation but capturing the call relation.

Lanza et al. [28,29] presented a software visualization technique enriched with metrics information, so-called polymetric views. This approach eases the process of understanding the structure of a software artifact and detects problems in the initial phases of a reverse engineering process. The actual visualization requires: (1) a layout considering the selected entities, relationships, and areas of interest into how they should be sorted and displayed (*e.g.*, a tree layout is better suited for the display of an inheritance hierarchy than a circle layout); (2) a set of metrics extracted from the source code entities, which heavily influence the resulting visualization, being suitable to control the state of a software system during development; and (3) a set of entities that are the parts of the system selected for visualization [29].

Wettel et al. [57] software visualization approach, adopted the urban domain—influenced by the role that civil architecture has on software engineering—as the central metaphor to abstract the different parts of the system. Several similarities can be seen between a city and a software system since both are conceived during a planning phase, in which requirements are the foundation; and then both are built incrementally and require constant maintenance.

Using this city metaphor, Wettel et al. present city elements (*e.g.*, buildings and districts) mapped to software system components (classes and packages respectively). Further, to enhance the visualization, the physical properties of the urban artifacts (*e.g.*, color, and dimensions) reflect attributes of the software components.

The concept of such visualization was implemented in *CodeCity* [57] (Fig. 2). As to validate the feasibility and utility of the approach, an empirical evaluation was carried on in a series of experimental runs spanned over six months. Wettel et al. conclude that for the program comprehension and design quality assessment, the city metaphor enabled the creation of efficient software visualizations. The experiments showed improved correctness 24% of the cases and reduced completion time in 12% over similar state-of-the-practice tools.

Merino et al. extended this vision and brought the concept of virtual reality into the idea of the *CodeCity*, the *CityVR* [38]. In *CityVR*, the city visual

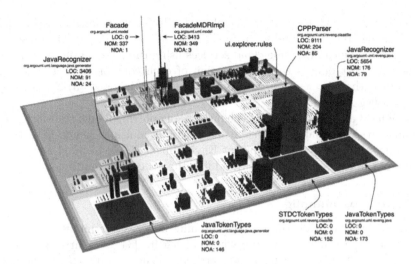

Fig. 2. A 3D representation of the ArgoUML software using the *CodeCity* concept by Wettel et al. [57].

metaphor is enhanced by allowing the developer to explore software pieces in an immersive 3D environment medium.

Other works explore the same idea, such as: (1) *ExplorViz*, a VR approach following the 3D city metaphor [18]; (2) *VR City*, a modification of the city metaphor in virtual reality environment, with a different layout technique that provides a higher level of detail and positioning oriented to the coupling between classes [56]; (3) *SwiftCity*, an application of the City visual metaphor to Swift projects [40]; and (4) Amaral et al. approach for a live development environment for Java using 3D and VR [2].

2.2   Model-Driven Engineering

Models raise the level of abstraction, revealing the big picture, or providing a focus on specific aspects of a system. Model-based approaches have been used as a way to specify the structure and behavior of a system for a long time. UML is one example of a modeling language that is methodology-independent and platform-independent [41]. Although not a visualization approach, but rather a visual notation, it is closely related to software visualization [57].

Sandobalin et al. [47] present ARGON, a solution to help the management of Infrastructure as Code (IaC), through a Domain-Specific Modeling Language (DSML). ARGON is a modeling tool for specifying the final state of the infrastructure and provisioning of cloud resources. The tool aims mainly on the automatic generation of infrastructure provisioning scripts. One of the advantages of this approach is the abstraction from the complexity of working with different cloud providers, resulting in a platform-independent metamodel and thus mitigating the vendor lock-in issue.

Mastelic et al. [33] take advantage of model-driven development for building and managing arbitrary cloud services in a cloud-agnostic manner. The presented CoPS metamodel can describe cloud services using three sequential models: (1) Component, that defines the configuration of each component of the service; (2) Product, that defines the arrangement of the service; and (3) Service, that defines services requirements.

Ardagna et al. [6] defends the same purpose of applying model transformation techniques to instantiate the system into possible multiple clouds. The result aims to be an Integrated Development Environment (IDE) to build and deploy applications in a cloud-agnostic way, adding the concept of multi-clouds.

2.3 Live Programming

As pointed by Sean McDirmid, "programming burdens our minds as we must imagine how the code will execute while editing it" [34,49]. Christopher Hancock [20] in his thesis compares this to archery: aiming an arrow (editing code) involves mentally simulating a physical system while shooting (debugging) provides discrete feedback for the next shot. In other words, to find the cause of errors in software, one should resort to debugging to get feedback about how the code behaves, and this causes a break in the mental flow and the editing process [34].

Live Programming is an idea pioneered by programming environments from the earliest days of computing, such as those for Lisp and Smalltalk. One thing they had in common is *liveness*: an always-available evaluation and nearly instantaneous feedback, usually focused on coding activities. Tanimoto targeted the "edit-compile-link-run" loop, proposing to blur it into a continuum, where the programmer and the system interact in a very tight way—*live* [52,53].

Back to Hancock's analogy, consider hitting a target with a stream of water: we keep correcting our aim until the target is hit, where, unlike archery, we receive continuous feedback on where we are shooting [49].

By unifying the gap between code editing and debugging [49], re-executing the program and providing continuous feedback while editing eases the burden of programming [34]. It is not a *silver-bullet* for software systems development, but potentially very important for some. While the ability to inspect and modify is taken for granted in most IDEs, adding liveness is an enhancement [53].

Examples of liveness can be observed in several IDEs that already provide continuous and responsive feedback on the lexical, syntactic, and type safety of the developer's code. Further, many *live* visual programming languages such as VIVA, Forms/3, Morphic, and PureData go beyond this by providing live feedback about how the program executes as the code is edited [34].

Some challenges to this concept have been pointed out on how feedback may be considered harmful, since that receiving continuous results with change can be potentially distracting in some cases, forcing the programmer to write in a particular order to *keep it live*. For live programming to succeed, it must enhance programming without restricting what the programmer can do, either beginner or expert [35].

Other frequent critics highlight the fact that the steps in between execution are the essential part of programming, and, the usage of *liveness* can result in hiding some critical parts of the flow of execution, with the developer only focusing on the program output [34]. Nevertheless, from a debugging perspective, live programming can address this concern combining editing and debugging, having debug results readily visible while editing, thus returning the focus to the program flow and how changes affect specific parts of execution [34].

Although the notion of *Live Programming* focuses on the particular activity of *programming*, there is nothing in its principles that cannot be applied to many other activities, such as: requirements analysis, design, testing, deployment, or maintenance. Therefore, Live Software Development concerns on achieving higher *liveness* in more development activities beyond programming [1].

2.4   Cloud Management

The trend has been to leverage clouds as complex, highly heterogeneous, and distributed architectures, including hybrid and multiclouds [31]. This growth has given rise to new challenges and technologies to deal with them, namely with governance, security, and management.

The process of obtaining services from the cloud, such as spawning computers or virtual hosts and tailoring its software and configurations, is known as *provisioning* [9]. Inspite of its close relation to deployment of services or applications, provisioning does not necessarily imply new deployments or *vice versa* [48].

The widespread use of cloud computing has been empowering the movement of DevOps—a software engineering culture aiming to unify software development (oriented to change) and software operation (oriented to stability) [4,15] – due to its benefits when comparing to traditional operations processes, namely:

Rapid Delivery. Quickly respond to customer needs and move a change into production [4,15].
Reliability. Ensure the quality of application updates and infrastructure changes through testing in practices such as continuous integration and continuous delivery (CI/CD) [4,15].
Scale. Automation and consistency help changing systems efficiently and with reduced risk [4].
Collaboration. Developers and operation engineers share responsibilities and combine workflows [4].

This movement has increased the responsibilities of developers beyond *programming*, having now an increasing role in the building, continuous integration, and fast delivery (building an effective pipeline of releases) of new services and applications. Thus, developers now need to focus more on the configuration management (*e.g.*, cloud configuration management), testing, and production of these systems [27].

Configuration Management. Configuration Management (CM) is a core part of the *provisioning* process, methodically handling changes to a system to maintain its integrity over time. Pressman et al. define such process as [45]:

> "A set of activities designed to manage change by identifying the work products that are likely to change, establishing relationships among them, defining mechanisms for managing different versions of these work products, controlling the changes imposed, and auditing and reporting on the changes made."

One can identify *automation*—the ability to automatically deploy new system versions in the existent infrastructure—as the most fundamental concept in configuration management. Thus, commonly, configuration management tools are presented as Automation Tools or IT Automation Tools [22]. Examples of CM tools include CHEF and PUPPET [5,46,58]. Both allow the specification of infrastructure as code (so-called *recipes*) by using a domain specific language.

Although these approaches spread a notion of controlled and reliable mutable oriented node configuration, it is important to consider the possibility of configuration drifts, over time, as each server builds a unique history of changes [8].

Infrastructure Orchestration. The main feature of configuration management tools is to install software on resources that already exist. Orchestration *per se* has a different purpose than CM. Orchestration tools are typically designed to enforce a particular workflow order to a set of automated tasks, such as the provisioning of those resources. However, both orchestration and CM categories are not mutually exclusive, with some orchestration tools extending its features to configuration and vice-versa [8].

Examples of Infrastructure Orchestration tools are CLOUDFORMATION, the AWS-based orchestration tool to describe and provision infrastructure as code, and TERRAFORM, a similar tool but cloud-agnostic, enabling the combination of multiple cloud service providers with a unified syntax [21]. Both tools focus on the definition of a blueprint for controlling and versioning resources configurations easily, which typically defaults to an immutable infrastructure paradigm.

As a summary, we conclude that most of the approaches and tools for managing cloud services prevail on the concept of infrastructure as code, with some following a kind of model-driven approach, namely to manage multiple cloud services and thus to avoid vendor lock-in. However, the existing tools only provide minimal, or even none, live support, one of the aspects we focus on exploring with this work.

3   CloudCity: The Approach

Resulting from the lack of resources and expertise on how to handle and manage different cloud services altogether [46], there has been an increasing interest in novel approaches to support infrastructure provisioning, orchestration and configuration management. Most of these approaches have requirements of automation and orchestration, due to the ever-growing complexity and scale of systems (*e.g.*, Internet-of-Things) [44, 54].

3.1 Overview

To tackle the current issues in cloud computing, while taking into account the existent requirements, our tool, named *CloudCity*, uses a 3D visualization approach for managing cloud infrastructures. The chosen visual metaphor, the city metaphor, was based on the work by Wettel et al. [57] in *CodeCity 3D* since the software engineering scientific community already validated it with good empirical results in what regards software visualization. Also, using a city to represent an infrastructure intends to help the user familiarizing with the domain by using already known city objects.

The need for metaphors arises from the fact that the cloud is not a physical entity. Thus, by nature, it cannot be purely synthesized into a straightforward, visually understandable mapping. However, it can be transposed into other dimensions, such as code (*c.f.* TERRAFORM and CLOUDFORMATION) or models as a way to ease the process of managing such infrastructures. Representing clouds with a validated metaphor, the city, enables users to gradually become familiar with the described architecture, due to the many similarities between the two domains.

CloudCity embraces the concept of *liveness*, underlying Live Software Development [1], allowing the developer to get continuous feedback on *how architectural* (instead of code) *changes affect the whole system*, going beyond a static 3D visualization of a cloud architecture.

In detail, the main objective of *CloudCity* is to allow the design and analysis of cloud compositions through a mostly-intuitive mapping between city objects (*i.e.*, houses, streets, skyscrapers) and cloud resources. Each one of the buildings contains a set of properties reflected from the cloud, which can be inspected or modified through simple user interaction. Relations between elements are depicted as curved lines between them, which can be filtered and inspected on-demand. The main difference from other model-driven approaches is that this environment does not reflect a static infrastructure mapping, but instead a live infrastructure showing the real-time state of each component—a metaphor that we introduce as, *the live city*. An example of *CloudCity*'s main environment is depicted in Fig. 3.

Regarding the tools provided to the developer, the user interface is composed of the interactive components listed below. All the panels are collapsible, triggered by a user action, to save visual space.

Information Panel. Acts as an inspector with information about the selected resource.

Resource Context Menu. Acts as a dynamic options menu, with several actions depending on the selected resource.

Fig. 3. CloudCity's main environment containing an small size example architecture, displaying all relations.

Plane Main Menu. Contains global infrastructure actions, such as spawning new resources.

Regarding the environment's background, it consists of a simple skybox chosen to increase the resemblance to a city's atmosphere.

3.2   Architecture

CloudCity follows a model-driven engineering philosophy, embracing the concept of models as a way to express the system and the relation between system parts.

CloudCity high-level architecture, depicted in Fig. 4, is composed of three core components, namely:

Cloud Service Providers API. Provides a connection to a specific cloud service provider, thus allowing to fetch and interact with the cloud architecture.

Importer. Periodically pools or checks the provider and detects changes in the infrastructure state, forwarding actions to update specific resources.

Resources. The elements correspond to different cloud services. These resources follow a composite pattern, *viz.* a group of resources can either contain a resource or another resource group. If it contains another group, the same applies recursively downwards the tree structure.

3.3   Proof-of-Concept

For the sake of simplicity, some technological decisions were made to ease the development of a proof-of-concept. In what regards Cloud Service Providers API integration, we focused only on Amazon Web Services among the existent

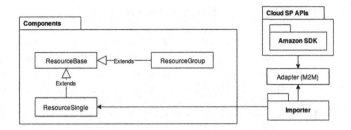

Fig. 4. CloudCity's architecture described in a package diagram [32].

options. Regarding the fetch of information from the cloud provider, we implemented a pooling approach instead of a more efficient one, such as event-driven, or publish-subscribe approach, due to limitations of the API of the provider itself.

However, even given the fact that the proof-of-concept integrates with only one cloud provider, the system is built in a modular way that allows the addition of new adapters to different cloud services providers, easing the process of integrating with other sellers such as Microsoft Azure. This capability is accomplished by dividing the *CloudCity* architecture into two decoupled layers:

Platform Independent Model. Illustrated in Fig. 5, this model is independent of any specific provider.

Platform Specific Model. This model is coupled with a specific provider and can be obtained with a model to model transformation.

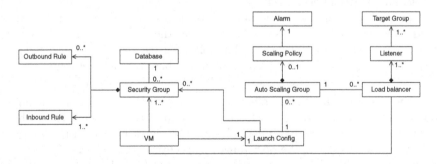

Fig. 5. Infrastructure metamodel (inspired by the abstract syntax presented by Sandobalin et al. [47]) [32].

The proof of concept was implemented using a multipurpose three-dimensional engine, Unity. This solution also opens doors for new features to be studied and provides support for Virtual/Augmented Reality, an exciting perspective also studied in other approaches using the City Metaphor [38,56].

4 CloudCity: The Live Environment

One of the key challenges was to find the most suitable abstractions—within the urban catalog of metaphors—to portray the cloud architecture infrastructure, while still being compatible with *live* features and easy to use and understand. To be able to achieve this, we decided to start by using the following metaphors:

Resource Mapping. Establishing a correspondence between the resources offered by cloud providers and the catalog of metaphors available (or permutations of those metaphors).

Layout. Defining a proper environment that lays out the different components in an understandable way and adjusts automatically as the cloud architecture is modified while remaining consistent throughout the process.

Updates and Interactions. Support the *live* aspects of the environment, *i.e.*, how to translate the infrastructure updates into a human-understandable notation in real-time.

The following subsections describe these three aspects in more detail.

4.1 Resource Mapping

The number of services offered by cloud providers is continuously growing. This growth is mostly driven by the necessity of providers to adapt their offer to clients, to maintain their position in a demanding market [51].

However, at any given point in time, there is a finite set of services and resources with properties known *a priori*. This fact allows the creation of an *alphabet*, which can be expanded accordingly to new services that can appear, with models for each one of the elements that need to be represented, rather than defining new models on-the-fly.

Even so, due to the current number of services in the portfolio of the cloud providers, we focused on creating models only for the most common and popular services across cloud providers [30]. The following list describes those services along with the respective model and their urban-based visual metaphor.

Security Group. Virtual firewalls to control instances (*e.g.*, virtual machines) inbound and outbound traffic. Each security group contains a set of rules which control the port range where traffic is allowed. The metric chosen for the building height varies according to the port range the security group covers. Due to the commonality of this element in cloud architectures (a VM instance can have from one up to five different groups), the building dimensions correspond to the *small* building type as depicted in Fig. 6, resulting in the Fig. 7b.

Virtual Machine. VMs are one of the most common elements in cloud computing since they provide scalable computation capacity in the cloud. Each instance has a pre-determined size depending on its hardware specifications. The metric for the building dimensions varies according to this attribute accordingly with Fig. 6, and their visual representation is given in Fig. 7a.

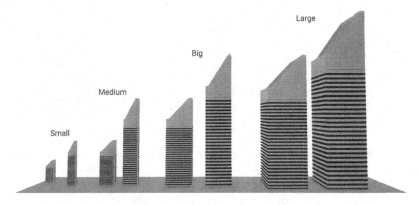

Fig. 6. CloudCity's reference building dimensions sorted in ascending order [32]. Nano VM instances are considered *small*, Micro and Small are considered *medium*, from Large to 8x Large are considered *big* and from 8x Large to 32x Large are considered *large*.

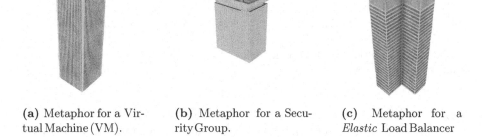

(a) Metaphor for a Virtual Machine (VM).

(b) Metaphor for a Security Group.

(c) Metaphor for a *Elastic* Load Balancer

Fig. 7. Visual notation for a Virtual Machine, Security Group and Load Balancer [32].

Load Balancer. Element that distributes traffic across multiple targets for achieving multi-tenancy and resource pooling. A Load Balancer can have multiple listeners that receive incoming connections and distribute them across multiple groups of targets. The building size fluctuates depending on the total number of rules that the load balancer takes into consideration when forwarding connections, depicted in Fig. 7c. It is part of the *big* buildings category since it is a central component between the point of entry and the targets.

Scaling Policy. Policies define how the scaling group increases or decreases the size, and according to which metrics. The building height varies depending on the scaling adjustment, Fig. 8a, and the building type falls in the *medium* buildings category since it can be considered a subset of the Auto Scaling Group.

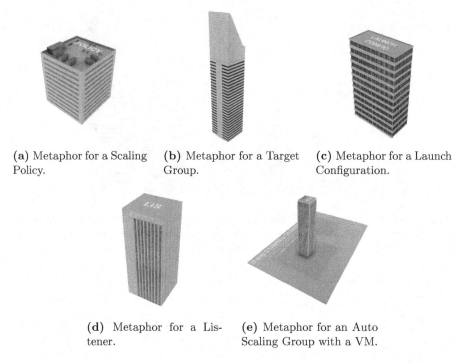

(a) Metaphor for a Scaling Policy.

(b) Metaphor for a Target Group.

(c) Metaphor for a Launch Configuration.

(d) Metaphor for a Listener.

(e) Metaphor for an Auto Scaling Group with a VM.

Fig. 8. Visual notation for a Scaling Policy, Target Group, Launch Configuration, Listener and Auto Scaling Group.

Target Group. A target group routes incoming listener requests to one or more registered targets. The building height varies depending on the number of instances registered in it, Fig. 8b. It is considered as part of the *medium* buildings category since this component can also be considered a subset of the load balancer.

Launch Configuration. This is a parental reference of machine specifications for a VM to be mirrored from, guiding the Auto Scaling Group as it expands the number of replicated instances. The building type chosen for this component depends on the instance type attribute (*c.f.* Fig. 6), and it is represented in Fig. 8c.

Listener. Listeners are responsible for checking for incoming requests on a specific port and forward them to a Target Group. The building height varies in consonance with the number of rules it takes consideration when forwarding a connection to a specific group of targets, Fig. 8d. The building is part of the *medium* buildings category.

Auto Scaling Group. This element is not depicted as a building since it is a group with multiple VMs and scales dynamically. The metaphor chosen was a plane with sufficient area to support the different availability zones and specific VM, visually represented on Fig. 8e.

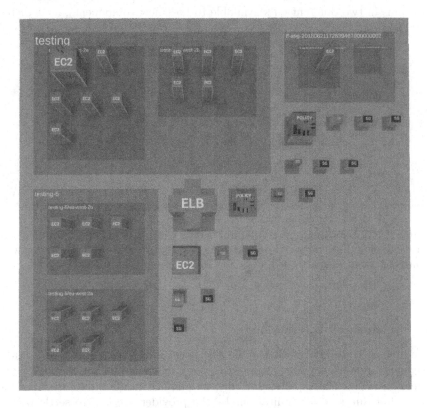

Fig. 9. An example of the rectangle packing layout for a considerable size infrastructure, composed of: three Auto Scaling Groups containing multiple size instances and two Scaling Policies; a stopped Virtual Machine; one Load Balancer and several Security Groups [32].

4.2 Layout

To be able to manage a cloud infrastructure in a live way, there is the need for a mechanism to layout and update components quickly in the tool's environment, as the architecture expands and is modified. It has to: (1) support laying out all the imported components of the infrastructure, with different dimensions, in an ordered and understandable manner; (2) optimize the number of buildings, not wasting much of the cities' real-estate [57]; (3) support grouping components according to a class.

The strategy picked for layering the elements is *CodeCity*'s rectangle packing algorithm proposed by Wettel et al. [57]. This approach starts with an empty rectangular space, large enough to host a set of exposed components. In each step, the elements are laid out in the best free space from a list of potential candidates. In case the element does not cover the full space, we recursively split the surplus in two different cuts available to host new components, as depicted in Fig. 9.

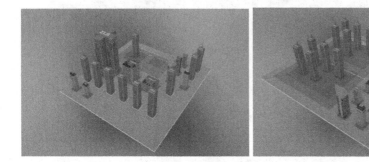

Fig. 10. Visualization of an infrastructural update when an auto-scaling group enters in action, scaling the number of instances from 1 to 10. As result nine new servers were spawned (left) and then attached inside the scaling group (right) [32].

4.3   Updates and Interactions

To be able to fetch information about the cloud infrastructure, as well as any subsequent updates, a pooling approach was implemented, that checks for differences between each response. Initially, we planned to use a publish-subscribe pattern, but due to some limitations by the provider, we had to settle with a poll mechanism.

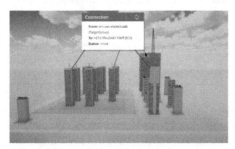

(a) Helper window that allows the inspection of links between elements.

(b) Selection of an element within the environment.

Fig. 11. Representation of some user interactions within the live environment.

Having communication-enabled and a method to detect the change, the next step is to refresh the infrastructure when changes happen. The most naive approach would be to destroy the whole infrastructure and rebuilt it. However, for efficiency reasons, we decided not to destroy any element except if it has been terminated. Instead, every time the layout needs to re-position elements, only the affected ones change position, as depicted in Fig. 10.

To avoid abrupt changes in the layout, all components change their position *slowly* (speed of 1 unit per second) to increase the response feedback (sliding in-between positions), making it easier for the developer to understand changes.

Relations are mapped as arcs beginning at one instance, or group, and ending in another. Both resources and their relations may contain a state depending on their nature; which can be inspected by clicking it, and filtered when a specific component is selected, as depicted in Fig. 11a. Cloud elements, represented as different buildings, can be selected (Fig. 11b) and configured with the aid of windows within the 3D environment.

5   Experiments and Results

There is a broad consensus in the software visualization community, and also in the broader information visualization community, that a lack of proper evaluation that can demonstrate the effectiveness of tools is detrimental to the development of the field [50].

Fig. 12. Different views of the stress test with 10 Auto Scaling Groups and 1000 Virtual Machines.

5.1   Sanity Checks

To test the visualization of a considerable sized infrastructure, we simulated an environment composed of 10 different Auto Scaling Groups and a total of 1000 servers, as in Fig. 12.

We concluded that having a large number of resources together in a unique model eventually becomes unnecessary and inefficient for considerably large infrastructures. Conversely, if we divided or collapsed large groups of resources by their Auto Scaling Group, availability zone, or even resource type, we would accomplish a higher-level analysis of a cloud architecture. Thus, avoiding updates in locations far away from our focus zone.

5.2   Controlled Experiment

We designed a controlled experiment to assert the feasibility of *CloudCity*. In this experiment, we focused on: (1) creating and managing a collection of related AWS resources; and (2) inspecting a running architecture and update it on-the-fly.

The population under survey consisted of 18 MSc students, ranging from those with experience in cloud computing to those with little or no knowledge of it. The experiment consisted in performing a similar set of tasks using three different tools. The goal was to evaluate the effect of the tools on the completion of the tasks.

The controlled experiment was designed to probe different perspectives, which were combined into two distinct phases: construction and analysis.

One of the objectives is to compare the feasibility of CloudCity when comparing with state-of-the-practice tools, namely AWS CLOUDFORMATION, which allows the specification of architecture in a blueprint file, providing a static visualization of it. However, AWS CLOUDFORMATION does not give the ability to inspect a running architecture, and, as such, an additional tool was used for fulfilling this aspect, namely AWS MANAGEMENT CONSOLE.

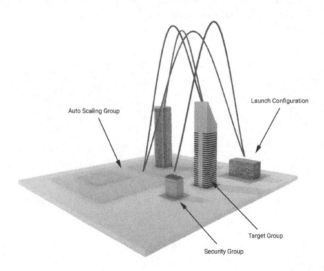

Fig. 13. An illustration of the resulting CloudCity model in the construction phase [32].

Although the data from the experiments are too scarce for definite and sound conclusions, we could assert the feasibility of the solution, and the experimental treatment represents a considerable improvement over some of the current practices, appointing the open potential of adding *liveness* to current cloud management tools.

Construction Phase. In the construction phase, the participants were asked to design a simple cloud architecture composed of four resources using CloudCity, namely: (1) an Auto Scaling Group with a minimum size of two instances; (2) a Launch Configuration for each new instance to be spawned inside the scaling group; (3) a Security Group; and (4) a Target Group to route incoming requests to the targets in the scaling group. The expected, resulting model is depicted in Fig. 13.

All of the participants were capable of fulfilling this task by using the provided *alphabet* and the environment, initially, identifying the right resources and then proceeding to configure and connect them according to the requirements.

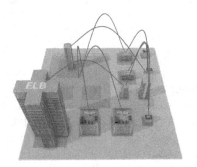 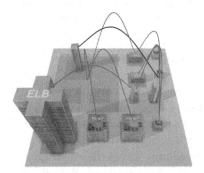

(a) The resulting model of the second phase of the experiment according to TERRAFORM's configuration plan.

(b) The result after the misconfiguration of a Security Group, for the purpose of identifying the resulting infrastructural changes (unhealthy VM instance).

Fig. 14. Resulting visualizations of the experiments. The connections between elements are representing connections and the floor gives information about the group/context of those elements. If everything is operating normally both the connections and floor colors are in green, otherwise the connections and/or floor colors of each element turn red (Color figure online) [32].

Analysis Phase. As for the analysis phase, it consisted of inspecting an existing infrastructure. In order to keep the experience randomized and create some independence between the two phases of the experiment, we previously prepared a similar infrastructure using TERRAFORM containing: (1) an Auto Scaling Group in two zones connected to the respective launch configuration; (2) two Scaling Policies; (3) a Load Balancer with respective Listener, Target Group and Security Group; and (4) a simple HTTP web service running on port 80 (Virtual Machine).

The rationale of the second phase was to simulate the occurrence of an unhealthy target, a common event in a cloud environment. In most cases, the cause is due to a failed/overloaded VM instance or Security Group misconfiguration. For that purpose, we misconfigured a Security Group (firewall) on purpose in one of the registered targets and disallowed any traffic coming from the Target Group. In consequence, the Target Group was not able to send health check requests, and consider the instance unhealthy. The goal is to locate that specific instance and analyze its cause, targeting *liveness* level three: informative, significant, and responsive [53]. Both the occurrences can be confirmed in Fig. 14a and b.

All of the participants were able to identify the issue by observing the red connection (failed health check) between the Target Group and the Virtual Machine instance. They were able to inspect it (by clicking on the connector) and, by tracing back the origin of the problem to the Security Group, they were able to create a new rule to allow the traffic.

6   Final Remarks

There are several issues with cloud management resulting from: (1) the cloud providers being always developing new services to keep up with a demanding market and as reaction to new paradigms (*e.g.*, IoT), and (2) the unavoidable increasing complexity when too many resources are under management in an overwhelming disheveled environment.

From the viewpoint of cloud management, the main contribution of this work is a development environment for cloud architectures, *i.e.*, an approach to analyze, architect and configure cloud compositions with a higher level of abstraction. This environment allows developers to focus more on their business logic and track the changes as the infrastructure evolves, and its complexity increases.

The *CloudCity* approach, resulting from a combination of strengths from several tools and methods for developing cloud architectures and software in general, explores the concept of Live Software Development [1] in the cloud domain, by shortening the feedback loop between the developer and the infrastructure, allowing them to quickly understand, almost immediately, how the infrastructure reacts to change.

As per the comparison to the current state-of-the-practice, we consider that increasing *liveness* improves the developers' experience in cloud architecture configuration tasks. The carried controlled experiment asserted the feasibility and sanity (*i.e.*, evaluate if the approach works as the cloud architecture scales) of the *CloudCity* approach, although further validation is needed to assert aspects such as the *efficiency*—achieving the results in a faster way compared to the traditional methods doing the same task—and overall developer experience. An empirical validation within an industrial case scenario would bring useful information about the *usefulness* of the approach.

During the development of this approach several future research directions where uncovered, such as (1) providing a modifiable layout technique—a user's ability to manually modify the position of a specific component; (2) explore other levels of liveness following the Tanimoto 6-level scale [53]; (3) investigate different metaphors beyond the one of Wettel et al. [57]; and (4) adding other services offered by cloud providers to the *alphabet* (*e.g.*, dealing with the new services related to IoT would bring new challenges such as how to deal with a mixture of virtual infrastructure and real infrastructure, *i.e.*, gateways, sensors, and actuators [12]).

References

1. Aguiar, A., Restivo, A., Figueiredo Correia, F., Ferreira, H.S., Dias, J.P.: Live software development: tightening the feedback loops. In: Conference Companion of the 3rd International Conference on Art, Science, and Engineering of Programming. Programming 2019 Companion (2019)
2. Amaral, D., Domingues, G., Dias, J.P., Ferreira, H.S., Aguiar, A., Nóbrega, R.: Live software development environment for Java using virtual reality. In: Proceedings of the 14th International Conference on Evaluation of Novel Approaches to Software Engineering. ENASE, vol. 1, pp. 37–46 (2019)
3. Amazon, A.: Announcing Amazon Elastic Compute Cloud (Amazon EC2) - beta (2006). https://aws.amazon.com/about-aws/whats-new/2006/08/24/announcing-amazon-elastic-compute-cloud-amazon-ec2---beta/. Accessed 07 2019
4. Amazon Web Services: what is devops? (2017). https://aws.amazon.com/pt/devops/what-is-devops/
5. Anicas, M.: Getting started with puppet code: manifests and modules (2014). https://www.digitalocean.com/community/tutorials/getting-started-with-puppet-code-manifests-and-modules
6. Ardagna, D., et al.: MODA CLOUDS: a model-driven approach for the design and execution of applications on multiple clouds. In: Modeling in Software Engineering, pp. 50–56 (2012)
7. Armbrust, M., Fox, A., Griffith, R., Joseph, A., Katz, R.H.: Above the clouds: a Berkeley view of cloud computing. Technical report, University of California, Berkeley, UCB, p. 1 (2009)
8. Brikman, Y.: Why we use Terraform and not Chef, Puppet, Ansible, SaltStack, or CloudFormation (2016). https://blog.gruntwork.io/
9. Buyya, R., Broberg, J., Goscinski, A.: Cloud Computing Principles and Paradigms. Wiley, Hoboken (2011)
10. Cachin, C., Schunter, M.: A cloud you can trust. IEEE Spectr. **48**(12), 28–51 (2011)
11. Microsoft Corporation: Microsoft Azure IoT Reference Architecture. Technical report, Microsoft Corporation (2016). https://azure.microsoft.com/de-de/updates/microsoft-azure-iot-reference-architecture-available/
12. Dias, J.P., Faria, J.P., Ferreira, H.S.: A reactive and model-based approach for developing internet-of-things systems. In: 2018 11th International Conference on the Quality of Information and Communications Technology (QUATIC), pp. 276–281, September 2018
13. Diehl, S.: Software Visualization: Visualizing the Structure, Behaviour, and Evolution of Software. Springer, Heidelberg (2007). https://doi.org/10.1007/978-3-540-46505-8
14. Dillon, T., Wu, C., Chang, E.: Cloud computing: issues and challenges. In: 2010 24th IEEE International Conference on Advanced Information Networking and Applications, pp. 27–33, April 2010

15. Edwards, D.: What is devops? (2010). http://dev2ops.org/2010/02/what-is-devops/

16. Erian, T.E.: The XaaS family: understanding IaaS, PaaS and SaaS (2018). https://www.ibm.com/blogs/cloud-computing/2014/10/31/xaas-family-iaas-paas-saas-explained/

17. Fittkau, F., Waller, J., Wulf, C., Hasselbring, W.: Live trace visualization for comprehending large software landscapes: the explorviz approach. In: 2013 First IEEE Working Conference on Software Visualization (VISSOFT), pp. 1–4, September 2013

18. Fittkau, F., Krause, A., Hasselbring, W.: Exploring software cities in virtual reality. In: 2015 IEEE 3rd Working Conference on Software Visualization, VISSOFT 2015 - Proceedings, pp. 130–134 (2015)

19. Fraser, S.D., et al.: No silver bullet reloaded: retrospective on essence and accidents of software engineering. In: Companion to the 22nd ACM SIGPLAN Conference on Object-Oriented Programming Systems and Applications Companion, pp. 1026–1030. ACM (2007)

20. Hancock, C.M.: Real-time programming and the big ideas of computational literacy. Ph.D. thesis, Massachusetts Institute of Technology (2003)

21. HashiCorp: Terraform vs. other software (2017). https://www.terraform.io/intro/vs/index.html

22. Heidi, E.: An introduction to configuration management (2016). https://www.digitalocean.com/community/tutorials/an-introduction-to-configuration-management

23. Junior, F.M.R., da Rocha, T.: Model-based approach to automatic software deployment in cloud. In: CLOSER, pp. 151–157 (2014)

24. Kapec, P.: Visualizing software artifacts using hypergraphs. In: Proceedings of the 26th Spring Conference on Computer Graphics - SCCG 2010, p. 27 (2010)

25. Kavis, M.J., et al.: Architecting the Cloud: Design Decisions for CloudComputing Service Models (SaaS, PaaS, and IaaS). Wiley, Hoboken (2013)

26. Kent, S.: Model driven engineering. In: Butler, M., Petre, L., Sere, K. (eds.) IFM 2002. Lecture Notes in Computer Science, vol. 2335, pp. 286–298. Springer, Heidelberg (2002). https://doi.org/10.1007/3-540-47884-1_16

27. Kerzazi, N., Adams, B.: Who needs release and devops engineers, and why? In: Proceedings of the International Workshop on Continuous Software Evolution and Delivery - CSED 2016, pp. 77–83 (2016)

28. Lanza, M.: CodeCrawler - Polymetric views in action. In: Proceedings - 19th International Conference on Automated Software Engineering, ASE 2004, pp. 394–395 (2004)

29. Lanza, M., Ducasse, S.: Polymetric views-a lightweight visual approach to reverse engineering. Trans. Softw. Eng. (TSE) **29**(9), 782–795 (2003)

30. Li, A., Yang, X., Kandula, S., Zhang, M.: CloudCmp: comparing public cloud providers. In: Proceedings of the 10th ACM SIGCOMM Conference on Internet Measurement, IMC 2010, pp. 1–14. ACM, New York (2010)

31. Linthicum, D.S.: Understanding complex cloud patterns. IEEE Cloud Comput. **3**(1), 8–11 (2016)

32. LourenÇo, P., Dias, J.P., Aguiar, A., Ferreira, H.S.: CloudCity: a live environment for the management of cloud infrastructures. In: Proceedings of the 14th International Conference on Evaluation of Novel Approaches to Software Engineering. ENASE, vol. 1, pp. 27–36 (2019)

33. Mastelic, T., Brandic, I., Garcia, A.G.: Towards uniform management of cloud services by applying model-driven development. In: 2014 IEEE 38th Annual Computer Software and Applications Conference, pp. 129–138 (2014)
34. McDirmid, S.: Usable live programming. In: Proceedings of the 2013 ACM International Symposium on New Ideas, New Paradigms, and Reflections on Programming & Software, Onward! 2013, pp. 53–62. ACM, New York (2013)
35. Mcdirmid, S.: The promise of live programming. In: LIVE Programming Workshop (2016)
36. Mell, P., Grance, T.: The NIST definition of cloud computing recommendations of the national institute of standards and technology. Technical report, NIST (2011)
37. Mens, T.: On the complexity of software systems. Computer **45**(8), 79–81 (2012)
38. Merino, L., Ghafari, M., Anslow, C., Nierstrasz, O.: CityVR: gameful software visualization. In: 2017 IEEE International Conference on Software Maintenance and Evolution (ICSME), pp. 633–637, September 2017
39. Janakiram, M.S.V.: AWS service sprawl starts to hurt the cloud ecosystem (2018). https://www.forbes.com/sites/janakirammsv/2018/01/08/aws-service-sprawl-starts-to-hurt-the-cloud-ecosystem/#44616e775c1f. Accesseed July 2019
40. Nunes, R., Reboucas, M., Soares-Neto, F., Castor, F.: Visualizing swift projects as cities. In: Proceedings - 2017 IEEE/ACM 39th International Conference on Software Engineering Companion, ICSE-C 2017, pp. 368–370 (2017)
41. Object Management Group, Inc.: Introduction to OMG's unified modeling language (2005). http://www.uml.org/what-is-uml.htm
42. Oladehin, O., Brett, F.: Core tenets of IoT. Technical report, Amazon Web Services (2017). https://d1.awsstatic.com/whitepapers/core-tenets-of-iot1.pdf
43. Opara-Martins, J., Sahandi, R., Tian, F.: Critical review of vendor lock-in and its impact on adoption of cloud computing. In: International Conference on Information Society (i-Society 2014), pp. 92–97. IEEE (2014)
44. Pinto, D., Dias, J.P., Sereno Ferreira, H.: Dynamic allocation of serverless functions in IoT environments. In: 2018 IEEE 16th International Conference on Embedded and Ubiquitous Computing (EUC), pp. 1–8, October 2018
45. Pressman, R.S., Maxim, B.R.: Software Engineering: A Practitioner's Approach. McGraw-Hill Education, New York (2015)
46. RightScale: State of the Cloud Report. Technical report, RightScale (2017)
47. Sandobalin, J., Insfran, E., Abrahao, S.: An infrastructure modelling tool for cloud provisioning. In: Proceedings - 2017 IEEE 14th International Conference on Services Computing, SCC 2017, pp. 354–361 (2017)
48. Sayers, D.: Configuration management vs. application release automation (2017). https://devops.com/configuration-management-vs-application-release-automation/
49. McDirmid, S.: Live programming as gradual abstraction. In: LIVE Programming Workshop (2017)
50. Sensalire, M., Ogao, P., Telea, A.: Evaluation of software visualization tools: lessons learned. In: 2009 5th IEEE International Workshop on Visualizing Software for Understanding and Analysis, pp. 19–26 (2009)
51. Serrano, N., Gallardo, G., Hernantes, J.: Infrastructure as a service and cloud technologies. IEEE Softw. **32**, 30–36 (2015)
52. Tanimoto, S.L.: VIVA: a visual language for image processing. J. Vis. Lang. Comput. **1**, 127–139 (1990)
53. Tanimoto, S.L.: A perspective on the evolution of live programming. In: 2013 1st International Workshop on Live Programming, LIVE 2013 - Proceedings, pp. 31–34 (2013)

54. Tosatto, A., Ruiu, P., Attanasio, A.: Container-based orchestration in cloud: state of the art and challenges. In: Proceedings - 2015 9th International Conference on Complex, Intelligent, and Software Intensive Systems, CISIS 2015, pp. 70–75 (2015)
55. Vaquero, L.M., Rodero-Merino, L., Caceres, J., Lindner, M.: A break in the clouds: towards a cloud definition. ACM SIGCOMM Comput. Commun. Rev. **39**(1), 50–55 (2008)
56. Vincur, J., Navrat, P., Polasek, I.: VR City: software analysis in virtual reality environment. In: 2017 IEEE International Conference on Software Quality, Reliability and Security Companion (QRS-C), pp. 509–516 (2017)
57. Wettel, R., Lanza, M., Robbes, R.: Software systems as cities. In: Proceeding of the 33rd International Conference on Software Engineering - ICSE 2011 (2011)
58. Wettinger, J., et al.: Integrating configuration management with model-driven cloud management based on TOSCA. In: CLOSER 2013 - Proceedings of the 3rd International Conference on Cloud Computing and Services Science, pp. 437–446 (2013)

Live Software Development Environment Using Virtual Reality: A Prototype and Experiment

Diogo Amaral[1], Gil Domingues[1], João Pedro Dias[1,2(✉)],
Hugo Sereno Ferreira[1,2], Ademar Aguiar[1,2], Rui Nóbrega[1,2],
and Filipe Figueiredo Correia[1,2]

[1] Faculty of Engineering, University of Porto, Porto, Portugal
[2] INESC TEC, Porto, Portugal
{diogo.amaral,gil.domingues,jpmdias,hugosf,
aaguiar,ruinobrega,filipe.correia}@fe.up.pt

Abstract. Successful software systems tend to grow considerably, ending up suffering from essential complexity, and very hard to understand as a whole. Software visualization techniques have been explored as one approach to ease software understanding. This work presents a novel approach and environment for software development that explores the use of *liveness* and virtual reality (VR) as a way to shorten the feedback loop between developers and their software systems in an interactive and immersive way. As a proof-of-concept, the authors developed a prototype that uses a visual city metaphor and allows developers to visit and dive into the system, in a live way. To assess the usability and viability of the approach, the authors carried on experiments to evaluate the effectiveness of the approach, and how to best support a *live* approach for software development.

Keywords: Software engineering · Virtual reality · Live Software Development · Live programming · Software visualization

1 Introduction

Much of the software created today is built incrementally from an initial prototype that evolves gradually through the addition of new features. Along this process, the dimension of the system increases, and the productivity is hampered by the comprehension tasks.

Software systems can achieve very high complexity, to a great extent due to their size, which can reach millions of lines of code [2]. Software engineers, when adding new functionality or merely performing maintenance tasks, should first understand the system [23,32], which can be challenging due to scalability and complexity [7,19,33].

We argue that this difficulty can be reduced in many cases by applying the idea of *liveness*, i.e., the ability to modify a system while it is running [30],

© Springer Nature Switzerland AG 2020
E. Damiani et al. (Eds.): ENASE 2019, CCIS 1172, pp. 83–107, 2020.
https://doi.org/10.1007/978-3-030-40223-5_5

allowing the developer to receive immediate *feedback* of changes made, with the system continually rerunning while being edited.

Additionally, visualizing and interacting with software in a virtual reality environment can increase comprehension by using real-world-based visual metaphors that represent software in a familiar context that can easily be identified by the programmer [32]. In a fully-immersive virtual environment, it is possible to get closer to reality, creating a simulation of a real or virtual world in which the user can be present, dive, touch and feel objects [29].

In the research work presented in this paper, our goal is to explore how software comprehension improves by allowing users to view and change the system in a live way using virtual reality. A prototype was developed for Java systems that receives information about the static and dynamic analysis of the system, using reverse engineering approaches, such as the ones presented by Fauzi et al. [8] and Guéhéneue et al. [12]. The tool allows visualizing the software using visual metaphors, in real-time and during the execution of the system. The interaction with the system in full execution is a crucial factor, to get closer to the experience of live programming and create a fluid feedback-loop between the program and the programmer. In this work, the approach of *Live Software Development* resorts to the virtual reality for the construction of an environment, through which it is possible to understand the system and visit it in an interactive and immersive way.

The work here presented expands on previous work from the authors in the *Live Software Development* paradigm [1,3,18] and provides a more detailed account of a user study that was performed to validate the merits of the approach.

The paper is structured as follows: Sect. 2 overviews the current state-of-the-art on live programming, software visualization, software analysis, and virtual reality; Sect. 3 overviews our approach towards live software development, including architecture details; Sects. 4 and 5 present the user study and its results; and, finally, Sect. 6 provides some final remarks and hints for future work.

2   Literature Review

This work involves different areas, such as *Live Programming, Software Visualization, Software Analysis* and *Virtual Reality.*

2.1   Live Programming

The fundamental notion of live programming is not having a traditional program development cycle involving four phases—*edit, compile, link, run*—but only one phase, at least in principle. This phase consists simply of having the program always running, continuously, even if various editing events occur [30].

Live programming embraces the concept of *liveness* to ease the programming task by executing a program continuously during editing (real-time programming). Looking back at Hancock's analogy, consider hitting a target with a stream of water: we *receive continuous feedback on where we are shooting*, whereas, with archery, we need to shoot (run the software) and rely on the discrete feedback (debugging) provided by the point the arrow hit, adjusting the aim if necessary [13,21].

Liveness is a notion originally observed in LISP machines and the Smalltalk language, as examples of live programming in the earlier days of computing. Liveness is closely related to visual programming, which provides a more straightforward and intuitive interface to develop and modify software.

2.2 Software Visualization

The software is inherently invisible, which does not help the task of understanding how it functions. Visualization tools are useful to associate a tangible representation to the code and the program execution. Visualizations are especially relevant in the maintenance, reverse engineering, and re-engineering cases [16].

Bassil et al. show evidence that the most common visualization methods are based on graphs, and there are plenty of examples in literature [4,26] that represent the relationships between levels of a system using graphs [5].

CodeCrawler [17] is a tool to visualize data retrieved from other reverse engineering tools, offering a visual encoding that allows representing five metrics per entity. For this type of visualization, we need to choose the layout, the five metrics out of a defined list [17], and the entities representing those metrics.

Jinsight is an example of a tool created to visualize program runtime data. It provides multiple views to increase the probability of the user detecting existing performance issues, unexpected behavior, or bugs. The *JVM* profiling agent [6] provides the data used by this tool.

While the most common software visualization methods are two-dimensional representations, some authors present a 3D representation of the architecture of software as a city, where the user can freely move around and observe and interact with the system [24,34]. This approach is a pure visualization system, and does not deal with real-time modifications of the running system.

Teyseyre et al. [31] discusses the use of 3D software representations and how they have been approach up until this point. Representations have mostly been in one of two ways: abstract visual or real-world representations. Abstract visual representations are graphs, trees, and other abstract geometric shapes, while an example of real-world representations is a city metaphor.

2.3 Static and Dynamic Analysis

The source code is the representation most familiar for developers. It is how software is built and modified. However, it is not necessarily the best when the goal is to ease software comprehension. For that purpose, different and higher levels of abstraction are useful to increase the developers' understanding of the software. *UML* is an example of a higher-level representation of a system's structure and behaviour [25], being amongst the most popular for object-oriented systems.

To develop a higher-level abstraction, firstly, it is required to obtain the existent structural information from the system. Feijs et al. [9] describe a model for analyzing architecture: Extract-Abstract-Present. *Extraction* consists of retrieving structural information from the system, *abstraction* is the derivation of new relationships between the components obtained in the earlier phase (i.e., further analysis of those components) and the *presentation* of that information through a graphical format.

Software Reverse Engineering. Fauzi et al. [8] identify reverse engineering as a valid approach to generate sequence diagrams that reflect a system's behavior.

Although one may assume reverse engineering makes use solely of static representations, such as source code or bytecode, this is not the case. There are several situations where the static and dynamic analysis must be combined. Guéhéneuc et al. [12] demonstrate how a mixture of static and dynamic models allows for a more precise automatic generation of class diagrams. Furthermore, Shi et al. [28] describe *PINOT*, a tool to automatically detect design patterns from both the source code and the system's behavior.

Abstract Syntax Trees. Abstract syntax trees (*AST*) are data structures used by compilers to create intermediate representations of the software that ignores unnecessary syntactic details [14]. This makes it an interesting starting point for analyzing the structure of a software system. Related works include visualizing the evolution of a software project by analyzing the *AST* between commits, as opposed to the typical *file diffs* done by version control systems [10].

Dynamic Analysis. Obtaining a software system's structure is not sufficient to understand how it behaves. There are multiple sources of variability that cannot be taken into account during static analysis, such as user input, the performance of shared resources and variable control flow paths [11].

To compensate for this lack of information, the system should be observed during runtime. For example, logging is a very common practice in software development to record dynamic information of a program's execution [36].

Dynamic analysis can be implemented in multiple ways. Gosain et al. [11] describe the different approaches and tools associated.

2.4   Virtual Reality

Virtual Reality (VR) is used to create real or virtual simulations, applies the theory of immersion in a 3D virtual space where the senses resemble the real world [29]. The presence of investments in the research and development of VR has been driven by the decrease in size and costs of VR equipment, such as headsets. For example, nowadays anyone can have a VR device, be it more sophisticated or cheap, created with a card.

Although still few software visualization tools use VR for comprehension tasks [22], some applications have already been developed. As an example, VR

City [32] uses an animation to demonstrate which classes and methods undergo changes in a sequence of commits, previously provided to the tool.

In general, the use of an immersive environment is an added value for visualization and interaction with the created representation of the software system.

3   Live Software Development Environment

This work aims at providing a Live Software Development environment for improving comprehension by visually representing the software structure and runtime behavior using VR. The overall architecture is depicted in Fig. 1.

To obtain relevant information about the software system under analysis, we developed an extraction and storage framework, which uses static and dynamic analysis strategies. The metadata extracted with the framework (both static and dynamic) is then used by the VR engine, which renders it following a city metaphor. The visualization provides different visual elements to help the developers to understand the software at hand, as, for example, representing class packages as city blocks and classes as city buildings.

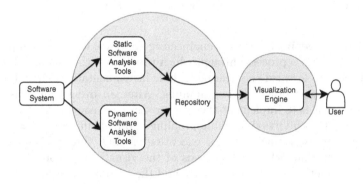

Fig. 1. Diagram of the idealized *Live Software Development* environment [3].

The framework is responsible for the extraction, storage, and provision of information about a software system, so far in Java. The information is extracted from the development environment, without the need to modify the source code itself, and stored in a repository. It is then possible to query this repository and be notified of any modifications in real-time.

As software comprehension is inherently tied to development and maintenance, we assume that the tools which request information from this framework will do so from within a development environment.

The environment allows the visualization of spatial and temporal content through the use of VR. Familiar metaphors allowing the 3D visualization and interaction favor the understanding of the information. At this point, the use of VR equipment, such as simple headsets and controls, allows the user to control the flow of software execution and to traverse the space created by the metaphor. The control of the execution visualization is in the hands of the user.

To develop the environment, the authors considered a series of design concerns, which we describe in the following sections.

3.1 General Approaches to Analyze Source Code

It was first defined how to best identify and analyze the structure and behavior of a *Java* system. This analysis focuses on the source code, and two main paths can be followed: *reverse engineering* and *forward engineering*.

Reverse Engineering. Through reverse engineering, higher-level representations of the software can be extracted, the basis of the static structural analysis. Two representations of a *Java project* are used. First, the *Java Model* used by the *Eclipse IDE*, containing information about the Java elements, such as compilation units, packages, and methods. Second, the AST of the software is used to overlook minor syntactic details of the code and arrive at an easier to understand representation of the source code structure, from package-level down to method-level. Combining these two representations provides the information on how the system is composed and empowers the next process.

Forward Engineering. Forward engineering supports lower-level representations of the system, a process through which we observe the system's behavior.

Approaches to forward engineering include instrumentation, virtual machine profiling, and aspect-oriented programming. After an overall analysis of how straightforward it is to implement these approaches, we concluded that the best fit was a mix of both virtual machine profiling and code instrumentation.

The approach was then used for execution tracing, through event logging, at a granularity that best fits the needs of the visualization component—e.g., logging called methods, the calling class, and the used arguments.

Monitoring would also be a viable option for relevant behavior information. We would need to define resource usage or function execution time thresholds so that an event is logged when one of those thresholds is violated.

3.2 Structural Analysis

The extraction of structural information regarding the software project focused explicitly on the *Java* language. The *Java* AST can be used to abstract syntactic details from the program and provides a structure of the elements considerably more straightforward to interpret than the code itself.

To have easier access to the AST, as well as some other structural details of a *Java* project, and given the assumption of a development environment, the software structure analysis was envisioned as a *IDE plug-in*. *Eclipse* is an *IDE* containing a set of *Java Development Tools* (JDT) which allows *plug-in* developers access to the internal representations of *Java* projects. For this reason, the structure analysis tool was developed as an *Eclipse plug-in*.

Sources of Program Structure. Before designing the internal representation of the workspace for the *plug-in*, it was necessary to understand the structures that *Eclipse JDT* provides access to: the abstract syntax tree (AST) and the *Java Model*. The AST is composed of *ASTNodes* that can be composed of other *ASTNodes*. Each *ASTNode* represents a *Java* source code construct, such as a name, type, expression, statement or declaration. Other classes exist that extend *ASTNode* to include attributes and methods specific to the source code construct that they represent.

Given its proximity with the source code, the *AST* allows fine-grained information about where elements are located in a source file. Nevertheless, the fact that the *AST* is a powerful representation of a project comes with a significant drawback. Due to its fine-grained structural nature, it is considerably more complicated to navigate than the *Eclipse Java Model*.

The *Java Model* is composed of the classes which model the elements that compose a *Java* program. These classes range from *IJavaModel*, which represents the workspace in question, *IJavaProject*, which represents the project itself, to *IMethod* and *IType*, which represent methods and classes respectively.

As the *Java Model* structure is considerably easier to traverse than the AST due to its coarser granularity, it was used as the primary source of information to build the internal model of the project.

Extraction of Program Structure. The actual process of extracting the structure of the projects in the workspace is based on a progressive descent through the *Java Model*. Before the *Java Model* can be analyzed, it has to be generated from the *IWorkspace* class, which represents the workspace in a language-agnostic manner. This is done by invoking *JavaCore* to create a method with the current *IWorkwspace* as an argument.

Once the *Java Model* is obtained, we analyze each project in the workspace. The analysis of an element of a certain level in the *Java Model* implies the analysis of all their child elements. For example, analyzing one project implies analyzing that project's package fragments, which further implies analyzing each package fragment's compilation units, and so on.

Although this process may seem trivial, there are some points worth noting regarding the extraction of the lower-level elements in the model. There are cases in which obtaining the child elements of a specific parent element is not as linear as calling a *getChildElements* method which returns an array of said child elements. This is the case when obtaining both the classes' methods and the method invocations within them.

The complexity in obtaining these two types of structural elements arises from being necessary to, in both cases, obtain information from the *AST*, to be used in conjunction with the information from the *Java Model*.

Live Changes. One of the crucial features of the *plug-in* developed for the statistical analysis is the ability to detect changes to the source code in real-time and reanalyzing the changed elements.

The *Eclipse JDT* provides the mechanism to implement an element change listener, which calls a predefined function once there is a change to a *Java* element inside the *Eclipse IDE*. The callback function will receive as an argument the *ElementChangedEvent*, from which we can obtain the *IJavaElementDelta* that contains information about the element changed.

As *IJavaElementDelta* informs us of the element changed, the representation of the project in the *plug-in* does not have to be rebuilt from the start. Processing time is thus saved by only analyzing the affected elements, from the *Project* level to the *Compilation Unit* level.

Although it would be interesting to allow modifications at the *Method* level, *Eclipse JDT* does not provide a notification of a change in a *IMethod* when the method body is changed, only a *ICompilationUnit* level notification. The lowest change listener implemented was therefore at the *Compilation Unit* level.

When communicating the result of this partial analysis to the repository, the *JSON* data sent is the part of the aforementioned *JSON* structure relevant to the element level analyzed. The request is then sent to the endpoint corresponding to the respective element: `/projects`, `/packages` or `/i-classes`.

Another critical factor in guaranteeing consistency is the analysis of the workspace when the *IDE* is launched. This compensates for any changes that may have been done to the source code from an external tool. Also, this establishes a mechanism to restore the projects' representations to a safe state if any inconsistency issues occur during the detection of live changes.

It is also important to note that if there are any issues with the analysis as a result of incorrect source code (i.e., invoking nonexistent functions), the model is not generated, and the changes are not propagated.

3.3   Runtime Analysis

The software's behavior upon execution is also important, to know how a piece of software functions.

However, a runtime analyzer should be minimally invasive—the logging concerns should be as decoupled from the software to be analyzed as possible. This concern excludes the case of merely implementing a logger as a class in the project and then calling a *log* method whenever it is relevant, adapting it to whichever context it is called.

AspectJ provides a way to achieve such segregation of concerns, by weaving *advices* into the original code. For the analyzer code to be weaved into the project in question, we need to choose the relevant *join points*, define the *pointcuts* and the *advices* [15].

The first concern is to choose the relevant **joint points**. These are the points in a *Java* project in which *AspectJ* allows us to introduce advice. Examples of *join points* are method calls, method executions, constructor calls, field reference, and exception handlers, among others. For our analyzer, however, we chose to only focus on method calls.

Secondly, it is necessary to define the **pointcuts**, that is, exactly what instances of the *joint points* are weaved with the *advice*. Since the goal is to build a generic method call logger, the conjunction of *pointcuts* must include all the calls of the system to be analyzed. The *pointcuts* used by the analyzer are the *call pointcut*, which gathers all method calls, and the *within pointcut*, to exclude all method calls from within the classes of the runtime analyzer itself.

Given the fact that the analyzer is provided as a *AspectJ* project, the user can add pointcuts to the existing advice. One possible application for this would be to select method calls originating from a specific class or package by using the *within* pointcut. Besides allowing for more targeted analysis, it would help the communication process run more smoothly since the amount of information being sent would be reduced.

Finally, we need to define the aspect **advice**, which specifies the code that is weaved into the original source code upon compilation, at each *pointcut*. As we want to have a notion of the order of method calls, the advice is weaved to run before the method calls.

Figure 2 shows the partial definition of the aspect used to monitor method calls (missing the rest of the advice). The joinpoint corresponds to *call*, while the rest of the pointcut specifies that the advice should not be weaved into method calls of the execution analyzer. Finally, the advice recovers information from the method call and hands it over to the communication interface to send the method call to the repository.

```
public aspect MethodInvocation {
    pointcut methodInvocation() :
        call(* *(..)) && (!within(MethodInvocation)) &&
            (!within(communication.Logger)) && (!within(communication.RepositoryInterface)) &&
            (!within(communication.Startup)) ; //&&
            //( insert other calls here || call);

    before() : methodInvocation(){
        System.out.println("NOW\n");

        Startup.getInstance();

        JSONObject event = new JSONObject();

        event.put("this", thisJoinPoint.getThis() == null ? "static" : "instance");
        event.put("target", thisJoinPoint.getTarget() == null ? "null" : "exists");
        event.put("kind",  thisJoinPoint.getKind());
```

Fig. 2. Definition of the aspect which monitors the execution [3].

A user-interface was not built for this, but a developer could easily modify the aspect where the comment *"insert other calls here"* is done in Fig. 2, and add *within* pointcuts to focus the extraction on classes or packages of interest. This reduces the toll on the repository and allows them to focus specifically on the particular method calls of a small set of classes.

Upon compiling the project, *AspectJ* instruments the resulting code by inserting the code defined in the advice in the points specified by the advice.

The main goal of this process is to extract the most valuable information without compromising the dimension of each *event*, considering there is a massive amount of method calls in a typical piece of software and that these *events* have to be handled by the repository.

The analyzer also obtains an array of the arguments used in the method call and for each stores its type (*type* field) and whether it is null or not (*value* field).

3.4   Communication

Communication is of utter importance, given the large amount of data it may transmit. To reduce the impact of the analysis and the latency with which *events* arrive at the repository, and, consequently, to the visualization engine, two approaches are adopted: *asynchronous requests* and *buffering*.

Fig. 3. Structure of the visualization using the engine tool on *JUnit* project [3].

Asynchronous requests are the most straightforward improvement that can be implemented, especially taking into account that no return information must be processed. As we favor reduced latency over the guarantee that all *events* are received, asynchronous requests avoid stopping the execution of the original software from sending a request and await the server's response. This significantly reduces the performance impact of the analyzer.

The second mechanism is buffering *events*, that is, storing events in an array and sending a request with all the stored events, clearing the array afterward, and repeating this process at a fixed time interval. The reasoning behind using buffering is to minimize the impact of the inherent latency of communicating with the server. Similarly to the reasoning behind sending the whole project structure in a single request, it is better to send one large request and allow the server to process it than to send a large batch of smaller requests.

Though buffering may affect the notion of *liveness*, it prevents unordered *events* and avoids, or at least reduces the likelihood of overwhelming the communication channel with massive amounts of small requests.

3.5   Visualization Engine

The visualization engine seeks to combine the best of both worlds: liveness and virtual reality. The virtual environment is responsible for visualizing static and dynamic content, while the use of liveness increases and improves the feedback of the software transmitted to the user. The VR feature for visualizing the 3D content is critical for the immersion. Figure 3 is a static sample of the tool's features.

City-Based Metaphor. The city-based metaphor was selected for this project due to its frequent appearance among different literature about software visualization. Further, this metaphor is easily recognized by a developer as it is based on city buildings, roads, and typical city blocks.

The mapping performs the conversion from packages, classes, and invocations information into districts, buildings, and connections. The whole environment is built using blocks. The dimensions and colors of the blocks are defined through metrics obtained from the software. Block allocation also follows a predefined rule, to minimize the total space required for the construction of the city, maintaining a rectangular space and instantiating the elements by dimension.

The tangibility created with the city metaphor allows us to take a different stance on code understanding.

Interaction Actions and Interface. Being a virtual live environment, the invocations that occur would be imperceptible, since they may happen in less than a millisecond. To view and analyze the software, the engine generates the connections when it receives them, and adds 3 s of duration so that the user has the necessary time to understand what is happening. Also, the user has in his possession other time controls in the environment menu.

Using the controllers and sensors of the VR devices, the user can perform several actions. **Pause**—block any changes in the environment, either with connections or with districts and packages. This is the ideal time for the user to make his analysis because he has total temporal freedom. **Start Live**—return to the live state, after a pause; i.e., back to real-time operation, ignoring everything that might have happened at the time it was paused. **Continue**—continue to execute at the next point to the one that was in the moment that paused the execution. All events that the engine received and were not viewed are cached and can thus be recovered. **Go back 1 second**—despite the intentional delay created in the changes that occur in the environment, the user may lose some detail, and may want to go *back in time*. This feature asks the server for the events that happened in the last second and returns to show them.

Navigating the virtual world is achieved by physically moving the user, or by using the *teleport* functionality.

The user interaction with the virtual environment is possible using only one monitor of a computer. However, the visualization loses its immersiveness and the interaction becomes impracticable due to the non-existence of controllers.

As a result, it is advised to use VR devices with hand controllers and sensors, such as HTC Vive or Oculus Rift.

4 User Study Design

The environment presented in Sect. 3 has the goal of reducing the effort of understanding a software system, hence shortening the length of the feedback loop required to change it or debug it. The controlled experiment detailed in this section has the goals of exploring the potential of the environment for understanding concrete software systems, and of validating the relative effectiveness and efficiency of developers when using it.

4.1 Guidelines

A user study should have into account multiple concerns to reach its goals. The following guidelines were considered when designing the experiment [34].

- **Pedagogical Goals.** As other empirical studies with students, there was the goal of aligning it with educational objectives and the learning process [35].
- **Software Development Experience.** The participant must be familiar with the mechanisms of understanding software systems. Thus, all participants should have experience in software development.
- **Participant Motivation.** Using new technologies as the case of virtual reality devices often arouses the interest of potential participants and is a motivation for signing up to participate in the experiment [27].
- **Familiarity with the Environment.** A reliable and fair comparison of the tool requires prior training with the goal of giving participants the basic knowledge to use the hardware and software. Such a tutorial should be done, if possible, sometime in advance from the experience [20,27,34].
- **Duration.** Participants should have a maximum length of time to perform the tasks and be informed about this limit [27].
- **Project Selection.** Identify student project cases to use in research without interfering with educational goals [35].
- **Prior Knowledge.** To maximize confidence in the results, the participants should have roughly the same experience using the environment [27].

4.2 Experimental Design

The guidelines described in the previous section were considered when designing the experiment, as detailed below.

Participants. The participants were 25 subjects from an academic context—students, researchers, and professors. All had strong programming training and participated freely and with the interest of knowing and exploring the tool.

Physical Environment. The experiment was carried out in a closed room in the Department of Informatics Engineering of the Faculty of Engineering of the University of Porto. The room had a computer screen, which showed what was visualized by the participant, and a free space of 3×3 m for the user's movement. If the participant approached the boundaries of free space, a bounding grid would appear in the virtual environment, prompting it to move away. For interaction with virtual reality, the *Oculus Rift* device was used.

Questionnaire. The experiment included filling out different parts of a questionnaire, one for each of the tasks described in Sect. 4.3. The questionnaire allowed to characterize the participants, to provide insights about the tasks, the interaction, and the usability of the environment.

The questions were designed using a Likert scale by dividing the possible answers into *Strongly Disagree, Disagree, I Have No Opinion, Agree* and *Strongly Agree*, or *Very difficult, Difficult, I have no opinion, Easy* and *Very easy*. For analysis, values from 1 to 5 were assigned, respectively, to the two previous scales, with 1 being the negative evaluation and 5 the most positive evaluation.

Duration. Participants could use the environment for 25 min. Having a hard limit for the duration of the experiment is valued by the participants as it allows them to manage their time better. It is also important because it creates the same time base for the completion of tasks for all participants. Sensalire et al. investigated the average duration of experiments taking up to several hours [27].

Exposure to the Environment. The participants received, before starting the experiment, a tutorial of use of the tool and its main functionalities. The first task had the goal of exposing the participant to all the features of the environment and obtaining feedback on the ease of interacting or visualizing elements of the software system. The time allowed for this first task was what was necessary for the participant to know and understand the functionalities.

Data Integrity. All participants were also informed of the project's authorship before the experiment started. To try to maximize criticism and reduce participants' generosity in responses, which would bias the data, criticism was encouraged by making all responses anonymous.

4.3   Tasks

A small project called *Maze* was selected as the target for the tasks. The project was developed by students in an undergraduate course and had the right dimension to make understanding attainable while still having some degree of architectural complexity, that is, it contains a reasonable number of each one of the structural elements (e.g., packages, classes).

The experiment consists of three tasks, accompanied by different sets of questions, to evaluate different factors in the virtual environment.

Task T1: **Learning to use the Virtual Environment.**

The participant must learn how to use the available features and controls of the VR device. After this introductory phase, the objective is to experience the visualization of all possible components and interactions. Figure 4 illustrates several participants performing T1 on their first exposure to the tool.

Fig. 4. Participants in the first exposure to the virtual environment (Task 1).

Task T2: **Identifying an Infinite Loop.**

The participant had the goal of identifying an infinite loop by using the virtual environment (Fig. 5). The invocations within the loop occur sequentially. The participant could not interfere with the loop, which had no possibility of being terminated. The participant is informed that on the IDE side, there is no error, and the system is blocked.

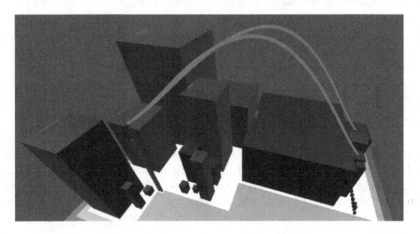

Fig. 5. Display of infinite loop invocations (Task 2).

Task T3: **Identifying a *null* Method Argument.**

The participant had the goal of identifying the class that made a method call with a *null* argument Fig. 6 shows such class. Its color flashes red, and an audible alert is triggered so that the participant is alerted of the event. The sound is useful when the class that performed the invocation is not in the participant's field of vision.

Fig. 6. Display of class performing an invocation with a null argument (Task 3). (Color figure online)

4.4   Data Sources

In addition to the answers in the questionnaires, two attributes of interest were collected throughout the experiment.

- **Duration.** Each of the three tasks was timed. This metric is important to compare participants and to calculate the mean.
- **Difficulty.** The perception obtained by a control agent—the first author—of the execution of each task. This perception is quantified from 0 to 5, with 5 corresponding to a task performed integrally and with a good performance.

  Participants had no notion of time in the virtual environment and weren't aware of the difficulty they showed in solving the tasks as perceived by the control agent. Duration is a quantitative attribute, easy to measure, and difficulty is a qualitative attribute, that was based on the opinion of the control agent.

5   Results

The data collected by the questionnaire and the control agent is analyzed and discussed hereafter.

5.1   Subject Characterization

The experiment had the participation of 19 male subjects and 6 female subjects. They included undergraduate students (12%), graduate students (72%), people with a master's degree (12%) and with a Ph.D. degree (4%). Ages range from 18 to 36 years ($\bar{x} = 23.44 \pm 3.15$).

All participants confirmed they had programming experience, with 88% of them programming practically daily. More than half of the participants confirmed that they often experienced some difficulty in understanding software systems (76%) and almost all use tools to help them understand them (92%), but 88% never used *visual* tools to aid in code comprehension.

5.2   Experience with the Oculus Rift

The familiarity of the participants with the device used to perform the tasks, the Oculus Rift VR Headset, in particular with its controls, is shown in Table 1.

Table 1. Number of participants with Oculus Rift experience.

Oculus rift experience	# of participants
None	18
Some	4
Considerable	3

Having previous experience with the device, either in the use of controllers or in the experience of immersing in virtual reality, could make the adaptation to the environment easier. A small number mentioned that this was their first experience with VR, but it's to be expected that many users in a broader context would also not have had previous access and experience with VR headsets.

5.3   Task 1 (T1)

The first of the three tasks (T1) is explained in Sect. 4.3. It exposed the participant for the first time to the virtual environment and its features.

Figure 7 presents the data collected via de questionnaire concerning T1, and shows a general agreement that it was easy to perform.

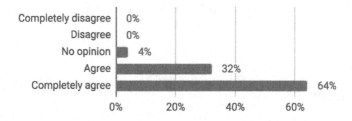

Fig. 7. Answers to T1.1—"Task 1 in general was easy to perform".

The easiness of the recognition and exploration activities of the major features of the environment were also classified. The answers to T1.2a and T1.2b can be seen in Figs. 8 and 9. The first of these figures shows that it's not as easy to think about packages. This is due to the small dimension of the system being used, which contained only 3 package levels—i.e., 3 district levels—and additionally, all buildings were at the same district level.

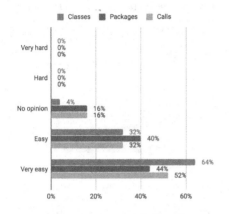

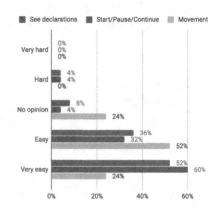

Fig. 8. Answers to T1.2a—"These activities were easy to perform" (identify classes; identify packages; identify method calls).

Fig. 9. Answers to T1.2b—"These activities were easy to perform" (see declarations; start/pause/continue execution; movement in the environment).

The T1.2b task required more interaction with the *headset* controllers, which created difficulties for participants who had less experience using Oculus. Physical movement was not used as much as it could, because the participants relied mostly on the teleport functionality.

The evaluation done by the experiment's control agent regarding the difficulty shown by participants when doing T1 had a mean of $\bar{x} = 4.56 \pm 0.65$. This value represents the agent's perception, scored from 1 to 5. This reflects the fact that the task was, in general terms, done positively and entirely by all participants.

In conclusion, the collected data highlights the low difficulty in using the environment by users that are exposed to it for the first time.

5.4 Task 2 (T2)

The focus of T2 was to debug an infinite loop, which blocked the system and the IDE without any error or warning. Upon concluding the task, most of the participants reported no difficulty in identifying the infinite loop (Fig. 10). Figure 11 shows the perception of participants regarding how easy it was to find the issue using the virtual environment when compared with an IDE. Participants found that finding the problem using the visualization was easier, as the IDE wouldn't provide feedback about what is happening and where it is happening, prompting the user to scrutinize the source code or use additional tools.

The controlling agent's assessment of the difficulty shown in solving Task 2 had an average rating of $\bar{x} = 4.24 \pm 0.78$. The average result is lower than that obtained by the participants in the previous task, possibly because it was intrinsically harder to accomplishment, requiring more reasoning.

In short, the participants considered it advantageous to use the virtual environment to perform this type of activity.

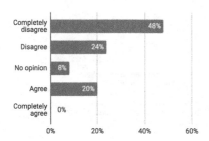

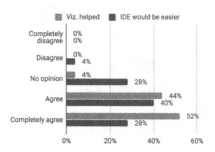

Fig. 10. Answers to T2.1—"I had difficult identifying the infinite loop".

Fig. 11. Answers to T2.2—"In my current IDE I would have a harder time finding the system locked in the loop".

5.5   Task 3 (T3)

Task 3 sought to determine the participants' ability to find a method call in which one of the arguments was *null*, leading to a `NullPointerException`. In the environment, this translated into a building with a flashing red color.

The solution would be to use the *scroll* feature to increase elevation. From the top of the tallest building, participants would not be able to see the object, so this strategy would not be enough to spot the building flashing red.

From the analysis of Figs. 12 and 13, we can conclude that most participants did not have difficulty in performing the task and consider that the visualization helped them to find the problem.

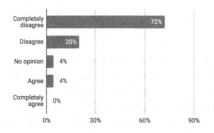

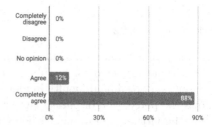

Fig. 12. Answers to T3.1—"I found it difficult to identify the invocation that threw the null exception".

Fig. 13. Answers to T3.2—"The visualization helped me find the problem".

Most participants eventually found the most practical solution and used the *scroll* functionality. Some others decided to walk all the streets of the city on the ground and took more time to find the object.

The controlling agent's assessment of the difficulty shown in solving T3 had an average rating of $\bar{x} = 4.84 \pm 0.37$. The task had a low difficulty, and this value is not higher because some participants didn't immediately realize that gaining a top view of the city was the most straightforward way to answer the task.

In conclusion, this feature was found helpful in debugging *null* exceptions. Even though the sound alert feature was not used in this experiment, we expect it to aid in determining the building's location, as the sound propagates in space and can be heard from farther or closer.

5.6   Virtual Environment Participant Assessment

After completing the tasks, participants evaluated their experience using the virtual environment (Figs. 14 and 15).

The set of questionnaire items A1.1a focused on the perception of static and execution information. The results are similar and positive for both scenarios, as participants were able to obtain the bits of information that they needed.

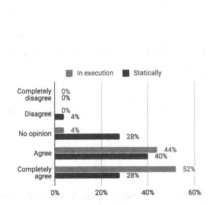

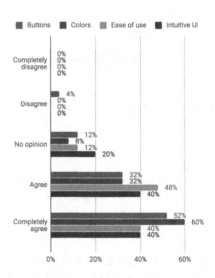

Fig. 14. Answers to A1.1a—"Experience using the virtual environment" (easy perception of static scenario; easy perception of execution scenario).

Fig. 15. Answers to A1.1b—"Experience using the virtual environment" (easy understanding of the use of color; button usefulness; intuitive user interface; ease of use). (Color figure online)

The set A1.1b consisted of four statements. The usefulness of the buttons was confirmed for the vast majority of participants except for one who considered that the buttons should not be in the virtual environment but should be physical buttons present in the Oculus controllers. The use of colors stood out positively because it is one more way of expressing information without requiring any inter-action with objects. Regarding ease of use and interface, despite the majority of positive responses, participants considered that a longer exposure time favored the use of the tool and interaction with the interface.

Regarding the participants' interest in using the tool again, 96% agreed, and only one participant did not express an opinion on this statement (Fig. 16).

This interest is positive because participants in the VR experience, in some cases in their first experience, felt no discomfort in using it and considered an idea with potential for use in real-world contexts.

Participants also expressed if they found the virtual environment beneficial to understanding software systems (Fig. 17). The results are encouraging to the objective of the virtual environment, due to the significant presence of positive responses compared to no negative ones.

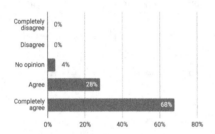

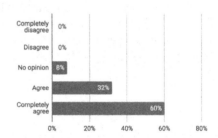

Fig. 16. Answers to A1-2—"Would use the tool again".

Fig. 17. Answers to A1-3—"I find the virtual environment beneficial in understanding software systems".

In conclusion, considering the overall assessment of the virtual environment, participants found advantages in using the tool.

5.7   System Usability Scale

Finally, the participants answered the system usability scale, which consists of 10 questions, to help us identify usability aspects that deserve further attention.

Figure 18 shows the percentage of answers given for each of the 10 questions. The colors used in the table are intended to reduce the effort to understand it, with values close to 0% being red and those around 100% green.

After analyzing the results and following the calculation of the System Usabil-ity Scale, a global rating of 83.8 was calculated, which translates into an A grade, i.e., the highest possible grade. Participants thus show interest in the usability of the tested tool.

	I think that I would like to use this system frequently.	I found the system unnecessarily complex.	I thought the system was easy to use.	I think that I'd need support of a technical person to use this system.	I found the various functions in this system were well integrated.	I thought there was too much inconsistency in this system.	I'd imagine that most people would learn to use this system very quickly.	I found the system very cumbersome to use.	I felt very confident using the system.	I needed to learn a lot of things before I could get going with this system.
Completely agree	40%	0%	52%	0%	56%	0%	44%	0%	44%	0%
Agree	48%	4%	44%	28%	32%	0%	52%	0%	48%	8%
No opinion	12%	4%	4%	16%	12%	4%	0%	8%	8%	16%
Disagree	0%	36%	0%	28%	0%	20%	4%	0%	0%	24%
Completely disagree	0%	56%	0%	28%	0%	76%	0%	0%	0%	52%

Fig. 18. Overall assessment of the virtual environment. (Color figure online)

5.8 Challenges

From the analysis of the presented data and the feedback received from the participants, their biggest challenge was the little experience they had using VR headsets. This issue represented some learning time and greater difficulty in interactions due to inadequate knowledge of how the controllers worked.

Figure 19 highlights that Oculus Rift's user experience has favored T1, reducing the time required to realize it, i.e., the exposure time required to explore the virtual environment reduced. The coefficient of determination was approximately 0.6339.

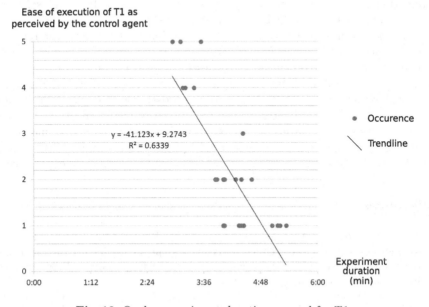

Fig. 19. Oculus experiment durations spread for T1.

The controlling agent of the experiment noticed an evolution in the ability to interact with the system throughout the experiment, suggesting that if there were additional tasks, or if the same participants would participate of future experiments, they would feel more confident in using the VR device and would achieve better results.

A similar analysis was performed for tasks T2 and T3, comparing the duration of the experiment to the Oculus usage experience, but no significant results emerged. That is, having more or less experience with the VR device had no impact on the time required to solve the problem. In T2, it may be more significant to compare participant programming practice with duration. However, as all are programmers, in particular, 88% of participants said they program practically daily, such an analysis would not produce meaningful results.

6   Conclusions

The contributions described in this paper consist of **(1)** a structural analysis tool for *Java* projects that can be included in any *JDT*-enabled *Eclipse IDE* as a plug-in, and is capable of recognizing changes to several levels of the *Java Model* tree; **(2)** an execution analysis tool for *Java* projects that can be included in the relevant workspace and added to a project with minimal required modifications to the concerning source code; **(3)** a software repository ready to receive information from the previously mentioned analysis tools, and provide it in real-time through a *API*; **(4)** a VR application for the live visualization of a software system that makes use of visual and spatial metaphors to facilitate software understanding; **(5)** a controlled experiment to directly validate the merits of the combined use liveness and VR visualization, and indirectly validate the remaining contributions.

The controlled experiment showed mostly agreement for the benefits and usefulness of this approach for visualizing software and provided some insights to be used in future work. Regarding future improvements, these include adding new spatial and temporal interactions, and two-way communication between the visualization, the repository, and the running system, which would allow modifications in the virtual environment to be passed to the running system more instantaneously, therefore improving the liveness of the developers experience.

References

1. Aguiar, A., Restivo, A., Figueiredo Correia, F., Ferreira, H.S., Dias, J.P.: Live software development – tightening the feedback loops. In: Conference Companion of the 3rd International Conference on Art, Science, and Engineering of Programming. Programming 2019 Companion (2019)
2. Alam, S., Dugerdil, P.: EvoSpaces: 3D visualization of software architecture. In: 19th International Conference on Software Engineering and Knowledge Engineering, vol. 7, pp. 500–505. IEEE (2007)

3. Amaral, D., Domingues, G., Dias, J.P., Ferreira, H.S., Aguiar, A., Nóbrega, R.: Live software development: an environment for Java using virtual reality. In: Proceedings of the 14th International Conference on Evaluation of Novel Approaches to Software Engineering, ENASE, vol. 1, pp. 37–46. INSTICC, SciTePress (2019). https://doi.org/10.5220/0007699800370046

4. Bartoszuk, C., Timoszuk, G., Dabrowski, R., Stencel, K.: Magnify - a new tool for software visualization. In: 2013 Federated Conference on Computer Science and Information Systems, pp. 1485–1488, September 2013

5. Bassil, S., Keller, R.K.: Software visualization tools: survey and analysis. In: Proceedings of the 9th International Workshop on Program Comprehension, IWPC 2001, pp. 7–17. IEEE Computer Society, Washington, DC (2001)

6. De Pauw, W., Jensen, E., Mitchell, N., Sevitsky, G., Vlissides, J., Yang, J.: Visualizing the execution of Java programs. In: Diehl, S. (ed.) Software Visualization. LNCS, vol. 2269, pp. 151–162. Springer, Heidelberg (2002). https://doi.org/10.1007/3-540-45875-1_12

7. Elliott, A., Peiris, B., Parnin, C.: Virtual reality in software engineering: affordances, applications, and challenges. In: Proceedings of the 37th International Conference on Software Engineering, ICSE 2015, vol. 2, pp. 547–550. IEEE Press, Piscataway (2015)

8. Fauzi, E., Hendradjaya, B., Sunindyo, W.D.: Reverse engineering of source code to sequence diagram using abstract syntax tree. In: 2016 International Conference on Data and Software Engineering (ICoDSE), pp. 1–6, October 2016. https://doi.org/10.1109/ICODSE.2016.7936137

9. Feijs, L., Krikhaar, R., Ommering, R.V.: A relational approach to support software architecture analysis. Softw. Pract. Exp. **28**(4), 371–400 (1998)

10. Feist, M.D., Santos, E.A., Watts, I., Hindle, A.: Visualizing project evolution through abstract syntax tree analysis. In: 2016 IEEE Working Conference on Software Visualization (VISSOFT), pp. 11–20, October 2016. https://doi.org/10.1109/VISSOFT.2016.6

11. Gosain, A., Sharma, G.: A survey of dynamic program analysis techniques and tools. In: Satapathy, S.C., Biswal, B.N., Udgata, S.K., Mandal, J.K. (eds.) Proceedings of the 3rd International Conference on Frontiers of Intelligent Computing: Theory and Applications (FICTA) 2014. AISC, vol. 327, pp. 113–122. Springer, Cham (2015). https://doi.org/10.1007/978-3-319-11933-5_13

12. Guéhéneuc, Y.G.: A reverse engineering tool for precise class diagrams. In: Proceedings of the 2004 Conference of the Centre for Advanced Studies on Collaborative Research, CASCON 2004, pp. 28–41. IBM Press (2004)

13. Hancock, C.M.: Real-time programming and the big ideas of computational literacy. Ph.D. thesis, Massachusetts Institute of Technology (2003)

14. Jones, J.: Abstract syntax tree implementation idioms. In: Proceedings of the 10th Conference on Pattern Languages of Programs (PLoP2003) (2003)

15. Kiczales, G., Hilsdale, E., Hugunin, J., Kersten, M., Palm, J., Griswold, W.G.: An overview of AspectJ. In: Knudsen, J.L. (ed.) ECOOP 2001. LNCS, vol. 2072, pp. 327–354. Springer, Heidelberg (2001). https://doi.org/10.1007/3-540-45337-7_18

16. Koschke, R.: Software visualization in software maintenance, reverse engineering, and re-engineering: a research survey. J. Softw. Maint. Evol.: Res. Pract. **15**(2), 87–109 (2003). https://doi.org/10.1002/smr.270

17. Lanza, M., Ducasse, S.: Polymetric views-a lightweight visual approach to reverse engineering. IEEE Trans. Softw. Eng. **29**(9), 782–795 (2003). https://doi.org/10.1109/TSE.2003.1232284

18. Lourenço, P., Dias, J.P., Aguiar, A., Ferreira, H.S., Restivo, A.: CloudCity: a live approach and environment for the management of cloud infrastructures. Commun. Comput. Inf. Sci. (2019)

19. Maalej, W., Tiarks, R., Roehm, T., Koschke, R.: On the comprehension of program comprehension. ACM Trans. Softw. Eng. Methodol. **23**(4), 31:1–31:37 (2014). https://doi.org/10.1145/2622669

20. Marcus, A., Comorski, D., Sergeyev, A.: Supporting the evolution of a software visualization tool through usability studies. In: 13th International Workshop on Program Comprehension (IWPC 2005), pp. 307–316, May 2005. https://doi.org/10.1109/WPC.2005.34

21. McDirmid, S.: Usable live programming. In: Proceedings of the 2013 ACM International Symposium on New Ideas, New Paradigms, and Reflections on Programming & Software - Onward! 2013, pp. 53–62. ACM Press, New York (2013). https://doi.org/10.1145/2509578.2509585

22. Merino, L., Ghafari, M., Anslow, C., Nierstrasz, O.: CityVR: gameful software visualization. In: 2017 IEEE International Conference on Software Maintenance and Evolution (ICSME), pp. 633–637, September 2017. https://doi.org/10.1109/ICSME.2017.70

23. Panas, T., Berrigan, R., Grundy, J.: A 3D metaphor for software production visualization. In: Proceedings on Seventh International Conference on Information Visualization, IV 2003, pp. 314–319, July 2003. https://doi.org/10.1109/IV.2003.1217996

24. Romano, S., Capece, N., Erra, U., Scanniello, G., Lanza, M.: The city metaphor in software visualization: feelings, emotions, and thinking. Multimed. Tools Appl. **78**, 1–37 (2019)

25. Rumbaugh, J., Jacobson, I., Booch, G.: Unified Modeling Language Reference Manual, 2nd edn. Pearson Higher Education (2004)

26. Sadar, A., Panicker, V.: DocTool - a tool for visualizing software projects using graph database. In: 2015 Eighth International Conference on Contemporary Computing (IC3), pp. 439–442, August 2015. https://doi.org/10.1109/IC3.2015.7346721

27. Sensalire, M., Ogao, P., Telea, A.: Evaluation of software visualization tools: lessons learned. In: 2009 5th IEEE International Workshop on Visualizing Software for Understanding and Analysis, pp. 19–26, September 2009. https://doi.org/10.1109/VISSOF.2009.5336431

28. Shi, N., Olsson, R.A.: Reverse engineering of design patterns from Java source code. In: Proceedings of the 21st IEEE/ACM International Conference on Automated Software Engineering, ASE 2006, pp. 123–134. IEEE Computer Society, Washington, DC (2006). https://doi.org/10.1109/ASE.2006.57

29. Singh, N., Singh, S.: Virtual reality: a brief survey. In: 2017 International Conference on Information Communication and Embedded Systems (ICICES), pp. 1–6, February 2017. https://doi.org/10.1109/ICICES.2017.8070720

30. Tanimoto, S.L.: A perspective on the evolution of live programming. In: Proceedings of the 1st International Workshop on Live Programming, LIVE 2013, pp. 31–34. IEEE Press, Piscataway (2013)

31. Teyseyre, A.R., Campo, M.R.: An overview of 3D software visualization. IEEE Trans. Vis. Comput. Graph. **15**(1), 87–105 (2009). https://doi.org/10.1109/TVCG.2008.86

32. Vincur, J., Navrat, P., Polasek, I.: VR city: software analysis in virtual reality environment. In: 2017 IEEE International Conference on Software Quality, Reliability and Security Companion (QRS-C), pp. 509–516, July 2017. https://doi.org/10.1109/QRS-C.2017.88
33. Wettel, R.: Software systems as cities. Ph.D. thesis, Faculty of Informatics of the Università della Svizzera Italiana, September 2010
34. Wettel, R., Lanza, M., Robbes, R.: Software systems as cities: a controlled experiment. In: Proceedings of the 33rd International Conference on Software Engineering, ICSE 2011, pp. 551–560. ACM, New York (2011). https://doi.org/10.1145/1985793.1985868
35. Wohlin, C.: Empirical software engineering: teaching methods and conducting studies. In: Basili, V.R., Rombach, D., Schneider, K., Kitchenham, B., Pfahl, D., Selby, R.W. (eds.) Empirical Software Engineering Issues. Critical Assessment and Future Directions. LNCS, vol. 4336, pp. 135–142. Springer, Heidelberg (2007). https://doi.org/10.1007/978-3-540-71301-2_42
36. Yuan, D., Park, S., Zhou, Y.: Characterizing logging practices in open-source software. In: 2012 34th International Conference on Software Engineering (ICSE), pp. 102–112, June 2012. https://doi.org/10.1109/ICSE.2012.6227202

Model-Based Risk Analysis
and Evaluation Using CORAS and CVSS

Roman Wirtz[✉] and Maritta Heisel

University of Duisburg-Essen, Duisburg, Germany
roman.wirtz@uni-due.de

Abstract. The consideration of security during software development is an important factor for deploying high-quality software. The later one considers security in a software development lifecycle the higher the effort to address security-related incident scenarios. Following the principle of security-by-design, we aim at providing methods to develop secure software right from the beginning, i.e. methods for an application during requirements engineering.

The level of risk can be used to prioritize the treatment of scenarios, thus spending the required effort in an efficient manner. It is defined as the likelihood of a scenario and its consequence for an asset. The higher a risk level, the higher the priority to address the corresponding incident scenario. In previous work, we proposed a method that allows to semi-automatically estimate and evaluate risks based on the Common Vulnerability Scoring System using a template-based description of scenarios. In the present paper, we show how the method can be integrated into an existing risk management process like CORAS. To relate the CORAS diagrams and the template, we provide a metamodel. Our model-based approach ensures consistency and traceability between the different steps of the risk management process.

Furthermore, we enhance the existing method with a questionnaire to improve the assessment of an incident scenario's likelihood.

Keywords: Security · Risk management · Risk analysis risk evaluation · CVSS · Requirements engineering · Model-based

1 Introduction

In the context of security, risks for software can be defined as the likelihood of an incident scenario and its consequence for an asset. An asset is anything of value for a stakeholder, e.g. customer data for a company. We focus on information security. Therefore, an asset is a piece of value that shall be protected with regard to confidentiality, integrity, or availability. The level of risk can be used to prioritize incident scenarios. Such prioritization helps security engineers to spend the effort of addressing security aspects in an efficient manner.

The principle of security-by-design aims at considering security as early as possible in a software development process. The later one considers such aspects,

© Springer Nature Switzerland AG 2020
E. Damiani et al. (Eds.): ENASE 2019, CCIS 1172, pp. 108–134, 2020.
https://doi.org/10.1007/978-3-030-40223-5_6

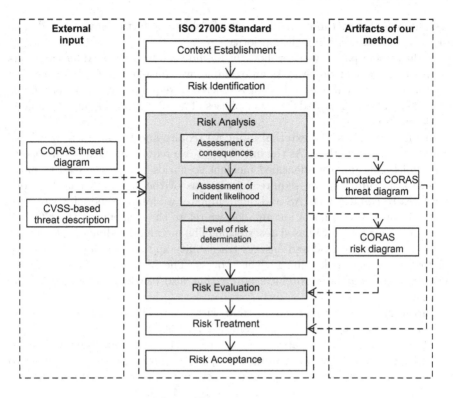

Fig. 1. ISO 27005 overview.

the higher the effort is to address any issue. Therefore, we aim at providing a risk management process that can be applied during requirements engineering.

The ISO 27005 standard [7] describes a framework for information security risk management. There are several steps to be carried out for which we provide an overview in Fig. 1. After establishing the context of software to be analyzed and identifying relevant risks, the risks need to be analyzed, e.g. to determine the corresponding likelihood and consequence. The step of risk evaluation provides activities to decide whether a risk level is acceptable or not. Unacceptable risks can then be treated in the following step by selecting appropriate controls. Last, there is a review of the whole process in which it has to be decided whether the risk treatment plan will be accepted and whether all risks have been reduced sufficiently.

In this paper, we contribute to the steps of risk analysis and risk evaluation which are marked in gray in Fig. 1. In previous work [21], we proposed a systematic method to estimate and evaluate risks during requirements engineering. The distinguishing features of that method are (1) to make consequences for different stakeholders explicit, and (2) to use a template-based description of incident scenarios as input [22]. The template is based on the *Common Vulnerability Scoring System (CVSS)*, which allows a semi-automatic evaluation of identified risks. As final outcome, the method provides a list of risks to be further investigated. The risks are ordered according their priority.

In the present paper, we show how the method can be embedded into an existing risk management process. As an example, we consider the CORAS method [13]. Since the CORAS method is not restricted to requirements engineering, our method can also be adapted for other phases of a software development process, e.g. design time.

In Fig. 1, we show the external input we require and the artifacts which we generate with our method. As the initial input, we require a CORAS threat diagram which contains the identified incident scenarios that might lead to harm for assets. In addition, we require descriptions of the scenarios based on our template. To connect CORAS and our template, we follow a model-based approach. By providing a novel metamodel, we relate the elements of the CORAS language to our template-based description. The metamodel allows to document the results of the method and ensures traceability and consistency between the different steps of a risk management process. The instantiation of the metamodel is supported by a graphical editor that also provides assistance for the application of our method.

Furthermore, we extend our method with a checklist that assists security engineers in assessing the incident scenario's likelihood.

The remainder of this paper is structured in the following way: In Sect. 2, we describe CORAS and our template to specify security incident scenarios. To combine both approaches, we propose a metamodel in Sect. 3. Our method to estimate and evaluate risks is described in Sect. 4, followed by a case study in Sect. 5. We discuss the achieved results in Sect. 6, and we state related work in Sect. 7. Section 8 concludes the paper with a summary and an outlook on future research directions.

2   CORAS and Incident Description

We make use of two basic concepts in this paper which we introduce in the following. First, we describe the CORAS risk management process along with its specific language [13]. Second, we introduce our template to specify security incident scenarios based on the CVSS [22].

2.1   CORAS

CORAS is a model-based method for risk management. It consists of a step-wise process and different kinds of diagrams to document the results. The method follows the ISO 31000 risk-management standard [10]. Each step provides guidelines for the interaction with the customer on whose behalf the risk management activities are carried out. The results are documented in diagrams using the CORAS language. The method starts with the establishment of the context and ends up with the suggestion of treatments to address the risk.

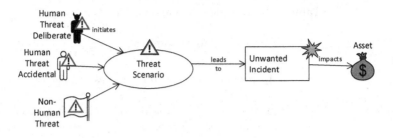

Fig. 2. CORAS threat diagram.

For our method, there are two types of diagrams we make use of. The first type is a so-called threat diagram for which we show an example in Fig. 2. A threat diagram consists of the following elements: An *Asset* is an item of value. There are *Human-threats deliberate*, e.g. a network attacker, as well as *Human-threats accidental*, e.g. an employee pressing a wrong button accidentally. To describe technical issues there are *Non-human threats*, e.g. malfunction of software. A threat *initiates* a *Threat scenario* with a certain likelihood, and a threat scenario describes a state, which may *lead to* an unwanted incident with another likelihood. An *Unwanted incident* describes the action that actually *impacts* an asset and therefore leads to a consequence for the asset.

The second type of diagram is a risk diagram for which we present an example in Fig. 3. There is a *Risk* for an asset. A path from a threat to an unwanted incident in a threat diagram represents a risk with a consequence for the asset. The risk level depends on the likelihood with which a threat initiates a threat scenario, on the likelihood with which a threat scenario leads to an unwanted incident, and the consequence for the asset.

In our method, we consider threat diagrams as input, and we use risk diagrams to document our results along with the security incidents.

2.2 Security Incident Description

In the present paper, we make use of the *Common Vulnerability Scoring System (CVSS)* [6] to estimate security risks. It consists of different metrics to calculate the severity of vulnerabilities. In the following, we describe the *Base Metric Group* which we consider for our method. For each metric, there is a predefined

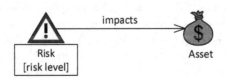

Fig. 3. CORAS risk diagram.

Table 1. Incident description: injection [22].

Basic information	
Name	*Injection*
Context	*Application that provides some user input to select or edit some data*
Description	*Data entered by users is not validated and used in queries to read or modify data, e.g. SQL queries. An attacker needs to be able to input data which is then used to query or modify data*
Vulnerability	*User input is not validated before execution*
Consequences	*Data is manipulated, deleted or disclosed by unauthorized persons*
Likelihood information	
Threat vector	☑ Network ☑ Adjacent ☑ Local ☐ Physical
Complexity	☑ Low ☐ High
Privileges required	☐ None ☑ Low ☐ High
User interaction	☑ None ☐ Required
Threat scope	☐ Unchanged ☑ Changed
Impact information	
Confidentiality impact	☐ None ☐ Low ☑ High
Integrity impact	☐ None ☐ Low ☑ High
Availability impact	☐ None ☐ Low ☑ High

qualitative scale. To each value of the scale, the CVSS assigns a numerical value. Those numerical values are then used in formulas to calculate the severity.

In previous work, we related the CVSS to the description of security incidents for an application during requirements engineering [22]. The proposed template can be used to further specify security incidents of a CORAS threat diagram. Table 1 shows the relevant excerpt of a template instance for the security incident *Injection*. There are three main sections for which we explain the different metrics and corresponding values in the following.

The first section contains some *Basic Information* about the incident, e.g. a name and informal descriptions.

Furthermore, we distinguish between a section for *Likelihood Information* and one for *Consequence Information*. The template describes the likelihood that a threat scenario successfully leads to an unwanted incident using different vectors. The *Threat Vector* (attack vector in CVSS) describes possible ways how to realize a threat. There are four different values: (1) *network*, which means access from an external network; (2) *adjacent*, which means a local network; (3) *local*, which means direct access to the computer; and (4) *physical*, which describes access to the hardware.

Fig. 4. Metamodel: CVSS datatypes.

The *Complexity* of a threat is defined by two possible values: *low* and *high*. A high effort is required when a threat agent needs some preparation to realize the threat and that the threat cannot be repeated an arbitrary number of times.

To state whether privileges are required to successfully realize the threat, we make use of the corresponding attribute. There are three possible values: (1) *None*; (2) *Low*, e.g. a user account; and (3) *High*, administrative rights.

A threat realization may require some *User Interaction*, for example by confirming the installation of malicious software.

The *Threat Scope* may change when a threat uses a component to reach other parts of the software.

For describing the impact, we focus on the three security properties confidentiality, integrity, and availability. The impact on those properties is defined by qualitative scales consisting of three values: *None, Low* and *High*.

To relate CORAS diagrams to the incident description, we provide a metamodel in Sect. 3.

3   Metamodel

To combine CORAS with our template, we provide an ECore metamodel based on the *Eclipse Modeling Framework (EMF)* [17]. Based on that metamodel, we also provide a graphical editor which enables security engineers to create model instances in a user-friendly way and to store the results of our method persistently.

The overall model consists of four parts which we present in the following.

3.1   CVSS Datatypes

Based on the template structure presented in Sect. 2.2, we define six different datatypes in form of enumerations. That part of the model is shown in Fig. 4. The possible values for all datatypes are given as literals. The enumerations *ThreatVector, Complexity, PrivilegesRequired, UserInteraction,* and *ThreatScope* belong to the likelihood specification. For describing the consequences with regard to confidentiality, integrity, and availability, the range of possible values is the same. Therefore, we define only one datatype called *ImpactScale* (given in gray).

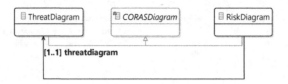

Fig. 5. Metamodel: CORAS diagrams.

3.2 CORAS Diagrams

As described in Sect. 2.1, we consider two types of CORAS diagrams in our approach which we show in Fig. 5. Both inherit from the abstract class *CORAS-Diagram*. The first is represented by the class *ThreatDiagram*, and the second one is represented by the class *RiskDiagram*. A risk diagram holds a reference to exactly one threat diagram from which it has been derived. In the following, we will specify the elements that are part of such diagrams.

3.3 CORAS Threat Diagram

In our metamodel, we make use of classes for all elements and relations contained in a CORAS diagram. In Fig. 6, we show the classes that are related to a threat diagram. There is an abstract class *Threat* from which the different threat types of the CORAS language inherit. Furthermore, there are classes for a threat scenario, an unwanted incident, and an abstract class for assets. That class is further refined into a direct and an indirect asset.

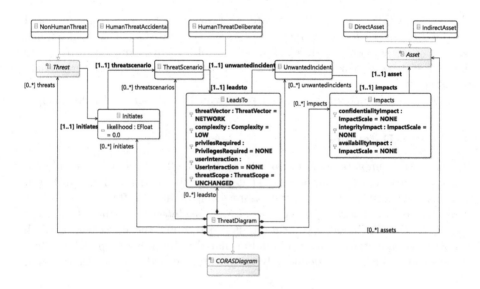

Fig. 6. Metamodel: CORAS threat diagram.

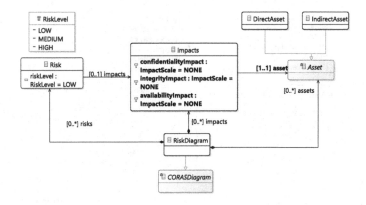

Fig. 7. Metamodel: CORAS risk diagram.

We distinguish three classes of relations: *Initiates*, *LeadsTo*, and *Impacts*. The likelihood that a threat initiates a threat scenario can be specified with a quantitative value, e.g. the occurrence per year. For a *leads to* relation, we make use of the previously presented datatypes to describe the likelihood that a threat scenario leads to an unwanted incident. The *impacts* relation provides attributes to specify the impact on confidentiality, integrity, and availability using the datatype *ImpactScale*.

3.4 CORAS Risk Diagram

Figure 7 shows the metamodel for a risk diagram. There is a new class *Risk* that has an attribute to specify its corresponding risk level. For that attribute, we define an additional enumeration called *RiskLevel*. Its qualitative scale consists of the values *LOW*, *MEDIUM*, and *HIGH*. By changing the metamodel, it is still possible to add more values later. Furthermore, the diagram contains an arbitrary number of the *Impacts* relations that connect a risk and the corresponding assets.

3.5 Graphical Editor

To instantiate the metamodel and to create CORAS diagrams, we provide a graphical editor[1] based on *Eclipse Sirius*[2]. The editor can be used to draw CORAS diagrams which document identified risks. For each diagram type, we defined a view on the model using the CORAS symbols. The created models are instances of the metamodel and therefore follow the defined semantics. Besides, it is possible to upload a template-based description for an identified incident scenario to automatically set the required attributes for likelihood and impacts. For that reason, we defined an XML-schema to express the template

---

[1] ProCOR - https://swe.uni-due.de/ (last access: August 14, 2019).

[2] Eclipse Sirius - https://www.eclipse.org/sirius/ (last access: August 14, 2019).

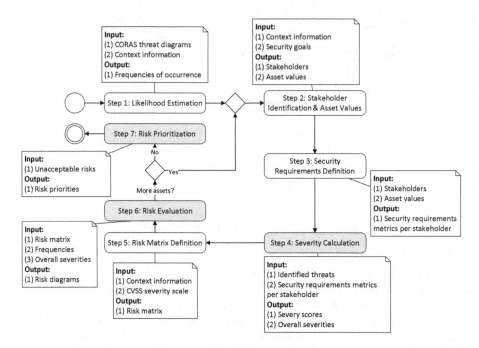

Fig. 8. Risk estimation method.

in a machine-readable way. Using that schema, it is possible to make the knowledge about incident scenarios reusable and to upload the corresponding files in different projects.

The model that can be created with the editor contains all threat diagrams along with the attributes and serves as the initial input for our method we describe in the following.

4   Risk Analysis and Evaluation Method

As shown in Fig. 1, our method contributes to the steps of risk analysis and risk evaluation. Overall, there are seven steps for which we provide an overview in Fig. 8. We marked those steps in gray that can be carried out automatically. The other steps need some manual effort, but all results can be stored in our model, and the documentation is supported by our tool. From the second to the sixth step, the method is carried out iteratively for all assets.

In the following, we describe each step in detail starting with the required external input.

4.1   Required Input

As mentioned in Sect. 2, the input for the risk analysis in CORAS are threat diagrams which document the results of the step of risk identification. Therefore, our method requires the following initial input.

1. **Assets:** Since our method focusses on information security, we consider an asset as a piece of information that shall be protected with regard to confidentiality, integrity, or availability. We assume that the definition of assets has already taken place during context establishment. Hence, we consider assets as given input which are part of the CORAS threat diagrams.
2. **Security Goals:** A security goal describes the aim to protect an asset with regard to confidentiality, integrity, or availability. We consider an unwanted incident in a CORAS threat diagram as the incident that actually impacts such security property for an asset.
3. **Incident Scenarios:** Relevant incident scenarios have been identified during risk identification and are therefore required input for the risk analysis. In addition to CORAS threat diagrams describing those scenarios, we also require a description for each scenario based on our template.

4.2 Step 1: Likelihood Estimation

For each threat that has been identified, it is necessary to estimate the likelihood that it leads to a threat scenario. We define that likelihood by its frequency of occurrence per year.

In contrast to the consequence of a threat, the occurrence of it is independent of any asset. Therefore, we estimate the values in the beginning.

To assist security engineers in estimating such likelihoods, we propose a checklist. The checklist provides items for each threat type: human-threat accidental, human-threat deliberate, and non-human threat. For each item, there is a numerical scale between zero and five. Furthermore, it is possible to state that an item is not relevant for software under investigation. A higher value reduces the likelihood that a threat may initiate a threat scenario. Not relevant means that this item is not relevant for software under investigation or for that combination of threat and threat scenario. Table 2 shows the current version of the checklist. We consider the checklist as not yet complete since we aim to extend it with additional items based on ongoing research. More items will improve the precision of the checklist and therefore of the derived likelihood.

Currently, the checklist has to be applied manually and serves as an indicator for security engineers to estimate likelihoods. The resulting likelihood can be annotated in the corresponding CORAS threat diagram using our graphical editor. We are evaluating different metrics that allow to automatically derive likelihoods from the filled checklist. The checklists, as well as the metrics, will later be embedded in our tool to automate this step of our method.

4.3 Step 2: Stakeholder Identification and Asset Values

The specific value of an asset with regard to a security property may differ for each stakeholder. For example, harming the integrity of health records may lead to death for a patient, whereas for a hospital, it leads to a loss of reputation. In existing risk management processes, e.g. CORAS [13], security engineers define

Table 2. Checklist for likelihood estimation.

Human threat accidental
(1) The application is used by experienced users ⦿ not relevant ○ 0 ○ 1 ○ 2 ○ 3 ○ 4 ○ 5
(2) Users will receive a training before using the software ⦿ not relevant ○ 0 ○ 1 ○ 2 ○ 3 ○ 4 ○ 5
(3) The graphical user interface follows style guidelines ⦿ not relevant ○ 0 ○ 1 ○ 2 ○ 3 ○ 4 ○ 5
(4) Users are aware of security, e.g. they know how to keep their credentials secret ⦿ not relevant ○ 0 ○ 1 ○ 2 ○ 3 ○ 4 ○ 5
Human threat deliberate
(5) Comparable software has not often been subject to attacks ⦿ not relevant ○ 0 ○ 1 ○ 2 ○ 3 ○ 4 ○ 5
(6) Processed information is of low value ⦿ not relevant ○ 0 ○ 1 ○ 2 ○ 3 ○ 4 ○ 5
(7) The attacker needs insider knowledge ⦿ not relevant ○ 0 ○ 1 ○ 2 ○ 3 ○ 4 ○ 5
(8) The attacker needs high skills ⦿ not relevant ○ 0 ○ 1 ○ 2 ○ 3 ○ 4 ○ 5
(9) The software provider complies to security standards ⦿ not relevant ○ 0 ○ 1 ○ 2 ○ 3 ○ 4 ○ 5
Non-human threat
(10) The underlying operating system is well protected against any type of virus, trojan horse, etc. ⦿ not relevant ○ 0 ○ 1 ○ 2 ○ 3 ○ 4 ○ 5
(11) The hardware and software is maintained by experienced persons ⦿ not relevant ○ 0 ○ 1 ○ 2 ○ 3 ○ 4 ○ 5
(12) External libraries can be considered as secure ⦿ not relevant ○ 0 ○ 1 ○ 2 ○ 3 ○ 4 ○ 5
(13) Users are not allowed to install own software ⦿ not relevant ○ 0 ○ 1 ○ 2 ○ 3 ○ 4 ○ 5

a single point of view to estimate risks. Doing so, consequences for some stakeholders may be omitted, which leads to incomplete risk estimations.

A distinguishing feature of our method is that we make all stakeholders explicit. For each identified stakeholder, we estimate the value of an asset with regard to confidentiality, integrity, and availability independently. Those values are defined independently of any threat. We consider three types of stakeholders:

Software Provider. Stakeholder or company that is responsible for the software, e.g. development and maintenance. Since all assets are related to the same piece of software, the software provider is the same for all assets.

Data Owner. Stakeholder to which the asset belongs, e.g. a patient is the data owner for his/her health record. The data owner may also be a company, for example when protecting business information.

Third Parties. Set of other stakeholders for which consequences might exist. We investigate each relevant third party independently of each other.

Using a detailed description of the context, in which the application shall be deployed, we identify data owner and relevant third parties for each asset. For each so identified stakeholder, we estimate the impact for each security property using the same unit, e.g. in terms of monetary impact. The monetary impact can also later be used to evaluate the costs of selected controls.

Currently, our method does not provide any specific method to elicit stakeholders. Using context patterns, e.g. the ones proposed by Beckers [3], security engineers can be assisted in identifying relevant stakeholders.

To document the stakeholders and the corresponding asset values, we extend our metamodel (cf. Sect. 3). We show that extension in Fig. 9. There is an abstract class *SecurityGoal* which refers to exactly one asset. It provides an attribute to specify a stakeholder's value for the specific asset. An asset can have an arbitrary number of security goals. A security goal can be of the class *Confidentiality*, *Integrity*, or *Availability*. There is also one class to model a *Stakeholder*. A stakeholder can have an arbitrary number of security goals. The attribute and datatype *SecurityRequirement* will be used in the next step of the method. There is a graphical editor to document the results in the model. We provide an example of the resulting diagram in Fig. 12.

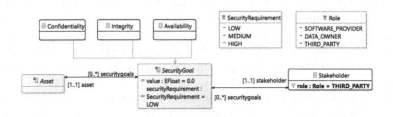

Fig. 9. Metamodel: security goals.

4.4   Step 3: Security Requirements Definition

Our template states the maximum impact on confidentiality, integrity, and availability independently of the concrete context and the asset's value for a stakeholder. In contrast to existing methods, we put a special focus on stakeholders and make them explicit during risk analysis. Therefore, it is necessary to adjust the importance of impact metrics according to the stakeholders' asset values.

To reweight the importance of impacts, the CVSS contains metrics to define security requirements. The metric is defined as a qualitative scale with the following values: *Not defined, Low, Medium,* and *High. Not defined* means that the asset has no value for the stakeholder. Using those metrics, we take the different stakeholders into account. We define security requirements for each stakeholder to reflect his/her specific value of the asset with regard to confidentiality, integrity, or availability.

In the second step of our method, we defined a monetary value for each asset. From those values, security engineers have to derive the qualitative values for security requirements. There is no specific algorithm for that. Therefore, the present step needs manual interaction. To document the security requirements in the model, we provide an additional metamodel extension which we also show in Fig. 9. The class for a security goal provides an attribute *securityRequirement*. For this attribute, we define a datatype *SecurityRequirement* as an enumeration. It provides all values defined by the corresponding CVSS metric, except *not defined* since this is implicitly given by the absence of a corresponding security goal in the model.

4.5   Step 4: Severity Calculation

In our method, we define the severity of an incident scenario as the likelihood that a threat scenario leads to an unwanted incident and the impact on a specific asset. Furthermore, we consider the previously defined security requirements as additional metrics.

Our method provides an easy and precise way to calculate the severity of each incident scenario. It needs to be calculated for each incident scenario that impacts the asset under investigation. Since the impact differs per stakeholder, we calculate the severity for each stakeholder using the security requirements metrics and the template. The CVSS defines formulas for the severity calculation [6], which we use for that task.

In case that a security requirement for a security property is not defined, it is necessary to adjust the related impact metric. Not defined means that harming the security property will not lead to value loss for the stakeholder. Thus, the severity of the incident scenario is reduced. To adjust the scenario description accordingly, we define a so-called modified base metric for that property which is set to *None*. During the severity calculation, a modified base metric overwrites the base metric provided by the scenario description. The calculation yields a set of severities per incident scenario. There is one severity per stakeholder.

Next, we combine the values of the set to derive the overall severity of an incident scenario to an asset. For this, we propose two different approaches:

1. Taking the maximal value of all severities.
2. Calculating the average of all severities.

In case that software provider and data owner are the same for the asset, we consider the corresponding severity only once since the impact for the stakeholder can also only happen once. For later prioritization of risks, the values have to be comparable for all assets. Therefore, the same approach has to be taken for all calculations.

As mentioned in Sect. 3, the information provided by the template can be stored in the model. Since we allow to add the security requirements to the model as well, the severities can be calculated based on the model. To do so, we implement functions in our tool based on the CVSS specification. The user of the tool can select between average and maximal severity per asset. Since the values for the calculation are part of the model, we do not provide a specific attribute to store the severity persistently.

4.6   Step 5: Risk Matrix Definition

When treating risks, it is important to focus on the most important ones. First, it is necessary to define risk levels that are considered acceptable or unacceptable. It is also possible to define further levels, e.g. risks to be monitored. Later on, only unacceptable risks need further inspection and hence, only those risks need to be prioritized. We make use of risk matrices to evaluate risks. That kind of matrix has already been used in other risk methods, for example in CORAS [13].

Define Scales. Prior to the definition of the risk matrix, it is necessary to define its scales. The CVSS score describes the severity of a threat. The severity is derived from conditions under which a threat can be successfully realized and its corresponding impact on an asset. The second dimension is the likelihood of the occurrence of a threat as mentioned in the first step of the method. For creating a risk matrix, we define intervals for the occurrence which we use to define a qualitative scale.

The likelihood scale is the same for all risk matrices and hence, for all assets. Therefore, it is only necessary to define it once during method execution.

In the CVSS specification document [6], there is an interval-based qualitative scale. It consists of the following values: *None, Low, Medium, High,* and *Critical.* The numerical severity values can be classified according to the provided intervals. Therefore, we make use of the qualitative scale in our risk matrices.

Define Risk Matrices. The acceptance threshold for risks highly depends on the importance of an asset. Therefore, it is necessary to provide a risk matrix for each asset. We annotate the severity scale horizontally and the likelihood scale vertically. For each cell of the matrix, it is necessary to define whether the risk level is acceptable or not. In a graphical representation, we mark acceptable values in green (white) and unacceptable values in red (gray). An example of such a risk matrix is shown in Table 8. Other categories of risks may be added, as well, e.g. for risks that do not need to be treated but which shall be monitored.

The likelihood scale might be reused from other software projects, but the definition of acceptance needs some manual interaction. Currently, our tool does not allow to define risk matrices in the model.

4.7   Step 6: Risk Evaluation

For each asset, we evaluate the acceptability of identified risks. The risk of an incident scenario for an asset is composed of the likelihood that a threat initiates a threat scenario (Step 1) and its severity (Step 4). Using these values, we fill the risk matrix for the corresponding asset which has been defined in the previous step.

As mentioned in Sect. 3, we distinguish three different risk levels:

Low. Risk with an acceptable level. No further investigation is necessary.
Medium. Risk with an acceptable level but which shall be monitored.
High. Risk with an unacceptable level. Risk treatment necessary.

The unacceptable risks will be prioritized in the next step.

To bridge the gap between the risk matrices and our model-based approach, we derive CORAS risk diagrams from the threat diagrams. There is one risk diagram per identified risk, i.e. one diagram for each path between threat and asset. Our tool generates those diagrams automatically from the underlying model. Since our tool currently does not support risk matrices, the user has to set the risk level attribute's value manually.

4.8   Step 7: Risk Prioritization

The final step of our method is the prioritization of unacceptable risks, i.e. those risks with a high risk level. A well-known concept for calculating risk levels is to multiply likelihood and impact [18]. We follow the same approach since both values are available from previous steps and are available in our model. By multiplying the numerical values for the likelihood (Step 1) and the overall severity of a risk (Step 4), we define risk priorities. The higher the value, the higher the priority.

The final step of our method takes all risks into account. The final outcome of our method is, therefore, a list of all unacceptable risks which are ordered according to their priority. The list ensures that risks can be treated in an effective manner by considering their priority.

Our tool automatically derives risk priorities for all risks at a high level. The corresponding priority is annotated at the risk element in a risk diagram. Furthermore, our tool provides a table that provides an overview of all risks including different values, e.g. priority.

5   Case Study

To illustrate our risk estimation and evaluation method, we make use of a smart home scenario. We first describe the scenario and the initial input, and then we execute the different steps of our method.

Remark: Since our tool does currently not support the export of vector graphics, we redrew the diagrams and tables for the printed version. In addition, we present the values contained in the underlying model in tables.

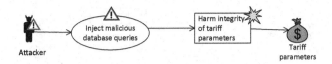

Fig. 10. Case study: CORAS threat diagram for *Injection*.

5.1   Scenario and Input

Our scenario is a smart grid which enables the energy supplier to measure a customer's power consumption remotely. The invoices are calculated automatically based on the measured values. The gateway at the customer's home is called *Communication Hub*, for which the software shall be developed. It is the bridge between energy supplier and measuring units. Customers can connect to the communication hub using a mobile app in the local area network to check the invoices or to change their personal data. The invoices are calculated based on the customer's tariff parameters, which are stored at the communication hub, as well as the personal data and the measured values. We consider the following two assets for our example:

Customer's Tariff Parameters. which shall be protected with regard to integrity.
Customer's Personal Data. which shall be protected with regard to confidentiality.

   In addition, we consider the incident scenarios *Injection* and *Inception* as risk that have been previously identified. We describe those scenarios in more detail in the following.

Injection. The CORAS threat diagram is given in Fig. 10, and the template instance has already been presented in Sect. 2.2 (cf. Table 1). An attacker (human-threat deliberate) may take the role of a user and uses the connection to the gateway via the app to inject malicious database queries and updates. The functional requirement only considers changing the customer's personal data. Since the tariff parameters are stored in the same database, it is possible to harm the integrity of the asset using malicious updates. Since the app can be used in the local area network, the threat vector is defined as *adjacent*. The complexity of injecting malicious queries is considered as low. The threat agent only needs user privileges to realize the threat, which leads to a low privilege value. There is no additional user interaction and the threat scope is changed, because the threat agent uses the software to manipulate the database. In general, an injection may have a high impact for all three security properties.

Interception. Figure 11 shows the CORAS threat diagram, and in Table 3 we show the corresponding template instance. An attacker (human-threat deliberate) may also intercept the local network connection (adjacent) to disclose

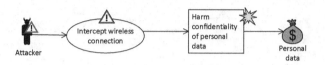

Fig. 11. Case study: CORAS threat diagram for *Interception*.

Table 3. Case study: description of *Interception* [21].

Basic information	
Name	*Interception*
Context	*Data transmission via an untrusted network connection, e.g. WLAN*
Description	*An attacker tries to intercept a network connection to disclose transmitted data*
Vulnerability	*Connection can be intercepted*
Consequences	*Data is manipulated, deleted or disclosed by unauthorized persons*
Likelihood information	
Threat vector	☐ Network ☑ Adjacent ☐ Local ☐ Physical
Complexity	☐ Low ☑ High
Privileges Required	☐ None ☐ Low ☑ High
User Interaction	☑ None ☐ Required
Threat scope	☑ Unchanged ☐ Changed
Consequence information	
Confidentiality impact	☐ None ☐ Low ☑ High
Integrity impact	☑ None ☐ Low ☐ High
Availability impact	☑ None ☐ Low ☐ High

transmitted data. Such incident scenario is relevant because customer's personal data can be transmitted via the WLAN. Hence, it may impact the confidentiality of personal data. The scenario has a high complexity and requires high privileges. Since the attacker intercepts the connection and only discloses data on that level, the scope remains unchanged. There is a high impact on confidentiality but no impact on integrity or availability.

Based on the initial input, we describe the application of our method in the following.

5.2   Step 1: Likelihood Estimation

Using our checklist we have shown in Table 2, we estimate the likelihood that an attacker initiates the threat scenario as *25 times a year*. That is, 25 times a year an attacker tries to inject malicious code to manipulate tariff parameters.

In the same way, we estimate the likelihood for the interception of a local network as *25 times a year*, too. We document both values in the model accordingly.

5.3   Step 2: Stakeholder Identification and Asset Values

The software provider in our scenario is the energy supplier, which is the same for all assets.

Tariff Parameters. The first asset are *tariff parameters*, which shall be protected with regard to integrity. Since tariff parameters are defined by the energy supplier, we consider that stakeholder as the data owner. We define an asset value per customer of 200 €, because invoices are generated automatically based on the tariff parameters, and not each invoice is checked for its correctness by the energy supplier. A lower invoice amount will lead to a loss of money, whereas a higher amount might harm the reputation of the company and also produces effort to correct the incorrect invoices manually. In case that the tariff parameters are not manipulated by customers themselves, we consider customers as a relevant third party. Manipulated tariff parameters lead to an incorrect invoice and may request the customer to pay more money than necessary. Since most customers check their invoices, we estimate an impact only at 50 €. Customers who check their invoices and find errors still have to spend some effort to get it sorted. Table 4 summarizes the results for the asset tariff parameters which have been added to the model. *SP* stands for software provider, *DO* for data owner and *TP* for third party. The corresponding diagram created with our editor is shown in Fig. 12.

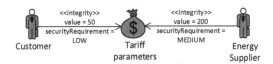

Fig. 12. Case study: stakeholders and asset values.

Personal Data. The second asset is the personal data of the customer who is the data owner. There are no other third parties. When personal data is disclosed, the software provider may be liable for damages. Therefore, we estimate a value of 400€ per customer. The personal data only consists of the customer's address to provide the invoice, which may also be accessible via the phone book. Therefore, we do not consider address data as highly sensitive information, and we estimate a relatively low value of 50€ for the data owner. Table 4 also summarizes the results for that asset.

Table 4. Case study: identified stakeholders and asset values.

Tariff parameters		Personal data	
Stakeholder	*Integrity*	*Stakeholder*	*Confidentiality*
(SP) Energy supplier	200€	(SP) Energy supplier	400€
(DO) Energy supplier	200€	(DO) Customer	50€
(TP) Customer	50€	–	–

5.4   Step 3: Security Requirements Definition

Tariff Parameters. For the asset tariff parameters, there is no impact on confidentiality and availability for both stakeholders. Therefore, there is no corresponding security requirement. Using the previously defined asset values, we define the impact on integrity for the energy supplier as *medium* and for customers as *low*. Using the graphical editor, the values can be added to the model as shown in Fig. 12.

Personal Data. For the second asset, there is only an impact on confidentiality. For the customer, we define the impact as *low*, whereas for the software provider, the impact is *medium*. We summarized the results in Table 5.

Table 5. Case study: stakeholders and security requirements.

Tariff parameters		Personal data	
Stakeholder	*Integrity*	*Stakeholder*	*Confidentiality*
(SP) Energy supplier	medium	(SP) Energy supplier	Medium
(DO) Energy supplier	medium	(DO) Customer	Low
(TP) Customer	Low	–	–

5.5   Step 4: Severity Calculation

In our example, there is one threat per asset for which we need to calculate its severity.

Tariff Parameters. For the asset *tariff parameters*, we identified the threat *Injection*. The formulas provided by the CVSS specification document [6] are filled with the base metrics contained in the instance of the threat pattern. In the third step of our method, we defined security requirements metrics. Since the metrics for confidentiality and availability have been set to *not defined*, we define corresponding modified base metrics which are set to *none*.

The severity needs to be calculated for the energy supplier and the customer independently. The results of the calculation are summarized in Table 6. The table states the severities for the energy supplier and the costumer, the maximum severity and the average severity. In our example, software provider and data owner are the same. Therefore, that stakeholder counts only once for calculating the average.

Table 6. Case study: severity for tariff parameters [21].

Stakeholder	Severity of injection
(SP) Energy supplier	6.8
(DO) Energy supplier	6.8
(TP) Customer	4.5
Average	5.65
Maximum	6.8

Personal Data. The severity of the threat *Interception* for the asset *personal data* is calculated in the same manner. We state the corresponding results in Table 7. Here, we do not have any third party. The average severity is only calculated based on software provider and data owner.

Table 7. Case study: severity for personal data [21].

Stakeholder	Severity of interception
(SP) Energy supplier	4.2
(DO) Customer	2.4
Average	3.3
Maximum	4.2

5.6   Step 5: Risk Matrix Definition

Likelihood Scale. We define a qualitative likelihood scale for the frequency of occurrences per year with the following values: *Never, Seldom* (up to 20 times a year), *Frequently* (up to 50 times a year), and *Often* (more than 50 times a year).

Risk Matrix. We define a risk matrix to evaluate whether a risk is acceptable or unacceptable. On the vertical axis, we annotate the previously defined likelihood scale and on the horizontal axis we annotate the CVSS severity score. The resulting matrix is shown in Table 8. Acceptable risks are shown in white and unacceptable risks are shown in gray. In the present example, we use the same matrix for both assets.

Table 8. Case study: risk matrix [21].

	None 0.0	Low 0.1–3.9	Medium 4.0–6.9	High 7.0–8.9	Critical 9.0–10.0
Never 0 times					
Seldom ≤ 20 *times*					
Frequently ≤ 50 *times*		$R2_{Avg}$	$R1_{Avg}$, $R2_{Max}$ $R1_{Max}$,		
Often > 50 *times*					

5.7 Step 6: Risk Evaluation

To evaluate the risks, we make use of the risk matrix shown in Table 8.

Tariff Parameters. For the asset *tariff parameters*, there is one risk concerning the threat *Injection*. In Table 8, we use **R1** as an abbreviation for the corresponding risk. *Max* indicates the risk level when using the maximal value of all severities, and *avg* indicates the average value. Both approaches lead to an unacceptable risk which is indicated by a gray cell.

Personal Data. For the asset *personal data*, there is a risk for the threat *Interception*. In Table 8, we use **R2** as an abbreviation for the corresponding risk. Using the risk matrix, we consider the risk as acceptable for using the average value for the severity, which is indicated by the green cell. The risk is unacceptable for using the maximum of all severities. Hence, further inspection of the threat is necessary for the asset *personal data* when taking the maximum severity.

Figure 13 shows the resulting CORAS risk diagrams that have been derived from the threat diagrams. For those diagrams, we only consider the maximal severity.

Fig. 13. Case study: risk diagrams.

5.8 Step 7: Risk Prioritization

To prioritize risks, we multiply likelihood and severity for each unacceptable risk. The higher the calculated value, the higher the priority of the risk.

Using the average of the severities, we only identified one unacceptable risk in the sixth step. Therefore, a prioritization is not necessary.

Using the maximum of the severities, there are two risks that need to be prioritized: **R1**, risk of injection for the asset tariff parameters; and **R2**, risk of interception for the asset personal data. The results of the calculation are summarized in Table 9. The risk of injection has a higher level, and hence will have priority during risk treatment.

In Fig. 13, we also annotate the risks' priorities in the diagrams.

Table 9. Case study: calculated risk levels [21].

Risk	Likelihood	Maximal severity	Risk level
R1	25	6.8	170
R2	25	4.2	105

6 Discussion

Based on the description of our method in Sect. 4 and the application for the case study in Sect. 5, we discuss the benefits and limitations of our method.

6.1 Usability

Incident scenarios that have been identified during risk identification are described in form of CORAS threat diagrams. Using our template format, we systematically make use of additional information about the identified scenarios. Limiting the effort for security engineers, the template allows to calculate the severity without collecting additional information about the scenario. Besides, the CORAS diagrams present the input and output of the method in a user-friendly way. For each step, we explicitly state input, output, and procedure which assists engineers in applying our method. By following a model-based approach, we ensure consistency and traceability between the different steps of a risk management process. Our tool, we describe in this paper, supports the application of our method and helps to document the results systematically.

Security engineers still need some specific expertise, for example in estimating the likelihood for a threat initiating a threat scenario. With our questionnaire, we aim to assist them in collecting and documenting the results in an effective and structured way.

6.2 Scalability

The complexity of our method mainly depends on the number of assets, threats and identified stakeholders. The complexity of the first step which deals with the likelihood estimation of identified threats cannot be improved. It is always necessary to estimate the likelihood of a threat depending on the concrete context.

Since we identify different stakeholders for estimating the severity of a threat, we increase the complexity of some steps. When omitting the stakeholders, we will improve the scalability of our method but the estimated risk levels will be less precise. Therefore, it is necessary to find a compromise between both limitations. We automated all steps as much as possible to limit the manual effort for engineers to perform those steps. The required calculation can be performed with our tool based on information stored in the model. For steps that need manual interaction, our tool guides security engineers.

6.3   Precision

To calculate the severity of an incident scenario concerning a specific asset, we use the CVSS. The defined metrics are widely accepted by the community and many industrial partners. For example, the system is used by the *National Vulnerability Database*[3], which is provided by the *National Institute of Standards and Technology*. Based on the template (cf. Sect. 2), we adapted the scoring system to estimate the severity of incident scenarios. The corresponding formulas to calculate the score have been defined by security experts based on real vulnerabilities. Although the metrics and formulas have been defined on sound expertise, there are limitations in their precision. The instances of the template do not consider the concrete context of the application, and the values for the metrics are qualitative. As mentioned above, predefined scales have the benefit of better usability. So there is still a compromise between usability and precision. We try to address the issue with a context-independent description by an explicit identification of stakeholders and by adjusting the base metrics with security requirements.

To evaluate risks, we make use of qualitative scales in risk matrices. Risk matrices are a well-known concept in the context of risk management, not only restricted to information security. We only use qualitative scales to define intervals for risk acceptance. The scales we use in this paper can be easily replaced by arbitrary ones with a more fine-grained resolution. For risk prioritization, we still consider quantitative scales to ensure precision in this stage.

7   Related Work

To identify related work, we performed a simplified literature using the search engine of Scopus[4]. We used the built-in search engine to identify relevant publications that either describe a risk estimation or risk evaluation method. Those methods should be applicable during requirements engineering and should put

---

[3] https://nvd.nist.gov/ - NVD by NIST (last accessed on 3 December 2018).

[4] www.scopus.com - Scopus (last access: December 4, 2018).

a special focus on security. Therefore, we defined the following search query: *(Requirements Engineering) AND ((Risk Estimation) OR (Risk Evaluation)) AND Security*. We performed the search on December 5, 2018. The initial result set contained 170 publications. We limited this set to the subject area *Computer Science* and to the language *English*. This limitation leaded to a subset of 97 relevant publications from 1996 to 2018.

From all of these publications, we read title and abstract to decide about the relevance. From the so identified 28 publications, we read the full text. When reading the full text, we focused on publications that (1) introduce or extend risk estimation or evaluation methods, (2) that evaluate such methods or (3) where such methods are referenced in their contributions. Additionally, we considered publications that may extend or support our work. In the following, we briefly state the relevant publications.

Argyropoulos et al. suggest to use the analytic hierarchy process (AHP) [16] in the context of security [2]. The AHP method allows to prioritize risks relatively to each other. The approach has a high precision but requires an overhead in terms of effort because all risks need to be compared pair-wise.

Llansó et al. considers the level of effort to realize a cyber attack as an important factor to determine the likelihood of the attack [12]. The authors propose a model-based algorithm to estimate such effort. In our approach, we consider the level of effort by some attributes of the CVSS, e.g. threat vector. The proposed algorithm may improve the precision of our method.

Using Bayesian Networks and agent-based simulation, other authors aim to provide a probabilistic approach to support risk analysis [19,20]. There, a risk level is defined as the percentage of failure for a functionality. Using the mentioned approaches, it is possible to analyze the propagation of risks throughout the system's components. There is no prioritization of risks, but the approaches may extend our method to analyze the dependencies between different risks.

ArgueSecure [8] is a method for argument-based risk assessment that does not rely on any quantitative estimation of risks. The proposed framework relies on a qualitative method that is performed in brainstorming sessions. The results are documented in a tree structure. The proposed graphical notation is designed for an application by non-experts, but there are no explicit risk levels, which makes it hard to evaluate the identified risks.

The CORAS [13] risk management process which we use in this paper performs risk analysis in form of a structured brainstorming session.

SERA [1] is a risk analysis framework with a special focus on social engineering attacks. The importance of human factors is also mentioned in other publications (e.g. [15]). Currently, neither the CVSS nor our method supports the consideration of social engineering.

Islam et al. propose an attribute-based estimation of risks which is based on the Common Criteria [4,9]. The attributes to define the likelihood are comparable to the CVSS, whereas the impact is not measured with regard to a specific security property. The values for the attributes need to be set manually, whereas we make use of existing pattern-based threat knowledge.

Elahi et al. make use of a qualitative method to analyze goal models [5]. The i*-notation has been extended to model attacks. The authors mention that the qualitative evaluation makes an application easier, but it is less precise.

Another approach is to combine threat trees with Monte Carlo models [14]. The risk is defined by a set of parameters, such as complexity and motivation of an attacker. The assigned values are used for a Monte Carlo simulation to estimate risk values. The method does not rely on existing threat knowledge and does not allow to prioritize risks.

Labunets et al. have carried out a study to compare graphical and tabular representations for security risk assessment [11]. The results of the study revealed that there is no significant difference between both representations with regard to the perceived efficacy. Our method relies on tabular descriptions for the results and does not contain any graphical notation. Since the study shows the equivalence of both notations, there is no need to add such a notation.

All other identified publications do not propose any specific risk estimation or evaluation method. Instead, they only rely on external expertise to deal with such risks.

In contrast to our method, none of the mentioned methods makes different stakeholders' perspectives explicit for estimating risks. To the best of our knowledge, it is a novelty in our method.

8   Conclusion and Outlook

Finally, we summarize our results and give an outlook on future research directions and improvements.

Summary. In this paper, we showed how our method to evaluate risks can be embedded into the CORAS risk management process. The method provides several benefits for users of the method: (1) It does not only focus on the impact of one stakeholder but makes the impact for different stakeholders explicit; (2) The template allows to systematically consider existing knowledge about incident scenarios for risk calculation; and (3) our method follows a systematic process which clearly defines required input and corresponding for each step.

Furthermore, we provide a questionnaire that systematically elicits knowledge to assess the likelihood that a threat initiates a threat scenario. The questionnaire distinguishes between the different threat types defined by the CORAS language.

By following a model-based approach, we ensure consistency and traceability between the different steps of our method. As a foundation for the models to be created, we defined a metamodel that combines CORAS diagrams with our template. Our graphical editor provides a user-friendly way to create CORAS diagrams and to carry out our method, which reduces the manual effort significantly.

Outlook. As future work, we plan to evaluate the usability of our tool in the form of an experiment. As participants, we consider security engineers that are familiar with the CORAS risk management process. After carrying out our method with the tool, we will systematically ask them for feedback based on a questionnaire. The results will not only be used to improve our tool, but also the method itself. Therefore, we will compare the results achieved with our method with a risk estimation without any assistance.

For the questionnaire for assessing the likelihood, we plan to elaborate metrics that allow to automatic derive likelihoods from the questionnaire's results.

The next step of the risk management process is risk treatment. The output of our method serves as the input for that step. For that reason, we will extend our method and our tool to suggest appropriate controls for the necessary risk reduction. By adjusting our method, we also plan to assist security engineers in evaluating their treatment plan.

References

1. Abeywardana, K., Pfluegel, E., Tunnicliffe, M.: A layered defense mechanism for a social engineering aware perimeter, pp. 1054–1062 (2016). https://doi.org/10.1109/SAI.2016.7556108

2. Argyropoulos, N., Angelopoulos, K., Mouratidis, H., Fish, A.: Risk-aware decision support with constrained goal models. Inf. Comput. Secur. **26**(4), 472–490 (2018). https://doi.org/10.1108/ICS-01-2018-0010

3. Beckers, K.: Pattern and Security Requirements - Engineering-Based Establishment of Security Standards. Springer, Cham (2015). https://doi.org/10.1007/978-3-319-16664-3

4. Common Criteria: Common Criteria for Information Technology Security Evaluation v3.1. Release 5. Standard (2017). http://www.iso.org/iso/catalogue_detail?csnumber=65694

5. Elahi, G., Yu, E., Zannone, N.: A vulnerability-centric requirements engineering framework: analyzing security attacks, countermeasures, and requirements based on vulnerabilities. Requirements Eng. **15**(1), 41–62 (2010). https://doi.org/10.1007/s00766-009-0090-z

6. FIRST.org: Common Vulnerability Scoring System v3.0: Specification Document (2015). https://www.first.org/cvss/cvss-v30-specification-v1.8.pdf

7. International Organization for Standardization: ISO 27005:2011 Information technology - Security techniques - Information security risk management. Standard (2011). http://www.iso.org/iso/catalogue_detail?csnumber=65694

8. Ionita, D., Kegel, R., Baltuta, A., Wieringa, R.: Arguesecure: out-of-the-box security risk assessment, pp. 74–79 (2017). https://doi.org/10.1109/REW.2016.19

9. Islam, M.M., Lautenbach, A., Sandberg, C., Olovsson, T.: A risk assessment framework for automotive embedded systems. In: Proceedings of the 2Nd ACM International Workshop on Cyber-Physical System Security, CPSS 2016, pp. 3–14. ACM, New York (2016). https://doi.org/10.1145/2899015.2899018

10. ISO: ISO 31000 Risk management - Principles and guidelines. International Organization for Standardization (2009)

11. Labunets, K., Massacci, F., Paci, F.: On the equivalence between graphical and tabular representations for security risk assessment. In: Grünbacher, P., Perini, A. (eds.) REFSQ 2017. LNCS, vol. 10153, pp. 191–208. Springer, Cham (2017). https://doi.org/10.1007/978-3-319-54045-0_15

12. Llansó, T., Dwivedi, A., Smeltzer, M.: An approach for estimating cyber attack level of effort. In: 2015 Annual IEEE Systems Conference (SysCon) Proceedings, pp. 14–19 (2015)
13. Lund, M.S., Solhaug, B., Stølen, K.: Model-Driven Risk Analysis. The CORAS Approach. Springer, Heidelberg (2010). https://doi.org/10.1007/978-3-642-12323-8
14. Pardue, H., Landry, J., Yasinsac, A.: A risk assessment model for voting systems using threat trees and monte carlo simulation. In: 2009 First International Workshop on Requirements Engineering for e-Voting Systems, pp. 55–60, August 2009. https://doi.org/10.1109/RE-VOTE.2009.1
15. Rajbhandari, L.: Consideration of opportunity and human factor: required paradigm shift for information security risk management. In: 2013 European Intelligence and Security Informatics Conference, pp. 147–150, August 2013. https://doi.org/10.1109/EISIC.2013.32
16. Saaty, T.L.: What is the analytic hierarchy process? In: Mitra, G., Greenberg, H.J., Lootsma, F.A., Rijkaert, M.J., Zimmermann, H.J. (eds.) Mathematical Models for Decision Support, pp. 109–121. Springer, Heidelberg (1988). https://doi.org/10.1007/978-3-642-83555-1_5
17. Steinberg, D., Budinsky, F., Paternostro, M., Merks, E.: EMF: Eclipse Modeling Framework 2.0, 2nd edn. Addison-Wesley Professional, Boston (2009)
18. Stonerburner, G., Goguen, A., Feringe, A.: Risk management guide for information technology systems, 2002 (NIST Special Publication 800-30) (2007)
19. Tundis, A., Mühlhäuser, M., Gallo, T., Garro, A., Saccá, D., Citrigno, S., Graziano, S.: Systemic risk analysis through se methods and techniques, vol. 2010, pp. 101–104 (2017). https://www.scopus.com/inward/record.uri?eid=2-s2.0-85038855133&partnerID=40&md5=513629eb20df7e1f564d579af6a655b8
20. Tundis, A., Mühlhäuser, M., Garro, A., Gallo, T., Saccá, D., Citrigno, S., Graziano, S.: Systemic risk modeling & evaluation through simulation & Bayesian networks, vol. Part F130521 (2017). https://doi.org/10.1145/3098954.3098993
21. Wirtz, R., Heisel, M.: CVSS-based estimation and prioritization for security risks. In: Proceedings of the 14th International Conference on Evaluation of Novel Approaches to Software Engineering - Volume 1: ENASE, pp. 297–306. INSTICC, SciTePress (2019). https://doi.org/10.5220/0007709902970306
22. Wirtz, R., Heisel, M.: A systematic method to describe and identify security threats based on functional requirements. In: Zemmari, A., Mosbah, M., Cuppens-Boulahia, N., Cuppens, F. (eds.) CRiSIS 2018. LNCS, vol. 11391, pp. 205–221. Springer, Cham (2019). https://doi.org/10.1007/978-3-030-12143-3_17

Towards GDPR Compliant Software Design: A Formal Framework for Analyzing System Models

Evangelia Vanezi$^{(\boxtimes)}$, Dimitrios Kouzapas, Georgia M. Kapitsaki, and Anna Philippou

Department of Computer Science, University of Cyprus, Nicosia, Cyprus
{evanez01,dimitrios.kouzapas,gkapi,annap}@cs.ucy.ac.cy

Abstract. Software systems nowadays store and process large amounts of personal data of individuals, rendering privacy protection a major issue of concern during their development. The EU General Data Protection Regulation addresses this issue with several provisions for protecting the personal data of individuals and makes it compulsory for companies and individuals to comply with the regulation. However, few methodologies have been considered to date to support GDPR compliance during system development. In this paper, we propose a process-calculus framework for formal modeling of software systems during the design phase, and validation of properties relating to the GDPR notion of Consent, the Right to Erasure, the Right to Access, and the Right to Rectification. Moreover, the framework enables the treatment of the notion of purpose through privacy policy satisfaction. Validation is performed with static analysis using type checking. Our work is the first step towards a framework that will implement Privacy-by-Design and GDPR compliance throughout the development cycle of a software system.

Keywords: GDPR · Privacy protection · Consent · Purpose · π-calculus · Static analysis · Privacy by design

1 Introduction

Software systems are nowadays becoming ubiquitous. To provide personalised, context-aware, or social-networking services, these systems store and process large amounts of personal data of individuals, thus rendering privacy protection a core issue during their development. This need has been well recognised with legislation being enacted to protect the privacy of individuals, a recent important example being the European Union's *General Data Protection Regulation* (GDPR) [16] in enforcement since May 2018. The GDPR defines several provisions regarding the collection and processing of EU residents personal data and all systems that in any way store and process such data are obliged to comply to the regulation. This obligation raises the challenge of designing and

© Springer Nature Switzerland AG 2020
E. Damiani et al. (Eds.): ENASE 2019, CCIS 1172, pp. 135–162, 2020.
https://doi.org/10.1007/978-3-030-40223-5_7

developing software systems that are guaranteed to adhere to expected privacy requirements, as enunciated by the GDPR.

Formal modeling schemes can be a facilitator in designing software system that comply to GDPR. In our recent work, we proposed the use of a formal methodology for the design and modelling of software systems that integrates provisions of the GDPR [46]. The methodology is based on the Privacy Calculus [33], a formal framework based on the π-calculus [35]. Our framework of [46] extends the Privacy Calculus with features for providing and withdrawing consent, and a type system that can validate that a system model conforms to associated GDPR provisions. Such a static-checking methodology can be thought of as an automated system, receiving as input the model and producing the result of the validation as output. A future objective of that work was to incorporate more GDPR provisions into the framework in order to support an almost fully compliant software model design and verification and, ultimately, to provide a rigorous framework for developing GRPR-compliant systems that can support the entire software development cycle, thus pursuing conformance to Data Protection by Design [41].

In the current work we embark on that objective by integrating a privacy policy mechanism within our framework. This addition enhances the framework by enabling the treatment of the notion of purpose, a central notion in the GDPR expressing that following consent, personal data must be processed according to a specific policy to which the user has provided consent. In order to achieve this, we build on the policy language of [33] with additional permissions as needed for the GDPR provisions under consideration. Furthermore, we define a type system that is now able to validate that models implement requirements associated with consent provision and withdrawal and, additionally, that following consent provision and before its withdrawal, processing of personal data conforms to a formally-defined privacy policy. A detailed case study at the end of this paper is used to present the complete approach of this work.

Outline. The remainder of the paper is organized as follows. In Sect. 2, we discuss some background work: we present the basic principles of the GDPR focusing on the ones relevant to our work, and continue to discuss the need of appropriate frameworks for developing GDPR-compliant systems, the role of formal methods towards this goal as well as related works in these areas. In Sect. 3 we review the process calculus from [46], an extension of the Privacy Calculus that incorporates the GDPR principles of lawfulness of processing by providing consent, consent withdrawal and right to erasure into the software's model. Section 4 presents an associated privacy policy language for specifying the privacy requirements of a data-processing system, whereas in Sect. 5 we develop a type system for guaranteeing compliance of a system to such a privacy policy. Section 6 illustrates the applicability of our methodology on a case study and, finally, Sect. 7 concludes the paper and discusses possible directions for future work.

2   Related Work

2.1   The General Data Protection Regulation

The GDPR was enforced in the European Union in May 2018 with the goal of unifying national laws and laying the rules for the protection of natural persons with regard to the processing of personal data where, according to GDPR Article 4(1), personal data is *"any information relating to an identified or identifiable natural person ('data subject')"*. This regulation constitutes a significant departure over previous regulations as it gives individuals increased rights on how their personal information is processed. Furthermore, compliance to the GDPR is compulsory and significant fines are imposed upon its violation.

The GDPR specifies a number of requirements and principles. In this work we aim to provide a framework that adheres to the following:

– According to Article 6(1a) (*"Lawfulness of Processing"*), and Recital 40 (*"Lawfulness of data processing"*), a system may collect and process personal data only upon the receipt of the respective user's explicit consent. This is also supported by Article 5(1) (*"Lawfulness, fairness and transparency"*), and specifically the principle of *Lawfulness* as any processing is considered to be lawful only in the case that the system has a lawful basis (under Article 6), one of them being consent.

– According to Article 17 (*"Right to erasure (right to be forgotten)"*) and Article 7(3) *"Conditions for consent"* the user has the right to withdraw her consent at any given time, and additionally have all of her personal data deleted from the system without undue delay.

– Article 5(1b) principle of *"Purpose Limitation"*, is discussing the notion of *Purpose*, defining that all *personal data* should be collected for specified, explicit and legitimate purposes, and be only used in a compatible way. A user's consent should be based on such purposes defined in the privacy policy, and the processing of data should conform to them. Also note that consent can be given for one or more specific purposes. The notion of purpose is implied in many other provisions of the GDPR, such as Article 5(1a) principle of *"Lawfulness, fairness and transparency"*, 5(1c) Principle of *"Data Minimisation"*, and 5(1e) principle of *"Storage Limitation"*.

– Article 15 *"Right of access by the data subject"* defines that the user has the right to access her personal data stored within a system at any time.

– Article 16 *"Right to Rectification"* and Article 5(d) principle of *"Accuracy"* defines the right of the owner to at any time rectify any inaccurate personal data, or complete any incomplete data.

A few works have already addressed GDPR issues such as the GDPR provisions for consent withdrawal and the right to forget, which are discussed in [38]. Moreover, a pattern catalog in order to help privacy regulation integration in systems is discussed in [26]. Another example is [40], which discusses GDPR in the framework of socio-technical systems.

2.2   Software Design and Modelling and the GDPR

Privacy by Design [41] or, as referred to in the GDPR Article 25(1) Data Protection By Design [16], is a widely discussed topic advocating that privacy should be incorporated into systems by default and should be a priority from the beginning of a system's design. By its definition, Data Protection by Design needs no specific distinct analysis, handling and mechanisms in order to be fulfilled. If all relevant principles and rights are embedded in a system's specifications model in the right way and are then transferred into the succeeding implementation, Data Protection by Design is guaranteed. Moreover, Data Protection by Design advocates the proactive consideration of privacy issues: ensuring a software's compliance should take place from the design phase and possible pitfalls should be anticipated and prevented before they can materialise, rather than remedied on a reactive basis.

Looking into the software engineering cycle, in the initial steps of the development of a software system, its specifications are drafted and subsequently a model of the software is created during the design phase reflecting these specifications at a proper level of abstraction. The software model can then be used both to check if the design of the system indeed represents the gathered specifications, and/or to produce a skeleton code for the actual system, using a Model Driven Engineering approach (MDE) [31,42]. For the modelling task, many modelling languages have been created and are widely used such as the Unified Modeling Language (UML) [19]. Furthermore, various extensions have been proposed to allow reasoning about security-related features, including UMLsec that allows to express security relevant information for a system specification [28], the Privacy-aware Context Profile (PCP) that can be exploited in context-aware applications [32], and the Privacy UML profile that can be used to capture the privacy policies of a software system [5].

As far as the GDPR is concerned, there have only been few attempts to understand the GDPR, mainly from the legal perspective, and even fewer discussing mechanisms to support GDPR compliance during system development [20,25]. Approaches include *PriS*, that integrates privacy requirements in the early stages of the system development process [29] focusing on organizational processes and suggesting implementation techniques and *privacyTracker*, taking into account the GDPR and proposing a framework that supports some of its basic principles such as data traceability [20]. Privacy in designing systems for Internet of Things is discussed in [37]. In [2] modelling is used to analyze the system design and propose security and privacy controls that can improve it, whereas other works rely on ontologies and modelling in the Web Ontology Language (OWL) or the Resource Description Framework (RDF), such as Linked USDL Privacy [30]. Finally, [17] proposes the use of tainting and other static analysis techniques to detect the potential leak of sensitive information at code level.

2.3   GDPR Software Compliance and Formal Methods

Another dimension towards the development of software systems is that of formal methods. Formal methods are mathematical tools and methodologies for the rigorous specification, modelling, development, and verification of systems. The use of formal methods is especially relevant for the development of dependable and safety-critical systems and can also prove useful for the development of systems handling private data, supporting Privacy by Design and GDPR compliance. In contrast to modelling languages such as UML, languages used for modelling in formal methods approaches possess formal semantics. Such semantics enable the enunciation of a system as a mathematical object on which exhaustive verification can be performed. Verification approaches include model-checking [12], which enables to verify that a system model satisfies specifications expressed as temporal logic properties, and type checking, via which properties of a system can be checked statically.

One formal framework that has been receiving increased attention, and on which our work is based, is the π-calculus [35]. The π-calculus is a process calculus that can act as a modelling language for systems and at the same time support validation of their properties. The π-calculus, being a formal language, has been used for formalizing aspects of the UML modelling language [34], as well as for transforming the basic workflow patterns of Business Process Model and Notation (BPMN) into equivalent π-calculus code [8]. It has also formed the theoretical basis of the Business Process Modeling Language (BPML) [21] and of Microsoft's XLANG [43].

Various extensions of the π-calculus have been proposed to reason about security and privacy properties. One such extension developed for describing and analyzing cryptographic protocols is the spi-calculus [1], whereas in [11] the π-calculus is extended with the notion of groups as types for channels which are used to statically prohibit the leakage of secrets. Type systems have also been employed in process calculi to reason about access control that is closely related to privacy. For instance, the work on the Dπ-calculus has introduced sophisticated type systems for controlling the access to resources advertised at different locations [22–24]. Furthermore, discretionary access control has been considered in [10] employing the π-calculus with groups, while role-based access control (RBAC) has been considered in [9,13,15]. In addition, authorization policies and their analysis via type checking has been considered in a number of papers [3,7,18]. Closest to our work is the Privacy Calculus of [33], a formal framework based on the π-calculus with groups accompanied by a type system for capturing privacy-related notions, and a privacy policy language for expressing privacy policies. Unlike other works the Privacy calculus focuses on considering privacy as a general notion and addresses a wider class of privacy violation such as aggregation and identification. Furthermore, our previous work of [46] extends the Privacy calculus by proposing a modelling language that incorporates the GDPR notions of consent provision and withdrawal. The present paper extends [46] by enabling the treatment of the GDPR notion of *purpose*, with the incorporation of the privacy policies of [33] appropriately extended, and by proposing a type system according to which a well-typed system satisfies an associated GDPR-compliant privacy policy.

Other formal methods relating to GDPR compliance include [44,45] where Markov Decision Processes are used to describe semantic requirements relating to the notion of purpose. Furthermore, in [4], the authors propose identifying a purpose with a business process, and using formal models of inter-process communication to audit or derive privacy policies whereas in [27], the authors define a semantic model for purpose-based privacy policies, a modal logic, and a corresponding model-checking algorithm to verify whether a particular system complies to them. Other related work includes [39], specifying purposes as work flows modeled by Petri nets and model-checked against actor models, and [14], proposing semantics of purpose-based privacy policies in temporal logic and defining a run-time monitoring methodology. The present work is distinguished from these approaches mainly in its aim to provide a methodology for modeling systems during the design phase of the software engineering cycle and for verifying that they satisfy GDPR-based privacy provisions. Furthermore, the verification is implemented via type checking, a static approach that does not suffer from the state-space explosion problem, being complementary to model-checking methodologies.

3   The Calculus

We propose the use of a process calculus [46], which is an extension of the Privacy Calculus [33], as a formal modelling language for systems. Privacy Calculus terms can be considered as black boxes that can be translated, manually or automatically, into code and/or code templates at the implementation phase of software development.

In the Privacy Calculus, system entities are modelled as distinct processes communicating and interacting with each other using channel-based message passing. Channels are referred to as *names*, and are dynamically created and passed between processes. We proceed to present this extended syntax and semantics, as defined in [46].

3.1   Syntax

Table 1 summarizes the proposed syntax including values and functionality. Assume a set of names $n \in N$ that are partitioned over names, a, and store references, r. Also, assume a set of constants $c \in C$, and a set of variables $x, y \in V$. Values ranged over by ι include identities, id, the hidden identity, $\_$, and variables, x, while values ranged over by δ include constants, c, the empty constant, $*$, and variables. Data structure $\mathsf{id} \otimes c$ associates an identity, id, with a personal data value, c, integrating the notion of personal data as required by our framework. It also enables the form $\_ \otimes c$, which associates data with an identity that is hidden, mapping to GDPR provision for anonymous personal data. Variable placeholders for private data are written as $x \otimes y$. We use meta-variable u to range over names or variables. Values, ranging over v, include names, private

Table 1. Extended syntax of the privacy calculus [46]

(identity values)	ι	$::=$ id $\mid$ $_-$ $\mid$ x
(data values)	δ	$::=$ c $\mid$ $*$ $\mid$ x
(private data)		$\iota \otimes \delta$ where $\iota \neq x \Rightarrow \delta = c$ and $\iota = x \Rightarrow \delta = y$
(identifiers)	u	$::=$ a $\mid$ r $\mid$ x
(terms)	t	$::=$ a $\mid$ r $\mid$ $\iota \otimes \delta$ $\mid$ d $\mid$ x
(constants)	v	$::=$ a $\mid$ r $\mid$ $\mathsf{id} \otimes d$ $\mid$ d
(placeholders)	k	$::=$ x $\mid$ $x \otimes y$ $\mid$ $_- \otimes x$
(processes)	P	$::=$ $\mathbf{0}$ $\mid$ $u!\langle t \rangle.P$ $\mid$ $u?(k).P$ $\mid$ $(\nu\, n)P$ $\mid$ $P \mid P$ $\mid$ $*P$
		$\mid$ $\mathsf{if}\ e\ \mathsf{then}\ P\ \mathsf{else}\ P$ $\mid$ $\bar{r} \triangleright [\iota \otimes \delta]$
		$\mid$ $u \triangleleft \mathsf{consent}(x).P$ $\mid$ $u \triangleright \mathsf{consent}(r).P$ $\mid$ $u \triangleleft \mathsf{withdraw}.P$
(systems)	S	$::=$ $\mathsf{G}[P]$ $\mid$ $\mathsf{G}[\{P\}_{\mathsf{id}}]$ $\mid$ $\mathsf{G}[S]$ $\mid$ $S \parallel S$ $\mid$ $(\nu\, n)S$

data, or data; placeholders, ranging over k, include the variable structures of the calculus, whereas terms, ranging over t, include both values and placeholders.

The Privacy Calculus is defined in two levels; processes and systems. At the process level the termination term, $\mathbf{0}$, defines the inactive process; the output term, $u!\langle t \rangle.P$, defines a process ready to send a message t on channel u and then proceed as P, while the input term, $u?(k).P$, defines a process that waits to receive a message on channel u, that will be substituted on variable k and then proceed as P. The name creation term, $(\nu\, n)P$, defines the creation and restriction of a new name n within the scope of process P. The parallel composition term, $P_1 \mid P_2$, defines the parallel execution of processes P_1 and P_2, proceeding either independently or interacting with each other. The replication term, $*P$, defines the option of creating multiple copies of process P. Moreover, the conditional construct, $\mathsf{if}\ e\ \mathsf{then}\ P_1\ \mathsf{else}\ P_2$, defines the evolution of the process based on the evaluation of the condition e, proceeding as a process P_1 if true or as process P_2 if not. The Privacy Calculus incorporates the additional store term $\bar{r} \triangleright [\mathsf{id} \otimes c]$, that defines a store holding and giving access to private data through reference r. Stores can be mapped into actual software as database table records, that can be accessed by any system entity through their unique key.

Our extension integrates consent-based terms on the Privacy Calculus. The consent term, $u \triangleleft \mathsf{consent}(x).P$, defines a process ready to provide consent on channel u and receive a new store reference on x. Term $u \triangleright \mathsf{consent}(r).P$, is dual to the consent term and defines a process receiving consent on channel u. Finally, term $u \triangleleft \mathsf{withdraw}.P$ defines a process that withdraws consent from store u.

At the system level, the Privacy Calculus processes and systems are organized using groups. System $\mathsf{G}[P]$ associates process P with group G. Similarly, system $\mathsf{G}[\{P\}_{\mathsf{id}}]$ associates a process with a user identity, id, and a group G. Associating an identity with the process allows for the abstract representation of individual system users and associates them with their personal data. A group hierarchy is created using system $\mathsf{G}[S]$, that associates system S with group G. New names can be created at the system level via system $(\nu\ n)(S)$. Finally, systems can be composed in parallel $S_1 \parallel S_2$.

Example 1 (Modelling a Bank Notification System). We provide the specification of a running example that will be used throughout the paper to demonstrate the modelling capabilities of our framework. Consider a system that monitors the transaction details of a user's bank account, in the form of a transactions log, and sends the user statistical information regarding these data once a month, with the following specifications:

1. The system handles the transaction logs of the users' bank accounts, classified as personal data.
2. The system cannot store or process any user personal data before the provision of the user's consent.
3. The user has to provide her consent to register to the service provided by the system.
4. Upon a new transaction, the accounting entity adds the transaction's details to the transactions log in the system's database.
5. The user may access and view her transactions log at any time.
6. Once a month the notifications entity is triggered and sends the user some statistical data, such as the amount spent and the amount earned, to the user.
7. The user has the option to withdraw her consent at any given time, and the data associated to her should be deleted from the system, and no further processing should be applied to them.

The Bank Notification system is identified as an entity composed by three subsystems: the Accounting subsystem, the Notification subsystem, and the Database. We also identify the User entity, as the data subject.

We illustrate how the Bank Notification System can be modelled in our calculus. To implement a system hierarchy, assume the existence of groups User, DBase, Accounting, Notification, System, and Network. To simplify the example, let us assume the existence of a single user, and the termination of the system functionality immediately after statistical data is sent once to the user.

$$U \overset{\mathrm{def}}{=} (\nu\ a)(\nu\ b)(\mathsf{User}[\{c!\langle a\rangle.a \vartriangleleft \mathsf{consent}(x).d!\langle b\rangle.b?(y).x \vartriangleleft \mathsf{withdraw}.\mathbf{0}\}_{\mathsf{id}}])$$

$$DB \overset{\mathrm{def}}{=} \mathsf{DBase}[c?(y).y \vartriangleright \mathsf{consent}(r).e!\langle r\rangle.f!\langle r\rangle.\mathbf{0}]$$

$$Acc \overset{\mathrm{def}}{=} \mathsf{Accounting}[e?(x). * (x!\langle id \otimes \mathsf{transaction\_data}\rangle.\mathbf{0})]$$

$$Not \overset{\mathrm{def}}{=} \mathsf{Notification}[d?(z).f?(x).x?(\_ \otimes y).z!\langle \mathsf{stats}(y)\rangle.\mathbf{0}]$$

$$Sys \overset{\mathrm{def}}{=} \mathsf{Network}[U \parallel \mathsf{System}[DB \parallel Acc \parallel Not]]$$

System U represents the user entity and is characterized by the group User. It is annotated with the user's unique identifier, id, which is linked to the user's personal data. The user creates channels a and b and shares them, via channel c and d, with the database system, DB, and the notification system, respectively.

The user provides her consent towards the database via channel a, that results in the user receiving the store reference substituted on name x. After, receiving data from the Notification system, the user withdraws her consent and terminates.

The database system, DB, is modelled using group DBase, and is responsible for receiving and storing the user's personal data. The database system receives a private communication channel from the user through the public channel c. Then, it receives consent from the private communication channel that will dynamically create a new private data store on reference r, which is associated with the identity of the user. Reference r is subsequently sent to the notification process, through channel e, and to the Accounting process, through channel f.

The Accounting system, Acc, is responsible to update the transactions log in the database through the reference to the store upon each new transaction occurrence. The Accounting system first receives the reference to the store of the transaction_data from the database via channel e, and then proceeds to append subsequent transaction data to the transactions log via the received reference. We abstract the creation of a transactions log by assuming that each time the process is updating the transaction_data, the new transaction details are appended to the previous transactions log.

The Notification system, Not is defined using group Notification. It first receives a private channel from the user via channel d, and subsequently the reference to the database store holding the personal data of the user, via channel f. It then reads the transaction_data from the store using the received reference, and calculates statistical transaction data via function stats. Finally, it sends the statistical data to the user through their private shared channel.

The complete system, Sys is realised by the group Network that is composed by the User system and the Bank Notification System, which is realised by group System and its subgroups DBase, Accounting and Notification.   □

3.2   Semantics

The calculus is accompanied by semantics prescribing the behavior of each construct, and consequently the behavior of a system. The semantics is defined using a *labelled transition relation*, $S \xrightarrow{\ell} S'$, denoting that system S can execute, i.e. observe, the action indicated by label ℓ, and evolve into system S'. Interaction between system components is enabled using dual actions. Two actions that are dual, i.e. labels that represent dual input and output actions, can be synchronised when they are observed on parallel systems. The synchronisation gives rise to interaction between parallel components of a system (cf. Example 2). Assuming that ℓ_1 dual ℓ_2 indicates that label ℓ_1 is dual to label ℓ_2, the rule that describes parallel interaction is defined as:

$$\frac{S_1 \xrightarrow{\ell_1} S_1' \quad S_1 \xrightarrow{\ell_2} S_2' \quad \ell_1 \text{ dual } \ell_2}{S_1 \mid S_2 \longrightarrow S_1' \mid S_2'}$$

The set of labels of the Privacy Calculus is extended with the following:

$$a \lhd \mathsf{consent}(r) \qquad a \lhd \mathsf{consent}(r)@\mathsf{id} \qquad a \rhd \mathsf{consent}(r)@\mathsf{id}$$
$$r \lhd \mathsf{withdraw} \qquad r \lhd \mathsf{withdraw}@\mathsf{id} \qquad \bar{r} \rhd \mathsf{withdraw}@\mathsf{id}$$

Label $a \lhd \mathsf{consent}(r)$ denotes the basic action for providing consent on channel a and receiving a reference on channel r, whereas label $a \lhd \mathsf{consent}(r)@\mathsf{id}$ is the same action lifted to a user identity, id. Dually action $a \rhd \mathsf{consent}(r)@\mathsf{id}$ is the acceptance of a consent on channel a and the creation of a new store with reference r and identity id. Withdraw labels are $r \lhd \mathsf{withdraw}$ that denotes a withdraw on reference r; $r \lhd \mathsf{withdraw}@\mathsf{id}$ that lifts a withdraw at the user level; and $\bar{r} \rhd \mathsf{withdraw}@\mathsf{id}$ that denotes the receipt of a withdraw on reference r with identity id. These labels give rise to the additional dual pairs of actions:

$$a \lhd \mathsf{consent}(r)@\mathsf{id} \quad \mathbf{dual} \quad a \rhd \mathsf{consent}(r)@\mathsf{id} \quad r \lhd \mathsf{withdraw}@\mathsf{id} \quad \mathbf{dual} \quad \bar{r} \rhd \mathsf{withdraw}@\mathsf{id}$$

A consent action, $a \lhd \mathsf{consent}(r)@\mathsf{id}$ may synchronise with $a \rhd \mathsf{consent}(r)@\mathsf{id}$, in order for a user to provide consent for the store of its private data. Symmetrically, a withdraw action $r \lhd \mathsf{withdraw}@\mathsf{id}$ may synchronise with action $\bar{r} \rhd \mathsf{withdraw}@\mathsf{id}$ in order for a user to withdraw its consent for storing its private data.

Table 2. Extension to privacy calculus labeled transition semantics.

$$[\mathsf{UCons}] \; a \lhd \mathsf{consent}(x).P \xrightarrow{a \lhd \mathsf{consent}(r)} P\{^r/_x\}$$

$$[\mathsf{SCons}] \; a \rhd \mathsf{consent}(r).P \xrightarrow{a \rhd \mathsf{consent}(r)@\mathsf{id}} P \mid \bar{r} \rhd [\mathsf{id} \otimes *]$$

$$[\mathsf{UWDraw}] \; r \lhd \mathsf{withdraw}.P \xrightarrow{r \lhd \mathsf{withdraw}} P \qquad [\mathsf{SWDraw}] \; \bar{r} \rhd [\mathsf{id} \otimes c] \xrightarrow{\bar{r} \rhd \mathsf{withdraw}@\mathsf{id}} \bar{r} \rhd [\_ \otimes *]$$

$$[\mathsf{SNOut}] \; \bar{r} \rhd [\_ \otimes *] \xrightarrow{\bar{r}!\langle\_\otimes*\rangle} \bar{r} \rhd [\_ \otimes *] \qquad [\mathsf{SNInp}] \; \bar{r} \rhd [\_ \otimes *] \xrightarrow{\bar{r}?(\mathsf{id}\otimes c)} \bar{r} \rhd [\_ \otimes *]$$

$$[\mathsf{SId}] \; \dfrac{P \xrightarrow{\ell} P'}{\mathsf{S}[\{P\}_{\mathsf{id}}] \xrightarrow{\ell@\mathsf{id}} \mathsf{S}[\{P'\}_{\mathsf{id}}]}$$

The labeled transition semantics are defined by the rules in Table 2. Rule [UCons] describes a process that provides consent on channel a by observing the $a \lhd \mathsf{consent}(r)$ label. Rule [SCons] defines the action of receiving consent, which is done via label $a \rhd \mathsf{consent}(r)@\mathsf{id}$. After the label is observed a new store, $\bar{r} \rhd [\mathsf{id} \otimes *]$ is created on reference r with identity id. Following the dual definition of labels, rules [UCons] and [SCons] can synchronise to create a new store and exchange the corresponding reference. Withdraw follows a similar fashion.

A process with a withdraw prefix observes a withdraw label $r \lhd$ withdraw, rule [UWDraw]. Rule [SWDraw] observes a store receiving a withdraw request via label $\overline{r} \rhd$ withdraw@id and as a result it deletes the corresponding private data and assigns the anonymous identity and the empty value to its memory. Rules [SNOut] and [SNInp] define the interaction of the empty store. Both interaction has no effect on the private data store. Finally, rule [SId] provides semantics to the system that associate a process with an identity, $G[\{P\}_{id}]$. Operation ℓ@id is defined as ℓ whenever $\ell \notin \{a \lhd \mathsf{consent}(r), t \lhd \mathsf{withdraw}\}$, $a \lhd \mathsf{consent}(r)$@id whenever $\ell = a \lhd \mathsf{consent}(r)$, and $a \lhd$ withdraw@id whenever $\ell = a \lhd$ withdraw.

Example 2 (Execution of the Bank Notification System). To further understand the Privacy calculus semantics, we provide an execution of the Bank Notification System defined in Example 1.

$$Sys \xrightarrow{\tau} (\nu\ a)(\nu\ b)(\mathsf{Network}[\mathsf{User}[a \lhd \mathsf{consent}(x).c!\langle b\rangle.b?(y).x \lhd \mathsf{withdraw}.\mathbf{0}]$$
$$\|\ \mathsf{System}[\mathsf{DBase}[a \rhd \mathsf{consent}(r).DB'] \| \mathsf{Acc} \| \mathsf{Not}]])$$
$$\xrightarrow{\tau} (\nu\ a)(\nu\ b)(\mathsf{Network}[\mathsf{User}[c!\langle b\rangle.b?(y).r \lhd \mathsf{withdraw}.\mathbf{0}]$$
$$\|\ \mathsf{System}[\mathsf{DBase}[DB' \mid \overline{r} \rhd [\mathsf{id} \otimes *]] \| \mathsf{Acc} \| \mathsf{Not}]])$$

As a first step we observe the synchronization between the User and the Database system, where the User sends a newly created channel a on public channel c to the Database, which is subsequently substituted on variable y. The next step, describes the synchronization for the User to provide consent for data storage to the Database, via channel a. This results in the creation of a new store on reference r, which is associated with the user identifier, id. The store is created within the Database system. Upon creation the User system receives a reference r substituted on name x.   □

4   Privacy Policy Language

As discussed, we extend our framework by enabling the treatment of the notion of *purpose* based on Privacy Policy satisfaction, i.e., entities in the system should process the data according to a defined privacy policy indicating the processing purpose. This work adopts the language used in the Privacy Calculus [33] to express privacy policies, by incorporating a subset of the Privacy Policy language permissions and extending them with an additional permission term, capturing the provision and withdrawal of consent. Note that we embed a set of possible permissions judged as essential, but our framework is able to accommodate additional permissions if needed. The Privacy Policy language is structured in such a way as to formally define the allowed and disallowed actions in the form of permissions, linked to specific agents distinguished by their roles, for specific types of private data. As such, the concepts of *types*, and *roles*, referred to as *groups*, are central for the definition of policies and are explained below. Data types will be used in policies, where we assume the following set of types to characterize values and channels used by the processes:

$$g\quad ::=\quad \mathsf{nat} \mid \mathsf{bool} \mid \ \ldots \qquad\qquad T\quad ::=\quad \mathsf{t}[g] \mid \mathsf{p}[g] \mid \mathsf{G}[T]$$

We assume a set of ground types, ranged over by g, which include primitive data types, e.g. natural numbers, booleans, etc. Type t[g] is used to characterise private data of the form id $\otimes$ c with c being of type g, and type p[g] is used to type constants c. Moreover, we can construct types of the form G[T] used to type channels that are able to communicate data of type T between processes belonging to group G.

The Privacy Policy language uses a set of permissions to describe, in regards to a specific private data type, the actions each group in a system is able to perform. The permissions we consider for handling private data are the following:

$$\text{prm} \quad ::= \quad \text{read} \mid \text{update} \mid \text{reference} \mid \text{disseminate } G \mid \text{store} \mid \text{readId}$$
$$\mid \quad \text{usage}\{p\} \mid \text{identify}\{t\} \mid \text{consent}$$

Permission read allows processes to read the private data. Permission update allows to update the private data content. Permission reference allows to gain access to the reference of the store holding the private data. Permission disseminate G defines that the reference to the store of the private data might be sent to processes of group G. Permission store allows the creation of a new store to hold private data. Permission readId allows access to the identifier of the private data. Permission usage\{p\} allows the matching of a private data with a constant of type p, and permission identify\{t\} allows the matching of private data against other private data. The additional permission consent, when associated with a type of private data and a group, indicates that processes of the specific group are allowed to provide/withdraw their consent for creating a store to collect private data of that type.

A Privacy Policy can now be defined as an assignment of permissions to a hierarchy of groups with respect to types of sensitive data and it is defined as follows:

$$\mathcal{P} \quad ::= \quad t \gg H \mid t \gg H; \mathcal{P} \qquad\qquad H \quad ::= \quad G\{\tilde{\text{prm}}\}[\tilde{H}]$$

where $\tilde{\text{prm}}$ is a set of permissions. A Privacy Policy has the form $t_1 \gg H_1; \ldots; t_n \gg H_n$ where t_i are the base types subject to privacy. Given a policy $\mathcal{P}$, we write $\mathcal{P}(t)$ for H_i where $t = t_i$. The components H_i, which we refer to as *permission hierarchies*, specify the group-permission associations for each base type. A permission hierarchy H has the form $G\{\tilde{\text{prm}}\}[H_1, \ldots, H_m]$ and it is structured in the same way as the group hierarchy of the Privacy Calculus system it is associated with. The permission hierarchy expresses that a process under the hierarchy of group G has permissions $\tilde{\text{prm}}$ towards the data in question. These permissions accumulate as we follow the Privacy Policy hierarchy. For a more detailed definition of the privacy policy language and the permissions, the reader is referred to the [33].

The next example illustrates the use of the Privacy Policy language by defining a Privacy Policy for the Bank Notification System.

Example 3 (Privacy Policy for the Bank Notification System). We define the Privacy Policy of the Bank Notification System in Example 1. The system has the following privacy specification:

1. Only the User, i.e. the data subject, can provide and withdraw consent regarding her transaction data being stored and processed by the system, This is based on the GDPR principle of *"Lawfulness of Processing"* and *"Right to erasure"*.
2. The user should be able to access and read her stored personal transaction data, conforming to GDPR *"Right of access by the data subject"*.
3. The user should not be able to update her personal transaction data, as they are documented by the actual transaction. If the user has an objection and requires rectification of the data then a distinct rectification mechanism should be triggered. The above are in compliance with GDPR *"Right to Rectification"* and principle of *"Accuracy"*.
4. The Notification entity should be able to access and read the transaction data.
5. The Notification entity should be able to use the transaction data for statistics purposes.
6. The Accounting entity should be able to update the transaction data, but should not be able to read neither the identifier nor the value of the stored data.
7. The Database entity is the only entity that should be able to store the personal transaction data. Additionally, the Database entity is able to distribute access to them to the Accounting and Notification entities.

Privacy requirements (4)–(7) even though not directly mapped to an explicit GDPR article, are comprising the processing purpose of the system, regarding personal data of the user, as needed, defined in the GDPR principle of *"Purpose Limitation"*. The above requirements are formally described using the following Privacy Policy:

```
transaction_data ≫ Network{}[
    User{consent, read, reference},
    System{}[
        DBase{store, disseminate Notification, disseminate Accounting},
        Accounting{reference, update}
        Notification{reference, read, readId, usage{statistics}}
    ]
]
```

The group hierarchy of the Privacy Policy follows the group hierarchy of the Bank Notification System in Example 1. The permissions assigned to each group formally describe the privacy requirements of the Bank Notification system.

The User has the permission to provide and withdraw consent regarding the storage and processing of her transaction log. The User also has the permission to gain access to the reference and read its private data store. The DBase has the permissions to create a store for storing the transaction log, and disseminate the reference for the transaction log store towards the Notification and Accounting system. The Accounting system has the permissions to receive a transaction store reference and to update its data. Finally, the Notification system has the permissions to receive the reference of the transaction data store. It can also read the transaction data and use them for statistical analysis. Moreover, it has the permission to read the identifier associated with the data.   □

5   Typing Policy Compliance

In this section, we present the developed type system, the mechanism within our framework that is able to validate whether a system model, defined in the calculus proposed, conforms to a defined privacy policy. As a consequence this mechanism can statically check for compliance to GDPR-based provisions. The type system can guarantee the compliance of a model by applying static type-checking techniques. Given the results of the type-checking analysis, no further testing is required to examine the system model. At the end of the section, we prove that well-typed processes do not present errors. Note that we only present the additional typing rules that we need to add to the Privacy calculus type system and we refer the reader to [33] for its complete exposition.

Example 4. Consider a system similar to the one in Example 1, that follows the exact same privacy policy (see Example 3), but is defined with a minor variation on the definition of the Accounting entity, as follows:

$$Sys \stackrel{\text{def}}{=} \texttt{Network}[U \parallel \texttt{System}[DB \parallel Acc \parallel Not]]$$

$$Acc \stackrel{\text{def}}{=} \texttt{Accounting}[e?(z).z?(x \otimes y).\mathbf{0}]$$

This model defines a system, where an Accounting Department entity tries to read the personal data of the user. The Privacy Policy in Example 3 assigns permissions for holding the store reference and for updating the stored value. Therefore, the above system violates the Privacy Policy because the `Accounting` role does not have a read permission. The type system is designed to perform static analysis in order to verify whether a system *satisfies* a privacy policy (Definition 2).   □

5.1   Type System

Our type system uses the following typing environments:

$$\Gamma \quad ::= \quad \Gamma, t : T \mid \emptyset \qquad \Lambda \quad ::= \quad \Lambda, \bar{r} \mid \Lambda, \text{id} \mid \emptyset \qquad Z \quad ::= \quad Z, \langle \text{id}, t \rangle \mid \emptyset$$

Γ associates values, t, with types, T. Γ_1, Γ_2 is defined as $\Gamma_1 \cup \Gamma_2$. Λ ensures that store references $\bar{r}$ and identity values id are unique within a system. Λ_1, Λ_2 is defined as $\Lambda_1 \cup \Lambda_2$, whenever $\Lambda_1 \cap \Lambda_2 = \emptyset$ and otherwise undefined. Similarly linear environment Z tracks identities and associated private data to track unique private stores for each identity. Z_1, Z_2 is defined as $Z_1 \cup Z_2$, whenever $Z_1 \cap Z_2 = \emptyset$, and otherwise undefined. In addition, we define the following environments:

$$\Delta \quad ::= \quad \Delta, t : \tilde{\text{prm}} \mid \emptyset \qquad \theta \quad ::= \quad \mathsf{G}[\theta] \mid \mathsf{G}[\tilde{\text{prm}}] \qquad \Theta \quad ::= \quad \Theta, t : \theta \mid \emptyset$$

Environment Δ maps private data types to a set of permissions. Structure θ provides a hierarchy for a set of permissions. Finally, environment Θ, called interface, maps private types to a set of permissions under a hierarchy. These environments assume a linear treatment and they are used by the typing system to extract information on how private data are being used. We use typing judgments of the following forms:

$$\Gamma \vdash t : T \triangleright \Delta \qquad \Gamma; \Lambda; Z \vdash P \triangleright \Delta \qquad \Gamma; \Lambda \vdash S \triangleright \Theta$$

The first judgment states that a variable or value t has a type T given a type environment Γ. At the same time we derive the permissions applied while processing this value, in permissions environment Δ. The second and third typing judgments state that given environments Γ and Λ process P or system S is well typed producing a permission environment Δ or an interface Θ respectively. Permissions environment Δ and interface Θ are following the same structure and rules as in the Privacy Calculus. We refer the reader there for more details.

$$[\mathsf{NVal}]\ \Gamma \vdash id \otimes * : \mathsf{t}[\mathsf{g}] \triangleright \emptyset$$

$$[\mathsf{TCons}]\ \frac{\Gamma; \Lambda; Z \vdash P \triangleright \Delta' \qquad \Gamma \vdash x : \mathsf{G}[\mathsf{t}[\mathsf{g}]] \triangleright \emptyset \qquad \Gamma \vdash u : \mathsf{G}'[\mathsf{G}[\mathsf{t}[\mathsf{g}]]] \triangleright \emptyset}{\Gamma \backslash x; \Lambda; Z \vdash u \triangleleft \mathsf{consent}(x).P \triangleright \mathsf{t} : \{\mathsf{consent}\} \uplus \Delta'}$$

$$[\mathsf{TCreate}]\ \frac{\Gamma; \Lambda; Z \vdash P \triangleright \Delta' \qquad \Gamma \vdash r : \mathsf{G}[\mathsf{t}[\mathsf{g}]] \triangleright \emptyset \qquad \Gamma \vdash u : \mathsf{G}'[\mathsf{G}[\mathsf{t}[\mathsf{g}]]] \triangleright \emptyset}{\Gamma; \Lambda, \overline{r}; Z, \langle id, \mathsf{t} \rangle \vdash u \triangleright \mathsf{consent}(r).P \triangleright \mathsf{t} : \{\mathsf{store}\} \uplus \Delta'}$$

$$[\mathsf{TWithdraw}]\ \frac{\Gamma; \Lambda; Z \vdash P \triangleright \Delta' \qquad \Gamma \vdash u : \mathsf{G}[\mathsf{t}[\mathsf{g}]] \triangleright \emptyset}{\Gamma; \Lambda; Z \vdash u \triangleleft \mathsf{withdraw}.P \triangleright \mathsf{t} : \{\mathsf{consent}\} \uplus \Delta'}$$

$$[\mathsf{TId}]\ \frac{\Gamma; \Lambda; Z \vdash P \triangleright \Delta \qquad \Theta = \{\mathsf{G}[\mathsf{t} : \tilde{\mathsf{prm}}] \mid \mathsf{t} : \tilde{\mathsf{prm}} \in \Delta\}}{\Gamma; \Lambda, \mathsf{id} \vdash \mathsf{G}[\{P\}_{\mathsf{id}}] \triangleright \Theta}$$

$$[\mathsf{Gr}]\ \frac{\Gamma; \Lambda; Z \vdash P \triangleright \Delta \qquad \mathsf{consent} \notin \Delta \qquad \Theta = \{\mathsf{G}[\mathsf{t} : \tilde{\mathsf{prm}}] \mid \mathsf{t} : \tilde{\mathsf{prm}} \in \Delta\}}{\Gamma; \Lambda \vdash \mathsf{G}[P] \triangleright \Theta}$$

Fig. 1. Typing rules.

Our typing system extends the Privacy Calculus typing system with the additional rules in Fig. 1. Typing rule [TCons] types the $u \triangleleft \mathsf{consent}(x).P$ term. It checks if channel x is of a store reference type and if channel u can carry x. Additionally it adds the consent permission to the permissions environment practiced by process P so far. Rule [TCreate] types the $u \triangleright \mathsf{consent}(r).P$ term, similarly to the [TCons] rule, except that permissions store is added to the permission environment of the process. Rule [TWithdraw] types the $u \triangleleft \mathsf{withdraw}.P$ term by checking that u is indeed a reference channel. The [TWithdraw] rule adds the consent permission in the environment. As discussed before, providing and withdrawing consent practice the same permission. Rule [TId] types the process annotated with an identifier. It adds the identifier in the linear Λ environment to ensure that it will not be used by another system. Environment Δ is lifted to environment Θ. Finally, Rule [Gr] types system G[P]. It ensures that process P is typed without a consent permission. This is because the consent permission is only allowed by systems associated with an identity.

Example 5. Consider the system in Example 4 that mishandles personal data with respect to the Privacy Policy in Example 3. Although the system is well typed, it fails to produce an interface that can satisfy the Privacy Policy. Process *Acc* when type-checked will produce permissions environment $\Delta = \{$readId, read, reference$\}$ for the process in the group Accounting. This does not check against the Privacy Policy, that contains permissions update and reference only.

Another case of a system that mishandles data in violation is the following:

$$\mathsf{User}[c!\langle id \otimes \mathsf{transaction\_data}\rangle.a \lhd \mathsf{consent}(x).P] \parallel \mathsf{Sys}[c?(x \otimes y).Q]$$

This system describes the situation where private data is sent (resp. received) via a non-reference channel before consent is provided by the user. However, this absence of consent violates the GDPR provisions. Therefore, this system should not satisfy any Privacy policy and should be characterized as ill-typed by the type system. Indeed, the system does not type-checked; the error in this case is captured by typing rule [TOut] (cf. [33]) checking that in an output action the type of the data sent must be compatible with the type of data that the channel can carry. Personal data can only be carried on reference channels, thus this process is not well-typed and is correctly characterized as non compliant with the consent provisions of the GDPR.

On the other hand, the system defined in Example 1 is well-typed deriving a permissions interface that fully matches the privacy policy permissions assignment.   □

5.2   Soundness and Safety

In this section we provide soundness and safety results for our framework. Our results extend those of the Privacy Calculus. Specifically, we prove Type Preservation (Theorem 1) that states that a well typed process, (resp. system), continues to be well typed if it is executed. Furthermore, based on Type Preservation we show that a well-typed system is Safe (Theorem 2): a system that complies to a privacy policy will never reach an error state, i.e., a state that violates the privacy policy requirements.

Prior to stating the Type Preservation Theorem we assume the environment inclusion relation, $\preceq$, as defined in [33, Definition 6.4]. The Type Preservation Theorem states the soundness of our typing system: given a well-typed process (resp. system), well-typedness is preserved by the labelled transition semantics relation.

Theorem 1 (Type Preservation). *Consider a process P and a system S.*

- *If $\Gamma; \Lambda; Z \vdash P \triangleright \Delta$ and $P \xrightarrow{\ell} P'$, then for some Λ', Z', Δ' we have $\Gamma; \Lambda'; Z' \vdash P' \triangleright \Delta'$ and $\Delta' \preceq \Delta$.*
- *If $\Gamma; \Lambda \vdash S \triangleright \Theta$ and $S \xrightarrow{\ell} S'$ then, for some Λ', Θ', we have $\Gamma; \Lambda' \vdash S' \triangleright \Theta'$ and $\Theta' \preceq \Theta$.*

Before we present the proof of the Type Preservation Theorem assume Weakening [33, Lemma 6.1], Strengthening [33, Lemma 6.2], and Substitution [33, Lemma 6.3] Lemmas, as well as [33, Proposition 6.8].

Proof. Similarly with the Privacy calculus, the proof is by induction on the inference tree for $\xrightarrow{\ell}$. We will be proving the theorem only for the labels added in this work. For all previously existing labels we the proof remains the same.

- Case: $a \triangleleft \mathsf{consent}(x).P \xrightarrow{a \triangleleft \mathsf{consent}(r)} P\{^r/_x\}$ and $\Gamma; \Lambda; Z \vdash a \triangleleft \mathsf{consent}(x).P \triangleright \Delta$. By the premise of typing rule [TCons] we get that $\Gamma; \Lambda; \vdash P \triangleright \Delta'$ with $\Delta = \mathsf{consent} \uplus \Delta'$. From the Weakening lemma and the Substitution lemma we get that for some Λ' we have $\Gamma, r : \mathsf{G}[\mathsf{t}[\mathsf{g}]]; \Lambda' \vdash P\{^r/_x\} \triangleright \Delta'$. The result is then immediate from [33, Proposition 6.8].

- Case: $a \triangleright \mathsf{consent}(r).P \xrightarrow{a \triangleright \mathsf{consent}(r)@\mathsf{id}} P \,|\, \overline{r} \triangleright [\mathsf{id} \otimes *]$, and $\Gamma; \Lambda, \overline{r} \vdash a \triangleright \mathsf{consent}(r).P \triangleright \Delta$. By the premises of the [TCreate] typing rule we get that $\Gamma; \Lambda_1 \vdash P \triangleright \Delta'$ with $\Delta = \mathsf{t} : \{\mathsf{store}\} \uplus \Delta'$, and $\Gamma \vdash r : \mathsf{G}[\mathsf{t}[\mathsf{g}]] \triangleright \emptyset$. By the typing rules [NVal] and [TSt] we get that $\Gamma; r : \mathsf{G}[\mathsf{t}[\mathsf{g}]]; \langle id, \mathsf{t} \rangle \vdash \overline{r} \triangleright [id \otimes *] \triangleright \emptyset$. By the [TPar] typing rule, we have $\Gamma; \Lambda_1; r : \mathsf{G}[\mathsf{t}[\mathsf{g}]]; \langle id, \mathsf{t} \rangle \vdash P \,|\, \overline{r} \triangleright [id \otimes *] \triangleright \Delta'$. The result is then immediate from [33, Proposition 6.8].

- Case: $r \triangleleft \mathsf{withdraw}.P \xrightarrow{r \triangleleft \mathsf{withdraw}} P$, and $\Gamma; \Lambda \vdash r \triangleleft \mathsf{withdraw}.P \triangleright \mathsf{t} : \{\mathsf{consent}\} \uplus \Delta$. By the premise of typing rule [TWithdraw] we get that $\Gamma; \Lambda \vdash P \triangleright \Delta'$ with $\Delta = \mathsf{t} : \{\mathsf{consent}\} \uplus \Delta'$. The result is then immediate from [33, Proposition 6.8].

- Case: $\overline{r} \triangleright [\_ \otimes *] \xrightarrow{\overline{r}!\langle \_ \otimes * \rangle} \overline{r} \triangleright [\_ \otimes *]$. The case is trivial.

- Case: $\overline{r} \triangleright [\_ \otimes *] \xrightarrow{\overline{r}?(\mathsf{id} \otimes c)} \overline{r} \triangleright [\_ \otimes *]$. The case is trivial.

- Case: $\mathsf{G}[\{P\}_{\mathsf{id}}] \xrightarrow{\ell} \mathsf{G}[\{P'\}_{\mathsf{id}}]$ and $\Gamma; \Lambda, \mathsf{id} \vdash \mathsf{G}[\{P\}_{\mathsf{id}}] \triangleright \Theta$. By the premise of the LTS rule [SId] and the typing rule [TId] we get: $P \xrightarrow{\ell} P'$ if $\ell \neq a \triangleleft \mathsf{consent}(r), r \triangleleft \mathsf{withdraw}$ and $\Gamma; \Lambda \vdash P \triangleright \Delta$. We know from the previous cases that $P \xrightarrow{\ell} P'$ preserves the types, thus we know that $\Gamma; \Lambda \vdash P' \triangleright \Delta'$ and $\Delta' \preceq \Delta$. We apply the typing rule [TId] to the latter and we get: $\Gamma; \Lambda, \mathsf{id} \vdash \mathsf{G}[\{P'\}_{\mathsf{id}}] \triangleright \Theta'$ and $\Theta' \preceq \Theta$.

- Case: $\bar{r} \triangleright [\mathsf{id} \otimes c] \xrightarrow{\bar{r} \triangleright \mathsf{withdraw}@\mathsf{id}} \bar{r} \triangleright [- \otimes *]$. The case is trivial because value $- \otimes *$ has no effect on permissions.

$\square$

We provide the notion of policy satisfaction for interfaces, Θ, and a Privacy Policy, $\mathcal{P}$. Intuitively, Θ satisfies $\mathcal{P}$ if Θ is a structural subset and a permission subset of $\mathcal{P}$.

Definition 1. *We define the satisfaction relation, denoted* $\Vdash$, *as:*

- *Consider a policy hierarchy* H *and an interface hierarchy* θ. *We say that* θ *satisfies* H, *written* $H \Vdash \theta$, *whenever:*

$$\frac{\exists k \in J : H_k = G' : \tilde{\mathsf{prm}}'[H_i]_{i \in I} \qquad G' : \mathsf{prm}' \uplus \tilde{\mathsf{prm}}[H_i]_{i \in I} \Vdash \theta}{G : \tilde{\mathsf{prm}}[H_j]_{j \in J} \Vdash G[\theta]} \qquad \frac{\tilde{\mathsf{prm}}_2 \preceq \tilde{\mathsf{prm}}_1}{G : \tilde{\mathsf{prm}}_1[] \Vdash G[\tilde{\mathsf{prm}}_2]}$$

- *Consider a policy* $\mathcal{P}$ *and an interface* Θ. Θ *satisfies* $\mathcal{P}$, *written* $\mathcal{P} \Vdash \Theta$, *whenever:*

$$\frac{H \Vdash \theta}{t \gg H; \mathcal{P} \Vdash t : \theta} \qquad \frac{H \Vdash \theta \qquad \mathcal{P} \Vdash \Theta}{t \gg H; \mathcal{P} \Vdash t : \theta; \Theta}$$

Definition 2 (Policy Satisfaction). *Consider* $\mathcal{P}$, *a type environment* Γ, *and system* S. *We say that* S *satisfies* $\mathcal{P}$, *written* $\mathcal{P}; \Gamma \vdash S$, *whenever there exist* Λ *and* Θ *such that* $\Gamma; \Lambda \vdash S \triangleright \Theta$ *and* $\mathcal{P} \Vdash \Theta$.

The main idea is to check whether a system satisfies a given a privacy policy under an environment that maps channels, constants, and private data to channel types, constant types, and private data types, respectively.

The Type Safety Theorem ensures that a System will not mishandle data with regards to a Privacy Policy given that our system satisfies that Privacy Policy according to Definition 2. To state the Type Safety Theorem we define the notion of the Error System displaying the cases where a system does not follow a given Privacy Policy.

Definition 3 (Error System). Assume $\tilde{G} = G_1, \ldots, G_n$, and consider a policy $\mathcal{P}$, an environment Γ, and a system:

$$\mathsf{System} \equiv G_1[(\nu \; \tilde{x}_1)(G_2[(\nu \; \tilde{x}_2)(\ldots (G_n[(\nu \; \tilde{x}_n)(P \mid Q)] \parallel S_n) \ldots)])] \parallel S_1$$

System System is an *error system* with respect to $\mathcal{P}$ and Γ, if there exists t such that $\mathcal{P} = t \gg H; \mathcal{P}'$ and at least one of the following holds:

1. $\mathsf{consent} \notin \mathsf{perm}(H_{\tilde{G}})$ and $\exists u$ such that $\Gamma \vdash u : G'[G[t[g]]] \triangleright \emptyset$ and $P \equiv u \triangleleft \mathsf{consent}(x).P'$ or $P \equiv u \triangleleft \mathsf{withdraw}.P'$.
2. $\mathsf{read} \notin \mathsf{perm}(H_{\tilde{G}})$ and $\exists u$ such that $\Gamma \vdash u : G[t[g]] \triangleright \Delta$ and $P \equiv u?(k).P'$.
3. $\mathsf{update} \notin \mathsf{perm}(H_{\tilde{G}})$ and $\exists u$ such that $\Gamma \vdash u : G[t[g]] \triangleright \Delta$ and $P \equiv u!\langle v \rangle.P'$.
4. $\mathsf{reference} \notin \mathsf{perm}(H_{\tilde{G}})$ and $\exists k$ such that $\Gamma \vdash k : G[t[g]] \triangleright \emptyset$ and $P \equiv u?(k).P'$.

5. disseminate $G' \notin \text{perm}(H_{\tilde{G}})$ and $\exists u$ such that $\Gamma \vdash u : G[t[g]] \rhd \emptyset$ and $P \equiv u'!\langle u \rangle.P'$.

6. readId $\notin \text{perm}(H_{\tilde{G}})$ and $\exists u$ such that $\Gamma \vdash u : G[t[g]] \rhd \Delta$ and $P \equiv u?(x \otimes y).P'$.

7. store $\notin \text{perm}(H_{\tilde{G}})$ and $\exists u$ such that $\Gamma \vdash u : G'[G[t[g]]] \rhd \emptyset$ and $P \equiv u \rhd$ consent$(r).P'$ or $P \equiv \bar{r} \rhd [\text{id} \otimes c]$.

8. usage$\{p\} \notin \text{perm}(H_{\tilde{G}})$ and $\exists c, c'$ such that $\Gamma \vdash c : p[g] \rhd \emptyset, \Gamma \vdash \iota \otimes c' : t[g] \rhd \Delta$ and $P \equiv \text{if } c' \text{ then } c \text{ else } P_1 P_2$.

9. identify$\{t'\} \notin \text{perm}(H_{\tilde{G}})$ and $\exists c, c'$ such that $\Gamma \vdash \iota \otimes c : t'[g] \rhd \emptyset, \Gamma \vdash - \otimes c' : t[g] \rhd \Delta$ and $P \equiv \text{if } c' = c \text{ then } P_1 \text{ else } P_2$.

□

We can now state the Type Safety Theorem.

Theorem 2 (Type Safety). *If $\mathcal{P}; \Gamma \vdash S \rhd \Theta$ and $S \xrightarrow{\tilde{\ell}} S'$ then S' is not an error with respect to policy $\mathcal{P}$.*

Proof. The proof is immediate by [33, Corollary 6.10] and [33, Lemma 6.13]. □

Neither system entities, $S1$ nor $S2$ are able to execute a computational step, as they are waiting for an input to be sent through channels c and r respectively, in order to be able to receive it. Thus, the user process, U, is the only one that can execute its functionality. It can proceed with restricting channel a in its scope and input it into the public channel c. At this point, it is the user process that will not be able to proceed, as the action of providing consent requires its dual action to be executed in order to interact with each other. $S2$ is still unable to proceed with reading from channel r as nothing was sent to that channel, so it is the turn of $S1$ to execute a computational step, i.e. input from channel c and substitute variable y with the received value, i.e. channel a. As a result, from this point on when $S1$ definition is using the variable y, the channel a will be referred. We can now observe that the dual action that U needed, is now able to be executed in $S1$, thus allowing their interaction that will result into the creation of a new store for U, associated with the user's identifier and simultaneously U will obtain a reference to the specific store, that will be held and referred from now on into variable x. $S1$ will then terminate any functionality, except from holding and managing the store. The only action that is able to be executed at this point, is the input-output interaction through the store reference, meaning U outputting into the store reference her personal data structure and the store in $S1$ receiving them and storing them.

We have now reached a crucial point of our system's execution. Both processes $S2$ and U are able to proceed with executing their actions: reading personal data from the store or withdrawing consent respectively. The model shall only permit the execution with the above mentioned order and not vice versa. If this is indeed the case, then $S2$ will proceed with inputting from the store reference, interacting with the store in $S1$ resulting in receiving the data and holding them into variable placeholder $x \otimes y$. Finally, U will proceed with withdrawing its consent on the store reference and terminate its execution. $S2$ can then send the notification to the received phone number.

The importance is on examining the case where U executes the consent withdrawing action, resulting in emptying the store, and after that $S2$ attempts to receive the data as it already holds the correct store reference. In such a case, the calculus semantics rule will allow the interaction with the store, sending as an output to $S2$ the empty data set and thus, no private data of the user.

6   Case Study: An Electricity IoT Service

In order to demonstrate our framework and methodology, we present a software system case study. Consider an *electricity IoT service* receiving, holding, and processing a set of electric consumption data about households. The data include the type of electric devices used, the exact date-time each device was used, and its consumption in power units. The data are gathered from several smart meters installed in several points of the house. All data are considered personal and are linked to the user's id, thus identifying the owner as the data subject. The service implements two different processing purposes: (i) to collect and store the electricity data of the user and to calculate the total fee that the user has to pay; and (ii) to keep a record of the user's fees for each billing period. The specification of the electricity IoT service is as follows:

Collecting Electricity Data

1. A user can register to this service by providing her consent.
2. Upon registration, the system creates a record to log the user's electricity data.
3. Each time an electrical device is used, the connected smart meter device updates the electricity data log with new consumption data.
4. The user is able to access and view the record kept for her.
5. At the end of each billing period, the electricity fee is calculated by the billing department, based on the records collected. The fees is then sent to the user.
6. The user can withdraw her consent at any time, and have her electricity data record erased from the system.

Keeping Fee Records

1. A user can register to this service by providing her consent.
2. Upon registration, the system creates an empty record for the user's fee log.
3. The billing department stores the calculated fee in the user's fee log.
4. The user can view her fees log.
5. The statistics department can read and compare the electricity data with a consumption threshold and extracts several statistical data based on the result.
6. The statistical data are sent to the user, and the user's fee is added to a graph, anonymously.
7. The user can withdraw her consent and have her fee data erased from the system. The anonymous data in the statistical graphs can be kept in the system.

The IoT Service System is identified as entity System, composed by the following subsystems/groups: the Database, DBase, the Smart Meter entities, SMeter, the Billing department, BillDept, and the statistics department, StatDept. We also identify a user entity of group Owner, that the user uses to interact with the System. To implement a system hierarchy, assume the existence of groups Owner, $DBase_1$, $DBase_2$, SMeter, BillDept, StatDept, System and IoT. For the purpose of simplifying the example, we will present the case of having a single smart meter sending information.

Privacy Policy. The Privacy requirements of the Electricity IoT Service are as follows:

1. Only the User, i.e., the data subject, can provide and withdraw consent regarding her electricity data being stored and processed by the system, This is based on the GDPR principle of *"Lawfulness of Processing"* and the *"Right to erasure"*.
2. The user should be able to access and read her stored electricity data, conforming to GDPR *"Right of access"*.
3. The user should not be able to update her electricity data, as they are mapping to the actual consumption. If the user has an objection and requires rectification of the data then a distinct rectification mechanism should be triggered. The above are in compliance with GDPR *"Right to Rectification"* and principle of *"Accuracy"*.
4. The databases are the only entities that should be able to store the electricity and fee data. Additionally, the Database entities are able to distribute access to them to specific subsystems: to the billing department and to the smart meter regarding electricity data.
5. The smart meters should be able to update the electricity data.
6. The Billing department should be able to access the electricity data, read them, and use them to calculate the fee. Furthermore, it should be able to access and read the fee data as well as update them with new calculated fees.
7. Finally, the Statistics department should be able to access and read the electricity fee data, and to compare them with a consumption threshold.

Privacy requirements (4)–(8) comprise the processing purpose of the system, defined in GDPR Principle of *"Purpose Limitation"*. The permission assignment for the electricity consumption data, in relation to each process group, is presented in the form of the entities electricity_data $\gg H_1$ and electricity_fee $\gg H_2$, as follows:

H_1 = electricity_data $\gg$ Network$\{\}[$
    Owner$\{$consent, reference, read$\}$,
    IoTService$\{\}[$
        DBase$_1\{$store, disseminate BillDept, disseminate SMeter$\}$,
        SMeter$\{$reference, update$\}$,
        BillDept$\{$reference, read, readId, usage$\{$feeSum$\}\}$,
        StatDept$\{\}$
    $]$
$]$

H_2 = electricity_fee $\gg$ Network$\{\}[$
    Owner$\{$consent, reference, read$\}$,
    IoTService$\{\}[$
        DBase$_2\{$store, disseminate StatDept, disseminate BillDept$\}$,
        SMeter$\{\}$,
        BillDept$\{$reference, read, readId, update$\}$,
        StatDept$\{$reference, read, usage$\{$threshold$\}$, usage$\{$stat_data$\}\}$
    $]$
$]$

The group hierarchy of the Privacy Policy follows the group hierarchy of the IoT Service System. In regards to the electricity_data the Owner has the permission to provide and withdraw consent, to gain access to the electricity_data store reference, and to read at any given time her electricity data. The database entity, DBase$_1$, has the permission to define a store for electricity_data, and to disseminate the store reference towards the billing department, BillDept, and the smart meter, SMeter. The smart meter, SMeter, has the permission to gain access to an electricity_data store reference and to update the electricity_data. The billing department, BillDept, has the permission to gain access to a reference to the electricity_data store, and read its data. Additionally, it can access the private data identifier to identify the user that should receive the billing fee. Finally, the statistics department, StatDept, has no permissions regarding the electricity_data.

In regards to the electricity_fee data, the owner has the same permissions as with the electricity_data. The database, DBase$_2$ has the permissions to create an electricity_fee data store and the permission to disseminate the electricity_fee store reference towards the billing department, BillDept, and the StatDept. The smart meter entity, has no permissions regarding the electricity_fee data. The billing department has the same permissions as with the electricity_data, and additionally the permission to update the value in the store with the calculated fee. Finally, the statistics department, StatDept, has the permissions to read and compare the electricity_fee value anonymously, against a constant threshold.

Modelling the System. The Electricity IoT Service is modelled as follows:

$$U \stackrel{\text{def}}{=} (\nu\ a)(\nu\ b)(\texttt{Owner}[\{cudb_1!\langle a\rangle.a \lhd \text{consent}(x_1).cudb_2!\langle b\rangle.b \lhd \text{consent}(x_2).$$
$$x_1?(y_1 \otimes z_1).x_2?(y_2 \otimes z_2).e?(w_1).j?(w_2).x_1 \lhd \text{withdraw}.x_2 \lhd \text{withdraw}.0\}_{\text{id}}])$$

$$DB_1 \stackrel{\text{def}}{=} \texttt{DBase}_1[cudb_1?(y).(\nu\ r_1)(y \rhd \text{consent}(r_1).d!\langle r_1\rangle.f!\langle r_1\rangle.0)]$$

$$DB_2 \stackrel{\text{def}}{=} \texttt{DBase}_2[cudb_2?(y).(\nu\ r_2)(y \rhd \text{consent}(r_2).g!\langle r_2\rangle.k!\langle r_2\rangle.0)]$$

$$SM \stackrel{\text{def}}{=} \texttt{SMeter}[d?(x). * (x!\langle \text{id} \otimes \text{electricity\_data}\rangle.0)]$$

$$BD \stackrel{\text{def}}{=} \texttt{BillDept}[f?(z_1).z_1?(x \otimes y).e!\langle feeSum(y)\rangle.k?(z_2).z_2!\langle \text{id} \otimes feeSum(y)\rangle.0]$$

$$SD \stackrel{\text{def}}{=} \texttt{StatDept}[g?(z).z?(x \otimes y).$$
$$\text{if } y \geq \text{threshold } \textbf{then } (j!\langle stat\_data(y)\rangle.graph!\langle\_ \otimes y\rangle.0) \textbf{ else}$$
$$(j!\langle stat\_data_2(y)\rangle.graph!\langle\_ \otimes y\rangle.0)]$$

$$Sys \stackrel{\text{def}}{=} \texttt{Network}[\{U\}_{\text{id}} \parallel \texttt{System}[DB_1 \parallel DB_2 \parallel SM \parallel BD \parallel Ad \parallel SD]]$$

The $\texttt{Owner}$ creates two new channels, a and b, and sends them to $\texttt{DBase}_1$ and $\texttt{DBase}_2$, respectively. Through a and b the $\texttt{Owner}$ provides her consent for the creation of two private data stores. The user uses the store reference to read her data. The user then receives the fee sent by the billing department, via channel e, and the statistical data sent by the statistics department, via channel j. She then proceeds with withdrawing both consents.

There are two database entities in the system: DB_1 is responsible for storing and providing access to the electricity_data and DB_2 for the electricity_fee. They both establish a private communication channel with the $\texttt{Owner}$. Upon receiving a consent from the $\texttt{Owner}$, they create two distinct stores for each type of personal data. Both store references are disseminates towards the smart meters via channel d, the billing department via channels f and k, and the statistics department via channel g.

The smart meter entity, $\texttt{SMeter}$, upon receiving the electricity_data store reference, updates its contents whenever a device usage occurs.

The Billing Department process, $\texttt{BillDept}$, receives the electricity_data store reference, reads the store data, and sends to the user the calculation $feeSum(y)$. It then receives the electricity_fee store reference, and then updates the store with the $feeSum(y)$ calculation. Function $feeSum(y)$ calculates the fee out of the electricity_data.

The Statistics department, $\texttt{StatDept}$, receives the electricity_fee store reference, reads from the stored data, and compares them with a threshold value. If the calculated fee is greater or equal to the threshold, then it sends a set of statistical data to the user, and adds the anonymous electricity_fee data to a graph prepared for statistical purposes. In the case that the condition is not true, it sends a different set of statistical data to the user and adds the anonymous electricity_fee data to a graph. Functions $stat\_data_1(y)$ and $stat\_data_2(y)$ calculate some statistical data taking as input the electricity_fee data.

Functionality, such as reading and writing data directly to the database store, or calculating the sum of the fee through an abstract function, can be considered as black boxes in the system's model. Such functionality is supposed to be fully implemented during the system development.

Systems DB_1, DB_2, SM, BD, and SD are composed under the System group to form the IoT service. Both the Owner and the System are composed under the IoT group to form the entire service.

By applying the rules of our type system we may show that $\Gamma; \emptyset \vdash$ System$\triangleright\Theta$, where:

$$\Theta = \text{electricity\_data} : \text{IoT}[\text{Owner}[\{\text{consent}, \text{reference}, \text{read}\}]]$$

$$\text{electricity\_data} : \text{IoT}[\text{System}[\text{DBase}_1[\text{store}, \text{disseminate BillDept}, \text{disseminate SMeter}]]]$$

$$\text{electricity\_data} : \text{IoT}[\text{System}[\text{SMeter}[\text{reference}, \text{update}]]]$$

$$\text{electricity\_data} : \text{IoT}[\text{System}[\text{BillDept}[\text{read}, \text{readId}, \text{usage}\{\text{feeSum}\}]]]$$

$$\text{electricity\_fee} : \text{IoT}[\text{Owner}[\{\text{consent}, \text{reference}, \text{read}\}]]$$

$$\text{electricity\_fee} : \text{IoT}[\text{System}[\text{DBase}_2[\text{store}, \text{disseminate BillDept}, \text{disseminate StatDept}]]]$$

$$\text{electricity\_fee} : \text{IoT}[\text{System}[\text{BillDept}[\text{reference}, \text{read}, \text{readId}, \text{update}, \text{usage}\{\text{feeSum}\}]]]$$

$$\text{electricity\_fee} : \text{IoT}[\text{System}[\text{StatDept}[\text{reference}, \text{read}, \text{usage}\{\text{threshold}, \text{stat\_data}\}]]]$$

We can check that Θ is compatible with the enunciated policy; therefore, the policy is satisfied by the system.

7   Conclusions and Future Work

In this paper, we have extended our previous framework of [46] based on the Privacy calculus of [33] enhanced with features to support the granting and withdrawal of consent by users, with privacy policies and permissions assignments as in [33]. Moreover, a type system was presented for the type checking of system models, to ensure satisfaction of requirements pertaining to the purpose of usage, i.e., indicated by the privacy policy, on top of validating the compliance of the system models to the under discussion GDPR provisions regarding consent, as in the previous work [46].

7.1   Potential Applications

Our vision is that a π-calculus-based framework can be developed and used by software engineers to model systems during the design phase, as well as in order to analyze and validate privacy-related properties, such as the GDPR-based provisions of *Lawfulness of Processing*, and the *Right to Erasure and Consent Withdrawal*. Analyzing and validating a system's specifications design model is a required step of software system creation. The modeling scheme introduced will provide information on conformance or may reveal any infringements found. We point out, however, that this process cannot guarantee that the software engineers will implement the system to precisely conform to its specifications design, unless MDE techniques relying on the Privacy calculus are employed. Potential MDE-based applications of our approach include:

- The transformation of the formal model in the extended Privacy calculus to source code and relevant configuration of the system, in conformance with GDPR. This process needs to be tailored to the needs of specific kinds of systems, e.g., mobile applications, and will provide the skeleton of the system code, whereas additional provisions will need to be added manually by the developers of the system.
- The same model can be utilized to drive the testing process of the software system for its privacy aspects, following the notion of test-driven development, where the tests are created before the actual system implementation [6].
- The documentation of the software system can be automatically generated using the formal model, targeting different user groups, such as the end user and the maintenance engineers.

7.2 Future Work

As future work, we intend to embed more GDPR provisions in our framework and treat the GDPR notion of purpose in a more specific and detailed manner. We will also work towards offering tools for easily expressing a system's specifications model in π-calculus-based formalism. Furthermore, tools for static checking actual code implementations by exploiting the ability of type-checking techniques at the coding level can be developed to assist GDPR compliance. Relevant work that does not capture privacy requirements but was developed in the context of the π-calculus and applies automated static analysis techniques to software code can be found in [36, 47].

Additionally, tools for formally translating verified models to verified developed systems can be created, thus assisting the transition from the design phase to the development phase towards the generation of GDPR compliant code. Thus, as future work we envision the development of the framework into programming semantics and analysis tools for supporting the software engineering development phase and the construction of privacy-respecting code following the Privacy by Design principle.

References

1. Abadi, M., Gordon, A.D.: A calculus for cryptographic protocols: the Spi calculus. Inf. Comput. **148**(1), 1–70 (1999)
2. Ahmadian, A.S., Strüber, D., Riediger, V., Jürjens, J.: Supporting privacy impact assessment by model-based privacy analysis. In: ACM Symposium on Applied Computing, pp. 1142–1149 (2018)
3. Backes, M., Hritcu, C., Maffei, M.: Type-checking zero-knowledge. In: Proceedings of the 2008 ACM Conference on Computer and Communications Security, CCS 2008, pp. 357–370 (2008)
4. Basin, D., Debois, S., Hildebrandt, T.: On purpose and by necessity: compliance under the GDPR. In: Proceedings of FC 2018 (2018)

5. Basso, T., Montecchi, L., Moraes, R., Jino, M., Bondavalli, A.: Towards a UML profile for privacy-aware applications. In: Proceedings of the IEEE International Conference on Computer and Information Technology; Ubiquitous Computing and Communications; Dependable, Autonomic and Secure Computing; Pervasive Intelligence and Computing (CIT/IUCC/DASC/PICOM 2015), pp. 371–378. IEEE (2015)

6. Beck, K.: Test-Driven Development: By Example. Addison-Wesley Professional, Boston (2003)

7. Bengtson, J., Bhargavan, K., Fournet, C., Gordon, A.D., Maffeis, S.: Refinement types for secure implementations. ACM Trans. Program. Lang. Syst. **33**(2), 8 (2011)

8. Boussetoua, R., Bennoui, H., Chaoui, A., Khalfaoui, K., Kerkouche, E.: An automatic approach to transform BPMN models to Pi-calculus. In: Proceedings of the International Conference of Computer Systems and Applications (AICCSA 2015), pp. 1–8. IEEE (2015)

9. Braghin, C., Gorla, D., Sassone, V.: Role-based access control for a distributed calculus. J. Comput. Secur. **14**(2), 113–155 (2006)

10. Bugliesi, M., Colazzo, D., Crafa, S., Macedonio, D.: A type system for discretionary access control. Math. Struct. Comput. Sci. **19**(4), 839–875 (2009)

11. Cardelli, L., Ghelli, G., Gordon, A.D.: Secrecy and group creation. In: Palamidessi, C. (ed.) CONCUR 2000. LNCS, vol. 1877, pp. 365–379. Springer, Heidelberg (2000). https://doi.org/10.1007/3-540-44618-4_27

12. Clarke, E.M., Grumberg, O., Peled, D.A.: Model Checking. MIT Press, Cambridge (2001)

13. Compagnoni, A.B., Gunter, E.L., Bidinger, P.: Role-based access control for boxed ambients. Theoret. Comput. Sci. **398**(1–3), 203–216 (2008)

14. De Masellis, R., Ghidini, C., Ranise, S.: A declarative framework for specifying and enforcing purpose-aware policies. In: Foresti, S. (ed.) STM 2015. LNCS, vol. 9331, pp. 55–71. Springer, Cham (2015). https://doi.org/10.1007/978-3-319-24858-5_4

15. Dezani-Ciancaglini, M., Ghilezan, S., Jakšić, S., Pantović, J.: Types for role-based access control of dynamic web data. In: Mariño, J. (ed.) WFLP 2010. LNCS, vol. 6559, pp. 1–29. Springer, Heidelberg (2011). https://doi.org/10.1007/978-3-642-20775-4_1

16. European Parliament and Council of the European Union: General data protection regulation. Official Journal of the European Union (2015)

17. Ferrara, P., Spoto, F.: Static analysis for GDPR compliance. In: ITASEC (2018)

18. Fournet, C., Gordon, A., Maffeis, S.: A type discipline for authorization in distributed systems. In: 20th IEEE Computer Security Foundations Symposium, CSF 2007, 6–8 July 2007, Venice, Italy, pp. 31–48 (2007)

19. Fowler, M.: UML Distilled: A Brief Guide to the Standard Object Modeling Language. Addison-Wesley Professional, Boston (2004)

20. Gjermundrød, H., Dionysiou, I., Costa, K.: privacyTracker: a privacy-by-design GDPR-compliant framework with verifiable data traceability controls. In: Casteleyn, S., Dolog, P., Pautasso, C. (eds.) ICWE 2016. LNCS, vol. 9881, pp. 3–15. Springer, Cham (2016). https://doi.org/10.1007/978-3-319-46963-8_1

21. Havey, M.: Essential Business Process Modeling. O'Reilly Media Inc., Sebastopol (2005)

22. Hennessy, M.: A Distributed Pi-Calculus. Cambridge University Press, Cambridge (2007)

23. Hennessy, M., Rathke, J., Yoshida, N.: safeDpi: a language for controlling mobile code. Acta Inform. **42**(4–5), 227–290 (2005)
24. Hennessy, M., Riely, J.: Resource access control in systems of mobile agents. Inf. Comput. **173**(1), 82–120 (2002)
25. Hintze, M., LaFever, G.: Meeting upcoming GDPR requirements while maximizing the full value of data analytics (2017)
26. Huth, D.: A pattern catalog for GDPR compliant data protection (2017)
27. Jafari, M., Fong, P.W., Safavi-Naini, R., Barker, K., Sheppard, N.P.: Towards defining semantic foundations for purpose-based privacy policies. In: Proceedings of CODASPY 2011, pp. 213–224. ACM (2011)
28. Jürjens, J.: UMLsec: extending UML for secure systems development. In: Jézéquel, J.-M., Hussmann, H., Cook, S. (eds.) UML 2002. LNCS, vol. 2460, pp. 412–425. Springer, Heidelberg (2002). https://doi.org/10.1007/3-540-45800-X_32
29. Kalloniatis, C., Kavakli, E., Gritzalis, S.: Addressing privacy requirements in system design: the PriS method. Requir. Eng. **13**(3), 241–255 (2008)
30. Kapitsaki, G., Ioannou, J., Cardoso, J., Pedrinaci, C.: Linked USDL privacy: describing privacy policies for services. In: 2018 IEEE International Conference on Web Services (ICWS), pp. 50–57. IEEE (2018)
31. Kapitsaki, G.M., Kateros, D.A., Pappas, C.A., Tselikas, N.D., Venieris, I.S.: Model-driven development of composite web applications. In: Proceedings of the 10th International Conference on Information Integration and Web-Based Applications and Services, pp. 399–402. ACM (2008)
32. Kapitsaki, G.M., Venieris, I.S.: PCP: privacy-aware context profile towards context-aware application development. In: Proceedings of the 10th International Conference on Information Integration and Web-Based Applications and Services, pp. 104–110. ACM (2008)
33. Kouzapas, D., Philippou, A.: Privacy by typing in the π-calculus. Log. Methods Comput. Sci. **13**(4) (2017)
34. Lam, V.S.: On π-calculus semantics as a formal basis for UML activity diagrams. Proc. Int. J. Softw. Eng. Knowl. Eng. **18**(04), 541–567 (2008)
35. Milner, R., Parrow, J., Walker, D.: A calculus of mobile processes, Parts I and II. Inf. Comput. **100**(1), 1–77 (1992)
36. Ng, N., de Figueiredo Coutinho, J.G., Yoshida, N.: Protocols by default - safe MPI code generation based on session types. In: Franke, B. (ed.) CC 2015. LNCS, vol. 9031, pp. 212–232. Springer, Heidelberg (2015). https://doi.org/10.1007/978-3-662-46663-6_11
37. Perera, C., McCormick, C., Bandara, A.K., Price, B.A., Nuseibeh, B.: Privacy-by-design framework for assessing internet of things applications and platforms. In: Proceedings of the 6th International Conference on the Internet of Things, pp. 83–92. ACM (2016)
38. Politou, E., Alepis, E., Patsakis, C.: Forgetting personal data and revoking consent under the GDPR: challenges and proposed solutions. J. Cybersecur. **4**(1), tyy001 (2018)
39. Riahi, S., Khosravi, R., Ghassemi, F.: Purpose-based policy enforcement in actor-based systems. In: Dastani, M., Sirjani, M. (eds.) FSEN 2017. LNCS, vol. 10522, pp. 196–211. Springer, Cham (2017). https://doi.org/10.1007/978-3-319-68972-2_13
40. Robol, M., Salnitri, M., Giorgini, P.: Toward GDPR-compliant socio-technical systems: modeling language and reasoning framework. In: Poels, G., Gailly, F., Serral Asensio, E., Snoeck, M. (eds.) PoEM 2017. LNBIP, vol. 305, pp. 236–250. Springer, Cham (2017). https://doi.org/10.1007/978-3-319-70241-4_16

41. Rubinstein, I.S.: Regulating privacy by design. Berkeley Technol. Law J. **26**, 1409 (2011)
42. Schmidt, D.C.: Model-driven engineering. IEEE Comput. **39**(2), 25 (2006)
43. Thatte, S.: XLANG: web services for business process design. Microsoft Corporation (2001)
44. Tschantz, M.C., Datta, A., Wing, J.M.: On the semantics of purpose requirements in privacy policies (2011). arXiv preprint arXiv:1102.4326
45. Tschantz, M.C., Datta, A., Wing, J.M.: Formalizing and enforcing purpose restrictions in privacy policies. In: Proceedings of SP 2012, pp. 176–190. IEEE Computer Society (2012)
46. Vanezi, E., Kapitsaki, G.M., Kouzapas, D., Philippou, A.: A formal modeling scheme for analyzing a software system design against the GDPR. In: Proceedings of the 14th International Conference on Evaluation of Novel Approaches to Software Engineering, ENASE 2019, pp. 68–79 (2019)
47. Yoshida, N., Hu, R., Neykova, R., Ng, N.: The Scribble protocol language. In: Abadi, M., Lluch Lafuente, A. (eds.) TGC 2013. LNCS, vol. 8358, pp. 22–41. Springer, Cham (2014). https://doi.org/10.1007/978-3-319-05119-2_3

Evaluation of Software Product Quality Metrics

Arthur-Jozsef Molnar[(✉)], Alexandra Neamţu, and Simona Motogna

Faculty of Mathematics and Computer Science, Babeş-Bolyai University,
Cluj-Napoca, Romania
{arthur,motogna}@cs.ubbcluj.ro
nais1841@scs.ubbcluj.ro

Abstract. Computing devices and associated software govern every-day life, and form the backbone of safety critical systems in banking, healthcare, automotive and other fields. Increasing system complexity, quickly evolving technologies and paradigm shifts have kept software quality research at the forefront. Standards such as ISO's 25010 express it in terms of sub-characteristics such as maintainability, reliability and security. A significant body of literature attempts to link these subcharacteristics with software metric values, with the end goal of creating a metric-based model of software product quality. However, research also identifies the most important existing barriers. Among them we mention the diversity of software application types, development platforms and languages. Additionally, unified definitions to make software metrics truly language-agnostic do not exist, and would be difficult to implement given programming language levels of variety. This is compounded by the fact that many existing studies do not detail their methodology and tooling, which precludes researchers from creating surveys to enable data analysis on a larger scale. In our paper, we propose a comprehensive study of metric values in the context of three complex, open-source applications. We align our methodology and tooling with that of existing research, and present it in detail in order to facilitate comparative evaluation. We study metric values during the entire 18-year development history of our target applications, in order to capture the longitudinal view that we found lacking in existing literature. We identify metric dependencies and check their consistency across applications and their versions. At each step, we carry out comparative evaluation with existing research and present our results.

Keywords: Software metric · Software quality · Descriptive statistics · Cross-sectional study · Longitudinal study

1 Introduction

Software development has experienced an exponential increase over the past decades, which can be observed in the variety of applications available (such as

© Springer Nature Switzerland AG 2020
E. Damiani et al. (Eds.): ENASE 2019, CCIS 1172, pp. 163–187, 2020.
https://doi.org/10.1007/978-3-030-40223-5_8

web, mobile, real time and so on), as well as in application size and complexity. Large-scale and enterprise applications are being developed over longer periods of time, using larger teams that are in many cases geographically distributed. In the same time frame, project management and software methodologies, available tools and development environments have evolved in an attempt to keep the pace with increasing requirements.

This increase in size and complexity raises another problem, namely the necessity to control the software development processes, and implicitly to measure it, as "you cannot control that which you cannot measure" [11]. In accordance, the domain of software metrics has evolved both as methodology as well as in terms of available software products, being influenced by the development of programming languages, paradigms and methodologies.

Software quality assurance is also an important aspect as software products have to satisfy user needs related to ease of use, security and reliability. Furthermore, development related needs such as maintainability, portability and testability must also be accounted for. The latest software quality models have undergone standardization processes, such as ISO standards 9126 and 25010, in order to establish a set of common criteria for software products. These standards can significantly benefit from data provided by software metrics, as there exists consistent research results that report the influence of software metrics on software quality factors [8, 17, 22, 25, 35].

However, additional data analysis is required before general models can be built [5]. Also, even if the influence of metrics on quality factors is well understood and accepted, there does not yet exist any general accepted method to evaluate software quality factors based on software metric values. As such, the relation between metric values and software quality factors remains an open problem. We aim to address this issue in the present paper. We carry out a comprehensive evaluation on values of software metrics that are widely associated with software product quality. We employ methodology and tooling compatible with existing results in order to enable comparative evaluation. We carry out a long-term study targeting three complex, open-source applications, and provide the following contributions:

(i) A clear description of our methodology, metric definitions and tooling used to extract metric values. Doing this ensures that our results can be used for comparative evaluation in future studies. We made all extracted metric values publicly available[1].

(ii) A quantitative evaluation of metric values is carried out and detailed for all target application versions.

(iii) A longitudinal exploratory study that examines the evolution of metric values over the course of 18 years of target application development.

(iv) Identification of statistical correlations between metric pairs. We identify both strongly correlated metrics as well as metrics that appear independent. We account for the confounding effect of class size and examine the stability of the correlation strength across application versions.

---

[1] http://www.cs.ubbcluj.ro/~se/enase2019/.

(v) A comparative evaluation of metric values and statistical correlations between target applications. We identify trends in metric values and correlations that are application-specific, together with those that hold across the target applications.

(vi) An evaluation of our obtained results in the context of existing research that uses the same methodology and software tools.

One of our study's key contributions lies in the selection of target applications. Existing studies are built around one of the following two approaches. The first one is where a number of applications are selected, and for each of them several versions are studied [17,32]. The second one considers a large number of target applications, that in many cases are automatically downloaded from open-source repositories [5], with a cross-sectional study including all of them [5,18,19]. Our approach aims to complement existing research. We select a number of three open-source applications developed on the same platform, having comparable complexity and scope, and include all their released versions in our study. This results in a large number of application versions that ensures statistical significance. More so, our approach includes both initial application versions, which are sometimes very simple functionality-wise and bug-prone. We also include the latest application versions, that appear polished, have extensive features sets and a consistent user base. This enables us to study how metric values evolve together with the target applications, as well as to identify any existing trends that might be influenced by application development status.

Another important contribution regards careful selection of software metrics and extraction tools. As detailed in our initial evaluation [26], we selected the evaluated metrics in order to cover complexity, inheritance, coupling and cohesion [2,22] as important characteristics of object-oriented software. In addition, the studied metrics can be found in existing literature studying software product quality [18,19,26,32]. Selection of the right tools for metric value extraction is also important, as most metrics have more than one definition [4,21]. As such, comparative evaluation can be carried out only with existing research that employs the same metrics, and that uses the same tooling to extract metric values.

In our initial evaluation [26], we employed the VizzAnalyzer tool[2], as it provides formal definitions of the extracted metrics. In addition, using VizzAnalyzer allows us to compare our results with those reported in [5], where authors use the same tool to carry out a cross-sectional study of 146 open-source applications. In our extensive literature survey, we identified [5] as the only paper that clearly detailed the study methodology and tooling in order to allow a comparative evaluation to be carried out. Since our present paper employs the same methodology and tooling as our initial evaluation [26], the obtained results are directly comparable. In addition, in the present paper we explore the effect class size has on metric correlations across our target applications. We show that metric variability is greatest in early versions, before application architecture is well

---

[2] http://www.arisa.se/vizz_analyzer.php.

established. Furthermore, we find that most significant changes to metric values occur across a small number of application versions, which we examine in detail.

2   Software Metrics

Evolution in the domain of software metrics was influenced by changes in the development of software, with increasingly specific metrics being proposed for the measurement of both software products as well as software processes. This is reflected in the appearance of software metric tools, both general and language dependent, stand-alone as well as integrated into IDEs in the form of plugins.

The oldest software metrics that remain widely used today include lines of code (LOC), number of functions or modules, and the number of comment lines. This was followed by proposed metrics to measure code complexity, such as cyclomatic complexity [23] and Halstead volume [14]. In turn, these were used to compute additional, more complex metrics such as the Maintainability Index [25]. The object oriented paradigm introduced new entities and relations, and these were reflected by several newly proposed metrics. The reference set of object-oriented metrics was defined by Chidamber & Kemerer (CK) [8], were implemented in most software metrics tools, and used in many subsequent studies. The lack of cohesion in methods (LCOM) metric deserves special mention, as it was refined from its original definition in [8] by Li and Henry [20], and then by Hitz and Montazeri [16]. While these changes were driven by a desire to better capture the essence of cohesion, LCOM values can only be compared when extracted using the same definition. Several tools are available to compute the CK metrics (and many more). Some of them are available as IDE plugins, such as Metrics2[3] for Eclipse, MetricsReloaded[4] for IntelliJ, NDepend[5] for .NET, or as standalone tools such as JHawk[6] or Sourcemeter[7]. Each of them employs its own implementation for metric computation, leading to different results for the same metric when extracted with different tools.

The metrics selected for our study were all computed using the VizzAnalyzer tool, that uses the definitions provided in [37]. Other studies [5,21] are based on the same tool, giving us the possibility to compare the obtained results. According to [22], object-oriented metrics measure one of the four internal characteristics essential to object orientation, namely coupling, inheritance, cohesion and structural complexity. We present the metrics used in our study, categorized according to the internal characteristics they aim to measure. We start with metrics dedicated to measuring **coupling**:

- *Coupling Between Objects* (**CBO**, $v_{CBO} \in [0, \infty) \cap \mathbb{Z}$) [28] - for class **c** is computed as the number of other classes that are coupled to it. Two classes

---

[3] http://metrics.sourceforge.net.
[4] https://plugins.jetbrains.com/plugin/93-metricsreloaded.
[5] https://www.ndepend.com/.
[6] http://www.virtualmachinery.com/jhawkprod.htm.
[7] https://www.sourcemeter.com/.

are coupled when methods declared in one class use methods or instance variables defined by the other class. CBO indicates the required effort to test and maintain a class.

- *Data Abstraction Coupling (**DAC**, $v_{DAC} \in [0, \infty) \cap \mathbb{Z}$)* [20] - measures when a class is used in the implementation of methods of another class or when it is the domain of its instance variables. VizzAnalyzer does not include platform classes in this measurement.
- *Message Pass Coupling (**MPC**, $v_{MPC} \in [0, \infty) \cap \mathbb{Z}$)* [28] - counts the number of methods from other classes that are called. It indicates the degree of dependency on the system's other classes.

The following metrics measure the **inheritance** characteristic:

- *Depth of Inheritance Tree (**DIT**, $v_{DIT} \in [0, \infty) \cap \mathbb{Z}$)* [28] - represents the length of the longest path from a given class to the root of the inheritance tree. DIT also accounts for multiple paths possible in the context of multiple-inheritance languages such as C++.
- *Number of Children (**NOC**, $v_{NOC} \in [0, \infty) \cap \mathbb{Z}$)* [28,31] - counts the immediate subclasses found in the inheritance tree for a given class.

System **cohesion** is measured using the following metrics:

- *Lack of Cohesion in Methods (**LCOM**, $v_{LCOM} \in [0, \infty) \cap \mathbb{Z}$)* [28] - represents the difference between the number of methods pairs that don't have, respectively have, instance variables in common. This uses the original definition of the metric [28].
- *Improvement to Lack of Cohesion in Methods (**ILCOM**, $v_{ILCOM} \in [1, \infty) \cap \mathbb{Z}$)* [16] - this employs the improved definition provided by Hitz and Montazeri. In several papers and software tools this is referred to as LCOM5.
- *Tight Class Cohesion (**TCC**, $v_{TCC} \in [0, 1] \cap \mathbb{Q}$)* [27] - defined as the ratio between the number of directly connected public methods in a class divided by the number of all possible connections between the public methods of that class.

We employ the following metrics that measure the **structural complexity** of classes:

- *Locality of Data (**LD**, $v_{LD} \in [0, 1] \cap \mathbb{Q}$)* [16] - represents the ratio between the data that is local to a class and all the data used by the class. VizzAnalyzer includes non-public and inherited attributes.
- *Number of Attributes and Methods (**NAM**, $v_{NAM} \in [0, \infty) \cap \mathbb{Z}$)* [28] - represents the total number of attributes and methods that are locally defined by the class. This includes static methods, but excludes constructors and inherited fields or methods.
- *Number of Methods (**NOM**, $v_{NOM} \in [0, \infty) \cap \mathbb{Z}$)* [28] - represents the number of methods locally defined in the class. $NAM - NOM$ gives the number of locally defined attributes.

- *Response For a Class (**RFC**, $v_{RFC} \in [0, \infty) \cap \mathbb{Z}$) [28]* - counts the number of methods that could be invoked as a response to a given message. RFC is the number of methods called by a given class.
- *Weighted Method Count (**WMC**, $v_{WMC} \in [0, \infty) \cap \mathbb{Z}$) [28]* - defined as the sum of the complexities of all methods of a given class. The complexity of a method is its McCabe cyclomatic complexity [23].

Finally, we also examine metrics related with code **documentation**:

- *Length of Class Name (**LEN**, $v_{LEN} \in [1, \infty) \cap \mathbb{Z}$)* - the length of the class name counted in characters.
- *Lack of Documentation (**LOD**, $v_{LOD} \in [0, 1] \cap \mathbb{Q}$)* - the ratio of missing comments in a given class. Each class should have one comment per class, and an additional one for each defined method. This metric ignores the structure and the content of the comments.

Beside these metrics, we also measured the Lines of Code (LOC), since it is considered a universal software metric that can be used across most programming languages and which gives basic information about the size of a project. The relation between object-oriented metrics and LOC is worthy of further investigation, especially as existing research showed that class size has a strong confounding influence on quality models based on metrics [12].

3   State of the Art

The increasing attention given to software metrics is proven by the large number of studies in this domain. In most cases, existing research is geared towards one of the following three main directions: definition and analysis of proposed software metrics, software metric application in refactoring, and studying the relation between software metrics and software quality models.

3.1   Metrics

New metrics are being defined in order to fine-tune the characteristics of software systems, and in order to better reflect the properties of source code and associated artefacts. Examples include approaches to improve estimation of the maintenance effort [30], in order to supersede existing measures such as the Maintainability Index [25] which was shown to be outdated [10,15,29]. Other studies propose new metrics to better capture system coupling or cohesion [1,9].

Special interest has been also given to studying inter-metric dependency and correlation. A large scale study [5] was carried out using 146 Java applications, with 16 metrics extracted using the VizzAnalyzer tool. Barkman et al. applied different descriptive statistic techniques in order to detect metric dependencies. Landman et al. [18] show that typical *getters* and *setters* can distort metric dependencies by artificially increasing dependency values. In [12], authors show that class size has a significant impact on metric correlation, using experimental data from a large scale telecommunication framework. These results illustrate that in order to validate strong conclusions derived from data analysis based on metric values, further research needs to be carried out. This is expected to be of special importance in the case of large-scale projects that were developed over a long period of time.

3.2 Refactoring

One of the first applications of software metrics was to use the recorded values in order to detect design flaws that could be solved through refactoring.

The impact of four refactoring methods on several metrics is described in [7], based on the source code's abstract syntax tree representation. Another significant study [34] refers to the impact 10 refactoring methods have on different metrics, including the Maintainability Index, cyclomatic complexity, DIT, class coupling and LOC. Changes to maintainability and modifiability after refactoring are presented in [34] through an empirical evaluation. The experimental evaluations included in the aforementioned studies illustrate that, in the case of complex systems, refactoring plays an important role for easing maintenance and keeping system complexity under control. The decision of where and how to refactor can be taken based on extracted values of suitable software metrics.

3.3 Software Quality Models

In recent years, several contributions attempted to connect software metrics with software quality factors. A software quality model is a hierarchical set of software quality factors or characteristics, that are further decomposed in subfactors or subcharacteristics. The first software quality model was introduced in 1976 by McCall, to which Boehm and Dromey later proposed important contributions. These initial contributions were later standardized by the ISO in the form of two families of standards: first, the ISO 9126, which expressed software quality as a function of six characteristics, that were comprised of 31 subcharacteristics. The 9126 standard was updated in the form of ISO 25010[8], which expands to the 8 characteristics shown in Fig. 1.

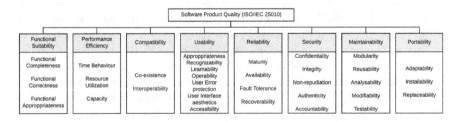

Fig. 1. ISO/IEC 25010 subcharacteristics hierarchy.

---

[8] https://iso25000.com/index.php/en/iso-25000-standards/iso-25010.

Some of the factors, like Maintainability, are known to be highly influenced by coupling and cohesion, such as evaluated by the CBO, TCC and LCOM metrics. However, in many other cases, dependencies remain to be proven.

The ARISA Compendium [2] offers an exhaustive study of the influence of over 20 metrics on the software quality characteristics of ISO 9126. The authors' approach is based on linking metrics with those source code entities that are involved in the metric's formal description. In [20], authors claim that metrics should be adapted for each programming paradigm. They introduce object oriented metrics for the maintenance effort and validate their approach on two commercial systems using 10 metrics. A complementary study was carried out in [6], where the CK metrics are assessed in regard to fault proneness, with experiments performed on eight C++ applications. The study concluded that LCOM, as defined in the CK suite is not evidential for fault detection, but that the other CK metrics are well suited for predicting faults. Also, the experimental data revealed an inverse relation between NOC and faults, a result confirmed also by the impact of reuse on fault proneness presented in [24].

Another study [33] regarding the relation between CK metrics and faults evaluated the efficient selection of testing techniques. Authors reported RFC and WMC as the most suited metrics for this task. A similar study was conducted in [13] for the open-source Mozilla web and e-mail suite. It concluded that CBO and LOC are good predictors for faults, while DIT and NOC can lead to false results. An analysis [35] of CK metrics on a NASA public data set revealed that LOC, WMC, CBO and RFC can be safely used for defect estimation. The conclusion of the study recommended further investigation on the relation between metric values and different dependent variables using statistical and AI techniques.

4   Evaluation

4.1   Target Applications

In order to carry out our evaluation, the first step was to select target applications. We first established several required criteria. First, we decided to target open-source applications developed in Java that were user interface driven and which did not have significant dependencies on external libraries or databases. We also searched for applications having long-term, consistent development history that were freely available. Our goals required a longitudinal study, an observational research method that consists in setting up and collecting metric data from each of the application versions. As detailed in [5], this can prove difficult in the case of open-source software, where development effort suffers interruptions, and where there are no guarantees that all software versions are complete and usable. As such, we selected three popular applications with long development histories, which had an established user base as well as public development repositories populated since project inception. We also ensured selected applications were free from complex dependencies. This allowed us to run them in order to check that functionalities worked as expected in all application versions.

The selected applications are the FreeMind[9] mind mapper, the jEdit[10] text editor and the TuxGuitar[11] tablature editor. The entire development history of these applications can be found on SourceForge[12].

FreeMind. Is a mind-mapping application that found many uses in productivity and content management. FreeMind was also employed in previous software research [3]. It is also a popular application with a solid user base, having over 465k[13] downloads in 2019. FreeMind includes a plugin ecosystem with many plugins available. However, only the source code of the base application was included in our study.

jEdit. Is an open-source text editor, developed entirely using the Java programming language. It is also a popular system under test for other research endeavours in software testing [3,36]. jEdit is one of the popular SourceForge applications, having over 59k downloads in 2019 and reaching over 8.9 millions downloads in its 19 years of existence. Similar to the case of FreeMind, plugin code was not included in our evaluation.

TuxGuitar. Is a free, open-source multitrack guitar tablature editor with an SWT-based user interface. It includes features like multiple format data import and export, tablature and score editing. TuxGuitar is also a popular application having over 131k downloads in 2019. In contrast with FreeMind and jEdit, where we disregarded the applications' plugin ecosystems, in the case of TuxGuitar functionalities related to data import and export itself were implemented in the form of a plugin, and were included in our evaluation.

Table 1 provides information about the earliest and latest application versions included in our evaluation, indicating their change of complexity during the considered period.

Table 1. First and last studied version of each target application (from [26]).

Application	Version	LOC	Classes
jEdit	2.3pre2	33,768	322
	5.5.0	151,672	952
FreeMind	0.0.3	3,722	53
	1.1.0Beta2	63,799	587
TuxGuitar	0.1pre	11,209	122
	1.5.2	108,495	1,618

---

[9] http://freemind.sourceforge.net/wiki/index.php/Main_Page.
[10] http://www.jedit.org/.
[11] http://www.tuxguitar.com.ar.
[12] https://sourceforge.net.
[13] Download data points taken on August 8th, 2019.

172   A.-J. Molnar et al.

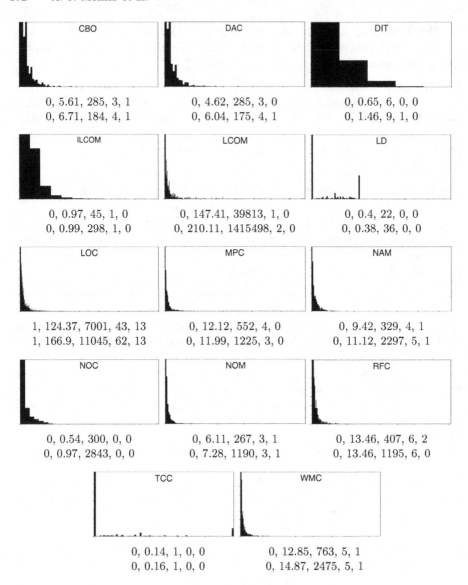

0, 5.61, 285, 3, 1
0, 6.71, 184, 4, 1

0, 4.62, 285, 3, 0
0, 6.04, 175, 4, 1

0, 0.65, 6, 0, 0
0, 1.46, 9, 1, 0

0, 0.97, 45, 1, 0
0, 0.99, 298, 1, 0

0, 147.41, 39813, 1, 0
0, 210.11, 1415498, 2, 0

0, 0.4, 22, 0, 0
0, 0.38, 36, 0, 0

1, 124.37, 7001, 43, 13
1, 166.9, 11045, 62, 13

0, 12.12, 552, 4, 0
0, 11.99, 1225, 3, 0

0, 9.42, 329, 4, 1
0, 11.12, 2297, 5, 1

0, 0.54, 300, 0, 0
0, 0.97, 2843, 0, 0

0, 6.11, 267, 3, 1
0, 7.28, 1190, 3, 1

0, 13.46, 407, 6, 2
0, 13.46, 1195, 6, 0

0, 0.14, 1, 0, 0
0, 0.16, 1, 0, 0

0, 12.85, 763, 5, 1
0, 14.87, 2475, 5, 1

Fig. 2. Code metric histograms. Data labels: minimum, mean, maximum, median, modus. Our results on top row, results from [5] on bottom row for comparison (data from [26]).

As a preparatory step, each studied version was imported into an IDE. We ensured that library source code was separated from actual application code in order to not affect our analysis. Since we employed Java 8, we encountered compilation errors with older versions of the applications that were developed using earlier versions of the Java platform. The issues were resolved taking into

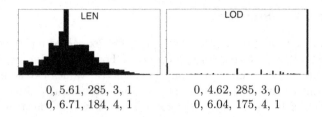

0, 5.61, 285, 3, 1   0, 4.62, 285, 3, 0
0, 6.71, 184, 4, 1   0, 6.04, 175, 4, 1

Fig. 3. Documentation metric histograms. Data labels: minimum, mean, maximum, median, modus. Our results on top row, results from [5] on bottom row for comparison.

account not to alter the results of metric extraction. We assured that for each application, all mandatory source code was included, testing all available functionalities in detail. The raw metric data that was extracted is available on our website[14]. Using this data, we developed a number of scripts in order to extract only the required metric values for our study for each application version as well as in aggregate form.

Data collection was helped by the fact that for each application, its complete development history was available on SourceForge. Furthermore, released versions were clearly marked, dated and had associated binaries and source code. In total, we included 38 versions of FreeMind, 43 for jEdit and 26 for TuxGuitar.

Table 2. Mean and median metric values per application.

	FreeMind	jEdit	TuxGuitar	[5]	FreeMind	jEdit	TuxGuitar	[5]
CBO	5.36	4.67	7.32	6.71	3.00	3.00	5.00	4.00
DAC	4.21	4.09	6.08	6.04	2.00	2.00	4.00	4.00
DIT	0.79	0.42	0.87	1.46	0.00	0.00	1.00	1.00
ILCOM	1.00	0.77	1.25	0.99	1.00	1.00	1.00	1.00
LCOM	197.62	124.83	130.81	210.11	2.00	1.00	2.00	2.00
LD	0.49	0.35	0.40	0.38	0.00	0.00	0.00	0.00
LEN	16.87	13.67	16.88	15.04	16.00	13.00	16.00	14.00
LOC	108.62	156.44	90.97	166.90	40.00	51.00	38.00	62.00
LOD	0.80	0.76	0.92	0.47	1.00	1.00	1.00	0.50
MPC	10.92	9.46	17.49	11.99	4.00	3.00	5.00	3.00
NAM	9.75	8.41	10.67	11.12	4.00	3.00	5.00	5.00
NOC	0.65	0.37	0.71	0.97	0.00	0.00	0.00	0.00
NOM	6.88	5.16	6.80	7.28	3.00	2.00	3.00	3.00
RFC	13.54	10.62	17.78	13.46	6.00	5.00	8.00	6.00
TCC	0.14	0.15	0.16	0.16	0.00	0.00	0.00	0.00
WMC	12.51	13.40	12.36	14.87	5.00	5.00	4.00	5.00
	Mean values ([26])				Median values			

---

[14] http://www.cs.ubbcluj.ro/~se/enase2019/.

4.2   Quantitative Statistics

In this section we provide an initial overview of the extracted metric values, and compare them with the results presented in [5]. For each of the target applications, we create its own data set, comprising metric values extracted from all studied versions of that application. This enables statistical comparison across applications in order to identify any existing trends. The data from all 107 application versions is coalesced into an aggregated data set. We compare the aggregated data against the results reported in [5], where authors carried out a cross-sectional study of 146 open-source Java applications.

Given the large number of data points recorded for our study[15], we detail those aspects that were found of most interest. We remind the interested reader that the entire metric data set is freely available on our website.

Histograms for code and documentation metric values in our aggregated data set are shown in Figs. 2 and 3. They also provide a faithful representation of the value distributions from the three target application data sets. This also holds when comparing our data with that presented in [5]. We find that histograms are similar even in the case of metrics having stand-out values, such as LD, LOD and TCC, where the value of 1 is frequent[16]. LEN appears to be the only metric with normal distribution.

Descriptive statistics for every metric in the aggregated data set, as well as corresponding ones from [5] are shown below the histograms in Figs. 2 and 3. We notice that in every case, the smallest recorded values are the minimal ones, which is 0 for all metrics with the exception of LOC, where it is 1. Maximal values are outliers and show much more variance, both across studied application versions and across the data sets. As such, our study will focus mostly around median and mean metric values, and detail extreme values only where it makes sense.

Examination of the mean, median and modus values proves to be of much more interest. Our first observation is that median and modus values are close across all the five data sets, for each of the 16 studied metrics. This is detailed in Table 2, where mean and median values for each application data set, as well as those recorded by Barkmann et al. [5] are shown. When examining these values, one must also consider the range for each metric, as detailed in Sect. 2. We observe that for CBO, NAM, NOM, TCC and WMC mean values are close across the data sets. Values for LEN and LOD show that while in most cases, the length of used identifiers is suitable, open-source applications appear to lack inline documentation. This is especially true in the case of our target applications, where more than 80% of methods remain undocumented. The data also illustrates the existance of application-specific trends. We observe that jEdit classes tend to be larger, as illustrated by higher LOC than FreeMind and TuxGuitar, being very close to the mean LOC reported in [5]. At the same time, jEdit shows a more flat inheritance hierarchy, illustrated by lower DIT and NOC values when compared

---

[15] 107 application versions x 16 studied metrics x 5 data points = 8,560 data points.
[16] In the case of TCC 1 is the maximal value.

Table 3. Metric dependencies in FreeMind (top row), jEdit (second row), TuxGuitar (third row) and as reported in [5] (bottom row). LEN and LOD metrics omitted as no strong dependencies were found. Data from [26].

Metric	CBO	DAC	DIT	ILCOM	LCOM	LD	LOC	MPC	NAM	NOC	NOM	RFC	TCC	WMC
DAC	**0.97**													
	0.98	1.00												
	0.96													
	0.98													
DIT	0.28	0.30												
	0.18	0.20	1.00											
	0.18	0.10												
	0.52	0.52												
ILCOM	0.46	0.49	0.08											
	0.44	0.46	−0.00	1.00										
	0.07	0.11	−0.29											
	0.53	0.41	0.39											
LCOM	0.53	0.56	0.05	0.55										
	0.55	0.56	−0.03	0.40	1.00									
	0.20	0.21	−0.12	0.37										
	0.53	0.55	0.40	0.47										
LD	0.20	0.22	0.07	0.40	0.11									
	0.18	0.21	0.15	0.56	0.07	1.00								
	0.03	0.06	−0.20	0.43	0.11									
	0.31	0.33	0.43	0.79	0.44									
LOC	0.58	0.61	0.09	0.56	0.77	0.25								
	0.77	0.78	−0.00	0.55	**0.84**	0.21	1.00							
	0.46	0.46	−0.14	0.34	0.66	0.16								
	0.58	0.60	0.14	0.47	0.58	0.32								
MPC	**0.83**	**0.81**	0.22	0.46	0.60	0.17	0.66							
	0.83	**0.82**	0.06	0.44	0.75	0.15	**0.87**	1.00						
	0.62	0.56	0.03	0.18	0.56	0.04	**0.82**							
	0.83	**0.81**	0.53	0.57	0.59	0.50	0.66							
NAM	0.69	0.72	0.11	0.72	**0.86**	0.32	**0.85**	0.71						
	0.71	0.72	−0.01	0.65	**0.85**	0.29	**0.94**	**0.82**	1.00					
	0.30	0.30	−0.23	0.57	0.78	0.29	0.78	0.59						
	0.51	0.53	0.16	0.63	0.68	0.46	**0.83**	0.62						
NOC	−0.01	0.02	−0.03	0.10	0.14	0.01	0.06	0.02	0.13					
	−0.04	−0.03	−0.05	0.02	0.01	−0.01	0.01	−0.02	0.01	1.00				
	−0.02	−0.03	−0.06	0.02	0.01	0.02	−0.02	−0.02	0.01					
	0.06	0.08	0.40	0.57	0.38	0.62	−0.11	0.21	0.06					
NOM	0.56	0.60	0.10	0.65	**0.91**	0.23	**0.82**	0.63	**0.95**	0.16				
	0.68	0.69	−0.05	0.59	**0.90**	0.20	**0.94**	**0.84**	**0.96**	0.03	1.00			
	0.32	0.33	−0.23	0.55	**0.83**	0.27	**0.83**	0.67	**0.92**	0.03				
	0.56	0.58	0.23	0.59	0.79	0.48	0.79	0.65	**0.91**	0.14				
RFC	0.74	0.74	0.18	0.62	**0.84**	0.23	**0.80**	**0.88**	**0.91**	0.11	**0.90**			
	0.83	**0.82**	0.02	0.53	**0.82**	0.18	**0.92**	**0.96**	**0.91**	−0.01	**0.93**	1.00		
	0.53	0.49	−0.02	0.32	0.62	0.12	**0.88**	**0.92**	0.73	−0.01	**0.82**			
	0.71	0.70	0.27	0.52	0.71	0.01	**0.80**	**0.81**	**0.83**	0.02	**0.90**			
TCC	0.02	0.02	0.02	0.11	−0.04	0.22	0.03	0.04	0.05	−0.02	0.02	0.04		
	0.05	0.07	0.05	0.25	−0.01	0.43	0.09	0.06	0.12	−0.04	0.08	0.08	1.00	
	0.08	0.09	−0.05	0.04	−0.05	0.25	0.03	−0.01	0.07	−0.05	0.02	0.01		
	0.33	0.35	0.54	0.78	0.46	**0.80**	0.26	0.51	0.41	**0.84**	0.45	0.36		
WMC	0.53	0.55	0.08	0.61	**0.86**	0.23	**0.89**	0.69	**0.90**	0.12	**0.93**	**0.90**	0.04	
	0.70	0.70	−0.04	0.53	**0.88**	0.16	**0.95**	**0.87**	**0.93**	0.01	**0.96**	**0.93**	0.08	1.00
	0.38	0.38	−0.17	0.37	0.72	0.16	**0.95**	**0.82**	0.79	−0.01	**0.88**	**0.88**	0.01	
	0.59	0.60	0.20	0.57	0.72	0.44	**0.84**	0.71	**0.88**	0.05	**0.93**	**0.93**	0.40	

to the other applications. As a matter of fact, our studied applications tend to have shallower inheritance trees than those from [5].

4.3   Metric Dependencies

Several metric value-based characterizations of software have been proposed in existing literature. However, many of them eschew a thorough study of the relations between numerical metric values. We believe that understanding existing correlations between metrics can further assist researchers in proposing and evaluating metric-based models. In this section we identify existing metric dependencies in the target applications and cross-check our data against [5].

As shown in Figs. 2 and 3, LEN is the only metric having a normal distribution. This, together with the difference in metric value ranges shown in Sect. 2, determined us to employ Spearman's rank correlation to determine metric dependency. Correlation data per application, including results from [5] are shown in Table 3. We establish a threshold of 0.8 in absolute value for *strong* correlations, which are highlighted and discussed below. In order to keep Table 3 readable, we did not include the LEN and LOD metrics, both of which appeared to be independent from other metrics as well as each other. The only exception is a weak correlation between DIT and LEN, which appeared in all studied applications, as well as [5]. It is explained by the tendency of derived classes in inheritance hierarchies to have more detailed names than those of base classes or interfaces.

Metric correlations in our target applications follow the trends identified by Barkman et al. [5]. We examine our results through the lens of the four characteristics of object-oriented software presented in Sect. 2.

We observe that strong and consistent correlations exist between coupling metrics CBO, DAC and MPC, as well as size-related metrics LOC, NAM and NOM. This was expected, as an increase in attributes or method count leads to increased class sizes when measured using metrics that predate object orientation. The same explanation covers the strong observed correlation between structural complexity RFC and WMC.

The NOM metric is also correlated with LCOM and NAM. This confirms that an increased method count usually leads to a lack of cohesion. As the number of class methods is a part of the NAM metric, this correlation was also expected. Inheritance metrics DIT and NOC remain uncorrelated in all data sets, challenging the expectation that classes at the base of the inheritance tree have more children.

An interesting result is that cohesion metrics LCOM, ILCOM and TCC do not show strong correlation in either of the studied data sets. LCOM shows a weak correlation with its improved variant in all data sets, showing that while they measure similar software aspects, there is enough differentiation between them. The result for TCC is more interesting, as the cross-sectional study in [5] showed much stronger correlation than observed by us. We believe this is a result of target application selection, which highlights the necessity of backing up any metric-based model with exploratory evaluation.

Table 4. Metric dependencies in FreeMind (top row - below Q1, middle row - interquartile range, bottom row - above Q3).

Metric	CBO	DAC	DIT	ILCOM	LCOM	LD	MPC	NAM	NOC	NOM	RFC	TCC	WMC
DAC	0.68												
	0.83	1.00											
	0.99												
DIT	0.34	0.59											
	0.42	0.55	1.00										
	0.26	0.25											
ILCOM	0.04	0.00	−0.10										
	0.04	0.17	−0.03	1.00									
	0.37	0.40	0.00										
LCOM	−0.10	−0.05	−0.12	−0.20									
	0.08	0.20	0.07	−0.01	1.00								
	0.49	0.51	−0.01	0.55									
LD	0.09	0.04	−0.07	**0.88**	−0.16								
	0.16	0.25	0.08	0.66	−0.07	1.00							
	0.04	0.06	−0.08	0.18	0.02								
MPC	0.67	0.21	−0.07	0.30	−0.13	0.36							
	0.78	0.59	0.32	−0.03	−0.05	0.14	1.00						
	0.81	0.79	0.20	0.36	0.56	−0.01							
NAM	−0.12	−0.12	−0.29	0.37	0.69	0.27	−0.03						
	0.13	0.32	0.10	0.53	0.64	0.41	0.03	1.00					
	0.65	0.68	−0.01	0.66	**0.89**	0.18	0.65						
NOC	−0.19	−0.04	−0.11	−0.11	0.33	−0.10	−0.26	0.26					
	−0.10	−0.04	−0.08	−0.03	0.22	−0.03	−0.17	0.19	1.00				
	0.02	0.02	0.08	0.22	0.21	0.04	0.05	0.18					
NOM	−0.08	−0.09	−0.25	0.07	**0.84**	0.00	−0.07	**0.88**	0.33				
	0.16	0.32	0.14	0.27	**0.80**	0.21	0.04	**0.90**	0.24	1.00			
	0.48	0.50	−0.04	0.59	**0.95**	0.07	0.55	**0.94**	0.23				
RFC	0.50	0.07	−0.24	0.23	0.44	0.24	0.71	0.53	0.02	0.57			
	0.66	0.61	0.29	0.15	0.45	0.25	0.74	0.58	0.06	0.63	1.00		
	0.68	0.68	0.09	0.54	**0.86**	0.04	**0.85**	**0.88**	0.18	**0.88**			
TCC	−0.13	−0.07	0.00	0.48	−0.11	0.27	−0.12	0.32	−0.03	0.18	0.00		
	−0.01	0.07	0.01	0.31	−0.14	0.35	0.05	0.27	0.00	0.14	0.16	1.00	
	−0.10	−0.12	−0.10	−0.15	−0.18	0.07	−0.09	−0.17	−0.03	−0.20	−0.16		
WMC	0.09	−0.01	−0.23	0.04	0.76	0.01	0.08	0.78	0.27	**0.90**	0.65	0.12	
	0.23	0.33	0.09	0.22	0.59	0.24	0.23	0.77	0.13	**0.83**	0.70	0.18	1.00
	0.42	0.43	−0.06	0.53	**0.88**	0.06	0.60	**0.86**	0.18	**0.91**	**0.87**	−0.13	

4.4 The Confounding Effect of Class Size

The confounding effect class size has on metric value-based measurements was reported by El Emam et al. [12]. Due to its significance, class size must be accounted for when studying metric dependencies. Authors of [12] showed that in many cases, metric dependencies could be explained by larger classes having higher metric values, which confounds data interpretation. As shown in Table 3, the LOC metric appears correlated with most of the metrics. The exceptions are DIT, LEN, LOD, NOC and TCC, which do not exhibit correlation with LOC, or other metrics.

Table 5. Metric dependencies in jEdit (top row - below Q1, middle row - inter-quartile range, bottom row - above Q3).

Metric	CBO	DAC	DIT	ILCOM	LCOM	LD	MPC	NAM	NOC	NOM	RFC	TCC	WMC
DAC	**0.82**												
	0.94	1.00											
	0.99												
DIT	0.34	0.50											
	0.33	0.39	1.00										
	0.09	0.09											
ILCOM	−0.06	0.01	0.05										
	−0.08	−0.02	−0.02	1.00									
	0.36	0.36	−0.13										
LCOM	0.07	0.08	−0.06	−0.12									
	−0.04	−0.02	−0.02	0.11	1.00								
	0.61	0.62	−0.09	0.47									
LD	−0.10	−0.02	0.04	0.78	−0.10								
	−0.11	−0.04	0.11	0.66	−0.03	1.00							
	−0.02	−0.01	0.16	0.23	0.00								
MPC	0.68	0.45	0.11	−0.09	0.01	−0.08							
	0.74	0.66	0.28	−0.03	−0.04	0.01	1.00						
	0.84	**0.83**	0.01	0.40	0.78	−0.03							
NAM	−0.15	−0.05	−0.21	0.40	0.39	0.38	−0.22						
	−0.10	−0.02	0.00	0.62	0.34	0.49	−0.01	1.00					
	0.70	0.70	−0.09	0.59	**0.91**	0.07	**0.82**						
NOC	−0.17	−0.08	−0.11	−0.08	0.16	−0.06	−0.21	0.04					
	−0.11	−0.07	−0.07	−0.04	0.11	−0.01	−0.14	0.00	1.00				
	−0.07	−0.06	−0.01	0.07	0.02	0.01	−0.04	0.00					
NOM	0.15	0.10	−0.09	0.06	**0.88**	0.03	0.09	0.33	0.17				
	−0.06	−0.02	−0.01	0.46	0.70	0.34	−0.02	0.65	0.08	1.00			
	0.68	0.68	−0.17	0.56	**0.94**	0.01	**0.83**	**0.97**	0.02				
RFC	0.56	0.30	−0.05	−0.05	0.44	−0.06	0.76	0.03	−0.06	0.60			
	0.59	0.52	0.21	0.15	0.26	0.14	**0.83**	0.22	−0.09	0.41	1.00		
	0.83	**0.82**	−0.07	0.49	**0.86**	−0.02	**0.96**	**0.92**	−0.02	**0.93**			
TCC	−0.07	−0.07	−0.03	0.21	−0.04	0.08	−0.04	0.15	−0.02	0.08	0.02		
	−0.08	−0.06	0.06	0.33	−0.13	0.44	−0.02	0.31	−0.05	0.26	0.07	1.00	
	−0.14	−0.15	−0.06	−0.09	−0.08	0.10	−0.07	−0.09	−0.08	−0.10	−0.09		
WMC	0.28	0.07	−0.19	−0.07	0.52	−0.09	0.40	0.08	0.00	0.67	0.71	0.03	
	0.27	0.21	−0.10	0.18	0.32	0.08	0.39	0.30	−0.08	0.55	0.63	0.13	1.00
	0.69	0.69	−0.14	0.49	**0.92**	−0.05	**0.87**	**0.93**	−0.01	**0.96**	**0.94**	−0.08	

To determine the effect class size has on metric dependencies, we partitioned all analyzed classes into quartiles using the LOC metric. We calculated the metric dependencies for each of our three data sets below the first quartile (below Q1), between the quartiles, and above the third quartile (above Q3). The detailed result is illustrated per application in Tables 4, 5 and 6. The LOC metric itself was omitted, as we had already used it to partition the data.

Table 6. Metric dependencies in TuxGuitar (top row - below Q1, middle row - inter-quartile range, bottom row - above Q3).

Metric	CBO	DAC	DIT	ILCOM	LCOM	LD	MPC	NAM	NOC	NOM	RFC	TCC	WMC
DAC	**0.92**												
	0.92	1.00											
	0.98												
DIT	0.64	0.60											
	0.60	0.53	1.00										
	0.10	0.05											
ILCOM	−0.26	−0.23	−0.32										
	−0.39	−0.32	−0.43	1.00									
	0.08	0.08	−0.15										
LCOM	−0.07	−0.01	−0.12	−0.12									
	−0.17	−0.15	−0.19	0.49	1.00								
	0.12	0.11	−0.14	0.41									
LD	−0.07	−0.04	−0.24	0.41	−0.11								
	−0.16	−0.07	−0.22	0.36	0.15	1.00							
	−0.08	−0.06	−0.18	0.42	0.06								
MPC	**0.82**	0.66	0.58	−0.25	−0.21	−0.02							
	0.77	0.60	0.44	−0.35	−0.14	−0.18	1.00						
	0.49	0.43	0.09	0.17	0.54	−0.13							
NAM	−0.10	−0.05	−0.20	0.30	0.66	0.09	−0.20						
	−0.19	−0.11	−0.30	0.60	0.52	0.30	−0.21	1.00					
	0.10	0.08	−0.18	0.51	**0.84**	0.15	0.52						
NOC	−0.16	−0.13	−0.16	−0.10	0.11	−0.07	−0.18	0.04					
	0.01	−0.02	−0.06	0.07	0.31	0.05	0.01	0.13	1.00				
	−0.06	−0.05	−0.08	0.27	0.12	0.20	−0.03	0.15					
NOM	−0.05	0.03	−0.17	0.12	**0.90**	−0.03	−0.22	0.75	0.13				
	−0.23	−0.17	−0.34	0.64	0.77	0.33	−0.15	0.70	0.21	1.00			
	0.16	0.14	−0.18	0.50	**0.88**	0.14	0.61	**0.92**	0.15				
RFC	0.79	0.66	0.47	−0.21	0.26	−0.10	**0.82**	0.18	−0.10	0.30			
	0.63	0.46	0.28	−0.03	0.26	−0.05	**0.83**	0.10	0.13	0.29	1.00		
	0.35	0.30	0.06	0.28	0.61	−0.06	**0.90**	0.65	0.03	0.77			
TCC	−0.14	−0.08	−0.20	0.24	−0.08	0.48	−0.12	0.12	−0.06	0.11	−0.10		
	0.05	0.13	−0.05	0.05	−0.18	0.32	−0.03	0.19	−0.05	0.13	−0.02	1.00	
	0.02	0.02	0.02	−0.14	−0.15	0.02	−0.11	−0.11	−0.09	−0.18	−0.14		
WMC	0.04	0.10	−0.13	0.09	**0.86**	0.00	−0.12	0.69	0.10	**0.95**	0.38	0.14	
	−0.12	−0.07	−0.34	0.45	0.59	0.32	0.04	0.54	0.17	**0.83**	0.40	0.13	1.00
	0.23	0.21	−0.10	0.29	0.72	−0.06	0.79	0.72	0.00	**0.84**	**0.85**	−0.17	

Immediately we observe that most of the strong metric dependencies occur in classes above the third quartile, which confirms El Emam et al.'s observation of the important role played by class size in metric dependencies. LCOM, NAM and RFC appear sensitive to class size across all target applications, showing strong dependencies for classes above Q3. An inverse relation is observed between DIT on one hand, and CBO and DAC on the other. In this case, we notice

Table 7. Extreme values for metric means for early (left) and *mature* application versions (right). Includes data from [26].

| Metric | FreeMind | | | | jEdit | | | | TuxGuitar | | | |
| | <1.0.0Alpha4 | | ≥1.0.0Alpha4 | | <4.0pre4 | | ≥4.0pre4 | | <1.0rc1 | | ≥1.0rc1 | |
	Min	Max	Min	Max	Min	Max	Min	Max	Min	Max	Min	Max
CBO	3.89	6.15	5.33	5.57	3.85	4.29	4.29	4.91	6.03	7.56	7.06	7.88
DAC	2.67	5.30	4.20	4.38	3.45	3.83	3.77	4.30	4.76	5.46	5.16	6.97
DIT	0.15	1.69	0.70	1.03	0.37	0.70	0.32	0.43	0.45	0.55	0.78	1.07
ILCOM	0.81	1.04	0.99	1.04	0.49	0.79	0.79	0.83	1.07	1.33	1.15	1.46
LCOM	84.85	193.25	196.85	237.90	43.44	117.75	126.79	149.31	90.94	130.49	117.15	176.79
LD	0.30	0.52	0.48	0.51	0.23	0.36	0.34	0.37	0.39	0.48	0.35	0.50
LEN	11.77	17.07	16.67	17.17	12.25	13.10	13.01	14.35	14.84	15.09	15.19	18.26
LOC	63.35	157.84	100.05	110.79	91.29	153.94	158.64	177.37	94.93	116.69	73.13	115.25
LOD	0.72	0.91	0.78	0.81	0.73	0.82	0.73	0.80	0.68	0.83	0.88	0.99
MPC	6.99	13.20	10.59	10.92	6.79	9.00	9.34	10.05	14.26	21.27	14.65	22.85
NAM	7.06	9.84	9.85	10.09	5.18	9.02	8.53	9.19	9.71	12.13	9.41	12.98
NOC	0.15	1.44	0.59	0.63	0.31	0.65	0.29	0.38	0.45	0.52	0.58	0.92
NOM	5.26	7.06	6.88	6.99	3.16	5.49	5.28	5.46	6.38	7.23	6.13	8.13
RFC	9.74	15.17	13.49	13.62	7.91	10.39	10.39	11.14	14.81	19.50	15.80	22.21
TCC	0.03	0.16	0.14	0.16	0.06	0.13	0.14	0.17	0.14	0.22	0.12	0.18
WMC	8.52	14.41	12.32	12.55	8.52	14.13	13.43	15.05	12.02	14.53	10.63	15.38

dependency strength decrease for larger class sizes. This is to be expected, as most metrics capture state and behaviour introduced by the class itself, disregarding inherited attributes. As such, many classes deep in inheritance hierarchies appear deceptively simple, as much of their complexity is hidden in base classes.

Even with class size accounted for, we still observe highly dependent metric pairs. Coupling metrics CBO and DAC, as well as complexity metrics NOM and WMC illustrate this best. In the same way, metric pairs that we observed to be independent in the previous section remain so even when partitioned according to class size. DIT, NOC and TCC showed no strong dependency in any of the data partitions.

4.5   Longitudinal Evaluation

This section is dedicated to an examination of the changes to metric values during application development. Data points illustrated in Figs. 2 and 3 are available for every metric and application version on our website. We found that values follow the illustrated distributions across all target application versions. As detailed in Sect. 4.2, maximum data points represent outliers, while minimal data points coincide with metric minimum values and are not interesting. As such, the present section is focused on discussing mean and median metric values. For the sake of brevity, we do not include all 8,560 data points. Our principle findings are that early application versions show more variability in metric values

Table 8. Application versions showing significant variance in metric values.

Application	Version	LOC	Classes
jEdit	2.6final	46,671	453
	3.0final	40,756	282
FreeMind	0.7.1	18,928	199
	0.8.0	84,199	718
	0.8.1	84,089	718
	0.9.0Beta17	56,752	577
TuxGuitar	1.2	77,056	736
	1.3.0	91,481	1,234

and that key application versions can be identified during which large changes to metric values occur.

Metric Variability in Early and Mature Versions. We examined the changes to metric values that occurred between consecutive versions of the same application. For all three target applications, we found that some of the most consistent changes occurred within early releases of the application. Of course, there exists no structured definition for an *"early version"*, especially not one that can be used across several applications. As such, we used our familiarity with the studied applications to identify the earliest version that we considered *mature*. In the case of our target applications, they were FreeMind 1.0.0Alpha4, jEdit 4.0pre4 and TuxGuitar 1.0rc1. These versions include most of the functionalities available in the latest version of the respective application, have the same look & feel as all subsequent versions and appear to be stable software releases. Table 7 illustrates minimum and maximum mean metric values in both early and *mature* application versions.

We observe that for all applications, metric variability is much higher for the earlier versions. As shown in Table 1, the first version of FreeMind consisted of 3,722 lines of code, fewer than the first version of TuxGuitar (11,209). In contrast, the first release of jEdit (33,768 LOC) was much more mature, and already contained the application's most important functionalities. On the other hand, once the application architecture is established and the principal functionalities set is implemented, we observe a significant reduction in the variability of metric values between versions. This is illustrated for each application, in the right-hand columns of Table 7. Furthermore, longitudinal examination also showed that specific trends can be identified for each application with regards to how object-oriented concepts such as coupling, inheritance and structural complexity are handled. It is our opinion that additional case studies presenting a longitudinal view are required before desirable metric ranges and most importantly, reliable metric-based characterisations can be established.

Table 9. Mean metric values for given application versions.

	FreeMind				jEdit		TuxGuitar	
	0.7.1	0.8.0	0.8.1	0.9.0Beta17	2.6final	3.0final	1.2	1.3.0
CBO	4.75	6.15	6.15	5.31	4.24	4.29	7.05	7.07
DAC	3.10	5.29	5.29	4.14	3.73	3.82	5.22	6.30
DIT	0.50	1.69	1.69	0.74	0.63	0.42	0.79	0.95
ILCOM	0.95	0.80	0.80	1.03	0.52	0.77	1.43	1.22
LCOM	179.54	152.56	152.56	189.32	47.95	114.37	176.79	130.11
LD	0.42	0.43	0.43	0.51	0.25	0.36	0.50	0.35
LEN	15.23	16.91	16.91	17.06	12.62	12.97	15.45	18.26
LOC	102.95	157.83	157.52	97.87	100.16	151.28	115.24	80.74
LOD	0.86	0.72	0.72	0.80	0.82	0.73	0.89	0.98
MPC	11.53	13.19	13.19	10.51	7.58	9.00	22.82	14.64
NAM	9.08	8.99	8.99	9.77	6.01	9.01	12.96	9.85
NOC	0.37	1.44	1.44	0.61	0.56	0.33	0.65	0.64
NOM	6.61	7.06	7.06	6.82	3.72	5.48	8.12	6.31
RFC	13.07	15.16	15.16	13.29	8.84	10.38	22.20	15.80
TCC	0.06	0.08	0.08	0.15	0.08	0.12	0.16	0.12
WMC	12.94	14.40	14.38	12.16	9.27	14.00	15.38	11.30

Causes of Large Variations in Metric Values. We also observed that metric values were consistent between most consecutive version pairs of the studied applications. At the same time, we could identify version pairs where metric values were greatly disrupted. We illustrate these pairs using Table 8. The table also includes information about LOC and the number of classes, in order to help understand the causes behind observed variations. For example, it is obvious that a large push in development between FreeMind 0.7.1 and 0.8.0 contributed to significant changes to metric values, as evidenced by the sharp increase in application LOC and class count. The same can be said about TuxGuitar version 1.3.0. The opposite however is true for jEdit 3.0final, as well as FreeMind 0.9.0Beta17. In these versions we observe important decreases in both LOC and class count, most likely a result due to refactoring.

Table 9 illustrates mean metric values for the highlighted application versions. For each version, we manually examined its source code in detail to identify the underlying changes leading to these variations.

FreeMind 0.8.0 contains major changes, as already evidenced by the sharp increase in LOC and class count. It is the first version to use external libraries for XML processing and input forms. During use, it is clear that FreeMind 0.8.0 is more complex and fully-featured, with many changes that are visible at UI level, including more complex application preferences and features for mind map and node management. Its scope remains apparent at source file level, with only 21 out of the 92 source files remaining unchanged from 0.7.1. The number of source files also increased greatly in the newer version, from 92 to 469. Much of the observed discrepancy between numbers of source files, classes and LOC between the versions can be explained by the newer application including 272 classes that were generated by the JAXB libraries encoding most of the actions that can be performed using the application. These classes contributed with 49,434 lines to the inflation of LOC witnessed between the studied versions. Between version 0.8.0 and 0.8.1, no source files were added or deleted, but many of them have undergone small updates. This includes all generated code, that was regenerated for version 0.8.1. FreeMind again underwent significant changes for version 0.9.0Beta17, an evolution from 0.8.1. Out of 469 source files in version 0.8.1, only 127 can be found in the newer version, and all of them have undergone changes. Version 0.9.0Beta17 also added 230 new Java source files, covering all functionality areas. Action source files generated using JAXB in version 0.8.0 were replaced with a smaller number of hand-written classes with similar naming and functionality. This explains most of the class count and LOC difference between versions 0.8.1 and 0.9.0Beta17.

In the case of jEdit, version 3.0final was the only one where mean metric values were disrupted. A possible contributor to this is that relatively, early analyzed versions were more mature than equivalent ones from the other applications. In the case of version 3.0final, we observed that the package *"org.gjt.sp.jedit.actions"*, which contained 153 event handler classes with low statement count and cyclomatic complexity was deleted. These were replaced with an XML file that provides action descriptors together with Java-like code snippets that are executed when the action is fired. Only 81 source files out of 341 remained unchanged between these versions.

In the case of TuxGuitar version 1.3.0, the *"org.herac.tuxguitar.gui"* package was split into **.app*, **.editor* and **.graphics* packages. Most packages were updated or refactored. New plugins were added, existing ones have seen source code changes. Only 62 out of the 650 source code files remained unedited between these versions. Version 1.3.0 introduced 930 new source files, most of which contain code for custom application actions in the form of small classes having low complexity, skewing the mean and median metric values.

The last observation is related to the expectation that mean metric values increase in more advanced application versions. Our data showed this to be true mostly in the case of FreeMind and jEdit, especially in the case of size metrics LOC, NAM and NOM. However, as we have shown in this section, this is alleviated by the refactorings that were carried out in some of the versions.

Our examination resulted in several conclusions. First, we observed that most of the significant metric variations occurred in early application versions. This was true both as highlighted in Table 9, as well as when manually identifying versions with significant metric variations. In addition, we feel that a more in-depth discussion is warranted regarding the effect that large numbers of small, relatively straightforward classes have on software quality characteristics. The importance and magnitude these classes should have when building metric-based models has yet to be clarified. In several cases, we observed Java source code being replaced with XML descriptors. This is an illustrative example of the inherent limitations of metric extraction tools and understanding of software based on metric values.

4.6   Threats to Validity

We carried out our study using the following steps, in order: preparing application versions, extracting metric data, processing the metric data and analysing it. We presented all the steps required to duplicate our study in detail. Extracted metric information, as well as aggregated data used for analysis is available on our website. Each target application version was manually examined in order to ensure that no factors that could influence metric values were present. We provided structured definitions for all metrics used, and extracted the data using a freely-available, cross-platform tool.

We selected three similar applications from a programming language and architecture standpoint. This helps limit external threats to validity related to application selection and generalization of results. This also allows comparing obtained results, as all three applications include the same layers. Application selection and metric extraction were finalized before data analysis, to eliminate selection bias. All results are presented both individually, per-application, as well as in aggregate form.

However, we believe one of our most important contributions was the comparative evaluation against a large-scale cross-sectional study that was carried out using the same methodology as ours. We believe this will help create a solid basis for additional studies towards a metric-based understanding of software quality and the software development process.

Among existing threats, we must include the limited number and types of studied applications. This means that additional research is required in order to draw conclusions about other types of software, such as non GUI-driven or mobile applications. Furthermore, as we only included open-source software, they might not be representative for other applications. As such, we believe that additional experimental evaluation is required in order to cover additional applications, programming languages as well as considered metrics.

5   Conclusions and Future Work

In this paper we establish a number of metrics that previous research has associated with software product quality. We select three open-source, user interface-driven applications developed in Java and analyze the values and relations between these metrics within each application's entire development history.

Each step of our evaluation is detailed and we employ open-source tooling to ensure that our evaluation is repeatable. At each step, we compare our results with a comparable large-scale evaluation, obtaining results from an aggregate of over 250[17] application versions. We believe these combined results provide a sound foundation to be used in further research.

---

[17] [5] evaluated 146 software projects.

We found that metric distributions, mean, median and modus values were consistent across the studies. Mean and median values prove stable once applications reach maturity, as evidenced in all three target applications. Comparing values across studied applications revealed the existence of trends in metric values, driven by the architecture and design of the underlying application.

With regards to identified metric dependencies, we could identify metric pairs showing strong correlation across applications and application versions, as well as certain metrics that did not show correlation with any others. We further investigated the confounding effect of class size in order to confirm our findings.

Our longitudinal approach also revealed that across many application version we could not witness significant changes to aggregated metric values. Where such changes occurred, they were mostly driven by application development as well as refactoring, and were reflected in object-oriented metric values.

An important avenue for further research regards a finer grained analysis, in order to detect significant changes at package and class levels, not just those that are visible at aggregated level. Our evaluation should be extended in order to cover other application types, including mobile and non user interface-driven software. We believe this type of research can lay the foundation for identifying suitable metric thresholds that point toward good design practices. Another aspect regards the role played by the programming language itself, as it too plays an influence on metric values.

The end goal of this research is represented by a characterization of good design and development practices, where software metrics will have an important role for understanding and controlling the software development process.

References

1. Al Dallal, J., Briand, L.C.: An object-oriented high-level design-based class cohesion metric. Inf. Softw. Technol. **52**(12), 1346–1361 (2010). https://doi.org/10.1016/j.infsof.2010.08.006
2. ARISA Compendium - Understandability for Reuse:. http://www.arisa.se/compendium/node39.html#property:UnderstandabilityR (2018). Accessed Nov 2018
3. Arlt, S., Banerjee, I., Bertolini, C., Memon, A.M., Schaf, M.: Grey-box GUI testing: efficient generation of event sequences. CoRR abs/1205.4928 (2012)
4. Bakar, N.S.S.A., Boughton, C.V.: Validation of measurement tools to extract metrics from open source projects. In: 2012 IEEE Conference on Open Systems, pp. 1–6, October 2012. https://doi.org/10.1109/ICOS.2012.6417648
5. Barkmann, H., Lincke, R., Löwe, W.: Quantitative evaluation of software quality metrics in open-source projects. In: 2009 International Conference on Advanced Information Networking and Applications Workshops, pp. 1067–1072, May 2009. https://doi.org/10.1109/WAINA.2009.190
6. Basili, V.R., Briand, L.C., Melo, W.L.: A validation of object-oriented design metrics as quality indicators. IEEE Trans. Softw. Eng. **22**(10), 751–761 (1996). https://doi.org/10.1109/32.544352
7. Du Bois B., Mens, T.: Describing the impact of refactoring on internal program quality. In: Proceedings of the 8th International Workshop on Evolution of Large-scale Industrial Software Applications, pp. 37–48 (2003)

8. Chidamber, S.R., Kemerer, C.F.: A metrics suite for object oriented design. IEEE Trans. Softw. Eng. **20**(6), 476–493 (1994). https://doi.org/10.1109/32.295895
9. Poshyvanyk, D., Marcus, A.: The conceptual coupling metrics for object-oriented systems. In: 2006 22nd IEEE International Conference on Software Maintenance, pp. 469–478 (2006). https://doi.org/10.1109/ICSM.2006.67
10. Dash, Y., Dubey, S.K., Rana, A.: Maintainability prediction of object oriented software system by using artificial neural network approach. Int. J. Soft Comput. Eng. **2**(2), 420–423 (2012)
11. DeMarco, T.: Controlling Software Projects: Management, Measurement, and Estimates. Prentice Hall PTR, Upper Saddle River (1986)
12. Emam, K.E., Benlarbi, S., Goel, N., Rai, S.N.: The confounding effect of class size on the validity of object-oriented metrics. IEEE Trans. Softw. Eng. **27**(7), 630–650 (2001). https://doi.org/10.1109/32.935855
13. Gyimothy, T., Ferenc, R., Siket, I.: Empirical validation of object-oriented metrics on open source software for fault prediction. IEEE Trans. Softw. Eng. **31**(10), 897–910 (2005). https://doi.org/10.1109/TSE.2005.112
14. Halstead, M.: Elements of Software Science. Elsevier North-Holland (1977)
15. Heitlager, I., Kuipers, T., Visser, J.: A practical model for measuring maintainability. In: IEEE Proceedings of 6th International Conference on the Quality of Information and Communications Technology, pp. 30–39 (2007)
16. Hitz, M., Montazeri, B.: Measuring coupling and cohesion in object-oriented systems. In: Proceedings of International Symposium on Applied Corporate Computing, pp. 25–27 (1995)
17. Kanellopoulos, Y., et al.: Code quality evaluation methodology using the ISO/IEC 9126 standard. Int. J. Softw. Eng. Appl. **1**(3), 17–36 (2010). https://doi.org/10.5121/ijsea.2010.1302
18. Landman, D., Serebrenik, A., Vinju, J.: Empirical analysis of the relationship between CC and SLOC in a large corpus of Java methods. In: Proceedings of the 2014 IEEE International Conference on Software Maintenance and Evolution, ICSME 2014, pp. 221–230. IEEE Computer Society, Washington, USA (2014). https://doi.org/10.1109/ICSME.2014.44
19. Lenhard, J., Blom, M., Herold, S.: Exploring the suitability of source code metrics for indicating architectural inconsistencies. Softw. Qual. J. **27**, 241–274 (2018). https://doi.org/10.1007/s11219-018-9404-z
20. Li, W., Henry, S.: Maintenance metrics for the object oriented paradigm. In: 1993 Proceedings First International Software Metrics Symposium, pp. 52–60, May 1993. https://doi.org/10.1109/METRIC.1993.263801
21. Lincke, R., Lundberg, J., Löwe, W.: Comparing software metrics tools. In: Proceedings of the 2008 International Symposium on Software Testing and Analysis - ISSTA 2008, pp. 131–142 (2008). https://doi.org/10.1145/1390630.1390648
22. Marinescu, R.: Measurement and quality in object-oriented design. In: 21st IEEE International Conference on Software Maintenance (ICSM 2005), pp. 701–704, September 2005. https://doi.org/10.1109/ICSM.2005.63
23. McCabe, T.J.: A complexity measure. IEEE Trans. Softw. Eng. **SE–2**(4), 308–320 (1976). https://doi.org/10.1109/TSE.1976.233837
24. Melo, W.L., Briand, L.C., Basili, V.R.: Measuring the Impact of Reuse on Quality and Productivity in Object-Oriented Systems. University of Maryland, Computer Science Department, Technical report (1995)
25. Molnar, A., Motogna, S.: Discovering maintainability changes in large software systems. In: Proceedings of the 27th International Workshop on Software Measurement and 12th International Conference on Software Process and Product

Measurement, IWSM Mensura 2017, pp. 88–93. ACM, New York (2017). https://doi.org/10.1145/3143434.3143447

26. Molnar, A., Neamţu, A., Motogna, S.: Longitudinal evaluation of software quality metrics in open-source applications. In: Proceedings of the 14th International Conference on Evaluation of Novel Approaches to Software Engineering, ENASE, vol. 1, pp. 80–91. INSTICC, SciTePress (2019). https://doi.org/10.5220/0007725600800091

27. Ott, L., Bieman, J.M., Kang, B.K., Mehra, B.: Developing Measures of Class Cohesion for Object-Oriented Software. Department of Computer Science, Michigan Technological University, Technical report (1970)

28. Rodriguez, D., Harrison, R.: An overview of object-oriented design metrics (2001)

29. Motogna, S., Vescan, A., Serban, C., Tirban, P.: An approach to assess maintainability change. In: 2016 IEEE International Conference on Automation, Quality and Testing, Robotics (AQTR), pp. 1–6 (2016). https://doi.org/10.1109/AQTR.2016.7501279

30. Saraiva, J.: A roadmap for software maintainability measurement. In: Proceedings of the 2013 International Conference on Software Engineering, ICSE 2013, pp. 1453–1455. IEEE Press, Piscataway (2013). http://dl.acm.org/citation.cfm?id=2486788.2487035

31. Sarker, M.: An overview of object oriented design metrics. Umeå University, Sweden (2005)

32. Silva, R., Costa, H.: Graphical and statistical analysis of the software evolution using coupling and cohesion metrics - an exploratory study. In: Proceedings - 2015 41st Latin American Computing Conference, CLEI 2015 (2015). https://doi.org/10.1109/CLEI.2015.7359472

33. Tang, M.H., Kao, M.H., Chen, M.H.: An empirical study on object-oriented metrics. In: Proceedings of the 6th International Symposium on Software Metrics, METRICS 1999, p. 242. IEEE Computer Society, Washington (1999). http://dl.acm.org/citation.cfm?id=520792.823979

34. Wilking, D., Farooq Kahn, U., Kowalewski, S.: An empirical evaluation of refactoring. e-Inform. Softw. Eng. J. **1**, 27–42 (2007)

35. Xu, J., Ho, D., Capretz, L.F.: An empirical validation of object-oriented design metrics for fault prediction. J. Comput. Sci. (2008). https://doi.org/10.3844/jcssp.2008.571.577

36. Yuan, X., Memon, A.M.: Generating event sequence-based test cases using GUI run-time state feedback. IEEE Trans. Softw. Eng. **36**(1), 81–95 (2010). https://doi.org/10.1109/TSE.2009.68

37. ARISA Compendium:. http://www.arisa.se/compendium/ (2020). Accessed Jan 2020

Model-Driven Development Applied to Mobile Health and Clinical Scores

Allan Fábio de Aguiar Barbosa$^{(\boxtimes)}$

Federal University of Maranhao, São Luís, Maranhao, Brazil
afabio@lsdi.ufma.br

Abstract. Clinical scores are a widely discussed topic in health as part of modern clinical practice. In general, these tools predict clinical outcomes, perform risk stratification, aid in clinical decision making, assess disease severity or assist diagnosis. However, the problem is that clinical scores data are traditionally obtained manually, which can lead to incorrect data and result. Besides, by collecting biological/health data in real-time from humans, the current mobile health (mHealth) solutions that computationally solve that problem are limited because those systems are developed considering the specificities of a single clinical score. This work addresses the productivity in developing mHealth solutions for clinical scores through the use of Model-Driven Development concepts. This paper focuses on describing DSML4ClinicalScores, a high-level domain-specific modeling language that uses the Ecore metamodel to describe a clinical score specification. To propose the DSML4ClinicalScores, we analyzed 89 clinical scores for defining the artifacts of this proposed Metamodel. From the concrete model created by the DSML4ClinicalScores, we apply model transformation techniques to automatically generate software components in the domains of mHealth and clinical scores. In the end, we evaluate the proposed approach through the modeling of eight different clinical scores for validating the DSML4ClinicalScores metamodel, and the development a practical case study using a specific clinical score for illustrating how to use the proposal in a clinical situation scenario.

Keywords: Clinical scores · Mobile health model-driven development · Domain-specific modeling language

1 Introduction

Clinical scores have been discussed as part of modern clinical practice in recent decades. In general, these tools have been created to predict clinical outcomes, perform risk stratification, aid in clinical decision making, assess disease severity or assist diagnosis [1]. In the medical literature, there are many formally defined clinical scores, in which each one of them deals with a specific type of disease, especially those considered as chronic. For example, there are clinical scores for heart diseases, infectious diseases, neurological diseases, and so on.

© Springer Nature Switzerland AG 2020
E. Damiani et al. (Eds.): ENASE 2019, CCIS 1172, pp. 188–203, 2020.
https://doi.org/10.1007/978-3-030-40223-5_9

Recently, the importance of scores for clinical practice within the hospital environment has been investigated with greater emphasis. For example, Aakre et al. [1,2] examined the feasibility of including these scores within the patient's electronic health record (EHR). In this context, clinical scores data are traditionally obtained in a manual way, which can lead to incorrect data and result, and they can also involve complex mathematical calculations. Initiatives in the mobile health (mHealth) field that currently arise to computationally solve the problem are limited because a software is developed considering the specificities of a particular clinical score.

In that scenario, the development process of mobile solutions for clinical scores using traditional approaches requires building a new software for each clinical score, even if they have similar characteristics, repeating all development steps, which limits productivity. To tackle this problem, we propose to use Model-Driven Development (MDD) concepts that helps to simplify the process of developing mHealth applications for clinical scores. In particular, we propose a Domain-Specific Modeling Language (DSML) for specifying clinical scores in general. Additionally, we apply Model Transformation techniques to generate software components from the specified clinical score (i.e., concrete model). The resulting software components describe an Internet of Things (IoT) application targeting the evaluation of a single clinical score.

This work presents the *DSML4ClinicalScores*, a high-level DSML that uses an Ecore metamodel to describe a clinical score specification. In general, a clinical score specification contains a section for defining its variables, a section for defining the rules for calculating its score, and a section for describing its evaluation models. Our *DSML4ClinicalScores* can cover all these particular features and generalizes specific details of different specifications. Thus, the clinical score modeled by the *DSML4ClinicalScores* is submitted to a model-to-text (M2T) transformation that generates an OWL ontology within the domains of mHealth and clinical scores.

The remaining of the paper is organized as follows. In Sect. 2, we present concepts related to this research. Section 3 reviews published mHealth solutions targeting the automation of clinical scores and discusses the issues that have motivated the development of our approach. Section 4 is an overview of the proposed approach components and technology. Section 5 evaluates the proposed approach and discusses its advantages and limitations. Finally, in Sect. 6, we drive our conclusions and perspectives for future work.

2 Background

2.1 Clinical Scores

According to Thompson [3], clinical scores are based on clinical prediction rules (CPRs), which are tools that use specific criteria to establish probabilities of outcomes or assist in management decisions. Falk and Fahey [4] summarize the critical element of CPR as follows: "CPRs quantify the contribution of symptoms, clinical signs, and available diagnostic tests, and stratify patients according to the probability of having a target disorder. The outcome of interest can be diverse and be anywhere along the diagnostic, prognostic, and therapeutic spectrum".

In this context, some researchers have classified three types of CPRs and, consequently, three models of clinical scores: (1) Diagnostic CPRs that focuses on factors related to the clinical diagnosis; (2) Prognostic CPRs that predicts outcomes; (3) Prescriptive CPRs that provides recommendations for clinical intervention. The format of a CPR is variable and depends on the purpose for which it is intended, but it should include three or more variables obtained from patient history, physical examinations, or necessary diagnostic tests [3]. The combination of these CPRs forms the clinical score specification skeleton.

The process of establishing a clinical score within the clinical practice is complex and requires considerable time. According to Adams and Leveson [5], only to prove a CPR, the following steps are necessary: development, validation, impact analysis and implementation. Development is the stage in which it is identified the predictors from an observational study. Validation is the stage in which it is tested the rule on a separate population to see if it remains reliable. Impact analysis is the stage in which it is measured the usefulness of the rule in a clinical setting concerning cost-benefit, customer satisfaction and time/resource allocation. Implementation is the stage that there are universal acceptance and adoption of the rule in clinical practice.

Table 1. CURB-65 Score specification, where BUN is blood urea nitrogen and BP is blood pressure.

Variable	Rule	Score
Confusion	Yes/No	+1
BUN > 19 mg/dL	Yes/No	+1
Respiratory rate ≥ 30	Yes/No	+1
Systolic BP < 90 mmHg or Diastolic BP ≤ 60 mmHg	Yes/No	1+1
Age ≥ 65	Yes/No	+1
Evaluation		Result
0.60% = Low risk; consider home treatment		0
2.70% = Low risk; consider home treatment		1
6.80% = Short inpatient hospitalization or closely supervised outpatient treatment		2
14.00% = Severe pneumonia; hospitalize and consider admitting to intensive care		3
27.80% = Severe pneumonia; hospitalize and consider admitting to intensive care		4 or 5

In general, a clinical score specification consists of variables, rules for calculation of the score and evaluation. Variables are precisely the predictors obtained in the development phase of the model. Rules define the punctuation of each variable in the specification according to the methodology used in the validation step of the model. Evaluation describes the interpretation of a clinical score according to the result obtained by applying the rules for calculating the score. For example, the well-known CURB-65 Score [6], which estimates mortality of pneumonia, has variables, rules for calculating score and evaluations as detailed in Table 1. It is possible to see in the Table 1 the declared variables, the set of rules associated with each specified variable and its respective score, and the two types of evaluation of this clinical score. We propose that mHeatlh applications can use a DSML to specify different clinical scores, in which transformation rules will be applied to generate executable code artifacts.

2.2   Model-Driven Development

In the software development process, the key element for MDD is the system modeling. The main focus of MDD consists of developing and refining a model of a specific domain, in order to produce a vocabulary for use in software development [7]. This approach is based on following two main concepts: Domain-Specific Languages (DSL) and model transformations. DSL is a programming language based on abstractions (text, symbol or graph) strongly connected to the domain for which this language is intended [8]. On the other hand, model transformation is the technique that allows a platform-independent model to be translated into another platform-specific model, enabling models to produce executable software artifacts [9].

In this context of MDD and DSLs, there is a special case of this language called DSML, which serves to formalize the structure, behavior, and requirements of an application through metamodels, whose representations define semantic relationships and constraints between concepts in a domain [10]. The definition of DSML usually begins with capturing and identifying the domain. The result of this activity produces the abstract syntax of the language, which corresponds to a metamodel with all concepts identified at the meta-domain level. The concrete syntax of the language refers to how it is understood and used by its users, or how the models are written or designed [11,12]. Moreover, we usually apply a model transformation technique for code generation. So, it is necessary to go through the abstract syntax tree (i.e., the specified concrete model) and generate code in a programming language or other text. As this resulting code is considered as pure text, there is no recognition of the language to be transformed [8]. This process is called M2T transformation.

3   Clinical Scores in mHealth

In the literature, there have been some initiatives involving mHealth and clinical scores in recent years. For example, Cook et al. [13] developed and evaluated a mobile application to improve asthma control through proactive actions and without the need for regular inputs (i.e., treatment plans, patient education and encouragement of self-care). The authors used the Asthma Control Test [14] (ACT) in this application to provide patients with a self-assessment questionnaire for controlling asthma, as well as making available a collection of educational archives on audio and video media. Aminian et al. [15] developed a mobile application that provides quick access to evidence-based risk calculators for decision-making regarding bariatric surgical procedures. The authors used the following three clinical scores to ensure the patient and physician understand the relative risk and benefit of surgery: Sleeve Gastrectomy Risk Calculator [16], Risk of Post-discharge Venous Thromboembolism after Bariatric Surgery [17], and Individualized Metabolic Surgery Score [18].

Stamate et al. [19] developed the cloudUDPRS application for clinical evaluation of the motor symptoms of Parkinson's Disease. The authors based the application on the well-known scores: Unified Parkinson's Disease Rating Scale [20] (UPDRS) and Parkinson's Disease Questionnaire [21] (PDQ39). Pereira-Azevedo et al. [22] created a mobile application for the Rotterdam Prostate Cancer Risk Calculator [23] (RPCRC). With the application, the authors improved the risk stratification of prostate cancer, avoiding unnecessary biopsies and reducing the time for diagnosis and unnecessary treatment.

All works described above tackle the problem of clinical scores in mHealth in a restricted way, developing a computational system for specific clinical scores. Their main focus is on solving the clinical score or using it to address a more significant problem in health domain. This paper presents an extension of what we exploited in [24] at ENASE Conference. In [24], we proposed a domain-specific modeling language to specify different clinical scores in mHealth domain. By modeling many clinical scores using a DSML, we standardize the requirements of any application that fits within this domain and can use the resulting code artifacts from our approach in future mHealth applications for different clinical scores. Once a clinical score is specified using the provided DSML, we takes it as input in order to apply a model-to-text transformation and generate software artifacts related to the clinical score evaluation.

4   Proposed Approach

Our approach focuses on the development of software to allow real-time remote patient monitoring using the processing of data streams generated from people and biomedical sensors. Unlike most previous works, which develop a computational system for each specific clinical score, our approach stands out by allowing the specification of several clinical scores and the automatic generation of software components through the use of model transformation techniques. The generated software components allow real-time remote patient monitoring according to the provided clinical score specifications. Figure 1 illustrates the proposed approach.

The first part of Fig. 1 (identified by the (1) label) corresponds to the automatic code generation. This step involves using a DSML (DSLM4ClinicalScores)

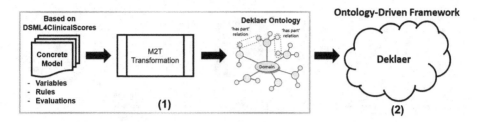

Fig. 1. The proposed approach.

to model different clinical score specifications. Based on the provided specification (concrete model), our approach applies an M2T transformation for the generation of OWL ontology classes, which are described according to the Deklaer language [25]. The generated ontology describes the rules that will be used for patient monitoring according to the provided clinical score specification. The second part of Fig. 1 corresponds to an ontology-driven framework, which semi-automates the creation of an IoT application comprising the evaluation of the previously specified clinical score. The process of an IoT application generation and the deployment of the its software components is described in Pinheiro et al. [25].

4.1 The DSML4ClinicalScores Design

DSML4ClinicalScores is a domain-specific language derived from our work [24]. This language allows the user to model different clinical score specifications using a DSML. This language allows the user to model different clinical score specifications using a DSML. To identify which concepts would be included as artifacts in this language, we adopted the work of Aakre et al. [2] as the initial reference for the *DSML4ClinicalScores* definition. In that work, the authors empirically evaluated 110 clinical scores regarding the importance of having the scores inserted automatically into the patient's electronic record. This evaluation was based on subjective criteria of US medical specialists, considering a classification divided in "VERY IMPORTANT", "NICE TO HAVE" or "NOT IMPORTANT". From that, we chose the clinical scores considered as VERY IMPORTANT and NICE TO HAVE. The resulting set had a total of 89 clinical scores, whose specifications were the basis for defining the *DSML4ClinicalScores* metamodel.

In this section, we present the *DSML4ClinicalScores* metamodel, as shown in Fig. 2. The only difference between this metamodel and the one presented in [24] consists of including clinical score results as input variables for a specification. The *DSML4ClinicalScores* was implemented on top of the Ecore metamodel and we used the Eclipse Modeling Framework[1] (EMF), a distribution of the Eclipse community, to edit and create case studies of clinical scores. EMF is a modeling framework and code generation facility for building tools and other

---

[1] https://www.eclipse.org/sirius/overview.html.

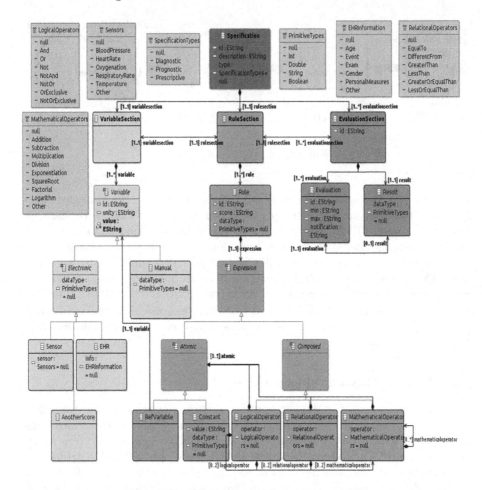

Fig. 2. The *DSML4ClinicalScores* metamodel.

applications based on a structured data model, in addition to providing an API
for the Ecore dialect to UML. Ecore describes models and runtime support for
the models, including change notification, persistence support with default XMI
serialization, and a very efficient reflective API for manipulating EMF objects
generically [26].

Therefore, the definition of the *DSML4ClinicalScores* metamodel is based on
the extracted concepts from those 89 previously mentioned clinical scores. It is
organized into four main classes (see Fig. 2) in order to separate the element
needed for identifying a clinical score specification (*Specification*) from those
related to each section model definition (*VariableSection, RuleSection* and *EvaluationSection*). The *Specification* class represents a single clinical score specification, including an identifier, a description and a type from the *SpecificationTypes*
class (*Diagnostic, Prognostic* or *Prescriptive*). The *VariableSection* class defines

all variables in a clinical score specification, and a variable can be obtained through sensors, information of the patient's EHR, interviews with the health professional or patient, or information from other clinical scores. The *RuleSection* class defines all rules for calculating the score of the clinical score, associated with each variable in the specification, and a rule can be represented by any possible expression (logical, relational or mathematical). The *EvaluationSection* class defines all possible evaluation models for a clinical score specification, and it can have more than one model described by one information associated with a result, identifying each one of them.

4.2 The Deklaer Language

Deklaer is a declarative language developed by Pinheiro et al. [25], which describes an IoT application that uses sensors and actuators through a set of ontologies. The vocabulary of this language is composed of the following classes: (1) *Entity*, which represents different entities (e.g., people, animals, or physical objects) of the system and each one of them has its identity; (2) *ActRule* represents class instances that describe an actuation into the environment; (3) *ActuationEffect* is in charge of grouping different forms of actuation; (4) *Notification* is a subclass of *ActuationEffect* and describes a text message and its recipient; (5) *Actuator* represents devices that can produce an action in the real world; (6) *Sensor* class represents sensors in the real world, in which an individual sensor can provide one or more type of information; (7) *SensorObs*, which describes what should be observed by a specific sensor, and it applies a logical condition associated with a mensuration value; (8) *ObsRule* combines one or more instances of *SensorObs* with one instance of ActRule to associate several observations with one response action; (9) *LogicalCondition* represents types of logical condition that can be applied to a *SensorObs*; and (10) *ObsActRule* class associates a set of *ObsRule* to a set of *ActRule* to associate several observations with several response actions.

4.3 M2T Transformation from DSML4ClinicalScores to Deklaer

The goal of the M2T transformation implemented by our approach is an OWL ontology described by the Deklaer language. To implement the M2T transformation, we used the Acceleo[2] tool, which is available as an EMF plug-in. Acceleo defines transformation rules through templates and queries. In Acceleo, a template defines a transformation stage (i.e., code text), and a query obtains values or collection of objects from the specified concrete model.

First, to understand the M2T transformation applied by our approach, it is necessary to identify which concepts the *DSML4ClinicalScores* metamodel is capable of generating for the *Deklaer* ontology. Table 2 shows the mapping between the concepts of these languages. For each specified instance of the type

---

[2] http://www.eclipse.org/acceleo.

Rule in the concrete model created by the *DSML4ClinicalScores*, the transformation uses its *id* attribute to generate corresponding data properties *has_id* for the *ActRule*, *ObsRule* and *ObsActRule* classes of the *Deklaer* ontology. At the same way, for each specified instance of the type *Rule* in the concrete model, the transformation uses its *score* attribute to generate corresponding data property *has_notificationText* for the *Notification* class of the *Deklaer* ontology. Finally, all object attributes of the type *Expression* in the concrete model produce all data properties for the *SensorObs* class of the *Deklaer* ontology.

Table 2. The mapping between the concepts of DSML4ClinicalScores and Deklaer.

DSML4ClinicalScores concepts	Deklaer concepts
Rule:id	*ActRule:has_id*
	ObsRule:has_id
	ObsActRule:has_id
Rule:score	*Notification:has_notificationText*
Rule:Expression	*SensorObs:has_valueOneRestriction*
	SensorObs:has_name
	SensorObs:isAbout
	SensorObs:has_numberOfValues
	SensorObs:has_logicalCondition
	SensorObs:has_unityOfMeasurement

The transformation process begins with the instantiation of the *Specification* object of the concrete model created by the *DSML4ClinicalScores*. After that, all specified objects of the type *Variable* and *Rule* within the concrete model are investigated by transformation rules, in order to find specified objects of the type *Sensor* and their rules. For each *Sensor* object found in the concrete model, our approach generates corresponding codes in the *SensorObs*, *ActRule*, *Notification*, *ObsRule*, and *ObsActRule* classes within the *Deklaer* ontology.

5   Evaluation

In this section, we describe how we evaluated our approach and the obtained results. The evaluation aimed: (1) to illustrate the expressiveness of the *DSML4Cli-nicalScores* language through the modeling of different concrete cases and (2) to demonstrate the effectiveness of the proposed approach through the development of a case study.

5.1   The DSML4ClinicalScores Validation

To illustrate the expressiveness of the *DSML4ClinicalScores* language, from those list of 89 clinical scores analyzed in the Sect. 4.1, we developed eight concrete case studies based on clinical scores that exploit different characteristics regarding variables, calculation rules and evaluations. The list of selected clinical scores is described in Table 3 and all specifications are available on the MD+Calc[3] platform. The *DSML4ClinicalScores* allowed correctly to model the proposed concrete cases. The plugins containing the *DSML4ClinicalScores* metamodel and the modeling of these mentioned concrete cases can be obtained through the following URL: http://www.lsdi.ufma.br/projetos/mdd4clinicalscores.

Table 3. List of clinical score used in the *DSML4ClinicalScores* validation.

Clinical score	Health domain
TIMI risk index	Acute coronary
HAS-BLED score	Bleeding risk
MEWS score	Degree of illness
CPIS score	Pneumonia
CURB-65 score	Pneumonia
Wells' criteria for PE	Pulmonary embolism
CHADS$_2$ score	Stroke
4Ts score	Thrombocytopenia

5.2 Case Study – CURB-65 Score

To demonstrate the effectiveness of our approach, we developed a case study for the CURB-65 score. The case study is a method that serves to evaluate a research theory, confirming that in one specific case this theory works [27]. Here we describe the process of generating a mHealth application focused on the evaluation of CURB-65 clinical score, involving all steps from the specification of its concrete model by the *DSML4ClinicalScores* to the production of the OWL ontology described according to the *Deklaer* language. The CURB-65 score specification is detailed in Table 1 at Sect. 2.1.

Creating the Concrete Model. The first step to create the *Deklaer* ontology focused on the CURB-65 score is the modeling of this specification according to the *DSML4ClinicalScores* metamodel. Figure 3 shows the concrete model of CURB-65 in a UML object diagram format. Because this clinical score has a complex specification and due to space limitations, the concrete model is only partially presented here. To start the modeling of CURB-65 score, the user declares a set of attributes (i.e., *id*, *description*, and *type*), which are part of the *Specification* object. After that, the user can define the CURB-65 score variables, rules for calculating the score and evaluations.

---
[3] https://www.mdcalc.com.

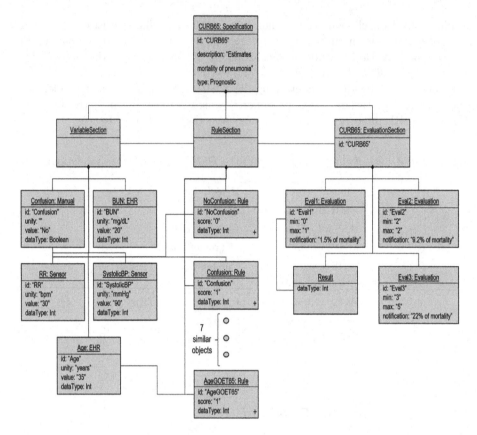

Fig. 3. The CURB-65 concrete model according to the *DSML4ClinicalScores* meta-model.

Figure 3 illustrates the modeling of variables, rules for calculating the score, and CURB-65 evaluations according to the *DSML4ClinicalScores* metamodel. The concrete model has 5 objects of the type *Variable* and respective attributes related to confusion, blood urea nitrogen (BUN), respiratory rate, systolic blood pressure, and age.

Additionally, we can also see in Fig. 3 examples of how to model the CURB-65 scoring rules, specifically those related to confusion and age variables of this clinical score. For example, to compose the rule of the type "does the patient have confusion?" with "String=NoConfusion" as identifier, the user can perform the following: (1) he/she creates a *RelationalOperator* of the type "EqualThan"; (2) from this relational operator, he/she creates one instance of *Constant* with value "False", and one instance of *RefVariable* associated with the variable with "Confusion" as identifier.

Finally, Fig. 3 shows only three possible objects of the type Evaluation, which are part of the CURB-65 evaluation, including their scoring range and respective

Fig. 4. The CURB-65 ontology according to the *Deklaer* language.

interpretation, and one object of the type Result, which represents the final result of the clinical score.

Generating the Deklaer Ontology. The second and last step to create the *Deklaer* ontology focused on the CURB-65 score is the submission of the concrete model of Fig. 3 to an M2T transformation implemented by our approach. Figure 4 shows the resulting ontology after this transformation. In detail, we see all generated individuals for *ActRule, Notification, ObsActRule, ObsRule,* and *SensorObs* classes. Both *ActRule* and *Notification* classes describe the possible scores for the defined rules. The *SensorObs* class detail the format of each specified rule. In turn, both *ObsActRule* and *ObsRule* classes associate each possible punctuation with its corresponding observation.

It is important to note that the *Deklaer* ontology in Fig. 4 doesn't have all the required concepts described by the *Deklaer* ontology. Therefore, this ontology should be edited manually in order to the *Deklaer* framework is capable of generating the mHealth application focused on the CURB-65 score. In this case, the edition refers to the inclusion of the data property *Sensor:has_sensorName* and the *Entity* class (e.g., an individual named Allan) and respective data and object properties. These data cannot be expressed at the *DSML4ClinicalScores* metamodel level because they are associated with each particular monitoring scenario.

5.3   Discussion

Analysis of the Results. To illustrate the expressiveness of the *DSML4Clinical-Scores* language, we modeled the eight concrete cases of different clinical scores. In these developed concrete cases, *DSML4ClinicalScores* allowed the user to correctly model different types of variables for a clinical score, regardless of whether they were manually inserted or electronically obtained. For example, it is possible to express manual data such as pain perception from the patient, as well as electronic data such as the age or gender of a patient and sensor measures. Additionally, *DSML4ClinicalScores* allowed the user to correctly model different formats of logical, relational, and mathematical rules. For example, it is possible to express a regular mathematical probability (i.e., mathematical format), as well as a complex rule involving composed relational expressions (i.e., logical and relational formats). Finally, *DSML4ClinicalScores* allowed the user to correctly model

Fig. 5. *ICare* application described in Pinheiro et al. [25].

several types of evaluation. For example, it is possible to express a single probability as evaluation such as a probability result, as well as more complex assessments, which define an evaluation into two or three layers, such as those defined by the Wells' Criteria for Pulmonary Embolism.

To demonstrate the viability of the proposed approach, we developed a case study involving the CURB-65 score. This case study encompassed all the activities necessary for modeling the clinical score specification and the transformation process of this specification into the *Deklaer* ontology. The M2T transformation implemented by our approach proved to be capable of generating concepts related to the *Deklaer* ontology. However, the resulting ontology is an incomplete version of that language. An example of an acceptable application is described in Pinheiro et al. [25], as shown in Fig. 5. Unlike the ontology of Fig. 4, this application describes the monitored individual (named *Dalva*) and the monitoring sensors (*ZephyrBloodPressure*, *ZephyrBpm* and *ZephyrTemperature*) used for remote patient monitoring.

Benefits of the Proposed Solution. In mHealth, the current solutions for automating clinical scores are limited. In this context, we propose to address the following problem related to the traditional development of mHealth applications for clinical scores: the development process of mobile solutions for clinical scores using traditional approaches requires to build a new software for each clinical score, even if they have similar characteristics, repeating all development steps, which limits productivity.

Concerning the productivity, our approach has contributed to the provision of *DSML4ClinicalScores*, which allows the user to specify clinical scores through a domain-specific language and, combined with the use of transformation rules, it semi-automatically generates a mHealth application for a provided score. The language provides a metamodel that embraces the main characteristics of the most relevant clinical scores described in the literature. To develop a new software for a specific clinical score, it is only necessary to adapt its specificities to the *DSML4ClinicalScores* metamodel and use its resulting software components. Thus, our approach allows to reduce or disregard some steps of the traditional software development process, such as requirements survey, system design and part of the implementation, when the application domain is the automation of clinical scores.

Limitations. Considering the methodology used in the development of the *DSML4ClinicalScores* language, our approach does not guarantee that other clinical scores, which are not included in the list of 89 clinical scores whose specifications were the basis for the definition of this metamodel, can be correctly modeled by that language.

6   Conclusion and Future Work

This paper presented an innovative approach applied in the domains of mHealth and clinical scores. For this purpose, we employed metamodeling and model transformation techniques proposed by Model-Driven Development. To specify different clinical scores, we used a domain-specific modeling language called *DSML4ClinicalScores*, which models the main characteristics of these specifications. Then, we perform a M2T transformation that creates an OWL ontology based on the *Deklaer* language. The proposed approach was evaluated considering the expressiveness of *DSML4ClinicalScores* through the modeling of eight clinical scores, and the viability of this approach through the development of case study for a specific clinical score.

Our approach proved to be a plausible solution for solving clinical scores in mHealth. It is an initial effort that can be improved in some of aspects. First, since the *DSML4ClinicalScores* metamodel uses Ecore, the Eclipse Modeling Framework provides an integrated development environment that allows the developer to create an authoring tool from an Ecore metamodel. An authoring tool can assist healthcare professionals to specify several clinical scores and, hence, support the clinical practice within hospital environments. Second, we plan to develop an application for managing the data from the *Deklaer* framework and providing the evaluation of a specific clinical score. This application will prove the integration viability between our approach and the *Deklaer* framework for automating clinical scores in mHealth.

References

1. Aakre, C., Dziadzko, M., Keegan, M., Herasevich, V.: Automating clinical score calculation within the electronic health record. Appl. Clin. Inform. **8**(2), 369–380 (2017)
2. Aakre, C., Dziadzko, M., Herasevich, V.: Towards automated calculation of evidence-based clinical scores. World J. Methodol. **7**(1), 16–24 (2017)
3. Thompson, G.: Clinical scoring systems in the management of suspected appendicitis in children. In: Lander, A. (ed.) APPENDICITIS, chapter 4, pp. 63–86. InTech, Rijeka (2012). https://doi.org/10.5772/25485
4. Falk, G., Fahey, T.: Clinical prediction rules. Br. Med. J. **339**(2), b2899 (2009)
5. Adams, S., Leveson, S.: Clinical prediction rules. Br. Med. J. **344**(1), 1–7 (2012)
6. Lim, W., et al.: Defining community acquired pneumonia severity on presentation to hospital: an international derivation and validation study. Thorax **58**(5), 377–382 (2003)
7. Gronback, R.: Eclipse Modeling Project: A Domain-Specific Language (DSL) toolkit, 1st edn. Addison-Wesley, Boston (2009)
8. Voelter, M.: DSL Engineering: Designing, Implementing and Using Domain-specific Languages (2010). http://dslbook.org. Accessed 21 Aug 2019
9. Kleppe, A.: Software Language Engineering: Creating Domain-Specific Languages Using Metamodels, 1st edn. Addison-Wesley, Boston (2008)
10. Schmidt, D.: Guest editor's introduction: model-driven engineering. IEEE Comput. **39**(1), 25–31 (2006)

11. Fowler, M.: Domain-Specific Languages, 1st edn. Addison-Wesley, Boston (2010)
12. Mernik, M., Heering, J., Sloane, A.: When and how to develop domain-specific languages. ACM Comput. Surv. **37**(1), 316–344 (2005)
13. Cook, K., Modena, B., Simon, R.: Improvement in asthma control using a minimally burdensome and proactive smartphone. J. Allergy Clin. Immunol. **13**(1), 730–737 (2016)
14. Schatz, M., et al.: Asthma control test: reliability, validity, and responsiveness in patients not previously followed by asthma specialists. J. Allergy Clin. Immunol. **117**(1), 549–556 (2006)
15. Aminian, A., Alberts, J., Clemence, S., Schauer, P.: Bariatric surgery decision-making calculator: a novel mobile app for evidence-based clinical practice. Surg. Obes. Relat. Dis. **13**(1), s147 (2017)
16. Aminian, A., Brethauer, S., Sharafkhah, M., Schauer, P.: Development of a sleeve gastrectomy risk calculator. Surg. Obes. Relat. Dis. **11**(1), 758–764 (2015)
17. Aminian, A., et al.: Who should get extended trhomboprophylaxis after bariatric surgery?: a risk assesment tool to guide indications for post-discharge pharmaco-prophylaxis. Ann. Surg. **265**(1), 143–150 (2017)
18. Aminian, A., et al.: Individualized metabolic surgery score: procedure selection based on diabetes severity. Ann. Surg. **266**(1), 650–657 (2017)
19. Stamate, C., et al.: The cloudUPDRS app: a medical device for the clinical assessment of Parkinson's Disease. Pervasive Mobile Comput. **43**(1), 146–166 (2018)
20. Goetz, C., et al.: Movement disorder society-sponsored revision of the unified Parkinson's disease rating scale (MDS-UPDRS): scale presentation and clinimetric testing results. Mov. Disord. **23**(1), 2129–2170 (2008)
21. Jenkinson, C., Fitzpatrick, R., Peto, V., Greenhall, R., Hyman, N.: The Parkinson's disease questionnaire (PDQ-39): development and validation of a Parkinson's disease summary index score. Age Ageing **26**(1), 353–357 (1997)
22. Pereira-Azevedo, N., Osório, L., Fraga, A., Roobol, M.: Rotterdam prostate cancer risk calculator: development and usability testing of the mobile phone app. JMIR Cancer **3**(1), e1 (2017)
23. Roobol, M., et al.: Importance of prostate volume in the european randomised study of screening for prostate cancer (ERSPC) risk calculators: results from the prostate biopsy collaborative group. World J. Urol. **30**(1), 149–155 (2012)
24. Barbosa, A., Silva, F., Coutinho, L., Santos, D., Teles, A.: A domain-specific modeling language for specification of clinical scores in mobile health. In: 14th International Conference on Evaluation of Novel Approaches to Software Engineering, pp. 104–113. SCITEPRESS, Heraklion (2019)
25. Pinheiro, V., Neumann, G., Endler, M., Silva, F.: An ontology-driven framework for generating IoT applications using ContextNet. In: IEEE Symposium on Computers and Communications, pp. 608–614. IEEE, Natal (2018)
26. Irawan, H.: Ecore (2010). https://wiki.eclipse.org/ecore. Accessed 22 Aug 2019
27. Yin, R.: Case Study Research: Designs and Methods, 5th edn. Sage, Thousand Oaks (2014)

Model-Driven Software Development Combined with Semantic Mutation of UML State Machines

Anna Derezinska[(✉)] [ID] and Łukasz Zaremba

Institute of Computer Science, Warsaw University of Technology,
Nowowiejska 15/19, 00-665 Warsaw, Poland
A.Derezinska@ii.pw.edu.pl

Abstract. The paper presents an approach to semantic mutation of state machines that specify class behavior in Model-Driven Software Development. The mutations are aimed at different variants of UML state machine behavior. Mutation testing of a target application allows to compare different semantic interpretations and verify a set of test cases. We present a notation of a process combining model-driven development with semantic mutation and semantic consequence-oriented mutations. Origin and details of the proposed mutation operators are discussed. The approach has been supported by the Framework for eXecutable UML (FXU) that creates a C# application from UML classes and state machines. The tool architecture has been reengineered in order to apply semantic mutation operators into the model-driven development process and realize testing on a set of semantic mutants. The tool and the implemented mutation operators have been verified in a case study on a status service for a social network.

Keywords: Model-Driven Software Development · State machine code generation · Mutation testing · Framework for eXecutable UML (FXU) · C#

1 Introduction

Improvement of test sets is a challenging task which can be assisted by mutation testing [1, 2]. Software artefacts could be modified in different approaches to mutation testing. Testing of resulting applications can be further verified against test sets in order to evaluate their quality and enhance with new test cases.

Mutation testing could be applied to any kind of software applications, in particular, those build in Model-Driven Software Development (MDSD) [3]. In this case, not only code-based, but also model-based mutations could be considered. Moreover, potential source models for MDSD could be, apart from structural models, like UML classes, also behavioral models, as state machines [4]. A proper behavior interpretation is in such case of the high importance, because behavior of these models could be directly and automatically reflected in operation of the target application.

In this paper, we address a problem of a process that combines MDSD with semantic mutation of state machine behavior. An important issue is to automate these

© Springer Nature Switzerland AG 2020
E. Damiani et al. (Eds.): ENASE 2019, CCIS 1172, pp. 204–226, 2020.
https://doi.org/10.1007/978-3-030-40223-5_10

activities and integrate them in a user friendly manner. One of challenges is automating of test execution for different semantic variants, preserving consistency of generated and supplemented code, as well as code of test cases.

This paper extends the work presented in the ENASE'2019 conference [5]. It discusses steps of the processes of concern and some formal issues. The proposed mutation operators are explained in more detail and supplemented with examples of the operator origin. We have also added more information about tool support, its architecture, notation of semantic specification, and realized process. Finally, we present a case study on a social service that has been used in experimental evaluation of the approach.

Within this paper, we focus on all state machine concepts approved in the UML specification [6]. A target application is built in an object-oriented programming language, especially in C#.

The rest of the paper is organized as follows: fundamentals and basic notions of the combined process are presented in Sect. 2. In Sect. 3, related work is discussed. The semantic mutation operators, their origin and meaning, are presented in Sect. 4. Information of the automatic support for the process are described in Sect. 5. In Sect. 6, a case study and the experimental results are discussed. Finally, Sect. 7 concludes the paper.

2   Process Fundamentals

The basic notions of mutation testing and processes of concern will be introduced.

2.1   Mutation Testing

A main goal of mutation testing is evaluation of quality of a test set and support for development of additional tests if necessary. A "standard" mutation testing approach refers to a program and its set of tests. Based on a given program, a set of its mutants is created. A *mutant* is a variant of the original program into which a simple change, so-called *mutation*, was introduced. A mutation is typically a simple syntactic change of the program. A mutated program should be syntactically correct, but its functionality can differ from the original program. This difference could be detected by appropriate test cases. In the mostly used first-order mutation, a change is injected into one program location per one mutant. A kind of a change, in fact a kind of a program transformation, is specified by a *mutation operator*. Different sets of mutation operators are specified for different programming languages [1].

The basic process of mutation testing can consist of the following steps:

1. Preparing an original program
2. Generation of a set of mutants for the program.
3. Running all program mutants against a set of test cases.
4. Evaluation of results, creation additional test cases if necessary (and repeat from step 3).
5. Optionally correcting faults in the original program (and repeat from step 1).

Apart from a typical code mutation, different source notations can be mutated, e.g., domain libraries, selected features of a paradigm – like concurrent mechanism, logical constraints, component contracts, UML models, and other specifications. According to a selected notation, corresponding mutation operators often imitate possible faults in the field of concern.

A special kind of mutation, discussed in this paper, is semantic mutation [7]. In this case a source notation can remain unchanged, but different mutants refer to different variants of semantic interpretations.

2.2 Model to Code Transformation

Model to code transformation is a core of Model-Driven Software Development. As a source of a transformation, structural models, e.g. class diagrams, as well as behavioral models, e.g. state machines, can be used. When a kind of complete behavioral specification is submitted, e.g. a complete state machine for each class, the target application could automatically operate as given in the input specification.

The basic MDSD process consists of the following steps:

1. Preparing of source models
2. Verification of models
3. Generation of code from models
4. Supplementing program with additional code, and building an executable project using additional standard and specialized libraries [result: code project].
5. Program execution and testing

In general, an MDSD process could be more complicated and cover many feedback loops. After model verifying or code testing the models could be improved, handwritten code can be reverse-engineered to models, modified models have to be transformed, new code can be supplemented, etc. Moreover, at different process stages some tests can be written or generated, e.g. prepared as models or code before source model development, after verification of models, based on the generated code, etc.

2.3 MSDS Process Combined with Mutation Testing

In general, mutation testing can be combined within an MDSD process in different ways. We can take into account various selection of:

– process stages at which mutations are applied,
– source artefacts into which mutations are introduced,
– types of software features that are mutated,
– process stages at which software behavior is evaluated,
– kinds of verification applied to the software.

When models and code are mutated, we can distinguish the following steps in a combined generic process. The main created artefacts are given in brackets.

1. Preparing of source models [result: a base model with its semantics].

2. Mutation of source models with structural mutation operators of models [result: mutated models, unchanged semantics].
3. Verification of mutated models against model constraints
4. Generation of code from models, and creation of mutants
5. Supplementing program with additional code, and building executable projects using additional standard and specialized libraries [result: code projects].
6. Creating of sets of mutants at a code level [result: code projects].
7. Running program and its mutants against a set of test cases.
8. Evaluation of results, creation additional test cases if necessary (and repeat from step 7).
9. Optionally correcting faults in the original model (and repeat from step 1).

In the above process, semantics does not change, therefore, it has not to be specially considered. Information about a mutant constitutes a set of models or a program code, in dependence of the process stage.

Different situation is in the case of semantic mutation. Below, we show the basic steps in a combined generic process in which models are not structurally mutated, but a model semantics is mutated.

1. Preparing of source models [result: a model with its base semantics].
2. Mutation of source models with semantic mutation operators of models [result: unchanged model, mutated semantics].
3. Verification of mutated models against model constraints
4. Generation of code from models, and creation of mutants
5. Supplementing program with additional code, and building executable projects using additional standard and specialized libraries [result: code projects].
6. Creating of sets of mutants at a code level [result: code projects].
7. Running program and its mutants against a set of test cases.
8. Evaluation of results, creation additional test cases if necessary (and repeat from step 7).
9. Optionally correcting faults in the original model (and repeat from step 1).

An important difference should be noticed in the considered artefacts. In the second variant of the combined generic process, the models are not modified, but variants of the base semantics are created.

In this paper, we will discuss realization of a subset of the latter proposed process. We focus on semantic mutation, therefore, the final application will be not mutated at code-level, i.e. step 6 will be omitted.

2.4   Basic Definitions

Semantic of state machines described in [6] builds on a state machine elements interpreted in a given manner. Determination of a practical semantics to be used in a MDSD process is, therefore, a selection of one of interpretations to each notion, taking into account possible combination of interpretations.

Let us denote by F – a set of all concepts of state machines. A concept or a set of concepts can be associated with a unique interpretation or with a set of possible semantic interpretations. We can assume that a set of interpretations applicable for a given concept or a group of concepts is countable and finite. Each element of a powerset of F, $\Pi(F)$ can be associated with a set of applicable interpretations $I(\Pi (F))$.

Therefore, in a context of a state machine, we can specify a semantics S, as a set of functions which map an element of $\Pi(F)$ into a selected interpretation from a set $I(\Pi(F))$.

In a code-based, or other structural mutation, a mutant is a single artefact, for example a modified program or model. In semantic mutation, a mutant that would be tested is specified by a tuple <P, S>, where P is a project code and S one of semantics.

3   Related Work

We discuss here work related to interpretation of state machine behavior, transformation of UML state machines and mutation testing.

3.1   Behavioral State Machines

UML has incorporated some existing modeling notions, as the well-known concepts of state machines. State machines are a kind of hierarchical, event-driven automata proposed by Harel [8]. They are a powerful modelling notion to describe behavior of classes or subsystems. State machines are widely used models in embedded system domain, and other application areas [9].

While interpreting behavior specified by a state machine, we can face many possible variants. The UML specification [6] provides the general boundaries of state machines accepted in UML models. However, it leaves open many unspecified issues and semantic variation points. Moreover, a precise semantics is not a part of the official specification. Therefore, different variants of state machine behavior within UML and apart can be met [10].

This situation might be acceptable during a model development, assuming that a model should cover various approaches. Though, in some cases this could lead to ambiguous interpretations. Higher precision is especially important when a model has to be interpreted or transformed to an executable application. Moreover, in most of implemented solutions, there are different interpretations of behavioral variants, but often without direct declarations about their semantics.

One of possibilities is leave to a user decision about behavioral variants. For example, event handling and queuing polices can be decided by a user of the Umple tool [11]. A similar approach, in which different variants are selected by a user were proposed by Chauvel and Jézéquel [12]. Prout presented another generic approach to creation of a code generator parametrized with semantic variants [13].

An MDSD tool can be associated with a primary selection of possible semantics. Therefore, during development of initial versions of the FXU tool, different problems of state machine interpretation have been resolved [14, 15]. In the case discussed in this paper, incorporation of different variants of state machine behavior into solutions offered to a user were considered as a mutation in mutation testing.

3.2   Transformation of UML State Machines

While considering UML models, class models are the main sources of transformations [16]. These structural models contain many notions which have direct mapping to basic structures used in object-oriented programming languages. Apart from structural models, behavioral models, especially state machines, are also common sources in model to code transformations [4]. Different methods are used to transform concepts of state machines into code, e.g., replication of states by attributes, applying state design patterns, and others, [11, 17–21].

An alternative to the code generation is an interpretation technique. It could be performed by direct execution of code [22]. Some case studies reported in [23] showed that interpreting UML state machine, although much slower, can give acceptable results in the context of network and system management.

It should be noted that the most of solutions dealing with state machines take into account only a restricted subset of UML notions. More advanced features, such as composite states, in particular with orthogonal regions, different pseudostates, including deep and shallow history, deferred events, entry/do/exit actions or internal transitions have often been omitted. This is, for example, in case of code generation supported by some commercial tools – as IBM Rational Software Architect Developer [24].

State machines taken into account in fUML (Foundation Subset for Executable UML) are also limited [25]. The seminal description of state machine coding in C++ also omits concurrency issues [18].

There are some approaches that try to cover state machine models in more comprehensive way. They considered composite states [11, 17], state machines labelled with constrains in the OCL language [21], or composite states with history [14].

Some solutions apply more complete set of state machine concepts, as IBM Raphsody [26], Umple [11], although most of them do not support the C# language. A distinguishing feature of a Framework for eXecutable UML (FXU) [27] is covering of full UML state machines with a target to the C# language.

3.3   Mutation Testing for Programs and Models

Mutation testing has been primarily applied as fault injection method for programs written in different programming languages, e.g. C, Fortran, Java, C++ [1, 2]. Mutation operators and tools have also been developed for programs in C# [28, 29].

Mutation testing approach has also been used to mutate specifications, constraints, and UML models [30], e.g. class models [31, 32].

Automata-based models were also considered as a mutation source in different approaches. Fabbri et al. focused on mutations in finite state machines [33] and hierarchical state charts [34]. Much research on state machines were dealing with syntactical changes of diagrams [35]. Some others related to syntactic changes of specification expressions labelling transitions in state machines. Those expressions were mutated in a similar way as any other programming code.

Another direction of mutation testing is semantic mutation. Semantic mutation has been specified for behavioral models, mainly state machines [7], in some variants called an implementation mutation [35, 36]. In semantic mutation, graph structure of a model is not changed, as in a "standard" mutation testing. In this approach, different semantic interpretations of a model are analyzed [37, 38].

4 Mutation Operators

Semantic mutation operators can be defined for different aspects of a state machine behavior.

4.1 Origin of Semantic Mutation Operators

In the code-based mutation testing [1, 2] many mutation operators were defined based on common mistakes performed by developers. Expert analysis of programming paradigm, e.g. object-oriented constructions, as well as specific features of different programming languages contributed also to specification of various mutation testing operators.

In case of semantic mutation of UML state machines, the primary source of mutation operators is the UML specification [6]. Operators can be driven from variants included in the specification and some ambiguities or issues left undefined.

Other variants of state machine behavior could be taken into account, exceeding the UML limitations. It could be, for example, original Harel-based statemachine as specified within the STATEMATE environment [39]. However, within this paper we would only discuss approaches that are consistent with the UML specification.

Many of UML specification variants correspond to orthogonal regions in a state machine. As an example, we consider entering a composite state using a history pseudostate. We examine the possible interpretations and show how one of semantic mutation operators was specified.

A composite state can be entered via a history pseudostate, as *State3* in Fig. 1. If *State3* were not active before, or its last active substate were a final state, then after entering *State3* the substate *State3_1* will be active.

This is determined by general specification rules. If (i) a composite state was not active before, or (ii) a last active substate included in this composite state was a final state, entering the composite state via a history pseudostate means entering via a *default history state*. However, specification of such a state in the model is not obligatory. This description is sufficient if a composite state has only single region.

Though, when a composite state comprises many orthogonal regions then entering via a history can be interpreted in different ways. This follows from various UML constrains:

- A composite state can include only one history pseudosate, regardless of the number of its regions.
- Only one transition can be outgoing a history pseudostate.
- Between substates included in different orthogonal regions of a composite state no transitions can be specified.
- Entering a composite state causes entering all its orthogonal regions.

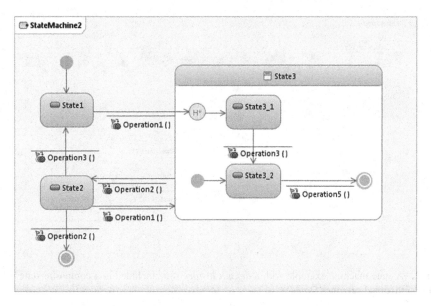

Fig. 1. A state machine example with a *default history state* included in a single region composite state (*State3*).

Therefore, a default history state can only be defined in one orthogonal region that includes the history pseudostate. The remaining orthogonal regions of this composite state have no default history states. Behavior of a region without its default history state can be specified in the following ways:

1. *Default Entry.* The region of the composite state is entered according to its default rule.
2. *Automatic Completion.* The region of the composite state is treated as realized and finished.
3. *Ill-formulation.* The model is considered to be ill-formulated. This situation could abandon processing of the state machine due to an error.

These interpretations are illustrated with an example (Fig. 2). We can consider a situation when *State2* is active and the next event is processing of *Operation2*. The transitions terminate the composite state *State3* using the history pseudostate. Therefore, for the upper region of *State3*, the default history state will be entered, in this case *State4_2*. For the bottom region of *State3* the default history state could not be specified, and one of the above interpretations could be selected. In case of the first interpretation, *State5_1* will be entered. In the second case, this region is counted to be completed. Finally, according to the third interpretation, the state machine is ill-formulated. The discussed interpretations are further used in a definition of a semantic mutation operator (IV.2 in Table 4).

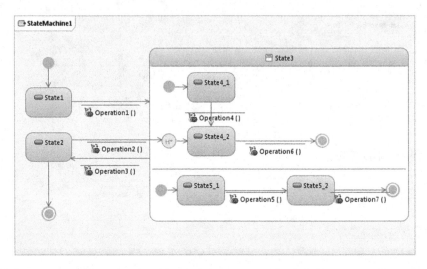

Fig. 2. A state machine example with a *default history state* included in a composite state with many orthogonal regions (*State3*).

4.2 Semantic Mutation Operators of State Machine Behavior

The proposed operators can be divided into several groups referring to different aspects of state machine behavior. In this section we discuss these operators that are summarized in tables (Tables 1, 2, 3 and 4).

Table 1. Semantic mutation operators dealing with event processing.

ID	Operator	Considered semantics
I.1	Queue policy for selection of events stored in an event pool for a state machine	(1) FIFO queue of events
		(2) FIFO queue of events, with exception of competition event and time events
		(3) Different priorities assigned to different event types (*MessageEvent*, *ChangeEvent*, *TimeEvent*). FIFO policy within events of the same type
		(4) Priority queue for all events
		(5) LIFO queue of events
I.2	Policy for detection of a change event trigger associated with an expression	(1) Evaluation of an expression value periodically for a given time interval, and its comparison
		(2) An expression is calculated and checked once during a single StateMachine step
		(3) An expression value is constantly monitored and its change (from *False* to

(continued)

Table 1. (*continued*)

ID	Operator	Considered semantics
		True) triggers immediately the corresponding change event
I.3	Policy of removal of a change event from a state machine event pool	(1) An event is removed from an event pool any time the expression associated with the event has changed to *False*
		(2) The corresponding expression is calculated during processing of the event. The event is removed from the queue if its expression amounts to *False*
		(3) Further changes of the associated expression have no impact the change event processing, are disregarded
I.4	Selection of handling of a deferred event for a state machine	(1) A deferred event is placed again in the corresponding event queue, as if the event has encountered once again
		(2) A deferred event is added to a special pool of deferred events, globally defined for the whole state machine
		(3) A deferred event is placed in a special pool of deferred events which is defined individually for each state
I.5	Queue policy for processing deferred events of a state	(1) FIFO queue of deferred events
		(2) Different priorities assigned to different event types (*MessageEvent*, *ChangeEvent*, *TimeEvent*). FIFO policy within events of the same type
		(3) Priority queue for all events
		(4) LIFO queue of deferred events

Mutation Operators of Event Processing. State machine behavior is defined by a notion of steps, as in a general labelled transition system. One of basic fundamentals of semantics of UML state machine is *run-to-completion step*. One single event is processed during a single step of a state machine behavior. Management of events is supported by a queue, *event pool*, that stores encountering events. The queue is specified for each state machine of a model.

Policy of a queue is not determined in the UML specification. Selection of five different queue strategies establishes the first operator (I.1 in Table 1).

There are different kinds of events that are considered in a state machine. One of them is a *change event*. A change event is associated with a Boolean expression. An event occurs any time when its value changes from False to True. However, the specification does not determine more details, i.e. when the expression is evaluated, what happens if the value changes back to False before an event is detected, etc. Different kinds of a change event management are considered in two mutation operators (I.2 and I.3 in Table 1). Operator I.2 covers three policies of detecting an expression change. A change event could be placed into an event pool and waits for processing. Operator I.3 determines policies whether and when the event should be removed from the queue if its value changes to False before processing of the event.

Moreover, some events can be *deferred* in a state. Occurrences of such an event remain in a queue until the event is no longer deferred for all active states from a current state configuration, or the deferred event is explicitly accepted in a trigger of a transition under concern. Two operators (I.4, I.5) deal with the semantics of deferred events. Policy of placing deferred events in a queue can be selected using operator I.4. Policy of selecting deferred event to be processed are considered in operator I.5.

Mutation Operators of Time Management. In the general UML specification there are only limited notions of time management. No time delay intervals between time events are established. Event processing time is not predefined neither bounded, by for example some minimal or maximal time. The time issues are open, in order to meet requirements of different semantic variants that could be associated with different application domains. Time concerns might be specified with the MARTE profile [40]. In this paper we have only referred to basic clocks defined in MARTE, logical clock and chronometric clock. Therefore, only one mutation operator for selection of a time processing strategy is proposed (Table 2). More details of MARTE are not considered in this paper.

Table 2. Semantic mutation operators dealing with time management.

ID	Operator	Considered semantics
II.1	Time processing policy in a state machine	(1) Time events are processed one after another
		(2) Logical clock is used for time evaluation and processing of time events
		(3) Chronometric clock is used for time evaluation and processing of time events

Mutation Operators of Handling Composite States with Orthogonal Regions. States in a state machine can be simple or composite. A composite state may have one or more orthogonal regions. Using many orthogonal regions, we can model concurrent behavior within a state. Semantic of transition realization into and from such a composite state undergoes the run-to-completion step principle. However, some details are left open in the UML specification.

One of unspecified issues is a kind of concurrency, i.e. how are performed actions considered to be executed simultaneously. The following three approaches have been taken into account. In "truly" concurrent execution, separate physical units are involved, as e.g. different cores of a processor. In this case actions can be realized in the same time. The second variant is a parallel execution, which could be implemented by separate parallel software units, e.g. processes or threads. These software units can be run on different physical units but also on a single core unit. The third approach corresponds to sequential interleaved execution of concurrent actions. These approaches are applied as semantic variants in operators III.1, III.2, and III.3 (Table 3). The operators are related to execution of actions associated with a transition connected to a state with orthogonal regions. Operator III.1 deals with execution of *exit* actions when many source states are left concurrently. Operator III.2 selects strategy for execution of actions of concurrent transitions. Finally, operator III.3 manages *entry* actions in many target states. The actions are supposed to be concurrently executed.

Another undefined issue concern entering a composite state with many orthogonal regions. In UML, a composite state can be entered via an internal initial pseudostate, or an internal substate can be used as a direct target of a transition. There might be a problem, when many orthogonal regions are used. We would call a region to be ambiguous, if it has no initial pseudostate, nor any substate is directly pointed as a starting point. Different strategies resolving this problem are specified in the mutation operator III.4 (Table 3). In this case it is also assumed that no history pseudostate is used.

Table 3. Semantic mutation operators dealing with composite states with orthogonal regions.

ID	Operator	Considered semantics
III.1	Execution policy of *exit* actions to be executed simultaneously	(1) Concurrent execution (physically true concurrent)
		(2) Parallel execution
		(3) Sequential execution
III.2	Execution policy of *transition* actions to be executed simultaneously	(1) Concurrent execution (physically true concurrent)
		(2) Parallel execution
		(3) Sequential execution
III.3	Execution policy of *entry* actions to be executed simultaneously	(1) Concurrent execution (physically true concurrent)
		(2) Parallel execution
		(3) Sequential execution
III.4	Policy for default entry to a composite state with at least one region without an initial pseudostate	(1) Abandonment of an ill-defined model
		(2) Behavior realization in ambiguous regions is omitted
		(3) Ambiguous regions are treated as executed (final sates are reached if appropriate)
		(4) Initial states are selected and entered in ambiguous regions

Mutation Operators of Handling History. Using of history in a composite state is a powerful modeling notion of UML state machines. However, if orthogonal regions are used, the situation might be interpreted in different ways. We propose two mutation operators related to history. The first one (IV.1) selects an interpretation of a default history pseudostate in orthogonal regions in which it is not defined explicitly. The second operator deals with entering an orthogonal state via a history pseudostate. This problem has been discussed in the previous section.

Table 4. Semantic mutation operators dealing with history pseudostates.

ID	Operator	Considered semantics
IV.1	Selection of an interpretation of a default history psudostate	(1) A history pseudostate refers to all regions of the composite orthogonal state in which it is included
		(2) A history pseudostate only refers to the region in which it is included
		(3) A history pseudostate refers to the region in which it is included, and also to other regions of its orthogonal state to which no concurrent direct entry exists
		(4) A history pseudostate is accepted to be valid only if there are concurrent direct entries to all other regions of the orthogonal state, in which it is included. Otherwise, the model is counted to be ill-modelled
IV.2	Default entry to an orthogonal state via a history pseudostate	(1) Default entering a region
		(2) A region is considered to be executed (a final substate is reached)

4.3 Operators for Semantic Consequence-Oriented Mutation

Mutation testing in general can be aimed at revealing weaknesses of test sets. A typical motivation derives from the fact that test cases could not detect all test data that should be determined as errors. In this section, we consider another weakness when test data that should be correct might be treated as errors.

In a level of state machine behavior, such tests could refer to consequences of dispatching the same sequence of events. For a given semantics, behavior of a state machine could be different in some random cases. However, it could be still correct and consistent with the semantics.

In particular, this situation can be observed for composite states with orthogonal regions. Many actions could be performed during one transition. The order of these actions is undefined. There are various correct flows that preserve appropriate order of *entry/exit* and transition actions within a single transition.

Mutation operators that are *oriented to semantic consequence* would generate mutants that reflect such different flows. Further, those mutants are used during testing in order to verify whether some test cases do not classify a correct sequence flaw as an erroneous one.

Realization of an operator for semantic consequence-oriented mutation depends of a selected variant of semantics. Three exemplary operators are shown in Table 5.

Table 5. Operators for semantic consequence-oriented mutation of state machines.

ID	Considered semantics	Operator
V.1	Parallel execution of *entry* actions while incoming orthogonal regions - Semantics (2) for operator III.3	Deterministic order of execution of *entry* actions
V.2	Parallel execution of transitions in orthogonal regions - Semantics (2) for operator III.2	Deterministic order of execution of transitions
V.3	Parallel execution of *exit* actions while outgoing orthogonal regions - Semantics (2) for operator III.1	Deterministic order of execution of *exit* actions

5 Architectural Support for Semantic Mutation

The Framework for eXecutable UML (FXU) has been designed and implemented as a support for a MDSD process targeted at the C# programming language [20]. Its distinguishing feature is consideration of all notions of UML state machines, including different types of events and actions, various pseudostates, history, orthogonal regions in composite states, etc. The framework consists of two main parts, FXU generator and FXU run-time library. The FXU generator translates UML class and state machine models into a corresponding source code. The FXU run-time library provides implementation for all concepts of state machines. The final application combines a generated code, the library, and additional application-specific code.

It is assumed that a state machine semantics is fixed and independent of an input model. The library includes all necessary interpretations of the state machine behavior. Code generated from a model was used for correct model structure and cooperation of appropriate library elements.

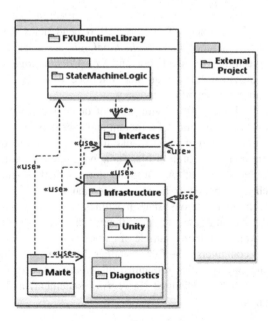

Fig. 3. FXU general architecture.

5.1   General Refactored Architecture

Introduction of semantic mutation has required refactoring of the framework architecture. One of the problems is a "code gap", concerning supplementary code added to the application [41]. When many final applications are created as mutants, the supplementary code should be applied to all the mutants automatically. Other issues concerns performance factors, as e.g. number of projects to be build, number of compilation runs, number of libraries. Four different architecture have been proposed and analyzed [42]. The approach based on configurable library proved to be the best solution. It required only single compilation run and one spot where the additional code should be placed for all generated mutants. It gives an easy extensibility with other semantic mutations and simple performing of iterative mutation testing. The selected approach has been implemented in the extended framework. New architecture allows to provide the mutations independently.

The new library includes the following main components: *StateMachineLogic, Interfaces*, and *Infrastructure* (Fig. 3). An *External Project* cooperates with the interfaces module. It contains a hierarchy of interfaces that corresponds to class hierarchy of different concepts of state machines. Using these interfaces, the state machine elements are accessible in the generated code. The *Interfaces* module includes also other interfaces to cooperate with the internal library objects.

5.2   Container-Based Specification of Mutant Semantics

The *Infrastructure* module consists of two parts: *Unity* and *Diagnostics*. The *Unity* submodule is responsible for dynamic binding of state machine objects according to an interface type or optionally a full name of a context class. The *Diagnostics* submodule provides classes for tracing execution of state machines.

Binding of classes is based on the *dependency injection* pattern realized with dedicated dependency containers. Therefore, all dependencies, except inheritance relations, among classes included in *StateMachineLogic* are deleted. No such dependencies are also between the generated code and *StateMachineLogic* classes. Selection of objects that are provided for a requested interface depends of objects that are registered in a current container of dependency.

A container should be initialized with a set of dependencies. Configuration of a single container represents semantics of a mutant and uses dependency injection based on constructors. It can be stored in an XML-like file. Configurations of all mutants can be specified in a common configuration file. An appropriate configuration has a name which is unique for each mutant. An original, non-mutated program has a default configuration, which corresponds to an unnamed container.

Within a single mutant, various state machines may have different semantics. Therefore, in a configuration of a container, different state machines of a model have to be distinguished. In Appendix I, an example of a configuration file is given. It includes configurations of two containers. The first container describes semantics of an original program. The second one specifies semantics of *Mutant1*. We can observe that the policy of event pool has been changed (in *register* statement) and mapped for one selected state machine.

5.3   Implementation of State Machine Concepts

Realization of different variants of all state machine notions is included in the *State-MachineLogic* module (Fig. 3). Different implementations of provided interfaces are given. This code can have only inheritance relations between classes. Different classes that implement the same interface relate to different semantics of the state machine concept.

For example, an interface of a service for default entry to a region is shown in Fig. 4. It is implemented by three classes. They correspond to different semantic policies realizing default entry.

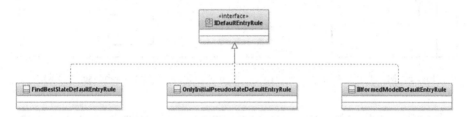

Fig. 4. Realization of different semantic variants.

Therefore, the module can be easily extended by new implementation variants for the interface, i.e. new semantic variants.

The *StateMachineLogic* module also realizes a required order of actions in orthogonal regions, according to a given configuration. Execution of a single transition is treated as an asynchronous task from a Task Parallel Library. Its status can be monitored on-line. The order of task execution follows the given semantic configuration or is concurrent if it is not specified explicitly. Events in a main event loop are handled in the similar way, disregarding a direct usage of threads.

A similar architecture has the *Marte* module (Fig. 3) that implements selected time concepts from the MARTE profile [40]. It has also been refactored to support semantic mutation, but application of MARTE is beyond the scope of this paper.

5.4   Realization of the Combined Process

General activity flows of code generation and mutation testing supported by the tool are shown in Fig. 5. Rounded shaded nodes present activities, and rectangular nodes state for input and output artefacts.

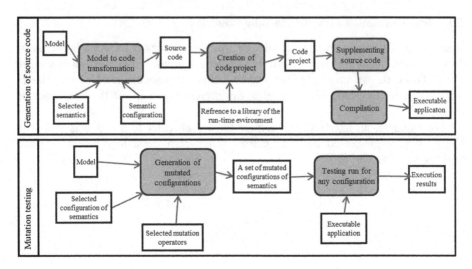

Fig. 5. Mutation testing process with configurable library (configurable semantics).

It could be noticed that only one compilation activity is performed regardless of the mutant numbers; models are input for two activities: code generation and generation of configurations; mutation operators influence only generation of configurations.

Mutation testing can be performed on two levels:

1. *Class Level.* Unit tests of classes are used for direct verification of classes. The class is specified with a state machine. The aim of testing is verification of a class and improvements of its test cases.
2. *Module Level.* Test cases are designed for a whole module modelled with classes and their state machines. The testing is focused on the module functionality.

In the first case, the testing should be performed independently for each class. Semantic operators can modify the whole model, but modification of only one state machine will be counted.

The process schema of module testing is similar to the class testing process. However, initial test cases should be focused of verification of the functionality of the whole module. The main difference is dealing with not only one but many state machines. Therefore, it is possible to mutate all state machines with the same mutation operators (i.e. using the same semantic variants), or to mutate each state machine behavior independently with different mutations.

6 Case Study Evaluation

The proposed approach has been evaluated by mutating a case study. The case study focused on a status service for a social network and was used in some previous research on MDSD [43]. The central part of the system is a presence server (PA) (Fig. 6). Status data of selected users is stored in the system. The services filter information in

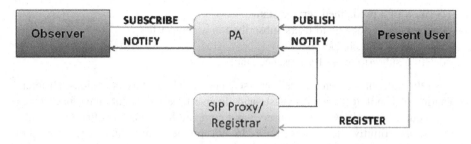

Fig. 6. General structure of the status service with a presence server.

accordance to various relationships among users. The presence server manages statuses of users, i.e. creates presence status, accepts and delates subscribers, notifies statuses to a list of subscribers, etc. The presence server can fetch a current status of a user from the SIP (Session Initial Protocol) service. The system is divided into three layers dealing with client communication, status management, and inter-system communication. Each layer has been modeled with a package including further subpackages and classes. Communication between modules has been modeled by appropriate adapters, that could correspond to mock solutions in the system execution.

The main part of the system, controller of the presence agent, consists of about twenty classes and interfaces. Each class has its state machine that specifies its behavior. In state machines, different modeling structures were applied, including history, *entry/do/exit* actions, transitions with guard conditions and triggers, parallel execution with *fork* and *join* pseudostates, composite states with one and many orthogonal regions, etc. Therefore, the comprehensive set of state machine notions has been practically used.

The status service model has been treated as an input model for the MDSD process combined with mutation testing following all its steps. All models have been transformed into code, and apart from code of state machines, some operations have been additionally implemented or mocked. The final project has been supplemented with the semantic configuration.

In experiments, all semantic and semantic consequence-oriented mutation operators have been applied, resulting in a set of corresponding mutants and their semantics.

The application has been tested at the code-level with a set of unit tests devoted to verification of particular classes and functionality of modules of the status service. The main tasks of the presence service have been tested, such as:

- creation of a predefined service status,
- publication of a status to users subscribed in a contact list,
- subscribing to a contact list,
- deleting subscriptions of a presence status.

All the tasks have been realized by a sequence of elementary operations. Different scenarios of handling various requests and diverse time constraints have been taken into account. In result, we could observe and compare behavior for different semantic variants, as primitive tests sometimes do not provide any differences in system behavior. The tests have not revealed any errors of the original application, but this application has been tested beforehand.

However, dealing with different semantic variant, we could verify our expectations of system behavior. Even though, this required creating adequate test scenarios. Consequently, considering semantic mutations encourages developers to build and improve comprehensive test scenario, although, this activity demands still many manual efforts.

7 Conclusion

A process that combines model-driven software development with mutation testing aimed at semantic mutation of behavioral state machines has been presented and realized in a tool support. To the best of authors' knowledge, there is no any other tool realizing semantic mutation for any kind of models. The appropriate architecture enables this kind of mutation operators to introduce efficiently. We have shown details of semantic mutation operators for state machines and their origin. The approach has been verified experimentally on a status service case study.

There are still some process steps that are too laborious, as preparation of semantic configuration, which could be facilitate by more comprehensive tool support. Another challenge to be taken up is assistance in creation of tests to run with mutants. Furthermore, the process support could be extended with other mutations, as structural mutation of models, and code-mutation of C# programs.

Appendix

Configuration File with a Set of Semantics

```
<container>
    <register type="IEventsPool" mapTo="PriorityEventQueue">
    <constructor>
     <param name="callEventPriority" value="1" />
     <param name="changeEventPriority" value="2" />
     <param name="signalPriority" value="3" />
     <param name="afterEventPriority" value="4" />
     <param name="completionEventPriority" value="5" />
    </constructor>
    </register>
    <register type="IDefaultEntryRule"
mapTo="RequiredExactlyOneInitialPseudostate">
    <constructor/>
    </register>
    <register type="IRegion" mapTo="Region">
    <constructor>
     <param name="defaultEntryRule" dependencyType="IDefaultEntryRule"/>
    </constructor>
    </register>
</container>
<container name="Mutant1">
    <register type="IEventsPool" mapTo="EventQueue">
    <constructor/>
    </register>
    <register name="PresenceAgent.utils.Status" type="IEventsPool"
mapTo="PriorityEventQueue">
    <constructor>
     <param name="callEventPriority" value="1" />
     <param name="changeEventPriority" value="2" />
     <param name="signalPriority" value="3" />
     <param name="afterEventPriority" value="4" />
     <param name="completionEventPriority" value="5" />
    </constructor>
    </register>
    <register type="IDefaultEntryRule" mapTo="UseMostAppropiateState">
    <constructor/>
    </register>
    <register type="IRegion" mapTo="Region">
    <constructor>
     <param name="defaultEntryRule" dependencyType="IDefaultEntryRule"/>
    </constructor>
    </register>
</container>
```

References

1. Jia, Y., Harman, M.: An analysis and survey of the development of mutation testing. IEEE Trans. Softw. Eng. **37**(5), 649–678 (2011). https://doi.org/10.1109/tse.2010.62

2. Papadakis, M., Kintis, M., Zhang, J., Jia, Y., Traon, Y.L., Harman, M.: Mutation testing advances: an analysis and survey. Adv. Comput. **112**, 275–378 (2019). https://doi.org/10. 1016/bs.adcom.2018.03.015

3. Liddle, S.W.: Model-Driven Software Development. In: Embley, D.W., Thalheim, B. (eds.) Handbook of Conceptual Modeling, pp. 17–54. Springer, Heidelberg (2011)

4. Domınguez, E., Perez, B., Rubio, A.L., Zapata, M.A.: A systematic review of code generation proposals from state machine specifications. Inf. Softw. Technol. **54**(10), 1045–1066 (2012). https://doi.org/10.1016/j.infsof.2012.04.008

5. Derezinska, A., Zaremba, Ł.: Mutating UML state machine behavior with semantic mutation operators. In: Damiani, E., Spanoudakis, G., Maciaszek, L. (eds.) Proceedings of the 14th International Conference on Evaluation of Novel Approaches to Software Engineering, ENASE, vol. 1, pp. 385–393. Scitepress, Setubal (2019). https://doi.org/10.5220/0007735003850393

6. UML (Unified Modelling Language) (2017). http://www.omg.org/spec/UML

7. Clark, J.A., Dan, H., Hierons, R.M.: Semantic mutation testing. Sci. Comput. Program. **78**(4), 345–363 (2013). https://doi.org/10.1016/j.scico.2011.03.011

8. Harel, D.: A visual formalism for complex systems. Sci. Comput. Program. **8**(3), 231–274 (1987)

9. Liebel, G., Marko, N., Tichy, M., Leitner, A., Hansson, J.: Model-based engineering in the embedded systems domain: an industrial survey on the state-of-practice. Softw. Syst. Model. **17**(1), 91–113 (2018). https://doi.org/10.1007/s10270-016-0523-3

10. Beeck, M.: A comparison of Statecharts variants. In: Langmaack, H., de Roever, W.-P., Vytopil, J. (eds.) FTRTFT 1994. LNCS, vol. 863, pp. 128–148. Springer, Heidelberg (1994). https://doi.org/10.1007/3-540-58468-4_163

11. Badreddin, O., Lethbridge, T.C., Forwared, A., Elaasar, M., Aljamaan, H., Garzon, M.A.: Enhanced code generation from UML composite state machines. In: Proceedings of the 2nd International Conference on Model-Driven Engineering and Software Development (MODELSWARD), pp. 235–245. SCITEPRESS - Science and Technology Publications, Setubal (2014). https://doi.org/10.5220/0004699602350245

12. Chauvel, F., Jézéquel, J.-M.: Code generation from UML models with semantic variation points. In: Briand, L., Williams, C. (eds.) MODELS 2005. LNCS, vol. 3713, pp. 54–68. Springer, Heidelberg (2005). https://doi.org/10.1007/11557432_5

13. Prout, A., Atlee, J.M., Day, N.A., Shaker, P.: Code generation for a family of executable modelling notations. Softw. Syst. Model. **11**(2), 251–272 (2012). https://doi.org/10.1007/s10270-010-0176-6

14. Derezińska, A., Pilitowski, R.: Interpretation of history pseudostates in orthogonal states of UML state machines. In: Feldman, Y.A., Kraft, D., Kuflik, T. (eds.) NGITS 2009. LNCS, vol. 5831, pp. 26–37. Springer, Heidelberg (2009). https://doi.org/10.1007/978-3-642-04941-5_5

15. Derezinska, A., Szczykulski, M.: Interpretation problems in code generation from UML state machines - a comparative study. In: Kwater, T. (ed.) Computing in Science and Technology 2011: Monographs in Applied Informatics, Department of Applied Informatics Faculty of Applied Informatics and Mathematics, Warsaw University of Life Sciences, pp. 36–50 (2012)

16. Batouta, Z.I., Dehbi, R., Talea, M., Hajoui, O.: Automation in code generation: tertiary and systematic mapping review. In: 4th IEEE International Colloquium on Information Science and Technology (CIST), pp. 200–205. IEEE (2017). https://doi.org/10.1109/cist.2016.7805042

17. Sunitha, E.V., Samuel, P.: Object oriented method to implement the hierarchical and concurrent states in UML state chart diagrams. In: Lee, R. (ed.) Software Engineering

Research, Management and Applications. SCI, vol. 654, pp. 133–149. Springer, Cham (2016). https://doi.org/10.1007/978-3-319-33903-0_10

18. Samek, M.: Practical statecharts in C/C ++: quantum programming for embedded systems. CMP Books (2002)
19. Wasowski, A.: Code generation and model driven development for constrained embedded software. Ph.D. thesis, University of Copenhagen (2005)
20. Pilitowski, R., Derezińska, A.: Code generation and execution framework for UML 2.0 classes and state machines. In: Sobh, T. (ed.) Innovations and Advanced Techniques in Computer and Information Sciences and Engineering, pp. 421–427. Springer, Dordrecht (2007). https://doi.org/10.1007/978-1-4020-6268-1_75
21. Iqbal, M.Z., Arcuri, A., Briand, L.: Environment modeling and simulation for automated testing of soft real-time embedded software. Softw. Syst. Model. 14(1), 483–524 (2013). https://doi.org/10.1007/s10270-013-0328-6
22. Burden, H., Heldal, R., Siljamaki, T.: Executable and translatable UML – how difficult can it be? In: 18th Asia-Pacific Software Engineering Conference, pp. 5–8. IEEE Computer Society, Washington (2011). https://doi.org/10.1109/apsec.2011.37
23. Hoefig, E.: Interpretation of behaviour models at runtime: performance benchmark and case studies. Ph.D. thesis, Berlin Institute of Technology (2011). http://dx.doi.org/10.14279/depositonce-2842. Accessed 08 Aug 2019
24. IBM RSA (Rational Software Architect). https://www.ibm.com/developerworks/downloads/r/architect. Accessed 08 Aug 2019
25. fUML: Semantics of a Foundation Subset for Executable UML models (2018). http://www.omg.org/spec/FUML/. 01 Dec 2018
26. IBM RRD (Rational Rhapsody Developer). https://www.ibm.com/developerworks/downloads/r/rhapsodydeveloper/. Accessed 08 Aug 2019
27. FXU (Framework for eXecutable UML). http://galera.ii.pw.edu.pl/~adr/FXU/. Accessed 08 Aug 2019
28. Derezińska, A., Szustek, A.: Object-oriented testing capabilities and performance evaluation of the c# mutation system. In: Szmuc, T., Szpyrka, M., Zendulka, J. (eds.) CEE-SET 2009. LNCS, vol. 7054, pp. 229–242. Springer, Heidelberg (2012). https://doi.org/10.1007/978-3-642-28038-2_18
29. Derezińska, A., Trzpil, P.: Mutation testing process combined with test-driven development in NET environment. In: Zamojski, W., Mazurkiewicz, J., Sugier, J., Walkowiak, T., Kacprzyk, J. (eds.) Theory and Engineering of Complex Systems and Dependability. DepCoS-RELCOMEX 2015. Advances in Intelligent Systems and Computing, vol. 365, pp. 131–140. Springer, Cham (2015). https://doi.org/10.1007/978-3-319-19216-1_13
30. Belli, F., Budnik, C.J., Hollmann, A., Tuglular, T., Wong, W.E.: Model-based mutation testing - approach and case studies. Sci. Comput. Program. 120(1), 25–48 (2016). https://doi.org/10.1016/j.scico.2016.01.003
31. Derezinska, A.: Object-oriented mutation to assess the quality of tests. In: Proceedings of the 29th Euromicro Conference, pp. 417–420 (2003). https://doi.org/10.1109/eurmic.2003.1231626
32. Strug, J.: Applying mutation testing for assessing test suites quality at model level. In: Proceedings of the 2016 Federated Conference on Computer Science and Information Systems, FedCSIS, Annals of Computer Science and Information Systems, vol. 8, pp. 1593–1596. IEEE (2016). https://doi.org/10.15439/2016f82
33. Fabbri, S.C.P.F., Delmaro, M.E., Maldonado, J.C., Masiero, P.C.: Mutation analysis testing for finite state machines. In: Proceedings of the 5th IEEE International Symposium on Software Reliability Engineering, pp. 220–229. IEEE Computer Society Press (1994). https://doi.org/10.1109/issre.1994.341378

34. Fabbri, S.C.P.F., Maldonado, J.C., Sugeta, T., Masiero, P.C.: Mutation testing applied to validate specifications based on statecharts. In: Proceedings 10th International Symposium on Software Reliability Engineering (Cat. No. PR00443), ISSRE 1999, pp. 210–219. IEEE Computer Society (1999). https://doi.org/10.1109/issre.1999.809326

35. Trakhtenbrot, M.: New mutations for evaluation of specification and implementation levels of adequacy in testing of Statecharts models. In: Proceedings of Testing: Academic and Industrial Conference Practice and Research Techniques – MUTATION, TAICPART-MUTATION 2007, pp. 151–160. IEEE (2007). https://doi.org/10.1109/taic.part.2007.23

36. Trakhtenbrot, M.: Implementation-oriented mutation testing of Statechart models. In: IEEE International Conference on Software Testing Verification and Validation Workshops (ICSTW), pp. 120–125. IEEE (2010). https://doi.org/10.1109/icstw.2010.55

37. Trakhtenbrot, M.: Mutation patterns for temporal requirements of reactive systems. In: IEEE International Conference on Software Testing, Verification and Validation Workshops (ICSTW), pp. 116–121. IEEE (2017). https://doi.org/10.1109/icstw.2017.27

38. Bartolini, C.: Software testing techniques revisited for OWL ontologies. In: Hammoudi, S., Pires, L.F., Selic, B., Desfray, P. (eds.) MODELSWARD 2016. CCIS, vol. 692, pp. 132–153. Springer, Cham (2017). https://doi.org/10.1007/978-3-319-66302-9_7

39. Harel, D., et al.: STATEMATE: a working environment for the development of complex reactive systems. IEEE Trans. Softw. Eng. **16**(4), 403–414 (1990). https://doi.org/10.1109/32.54292

40. Object Management Group: UML Profile for MARTE: Modeling and Analysis of Real-Time Embedded Systems (2018). http://www.omg.org/spec/MARTE/

41. Derezińska, A., Redosz, K.: Reuse of project code in model to code transformation, In: Borzemski, L., et al. (eds.) Information Systems Architecture and Technology, Contemporary Approaches to Design and Evolution of Information Systems, pp. 79–88. Oficyna Wydawnicza Politechniki Wroclawskiej, Wroclaw (2014)

42. Derezinska, A., Zaremba, Ł.: Approaches to semantic mutation of behavioral state machines in model-driven software development. In: Proceedings of the 2018 Federated Conference on Computer Science and Information Systems, ACSIS, vol. 15, pp 863–866 (2018). https://doi.org/10.15439/2018f313

43. Derezinska, A., Szczykulski, M.: Towards C# application development using UML state machines: a case study. In: Sobh, T., Elleithy, K. (eds.) Emerging Trends in Computing, Informatics, System Sciences, and Engineering. LNEE, vol. 151, pp. 793–803. Springer, New York (2013). https://doi.org/10.1007/978-1-4614-3558-7_68

Model-Driven Automatic Question Generation for a Gamified Clinical Guideline Training System

Job N. Nyameino[1,4]([✉]), Ben-Richard Ebbesvik[1], Fazle Rabbi[1,2],
Martin C. Were[3,4], and Yngve Lamo[2]

[1] University of Bergen, Bergen, Norway
jbngena@gmail.com
[2] Western Norway University of Applied Sciences, Bergen, Norway
[3] Vanderbilt University Medical Center, Nashville, TN, USA
[4] Institute of Biomedical Informatics, Moi University, Eldoret, Kenya

Abstract. Clinical practice guidelines (CPGs) are a cornerstone of modern medical practice since they summarize the vast medical literature and provide care recommendations based on the current best evidence. However, there are barriers to CPG utilization such as lack of awareness and lack of familiarity of the CPGs by clinicians due to ineffective CPG dissemination and implementation. This calls for research into effective and scalable CPG dissemination strategies that will improve CPG awareness and familiarity. We describe a model-driven approach to design and develop a gamified e-learning system for clinical guidelines where the training questions are generated automatically. We also present the prototype developed using this approach. We use models for different aspects of the system, an entity model for the clinical domain, a workflow model for the clinical processes and a game engine to generate and manage the training sessions. We employ gamification to increase user motivation and engagement in the training of guideline content. We conducted a limited formative evaluation of the prototype system and the users agreed that the system would be a useful addition to their training. Our proposed approach is flexible and adaptive as it allows for easy updates of the guidelines, integration with different device interfaces and representation of any guideline.

Keywords: Clinical practice guidelines · Model driven engineering gamification

1 Introduction

The rate at which medical knowledge is produced is accelerating and it is estimated that in 2020, the doubling rate of medical knowledge will be 73 days down from 7 years in 1980 [9]. At this rate it is virtually impossible for clinicians to

---

Supported by the HITRAIN project (Norad: Project QZA-0484).

E. Damiani et al. (Eds.): ENASE 2019, CCIS 1172, pp. 227–245, 2020.
https://doi.org/10.1007/978-3-030-40223-5_11

keep up with new knowledge [14]. Clinical practice guidelines (CPGs) provide a promising solution to this problem. CPGs are systematically developed statements that assist practitioners and patients to make decisions about appropriate health care for specific circumstances [21]. They are a comprehensive summary of the available evidence about medical conditions and provide recommendations for the management of those conditions [15]. A well-developed guideline reduces variations in care, improves diagnostic accuracy, promotes effective therapy and discourages ineffective therapies all which contribute to improved quality of care [37]. The mere availability of guidelines does not necessarily mean that the recommendations will be used in actual care. Indeed, there has been a reported gap between recommended care according to the evidence base and actual practice leading to preventable errors in practice [2,12]. This gap can be attributed to several barriers to guideline dissemination and implementation which include: internal barriers (lack of awareness, lack of familiarity, lack of agreement with the guideline content, and the inability to overcome the inertia of previous practice) and external barriers (i.e., patient, environmental, and guideline related factors such as ease of use and complexity of the guideline) [7].

The nature of guideline development means that published guidelines are well-researched, comprehensive documents that can be prohibitively voluminous. For example, the National Heart, Lung, and Blood Institute (NHLBI) 2007 Guidelines for the Diagnosis and Management of Asthma full report is 440 pages long [24] while the National Institute for Health and Care Excellence (NICE) guidelines for the diagnosis monitoring and management of chronic asthma (2017) report is 39 pages long [25]. Such large texts are impractical for use at the point of care. Additionally, poor guideline presentation has been identified as a factor in the lack of physician familiarity as some of the guidelines have been described as being tedious, repetitive, confusing, and unclear [6].

To mitigate some of the barriers to knowledge acquisition of guideline content, new dissemination strategies aimed at improving awareness and familiarity of guideline content are required. Active guideline dissemination strategies have been found to be more effective than passive strategies at improving the application of evidence based recommendations in patient care [16]. In particular, educational interventions (e.g. distribution of printed guidelines, educational meetings and outreaches) strengthen the effect of clinical educational material. Further, the more intensely the information is provided through these interventions, the greater its effect on the recipients [23]. Research into active strategies for clinical guideline dissemination are timely and relevant as they will potentially help to plug the gap between recommended and actual clinical practice.

One potentially useful active educational intervention is in the distribution of gamified guidelines. Gamification is the use of game design elements in non-game contexts [10,11]. It uses game based mechanics, aesthetics and thinking to engage people, motivate action, promote learning and solve problems [18]. The concept of Gamification is relatively new and has been used to describe the use of game-based concepts and techniques, with the goal of increasing the motivation and engagement of the participants and improving the results.

The implementation of guideline summaries as interactive, gamified flowcharts on a mobile platform will potentially mitigate the problems of guideline complexity and presentation that plague the effective dissemination of guideline content. In this paper we present a formal model driven approach to gamification of clinical practical guidelines. To illustrate the approach, we present three models, an entity model of the clinical encounter domain, a workflow model for the clinical processes and a game model all of which will be integrated to create our gamified system. We then describe a prototype mobile-based guideline app that incorporates these models to present a gamified interactive guideline training tool. Finally we conduct a limited formative evaluation of the prototype to get user feedback that will inform future improvements of the system. This paper extends the work presented in an earlier paper by Nyameino et al. [26]. In this extended version we elaborate on MDE concepts being used in the development of domain models for gamification, we present an evaluation of our approach and a discussion on its implications. Finally we present a revised related work section where we compare our work with existing automated elearning and gamification approaches. The results indicate the potential of our approach in developing e-learning tools with MDE techniques.

2   Method

2.1   Diagram Predicate Framework (DPF)

In this work we use a formal diagrammatic approach to model driven software engineering (MDE), called Diagram Predicate Framework (DPF) [35]. DPF formalizes software development activities such as metamodelling [35] and model transformations [36]. It is based on category theory [3] and graph transformations [22]. We can use DPF to formalize clinical guidelines in the form of diagrammatic specifications of clinical domain models at different abstraction levels. The diagrammatic nature of DPF also facilitates visual representations of guidelines that can be presented at different level of abstraction. A model in DPF is represented by a diagrammatic specification $\mathfrak{S} = (\mathcal{S}, C^{\mathfrak{S}} : \Sigma)$ which consists of a graph $\mathcal{S}$ and a set of constraints $C^{\mathfrak{S}}$ specified by a predicate signature Σ.

The predicate signature is composed of a collection of predicates, each having a name and an arity (shape graph). A constraint consists of a predicate from the signature together with a binding to the subgraph of the model's In order to apply DPF for the modeling of a gamified training system that operates over clinical practice guidelines we need to formalize the concepts of a guideline using DPF and also model the gamification concepts with DPF.

2.2   Model Driven Engineering

Model Driven Engineering (MDE) is a system development paradigm that promotes the use of models as the primary artefacts that drives the whole development process. In MDE models are specified using a modelling language whose syntax and semantics are defined by a metamodel [38]. This allows for the development of domain-specific modelling languages (DSLs) using notations and abstractions that are unique to a given domain. The use of DSLs allows for the development of more expressive models and ease of use by domain experts. A metamodel architecture introduces a generic pattern of metamodeling hierarchy in which models at each level are specified by a modeling language at the level above and conform to the corresponding metamodel of the language. Figure 1 illustrates a metamodeling hierarchy where a model M_i at a certain level i conforms to a metamodel M_{i+1} at the level above until a model M_j has itself as metamodel, called a *reflexive model*.

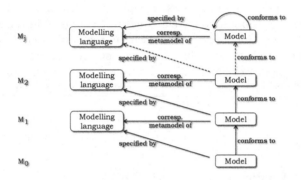

Fig. 1. Generic pattern: modeling languages and metamodels [34].

According to the traditional metamodeling architecture, proposed by OMG, a metamodeling architecture is organized in 4 meta-levels $M_0 - M_3$, known as the Object Management Group (OMG) 4-layered hierarchy [5]. A possible interpretation of the hierarchy is summarized as follows:

- The bottom layer M_0 is called the user object layer and it contains the data of the application (e.g. the instances populating an object- oriented system at run-time).
- The M_1 layer contains models (e.g. a UML class diagram of a software system).
- The M_2 layer contains metamodels that captures the language (e.g. UML class diagrams or statechart diagrams).
- The M_3 layer is the meta-meta layer that contains the meta-metamodel MOF. This layer describes the properties of all metamodels.

In the next few paragraphs we are going to describe the different models we propose to use. First an entity model for the clinical encounter domain, a workflow model, a game model and an integrated multi-metamodel that incorporates the entity and CPG workflow models.

Entity Model. In Fig. 2 we present an entity model from the clinical domain. The model contains the main entities in the clinical domain, their attributes and the relationships between them. This is illustrated in Fig. 2 where we have entities such as *Patient* with the attributes *name, age* and *weight* and corresponding relationships with other entities such as *Patient* **undergoes** *Investigation* and **receives** *Treatment*.

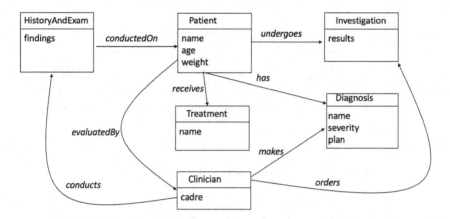

Fig. 2. A simplified entity model of the clinical encounter domain.

Workflow Model. Clinical practice guidelines are often summarized in algorithmic workflows showing the flow of management. Workflow models may be used to represent the flow and corresponding branching conditions of a clinical guideline In Fig. 3 we present an example metamodel (M_2) for behavioural models which specifies that instances of Task can be connected by Flow edges. On the next abstraction level (M_1) we see a generic treatment model that is typed by the elements from metamodel M_2. The treatment model has three tasks Assessment and Diagnosis, Treatment and Evaluation. Finally, at (M_0) we see an instance of the treatment workflow of a severe asthma diagnosis.

Game Model. Games are goal-oriented activities with reward and progress tracking mechanisms. These core gamification concepts should be under consideration in the design of gamified e-learning systems. In our system, a game engine will automatically generate questions from the entity and workflow models to instantiate a training module. The questions are categorized according to the learner's skill level (beginner, intermediate, advanced) and each question has a reward in the form of points. A game model should also specify a learner profile that tracks the learner's activities.

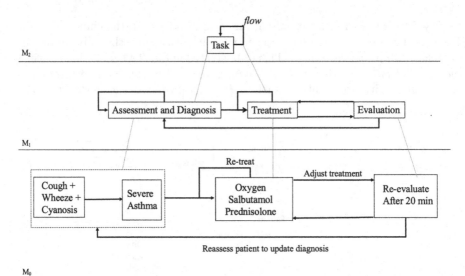

Fig. 3. The workflow model with its metamodel [26].

Gamification Elements. The core concepts of games that should inform the design of gamified e-learning systems are goal oriented activities with reward mechanisms and progress tracking [39]. In the training of guideline content, the main goal is for the trainees to learn how to treat different aspects of a disease as described in the guideline. The reward mechanisms and progress tracking aid in increasing the users engagement and motivation [4]. We describe the game elements below.

– **Category:** a guideline is developed for a specific medical condition. The quiz category will be the medical condition for which a guideline has been developed.
– **Level:** This is the difficulty level of the question.
– **Passing Condition:** This is the minimum number of points a student needs to score to successfully complete a specific difficulty level and be allowed to move to the next level.
– **Entity Instance:** a pointer to an instance of an entity graph. It is used together with a template to generate text.
– **Question:** a pointer to a template model. By using a template model, we can reuse templates on many entity instances.
– **Alternative:** or distraction. It is one of the answer alternatives for a question.
– **Reward:** a reward or penalty is given based on the correctness of the choice chosen by the student. A correct choice is rewarded while a wrong choice is penalised.

Model Integration. Separation of concern is a potential way to reduce the complexity of software systems. To raise the level of abstraction of complex software systems, we may require to model various aspects of a system in different models. However, to understand the functionality of the system as a whole we need to study the integrated system. One of the major problem of integrating complex information system is the heterogeneity of its subsystems. Requirements for integrating heterogeneous distributed systems are increasing with the rapid technological advancements. The study of integrating heterogeneous system is a complex process consisting of information, expert knowledge management, decision making support. In this paper we study model integration for constructing e-learning modules. The training model is built by the integration of the entity and workflow models based on the principles introduced by Rabbi et al. [27]. The states of the training module TM are defined by a set of elements that include a pair of workflow instance WI and an entity instance EI: $TM_i = <EI_i, WI_i>$ where i is a natural number. This integration of models is shown in Fig. 4 and the concept is discussed in more details in Subsect. 2.3. In Fig. 4, we show a section of the entity model with values from a given scenario where based on the *History & Examination findings*, a *Diagnosis* of Severe Asthma is made and its *Treatment* specified The flow of how this process should happen is shown in the workflow model.

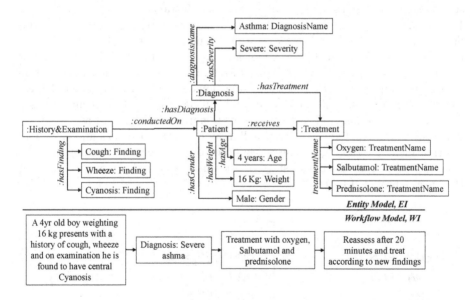

Fig. 4. Integrated entity and workflow models [26].

2.3 Training Modules

Rabbi et al. presented an approach where different aspects of a system were coordinated by means of multiple metamodels [27,28]. The approach is based on the foundation of DPF.

In the multi-metamodeling approach, a workflow model is integrated with an entity model by means of metamodel coordination. A workflow metamodel is used to design the flow of a system and an entity metamodel used to design the entities and relationship of a domain. A workflow model can be used to represent an abstraction of a CPG but we need to incorporate the detailed domain knowledge in our modelling. In this paper we exploit the use of the multi-metamodeling approach to represent the domain knowledge of a clinical guideline and the clinical process and apply them to execute a training session. The idea of using the workflow model is to control the flow of the game such that the user is interacting with the right gaming element at the right time.

In this subsection we describe a training module which consist of one or more workflow models and one or more entity models. The states of the training module TM are defined by a set of elements that include a pair of guideline workflow instance and an entity model instance that represents the entities within a domain and relationships between them. Figure 5 illustrates an example of two states TM_1 and TM_2 of a training module. The state TM_1 consists of a set of elements that include a pair of workflow instances and entity instances: $\{<WI_0, EI_0>, <WI_1, EI_1>, .. < WI_n, EI_n\}$ where $WI_1, WI_2, ..WI_n$ are workflow instances and $EI_0, EI_1, ..EI_n$ are DPF entity instances. Figure 6 shows a training session flow which consists of a sequence of states of training module i.e., $Training_{Flow1} := <TM_1, TM_2, ...TM_k>$. In Fig. 6 the game engine instantiates a training session by generating questions based on the entity model and the workflow model. For example, it could initially generate a scenario based on the patient details and history and examination findings and ask what the diagnosis is. If answered correctly, it will move on to the next task and ask about the treatment. A training session is composed of a sequence of training modules and is evolved from the initial state of a training flow and progresses based on the answer provided by the user.

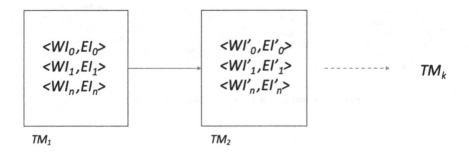

Fig. 5. States of training module [26].

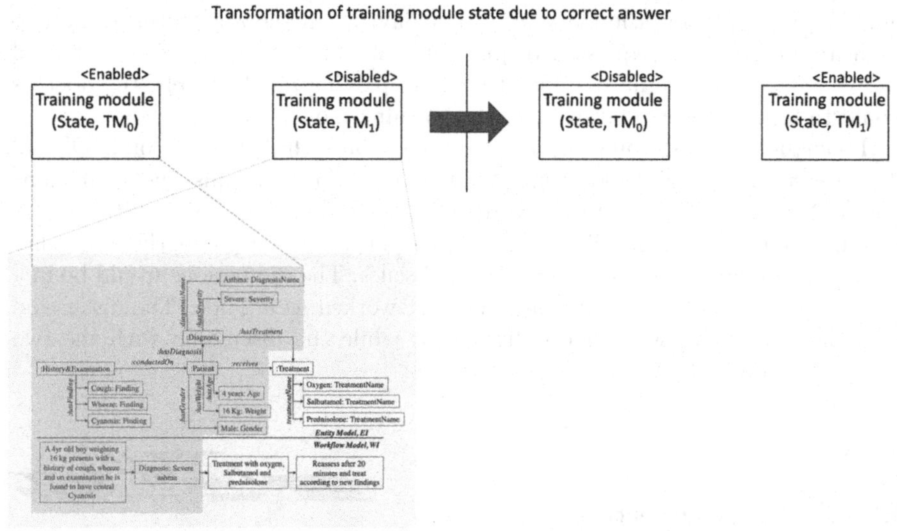

Transformation of training module state due to correct answer

Fig. 6. Progression of the states of training module.

In our approach a training session is evolved from the initial state of a training flow and progresses based on the answer provided by the user. Figure 6 illustrates the idea of the progression of the states of training session. Depending on the answer given by the user, a game engine consults with the training flow and evolves the state of the training session. We use two DPF predicates $<Enabled>$, $<Disabled>$ to represent the current status of the training modules. A training module TM_0 when annotated with the $<Enabled>$ predicate indicates that the training module is currently active and is being considered for training.

2.4 Formative Evaluation

Formative evaluations involve evaluating a product or service during development, often iteratively, with the goal of detecting and eliminating usability problems [31].

An evaluation of the application was done with two cadres of clinicians. We recruited two medical doctors and two specialist nurses through purposive sampling to participate in our evaluation. Both of the specialist nurses are employees at the polyclinic for pulmonary diseases at a university hospital in Western Norway. One of the nurses is a specialist in sleep apnea whose masters thesis was on developing clinical guidelines for sleep apnea. The other nurse is a specialist in asthma, but in adult medicine. The two doctors are general practitioners and researchers.

The evaluation methods were a combination of a cognitive walkthrough and a usability test with follow-up questions. Specifically, the nurses were asked to play the most difficult level of the game and to speak out loud on what they were thinking when playing the game and manoeuvring in the application. The two medical doctors were requested to play the entire game, from the easiest level and to completing the most difficult one. By playing all the levels, the doctors would to far greater extent evaluate the learning model.

Discussion points would arise as the clinicians thought out loud. One of the researchers would observe and take notes when problems and confusions occurred, or when the clinician expressed emotions such as joy, excitement or disappointment. After the clinicians had played through the game, the researcher would go through a check-list of topics to discuss. The discussions would be in a semi-structured format, where the check-list worked as a guide. The discussion with the two nurses was done individually, while the discussion with the two doctors was done in a small focus group.

3 Results

3.1 System Architecture

We propose to use a generic architecture based on the idea of multilevel-metamodeling and their coordination. Figure 7 shows an overview of the system. The 'Game Engine' controls the training flow, maintains the status of the trainee, produces dialogues and controls the order of the questions The user should be able to interact with the game engine via the presentation layer. We describe the different components of the architecture shown in Fig. 7 below.

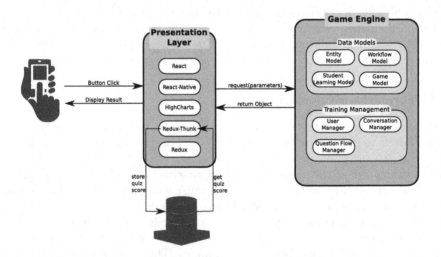

Fig. 7. Overview of the proposed system architecture.

Presentation Layer: The presentation layer is what the user sees and interacts with when using the application. React Native [30] is a JavaScript framework, used to build cross platform mobile applications for Android, iPhone and UWP. It is based on React [29], where it uses React components to build user interfaces for mobile applications.

For managing the state of the application, we use another JavaScript framework, Redux [32]. It is sort of a repository of functions and variables. When the student clicks on a button in the application, it will trigger a function in the Redux repository. The function can send a request to the Game Engine or do some calculations on its own. Then update a variable in the repository which is connected to a variable in the React Component, and the result is shown on the student's phone.

As the Redux repository is synchronous, we need the framework Redux-Thunk [33] to make asynchronous calls. A student's scores for a quiz is stored in the database on the student's phone. The game engine uses the scores to find questions at the right difficulty level for the student. As database calls are asynchronous, we need Redux-Thunk to make functions which can do asynchronous communication between Redux and the database.

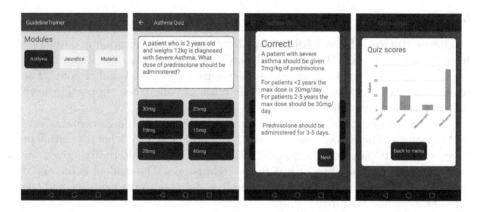

Fig. 8. Flow of the mobile application [26].

The presentation layer can be implemented in different interfaces such as in a mobile application as in this case or virtual assistants such as Google assistant as in Fig. 9.

HighCharts [17] is a JavaScript framework used for making interactive charts. We use it to visualize how well the user performed, and how far he is from advancing to more difficult questions.

Question Flow Manager: The question flow manager selects the questions to be asked depending on the level of difficulty of a training session. It maintains the order of questions to be shown to the user. For example, user-A has skill level 1 and chose to go through the beginning session. While randomly selecting questions that falls under the difficulty of 'Beginner', it also looks into the questions that has been used before for user-A. It puts more emphasize on the questions that the user has been struggling with.

Conversation Manager: The conversation manager keeps track of the conversation and manages the context of the conversation. For example, if there are three questions to be asked that is related to a child who is 2 years old, then the conversation manager produces a context for three questions and starts the conversation saying "A 2 year old child comes to the emergency department with <some condition>, answer to the following questions:". Afterwards it asks the first question, followed by the 2nd and 3rd questions.

User Management: The user management module keeps track of the trainees skill, progress and effort. The user management module is also used to produce visualization showing the performance of a population. If a group of trainee is particularly struggling with a set of questions or question category then the user management module will produce a report and the trainer will be able to monitor it.

3.2   Prototype

Implementation of the Mobile Application. The application is developed using React-Native and JavaScript. React-Native is based on the React framework, and is used to build mobile applications for Android and iPhone. The motivation for using such a framework is reuse of code when supporting both mobile platforms as well as the web.

The game consists of a collection of quizzes, where each quiz contains several questions. These questions are based around a scenario, where the student is presented with answer alternatives. Picking an answer alternative gives the student points for how close he was to the right action. The student is presented with the answer key, an explanation, as well as pointers to the evidence and the relevant guideline for further study.

The quiz conclude with a summary, giving feedback and statistics on students performance. The quiz should have a passing condition to unlock quizzes at a higher difficulty level. This is illustrated in Fig. 8.

Question Generation. To generate questions, the game engine first reads instances of the entity models using a model parser. We then link the parsed model instances with pre-written scenario questions in the form of narrative templates where we use tags to refer to variables in the entity model. The tag refers to a path in the entity graph. The application will traverse through the graph and return the value of the given vertex.

THe game engine then populates the tags with values from the entity model instances thereby creating the question as illustrated below. The correct answer is inferred from the corresponding entity model instance.

```
<%Ben.name%> arrives at the emergency
department.
He <%Ben.hasConsciousness.value.name%>.
```

translates to

```
Ben arrives at the emergency
department.
He is not alert and not verbal,
but responds to pain.
```

Alternate User Interfaces. As described earlier, the modular architecture allows for the implementation of different user interfaces in the presentation layer of the architecture (see Fig. 7). This allows flexibility to accommodate the various learning styles of trainees. For example, in Fig. 9 we see a sample conversation from the asthma guideline training using Google assistant. We use the google account for registering the participant to our system and we plan to use OAuth 2.0 protocol for authenticating the user from the mobile application to the participants Google account. It will allow the user to switch from one device to another. While the participant is using the mobile application they get more feature such as browsing the guideline.

Fig. 9. Sample flow of conversation from the asthma guideline training [26].

3.3   Formative Evaluation Results

As part of the usability evaluation and cognitive walkthroughs, we asked the respondents follow-up questions after they used. We present the responses below.

1. Can the application be a useful learning tool for medical students, nurses and doctors?
   - **Nurse1:** *Very useful indeed. It would be nice to take a test after a lecture about asthma or after having read about asthma to see how much I have learnt and remember. A quiz is far more fun than a check list in paper format. The application is also good for scalability, as you can train a lot of clinicians without adding any resources. Also great if a course leader can see the progress or the level of his students.*
   - **Nurse2:** *Absolutely useful, and I feel I have learnt a lot by just doing this quiz. The nurse found the game to be very engaging, cheering when getting a correct answer.*
   - **Doctors:** *For medical doctors, the quiz will be too basic. For nurses it might be good. For medical students it will be very good, as it fits with how the students works and how they will be tested for exams.*
2. How is the flow of the questions? Is the idea of scenarios where we go from assessment, diagnosis, management and follow-up a good approach?
   - **Nurse1:** *Happy with the flow and the use of scenarios.*
   - **Nurse2:** *Very happy with the flow, being able to follow the patient from the start to the end of the treatment.*
   - **Doctors:** *The categories weren't very clear. The questions are floating into each other. One suggestion is to have oxygen and antibiotic adminis-tration as own categories. Then you can measure how well they perform in these categories and ask them to repeat the basics if they perform poorly.*
3. Is the detail level the element to adjust for the difficulties of questions?
   - **Nurse1:** *Yes, but would like to have an even harder level with more details.*
   - **Nurse2:** *Yes, it seems like a right approach. The target group of users is relevant here, that this is meant for the emergency clinic.*
   - Doctors: *Yes, but the detail level of the questions need to be much harder. One example of going to higher detail level could be "what oxygen admin-istration device would you initially use to a neonate?" to "administering oxygen using nasal prong to a neonate doesn't work. What do you do?".*
   In Norway, the patients will visit the hospital with a lot more variation of illnesses and with a higher frequency of less severe diagnoses. Then differ-ential diagnoses gets more important and to represent a lot more clinical conditions as quizzes. The clinicians also work a bit different in Norway. If a patient comes into the hospital with symptoms of severe asthma, they will usually just treat and stabilize the really alarming symptoms and not go through a whole list of treatments.

4. How are the answer key explanations?
  - **Nurse2:** *I like how the measurements corresponds and are calculated with the scenario and the patient they are presented with. The answer key explanations gives relevant answers to the questions asked.*
  - **Doctors:** *The answer key explanations are good. We like that we get an explanation when we answer correctly. We preferred to try until getting the answer correctly rather than clicking "learn more" and proceed to next question. It could be nice to get an explanation why the answer was wrong, but we are rather impatient, we want to proceed and find the correct answer quickly.*

4   Discussion

We have presented a model-driven approach to the design and development of a gamified system for clinical guideline training. We have also conducted a limited formative evaluation to get user feedback on the prototype. Our modular approach provides several advantages. First, it makes it easier to separate concerns and thus updating guidelines requires changes to parts of the entity and workflow models change while the rest of the system remains unchanged. Second, the separation of the game engine from the presentation layer allows for integration with various devices supporting different means of user-interaction.

The user evaluation provided valuable feedback on the system. Overall, the respondents thought that the application was useful to clinical workers especially nurses and medical students as a complement to traditional learning methods. From the respondents, the training tool as it is now generate relatively basic questions and may not be very useful to experienced doctors. Both cadres of respondents (nurses and doctors) agreed that more difficult levels may need to be incorporated into the system to make it more useful.

There are a number of limitations to the gamified elearning system we describe in this work. First, full training of some guideline content requires the learning of some physical skills - such as performing cardiopulmonary resuscitation (CPR). This is a limitation as our system can only train on guideline content that does not require hands on training. Secondly, our system cannot automatically generate the wrong choices (distractors) for the questions and we are currently working on distraction generation strategies to make the system complete.

In the near future, we plan to enhance our conduct a more comprehensive evaluation of the quality of the questions generated by our system. We will also evaluate the acceptability and effectiveness of the proposed technique as a dissemination strategy for clinical guidelines within resource-limited settings.

5   Related Work

Leo et al. presented an ontology based automatic multiple-choice question (MCQ) generation system that exploits classes and existential restrictions to generate case-based questions [20]. Their aim is to develop questions with complex stems that are suitable for scenarios beyond mere knowledge recall. Their system used question templates to generate four types of questions i.e. *What is the most likely diagnosis?*, *What is the drug of choice?*, *What is the most likely clinical finding?* and *What is the differential diagnosis?*. Our narrative templates are more varied and can generate a wider variety of questions.

Farkash et al. presented a model-driven approach to formalize clinical guidelines using natural rule language (NRL) [13]. They specified the constraints of a CPG with an English-like rule language to reduce the gap of the representation and processing of guidelines. The authors presented a set of software components that support the representation, interpretation of CPGs using NRL and that can also be applied directly to a patient's EHR data for analysis. Their approach is supported by a proof-of-concept implementation for a simple essential hypertension guideline directive. Our approach is different with their approach as we use a graph based modeling technique and the main contribution of our approach is to support the training of a guideline by means of gamification.

Kristensen et al. presented a conceptual model for e-learning where the learning materials are divided into atomic units and organized in several graph based models such as 'Knowledge map', 'Learning map' and 'Student map' [19]. These conceptual models provide structure for representing an e-learning environment and an easy-to-use navigation interface for existing learning materials. We adopted concepts from this paper for representing CPGs and game elements by means of Diagram Predicate Framework and multi-metamodelling approach.

In Portugal Del Cura-Gonzalez et al. conducted a study to assess the effectiveness of a teaching strategy for the implementation of clinical guidelines using educational games [8]. They presented the findings for the use of an e-learning game EDUCAGUIA to improve knowledge and skills related to clinical decision-making by residents in family medicine. The system consisted of educational games with hypothetical clinical scenarios in a virtual environment. To evaluate the effectiveness of teaching strategies through e-learning, they proposed an average score comparison of hypothetical scenario questionnaires between the EDUCAGUIA intervention group and the control group. Such evaluation is very important and it reflects the usefulness of utilizing games in teaching guidelines. We plan to conduct similar evaluation of our gamification approach with healthcare professionals in future [8].

Aouadi et al. used Technology-Enhanced Learning standards to develop serious games which can be used in technological, professional or academic fields for learning. Their goal was to develop a scenario-building approach, built upon a model driven architecture [1]. Their system includes a health course with demonstrative videos and evaluation quizzes with each course having a passing condition. The game is also demonstrated as a 3D game in a context of medical training. In their approach, they used a platform independent model for the development of game components which was transformed into a platform specific model by means of ATL transformation. While their approach is very close to our proposed method, they lack modularization and separation of concerns.

In our approach we not only apply multilevel metamodelling but also the integration of different modeling hierarchies which allows us to conveniently articulate various aspects of an e-learning system.

6   Conclusion

In this work, we have presented a model-driven approach to the design and development of a gamified system for clinical guideline training. We also present a prototype mobile gamified e-learning system that utilized our design approach in its development. Finally we present the findings of a limited formative evaluation of the prototype system which received a good response from the users as being useful and scalable. We plan to incorporate the user feedback to improve the system and subject it to further more comprehensive evaluations.

References

1. Aouadi, N., Pernelle, P., Amar, C.B., Carron, T., Talbot, S.: Models and mechanisms for implementing playful scenarios. In: 2016 IEEE/ACS 13th International Conference of Computer Systems and Applications (AICCSA), pp. 1–8. IEEE, November 2016. https://doi.org/10.1109/AICCSA.2016.7945774. http://ieeexplore.ieee.org/document/7945774/
2. Baker, A.: Crossing the quality chasm: a new health system for the 21st century. BMJ: Br. Med. J. **323**(7322), 1192 (2001)
3. Barr, M., Wells, C.: Category Theory for Computing Science, vol. 49. Prentice Hall, New York (1990)
4. Bernik, A., Bubaš, G., Radošević, D.: Measurement of the effects of e-learning courses gamification on motivation and satisfaction of students. In: 41th International Convention-Mipro (2018)
5. Bezivin, J., Gerbe, O.: Towards a precise definition of the OMG/MDA framework. In: Proceedings 16th Annual International Conference on Automated Software Engineering (ASE 2001), pp. 273–280, November 2001. https://doi.org/10.1109/ASE.2001.989813
6. Cabana, M.D., Ebel, B.E., Cooper-Patrick, L., Powe, N.R., Rubin, H.R., Rand, C.S.: Barriers pediatricians face when using asthma practice guidelines. Arch. Pediatr. Adolesc. Med. **154**(7), 685–693 (2000). https://doi.org/10.1001/archpedi.154.7.685
7. Cabana, M.D., et al.: Why don't physicians follow clinical practice guidelines?: A framework for improvement. JAMA **282**(15), 1458–1465 (1999)
8. Del Cura-González, I., et al.: Effectiveness of a strategy that uses educational games to implement clinical practice guidelines among Spanish residents of family and community medicine (e-EDUCAGUIA project): a clinical trial by clusters. Implement. Sci. **11**, 71 (2016). https://doi.org/10.1186/s13012-016-0425-3
9. Densen, P.: Challenges and opportunities facing medical education. Trans. Am. Clin. Climatol. Assoc. **122**, 48 (2011)
10. Deterding, S., Dixon, D., Khaled, R., Nacke, L.: From game design elements to gamefulness: defining gamification. In: Proceedings of the 15th International Academic MindTrek Conference: Envisioning Future Media Environments, pp. 9–15. ACM (2011)

11. Deterding, S., Sicart, M., Nacke, L., O'Hara, K., Dixon, D.: Gamification using game-design elements in non-gaming contexts. In: CHI 2011 Extended Abstracts on Human Factors in Computing Systems, pp. 2425–2428. ACM (2011)
12. Donaldson, M.S., Corrigan, J.M., Kohn, L.T., et al.: To Err is Human: Building a Safer Health System, vol. 6. National Academies Press, Washington (2000)
13. Farkash, A., Timm, J.T.E., Waks, Z.: A model-driven approach to clinical practice guidelines representation and evaluation using standards. Stud. Health Technol. Inform. **192**, 200–204 (2013). http://europepmc.org/abstract/MED/23920544
14. Fervers, B., Carretier, J., Bataillard, A.: Clinical practice guidelines. J. Visceral Surg. **147**(6), e341–e349 (2010)
15. Goud, R., et al.: Effect of guideline based computerised decision support on decision making of multidisciplinary teams: cluster randomised trial in cardiac rehabilitation. BMJ **338**, b1440 (2009)
16. Grimshaw, J.M., et al.: Disseminating and Implementing Guidelines. Proc. Am. Thorac. Soc. **9**(5), 298–303 (2012). https://doi.org/10.1513/pats.201208-066ST. https://www.atsjournals.org/doi/full/10.1513/pats.201208-066ST
17. Highsoft: Interactive JavaScript charts for your webpage—Highcharts. https://www.highcharts.com/
18. Kapp, K.M.: The Gamification of Learning and Instruction: Game-Based Methods and Strategies for Training and Education. Wiley, Hoboken (2012)
19. Kristensen, T., Lamo, Y., Hinna, K.R.C., Hole, G.O.: Dynamic content manager – a new conceptual model for e-learning. In: Liu, W., Luo, X., Wang, F.L., Lei, J. (eds.) WISM 2009. LNCS, vol. 5854, pp. 499–507. Springer, Heidelberg (2009). https://doi.org/10.1007/978-3-642-05250-7_52
20. Leo, J., et al.: Ontology-based generation of medical, multi-term MCQs. Int. J. Artif. Intell. Educ. (2019). https://doi.org/10.1007/s40593-018-00172-w
21. Lohr, K.N., Field, M.J., et al.: Guidelines for Clinical Practice: From Development to Use. National Academies Press, Washington (1992)
22. Löwe, M.: Algebraic approach to single-pushout graph transformation. Theoret. Comput. Sci. **109**(1–2), 181–224 (1993)
23. Marriott, S., Palmer, C., Lelliott, P.: Disseminating healthcare information: getting the message across. BMJ Qual. Saf. **9**(1), 58–62 (2000)
24. NHLBI: Expert panel report 3: guidelines for the diagnosis and management of asthma. No. 97, DIANE Publishing (2007)
25. NICE: Asthma: diagnosis, monitoring and chronic asthma management. Nice Guideline 80 (2017)
26. Nyameino, J.N., Rabbi, F., Ebbesvik, B., Were, M.C., Lamo, Y.: A model driven approach to the development of gamified interactive clinical practice guidelines. In: Damiani, E., Spanoudakis, G., Maciaszek, L.A. (eds.) Proceedings of the 14th International Conference on Evaluation of Novel Approaches to Software Engineering, ENASE 2019, Heraklion, Crete, Greece, May 4–5, 2019, pp. 147–158. SciTePress (2019). https://doi.org/10.5220/0007736401470158
27. Rabbi, F., Lamo, Y., MacCaull, W.: Co-ordination of multiple metamodels, with application to healthcare systems. In: The 5th International Conference on Emerging Ubiquitous Systems and Pervasive Networks (EUSPN-2014)/ The 4th International Conference on Current and Future Trends of Information and Communication Technologies in Healthcare (ICTH 2014)/ Affiliated Workshops, September 22–25, 2014, Halifax, Nova Scotia, Canada. Procedia Computer Science, vol. 37, pp. 473–480. Elsevier (2014). https://doi.org/10.1016/j.procs.2014.08.071

28. Rabbi, F., Lamo, Y., MacCaull, W.: A flexible metamodelling approach for health-care systems. In: Jaatun, E.A.A., Brooks, E., Berntsen, K.E., Gilstad, H., Jaatun, M.G. (eds.) Proceedings of the 2nd European Workshop on Practical Aspects of Health Informatics, Trondheim, Norway, May 19–20, 2014. CEUR Workshop Proceedings, vol. 1251, pp. 115–128. CEUR-WS.org (2014). http://ceur-ws.org/Vol-1251/paper11.pdf
29. React: React - A JavaScript library for building user interfaces. https://reactjs.org/
30. React-Native: React Native · A framework for building native apps using React. https://facebook.github.io/react-native/
31. Redish, J.G., Bias, R.G., Bailey, R., Molich, R., Dumas, J., Spool, J.M.: Usability in practice: formative usability evaluations-evolution and revolution. In: CHI 2002 Extended Abstracts on Human Factors in Computing Systems, pp. 885–890. ACM (2002)
32. Redux: Redux · A Predictable State Container for JS Apps. https://redux.js.org/
33. ReduxJS-thunk: reduxjs/redux-thunk: Thunk middleware for Redux. https://github.com/reduxjs/redux-thunk
34. Rutle, A.: Diagram predicate framework: a formal approach to MDE (2010)
35. Rutle, A., Rossini, A., Lamo, Y., Wolter, U.: A diagrammatic formalisation of MOF-based modelling languages. In: Oriol, M., Meyer, B. (eds.) TOOLS EUROPE 2009. LNBIP, vol. 33, pp. 37–56. Springer, Heidelberg (2009). https://doi.org/10.1007/978-3-642-02571-6_4
36. Rutle, A., Rossini, A., Lamo, Y., Wolter, U.: A formal approach to the specification and transformation of constraints in mde. J. Logic Algebraic Program. **81**(4), 422–457 (2012)
37. Shiffman, R.N., Michel, G., Essaihi, A., Thornquist, E.: Bridging the guideline implementation gap: a systematic, document-centered approach to guideline implementation. J. Am. Med. Inform. Assoc. **11**(5), 418–426 (2004). https://doi.org/10.1197/jamia.M1444. http://www.ncbi.nlm.nih.gov/pmc/articles/PMC516249/
38. da Silva, A.R.: Model-driven engineering. Comput. Lang. Syst. Struct. **43**(C), 139–155 (2015). https://doi.org/10.1016/j.cl.2015.06.001
39. Strmečki, D., Bernik, A., Radošević, D.: Gamification in e-learning: introducing gamified design elements into e-learning systems. J. Comput. Sci. Technol. **11**(12), 1108–1117 (2015)

New Method to Reduce Verification Time of Reconfigurable Real-Time Systems Using R-TNCESs Formalism

Yousra Hafidi[1,2,3,4]($\boxtimes$) (iD), Laid Kahloul[2], Mohamed Khalgui[3,4] (iD),
and Mohamed Ramdani[1,2,3,4]

[1] University of Tunis El Manar, Tunis, Tunisia
ramdani.moh19@gmail.com, yousra_hafidi@hotmail.com
[2] LINFI Laboratory, Computer Science Department, Biskra University,
Biskra, Algeria
laid.k.b@gmail.com
[3] LISI Laboratory, National Institute of Applied Sciences and Technology,
University of Carthage, 1080 Tunis, Tunisia
khalgui.mohamed@gmail.com
[4] School of Electrical and Information Engineering,
Jinan University, Guangzhou, China

Abstract. Nowadays, several systems like manufacturing, aerospace, medical, and telecommunication ones face new challenges such as fault-tolerance, response in time, flexibility, modularity, etc. To deal with these requirements, systems had to include new abilities. Consequently, systems become more complex, and their verification becomes expensive in terms of computation time and memory. Reconfigurable real-time systems are ones of those complex systems that encompass reconfigurability constraints and subject to real-time requirements. Their verification is often a hard task due to their complex behavior. In this paper, we formally model these systems using reconfigurable timed net condition/event systems (R-TNCESs) formalism, which is a Petri net extension for reconfigurable systems. Then, we propose a new methodology to efficiently verify real-time properties by avoiding redundant computations. An application of the paper contributions is carried out on a benchmark manufacturing system, a performance evaluation is achieved to demonstrate it and to compare it with other related works.

Keywords: Real-time system · Reconfiguration · Formal verification
model-checking · CTL

1 Introduction

With the continuous development of technology, several systems like manufacturing, aerospace, medical, and telecommunication ones face new challenges. To deal with today's requirements such as: fault-tolerance, response in time, flexibility, modularity, etc., systems should comprise new abilities. By including new

© Springer Nature Switzerland AG 2020
E. Damiani et al. (Eds.): ENASE 2019, CCIS 1172, pp. 246–266, 2020.
https://doi.org/10.1007/978-3-030-40223-5_12

abilities, systems become complex and their design contains more constraints. An indispensable requirement is also having a correct behaviour behind of these complex systems. Actually, any problem that a critical system may face during its execution can cause serious consequences like loss of life in safety critical systems [8]. If it is not a loss of life, failures results can be economically serious. Most problems of critical systems are due to a faulty and an unreliable design [26]. Formal verification techniques can play an important role in addressing such issues. Therefore, many academic researchers as well as industrial companies tackle systems reliability by formal verification [2,12,14,16,24,31].

Formal verification methods exploit techniques based on mathematical and logical proofs to check whether a system meets the requirements of its initial specification. Indeed, system requirements are usually specified in a temporal logic like computational tree logic (CTL), and/or its extensions: extended CTL (eCTL), timed CTL (TCTL), etc. The system design is carried out using one of the existing formal languages such as *Petri Nets* and their extensions. Many system properties including safety, deadlock-freedom and liveness that are specified by a temporal logic can be verified using model-checking [1,4]. Model-checking is the process that takes as inputs a model (typically a state/transition system) and a property (typically written in a temporal logic), then proves that the system satisfies the given property or provides a counterexample of the execution that falsifies it.

Reconfigurability is the ability of systems to transform their selves and their working process in order to adapt to a changed inner/outer environment, respond to user requirements, prevent malfunctions when hardware failures occur during the process, etc. Reconfigurable real-time systems are systems that encompass reconfigurability constraints [20,21,31,33,34] and they subject to real-time requirements [29,30].

By the inclusion of some new skills, reconfigurable real-time systems become more complex, i.e., their design includes more details, and their verification becomes more expensive in terms of computation time and memory. Researchers have tried to deal with the formal modeling and verification of discrete event systems using *Petri nets* and their extensions. Badouel *et al.* [3] proposed reconfigurable Petri nets which are considered as high level Petri nets with special abilities of self reconfiguration. Biermann *et al.* [7] proposed reconfigurable object Petri nets (RONs) that are used to design reconfigurable manufacturing systems as demonstrated in [15]. RONs formalism has two types of places (1) net places that contain ordinary Petri nets as tokens, and (2) rule places that contain rules as tokens. Also, two types of transitions (1) firing transitions that model the simple firing of Petri nets, and (2) transform transitions that model the reconfiguration of the system. Rausch and Hanisch [9,17,27] proposed net condition/event systems (NCESs) formalism which is a modular Petri nets extension enriched with event/condition signals that models interactions among system modules. NCESs are developed through the last years to timed net condition/event systems (TNCESs) [13] involving time constraints on arcs. Zhang *et al.* [6,10,11,19,25,32,35] proposed reconfigurable timed net condition/event systems (R-TNCESs) which is an enriched extension of Petri nets formalism that supports reconfiguration constraints. In R-TNCESs formalism [5,6,10,18], the system is represented by a couple $Sys(B_{sys}, R_{sys})$ such that (1) B_{sys} is a set of TNCESs that represent the behavior module, and (2) R_{sys} is a set of reconfiguration rules that represent the control module. All of those research works are important because they are building convenient formal models. However, these models face important problems when they are used to verify complex reconfigurable real-time systems.

The formal verification of reconfigurable real-time systems is a hard computationally problem that requires so much time and memory, and it is identified as a very expensive task. Consequently, proposing a new methodology for ensuring the safety of these systems as well as controlling the complexity of their verification is an important research area. In this paper, we model reconfigurable real-time systems using R-TNCESs formalism. In fact, R-TNCESs formalism is like the well-known formalism timed net condition/event systems (TNCESs) [13] such that R-TNCESs formalism does not change the semantic of TNCESs but it just gives functional structure and a pattern for reconfigurable systems in terms of (B_{sys}, R_{sys}). R-TNCES is a suitable model because it provides modularity, time and reconfiguration abilities. However, many computations and redundancies can be encountered during R-TNCESs verification process. To deal with the complexity problem, we propose a method that benefits from the similarities between the system's configurations to avoid unnecessary and repetitive calculations. Indeed the paper proposes a method that generates an accessibility graph from another one according to the system's reconfiguration. Given an R-TNCES $Sys(B_{sys}, R_{sys})$, where (1) $B_{sys} = \{C_1, C_2\}$ is the set of system configurations, (2) $R_{sys} = \{rule_{C_1C_2}\}$ is the set of possible reconfiguration rules such that $rule_{C_1C_2}$ transforms the configuration C_1 to C_2, and (3) $tAG(C_0)$ is the timed accessibility graph of the configuration C_0. The proposed method, in this paper, shows how to generate $tAG(C_2)$ from $tAG(C_1)$ according to $rule_{C_1C_2}$, (i.e., rather than computing the whole accessibility graph $tAG(C_2)$ from zero, the new method applies the corresponding graph modifications such as adding/removing a state/arc in $tAG(C_1)$ in order to obtain $tAG(C_2)$).

Hafidi et al. [11] propose a methodology that improves the modeling and the verification of reconfigurable discrete event control systems using R-TNCESs formalism. The authors main contribution is efficient for the verification of functional properties in R-TNCESs, i.e., the performance evaluation in [11] demonstrates an important gain in terms of verification time and used memory. However, the suggested methodology cannot be used for systems under reconfigurability and real-time.constraints. That is in [11], authors do not consider the verification of real-time properties. The main difference between the paper's methodology and the one presented in [11] is that it shows how to generate an accessibility graph from another one when a reconfiguration on real-time constraints occurs which is not considered in other works. In this work, we assume that functional properties are already verified in the system, we focus on real-time properties, reconfiguration properties, their modeling in R-TNCES formalism and their efficient verification.

The main contributions of this paper are summarized as:

- The enrichment of R-TNCESs with new real-time reconfiguration forms such that modifying the earliest/latest firing times on the timed arcs are included, i.e., new structure modification instruction for the new reconfiguration forms;
- The proposition of new rewriting rules that generate a new graph from a given one, according to the reconfiguration on time applied by the system, i.e., this is used to control the complexity of the verification task.
- The proposition of an algorithm that describes a methodology for R-TNCESs verification using the suggested method of graph generation.

The originality of this research work can be founded from two general parts, i.e., the formal modeling and the improved verification of reconfigurable real-time systems using R-TNCESs. To the best of our knowledge, this is the first study that deals with the enrichment of R-TNCESs modeling by the new reconfiguration form of real-time systems, i.e., the modification of time constraints on timed arcs. In addition, no previous research works have tackled with the complexity control and optimization of the verification task. The performance evaluation proves that the complexity of the verification task increases exponentially if it is not controlled such as in the blind method which constructs the whole accessibility graph of the system after each reconfiguration step. However, by using the proposed method in this paper, significant gains in computation time are achieved for the same verification result as in the classical algorithm. The experimentation and the performance evaluation results are compared using the model checker SESA [24, 28] which analyses TNCESs models and computes their accessibility graphs.

The present paper is an extended version of our previous paper [12], presented at ENASE'2019 conference. The methodology is improved by detailing content and yielding results. For better comparison, a real experimental case study (i.e., benchmark production system) was used: in order to illustrate the results of the conference paper.

The remainder of the paper is organized as follows. Section 2 outlines the definition of R-TNCES formalism and explains its enrichment with the new time reconfiguration forms. Section 3 defines the proposed method for improving the verification of real-time and reconfiguration properties in R-TNCESs. Section 4.3 shows the performance of the proposed method on a case study. Section 5 concludes the paper with the limitations and perspectives for future works.

2 Reconfigurable Timed Net Condition/Event Systems (R-TNCESs)

Reconfigurable timed net condition/event systems (R-TNCESs) are an extension of Petri nets, firstly introduced in 2013 [35], used for formal specification of reconfigurable discrete event control systems (RDECSs). An RDECS may encompass a set of configurations, where each one is modeled by a TNCES. A TNCES is a set of modules graphically represented as depicted in Fig. 1. To model an RDECS, we use the concept of control components (CCs) introduced in [16], i.e., the interconnected modules communicating with signals that compose each TNCES are called control components (CCs). The syntax and semantics of the previous structures are explained in this subsection.

2.1 Syntax

R-TNCESs are formally defined in [35] as a couple $RTN = (B, R)$ where B (respectively, R) is the behavior (respectively, the control) module of a reconfigurable discrete event control system (RDECS). B is a union of multi-TNCESs represented by

$$B = (P, T, F, W, CN, EN, DC, V, Z_0)$$

where,

- P (respectively, T) is a finite set of places (respectively, transitions);
- $F \subseteq (P \times T) \cup (T \times P)$ is a superset of flow arcs;
- $W : (P \times T) \cup (T \times P) \longrightarrow \{0, 1\}$ maps a weight to a flow arc;
- $W(x, : y) > 0$ if $(x, y) \in F$, and $W(x, y) = 0$ otherwise, where $x, : y \in P \cup T$, (iv) $CN \subseteq (P \times T)$ (respectively, $EN \subseteq (T \times T)$) is a superset of condition signals (respectively, event signals);
- $DC : F \cap (P \times T) \rightarrow \{[l_1, h_1], \ldots, [l_{|F \cap (P \times T)|}, h_{|F \cap (P \times T)|}]\}$ is a superset of time constraints on transition's input flow arcs, where $\forall i \in [1, | F \cap (P \times T) |]$, $l_i, h_i \in \mathbb{N}$ and $l_i < h_i$, (vi) $V : T \longrightarrow \{\vee, \wedge\}$ maps an event-processing mode (AND or OR) for every transition;
- $Z_0 = (M_0, D_0)$, where $M_0 : P \longrightarrow \{0, 1\}$ is the initial marking, and $D_0 : P \longrightarrow \{0\}$ is the initial clock position.

R is a set of reconfiguration rules such that rule r is a structure represented by

$$r = (Cond, s, x)$$

where,

- $Cond \rightarrow \{True, False\}$ is the pre-condition of r, i.e., r is executable only if $Cond = True$;
- $s : TN(^\bullet r) \rightarrow TN(r^\bullet)$ is the structure-modification instruction such that $TN(^\bullet r)$ (respectively, $TN(r^\bullet)$) represents the structure before (respectively, after) applying the reconfiguration r;
- $x : last_{state}(^\bullet r) \rightarrow initial_{state}(r^\bullet)$ is the state processing function.

In this paper, we denote by r_{ij} the reconfiguration rule that transforms $TNCES_i$ to $TNCES_j$.

As reported in [35], the basic possible structure-modification instructions for R-TNCESs are summarized by adding/removing signals (i.e., condition signals or event signals) between or among modules. However, other possible reconfiguration forms should be considered in this paper to express the transformation

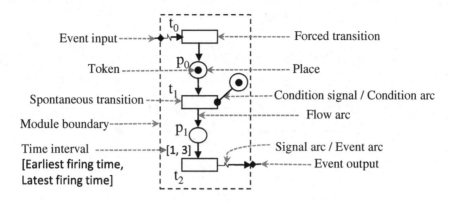

Fig. 1. RTNCESs module graphical model.

of time constraints. Therefore, we present in Table 1 [12] a new time structure-modification instructions for R-TNCESs. We denote by p a place, t a transition, eft the earliest firing time, lft the latest firing time, $\mathbb{N}^+ = \{1, 2, ...\}$ the set of positive natural numbers, and $\mathbb{N} = \mathbb{N}^+ \cup \{0\}$ the set of all natural numbers.

Table 1. Time structure-modification instructions [12].

Instruction	Symbol
Modify the earliest or/and the latest firing time value in the time interval of the flow arc (p, t)	$mtime((p, t), [eft, lft])$
$eft \in \mathbb{N}^+ \wedge lft, \omega \in \mathbb{N} \wedge eft < lft < \omega$	

eft: the new earliest firing time;
lft: the new latest firing time;
$mtime$: symbol of the instruction that modifies time constraints.

2.2 Semantics

The behavior of an R-TNCES $RTN(B_{RTN}, R_{RTN})$ is described by the dynamism of tokens inside of each $TNCES \in B_{RTN}$ (i.e., its behavior is affected by the firing conditions of transitions in TNCESs), and the transformations applied by each reconfiguration rule $rule \in R_{RTN}$. There exist two types of transitions in TNCESs formalism: spontaneous and forced. Forced transitions have at least an incoming signal arc from a forcing transition contrarily to spontaneous ones that do not have any incoming signal arcs. To be enabled, every transition should have token concession and condition concession which are described in Table 2. In addition, the forcing transitions with input flow arcs that are associated by time interval $[eft, lft]$ should fire after a duration d since it became

Table 2. Firing rules.

Firing rules	t is a spontaneous transition	t is a forced transition	Preconditions (conditions before firing t)	Post-conditions (results after firing t)
Token concession	Requires	Requires	$\forall p \in {}^{\bullet} t, \ M(p) = 1$	(1) $\forall p \in {}^{\bullet} t, \ M(p) = 0$ (2) $\forall p \in t^{\bullet}, \ M(p) = 1$
Condition concession	Requires	Requires	$\forall p \in {}^{-} t, \ M(p) = 1$	X^a
Requirement to forcing transition's firing	Does not require	Requires	(1) $V(t) = \wedge \rightarrow \forall t' \in {}^{\sim} t, \ fired(t')$; (2) $V(t) = \vee \rightarrow \exists t' \in {}^{\sim} t, \ fired(t')$	X^a

^{a} No conditions.

enabled such that $eft \le d \le lft$. In Table 2 and in the rest of this paper, we denote by

- $^{\bullet}t$ (resp, $t^{\bullet}$) the set of input (resp, output) places of the transition t;
- ^{-}t the set of input places that are connected to t through a condition signal;
- $M(p)$ the sum of tokens in the place p;
- $fired : T \rightarrow \{True, False\}$ the function that returns $True$ if the transition is fired, otherwise $False$;
- $^{\sim}t$ the set of forcing transitions of t (i.e., input transitions that are connected to t through an event signal).

A reconfiguration rule $rule(cond, s, x)$ has the priority to be applied first when its condition is verified, i.e., $cond = True$. In this case, the enability of transitions falls down and only the reconfiguration rule is applied. A reconfiguration rule r_{st} transforms a TNCES source TNS_s to a TNCES target TNS_t. $last_{state}(^{\bullet}r_{st})$ denotes the last state where the simulation among TNS_s ends (i.e., the dynamism of tokens), it also denotes the source state where the reconfiguration rule is applied. $initial_{state}(r_{st}^{\bullet})$ denotes the initial state where the simulation among TNS_t starts, it also denotes the target state after applying the reconfiguration rule.

3   Verification of Time Constraints in Reconfigurable Systems Using TAG

This section deals with the checking whether the modeled system (R-TNCES) meets the temporal requirements. In this task, we specify system properties using TCTL, we compute the accessibility graphs, and we use model-checking to check whether temporal properties are satisfied or not. Classical accessibility graphs (AGs) are extended to timed accessibility graphs (TAGs) and a new method is proposed to optimize the calculation of these last ones.

3.1   Formalization: TAG

Timed accessibility graph (TAG) of a TNCES TNS is a structure tAG given by

$$tAG(St,\ Ed,\ s_0)$$

where,

- St denotes the set of reachable states;
- $Ed : St \rightarrow St$ denotes the set of edges that defines state-transitions such that each edge is labeled by the executed step;
- s_0 denotes the initial state.

A state $s \in St$ is a structure given by

$$State(Mp,\ Pclocks,\ D)$$

where,

- Mp is the set of marked places in TNS;
- $Pclocks$ is a vector of integers representing places clock positions;
- D is the delay of the state which denotes the minimal number of time units after which at least one step becomes enabled.

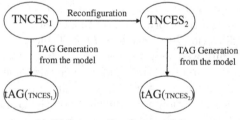

(a) TAG generation from model.

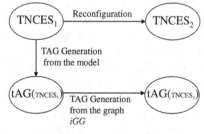

(b) TAG generation from graph.

Fig. 2. TAG generation from graph [12].

3.2   TAG Generation from a Graph (Contribution)

Given two TNCESs $TNCES_1$ and $TNCES_2$ such that $TNCES_2$ is obtained from $TNCES_1$ by applying a time modification instruction. Classically, $tAG(TNCES_1)$ (respectively, $tAG(TNCES_2)$) the timed accessibility graph of $TNCES_1$ (respectively, $TNCES_2$) is computed using the classical algorithm explained in [28], where the whole accessibility graph of each structure is computed from zero (Fig. 2(a)) [12].

Actually, $tAG(TNCES_1)$ and $tAG(TNCES_2)$ share some similar parts (subgraphs) that should not be recomputed again while generating $tAG(TNCES_2)$. Consequently, the complexity of the accessibility graphs generation can be optimized if these repetitive computations are avoided. In this paper as depicted in Fig. 2(b) [12], we propose an improved graph-generation method iGG that computes $tAG(TNCES_2)$ from the graph $tAG(TNCES_1)$ rather than computing $tAG(TNCES_2)$ from the model. The proposed iGG method then, considers the already computed parts and does not recalculate them.

3.3   The Improved Graph-Generation Method iGG (Contribution)

In order to verify system properties in an R-TNCES model $RTN(B, R)$, the timed accessibility graph of each TNCES $TS \in B$ should be generated using the classical method described in [28], i.e., the algorithm is therefore executed $| B |$ times. Consequently, the operation requires more time and memory.

Given two TNCESs structures $TNCES_a$, $TNCES_b$, where tAG_a is the timed accessibility graph of $TNCES_a$. The TNCES $TNCES_b$ is obtained from $TNCES_a$ after applying a transformation of time constraints which is described by the structure modification instruction SMI in Tables 1 and 3. The new proposed method iGG (improved graph generation) takes as an input tAG_a then transforms it into a new graph tAG_b by adding/removing some states/edges from tAG_a. Therefore, the complexity of iGG is $\mathcal{O}(1)$ in its best case where $\mathcal{O}(1)$ is the complexity of each instruction of modification on the graph. The complexity in the worst case is $\mathcal{O}(e^m)$, such that $\mathcal{O}(e^m)$ is the complexity of accessibility graphs computations as reported in [22]. The resulting graph is exactly the timed accessibility graph of $TNCES_b$ except that by using iGG method, there are less computed states, i.e., no repetitive calculations for the similar parts.

Table 3 [12] introduces the proposed rewriting rules on timed accessibility graphs (TAGs) related to the new time structure modification instructions (SMI) proposed in this paper. We denote by e a TAG edge, t a transition, Ed the set of edges in a TAG, s a state in a TAG, St the set of states in a TAG, $sc(e)$ the function that returns the source state of an edge e in a TAG, and $Label(e)$ the function that returns the label of the edge e in a TAG.

iGG method is applied in the case of having n SMIs to get tAG_b as follows.

$Step_0$ Copy tAG_a to tAG_b, i.e., initially, tAG_b is a copy of tAG_a;
$Step_1$ For every structure modification instruction SMI apply the indicated rewriting rules (Table 3) on tAG_b;
$Step_2$ Delete all unreachable states in tAG_b.

Table 3. Rewriting rules on TAG [12].

SMI	Rewriting rules on TAGs	Comments
$mtime((p,\ t),\ [eft,\ lft])$	(a) $\forall e \in Ed,\ t \subset Label(e) ::= St \leftarrow St \setminus \{sc(e)\};$	(a) Remove all source states of edges labeled by t in TAG;
	(b) $\forall s \in St ::= SimulationFrom(s)$	(b) Continue the simulation from each state

3.4 $iGG_{generalized}$: iGG for R-TNCESs (Contribution)

Algorithm 1 [12] deals with the application of iGG in the case when having n TNCESs. The proposed algorithm is recursive and composed of a parallel part that computes the TAGs of reachable TNCESs in the same time when possible. The algorithm stops in two cases: (1) if the behavior of a configuration is not validated by the verification, or (2) if it reaches a configuration that has been already verified before, i.e., to avoid redundant computations. In Algorithm 1, we denote by: (1) $NextConfigs(tAG, R)$ the function that from the TAG tAG of the current TNCES and a set of possible reconfiguration rules R returns the set of reachable TNCESs resulted from reconfigurations (2) $newTN(TNCES_i)$ the Boolean function that returns $True$ if $TNCES_i$ has not been verified before, otherwise it returns $False$, (3) $iGG(tAG, TNCES_i)$ the function that generates and returns the TAG of $TNCES_i$ from the TAG tAG (already explained in previous subsections), and (4) $verifyPropertiesIn(tAG_i, p)$ the Boolean function that returns $True$ if the system indicated properties p are verified on tAG_i, otherwise it returns $False$.

Algorithm 1. $iGG_{Generalized}$.

Input: $RTN(B$: Set of TNCESs, R : Set of Reconfiguration Rules): R-TNCES;
  $\quad\quad tAG_{current}$: TAG; p: Set of Properties;
Variables : tAG: TAG; $isCorrect$: Boolean; $ToVerify$: Set of TNCESs;
1 $tAG \leftarrow tAG_{current}$;
2 $ToVerify \leftarrow NextConfigs(tAG, R)$;
3 **foreach** $TNCES_i \in ToVerify$ **in parallel do**
4 $\quad$ **if** $newTN(TNCES_i)$ /* New TNCES: if its TAG has not been computed yet $\quad\quad$ */
5 $\quad$ **then**
6 $\quad\quad$ $tAG_i \leftarrow iGG(tAG, TNCES_i)$;
7 $\quad\quad$ $isCorrect \leftarrow verifyPropertiesIn(tAG_i, p)$;
8 $\quad\quad$ **if** $isCorrect == True$ **then**
9 $\quad\quad\quad$ $iGG_{Generalized}(RTN(B, R), tAG_i, p)$;
10 $\quad\quad$ **end**
11 $\quad$ **end**
12 **end**

3.5   Automatic Tool for R-TNCESs: SESA

SESA [24,28] is an automatic model checker for TNCESs formalism. SESA model-checker is an effective tool to compute the set of reachable states of a TNCES. It can also verify functional and temporal properties specified using CTL and its extensions. In this research work, we use SESA to model the different configurations of R-TNCESs. After that, we compute the state space of each configuration automatically using the tool. We use SESA outputs to validate the results given by our methodology. At this stage of our work, we use comparaison method to check that informations on behaviour are not lost when including the proposed methods for improved graph generation.

4   Experimentation

In this section, we apply the proposed method on a hypothetical manufacturing plant in order to illustrate it. After that, we evaluate its performance on large scale systems using factors like redundancy rate.

4.1   Running Example: Benchmark Production System

A hypothetical manufacturing system MS is physically composed of a set of interconnected units. Each unit is a set of components that work together in order to achieve a system task in a known time interval. MS is a reconfigurable real-time system, i.e., all its components are subjected to real-time and reconfigurability constraints. MS can run in several modes, and it can switch from a mode to another during its working process according to predefined conditions. This dynamism allows the system to be flexible to manufacturing demands or to prevent from malfunctions when hardware failures occur during its working process.

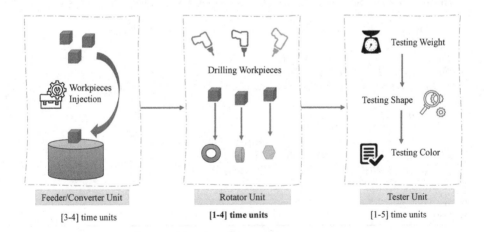

Fig. 3. MS working process.

Figure 3 represents MS working process and components. MS has three main units,

- Feeder/Converter unit: composed of a feeder that injects workpieces to the system, and a converter that converts then elevates them to the rotator unit;
- Rotator unit: composed of a rotator that rotates workpieces and drilling machines that drills them to perform the required shape;
- Tester unit: composed of sensors that receive workpieces from the rotator unit and test if they respect required weight, shape and color. After that, it transfers workpieces to other system units to continue the process of manufacturing.

Each system unit is associated by an interval of time. This interval of time described the earliest and the latest time units that each workpiece takes to leave that unit. MS has two modes: $mode_1$ and $mode_2$. MS switches from: $mode_1$ to $mode_2$ when precondition 2 is fulfilled, and from $mode_2$ to $mode_1$ when precondition 1 is fulfilled. By switching from $mode_1$ to $mode_2$, the system MS changes its time properties, i.e., time interval of Rotator unit becomes [0–4]. MS system can make this change in order to increase/decrease system performance, avoid some malfunctions that are due to material failure, minimize the used energy or cost, etc. This is actually done according to manufacturing demands and needs.

System Encoding. To apply the proposed methods, MS should be modeled using a formalism. MS is a reconfigurable real-time system composed of two configurations (i.e., configurations represent system modes: $mode_1$ and $mode_2$) and two reconfigurations (i.e., reconfigurations represent system switching from a mode to another), can be modeled using R-TNCESs formalism as follows. MS is an R-TNCES $RMS(B_{RMS}, R_{RMS})$ such that $B_{RMS} = \{conf_1, conf_2\}$ is the behavior module containing all possible configurations and $R_{RMS} = \{rec_{12}, rec_{21}\}$ is the control module containing all possible reconfigurations. Configuration $conf_1$ represents $mode_1$ and configuration $conf_2$ represents $mode_2$ of MS system. MS system units are presented by R-TNCESs modules in RMS. $conf_1$ is the initial configuration of MS system, and it is graphically presented as in Fig. 4.

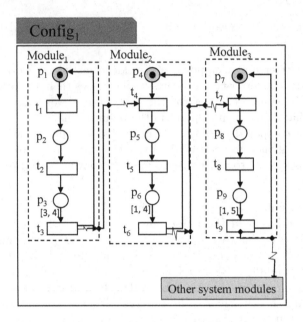

Fig. 4. $RM\overset{*}{S}$: $Config_1$ graphical presentation.

Possible system reconfigurations are: $conf_1 \rightarrow conf_2$ which is described by the reconfiguration rule rec_{12} and $conf_2 \rightarrow conf_1$ which is described by the reconfiguration rule rec_{21} in the control module R_{RMS}. Reconfiguration rules elements are described in Table 4.

Table 4. RMS system reconfiguration rules.

Reconfiguration rule	Precondition	s function	x function
rec_{12}	$True$	$\{mtime((p_6, t_6), [0, 4])\}$	$\{(S_9, config_1), (S_1, config_2)\}$
rec_{21}	$True$	$\{mtime((p_6, t_6), [1, 4])\}$	$\{(S_{16}, config_2), (S_1, config_1)\}$

By applying the transformations described by rec_{12} on the initial configuration $config_1$, we obtain $config_2$ model as described in Fig. 5.

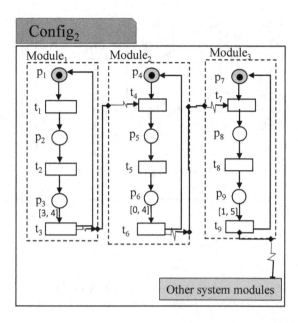

Fig. 5. RMS: $Config_2$ graphical presentation.

System Verification. In this research work, we focus on real-time properties verification. Thus, we consider that all other functional properties are already verified in the system RMS. Reconfigurations run spontaneously when their conditions are fulfilled, i.e., there are no time constraints on reconfiguration scenarios. Therefore, the control module R_{RMS} is not considered by the verification of real-time properties. Contrarily, the behavior module B_{RMS} contains a set of TNCESs which are timed and should be validated by checking real-time properties. Note that in the behavior module B_{RMS}, there exist similar parts between both configurations $conf_1$ and $conf_2$, e.g., $module_1$ in $conf_1$ is similar to $module_1$ in $conf_2$ and $module_3$ in $conf_1$ is similar to $module_3$ in $conf_2$. That because in reality, only some parts are transformed in reconfigurable systems, other parts are still the same in all process. The repetitive calculations on those similar parts are considered as redundancies that make of the verification a complex task.

In this subsection, we try to apply the proposed method to verify the R-TNCES $RMS(B_{RMS}, R_{RMS})$ efficiently by avoiding as much as possible unnecessary computations. The timed accessibility graph of the initial structure $conf_1$ is computed classically using SESA tool. The resulted graph $tAG(conf_1)$ is depicted in Fig. 6.

To compute $tAG(conf_2)$ from $tAG(conf_1)$ we use the improved graph-generation method iGG as following:

$Step_0$ Copy $tAG(conf_1)$ to $tAG(conf_2)$;
$Step_1$ Apply the rewriting rules (Table 3) on tAG_{conf_2} as in $Step_{11}$ and $Step_{12}$;

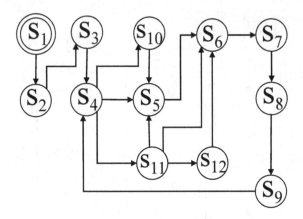

Fig. 6. $tAG(conf_1)$ [12].

$Step_{1.1}$ $(\forall e \in Ed_2, t_6 \subset Label(e) ::= St_2 \leftarrow St_2 \setminus \{s_6\}) \Rightarrow St_2 \leftarrow St_2 \setminus \{s_6\}$.
Ed_2 (respectively, St_2) represents the set of edges (respectively, states) in $tAG(conf_2)$;

$Step_{1.2}$ $\forall s \in St ::= SimulationFrom(s)$. By the simulation, new states are created: $St_2 \leftarrow St_2 \cup \{S_6, S_{13}\ S_{14}\ S_{15}\ S_{16}\ S_{17}\ S_{18}\}$;

$Step_2$ Delete all unreachable states in $tAG(conf_2)$: $St_2 \leftarrow St_2 \setminus \{S_7,\ S_8\ S_9\ S_{15}\}$.

After following the previous steps, $tAG(conf_2)$ the new accessibility graph of $conf_2$ is achieved.

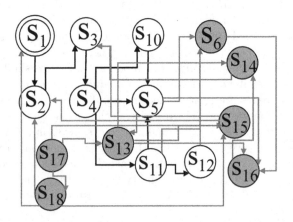

Fig. 7. $tAG(conf_2)$ [12].

$tAG(conf_2)$ is depicted in Fig. 7 where the colored states among it denote the new computed ones.

Note that the studied system RMS has 12 states in the configuration $conf_1$, and 15 states in the configuration $conf_2$ where only 7 states are computed using the improved graph-generation method iGG, i.e., the other states are kept from the first TAG $tAG(conf_1)$. Therefore, iGG has avoided the unnecessary repetitive computations and optimized RMS accessibility graphs generation by more than 50% calculations.

4.2   Concept of Redundancies

We define the function $RRedun(TNCES_a, TNCES_b)$ that takes two TNCESs $TNCES_a$, $TNCES_b$ and gives the redundancy rate between them.
$RRedun(TNCES_a, TNCES_b)$ is computed as follows

$$RRedun(TNCES_a, TNCES_b) = \frac{\#similarStates}{\#States}$$

where (1) $\#similarStates$ is the number of similar states that appear in both graphs $tAG(TNCES_a)$ and $tAG(TNCES_b)$, and (2) $\#States$ is the total number of states in $tAG(TNCES_b)$.

We denote by: (1) low redundancy rate LRR the systems with $RRedun \leq 30\%$, (2) medium redundancy rate MRR the systems with $30\% < RRedun < 80\%$, and (3) high redundancy rate HRR the systems with $RRedun \geq 80\%$, e.g. in the previous running example $RRedun(conf_1, conf_2) = \frac{8}{15} = 53\%$ is the redundancy rate of RMS which denotes that RMS is in MRR systems. This concept will be used in performance evaluation part as a factor.

4.3   Evaluation

The proposed method has proven benefits in the experimentation of the previous running example. We want to study its efficiency in larger systems by measuring computed states where a parameter namely redundancy rate is used as a factor to held the performance evaluation in different kinds of problems.

The 3D surfaces in Fig. 8 [12] depict the number of computed states resulted from the analyzes held on R-TNCESs with: (1) different redundancy rates, and (2) different numbers of nodes. The study is performed in two cases, the former by using the proposed iGG method while computing the TAGs, the latter using the classical method and without any improvement. The surfaces show that the number of computed states using iGG reduces when the $RRedun$ is higher, i.e., in HRR systems. Therefore, iGG method performs best for HRR systems verification regardless the number of nodes. The surface presented in Fig. 8(a) [12] matches to the surface depicted in Fig. 8(b) [12] when $RRedun = 0$. Thus, iGG method turns to classical verification methods when the redundancy rate is very low, i.e., the method is in its worst case (Table 5).

Table 5. RMS reachable states markings and clock positions [12].

State		P_1	P_2	P_3	P_4	P_5	P_6	P_7	P_8	P_9	D
S_1	Mp	1	0	0	1	0	0	1	0	0	0
	$Pclocks$	0	0	0	0	0	0	0	0	0	
S_2	Mp	0	1	0	1	0	0	1	0	0	0
	$Pclocks$	0	0	0	0	0	0	0	0	0	
S_3	Mp	0	0	1	1	0	0	1	0	0	2
	$Pclocks$	0	0	0	0	0	0	0	0	0	
S_4	Mp	1	0	0	0	1	0	1	0	0	0
	$Pclocks$	0	0	0	0	0	0	0	0	0	
S_5	Mp	0	1	0	0	0	1	1	0	0	0
	$Pclocks$	0	0	0	0	0	0	0	0	0	
S_6	Mp	0	0	1	0	0	1	1	0	0	1
	$Pclocks$	0	0	0	0	0	0	0	0	0	
S_7	Mp	0	0	1	1	0	0	0	1	0	0
	$Pclocks$	0	0	1	0	0	0	0	0	0	
S_8	Mp	0	0	1	1	0	0	0	0	1	0
	$Pclocks$	0	0	1	0	0	0	0	0	0	
S_9	Mp	0	0	1	1	0	0	1	0	0	2
	$Pclocks$	0	0	1	0	0	0	0	0	0	
S_{10}	Mp	1	0	0	0	0	1	1	0	0	0
	$Pclocks$	0	0	0	0	0	0	0	0	0	
S_{11}	Mp	0	1	0	0	1	0	1	0	0	0
	$Pclocks$	0	0	0	0	0	0	0	0	0	
S_{12}	Mp	0	0	1	0	1	0	1	0	0	0
	$Pclocks$	0	0	0	0	0	0	0	0	0	
S_{13}	Mp	0	1	0	1	0	0	0	1	0	0
	$Pclocks$	0	0	0	0	0	0	0	0	0	
S_{14}	Mp	0	0	1	1	0	0	0	0	1	0
	$Pclocks$	0	0	0	0	0	0	0	0	0	
S_{15}	Mp	0	1	0	1	0	0	0	0	1	0
	$Pclocks$	0	0	0	0	0	0	0	0	0	
S_{16}	Mp	0	0	1	1	0	0	0	1	0	0
	$Pclocks$	0	0	0	0	0	0	0	0	0	
S_{17}	Mp	0	0	1	0	0	1	1	0	0	0
	$Pclocks$	0	0	0	0	0	0	0	0	0	
S_{18}	Mp	1	0	0	1	0	0	0	1	0	0
	$Pclocks$	0	0	0	0	0	0	0	0	0	

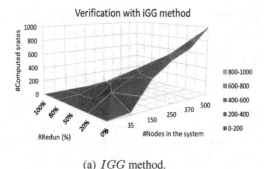

(a) *IGG* method.

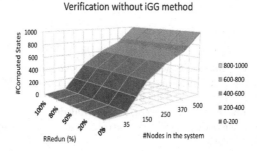

(b) Classical method.

Fig. 8. *iGG* efficiency [12].

5   Conclusion

In this paper, we deal with the formal modeling and verification of reconfig-urable real-time systems using reconfigurable timed net condition/event systems (R-TNCESs) formalism. We enrich the modeling with new possible reconfigu-ration forms: the modification of the earliest/latest firing time in the intervals associated to flow arcs. We suggest a new method for efficient verification of R-TNCESs when reconfigurations in time occur in the system. The proposed method *iGG* showed how to generate a TAG from another one to avoid repeti-tive computations when the two TAGs have some similar parts.

We applied the paper contribution on a benchmark manufacturing system. According to case study and performance evaluation results, it is shown that the verification task of temporal properties has been improved in terms of computing time and memory. In addition, it is shown that the proposed method performs best for *HRR* systems. The proposed method is less beneficial in *LRR* sys-tems. Actually in RDECSs reconfigurations, the transformation includes only some modules and others will still be identical as those in the source model, which gives a high similarity between models and makes most of them *HRR* systems. Therefore, the proposed methodology is suitable for RDECSs improved verification. Compared with the previous related works, this work presents a new reconfiguration form to the R-TNCES formalism, a method to verify real-time properties where the correctness of the system is considered and also the complexity of its verification is controlled.

Future works will (1) provide a formal proof of correctness proving that information on the system's behavior are not lost or corrupted after applying the proposed improvement method, (2) consider probabilistic constraints in the verification task, and (3) involve new techniques to reduce the system properties and TAGs in order to improve the model-checking on R-TNCESs, and (4) include the proposed improvement method in a model-checker in order to automatize it and profit from its gain. Finally the proposed techniques will be generalized to be considered in other formalisms like reconfigurable Petri nets [23].

References

1. Aichernig, B.K., Schumi, R.: Statistical model checking meets property-based testing. In: Proceedings IEEE International Conference on Software Testing, Verification and Validation ICST, pp. 390–400. IEEE (2017)
2. Arcaini, P., Riccobene, E., Scandurra, P.: Formal design and verification of self-adaptive systems with decentralized control. ACM Trans. Auton. Adapt. Syst. (TAAS) 11(4), 25 (2017)
3. Badouel, E., Oliver, J.: Reconfigurable nets, a class of high level Petri nets supporting dynamic changes within workflow systems. Ph.D. thesis, Inria (1998)
4. Baier, C., Katoen, J., Larsen, K.: Principles of Model Checking. MIT Press, Cambridge (2008)
5. Ben Salah, H., Benzina, A., Khalgui, M.: Verification of reconfigurable NoC under quality of service constraints. In: Proceedings IEEE 40th Annual Computer Software and Applications Conference (COMPSAC), pp. 329–334. IEEE (2016)
6. Ben Salem, M.O., Mosbahi, O., Khalgui, M., Jlalia, Z., Frey, G., Smida, M.: BROMETH: methodology to design safe reconfigurable medical robotic systems. Int. J. Med. Robot. Comput. Assist. Surg. 13(3), 1786 (2016). https://doi.org/10.1002/rcs.1786
7. Biermann, E., Modica, T.: Independence analysis of firing and rule-based net transformations in reconfigurable object nets. Electron. Commun. EASST 10 (2008)
8. Clarke, E.M., Henzinger, T.A., Veith, H., Bloem, R.: Handbook of Model Checking. Springer, Heidelberg (2016)
9. Dubinin, V., Vyatkin, V., Hanisch, H.M.: Synthesis of safety controllers for distributed automation systems on the basis of reverse safe net condition/event systems. In: Proceedings IEEE Trustcom/BigDataSE/ISPA, vol. 3, pp. 287–292, August 2015
10. Guellouz, S., Benzina, A., Khalgui, M., Frey, G.: ZiZo: a complete tool chain for the modeling and verification of reconfigurable function blocks. In: UBICOMM 2016: the Tenth International Conference on Mobile Ubiquitous Computing, Systems, Services and Technologies, 10 2016 (2016)
11. Hafidi, Y., Kahloul, L., Khalgui, M., Li, Z., Alnowibet, K., Qu, T.: On methodology for the verification of reconfigurable timed net condition/event systems. IEEE Trans. Syst. Man Cybern. Syst. 99, 1–15 (2018)

12. Hafidi, Y., Kahloul, L., Khalgui, M., Ramdani, M.: On improved verification of reconfigurable real-time systems. In: Proceedings of the 14th International Conference on Evaluation of Novel Approaches to Software Engineering - Volume 1: ENASE, pp. 394–401. INSTICC, SciTePress (2019). https://doi.org/10.5220/0007736603940401

13. Hanisch, H.M., Thieme, J., Luder, A., Wienhold, O.: Modeling of PLC behavior by means of timed net condition/event systems. In: Proceedings 6th International Conference on Emerging Technologies and Factory Automation Proceedings, pp. 391–396. IEEE (1997)

14. Hasan, O., Tahar, S.: Formal verification methods. In: Encyclopedia of Information Science and Technology, 3rd (edn.), pp. 7162–7170. IGI Global (2015)

15. Kahloul, L., Bourekkache, S., Djouani, K.: Designing reconfigurable manufacturing systems using reconfigurable object Petri nets. Int. J. Comput. Integr. Manuf. **29**(8), 889–906 (2016)

16. Khalgui, M., Mosbahi, O., Li, Z., Hanisch, H.M.: Reconfigurable multiagent embedded control systems: from modeling to implementation. IEEE Trans. Comput. **60**(4), 538–551 (2011)

17. Khalgui, M.: NCES-based modelling and CTL-based verification of reconfigurable embedded control systems. Comput. Ind. **61**(3), 198–212 (2010)

18. Khlifi, O., Mosbahi, O., Khalgui, M., Frey, G.: GR-TNCES: new extensions of R-TNCES for modelling and verification of flexible systems under energy and memory constraints. In: Proceedings 10th International Joint Conference on Software Technologies (ICSOFT), vol. 1, pp. 1–8. IEEE (2015)

19. Khlifi, O., Mosbahi, O., Khalgui, M., Frey, G.: New verification approach for reconfigurable distributed systems. In: Proceedings 12th International Conference on Software and Data Technologies ICSOFT, pp. 355–362, 01 2017 (2017)

20. Lakhdhar, W., Mzid, R., Khalgui, M., Li, Z., Frey, G., Al-Ahmari, A.: Multiobjective optimization approach for a portable development of reconfigurable real-time systems: from specification to implementation. IEEE Trans. Syst. Man Cybern. Syst. **49**, 623–637 (2018)

21. Lyke, J.C., Christodoulou, C.G., Vera, G.A., Edwards, A.H.: An introduction to reconfigurable systems. Proc. IEEE **103**(3), 291–317 (2015)

22. Murata, T.: Petri nets: properties, analysis and applications. Proc. IEEE **77**(4), 541–580 (1989)

23. Padberg, J., Kahloul, L.: Overview of reconfigurable Petri nets. In: Heckel, R., Taentzer, G. (eds.) Graph Transformation, Specifications, and Nets. LNCS, vol. 10800, pp. 201–222. Springer, Cham (2018). https://doi.org/10.1007/978-3-319-75396-6_11

24. Patil, S., Vyatkin, V., Pang, C.: Counterexample-guided simulation framework for formal verification of flexible automation systems. In: Proceedings IEEE 13th International Conference on Industrial Informatics (INDIN), pp. 1192–1197, July 2015

25. Ramdani, M., Kahloul, L., Khalgui, M.: Automatic properties classification approach for guiding the verification of complex reconfigurable systems. In: Proceedings of the 13th International Conference on Software Technologies - Volume 1: ICSOFT, pp. 591–598. INSTICC, SciTePress (2018). https://doi.org/10.5220/0006863005910598

26. Ramdani, M., Kahloul, L., Khalgui, M., Hafidi, Y.: R-TNCES rebuilding: a new method of CTL model update for reconfigurable systems. In: Proceedings of

the 14th International Conference on Evaluation of Novel Approaches to Software Engineering - Volume 1: ENASE, pp. 159–168. INSTICC, SciTePress (2019). https://doi.org/10.5220/0007736801590168

27. Rausch, M., Hanisch, H.M.: Net condition/event systems with multiple condition outputs. In: Proceedings Emerging Technologies and Factory Automation, vol. 1, pp. 592–600. IEEE (1995)
28. Starke, P.H., Roch, S.: Analysing Signal-Net Systems. Citeseer, New York (2002)
29. Wang, C., Pastore, F., Briand, L.: System testing of timing requirements based on use cases and timed automata. In: Proceedings IEEE International Conference on Software Testing, Verification and Validation ICST. IEEE (2017)
30. Wang, X., Li, Z., Wonham, W.M.: Dynamic multiple-period reconfiguration of real-time scheduling based on timed DES supervisory control. IEEE Trans. Ind. Inf. **12**(1), 101–111 (2016). https://doi.org/10.1109/TII.2015.2500161
31. Yanase, R., Sakai, T., Sakai, M., Yamane, S.: Formal verification of dynamically reconfigurable systems. In: Proceedings IEEE 4th Global Conference on Consumer Electronics (GCCE), pp. 71–75, October 2015
32. Zhang, J., Frey, G., Al-Ahmari, A., Qu, T., Wu, N., Li, Z.: Analysis and control of dynamic reconfiguration processes of manufacturing systems. IEEE Access **6**, 28028–28040 (2017)
33. Zhang, J., et al.: Modeling and verification of reconfigurable and energy-efficient manufacturing systems. Discret. Dyn. Nat. Soc. **2015**, 14 (2015)
34. Zhang, J., Khalgui, M., Li, Z., Frey, G., Mosbahi, O., Salah, H.B.: Reconfigurable coordination of distributed discrete event control systems. IEEE Trans. Control Sys. Techn. **23**(1), 323–330 (2015)
35. Zhang, J., Khalgui, M., Li, Z., Mosbahi, O., Al-Ahmari, A.: R-TNCES: a novel formalism for reconfigurable discrete event control systems. IEEE Trans. Systems Man Cybern. Syst. **43**(4), 757–772 (2013)

On Improving R-TNCES Rebuilding for Reconfigurable Real-Time Systems

Mohamed Ramdani[1,2,3,4]($\boxtimes$), Laid Kahloul[2], Mohamed Khalgui[3], and Yousra Hafidi[1,2,3,4]

[1] LISI Laboratory, National Institute of Applied Sciences and Technology, University of Carthage, 1080 Tunis, Tunisia
ramdani.moh19@gmail.com
[2] LINFI Laboratory, Computer Science Department, Biskra University, Biskra, Algeria
laid.k.b@gmail.com
[3] School of Electrical and Information Engineering, Jinan University, Guangzho, China
khalgui.mohamed@gmail.com
[4] University of Tunis El Manar, Tunis, Tunisia
yousra_hafidi@hotmail.com

Abstract. This paper deals with improved verification of real-time systems that extend the classical formal verification with the rebuilding of reconfigurable timed net condition event systems (R-TNCESs). Indeed, previous computation tree logic (CTL) model repair approaches make the model checking eligible for generating a new correct model from a faulty one at the debugging level. We propose R-TNCESs rebuilding method, which allows both verification and modification of real-time system models. The proposed approach generates from an incorrect model a new one that satisfies a given computation tree logic/Timed computation tree logic formula. Temporal logic formulas (CTL/TCTL) are defined to deal with the system functional/temporal properties specification respectively. This paper provides an efficient algorithm with a set of transformation rules to achieve the rebuilding phase. Finally, FESTO MPS platform is used as a case study to demonstrate the proposed rebuilding method for real-time system models. The obtained results show the efficiency of our contribution and its scalability in large complex systems.

Keywords: Real-time systems · Reconfigurable discrete-event system · Reconfigurable timed net condition event system · Computation tree logic · Model rebuilding

1 Introduction

The explosion of functionalities in asynchronous and non-deterministic systems and the auto-control deployment in such systems have created a new class of systems called: reconfigurable discrete event/control systems (RDECSs). RDECSs

© Springer Nature Switzerland AG 2020
E. Damiani et al. (Eds.): ENASE 2019, CCIS 1172, pp. 267–285, 2020.
https://doi.org/10.1007/978-3-030-40223-5_13

can work under various conditions: concurrency, control, communication, etc. Such class of systems includes manufacturing systems [16], real time systems [9], and embedded systems [7], etc. RDECSs represent a class of systems that adapts the set of internal changes dynamically and timely to the external changes and user requirements (reconfiguration). This adaptation can be inside the structure, functionality, or control algorithms [18]. There are two types of reconfiguration: static reconfiguration at the design time and dynamic reconfiguration at the runtime [8].

Model-checking is an effective technique for the automatic verification of functional and nonfunctional (time constraints) properties of RDECSs. In spite of the complexity of RDECSs, model-checking verifies the satisfaction between a formal model and a functional/nonfunctional property, which is specified by a temporal logic (CTL, TCTL, etc.). To deal with reconfigurable systems, it is necessary to develop new methods, formalisms, and tools to reduce the complexity of computation and to facilitate the design phase. Therefore, many formalisms are proposed and extended. Petri net is one of the most used formalism developed to cope with reconfigurability (reconfigurable Petri nets [13]). Reconfigurable time net condition/event systems (R-TNCES) are one of their extensions [17].

In the last decade, model-checking is also taking its share from the evolution and the improvement. It becomes more efficient in the debugging of errors and their auto-correction. The computation tree logic (CTL) *update* method proposed by [5] is one of these progressions, it modifies the system model in order to satisfy a given formula. In such context, different works of model modification are developed. Ding and Zhang in [5,19] proposed an algorithm based on a set of basic operations and minimal change criteria. Carrillo and Rosenblueth proposed another algorithm and introduced the protection concept in [4]. Martinez and Lopez proposed a CTL repair methodology for different classes of Petri nets, [10] for labeled state machines (LSM), [11] for bounded and deadlock free Petri nets, and [12] for open work-flow nets (oWFN). [14] have developed a new method to rebuild reconfigurable systems models using R-TNCESs models.

In the previous verification techniques of reconfigurable models, [14] covers the impotence of the layer-by-layer verification proposed in [17] and the formal verification proposed in [6] for automatizing the correction of a model which does not satisfy a property formula. Unfortunately, all the proposed methods overlook the nonfunctional properties, which are the time constraints. Indeed, with the system complexity, the high number of properties to be checked and the absence of a technique that facilitates the debugging task make the verification phase of R-TNCESs a hard task.

In this paper, we deal with the verification and model repair of reconfigurable systems modeled with R-TNCESs according to functional and temporal properties. We propose a new methodology called R-TNCESs rebuilding. First, we compute a Timed automata model from the behavior module of R-TNCES. Second, based on the original formula to be verified on the R-TNCES, we extract a CTL/TCTL formula to be verified in the computed automaton with the same semantic value. Using the five primitives of Ding and the minimal change criteria [5], the error will be localized and corrected at the automaton level using Uppaal model checker [2] in the verification of CTL or TCTL formula. Finally, according to the equivalence between the changes in the timed automata model and the modification instructions of the R-TNCESs formalism, we apply the reverse operation to get the new model of the R-TNCES which satisfies the given property.

To validate our methodology and to illustrate the virtue of the contribution, we use an academic case study FESTO MPS [17], which is a lab-scale station. The behavior module of FESTO MPS is deployed to show the performance of the different algorithms and to check the functional properties (properties of broadcasting and synchronizations) and the nonfunctional properties (properties of time constraints). The model-checker Uppaal is used to check CTL/TCTL properties of the timed automata. It is a toolbox for verification of real-time systems [2]. SESA model checker [15] is used to confirm the result of R-TNCESs rebuilding. Indeed, SESA is a software to analyze TNCESs and to compute the exact reachable set of states.

To address the correctness of the system, our proposition aims to ensure the viability of the R-TNCES model by checking properties on the broadcasting and its synchronization and by ensuring the respect of the time limits constraint. In this research, we provide a generalization of CTL model update approach from Petri nets formalism to R-TNCESs formalism to ensure the corrections in a complex system (i.e., RDECSs). We present an approach for reconfigurable models rebuilding, which it is able to generate a new model that satisfies requirements specified by a CTL/TCTL formula while respecting the original model and the minimal changes stated by Ding [5]. We have developed an algorithm to compute a timed automaton from an R-TNCES model, and another algorithm to adapt a temporal logic formula CTL/TCTL to a timed automaton verification without losing information.

The paper is organized as follows. Section 2 presents the preliminary concepts used throughout the paper. Section 3 contains the methodologies of the rebuilding operation for reconfigurable systems. In Sect. 4, experimental results are showcased through an academic case study. Finally, Sect. 5 concludes the paper and presents our future research directions.

2   Preliminaries

This section presents the basic concepts and notations used in this paper.

2.1   Reconfigurable Time Net Event Condition Systems

R-TNCESs represent a formalism which was proposed in [17] to specify and verify reconfigurable discrete event control systems (RDECSs). An R-TNCES RTN is a couple $RTN = (B, R)$. B is the behavior module such that, $B = (Conf_1, \ldots, Conf_n)$ (n configurations, each one is a TNCES, possibly redundant). R is the control module such that, $R = (r_1, \ldots, r_m)$ (set of reconfiguration functions with $n, m \in \mathbb{N}$). Formally, the behavior module is a tuple, defined as follows.

$$B = (\mathbb{P}, \mathbb{T}, \mathbb{F}, W, \mathbb{CN}, \mathbb{EN}, \mathbb{DC}, V, Z_0) \tag{1}$$

where, $\mathbb{P}$ (resp, $\mathbb{T}$) is a superset of places (resp. transitions), $\mathbb{F}$ is a superset of arcs, $W : (P \times T) \cup (T \times P) \rightarrow \{0,1\}$ maps a weight to a flow arc, $\mathbb{CN}$ (resp. $\mathbb{EN}$) is a superset of condition signals (resp. event signals), $\mathbb{DC}$ is a superset of clocks on output arcs, $V: T \rightarrow \{AND, OR\}$ maps an event processing mode for every transition, and $Z_0 = (M_0, D_0)$, where M_0 is the initial marking, and D_0 is the initial clock position.

Definition 1. (Control component CC) is a logical software unit [8], which represents the data-flows and actions of sensors/actuators (algorithms, extraction or activation). Every CC resumes the physical process in three actions: activation, working, and termination. Figure 1 shows a generic model of a CC.

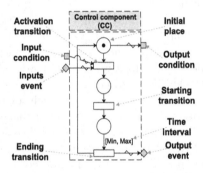

Fig. 1. The generic model of a control component [14].

Definition 2. (Time Net Condition/Event System TNCES) is a set of CCs interconnected by signals. The order of CCs describes the desired behavior of the TNCES.

2.2   Timed Automata

A Timed Automaton with Guards, denoted by G_{TA}, is a six-tuple

$$G_{TA} = (X, E, C, Tra, Inv, x_0) \tag{2}$$

where:

- X is the set of states.
- E is the finite set of events.
- C is the finite set of clocks, $c_1, ..., c_n$, /with $c_i(t) \in R^+$.
- Tra is the set of timed transitions of the automaton.
- Inv is the set of state invariants.
- x_0 is the initial state.

2.3   Temporal Logic

Computation Tree Logic. The model-checking of R-TNCESs is an automatic verification technique of a system using finite-state systems and their reachability graphs. The properties, to be checked, are specified using one temporal logic such as CTL and its extensions (Timed CTL, extended CTL or Probabilistic CTL). CTL [1] is used to specify the functional properties. The time is not explicitly expressed using CTL, but it is possible to say if a property will frequently/infrequently be verified or will never be verified. CTL offers facilities for the specification of properties that must be fulfilled by the system, like safety, liveness, reachability, etc. A formula holds in the system if it is proved true in the initial state of that system. The set of Computation Tree Logic formulas is defined inductively in [1] by the following grammar.

$$\Phi ::= true \mid a \mid \Phi_1 \wedge \Phi_2 \mid \neg\Phi \mid \exists\varphi \mid \forall\varphi \tag{3}$$

where a is an atomic proposition and φ is a path formula with the following syntax ($E \equiv \exists$ and $A \equiv \forall$):

$$\varphi ::= EX\Phi \mid AX\Phi \mid EF\Phi \mid AF\Phi \mid EG\Phi \mid AG\Phi \mid E\Phi_1 U\Phi_2 \tag{4}$$

where, Φ, Φ_1 and Φ_2 are CTL state formulas.

Timed Computation Tree Logic. TCTL is an extension of CTL which offers the possibility to specify qualitative temporal assertions with a time interval (delay D) which denotes the number of time units that have to elapse before firing a transition [3]. The relation $z_0 \models \phi$ for a TCTL formula is given by:

- $z_0 \models EX_{[Min,Max]}\phi$: If there exists a successor state z_1 such that there is an edge (z_0, z_1) with delay $D \in [Min, Max]$ and $z_1 \models \phi$ holds.
- $z_0 \models EF_{[Min,Max]}\phi$: It holds True if there exists a future state z_j when $z_j \models \phi$ holds with the path (z_0, z_j) and with delay $D \in [Min, Max]$.

2.4   Computation Tree Logic Update Method

Ding and Zhang have developed a formal approach for computation tree logic model update based on minimal change criteria over Kripke structure models [5]. CTL model update is an approach for the automatic verification and modification of system models. The principle used is to generate admissible models that represent the correct design [19] in order to repair software errors. The model updater functions modify the models using five primitives $(PU1, \ldots, PU5)$. These primitives are described in their simplest forms as follows.

- PU1: Adding a relation.
- PU2: Removing a relation.
- PU3: Changing the label of one state or onr relation.

- PU4: Adding a state and its associated relations.
- PU5: Removing a state and its associated relations.

The semantics of the above primitives and of the minimal changes principle are detailed in [19].

Fig. 2. Working process of FESTO MPS.

2.5   Benchmark Production System: FESTO MPS

FESTO modular production system (FESTO MPS) as shown in Fig. 2 is a lab-scale production line simulating the functions of production system (distribution, testing, and processing). The distribution function represents the transport unit, the testing is responsible for checking the color, material, and height of workpieces and the processing represents the drilling of workpieces.

The whole system is composed by 12 physical processes (Election, convert, Test, Test failed, Evaluate, Rotate, Drill1, Drill2, Drill1 OR Drill2, Drill1 And Drill2, Checker, Evacuation) each one is modeled by one control component (CC). FESTO achieves the physical processes sequentially and executes them in configurations $(Config_1, Config_2, Config_3, Config_4)$ and every configuration $Config_i$ has one control chain (C_{chain_i}). The control chains describing the physical process are as following.

- $C_{chain_1} = (CC_1, CC_2, CC_3, CC_4)$, when $Test failed$ is executed.
- $C_{chain_2} = (CC_1, CC_2, CC_3, CC_5, CC_6, CC_7, CC_9, CC_{10})$, when $Drill1$ is executed.
- $C_{chain_3} = (CC_1, CC_2, CC_3, CC_5, CC_6, CC_8, CC_9, CC_{10})$, when $Drill2$ is executed.
- $C_{chain_4} = (CC_1, CC_2, CC_3, CC_5, CC_6, CC_{11}, CC_9, CC_{10})$, when workpieces alternatively drilled $Drill1$ or $Drill2$.
- $C_{chain_5} = (CC_1, CC_2, CC_3, CC_5, CC_6, CC_{12}, CC_9, CC_{10})$, when workpieces intensively drilled $Drill1$ and $Drill2$.

The behavior of the FESTO MPS was modeled graphically by [17] (as shown in Fig. 3). FESTO MPS is well described and detailed in [17].

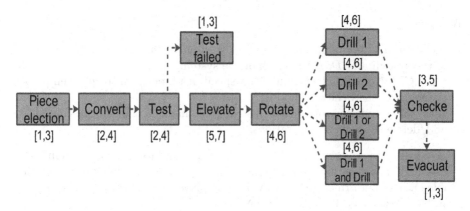

Fig. 3. Working process of FESTO MPS.

3 Rebuilding Operation for Reconfigurable Models

3.1 Formalization

Given a system model M with s_0 its initial state and a Temporal logic formula ϕ such that $(M, s_0) \nvDash \phi$, the rebuilding problem can be defined as finding a new model M' such that $(M', s_0') \vDash \phi$. M' is the repaired model of M, otherwise, there is a problem in the specification of the model/property (inconsistency). M' must respect the good specification and must conserve the good requirements of the system with minimal changes. Figure 4 illustrates the general problem of checking and rebuilding.

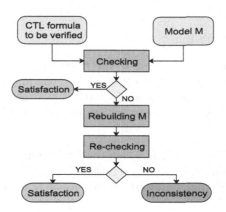

Fig. 4. General problem [14].

Rebuilding operation (RO) can be formalized as follow:

$$RO = (Z_0, \phi, I) \tag{5}$$

Where,

- $Z_0 = (m_i, D_i)$ is the initial state of the system, such that m_i is the marking of the system and D_i is the clock of the system.
- ϕ is a CTL (rep. TCTL) formula that specifies a functional (resp. a temporal) property on the behavior module.
- I is the rebuilding operation instruction chain. I can be restricted to add/delete components operations.

According to Ding's primitives in the CTL update approach [5]and the R-TNCES's modification instructions [17], we define the following dualities (Table 1). The performed dualities will be deployed in the rebuilding of reconfigurable systems specified using R-TNCESs.

Table 1. Equivalence between Ding primitives and R-TNCES rebuilding modifications [14].

	R-TNCES rebuilding modifications	Modification instruction
$PU1$	Add event signal	$Cr(ev(t,t'))$
$PU2$	Delete event signal	$De(ev(t,t'))$
$PU3$ on state	Add/Delete condition signal	$Cr(cn(p,t))/De(cn(p,t))$
$PU3$ on relation	Update the time limits constraint of CC	$De(CC))$ then $Cr(CC))$
$PU4$	Add control component	$Cr(CC))$
$PU5$	Delete control component	$De(CC))$

3.2   TNCESs Rebuilding

Given a TNCES TN and a formula ϕ, the rebuilding operation (RO) consists of synchronization verification between CCs, i.e., checking the synchronization faults between transitions in different CCs (the broadcasting correctness) then to repair the TNCES model if necessary. We can resume (RO) of a TNCES as follows.

1. Structural rebuilding of signals which consists to enable/disable one control component by adding/deleting its signals.
2. Update of TNCES (configuration) which consists of adding/deleting a whole CC (or set of CCs).
3. Temporal constraints update which consists of adjusting the time limits in a CC (or a set of CCs).

We denote by $EN(^{\bullet}T)/EN(T^{\bullet}))$ the set of entering/exiting events of transition T. Table 2 recapitulates the above faults and their correction.

Table 2. Table of synchronization faults and their corrections.

Faulty results	Correction	Explication graphic
$\exists t_i \in EN(^\bullet T)/W(t_i,T)=0$	$Cr(ev(T,t_i))$	
$\exists t_i \in EN(T^\bullet)/W(T,t_i)=0$	$Cr(ev(t_i,T))$	
$\forall t_i \in EN(^\bullet T)/W(t_i,T)=0$	$\forall t_i Cr(ev(t_i,T))$	
$\forall t_i \in EN(T^\bullet)/W(T,t_i)=0$	$\forall t_i Cr(ev(T,t_i))$	
$\exists t_i \in EN(T)/W(t_i,T')=1$	$De(en(t_i,T'))+Cr(ev(t_i,T))$	

Illustrative Example. Let's consider the TNCES shown in Fig. 5. As a functional property, CC_2 and CC_3 should not be joined in the same execution. Trivially, the CTL formula 6 is not satisfied by this TNCES, so that we need to rebuild the TNCES to be adequate for the required functional property.

$$\phi = AF(p_6 \rightarrow \neg EF p_9) \tag{6}$$

The rebuilding operation RO, in this case, can be achieved by deleting the synchronization signal between CC_2 and CC_3. Formally:

$$RO = (Z, \phi, I = (De(ev(t_6,t_7)))) \tag{7}$$

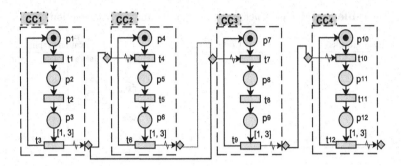

Fig. 5. Illustrative example.

For TNCES update, let's suppose that the designer needs to substitute CC_3 by CC_5 and to add a new process after CC_4. Formally, instructions chain of this RO is described as: $I = De(ev(t_3, t_7)) + De(CC_3) + De(ev(t_9, t_{10})) + Cr(CC_5) + Cr(ev(t_3, t_{13})) + Cr(ev(t_{15}, t_{10})) + Cr(CC_6) + Cr(ev(t_{12}, t_{16}))$.

Figure 6 depicts the TNCES update result.

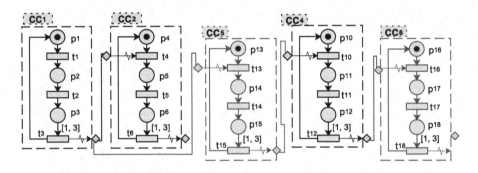

Fig. 6. TNCES update illustrative example.

3.3 Generalization of TNCES Rebuilding

Given M an R-TNCES and Φ a set of functional/temporal properties written in CTL, TCTL respectively. The verification process of M according to those formulas can be performed in two steps, so that exactitude of the first step initiates the second, as follows:

1. Check the functional properties and apply the rebuilding if needed.
2. Check the temporal properties of the behavior module and apply the rebuilding if needed.

Rebuilding an ordinary Petri net consists in adding/deleting place/transition [4]. Whilst, control module rebuilding, in R-TNCESs, consists in enable/disable one configuration by adding/deleting of signals or adding/deleting an entire configuration of the control module (according to the fundamental structure modification instructions of R-TNCES [17]).

Assumption 1. In this work, we assume that the control module is not faulty and represents the desired behavior, i.e., the reachability of each configuration is covered by the control module.

Assumption 2. Every CC respects the good requirements of the designer and it is not in a faulty case.

In this work, we focus on the deployment of the rebuilding of the behavior module according to the functional and temporal properties. We concentrate on the behavior module response when a reconfiguration is requested or an error occurs. Figure 7 illustrates the verification steps of an R-TNCES.

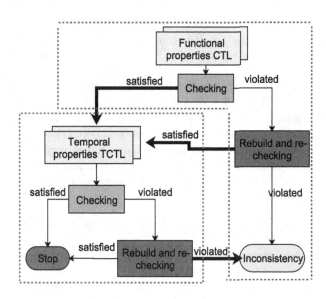

Fig. 7. The verification process of R-TNCES.

3.4   R-TNCES Rebuilding

Rebuilding operation (*RO*) of an R-TNCES reposes on two basic sub-processes that assure the needed abstraction of both model and formula to facilitate the CTL update process. The first one is the computation of a new timed automaton model from the behavior module *B* using Algorithm 1. Indeed, each control

---

Algorithm 1. TA generation.

Input: $B = \sum TNCES$;
Output: TA;

  for *each control component* $CC_i, i=1..n$ **do**
     Create state $s_i \in S$;
     Create label $L : s_i \rightarrow (cc_i)$;
     if $(\exists ev(t_j, t_k)/t_j \in CC_i$ *and* $t_k \in CC_k)$ **then**
        Create relation $(s_j, s_k) \in R$;
        if $(\exists$ *Time interval* $[l, h]$ *in* $(t_j))$ **then**
          | **Create clock** $C_i : [l, h] \rightarrow (s_j, s_k) \in R$;
        end
     end
     if $(\exists cn(p_j, t_k)/p_j \in CC_i$ *and* $t_k \in CC_k)$ **then**
        | **Create label** $L : s_k \rightarrow (cc_j)$;
     end
  end
  $s_0 \leftarrow s_1$;/*CC_1 is the 1st physical process*/
  Return (TA);

---

component (resp, event signal) in B becomes a state (resp, relation) in the timed automaton. The Time intervals at each CC will become a clock $C_i : [l, h]$ at the out put relation of its stat.

The second sub-process consists in the transformation of a CTL (resp. TCTL) formula expressed in R-TNCES to adapt it for the timed automaton verification. This transformation preserves path formulas and expresses state's formulas according to their CCs. Algorithm 2 computes the abstraction of CTL formulas without any loss of information for the timed automaton verification.

Given $RTN = (B, R)$ an R-TNCES to be checked according to the formula ϕ, we can define a *six steps* methodology for automatizing the rebuilding of behavior modules as follows.

1. Generate a timed automaton G from the behavior module B using Algorithm 1.
2. Abstract the formula ϕ to adapt its semantic value of the verification to the generated automaton using Algorithm 2.
3. Using Uppaal, check the satisfaction of $G \vDash \phi$. If $G \vDash \phi$, then the model is well specified, otherwise, go to the next step.
4. Modify G according to CTL model update approach [19]; action to be supervised by the designer.
5. Re-check the satisfaction of the modified model $G' \vDash \phi$. If $G' \vDash \phi$, then the model is well modified, otherwise, there is an inconsistency in the specification (formula/model or both).
6. Rebuild B using primitives that are equivalent to those executed in the 4th step. Table 1 presents the equivalence between CTL update primitives and R-TNCES rebuilding.

Algorithm 2. Formulas transformation.

Input: Φ expressed on R-TNCES;
Output: Φ' expressed on TA;
  for *each sub-formula $\phi \in \Phi$* **do**
    if *(ϕ is a path formula)* **then**
     | **CTL transformation**(ϕ, Φ'); ... /*Recursivity*/
    end
    else
      if *(ϕ is a state formula)* **then**
        for *each p_i, t_i expressed in ϕ* **do**
         | **Replace** $(p_i, s_i)/p_i \in CC_i$; ... /*repalce p_i by s_i*/
         | **Replace** $(t_i, s_i)/t_i \in CC_i$; ... /*repalce t_i by s_i*/
        end
      end
    end
  end
  Return (Φ');

Figure 8 resumes the rebuilding operation RO for an R-TNCES model.

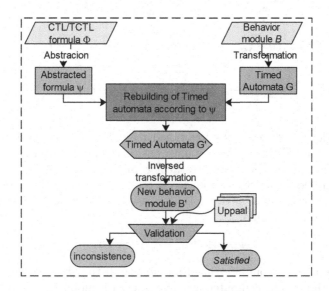

Fig. 8. Methodology of R-TNCES rebuilding.

4 Experimental Study

4.1 Case Study

To validate and to demonstrate the gain of the proposed contribution, let us consider the R-TNCES model shown in Fig. 9. It is a faulty model of behavior module of FESTO MPS.

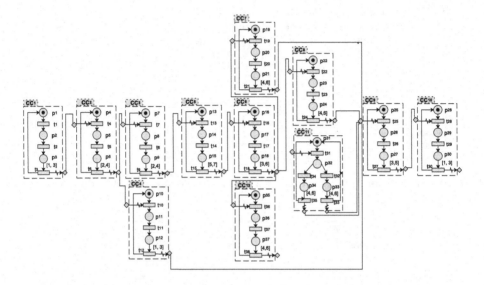

Fig. 9. Behavior module B of FESTO MPS.

The model must satisfy the functional requirements and must respect the quality guidelines. In particular, we must ensure the product quality (i.e., Every workpiece that fails in the quality test: color, material, and height of workpieces cannot be drilled). Once the workpiece is rejected at the quality test, it is not allowed to proceed to the next steps. To check this functional property, we use the following CTL formula:

$$\Phi := AG(p_{12} \rightarrow AF(\neg p_{26})) \tag{8}$$

First, we need to compute timed automaton of the above behavior module using Algorithm 1. The computed automaton G_{TA} is modeled using Uppaal and the result is shown in Fig. 10.

By applying Algorithm 2, we give the CTL transformation of Φ as follow.

$$\Phi := AG(cc_4 \rightarrow AF(\neg C_9)) \tag{9}$$

Formula 9 is written as a reachability query in Uppaal and is proven to be *False*. To rebuild the model according to this formula, we select each path has a state with C_9 in the model and satisfies $AF(C_9)$ as following:

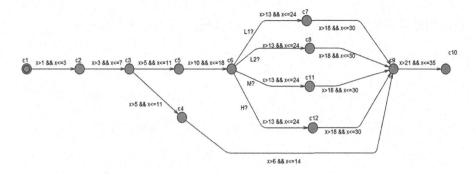

Fig. 10. Uppaal model of the computed timed automaton.

- $\pi_1 = [C_1, C_2, C_3, C_5, C_6, C_7, C_9, C_{10}]$;
- $\pi_2 = [C_1, C_2, C_3, C_5, C_6, C_8, C_9, C_{10}]$;
- $\pi_3 = [C_1, C_2, C_3, C_5, C_6, C_7, C_9, C_{10}]$;
- $\pi_4 = [C_1, C_2, C_3, C_5, C_6, C_{12}, C_9, C_{10}]$;
- $\pi_5 = [C_1, C_2, C_3, C_4, C_9, C_{10}]$;

Then, we select the path which have C_9 and C_4 ($\pi_5 = [C_1, C_2, C_3, C_4, C_9, C_{10}]$;).
According to Ding, eventually we need to update G_{TA}. We apply $PU2$ to remove
the transition (C_4, C_9). Thus, we obtain a new model G'_{TA}, which simply states
that no transition from state C_4 to state C_9 is allowed. Temporal constraints of
the model must be checked by assuring the lower and upper bounds of the execution for each control component. Indeed, we investigate that every CC respects
its activation constraint ensured by the TCTL based temporal properties. The
following Formula check that the drill machine can be activated in at least 14
time units after the system starts whatever the production mode.

$$\phi := AF[14, 24](p_{20} \vee p_{23} \vee p_{32} \vee p_{36}) = 1. \tag{10}$$

By applying Algorithm 2, we give the TCTL transformation as follows.

$$\Phi := AF[14, 24](C_7 \vee C_8 \vee C_{11} \vee C_{12}) = 1. \tag{11}$$

Using Uppaal, the property is proven to be *False* (Fig. 11(a)). The model
rebuilding will be deployed by adjusting the execution limit of the appropriate
CC with property limits (Fig. 11(b)). The result of those updates is depicted in
Fig. 12.

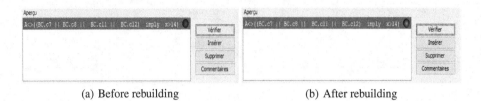

(a) Before rebuilding   (b) After rebuilding

Fig. 11. A screen-shot on TCTL formula verification.

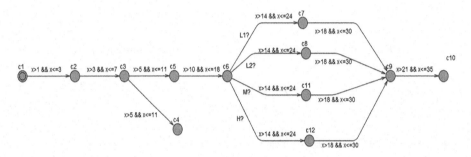

Fig. 12. The new model G'_{TA}.

Finally, we apply the equivalent R-TNCES rebuilding modifications of $PU2$ on the module behavior to get a new correct module, i.e., we delete event signal $ev(t_{12}, t_{25})$ by modification instruction $De(ev(t_{12}, t_{25}))$. For the second modification, we delete the cc_6 by applying the instruction $De((cc_6)$ and we create a new one with a new time limit. Results are shown in Fig. 13.

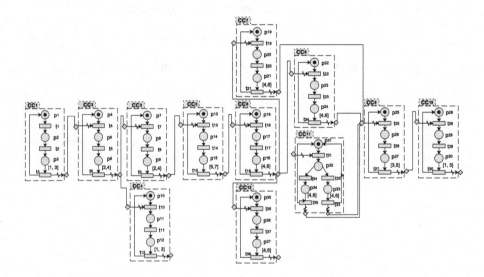

Fig. 13. Behavior module B of FESTO MPS after rebuilding.

The exact reachability graph is computed using the SESA model checker [15], thus 85493 sates are obtained as shown in Fig. 14(a). The computed graph is finite and it has no dead reachable states. SESA is applied automatically to verify the deadlock and boundedness properties and it is applied manually to check functional and temporal properties. Firstly, we check that the new model satisfies the functional property of quality ($\Phi := AG(p_{12} \rightarrow AF(\neg p_{26}))$). This formula is proven to be *True* (see. Fig. 14(b)). Then, we verify that it time constraint update is correctly applied. The TCTL formula P_8 is proven to be *True* at the new obtained R-TNCES as shown in Fig. 14(c).

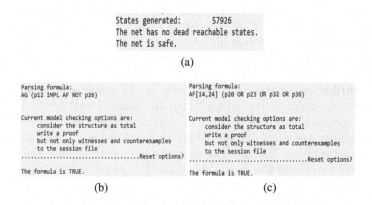

Fig. 14. A screen-shot on SESA verification.

4.2 Discussion

For real-time reconfigurable systems, there is no study in the rebuilding and model correction. However, our proposed methodology facilitates the process of synchronization properties and temporal constraint verification. Thus, the classical verification of R-TNCES checks these properties based on the whole

Table 3. Qualitative comparison with some related works.

Work	Formalism used	Reconfiguration	Timed model	Model repair
[5, 19]	Kripke structure	No	No	Yes
[4]	Kripke structure	No	No	Yes
[10–12]	Petri nets	No	No	Yes
[17]	R-TNCESs	Yes	Yes	No
[6]	R-TNCESs	Yes	Yes	No
[14]	R-TNCESs	Yes	Yes	No
Our work	R-TNCES	Yes	Yes	Yes

model, contrariwise, the R-TNCESs rebuilding (RO) provides a verification of an abstract model with model checking to ensure the correctness of functional and temporal properties. Table 3 describes a short qualitative comparison between the proposed contribution and the most recent related works.

5 Conclusion

This research deals, with a new method for the automatic rebuilding of reconfigurable systems with hard real-time constraints modeled by R-TNCESs.

In this paper, we have presented a functional/temporal rebuilding methodology for reconfigurable systems modeled with reconfigurable timed net condition/event systems (R-TNCESs). We define a method that deals with the modification of reconfigurable system models according to CTL and TCTL formulas that express functional and temporal exigences. Our method is based on the CTL update and models correction proposed by Ding around Kripke structure.

Our contribution reposes on a round-trip in the granularity passage. First, we deploy an algorithm to compute a timed automaton based on the R-TNCES and a new technique to transform a CTL formula expressed in the R-TNCESs model to another one expressed on the computed timed automaton keeping the same verification value. Second, The property is used to localize the source of the fault and to rebuild the model using the five primitives of Ding. Then, a reciprocal process will take place to return the corrected model to the original version (R-TNCES) using equivalence between Ding primitives and R-TNCESs rebuilding modification instructions. At the end, the platform FESTO modular production system is used as an experimental case study to confirm the result of R-TNCES rebuilding and to show the virtue of the contribution. To validate the final result, the SESA model checker is applied.

Contrary to the existing works on the verification and updating of models, our technique repairs the system model according to the functional and temporal properties directly to result in the gain of design time and effort. Using the contribution of this paper, the debugging cycle for each violated functional/temporal property is automatically assisted to be repaired on less complex models.

This work opens several possible avenues for future researches. Now, to extend the current research, we are planning to deal with reconfigurable systems with distributed behaviors and implementing real large case studies with different kind of properties.

References

1. Baier, C., Katoen, J.P., Larsen, K.G.: Principles of Model Checking. MIT Press (2008)
2. Behrmann, G., David, A., Larsen, K.G.: A tutorial on UPPAAL. In: Bernardo, M., Corradini, F. (eds.) SFM-RT 2004. LNCS, vol. 3185, pp. 200–236. Springer, Heidelberg (2004). https://doi.org/10.1007/978-3-540-30080-9_7
3. Bouyer, P.: Model-checking timed temporal logics. Electron. Notes Theor. Comput. Sci. **231**, 323–341 (2009)

4. Carrillo, M., Rosenblueth, D.A.: CTL update of Kripke models through protections. Artif. Intell. **211**, 51–74 (2014)
5. Ding, Y., Zhang, Y.: System modification case studies. In: 2007 31st Annual International Computer Software and Applications Conference, COMPSAC 2007, vol. 2, pp. 355–360. IEEE (2007)
6. Hafidi, Y., Kahloul, L., Khalgui, M., Li, Z., Alnowibet, K., Qu, T.: On methodology for the verification of reconfigurable timed net condition/event systems. IEEE Trans. Syst. Man Cybern.: Syst. 1–15 (2018). https://doi.org/10.1109/TSMC.2018. 2855209
7. Housseyni, W., Mosbahi, O., Khalgui, M., Li, Z., Yin, L.: Multiagent architecture for distributed adaptive scheduling of reconfigurable real-time tasks with energy harvesting constraints. IEEE Access **6**, 2068–2084 (2018). https://doi.org/10.1109/ ACCESS.2017.2781459
8. Khalgui, M., Hanisch, H.M.: Automatic NCES-based specification and sesa-based verification of feasible control components in benchmark production systems. Int. J. Model. Identif. Control. **12**(3), 223–243 (2011)
9. Lakhdhar, W., Mzid, R., Khalgui, M., Li, Z., Frey, G., Al-Ahmari, A.: Multiobjective optimization approach for a portable development of reconfigurable real-time systems: from specification to implementation. IEEE Trans. Syst. Man Cybern.: Syst. **49**(3), 1–15 (2018). https://doi.org/10.1109/TSMC.2017.2781460
10. Martínez-Araiza, U., López-Mellado, E.: A CTL model repair method for Petri nets. In: 2014 World Automation Congress (WAC), pp. 654–659. IEEE (2014)
11. Martínez-Araiza, U., López-Mellado, E.: CTL model repair for bounded and deadlock free Petri nets. IFAC-PapersOnLine **48**(7), 154–160 (2015)
12. Martinez-Araiza, U., López-Mellado, E.: CTL model repair for inter-organizational business processes modelled as oWFN. IFAC-PapersOnLine **49**(2), 6–11 (2016)
13. Padberg, J., Kahloul, L.: Overview of reconfigurable Petri nets. In: Heckel, R., Taentzer, G. (eds.) Graph Transformation, Specifications, and Nets. LNCS, vol. 10800, pp. 201–222. Springer, Cham (2018). https://doi.org/10.1007/978-3-319-75396-6_11
14. Ramdani, M., Kahloul, L., Khalgui, M., Hafidi, Y.: R-TNCES rebuilding: a new method of CTL model update for reconfigurable systems. In: Proceedings of the 14th International Conference on Evaluation of Novel Approaches to Software Engineering - Volume 1: ENASE. INSTICC, pp. 159–168. SciTePress (2019). https://doi.org/10.5220/0007736801590168
15. Starke, P.H., Roch, S.: Analysing Signal-Net Systems. Professoren des Inst. für Informatik (2002)
16. Zhang, J., Frey, G., Al-Ahmari, A., Qu, T., Wu, N., Li, Z.: Analysis and control of dynamic reconfiguration processes of manufacturing systems. IEEE Access **6**, 28028–28040 (2018). https://doi.org/10.1109/ACCESS.2017.2757044
17. Zhang, J., Khalgui, M., Li, Z., Mosbahi, O., Al-Ahmari, A.M.: R-TNCES: a novel formalism for reconfigurable discrete event control systems. IEEE Trans. Syst. Man Cybern.: Syst. **43**(4), 757–772 (2013). https://doi.org/10.1109/TSMCA.2012. 2217321
18. Zhang, J., Khalgui, M., Li, Z., Frey, G., Mosbahi, O., Salah, H.B.: Reconfigurable coordination of distributed discrete event control systems. IEEE Trans. Control Syst. Technol. **23**(1), 323–330 (2015)
19. Zhang, Y., Ding, Y.: CTL model update for system modifications. J. Artif. Intell. Res. **31**, 113–155 (2008)

Towards the Efficient Use of Dynamic Call Graph Generators of Node.js Applications

Zoltán Herczeg[(✉)], Gábor Lóki, and Ákos Kiss

Department of Software Engineering, University of Szeged,
Dugonics tér 13, Szeged 6720, Hungary
{zherczeg,loki,akiss}@inf.u-szeged.hu

Abstract. JavaScript is the most popular programming language these days and it is used in many environments such as *node.js*. The *node.js* ecosystem allows sharing JavaScript code easily, and the shared code can be reused as building blocks to create new applications. However, this ever growing environment has its own challenges as well. One of them is security: even simple applications can have many dependencies, and these dependencies might contain malware software. Another challenge is fault localization: finding the reason of a fault could be difficult in a software with many dependencies. Dynamic program analysis can help solving these problems. In particular, dynamic call graphs were used successfully in both cases before. Since no call graph generators were available for *node.js* before, we created them. In this paper, we compare the call graphs constructed by our generator tools. We show that a large amount of engine-specific information is present in the call graphs and filtering can efficiently remove it. We also discuss how the asynchronous nature of JavaScript affects call graphs. Finally, we show the performance overhead of call graph generation and its side effects on module testing.

Keywords: JavaScript · Node.js · Call graph · Security

1 Introduction

Similarly to the previous years, JavaScript is still the most popular [24] programming language. Its first version was developed in 1995 and the aim of the new language was to enrich static web pages with interactive features. Due to its growing popularity, JavaScript appeared in other areas, such as server side scripting and embedded systems [22]. JavaScript fits quite well in these event-driven environments because of its function model. JavaScript functions are objects, which are created from a source text and a lexical environment. The lexical environment allows sharing variables between several functions, and this variable collection is always available to a function even if it is called by an event handler. Therefore, developers can create private contexts from variables and functions to solve a given task, and the functions can rely on these contexts since they

E. Damiani et al. (Eds.): ENASE 2019, CCIS 1172, pp. 286–302, 2020.
https://doi.org/10.1007/978-3-030-40223-5_14

cannot be modified by external code. Although these private contexts can be emulated by classes, protected members, and inheritance in other languages, the JavaScript syntax is considerably simpler. The function model is a core concept of JavaScript, even JavaScript classes are specialized functions, so their analysis is important for understanding the behaviour of JavaScript programs.

Improving security is among the aims of program analysis. JavaScript can be easily extended with various application programming interfaces (APIs), and many APIs provide access to system resources such as file systems, network connections, cameras, or private user data. These resources should be protected from harmful uses. Enforcing security policies [2,10,29] can prevent certain attacks, although it could also limit the application developers as well. Another approach can be the dynamic analysis of JavaScript code in order to detect harmful actions. Most *node.js* [14] applications depend on JavaScript modules which are downloaded from software registries such as *npm* [19] where anybody can upload their code without any preliminary security checks. Injecting a vulnerability into a dependency can cause unexpected security threats. Analyzing the call information of a software can be used to detect harmful behaviour. One form of call information is call graphs, which have already been successfully used for malware detection on both mobile [8] and non-mobile systems [5] to detect both known and unknown threats.

A call graph [21] is a directed graph which represents calling relationships between functions of a program. Each called function has a corresponding node in the graph and the function calls are represented by edges between nodes, where the direction of an edge points toward the callee. Call graphs can be constructed without executing a program or during the execution. The former is called static call graph and it is a well-researched topic [6,7,13,16]. The latter is called dynamic call graph and we focus on them to pave the way for dynamic security analysis of JavaScript programs.

Another area where call graphs were successfully used is fault localization [20,27]. Finding the reason of test failures without human intervention can significantly reduce the time and costs for fixing issues. Call graphs can be used to find those functions which are likely responsible for the fail and developers can focus only on these functions. Usually, these methods compare the call graphs of successful and unsuccessful tests and rank the functions based on the probability of containing an implementation error.

This work is an extension of paper [12], which we improved in several ways. We improved the call graph generators and the tool that finds the same nodes in different call graphs. Furthermore, we compared the nodes of the generated call graphs, not just their edges. We also extended our benchmark set to twelve modules and these new modules revealed new differences in the call graphs. We also investigated the performance overhead of constructing call graphs.

In this paper, we investigate the differences of dynamic call graphs constructed by two call graph generators. The rest of the paper is organized as follows. In Sect. 2, we introduce the two call graph generators and describe how we improved them. In Sect. 3, we compare the nodes and edges of the generated

Table 1. Running time and disk space consumed by the *express* module (adapted from paper [12], p 474, Table 1).

	Nodejs with tracing enabled	nodejs-cg
Running time	48 s	5 s
Disk space	161 MB	0.9 MB

call graphs on a popular JavaScript benchmark. In Sect. 4, we continue our comparison with call graphs generated from twelve *node.js* modules, and also investigate the performance overhead of call graph construction. In Sect. 5, we review related work, and finally, conclusions and future works are discussed in Sect. 6.

2   Call Graph Generator Tools

In this section, we present two call graph generator tools, which were introduced in paper [12]. The paper also introduced a third tool that used the *Jalangi2* [23] framework. However, Jalangi 2 only supports an outdated version of JavaScript called ECMAScript 5.1 [3] and cannot be used for analysing newer *node.js* modules. In the following subsections, we describe the selected two call graph generators, which produce call graphs in different ways so their results can be validated against each other.

2.1   Nodeprof.js Framework

The first call graph generator tool is based on *nodeprof.js* [25], which is a dynamic program analysis framework for *node.js* applications. This framework is built on top of the *Graal-nodejs* project, which allows running *node.js* applications using the *Graal.js* [28] ECMAScript 2017 [4] compatible engine. Compared to our earlier work [12], we use a newer version of *nodeprof.js* that supports a larger subset of ECMAScript 2018 specification. The newer version also affects our results, so they cannot be directly compared to results presented in [12]. In fact, some changes have a large impact on them. For example, the function, which represented all built-in functions in the previous version is removed, and the repercussion of this removal is discussed in Sect. 3.3.

To analyze programs, *nodeprof.js* modifies the abstract syntax tree (AST) representation created from JavaScript source code. The purpose of these modifications is to notify *nodeprof.js* when certain events (e.g., variable assignment, function call) occure, and *nodeprof.js* passes these event notifications to custom JavaScript programs called analyses.

To support existing analyses, *nodeprof.js* adopted the public API of *Jalangi2* with minor modifications. The *Jalangi2* analyses are JavaScript programs because *Jalangi2* itself is written purely in JavaScript. This analysis concept

```
class ClassWithConstructor {
    constructor(arg) {
        // Prints the "arg" argument.
        console.log(arg);
    }
}
```

Fig. 1. An example for defining a class with an explicit constructor.

offers a great flexibility: analyses can subscribe to events supported by *Jalangi2* and may run any JavaScript code as a response to that event. The JavaScript code may even affect certain events, e.g., change the return value of a function. From *nodeprof.js* perspective, the call graph generator is an analysis, which is subscribed to function entry and exit events.

Unlike the other tool in this section, *nodeprof.js* framework modifies the AST representation to capture events and pass these events to custom analyses.

2.2 Nodejs-cg – A Modified Node.js

The second tool is a customized *node.js* called *nodejs-cg* [15]. The *V8* [9] engine is the default JavaScript interpreter of *node.js*, and this engine has built-in support for execution tracing. When tracing is enabled, the *V8* engine captures when the JavaScript exection enters or leaves a function and writes this information to the console. *Nodejs-cg* replaces this tracing mechanism with a call graph generator. The generator is mostly the same as introduced in our previous work [12], but a few bugfixes and improvements were made.

The call graph generator records all nodes and edges when a *node.js* application is executed and dumps the whole graph when *node.js* terminates. This approach is much faster and requires far less space than parsing the output of tracing. Table 1 shows that generating the call graph directly can be ten times faster and requires a hundredth of disk space than post-processing the tracing output. The *express* module referenced by the Table is among the benchmark programs in Sect. 4.

Compared to the other generator, the call graph is directly generated by the JavaScript engine of *nodejs-cg* without modifying the source code or the intermediate representation. Furthermore, this tool is a pure call graph generator, it does not support other custom analyses.

3 SunSpider Call Graphs

In this section, we compare the call graphs generated from the widely used *Sun-Spider* [1] performance benchmark suite in order to examine the basic characteristics of the generated call graphs. Version 1.0.2 of the suite contains twenty-six programs, which are executed one-by-one by a driver application.

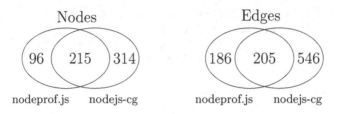

Fig. 2. Number of call graph nodes and edges on SunSpider.

3.1 Node Identification

To compare multiple call graphs of the same program generated by different tools, the same nodes need to be identified in all call graphs. This identification can be done by assigning a unique identifier to each node, which is independent from the current execution of the program. Such identifier can be created from the absolute path of the file where the function is defined and the source code location of the function start. However, the location provided by *nodeprof.js* and *nodejs-cg* are often different: *nodejs-cg* gives the start of the function argument list while *nodeprof.js* gives the start of the function. To identify the same nodes in the call graphs returned by these two tools, first the locations returned by *nodeprof.js* are converted to the locations that would be returned by *nodejs-cg* using the source code.

A notable improvement compared to previous work [12] is that explicit constructor nodes are also identified as same nodes. Figure 1 shows an explicit constructor in JavaScript. When this constructor is called, the locations provided by *nodeprof.js* and *nodejs-cg* are the starting position of the *class* keyword and the starting position of the *constructor* arguments, respectively. These locations are also converted in the call graph constructed by *nodeprof.js*.

We have to note that JavaScript supports dynamic script evaluation where scripts are not stored in files, but are strings constructed at run-time. As a result, they have no path information. Some heuristics could be designed to try and add unique identifiers for these strings, but the identification of an element in such a dynamic code is a complex task. Currently, all of these scripts are assigned to a single node with *<eval>* identifier.

3.2 Comparison of Found Nodes and Edges

Figure 2 shows the Venn diagrams of all call graph nodes and edges encountered during the execution of the *SunSpider* benchmark suite. The number of nodes and edges found by each generator tool is shown inside a circle corresponding to each tool. The intersection of the two circles contain the number of those nodes and edges that are found by both tools. These are called common nodes and edges in the rest of the paper. By contrast, unique nodes and edges that are found by a single tool only are shown in the non-intersected regions of the circles. If the call graphs generated by both generators had been the same, the

Table 2. Call graph node and edge groups by nodeprof.js.

Group name	Number of nodes		Number of edges	
Common	215	(69.1%)	205	(52.4%)
JS built-ins	0	(0.0%)	0	(0.0%)
Node.js init	91	(29.3%)	117	(29.9%)
Module loading	5	(1.6%)	69	(17.7%)
Total	311	(100.0%)	391	(100.0%)

Table 3. Call graph node and edge groups by nodejs-cg.

Group name	Number of nodes		Number of edges	
Common	215	(40.7%)	205	(27.3%)
JS built-ins	17	(3.2%)	29	(3.8%)
Nodejs init	290	(54.8%)	452	(60.2%)
Module loading	7	(1.3%)	65	(8.7%)
Total	529	(100.0%)	751	(100.0%)

number of unique nodes and edges would have been zero. However, Fig. 2 shows a large number of unique nodes and edges.

For further analysis, the nodes and edges in Fig. 2 are divided into four groups. Tables 2 and 3 show these groups and the number of nodes and edges that belong to these groups for the two call graph generators. The *common* group represents the common nodes and edges, and its values are the same as the values in the intersected regions of the circles in Fig. 2. In the following subsections, we focus on the other groups, which represent the differences between these two call graphs.

3.3 JavaScript Built-ins

The first group, which contains unique nodes and edges in Tables 2 and 3 is called *JS built-ins*. The ECMAScript standard defines many built-in functions [3, Sect. 15] and some of them are used by SunSpider. For example, the *string-tagcloud.js* benchmark program sorts the elements of an array with the help of the *sort()* built-in method. Figure 3 shows an example for using this built-in method.

A JavaScript engine may implement a built-in function either in JavaScript or as a native function. (Native functions are non-JavaScript functions, which can be called from JavaScript.) If a function is implemented in JavaScript, the call graph generator can construct a node for it and the appropriate edges are added to the call graph when this function is called or it calls other functions. However, native built-in functions are often not part of the call graph, because these functions usually do not notify the engine when they are called.

```
function compare(a, b) {
    if (a < b) {
        return -1;
    }
    return (a > b) | 0;
}

function doSort(arr) {
    arr.sort(compare);
}

doSort([3, 2, 1])
```

Fig. 3. An example for sorting an array.

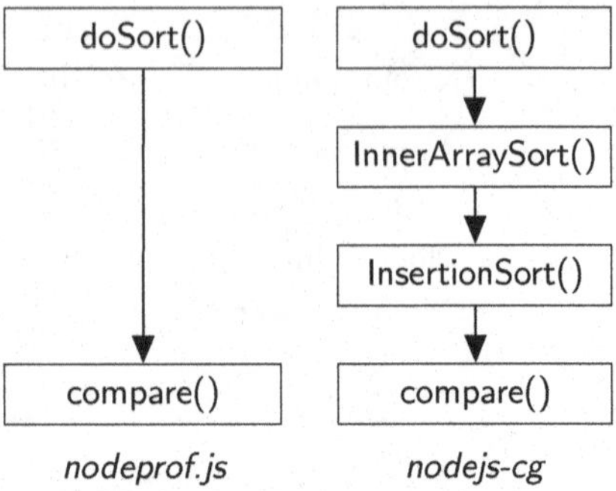

Fig. 4. Subgraphs from Fig. 3 example.

Figure 4 shows two different subgraphs where the nodes assigned to the *doSort()* and *compare()* functions declared in Fig. 3 are connected by a directed path. There is a direct edge between these two nodes on the left subgraph because the *sort()* function is implemented as a native function in *nodeprof.js* and its calls are not tracked. Earlier versions of *nodeprof.js* captured the call of native functions and assigned the same *<built-in>()* source file name for them, but this feature is removed from newer versions.

The *sort()* method in *nodejs-cg* is implemented in JavaScript and calling this function is visible on the right subgraph of Fig. 4. This subgraph reveals that the *compare()* function is indirectly called by *doSort()*. However, most built-ins are also native built-ins in *nodejs-cg*, so these two call graph generators provide little information about the built-in usage of a module at the moment. This situation could be improved in the future by adding function entry/exit notifications to native functions.

3.4 Module Initialization

The next group after *JS built-ins* in Tables 2 and 3 is the *nodejs init* group. The nodes and edges in this group are part of every call graph regardless of the program.

The *node.js* initialization process, called bootstrap, is partly implemented in JavaScript. During bootstrap, *node.js* runs several core modules, which initialize the module loading system, message queues, timers, etc. Unlike external modules, these core modules are part of the *node.js* binary to ensure that they cannot be changed and *node.js* can always rely on them.

As for *nodejs-cg*, sixty-four modules are loaded and nearly three hundred functions are executed during the initialization process. These functions are represented as nodes in the call graph and their precise number can be seen in the *nodejs init* group of Table 3. These numbers are much smaller for *nodeprof.js*: it only loads nineteen modules and executes nearly a hundred functions as shown

```
console.log('Hello!');
```

(a) Original source code

```
(function(exports, ...) {
console.log('Hello!');
})
```

(b) Wrapped source code

Fig. 5. Example for source code wrapping.

in Table 2. The reason for these lower numbers is that *nodeprof.js* loads the analyses at a later stage of the *node.js* initialization and the call graph generator cannot capture function calls that happened before it is loaded.

3.5 Module Loading

The last group in Tables 2 and 3 is the *module loading* group. The number of nodes in this group is low because a large part of the module loading system is used during the initialization process and only a few more helper functions are needed to load other modules.

Although SunSpider consists of only twenty-six single-file programs, there are more than sixty edges in this group in both tables. The programs of the SunSpider benchmark suite are loaded as modules by the test driver. The first step of module loading is wrapping the source code into a function expression as seen in Fig. 5. (Actually, the function expression has several arguments but only the first one is shown in the figure and the rest are represented by ellipses.) The wrapped source code is evaluated by the JavaScript engine of *node.js* which creates an internal function from the source code and executes it. This operation is captured by the call graph generators, and a new edge is appended to the call graph. Because of wrapping, the internal function simply returns with another function object. The returned function object is called by *node.js* later, which makes the generators add another edge to the call graph. Therefore, at least two new edges are created when a module is loaded, which explains the large number of edges in the *module loading* group.

The conclusion of this section is that although the call graphs generated by *nodejs-cg* and *nodeprof.js* have many common edges, they contain a large amount of unique edges as well. For example, only twenty-seven percent of the edges belong to the common group from the call graph generated by *nodejs-cg*. This ratio is lower than the common edge ratio of *nodeprof.js*, where it was around fifty percent. Hence, the call graphs constructed for the *SunSpider* benchmark suite reveal more information about the internal workings of *node.js* than about *SunSpider*. In Sect. 4, we show how filtering can effectively reduce these differences between call graphs.

4   Call Graphs of Real-World Programs

In the previous section, we compared the nodes and edges of multiple call graphs generated from the *SunSpider* benchmark suite. We found that these call graphs have a large amount of unique nodes and edges, e.g., seventy-three percent of the edges are unique in the call graph generated by *nodejs-cg*. However, *SunSpider* is a relatively small benchmark suite, so it would be beneficial if additional investigation was done with other applications before drawing conclusions.

Table 4. Number of call graph nodes found by nodeprof.js and nodejs-cg.

Name	All call graph nodes			Module call graph nodes		
	nodeprof.js	Common	nodejs-cg	nodeprof.js	Common	nodejs-cg
Bower	804	9604	996	1	9604	2
Doctrine	372	1954	581	7	1954	1
Eslint	571	15898	781	15	15898	17
Express	727	5239	928	0	5239	1
Hessian	437	2103	648	0	2103	1
Hexo	541	10076	749	2	10076	1
Jshint	412	2299	627	0	2299	1
Karma	828	9363	1019	0	9363	1
Mongoose	708	12508	890	2	12506	5
Pencilblue	539	6265	745	1	6265	6
Request	876	3675	1067	1	3675	3
Shields	773	9544	976	0	9544	2

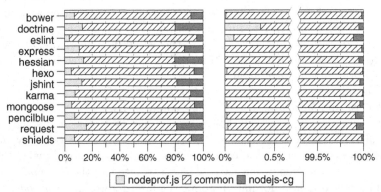

In this section, we compare the call graphs generated from twelve *node.js* modules. Nine modules are taken from the *BugsJS* [11] framework while the rest were used in a previous paper [12]. We chose the *BugsJS* variant of those four modules which were presented in the previous paper and available in the *BugsJS* framework as well. The *BugsJS* framework has one more module, called *node-redis*, which is excluded from this comparison. Further details about why this module was omitted are provided in Sect. 4.3.

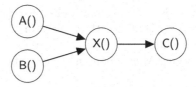

Fig. 6. Call graph filtering problem: if the node marked with *X()* is removed, it cannot be decided whether *C()* node is transitively called from *A()* or *B()* or both.

Each module has its own testing system, which runs *node.js* instances to do the testing. The call graph generators are also working *node.js* binaries, which can run these tests and construct the JavaScript call graphs at the same time. After the testing is completed, a final call graph, which is the union of the produced call graphs, is built. The final call graph contains all function calls that performed during testing including the internal calls of *node.js* and the JavaScript engine.

4.1 Comparison of Nodes

Table 4 shows the number of nodes recorded for each *node.js* module. The table is divided into two subtables: the left half contains all encountered nodes and the right half contains those nodes that remain after a filter is applied. Similar to the method described in our previous work [12], the filtering is done during testing and makes the generators to ignore the internal JavaScript functions of the JavaScript engine and *node.js*. Although the nodes could be filtered out after the testing is completed, this is not true for the call graph edges as shown in Fig. 6. When the filter is applied, only the application-related functions and their relationships remain in the call graph, e.g., core module functions, functions related to testing, and functions provided by various external dependencies installed by the package manager.

Both halves of Table 4 are further divided into three columns. The center column shows the number of those nodes, which are found by both *nodeprof.js* and *nodejs-cg*, while the columns on each side contain the number of those unique nodes which were captured by one generator only.

The values in the center columns of the two table halves are nearly always equal, which means that the filter improves the similarity of these call graphs because it only removes unique nodes. The exception is the *mongoose* module: we observed that test cases may disappear when running the tests of *mongoose* and *karma* modules. Further details about the missing tests is discussed in Sect. 4.3. Nodes represent the functions belong to these tests are also missing from the call graphs which reduces the number of common nodes.

Table 4 also reveals that several unique nodes are present in the call graphs when the filter is not applied. However, this difference is greatly reduced, to a single digit, after the filter is applied (except for *eslint*). Hence, most nodes in the side columns of the left subtable represent internal functions of both the

JavaScript engine and *node.js*. As for *eslint*, it creates temporary directories and runs JavaScript source files placed into these directories. Since the source code of these functions is not available later, they are currently not idenitified as same nodes in the two call graphs. More about node identification was discussed in Sect. 3.1.

The rest of the differences will be explained in the next subsection where we focus on the call graph edges.

Table 5. Number of call graph edges found by nodeprof.js and nodejs-cg.

Name	All call graph edges			Module call graph edges		
	nodeprof.js	Common	nodejs-cg	nodeprof.js	Common	nodejs-cg
Bower	8302	12250	8734	4	18849	6
Doctrine	1751	2788	2237	12	3572	1
Eslint	8153	24093	8791	124	29436	73
Express	4023	9988	4451	0	11455	1
Hessian	2346	2503	2735	0	3399	1
Hexo	6904	15460	7578	2	19856	1
Jshint	2084	2251	2493	0	3189	1
Karma	8463	10787	8892	3	15864	2
Mongoose	9468	28889	10735	148	31859	875
Pencilblue	5358	6856	5811	4	10000	12
Request	4662	3892	5059	9	5776	9
Shields	8329	8400	9035	39	13489	259

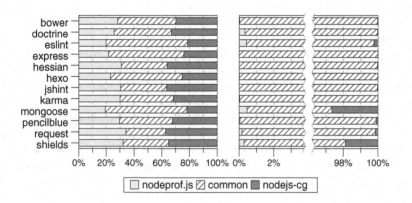

4.2 Comparison of Edges

Table 5 shows the number of edges recorded for each *node.js* module. Similar to Table 4, this table is also divided into two halves: the left half contains the

```
function f () {
    return 1;
}

function* g () {
    yield f ();
}

function h () {
    g ().next ();
}

h ();
```

```
function f () {
}

function r (res, rej) {
    res ("Resolved");
}

var p = new Promise (r);

async function g () {
    await p;
    f ();
}
g ();
```

Fig. 7. An example for JavaScript generator functions.

Fig. 8. An example for using Promises and await keyword.

number of all and the right half contains the number of filtered edges. The filter is the same as in Sect. 4.1.

Following the structure of the previous subsection, we discuss the effects of filtering first. Table 5 shows that after the filter is applied, the number of common edges increased and the number of unique edges decreased significantly. In sixteen out of twenty-four cases, the number of unique edges dropped to a single digit, which is less than 0.1% of the edges in the corresponding call graph. In Sect. 4.1, we showed that the unique nodes of the filtered call graphs are also very low, so we can conclude that the filtered call graphs generated by *nodeprof.js* and *nodejs-cg* are very similar.

However, there are two modules where the filtered call graphs have hundreds of unique edges. The call graphs of the *mongoose* module have the most unique edges, which is caused by JavaScript generator functions. Figure 7 shows an example for the use of a generator function. When the *g()* generator function is called, both call graph generators record a function call, although the body of the *g()* function is not executed at all. Instead, an object is created, which has a *next()* method. When this *next()* method is invoked, the body of the generator function is executed until a yield operator is processed or the function returns. Therefore, the *f()* function in Fig. 7 is called only when the *next()* method is invoked and the *nodejs-cg* tool correctly records this as a function call from *g()* to *f()*. On the contrary, the call graph generator based on *nodeprof.js* is not aware that the execution is entered into the body of the *g()* function and it records a function call from *h()* to *f()*. This difference may affect the number of edges considerably. For example, many tests of the *mongoose* module are implemented as generator functions, which call the same API functions with various parameters. If the generator functions represent these tests are ignored, the test driver becomes the caller of the API functions. Obviously, far less edges

Table 6. Performance overhead of generating call graphs.

Name	Times as slow without filtering		Times as slow with filtering	
	nodeprof.js	nodejs-cg	nodeprof.js	nodejs-cg
Bower	1.58	2.40	1.37	2.15
Doctrine	1.99	2.59	2.14	1.78
Eslint	2.76	8.80	2.53	8.70
Express	1.29	1.25	1.13	1.41
Hessian	1.61	4.06	1.57	3.51
Hexo	1.36	2.51	1.57	2.42
Jshint	1.71	1.79	1.50	1.63
Karma	1.20	2.30	1.20	1.14
Mongoose	1.41	2.33	1.02	2.10
Pencilblue	1.35	1.58	1.03	1.58
Request	1.52	1.45	1.03	1.17
Shields	1.60	4.45	1.55	4.15
Average	1.62	2.96	1.47	2.65

are created in this case, which explains why the call graph generated by *nodejs-cg* has six times more unique edges.

The call graph generator based on *nodeprof.js* could be improved in the future to detect function calls performed by generator functions. This is not a trivial change though because *nodeprof.js* only provides the source code location of the call site, not the source code location of the caller function and the generator should search the corresponding function for each site.

The call graphs of the *shields* module have the second biggest number of unique edges. However, this difference is not caused by generator functions, although the reason is somewhat similar. The *await* expression suspends the execution of an asynchronous JavaScript function until a *Promise* object is completed, as seen in Fig. 8. When function $g()$ is called, it runs until the *await* expression is reached and the function returns with a *Promise* object. The return value of a function declared with the *async* attribute is always a *Promise* object even if the function returns normally. When the *Promise* argument of the *await* expression in the $g()$ function is resolved, the $g()$ function continues its execution and calls the $f()$ function. Similarly to the generator functions, the call graph generator based on *nodeprof.js* is not aware that the $g()$ function execution is resumed, and it reports that the $f()$ function is called by the *Promise* callback executor, which leads to differences between the call graphs.

The rest of the call graph differences (both nodes and edges) are related to some test failures and the version of *node.js* used by the call graph generator. Every module in our benchmark set checks the versions of *node.js* and its sup-

```
// shorthand for: let f = function () { ... }
function f() { return true; }

f = function() { return false; }
```

Fig. 9. An example for redirecting a JavaScript function.

ported command line options, which triggers a slightly different initialization steps on different versions of *node.js*. Furthermore, there are a few test failures, which occure only with *nodeprof.js*. We have disabled those tests, which caused engine crashes, because the test systems cannot resume testing after a crash and a large part of the call graph would be missing.

4.3 Performance Overhead

Now, we discuss the performance overhead of constructing call graphs. Table 6 shows the overhead when *node.js* is replaced by a call graph generator. The slowdown is not negligible, the execution is eight times slower on *eslint* with *nodejs-cg*. Overall, the relative slowdown on *nodeprof.js* is smaller, although *nodeprof.js* runs around ten times slower than *nodejs-cg*. Not surprisingly, filtering speeds up the call graph construction although the difference is only 10%.

Normally, the mentioned slowdown has no negative effect on testing except for three modules from the *BugsJS* framework, namely *mongoose*, *karma* and *node-redis*. We observed that some tests may be skipped during testing and the nodes and edges related to these tests are also missing from the call graphs. This issue might even occure when an unmodified *node.js* runs the tests, albeit rarely. However, when the call graph generators are used, we observed more frequent test disappearences. Usually only a few tests disappear but sometimes 80% of the test cases are missing.

The aforementioned modules communicate with external tools: *mongoose* and *node-redis* control a database server, and *karma* controls a web browser. When an error occures during the communication, the test system captures this error and aborts the execution of the current batch of tests. Those tests which have not run yet are not counted as successful or failed tests, they are simply ignored, and the test system continues the testing with the next batch of tests. As for *mongoose* and *karma* modules, the call graph generators can often run nearly all of their tests successfully, but *node-redis* looses its network connection way too frequently so we decided to omit this module from the comparison. We suspect that the overhead of call graph construction causes this issue since *node-redis* runs several timing sensitive tests.

5   Related Work

Call graphs can be constructed statically or dynamically. Several tools are available for generating static call graphs from JavaScript code [6,7,13,16]. They can process JavaScript code regardless of the target platform, which can be a web browser, *node.js*, or anything else. However, their precision is limited because JavaScript is a highly dynamic language. Functions are objects, so they can be kept in any JavaScript value. Even when a function is declared with a name it is just a shorthand for assigning that function object to a local variable and this variable can be changed later, as seen in Fig. 9. Tracking which variable refers to which function object can be difficult for static analyzers.

Some static analyzers try to improve their prediction by supporting well-known APIs. For example, the event emitter API of *node.js* allows emitting named events, and these events can be captured by listener functions. The listener functions activated by a named event can be predicted statically [17] as long as certain conditions apply, e.g. the names of the events are string literals.

Besides *nodeprof.js*, there are other frameworks [18,23], which can be extended with dynamic call graph generators. They provide an API to capture events and run custom JavaScript code as a response. Although *nodeprof.js* provides an example analysis for generating call graphs, it connects call sites to called functions rather than two functions. Strictly speaking, this analysis is not a call graph generator.

There is a dynamic call graph generator [26] for web applications. They run the tests of a web application and collect method level execution traces. From these traces they build a call graph. Compared to our work, they focus on browser based web applications rather than *node.js*.

6   Summary

In this paper, we have compared two dynamic call graph generator tools. One of them is using the *nodeprof.js* framework, while the other is a modification of *nodejs*. These generator tools were originally introduced in paper [12], but we have improved both of them. We have also enhanced the node identification process to support the correct pairing of explicit class constructors.

First, we compared the generated call graphs for the SunSpider benchmark suite. Similarly to [12], we have found that a large number of edges are unique in these call graphs. We have shown that this is true for nodes as well. We have validated the unique nodes and edges by hand, and organized them in groups. We have compared these groups and explained the reason of their differences between call graphs.

To extend our comparison, we have compiled a set of modules from the BugsJS dataset and the modules used in [12]. We compared the call graphs generated for this module set with and without applying a filter. Compared to [12], we have identified new sources of differences. JavaScript supports suspending the execution of functions and the generators are handled differently when the execution of a function is resumed. We have also investigated the runtime overhead of the call graph generators and found that it can slow down the execution up to eight times. Due to this slowdown, unexpected test failures are more frequent for those modules which control external tools, e.g., database servers or web browsers.

One direction for future work is fixing the known issues of the tools: improve the performance of the call graph generators (e.g., by caching the last seen edges), or support resuming function execution in the *nodeprof.js*-based call graph generator. We also plan to support the comparison of dynamic code evaluation and JavaScript code stored in temporary files.

Another direction for extending this research is to use the call graphs for detecting unusual program activities or for performing fault localizations. We also plan to generate and investigate more detailed call information, e.g., call chains.

Acknowledgments. This research was supported by the EU-supported Hungarian national grant GINOP-2.3.2-15-2016-00037 and by grant TUDFO/47138-1/2019-ITM of the Ministry for Innovation and Technology, Hungary.

References

1. Apple: SunSpider benchmark suite. https://webkit.org/perf/sunspider/sunspider.html

2. Bielova, N.: Survey on JavaScript security policies and their enforcement mechanisms in a web browser. J. Log. Algebraic Program. **82**(8), 243–262 (2013). https://doi.org/10.1016/j.jlap.2013.05.001

3. Ecma International: ECMAScript Language specification 5.1 edition (2011). https://www.ecma-international.org/ecma-262/5.1

4. Ecma International: ECMAScript 2017 language specification (2017). https://www.ecma-international.org/ecma-262/8.0

5. Elhadi, A., Maarof, M., Hamza Osman, A.: Malware detection based on hybrid signature behaviour application programming interface call graph. Am. J. Appl. Sci. **9**, 283–288 (2012)

6. Feldthaus, A., Schäfer, M., Sridharan, M., Dolby, J., Tip, F.: Efficient construction of approximate call graphs for JavaScript IDE services. In: Proceedings of the 2013 International Conference on Software Engineering (ICSE 2013), pp. 752–761. IEEE Press (2013)

7. Fink, S., Dolby, J.: WALA-The TJ Watson Libraries for Analysis (2012). http://wala.sourceforge.net

8. Gascon, H., Yamaguchi, F., Arp, D., Rieck, K.: Structural detection of Android malware using embedded call graphs. In: Proceedings of the 2013 ACM Workshop on Artificial Intelligence and Security (AISec 2013), pp. 45–54. ACM (2013). https://doi.org/10.1145/2517312.2517315

9. Google: V8 JavaScript engine. https://developers.google.com/v8/

10. Guarnieri, S., Livshits, V.B.: Gatekeeper: mostly static enforcement of security and reliability policies for JavaScript code. USENIX Secur. Symp. **10**, 78–85 (2009)

11. Gyimesi, P., et al.: BugsJS: a benchmark of JavaScript bugs. In: 12th IEEE International Conference on Software Testing, Verification and Validation (2019). https://github.com/bugsjs

12. Herczeg., Z., Lóki., G.: Evaluation and comparison of dynamic call graph generators for JavaScript. In: Proceedings of the 14th International Conference on Evaluation of Novel Approaches to Software Engineering - (ENASE 2019), vol. 1, pp. 472–479. INSTICC, SciTePress (2019). https://doi.org/10.5220/0007752904720479

13. Jensen, S.H., Møller, A., Thiemann, P.: Type analysis for JavaScript. In: Palsberg, J., Su, Z. (eds.) SAS 2009. LNCS, vol. 5673, pp. 238–255. Springer, Heidelberg (2009). https://doi.org/10.1007/978-3-642-03237-0_17
14. Joyent: Node.js JavaScript runtime. https://nodejs.org/
15. Lóki, G., Herczeg, Z.: Dynamic call graph generators for JavaScript. https://github.com/szeged/js-call-graphs/tree/call-graphs (2019)
16. Madsen, M., Livshits, B., Fanning, M.: Practical static analysis of JavaScript applications in the presence of frameworks and libraries. In: Proceedings of the 2013 9th Joint Meeting on Foundations of Software Engineering, pp. 499–509. ACM (2013)
17. Madsen, M., Tip, F., Lhoták, O.: Static analysis of event-driven node.js JavaScript applications. SIGPLAN Not. **50**(10), 505–519 (2015). https://doi.org/10.1145/2858965.2814272
18. Maier, F.: Iroh a dynamic code analysis for JavaScript (2017). https://maierfelix.github.io/Iroh/
19. npm Inc.: npm public registry. https://www.npmjs.com/
20. Ren, X., Ryder, B.G.: Heuristic ranking of java program edits for fault localization. In: Proceedings of the 2007 International Symposium on Software Testing and Analysis (ISSTA 2007), pp. 239–249. ACM, New York (2007). https://doi.org/10.1145/1273463.1273495
21. Ryder, B.: Constructing the call graph of a program. IEEE Trans. Softw. Eng. **5**, 216–226 (1979). https://doi.org/10.1109/TSE.1979.234183
22. Samsung, University of Szeged: JerryScript: A JavaScript engine for internet of things. https://jerryscript.net/
23. Sen, K., Sridharan, M., Adamsen, C.Q.: Jalangi2 dynamic analyses framework for JavaScript (2015). https://github.com/Samsung/jalangi2
24. Stack Overflow: Stack Overflow annual developer survey (2019). https://insights.stackoverflow.com/survey/2019
25. Sun, H., Bonetta, D., Humer, C., Binder, W.: Efficient dynamic analysis for node.js. In: Proceedings of the 27th International Conference on Compiler Construction (CC 2018), pp. 196–206. ACM (2018). https://doi.org/10.1145/3178372.3179527
26. Toma, T.R., Islam, M.S.: An efficient mechanism of generating call graph for JavaScript using dynamic analysis in web application. In: 2014 International Conference on Informatics, Electronics Vision, pp. 1–6, May 2014. https://doi.org/10.1109/ICIEV.2014.6850807
27. Turhan, B., Kocak, G., Bener, A.: Software defect prediction using call graph based ranking (cgbr) framework. In: Proceedings of the 2008 34th Euromicro Conference Software Engineering and Advanced Applications (SEAA 2008), pp. 191–198. IEEE Computer Society, Washington, DC, USA (2008). https://doi.org/10.1109/SEAA.2008.52
28. Wuerthinger, T., et al.: Practical partial evaluation for high-performance dynamic language runtimes. ACM SIGPLAN Not. **52**, 662–676 (2017). https://doi.org/10.1145/3140587.3062381
29. Yu, D., Chander, A., Islam, N., Serikov, I.: JavaScript instrumentation for browser security. SIGPLAN Not. **42**(1), 237–249 (2007). https://doi.org/10.1145/1190215.1190252

Comparison of Computer Vision Approaches in Application to the Electricity and Gas Meter Reading

Maria Spichkova[(✉)], Johan van Zyl, Siddharth Sachdev, Ashish Bhardwaj, and Nirav Desai

School of Science, RMIT University, Melbourne, Australia
`maria.spichkova@rmit.edu.au`

Abstract. This chapter presents comparison of computer vision approaches in application to the meter reading process for the standard (non-smart) electricity and gas. In this work, we analyse four techniques, Google Cloud Vision, AWS Rekognition, Tesseract OCR, and Azure's Computer Vision. Electricity and gas meter reading is a time consuming task, which is done manually in most cases. There are some approaches proposing use of smart meters that report their readings automatically. However, this solution is expensive and requires both replacement of the existing meters, even when they are functional and new, and extensive changes of the whole meter reading system dealing.

Keywords: Software engineering · Computer vision · Google Cloud Vision · Aws Rekognition

1 Introduction

To collect readings of gas and electricity meters manually is a time-consuming task. For that reason we conducted a project in collaboration with Energy Australia, which is an electricity and gas retailing private company that supplies electricity and natural gas to more than 2.6 million residential and business customers throughout Australia. Their current solution involves consumers using updating their utility reading through using an online portal, which is inconvenient for consumers as they (1) need to provide intricate entry details, (2) are required to calculate their utility reading from their meter. Our goal was to analyse the possibility of providing a convenient alternative method for their current meter reading updating system. The proposed solution is to use computer vision techniques for capturing readings.

One of the alternative solutions would be to use smart meter readings. There are many approaches elaborating on the advantages of smart devices for several types of utilities, see e.g., [5,15,55]. The core property of the smart meters is the ability to record energy consumption and to send the corresponding data automatically to the electricity supplier for monitoring and billing purposes. This

© Springer Nature Switzerland AG 2020
E. Damiani et al. (Eds.): ENASE 2019, CCIS 1172, pp. 303–318, 2020.
https://doi.org/10.1007/978-3-030-40223-5_15

solution is definitely useful and has many advantages, including the potential to increase the sustainability of the energy consumption. The core disadvantage of this solution is its costs. For example, the costs of the transition program for Australia were estimated to be a total of $ 1.6 billions. In Australia, the customers have to pay for the upgrade to a smart version from the non-smart meters, which they are currently using: different energy providers may have different approaches to how they charge their customers for this change – either as a lump sum that is added to the first bill after the upgrade or a higher monthly fee. This leads to the situation that many customers prefer to avoid the upgrade. On the other hand, the use of smart meters raised privacy concerns: as the smart meters typically record energy consumption on the hourly basis or even more frequently, and report it to the system at least daily, this information might be used to identify whether the residences are at home or not, etc., which is seen by some consumers as privacy violation.

By the above reasons, many countries delay the transition to the smart meter systems or purpose a partial transition, even when the smart meters cold help to have a more sustainable energy consumption. For example, an analysis of on vulnerability and resistance in the United Kingdom's smart meter transition was presented in [38], where an analysis of acceptance and engagement with smart meters in the United States was discussed in [6]. Thus, until the transition to the smart meters is completed, another solution is required. In our project, we investigated the possibility of application computer vision techniques to allow for an easy way for customers to upload meter readings to their system. The proposed solution is to use a mobile application for capturing readings, a cloud-system to manage readings and a blockchain technology, see [30, 45, 56], to store reading securely.

Research Embedded in Teaching: The system was elaborated within a research project at the RMIT University (Melbourne, Australia) under the initiative *Research embedded in teaching*, see [36, 42]. The aim of this initiative is to encourage curiosity of Bachelor and Master students to the research in Computer Science, IT and Software Engineering. We include research and analysis components as a bonus task within the Software Engineering projects (SEPs) conducted in collaboration with industrial partners. The largest student cohorts were presented by the following courses:

– *COSC 2616 Postgraduate Software Engineering Project*, taught for Master of IT and Master of Computer Science students), and
– *COSC 2410/ 2411 Software Engineering Project*, taught for the Bachelor of Software Engineering students.

Short research projects have been sponsored by industrial partners and focused on the topics related to the project to conduct within semester. These have to be conducted after the semester end, focusing on research prospective and deeper analysis of the semester task, see for example [12–14, 21, 39–41, 44].

Contributions: The results presented in this chapter extend our work introduced at the 14th International Conference on Evaluation of Novel Software

Approaches to Software Engineering [43]. This current results introduce the improved architecture and implementation details of the proposed solution, as well as the comparison of several computer vision technologies, Google Cloud Vision[1], Amazon Web Services (AWS) Rekognition[2], Tesseract OCR [37], and Azure's Computer Vision[3], applied for recognition in utility meter readings. As the majority of the currently used meters have digital displays (the old versions were of dial type) we focused on this type of displays as well as on digit recognition analysis.

Outline: The rest of the chapter is organised as follows. The proposed comparison methodology as well as the results of the conducted study to compare the AWS Rekognition and Google Cloud Vision technologies, are introduced in Sect. 2. Section 3 introduces the results of the conducted study on Tesseract OCR and Azure's Computer Vision. The proposed system is presented in Sect. 4, where Sect. 5 discusses related work. Finally, Sect. 6 summarises the paper and proposed future work directions.

2   Case Study: AWS and Google Solutions

We analysed two computer vision technologies, AWS Rekognition vs. Google Cloud Vision in application to the data sets specific to the meter reading. The data sets were elaborated taking into account also specific challenges that we have to deal within this application domain, which include reflection from the meters' glass, clipped digits, additional text on the meter that does not belong to the actual meter reading, blur, noise, as well as cases, where a meter has digital representation style for some readings but dial representation for other. These challenges are discussed in details in Sect. 2.1.

The accuracy of recognition was calculated according to the standard formula (we measure the accuracy in percents, where 100% means a totally accurate recognition):

$$Accuracy = \frac{CorrectResults}{Total} * 100 \qquad (1)$$

where
CorrectResults is the number of results that match with the original readings completely,
Total presents the total number of images in data set. In our study, we had 30 images in each of the data sets.

The results of the comparison are then discussed in Sect. 2.2.

2.1   Data Sets

Images for the evaluation data set were selected based on their "uniqueness" – images with unique meters or images with unique lighting. A total of 30 images

---

[1] https://cloud.google.com/vision.
[2] https://aws.amazon.com/rekognition.
[3] https://docs.microsoft.com/en-us/azure/cognitive-services/computer-vision.

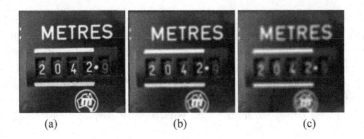

(a)   (b)   (c)

Fig. 1. Blurring effect: (a) 30BLUR, (b) 60BLUR, (c) 90BLUR.

were selected. This set of images were duplicated and modified with various effects in order to test the limitations of the different technologies. These effects are:

- *Scaling:* The data set was scaled in steps of 0.1 ranging from a scale of 0.1 to 0.9 (10% to 90%) of the original data set.
- *Blurring:* Blurring was done in steps of 10 from 10 to 90 with an open source blur algorithm that is based on the normalised box filter, see [32]. The algorithm uses a normalised box filter, the numeral value adjusts the kernel size. Figure 1(a)–(c) present examples of blurring application with 30BLUR, 60BLUR, and 90BLUR, respectively.
- *Gamma:* The gamma algorithm was used with an open source lookup table algorithm [32]. The gamma correction to simulate different lightning conditions. Figure 2(a)–(c) present examples of gamma algorithm application with 0.25GAMMA, 1.5GAMMA, and 3.0GAMMA, respectively.
- *Noise:* The noise algorithm is based upon the salt and pepper noise algorithm that adds sharp and sudden disturbances in the image in the form of sparsely occurring white and black pixels, see [22]. This algorithm was included to further test the performance of the various technologies as noise arguably emulates "dirt" on meters.

(a)   (b)   (c)

Fig. 2. Gamma correction effect: (a) 0.5GAMMA, (b) 1.5GAMMA, (c) 3.0GAMMA.

2.2   Discussion of the Comparison Results

Figure 3 summarises the comparison of the case study results for Google Cloud Vision and AWS Rekognition. The bar *Original* presents the recognition results for the original data set. For this case, Google Cloud Vision has performed slightly better than AWS Rekognition having a 3% higher accuracy. In the rest of the section we discuss the comparison of the data sets in details. Nevertheless, the achieved accuracy is definitely not enough for fully stable solution, which makes it necessary to search for further techniques and to provide an option for a manual adjustment of the recognised data.

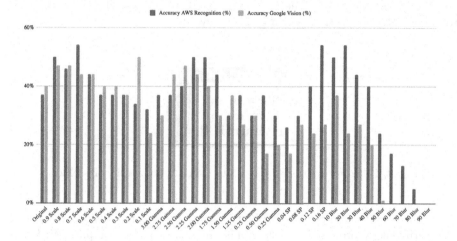

Fig. 3. Accuracy comparison: AWS Recognition and Google Cloud Vision.

Scale Data set: There is a variation of 10% in the accuracy of the two models. AWS Rekognition has an overall higher efficiency than Google Cloud Vision with the former performing 10% better than the latter in every iteration. As the value of scaling is increased, accuracy is also increasing.

Gamma Dataset: The variation between the two, in this case, is almost negligible, as both provide an accuracy of approx. 40%. SP Dataset: AWS Rekognition outperforms Google Cloud Vision with over 20% margin in accuracy. As the value of SP increases, so does the accuracy.

Blur Dataset: This dataset proved to be a challenge for both the models, with AWS Rekognition reaching a top accuracy of 50% whereas the Google Cloud Vision only reached around 37% when blur level is 10. It dropped down to almost 0% when it reached around 40% blur in Google Cloud Vision and 90% blur in the case of AWS Rekognition. Even with higher blurred images, AWS Rekognition is able to detect some readings, unlike Google Cloud Vision where accuracy is 0%.

Thus, on average, AWS Rekognition was able to perform approx. 7% better than Google Cloud Vision when same data set was provided.

3   Case Study: Tesseract OCR and Azure's Computer Vision

As we were not fully satisfied with the results of the first case study, we decided to investigate two other techniques, Tesseract OCR, an optical character recognition (OCR) engine [37], and Azure's Computer Vision[4].

The applied version of the Tesseract OCR was an untrained version 4.0. Thus, at the beginning of the case study, Tesseract 4.0 OCR was used to recognise digits from utility meters. Without training the OCR, it provided no results in recognising the images from the input dataset for utility meters, see Figure 4. However, in application to the computer generated images, Tesseract was able to identify the text with a very high accuracy.

Fig. 4. Failed recognition of the utility meters' photos using Tesseract.

To analyse the results provided by the Azure's Computer Vision, we applied the methodology proposed in Sect. 2. The limitation of the Computer Vision is that it can process only images up to 4 MB in size, which is a huge drawback compared to other cloud technologies like, e.g., Google Cloud Vision that has the limitation of 20MB for APIs and 10MB for JSON Objects. Thus, all the images were scaled to 1000 pixels with and relative height, before the calls to the API were made. The analysis of the data demonstrated that all results were fully or partially incorrect, which means 0% accuracy. In many cases, results were either non numeric or was not received at all, which is considered as technology failure for this application domain. To improve the results of image recognition, we also applied several image filtering techniques, which allowed us to improve the results slightly, but the overall accuracy was still 0%.

Thus, both techniques Tesseract OCR and Azure's Computer Vision were considered as inappropriate to our application domain.

4   Proposed System

Figure 5 presents the proposed process of using the elaborated system, where the high-level system architecture is presented in Fig. 6.

---

[4] https://docs.microsoft.com/en-us/azure/cognitive-services/computer-vision.

Fig. 5. Proposed process.

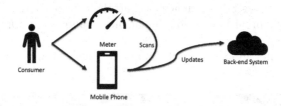

Fig. 6. Proposed high-level system architecture.

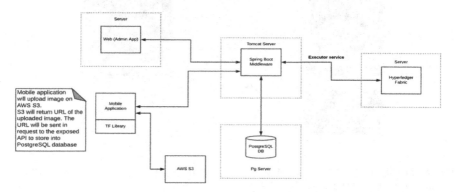

Fig. 7. Solution architecture.

Figure 7 presents the solution architecture for the proposed system, where computer vision approaches are applied to capture meter readings using mobile phones. These readings should then be passed on to the core system to update consumer utility-charges accordingly. Consumers should then be able to view their renewed charges and usages in an internet browser. Thus, the mobile application is used to capture, upload and store an image of the meter to the system. The system will then analyse this image to identify meter readings and return the readings' values back to the user for confirmation. Once the user has confirmed the meter reading, it will be stored on a blockchain.

The proposed system has two core components providing interfaces for two user types:

– an Android application developed for customers; the application was built using React Native, which provides cross-platform compatibility between Android and iOS platforms (thus, development of an iOS version of the app will be less time-consuming);

– a Web application developed using ReactJS for admin users to audit the
meter readings.

Mobile application and web application acts as a clients and call back-end APIs
(application programming interfaces) running of Spring Boot. Which is deployed
on Amazon Web Services Elastic Beanstalk [35]. AWS Elastic Beanstalk reduces
complexity without restricting choice or control, as it automatically handles the
details of capacity provisioning, load balancing, scaling, and application health
monitoring.

Figure 8 presents an examples of the mobile application pages.

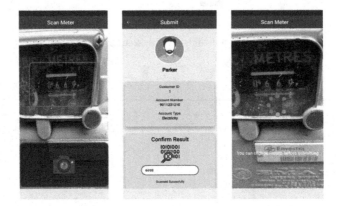

Fig. 8. Mobile application (Customer View): capturing an image of a meter, scanning
the image, and confirming the results.

Spring Boot APIs are secured using JSON Web Token OAuth 2.0 security.
The back-end uses PostgreSQL and Hyperledger Blockchain[5] to store data. Amazon Web Services (AWS) Rekognition is used to get the meter reading from the
meter image. The choice of the computer vision technology is justified by the
study presented in Sects. 2 and 3.

When a customer using the mobile application clicks an image of the meter
(the application uses viewfinder technology as shown in Fig. 8), a Spring Boot
API will be called to filter out the meter readings from the image and to forward
the result to AWS Rekognition, which returns all the text at the Spring Boot
level. Figure 9 presents an algorithm we elaborated to filter out all irrelevant
data and return only the relevant results back to the mobile application. The
API takes the image URL and the storage bucket (S3) name from the client
and returns the meter reading. Firstly, image is fetched from the URL and the
bucket name, then the image is passed to the AWS Rekognition library, which is
applied to identify all the text on the image. The algorithm further filters out all
irrelevant text by considering the user's last meter reading or the initial meter

---

[5] https://www.hyperledger.org.

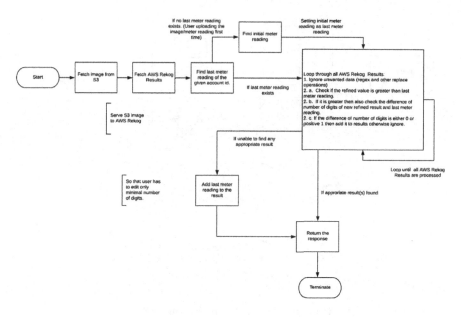

Fig. 9. Results refinement algorithm for image recognition [43].

reading, which was added to the system when the corresponding account was created. If the algorithm unable to return the scanned meter reading, it simply returns the last meter reading to the user, so that user has to change only the minimal number of digits.

If the customer is satisfied with the image recognition results, the customer submits the meter reading, thus, another API will be called which stores the immutable data into Blockchain and mutable data into PostgreSQL database. The administrator can use the Web application to audit the meter readings at any time. Web application also calls Spring Boot APIs to get all customer details and their meter readings.

The blockchain also contains an interface from which the cloud-system can interact with. The cloud-system provides a portal for administrators, where they can review customer meter readings through displaying previously uploaded images along with their respective geo-location coordinates. These features provide Energy Australia with a manual method of detecting falsified readings.

The blockchain component consists of three nodes, see Fig. 10: Customer Node, EA (Energy Australia) Node and Orderer Node; deployed using docker containers on three individual EC2 instances running on Ubuntu 16.04 Xenial Xerus. The peers are part of the Fabric and represent the node on the blockchain. Each Node has its own version of the Ledger using LevelDB. Each node also consists of MSP (Membership service provide) docker container used to provide signatures and certificates to new joining entities. Node.js is used on all the instances to expose the APIs for backend to interact with the Network.

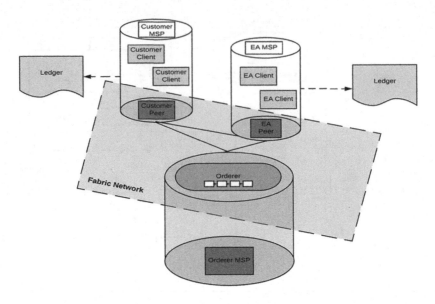

Fig. 10. Blockchain architecture [43].

When an update is made to the meter reading by a customer, it is sent by the customer node to the channel for verification. The EA node in this case acts as an endorser to verify the validity of the transaction. The requested transaction is executed on the endorsers' version of the ledger. Once it is successful, the transaction for meter reading update is signed and sent back to the customer node. This signed transaction is then sent to Orderer. Orderer will verify the endorsed signature and wait for the next block to come up. Once a block is available it will update the meter reading and attach this block to the ledger. The block is then sent to all the nodes for inclusion in the Ledger.

Docker[6] containers were used to launch the instances on to AWS EC2 instances. In this case, a docker container consist of six docker images: for Customer, for EA (Energy Australia), for Orderer, for Chaincode, for EAMSP (Energy Australia Membership Service Provider) and for Customer Membership Service Provider. The Chaincode docker consists of the channel on which the nodes are interacting and the latest version of Chaincode installed and instantiated. A simple web page is hosted to display the amount of transaction that have been committed to the ledger along with other network specifications. A shell bash script was written for each AWS EC2 instance to quickly generate all the artefacts required for Blockchain, to quickly setup and tear down the network for testing and development and finally for deployment.

---

[6] https://www.docker.com.

5 Related Work

The research on automated and remote meter reading was actively conducted over the last 20 years. A number of corresponding patents is available. For example, an automated meter reading system with distributed architecture was patented by [25]. This system aims to collect and manage data from energy meters and route this data automatically to upstream systems for a further analysis.

A automatic meter reading data communication system was patented by [31]. It has an integrated digital encoder and two-way wireless transceiver that is attachable to a wide variety of utility meters for meter data collection and information management. Many other systems with similar ideas were patented [16,24,27], but the research area is still very active, see e.g., [23,48].

However, the majority of works in this area last years focus on the following aspects:

– *Application of the data mining and data analytics techniques on the meter reading data.*
  Thus, an electricity consumption analysis was presented in [33]. The approach focuses on for consumers, and applies to meter reading data several data mining techniques.
  An approaches to recognise energy theft based on the analysis of meter data was proposed in [49].
  The load profiles of energy consumption to infer household characteristics using smart meters were analysed in [20].
– *Design of smart energy meter for the smart grid,* where a smart greed is a next generation power grid having a two-way flow of electricity and information, see [52] for more details on smart grids.
  An overview of typical smart meter's aspects and functions wrt. smart grid aspects was presented in [55].
  A survey on the energy meters evolution in smart grids was presented in [3].
  An approach on the energy theft detection with energy privacy preservation in the smart grid was introduced in [54]. Communication network requirements for smart grid applications were analysed in [28].
  An approach on automatic meter reading in the smart grid using contention based random access over the free cellular spectrum was proposed in [50].
  A study on design and development of smart energy meter for the smart grid was described in [2].
– *Privacy and security aspects of smart meters* are studied especially intensively over the last years, as the privacy and security concerns provide one of the biggest obstacles for the (potential) users of smart meters.
  A security protocol for advanced metering infrastructure in smart grid was proposed in [51]. A theoretical framework to analyse privacy aspects of smart meters was introduced in [34].
  The question on what the consumption patterns derived using the smart meters might say about the consumers, was discussed in [1] and [4].

An approach for non-intrusive occupancy monitoring using smart meters was discussed in [8]. This work aimed to implement energy-efficiency optimizations based on the information of home's occupancy. Other approaches for occupancy detection from electricity consumption data were proposed in [11,26,29,53] and [47].

A solution to increase the smart meter privacy through energy harvesting and storage devices was suggested in [46].

The influence of data granularity on smart meter privacy was analysed in [18]. The authors also analysed what granularity should be used to prevent the interference of personal data from load profiles by using non-intrusive appliance load monitoring methods. Another approach for preventing occupancy detection from smart meters was proposes in [9,10].

A set of use cases for Smart Metering was elaborated in [19].

A study on holiday detection from energy consumption data based on low-resolution smart meter data was presented in [17].

A study where swimming pools were detected through their filter pumps in load data with the 15 min granularity prescribed by the European Union for smart meters, was presented in [7]. It demonstrated how vulnerable the private information might be through access to the meter readings data.

6   Conclusions

In this chapter, we presented the core results of a research project conducted in collaboration with Energy Australia, an Australian electricity and gas retailing company. The project was conducted at the RMIT University (Melbourne, Australia) under the initiative *Research embedded in teaching*, which aim is to familiarise Bachelor and Master students with the applied research in Computer Science, IT and Software Engineering, and encourage their curiosity for these topics.

The goal of our project was to provide a convenient alternative method for their current meter reading updating system focusing on non-smart meters. We conducted a study to compare four approaches: Google Cloud Vision, AWS Rekognition, Tesseract OCR, and Azure's Computer Vision, where the last two were found completely inappropriate for our application domain. Google Cloud Vision and AWS Rekognition, applied for recognition in utility meter readings. The study demonstrated that AWS Rekognition provides better results for our application domain. Thus, AWS Rekognition was applied within the proposed system.

The developed system applies computer-vision technology to identify the meter readings automatically and has two interfaces:

- a mobile application for customers to allow for automated capturing meter readings and managing the account details and the essential details on the electricity and gas meters belonging to the customer;
- a web application for administrators to allow for management customers' accounts and the details on the electricity and gas meters, including the geolocation of the meters.

Future Work: We consider two directions for our future work. First of all, as the average accuracy values of Google Cloud Vision and AWS Rekognition applied for recognition in utility meter readings were not high, we would like to fins a solution that would provide a higher accuracy. We consider to conduct a study to analyse further technologies in application to the utility meter readings, for example an open-source solution Tensorflow and a commercial solution Anyline. We also consider extending the proposed system to allow incorporation of data from smart meters.

Acknowledgements. We would like to thank Shine Solutions Group Pty Ltd for sponsoring this project under the research grant RE-03615. We also would like to thank Energy Australia for collaboration in this project. We also would like to thank the experts from the Shine Solutions Group, especially Aaron Brown and Alan Young for numerous discussions as well as their valuable advice and feedback.

References

1. Albert, A., Rajagopal, R.: Smart meter driven segmentation: what your consumption says about you. IEEE Trans. Power Syst. **28**(4), 4019–4030 (2013)
2. Arif, A., Al-Hussain, M., Al-Mutairi, N., Al-Ammar, E., Khan, Y., Malik, N.: Experimental study and design of smart energy meter for the smart grid. In: 2013 International Renewable and Sustainable Energy Conference (IRSEC), pp. 515–520 (2013)
3. Avancini, D.B., Rodrigues, J.J., Martins, S.G., Rabêlo, R.A., Al-Muhtadi, J., Solic, P.: Energy meters evolution in smart grids: a review. J. Cleaner Prod. **217**, 702–715 (2019)
4. Beckel, C., Sadamori, L., Staake, T., Santini, S.: Revealing household characteristics from smart meter data. Energy **78**, 397–410 (2014)
5. Benzi, F., Anglani, N., Bassi, E., Frosini, L.: Electricity smart meters interfacing the households. IEEE Trans. Ind. Electron. **58**(10), 4487–4494 (2011)
6. Bugden, D., Stedman, R.: A synthetic view of acceptance and engagement with smart meters in the united states. Energy Res. Soc. Sci. **47**, 137–145 (2019)
7. Burkhart, S., Unterweger, A., Eibl, G., Engel, D.: Detecting swimming pools in 15-minute load data. In: 17th IEEE International Conference on Trust, Security and Privacy in Computing And Communications/12th IEEE International Conference On Big Data Science And Engineering (TrustCom/BigDataSE), pp. 1651–1655. IEEE (2018)
8. Chen, D., Barker, S., Subbaswamy, A., Irwin, D., Shenoy, P.: Non-intrusive occupancy monitoring using smart meters. In: Proceedings of the 5th ACM Workshop on Embedded Systems For Energy-Efficient Buildings, pp. 1–8. ACM (2013)
9. Chen, D., Irwin, D., Shenoy, P., Albrecht, J., et al.: Combined heat and privacy: preventing occupancy detection from smart meters. In: 2014 IEEE International Conference on Pervasive Computing and Communications (PerCom), pp. 208–215. IEEE (2014)
10. Chen, D., Kalra, S., Irwin, D., Shenoy, P., Albrecht, J.: Preventing occupancy detection from smart meters. IEEE Trans. Smart Grid **6**(5), 2426–2434 (2015)
11. Chen, Z., Jiang, C., Xie, L.: Building occupancy estimation and detection: a review. Energy Build. **169**, 260–270 (2018)

12. Christianto, A., et al.: Enhancing the user experience with vertical transportation solutions. Proc. Comput. Sci. **126**, 2075–2084 (2018)
13. Chugh, R., et al.: Automated gathering and analysis of cannabinoids treatment data. In: 23st International Conference on Knowledge-Based and Intelligent Information & Engineering Systems. Elsevier Science Publishers BV (2019). p. (to appear)
14. Clunne-Kiely, L., et al.: Modelling and implementation of humanoid robot behaviour. In: 21st International Conference on Knowledge-Based and Intelligent Information & Engineering Systems, pp. 2249–2258. Elsevier Science Publishers BV (2017)
15. Depuru, S.S.S.R., Wang, L., Devabhaktuni, V., Gudi, N.: Smart meters for power grid. challenges, issues, advantages and status. In: 2011 IEEE/PES Power Systems Conference and Exposition, pp. 1–7. IEEE (2011)
16. Ehrke, L.A., Nap, K.A., Dresselhuys, D.R.: Electronic electric meter for networked meter reading (2003). US Patent 6,538,577
17. Eibl, G., Burkhart, S., Engel, D.: Unsupervised holiday detection from low-resolution smart metering data. In: 4th International Conference on Information Systems Security and Privacy (ICISSP), pp. 477–486 (2018)
18. Eibl, G., Engel, D.: Influence of data granularity on smart meter privacy. IEEE Trans. Smart Grid **6**(2), 930–939 (2015)
19. Eibl, G., Engel, D., Neureiter, C.: Privacy-relevant smart metering use cases. In: 2015 IEEE International Conference on Industrial Technology (ICIT), pp. 1387–1392. IEEE (2015)
20. Fahim, M., Sillitti, A.: Analyzing load profiles of energy consumption to infer household characteristics using smart meters. Energies **12**(5), 773 (2019)
21. Gaikwad, P., Jayakumar, C., Tilve, E., Bohra, N., Yu, W., Spichkova, M.: Voice-activated solutions for agile retrospective sessions. In: 23st International Conference on Knowledge-Based and Intelligent Information & Engineering Systems, Elsevier Science Publishers BV (2019). p. (to appear)
22. Gonzalez, R.C., Woods, R.E.: Digital Image Processing, 2nd edn. Addison-Wesley Longman Publishing Co., Inc., Boston (2001)
23. Grady, B.D., Vaswani, R., Pace, J.: Method and system of reading utility meter data over a network (2016). US Patent 9,464,917
24. Jenney, W.P., Szydlowski, L.G., Ferguson, R.D., Potaczala, C.A.: Automatic meter reading system (1999). US Patent 5,897,607
25. Kelley, R.H., Carpenter, R.C., Lunney, R.H., Martinez, M.: Automated meter reading system (2000). US Patent 6,088,659
26. Kleiminger, W., Beckel, C., Staake, T., Santini, S.: Occupancy detection from electricity consumption data. In: Proceedings of the 5th ACM Workshop on Embedded Systems For Energy-Efficient Buildings, pp. 1–8. ACM (2013)
27. Knight, N.E., Banks, D.M.: Remote meter reading system (1998). US Patent 5,852,658
28. Kuzlu, M., Pipattanasomporn, M., Rahman, S.: Communication network requirements for major smart grid applications in HAN, NAN and WAN. Comput. Netw. **67**, 74–88 (2014)
29. Masoudifar, N., Hammad, A., Rezaee, M.: Monitoring occupancy and office equipment energy consumption using real-time location system and wireless energy meters. In: Simulation Conference (WSC), 2014 Winter, pp. 1108–1119. IEEE (2014)
30. Michael, J., Cohn, A., Butcher, J.: Blockchain technology. Journal (2018)

31. Nap, K.A., Ehrke, L.A., Dresselhuys, D.R.: Automatic meter reading data communication system (2001). US Patent 6,246,677
32. OpenCV: Open source computer vision (2018). https://docs.opencv.org/3.1.0
33. Rathod, R.R., Garg, R.D.: Regional electricity consumption analysis for consumers using data mining techniques and consumer meter reading data. Int. J. Electr. Power Energy Syst. **78**, 368–374 (2016)
34. Sankar, L., Rajagopalan, S.R., Mohajer, S.: Smart meter privacy: a theoretical framework. IEEE Trans. Smart Grid **4**(2), 837–846 (2013)
35. Services, A.W.: AWS Elastic Beanstalk: Developer Guide. Amazon Digital Services LLC, Seattle (2018)
36. Simic, M., Spichkova, M., Schmidt, H., Peake, I.: Enhancing learning experience by collaborative industrial projects. In: ICEER 2016, pp. 1–8. Western Sydney University (2016)
37. Smith, R.: An overview of the tesseract ocr engine. In: Ninth International Conference on Document Analysis and Recognition (ICDAR 2007), vol. 2, pp. 629–633. IEEE (2007)
38. Sovacool, B.K., Kivimaa, P., Hielscher, S., Jenkins, K.: Further reflections on vulnerability and resistance in the United Kingdom's smart meter transition. Energy pol. **124**, 411–417 (2019)
39. Spichkova, M.: Industry-oriented project-based learning of software engineering. In: 24th International Conference on Engineering of Complex Computer Systems. IEEE (2019). p. (to appear)
40. Spichkova, M., Bartlett, J., Howard, R., Seddon, A., Zhao, X., Jiang, Y.: SMI: stack management interface. In: 23rd International Conference on Engineering of Complex Computer Systems (ICECCS), pp. 156–159 (2018)
41. Spichkova, M.: Automated analysis of the impact of weather conditions on medicine consumption. In: 2018 25th Australasian Software Engineering Conference (ASWEC), pp. 166–170. IEEE (2018)
42. Spichkova, M., Simic, M.: Autonomous systems research embedded in teaching. In: De Pietro, G., Gallo, L., Howlett, R.J., Jain, L.C. (eds.) KES-IIMSS 2017. SIST, vol. 76, pp. 268–277. Springer, Cham (2018). https://doi.org/10.1007/978-3-319-59480-4_27
43. Spichkova, M., van Zyl, J., Sachdev, S., Bhardwaj, A., Desai, N.: Easy mobile meter reading for non-smart Meters: comparison of AWS rekognition and google cloud vision approaches. In: Proceedings of the 14th International Conference on Evaluation of Novel Approaches to Software Engineering , vol. 1, pp. 179–188. INSTICC, SciTePress (2019)
44. Sun, C., et al.: Software development for autonomous and social robotics systems. In: De Pietro, G., Gallo, L., Howlett, R.J., Jain, L.C., Vlacic, L. (eds.) KES-IIMSS-18 2018. SIST, vol. 98, pp. 151–160. Springer, Cham (2019). https://doi.org/10.1007/978-3-319-92231-7_16
45. Swan, M.: Blockchain: Blueprint for a New Economy. O'Reilly Media Inc., Newton (2015)
46. Tan, O., Gunduz, D., Poor, H.V.: Increasing smart meter privacy through energy harvesting and storage devices. IEEE J. Sel. Areas Commun. **31**(7), 1331–1341 (2013)
47. Tang, G., Wu, K., Lei, J., Xiao, W.: The meter tells you are at home! non-intrusive occupancy detection via load curve data. In: 2015 IEEE International Conference on Smart Grid Communications (SmartGridComm), pp. 897–902. IEEE (2015)
48. Winter, D.: Methods and systems of reading utility meters and methods and systems of transmitting utility meter data (2017). US Patent 9,752,895

49. Xiao, Z., Xiao, Y., Du, D.H.C.: Exploring malicious meter inspection in neighborhood area smart grids. IEEE Trans. Smart Grid 4(1), 214–226 (2013)
50. Yaacoub, E., Abu-Dayya, A.: Automatic meter reading in the smart grid using contention based random access over the free cellular spectrum. Comput. Netw. 59, 171–183 (2014)
51. Yan, Y., Hu, R.Q., Das, S.K., Sharif, H., Qian, Y.: An efficient security protocol for advanced metering infrastructure in smart grid. IEEE Netw. 27(4), 64–71 (2013)
52. Yan, Y., Qian, Y., Sharif, H., Tipper, D.: A survey on smart grid communication infrastructures: motivations, requirements and challenges. IEEE Commun. Surv. Tutor. 15(1), 5–20 (2013)
53. Yang, L., Ting, K., Srivastava, M.B.: Inferring occupancy from opportunistically available sensor data. In: 2014 IEEE International Conference on Pervasive Computing and Communications (PerCom), pp. 60–68. IEEE (2014)
54. Yao, D., Wen, M., Liang, X., Fu, Z., Zhang, K., Yang, B.: Energy theft detection with energy privacy preservation in the smart grid. IEEE Internet Things J. (2019)
55. Zheng, J., Gao, D.W., Lin, L.: Smart meters in smart grid: an overview. In: Green Technologies Conference, pp. 57–64. IEEE (2013)
56. Zheng, Z., Xie, S., Dai, H.N., Chen, X., Wang, H.: Blockchain challenges and opportunities: a survey. Int. J. Web Grid Serv. 14(4), 352–375 (2018)

Expanding Tracing Capabilities Using Dynamic Tracing Data

Dennis Ziegenhagen[1,2(✉)], Andreas Speck[2], and Elke Pulvermueller[1]

[1] Institute of Computer Science, Osnabrück University,
Postfach 4469, 49069 Osnabrück, Germany
[2] Department of Computer Science, Christian-Albrechts-University Kiel,
24098 Kiel, Germany
`{dez,aspe}@informatik.uni-kiel.de`

Abstract. Software traceability enables gaining insight into artifact relationships and dependencies throughout software development. This information can be used to support project maintenance and to reduce costs, e.g. by estimating the impact of artifact changes. Many traceability applications require manual effort for creating and managing the necessary data. Current approaches aim at reducing this effort by automating various involved tasks. To support this, we propose an enrichment of tracing data by capturing interactions that influence the artifacts' lifecycle, which we refer to as *dynamic tracing data*. Its purpose is to expand capabilities of traceability applications and to enable assistance in development tasks. In this paper, we present our research methodology and current results, most importantly a flexible and modular framework for capturing and using dynamic tracing data, as well as an example scenario to demonstrate a possible implementation and usage of the framework.

Keywords: Traceability · Developer-tool interaction · Automation

1 Introduction

Potential benefits and positive effects of using traceability in software project development have been described and cited in the past decades. Examples are quality improvements of software systems which may be achieved by using traceability information for maintenance and evolution [32]. Another usage is cost estimation: traceability can be used to analyze the impact of artifact changes and thus helps in deciding whether the associated costs are acceptable [33]. Amongst others, additional descriptions of how tracing links may support software engineering tasks are provided by Antoniol et al. [3]. Besides general advantages, traceability can also be *required* in specific cases, e.g. for developing safety-critical systems [20].

This work is supported by the InProReg project. InProReg is financed by Interreg 5A Deutschland-Danmark with means from the European Regional Development Fund.

© Springer Nature Switzerland AG 2020
E. Damiani et al. (Eds.): ENASE 2019, CCIS 1172, pp. 319–340, 2020.
https://doi.org/10.1007/978-3-030-40223-5_16

Various tools and methods exist for creating and managing the necessary data. These range from manual approaches to automated data generation and combinations of both. An example for the first type are manually edited lists and tables in office applications, while information retrieval methods are often the basis for automation. However, when traceability data is available in either way, its purpose and actual *usage* is often to analyze the current project state: gaining comprehensive insights and answering higher, more abstract questions. Typical examples are the previously mentioned change impact analysis and the verification of requirement fulfillments.

Although tools, methods and years of research exist in the field of traceability, it is not broadly used yet and current analyses state necessary research and problem areas [6]. Rempel and Mäder give a possible explanation for the low usage and acceptance of traceability: missing evidences regarding actually achieved benefits [24]. Furthermore, the return on investment has been described as a key challenge of traceability [5]. Before any benefits could be gained from it, traceability has to be planned and tailored carefully. According to the specific organization, project and/or team, an appropriate set of tools and methods has to be selected. Additionally, a *traceability information model* has to be created, which requires knowledge and decisions about the types and amount of captured artifacts, relationships and processes. This modeling step should also be guided by the individual goals: which questions should be answered using the tracing data? More precisely, it is necessary to design the information model in a way that the actual *traces* are covered. The expense in connection with planning, setting up and managing traceability also depends on the importance and desired correctness of its data. Safety-critical systems, on the one hand, require higher efforts in order to prove the fulfillment of crucial requirements and functionalities. On the other hand, lower effort is possible by automating individual tasks, e.g. the generation of tracing link candidates. A potential disadvantage of automating algorithms like information retrieval methods may be less "correct" data by missing artifact links or producing false ones. But this can be acceptable if the tracing data's main purpose is in a more supportive manner, e.g. to facilitate the developer's work by enabling navigation to related artifacts, provided that the number of "errors" is below a certain threshold.

The approach proposed in this paper is mainly intended to enable software traceability of the second type. Amongst others, the goals are supporting program comprehension, system understanding and decision-making throughout the development. Thus, we consider typical processes, tools and the life-cycles of artifacts from different perspectives. From a technical viewpoint, we focus on ways to access artifact data, e.g. using the tools' application programming interfaces (APIs) and storage possibilities, e.g. file systems, databases and repositories. Furthermore, we utilize these in order to receive information about interactions which influence traced artifacts. Thus, we enrich tracing data with details on how they are changed during development. In our approach, changing an artifact leads to an automated updating of the respective tracing data. For this reason, we call this enrichment *dynamic tracing data*. Of course, in current traceability applications the data also changes over time, but we use this denomination to emphasize the fundamental idea of combining artifacts, their relations and developer-tool interactions which influence them.

Capturing this data allows to integrate various existing approaches and findings on the interactions between developers and their tools. Amongst others, these include supporting the developer by providing helpful information for accomplishing a specific *task* [16] and suggesting *error solving solutions* [13]. Another example usage is the detection of correlating properties across tool boundaries, e.g. interdependent real-time constraints which are modeled using different tools [22]. Besides an extension of traceability features, the goal is to use *dynamic tracing data* in order to enable further analysis, research, and finally to better assist development tasks.

Another information we gain from the gathered data is about the relationship between tools involved in specific tasks. This, among with other related data, is also known as a task's *context* [16]. By recording interaction timestamps, it is possible to identify and present interconnections in the time domain. This enables including and benefiting from methods in the field of interaction and usage analysis, e.g. as described by Snipes et al. [31]. Furthermore, data about the origin of artifact changes and similar contextual relationships is intended to help understanding, analyzing and improving actual development processes. These are usage examples for which our framework provides a possible basis.

This paper extends our previous publication [37] by presenting more information about the research methodology and current results. We discuss the relation to existing work in Sect. 2. The main contribution is contained in Sect. 3, in which we provide more details on the overall approach, along with the research methodology and results to each of its tasks. Furthermore, we extend the example scenario of our previous work in Sect. 4 by adding details on its implementation. The presented results and future work are discussed in Sect. 5.

2   Related Work

This section contains an overview of related research in order to indicate the scope and boundaries of our approach. Additional existing work is described as part of our research results in Sect. 3.2.

2.1   Traceability

The basic idea of updating tracing data automatically when artifacts are changed has been presented by Mäder and Gotel [21]. Their approach focuses on a UML modeling tool and captures changes of model elements. Depending on the captured events, model traces are updated automatically. To our knowledge, this is one of only a few approaches that consider *changes* of traced artifacts as a basis. Although our approaches share this basic idea, fundamental differences exist. First of all, Mäder and Gotel use elementary change events primarily to trigger trace updates and to recognize development activities. Tracing data is updated when a detected activity shows the respective necessity. In our approach, the underlying elementary changes are *part* of the tracing data and integrated in a way common interaction analyses do. Furthermore, this enriched tracing data is provided for further applications in our approach. Amongst others, the identification of development activities is an example for this. Another difference can be found in the quality of tracing links. Their approach focuses on a specific tool along with a respective traceability definition, which enables a high quality of tracing links in terms of correctness and validation. We instead aim at a broader usage of data captured from multiple tools in order to provide a basis for various traceability applications and analyses. Therefore, we accept seemingly "unnecessary" tracing data which may not be used by all integrated applications. In fact, our framework is designed to enable various previously unknown usages, and thus cannot rely on predefined traceability.

Sanchez presents an approach which shares another of our motivations by considering inter-tool relationships of artifacts and including *contexts* [28]. The main goal is to design a declarative language for capturing semantic model relationships, along with an architecture using this language in order to automate model management tasks. While the solution proposed by the author also takes artifact-related contexts across tool boundaries into account, developer-tool interactions are not explicitly considered.

An overview of retrospective and prospective software traceability is provided by the work of Asuncion et al. [4]. The authors combine these techniques by applying topic modeling to tracing data which is recorded using various tool adapters. A difference to our approach can be found in the way working with multiple projects is integrated. While Asuncion et al. aim at separating the tracing data of each project from other projects, we instead use it to identify cross-project relations and e.g. to provide developers with problem solutions from other projects.

"SAT Analyzer" [23] is an example for comprehensive traceability management environments. By including DevOps practices, it is able to track artifact changes between builds and to create tracing data based on these changes semi-automatically. In contrast to our work, the tool focuses on a predetermined set of artifact types and provides respective, specialized functionalities, e.g. change impact analyses.

2.2 Developer-Tool Interaction

Extending traceability with a developer action has been realized by Mahmoud and Niu [19]. The authors analyze the impact various types of refactoring have on the traceability of a software project. Depending on the type, they observed both, positive and negative effects during refactoring. This confirms our assumption that considering developer interactions may be a valuable extension to the tracing methodologies.

Research on developer-interaction-analysis can roughly be divided into "offline" methodologies, i.e. understanding the developer's work by analyzing usage logs, and "online" approaches which directly monitor interactions when they occur. Examples for the first type are provided by Snipes et al. [31] and Damevski et al. [7], who utilize data collected by IDEs. Roehm and Maalej [27] show an example for the second type. The authors, along with others, also present an application to support developers by using the monitored data [26]. Although these approaches do not focus on traceability, we compare and analyze them in order to detect possible generalizations for enriching traceability data.

Recommendation systems are an example for supporting development tasks based on interaction data. An overview of this field is provided by Robillard et al. [25]. Common assistance functions which we consider in our work are recommending artifacts and other data which is related to the element the developer currently interacts with. Amongst others, representative applications are provided by Mäder and Egyed [17], Singer et al. [30] and Maalej et al. [15]. Research on the visualization of traceability data with focus on task contexts is provided by Li and Maalej [14]. Their findings also show insights in how developers interact with artifacts in various tasks, e.g. during design, implementation and testing. In our approach, such visualizations techniques are also used for providing assistance throughout development tasks.

3 Approach

This section contains information about the approach in addition to our previous work [37]. First of all, we specify the scope of our work and the type of traceability which it is based on. Afterwards, we describe the research methodology along with its structure, tasks and current results. Of main importance are the motivation and definition of *dynamic tracing data*, as well as a framework for capturing, providing and using it. An example scenario is described in Sect. 4, focusing on the implementation of its main components.

3.1 Scope and Background

Although an important goal is to support the developer's activities, it is necessary to consider various other roles of project members and their work during different phases of software development. Additionally, we want to include a wide variety of project types, development models, tools and methods. To enable this, we use a broad definition of the term "traceability", which Aizenbud-Reshef et al. propose: "We regard traceability as any relationship that exists between artifacts involved in the software-engineering life cycle" [1]. In addition to this, we use terms and definitions provided by Gotel et al. [10]. For example, the authors describe *requirements traceability* as a specialized form of general *traceability*. This specialization is achieved by delineating the artifact type which is of main interest. Relating to this methodology, our approach is mostly concerned with the *general* traceability term. The authors also include a more detailed definition of *requirements traceability*, which originates from Gotel and Finkelstein in 1994 [11] as the "ability to describe and follow the life of a requirement [...] through its development [...] and through periods of ongoing refinement and iteration" [10].

Here, we use this in order to clarify, differentiate and further characterize our term *dynamic tracing data*. At first glance, this may seem to already cover our approach: focusing on the *life* of artifacts; in this case especially requirements. So what are the differences to our work? Most notably, they use the specialization to one specific artifact type as the starting point for tracing, as many requirement engineering methods do. Additionally, and much more important, there is a strong difference in what actually substantiates the artifact's *life*. In their case, it is a compilation of other artifacts and the trace links which connect them to a requirement. For example, a related diagramming artifact may show how the implementation of a requirement is *designed*. Then, a linked source code artifact could contain the *implementation* of this design, and so forth. These artifacts, which can potentially be traced starting from a requirement, represent its life throughout the development process and phases. In contrast to this, we consider the changes of artifact contents, i.e. actual data modifications, as part of its life. Examples are source code edits or diagram modeling steps. Compared to the "life" in the *requirements traceability* definition, the changes which we consider are more fine-grained and create new variations or versions of an artifact.

The scope defined in this section enables demonstrating the relation to existing traceability approaches which are part of our research tasks.

3.2   Research Methodology

In order to examine possibilities for extending current tracing data with developer-tool interactions, we used the following procedure:

Task 1 Collect and analyze tools and approaches in the field of traceability.
Task 2 Collect and analyze work about developer-tool interactions with possible connections to tracing data and methods.
Task 3 Use the results of tasks 1 and 2 to compare the involved data (models) and processes.
Task 4 Draft example scenarios in which the results of tasks 1 and 2 can potentially benefit from each other and which make use of the results of task 3.
Task 5 Design and implement a framework for enabling a reusable, flexible implementation of the scenarios.
Task 6 Use the framework and the scenario implementations for the purpose of further research.

For each task, we will summarize main findings and highlight results which play an important role for our research and the envisaged framework in particular.

Results of Task 1 (Traceability Approaches). The first task has a focus on reusable aspects, especially components which are capable of being integrated into other applications. Thus, those containing generally applicable algorithms or open implementations are most interesting. We determined that the results can be categorized:

1. Comprehensive frameworks and tool collections that cover the overall traceability process.
2. Algorithms for generating tracing data:
   (a) Extracting artifacts and artifact data.
       Examples: Requirements, modeling elements, source code.
   (b) Retrieving link candidates
       Example: Requirement-to-code links.
3. Applications for *using* the generated tracing data.
   Examples: Analyzing methods, visualizations.

While the researched frameworks in category 1 enable performing multiple tasks, e.g. generating, managing and analyzing tracing data, we also found limitations. "SAT Analyzer" [23], for example, offers various functionalities from data generation to analyses, but in return relies on predetermined artifact types. Nevertheless, common proceedings of traceability frameworks can be found. We identify and summarize the following steps which are most relevant to our approach:

- Extract artifact data from the actual project contents (e.g. requirement documents or source code).
- Data equalization, i.e. transforming the various artifact data models to a common traceability data model.
- Dependency detection, i.e. generation of candidates for artifact link.
- Supervision by the user, e.g. correction of the automatically generated data.
- Usage of the corrected data, e.g. analyzing it with the purpose of assessing coverage aspects, executing trace queries or applying visualization techniques.

In addition to "SAT Analyzer", other frameworks following these steps are the "AMPLE Traceability Framework" [2] and the tool presented by Wijesinghe et al. [36]. Our approach and especially the framework's concept make strong use of the categorized traceability functions and steps. For our work, they also route the flow of tracing data: Its generation, followed by intermediate processes, e.g. supplementation, refinement or revision, up to its usage, e.g. for analyses. Of course, this is a simplified view on the tracing data's flow and in practice, there will be multiple iterations, for example further refinements and additions of missing data after visualizing or analyzing the current state. But for our approach, this is a rough guideline for classifying traceability functions, which is also the basis for our framework's architecture, as described in the results of task 5. In recent developments and research during this task, we notice a trend towards increasing automation of the above steps, which encourages our approach.

Results of Task 2 (Developer-Tool Interaction). Regarding existing research on interactions between developers and their tools, we differentiate approaches which either (a) analyze previously recorded data or (b) react to events when they occur. We interpret approaches of category (a) as "offline", because the analyses don't require simultaneously running tools for generating interaction data. But this is the case for category (b), so we attribute these approaches as "online". Typical data sources of the first category are IDE log files. Often, the goal is to detect interaction sequences or reoccurring patterns [7]. The second category is characterized by monitoring developer actions and tool events in order to provide immediate support and assistance. Examples are suggesting artifacts which are relevant to the current task and context [16], as well as recommending solutions to error messages [13]. From a technical view, both categories may share functions like custom data capturing, e.g. by attaching event listeners. Also, results of the second category often utilize data recorded in the past, too, but rather aim at supporting the current development work instead of enabling in-depth analyses. For our approach, the first category provides sources with regard to data models and characteristics of interaction sequences. The second category is especially interesting for providing example applications and potential use cases.

Analyses often include information about the involved GUI elements, e.g. GUI widgets as targets of user actions or the location of mouse events on the screen. An example for this is the work of Damevski et al. [7]. The information is used for aggregating consecutive messages of the analyzed dataset. Furthermore, the structure of these messages is a good example for typical interaction log files, as it consists of an action type (e.g. "Edit.Paste" or "View.SolutionExplorer"), a category (e.g. "Command" or "View"), a timestamp and an user id in order to distinguish the actions of different developers. It is notable that information regarding involved artifacts or their type is *not* included. This applies to other approaches as well, for example Roehm et al. [26]. The interaction data presented in their work uses the terms "Artifact Type" and "Artifact Id", but not in the sense traceability methods do. Instead, the terms are more related to GUI elements, e.g. text fields. However, such elements can actually *be* typical tracing artifacts, as it could be the case for interactions with model elements like a UML class. Other information which the authors collect in their approach is similar to the messages Damevski et al. use, e.g. an event type, a timestamp and a "Machine Id" for distinguishing events which occur on machines of different developers.

As mentioned in Sect. 2, recommendation systems are examples for applications which use interaction data in order to support development tasks. This domain is also referred to as "recommendation systems in software engineering" (RSSE) [25]. Maalej et al. [15] present a concept model for interaction data in RSSE which fits our approach quite well, as it considers interactions to directly concern specific artifacts. A difference to our approach can be found in the definition of the term "context". The authors describe it as the *circumstances* in which interactions are performed, e.g. the developers intention, or a specific task or issue. In our approach, these do not primarily define the context, but can rather be part of it. We instead consider the involved artifacts and tools to be essential context elements. The author's view has advantages because it enables to add structure and purpose to sequences of interaction data. While this can be important depending on the actual goal, our approach can not require the availability of the necessary information. Thus, we are in accordance with Gasparic et al. [9], who replace the "task" aspect of Maalej's model with *activities*, for example reading, navigating, editing, debugging, using version control and reviewing code.

Results of Task 3 (Data Comparison). In order to form a concept for "dynamic tracing data", we analyze and compare main characteristics of both, current tracing data and interaction data. Of main interest are possible generalizations of how the data is tailored for particular projects, along with usage aspects and the handling of different granularities.

At least in the scope which we defined for our approach, it is possible to abstract "static" tracing data to a most basic view: artifacts with relations to other artifacts [18]. Traceability applications usually add semantics to this basic model by defining types of artifacts and how they generally are able to relate to each other. For example, such a model could contain an artifact type "Requirement" and a link type "derived from", indicating possible dependencies between actual requirement artifacts. These meta models are often referred to as *traceability information models* (TIM) [6], including rules and constraints for modeling elements. Project-specific definitions and usages of TIMs are getting attention due to missing universally accepted reference models [6]. But without suitable and accepted standards, TIMs may be less reusable and probably incompatible in practice. Thus, we prefer the described abstract data model as a common basis, which enables to add semantics later instead of predefining them.

As mentioned in the results of task 2, interaction analyses often assign developer actions to higher tasks or intentions like implementing a specific functionality, debugging or refactoring. While some of these tasks are able to be automatically identified, e.g. the starting of an IDE's *debug mode* by attaching a respective listener, this is not generally possible. We examine such automated task identifications and may include them in the future, but currently a more basic handling shows to be more suitable. Thus, we categorize interactions using the CRUD functions: create, read, update and delete. For us, performing these functions using a tool mainly influences and determines an artifacts *life*; from its creation, to various accesses and modifications and possibly to its deletion. In a similar way to the subsequent addition of semantics to abstract tracing data described above, our approach includes the optional possibility to assign CRUD events to higher tasks, like *bug fixing* or *refactoring*, and thus adding semantic meanings to interaction events, too. Throughout the development, sequences of artifact-related interactions happen, which we interpret as a stream of events more or less continuously changing the tracing data. This denotes our use of the term "dynamic tracing data".

We already determined the minimal granularity of interaction data for our approach by considering CRUD functions. In our previous paper [37], we discussed further options, e.g. capturing single keystrokes, along with the typical frequencies in which they typically occur during development. Similar considerations are presented by Roehm et al. [26] and Maalej et al. [15]. A common assumption is that there has to be a trade-off between the level-of-detail in which data is captured, and the amount of information which is necessary for analyses or for providing assistance. Such considerations regarding static tracing data can also be found in the work of Egyed et al., who additionally explain missing literature on this topic by "the fact that it is unknown in advance which trace links will be used" [8]. This completely meets our research results and confirms the difficult, maybe even impossible existence of any generally applicable traceability.

With regard to the results summarized up to this point, the core of our approach can be formulated in the following way: **Dynamic tracing data covers the life cycle of artifacts, which is mainly influenced by developer-tool interactions.** We regard dynamic tracing data as an extension of current "static" data and aim at providing compatibility with current traceability methods on the one hand. On the other hand, we examine non-compatible usages which, in return, offer valuable functionalities that would not be possible otherwise.

Results of Task 4 (Example Scenarios). For creating the initial example scenarios, existing applications in the fields of traceability and interaction-based support are considered. Their functionalities are decomposed and integrated into the scenarios according to the results of the previous tasks, e.g. by using the steps described in the results of task 1 as a pattern. We examine what data is actually used, how it is generated and which are the goals users typically try to accomplish. The drafted scenarios are substantively characterized by automating most tasks if possibly, e.g. data extraction and link candidate generation. A basic scenario has been summarized in our previous work [37]. Additionally, we outline the detection of possible relations in dynamic tracing data by focusing on interactions with artifacts. Examples for detecting relations based on interaction data are:

- Creating a class which has the same name as an element in a UML diagram. (Possible relation because of similar artifact names.)
- Reading a requirement, followed by implementing a new method. (Possible relation because of interactions occurring close to each other.)
- Successfully building a previously erroneous project after using the browser. (Possible relation between an error and a website containing a solution.)

Methods for detecting such relations are part of existing applications. We integrate similar methods in our approach, as described in the example scenario (see Sect. 4).

Results of Task 5 (Framework Design and Implementation). As a conclusion of the previous tasks, we define the following goals for our framework:

1. Create a flexible, reusable and easily expandable infrastructure for integrating approaches according to the traceability steps identified in task 1.

2. Use *dynamic tracing data* as a basis and keep as much compatibility to static tracing data and interaction data as possible.
3. Provide two operational modes:
   (a) Immediate data usage, e.g. a prompt reaction to changes for enabling recommendations or similar assistance.
   (b) In-depth data usages, e.g. complex or comprehensive analyses.

To give an overview of the framework design, we refer to the data flow and steps described in the results of task 1 and arrange the components accordingly, as shown in Fig. 1. The traceability steps are represented as architectural layers in the figure, and thus enable a logical view on the components and their relations. As indicated at the right side of the figure, tracing data basically flows from the bottom components (e.g. artifact extraction) to the ones at the top (e.g. visualizations or analyzes). The functionalities and interfaces provided by the framework enable the integration of exchangeable components for specific tasks, i.e. extracting artifacts, generating link candidates and using the dynamic tracing data. In Fig. 1, these exchangeable components are indicated by a dashed border. By integrating the components, the framework forms a comprehensive system. Thus, it is specialized for specific usages by combining the generally provided functions with suitable components, e.g. tool adapters or link generators. The scenario described in Sect. 4 provides examples for such components and how they are integrated.

The general usage of the framework start with extracting artifact data from the adapted tools (bottom layer in Fig. 1). Usually, these adapters are also used to monitor interactions which influence these artifacts. The extracted and captured data is sent to the framework core, which then enables accessing it in a unified way (*data access provision* layer). The subsequent components are mostly link candidate generators which analyze the provided data. Generated links are sent to the framework, which enables an optional revision of the stored tracing data. In order to support automated usages in the application layer, the revision is not required. Therefore, it is up to the traceability applications whether they use unrevised, potentially incorrect data, or require revision by the user.

The framework infrastructure forms a distributed system and provides a RESTful API for connecting the exchangeable components. At the current state, multi-user usage is handled in a basic way. The framework doesn't implement an explicit user management, but as components access framework functions via the RESTful API, it is possible to distinguish the respective callers - i.e. the developer's devices - by using data of the underlying protocols, e.g. IP addresses.

As already mentioned, Fig. 1 contains a *logical* view. Indeed, examples exist in which it is reasonable to implement an artifact extractor together with a corresponding link generator inside the same physical component, e.g. an IDE plugin. This is especially the case when such implementations allow an easier access to necessary data compared to exclusively rely on the framework's functions.

Results of Task 6 (Usage and Experiences). This task is currently ongoing work. One notable result of the implementation and usage so far is the ability

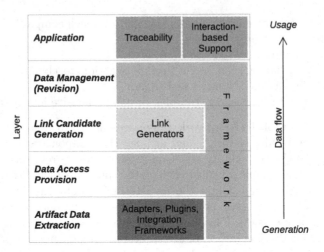

Fig. 1. Logical view on the framework layers (rows) and components (colored boxes). The framework connects the exchangeable components across the layers and enables the tracing data flow from its generation in the bottom layer to the applications in the top layer. (Color figure online)

to reproduce dynamic tracing data. Amongst other purposes, we use this for testing and proving the correct integration of interaction-based methods. Furthermore, it enables to compare different *versions* of tracing data, e.g. in terms of the previously discussed levels of abstraction and granularity. In order to (re) create interactions beyond a simple replay of explicitly recorded events, we created an approach based on GIT repositories of existing projects. The differences between consecutive repository states, i.e. commits, are used to simulate step-by-step modifications of artifacts. This procedure is likely to miss the original order of changes which occurred between repository versions, because this information is not part of a commit history. But it offers a simple mechanism of including a variety of project types and contents. Furthermore, we use this as a chance and take advantage of the unknown order of changes by creating respective sequences using pseudo-random number generators, and thus achieving additional variations of artifact changes. This allows us to reproducibly test many sequences of modifications.

Another possible source for reproducing and simulating interactions are log files of development tools. But most of the available datasets which we examined do not cover the necessary information, especially regarding the involved artifacts. Generally, interaction logs which refer to specific git repositories could be a valuable extension for our approach.

With regard to the results presented up to this point, we describe one of the example scenarios in the following section, focusing on the implementation and usage the components which are integrated using the framework.

4   Example Scenario

In our previous publication [37], we presented the scenario by describing the usage of static and dynamic tracing data, and how the latter builds upon the other. Furthermore, we described generally reusable components, for example a *Generic File Adapter* which monitors project-related data using the file system and forwards observed events to the framework API. Here, we add more details on the scenario's implementation. In our approach, this is *one* possible prototype, and we consider realizing the same scenario in different ways, e.g. by exchanging the adapted tools. For example, the current prototype connects the Eclipse IDE via its plugin API. It would also be possible to adapt any other Java IDE at this point, e.g. NetBeans. We assume that creating exchangeable prototype components will give us a better understanding of how to precisely divide logical and conceptional aspects from the necessary technical realization, and how the framework could possibly support adapting various tools.

4.1   Description

The example scenario focuses on a simplified software development environment. The main traceable artifacts are (a) requirement specifications, (b) UML class diagrams which are designed for their fulfillment and (c) Java classes which implement the UML designs. The respective development tools are an office application for writing requirement documents, a UML diagramming tool and a Java IDE for implementing the designed system. While the UML and Java tools can be connected using APIs, the office application does not provide a suitable interface. Thus, the generic file adapter is used, along with a specialized requirement file handler. It is able to parse the documents and to extract requirement artifacts. Besides the extracting artifact data, these adapters also generate tool-specific artifact links. Amongst others, these are dependencies between requirements and object-oriented associations contained in diagrams. Furthermore, generators for recovering the *cross-tool* artifact links are included. These automatically generate *requirement-to-diagram* and *diagram-to-code* link candidates when certain artifact changes are detected. The generated tracing data is stored using the framework's data management core, as well as subsequent interaction events related to the artifacts. Applications use this data to dynamically visualize the context of the currently edited artifact and to provide additional assistance, which is described more detailed in the following section.

4.2   Implementation

In this section, we firstly give an overview of all components which are part of the scenario. This includes their (inter-) connection from logical and technical perspectives. Afterwards, we describe the implementation of each component in a more detailed way.

Figure 2 shows the scenario's components, using the general framework structure presented in Fig. 1 as a template. To give more details on the actual implementation, two more layers are added at the bottom of Fig. 2. The components contained in the *integration* layer provide the technical access to the actual data sources, e.g. the plugin which adapts to the IDE's API. Thus, the *integration* components enable elements of the *extraction* layer to use and analyze the currently available contents of the *tools* (bottom layer). The extracted artifact data is send to the framework core, which is represented by the green rectangles between the layers in Fig. 2. Additionally, subsequent CRUD events which are related to the extracted artifacts and captured at the *integration* layer are also send to the framework. After receiving such artifact-related events, the framework informs the link candidate generators, so that they are able to react to the changing data. The current prototypic implementation uses a simple publish/subscribe mechanism in order to control the amount of notifications and messages between the components. The "requirement-to-diagram" link generator, for example, doesn't need to be informed about source code changes. A similar mechanism is used to update the applications which are connected to the framework in the top layer.

In the following, the components are described in the order according to the steps identified in task 1 in Sect. 3.2, from extracting data at the tools' interfaces up to its usage in sample applications.

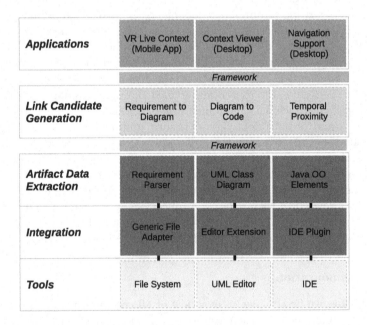

Fig. 2. Logical view on the scenario implementation. The framework integrates the components (colored boxes) and provides data from components of the bottom layers to the layers above. (Color figure online)

Data Extraction. The descriptions in this section cover components of the *artifact data extraction* and *integration* layer shown in Fig. 2. The separation of the layers is primarily to be understood from a logical view, while their components may technically be implemented close to each other.

The **Java IDE Plugin** analyses projects which are opened in the IDE. As a starting point, the files contained in a Java project are classified as artifacts. This information is sent to the framework core via its RESTful API, as well as following extracted or generated tracing data. Listeners are attached to the project, which enable to detect a) project-wide changes, e.g. adding or deleting files, and b) artifact-related events, e.g. source code edits. The plugin implements the strategy pattern in order to enable a specialized handling for artifact types, if available. Java classes, for example, are further analyzed to gather dependencies to other classes, which are subsequently treated as link candidates. This is an example for the separation of logical and technical views as described in Sect. 3.2.

In case no suitable strategy exists for an artifact, the *default handler* forwards basic information to the framework, without deeper analyses. Figure 3 illustrates the use of the strategy pattern along with implemented handlers, some of which are described in the following.

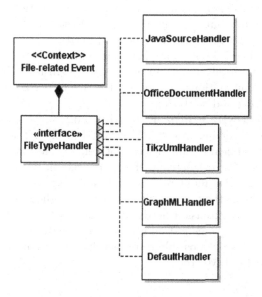

Fig. 3. The strategy pattern enables specialized artifact file handling in the IDE adapter plugin.

In this scenario, requirement documents are created and edited using an office tool that does not provide a suitable interface for directly attaching an adapter. Thus, data related to requirements is extracted using the *generic file adapter* in combination with the previously described strategy pattern implementation. The resulting component is the **Requirement File Adapter**. This may seem redundant, but enables covering different usages and interaction scopes. On the one hand, the artifact handler of the IDE plugin allow accessing further information via the plugin API, e.g. detailed interaction data. But on the other hand, this requires additional efforts on the implementation, along with respective knowledge about the interface. Using the *generic file adapter* approach reduces the necessary efforts, but offers less possibilities to monitor developer interactions.

The file adapter monitors activities related to contents of project directories and applies the strategy handlers depending on the file type. To avoid massive performance issues and overhead, the adapter provides both, a whitelist and a blacklist mode. Thus, it can either explicitly include or exclude specific files or file types. The monitoring implementation uses the *WatchService* which is part of Java NIO.2 APIs and therefore applicable for various file systems.

The office document handler analyses file contents in order to extract structured data. The current purpose is to receive requirements, but the same proceeding could generally be applied to other structured documents. For identifying requirement data, i.e. names, ids, descriptions and relations to other requirements, we implement a simple, configurable parser. Tools which provide similar functionalities, e.g. Rational DOORS, have been evaluated by Shahid et al. [29].

A general assumption of this scenario is that artifacts are to be handled close to the respective tools, but without *limiting* artifact types to specific applications. A Java source file may primarily be used inside an IDE, but technically it is also possible to open it in other applications, e.g. a basic text editor. Thus, we include these non-primarily usages in our approach. In fact, situation in which such exceptional combinations of tools and artifacts occur may be especially interesting for tracing and analyzing.

The prototypic **UML Editor Extension** adds an adapter to the open-source, Java-based modeling tool "Violet UML Editor"[1]. The extension monitors the creation, modification and deletion of elements, as well as non-modifying usages, e.g. selection. The extracted artifacts are class diagrams and their classes. Furthermore, information about modeled relations, e.g. dependencies and associations, is forwarded to the framework core as link candidates. Compared to the IDE plugin, the editor extension needs to be more specialized to the tool. For example, the editor's implementation uses a custom data structure for modeling elements and thus it is not possible to re-use this extension for other purposes, e.g. for adapting other UML tools.

Link Candidate Generation. The prototypic *Requirement-to-Diagram* (R2D) and *Diagram-to-Code* (D2C) link generators implement methodologies based on existing approaches. The work of Antoniol et al. [3] is a representative example for a similar, more comprehensive solution. The D2C component performs a very simple matching of diagram elements and source code elements by comparing names and hierarchies, i.e. classes and their methods. The R2D component generates link candidates based on simple information retrieval methods. The same

---

[1] http://violet.sourceforge.net/.

approach could potentially be used for generating *Requirement-to-Code* link candidates, as Antoniol et al. describe [3], but it is purposely limited in order to keep a strict scope for the scenario's implementation.

While the R2D and D2C link candidate generators provide typical traceability functionalities, the *Temporal Proximity* component includes time-related data for detecting possible artifact relationships. For this, it monitors all CRUD events which are sent to the framework and creates a link between artifacts when the events occur close to each other. The respective time window is configurable. A main purpose of the *temporal proximity links* is to examine possible advantages of having regularly updated link candidates available instead of explicitly performing larger analyses.

The link candidate generators in this scenario are designed to be executed automatically and frequently, i.e. when the framework detects respective artifact changes. Thus, there is a trade-off between the degree of "correctness" and the necessary execution time. We currently prefer a faster, more simple usage as the framework is intended to support the developer's work. In contrast to this, traceability applications which require correct and validated data, e.g. safety-critical systems, will need other, suitable link generators and/or additional validation.

Applications. The applications implemented for this scenario provide a general usage of all available artifacts and types. The *context viewer*, for example, enables the user to view data related to the currently "used" artifact in a desktop application. These relationships can either be typical tracing links, e.g. those between a requirement and a UML diagram, but also time-related in order to link artifacts which have previously been used at the same time as the selected one. At "the same time" means that interaction events related to these artifacts occurred inside a configurable time span. As a starting point, the information generated by the *temporal proximity* component is used. The user is also able to view the past evolution of the context on a timeline. The application automatically adapts to data updates provided by the framework and shows the context of the artifact which the developer most recently interacted with. This automation can be turned off in order to focus on a specific artifact.

The second application builds upon the previous, but is limited to the IDE. It enables navigation to those artifacts which are part of the current context *and* accessible in the IDE. "Navigation", in this case, means that the user is able to select a related artifact in the application and remotely open and focus it inside the IDE. This functionality can be compared to tools like "NavTracks" [30]. Note that this "return path", i.e. the additional usage of the plugin API, is up to the application itself and not part of the framework. But it makes use of data provided by the framework, e.g. the artifact's id which the IDE uses internally.

The third application makes further use of the framework's distributed infrastructure. We implemented a mobile application which presents the current context using virtual reality technologies. For this, the application communicates with the framework API using asynchronous HTTP requests and automatically arranges objects representing the received artifacts in a 3D scene. Distances between the objects are calculated using the relationships available in the current context. The scene is displayed in a stereoscopic view, enabling the mobile device to be used in a suitable VR headset like Google Cardboard. While the current implementation of this application provides a basic and generic view of the current context, we examine possibilities to further benefit from the 3D view to better visualize *dynamic* data and especially time-related aspects. First ideas are inspired from tools like *Gource*[2].

While the applications presented in this scenario are available for most artifact types, others are more specialized. To give an example, we implemented an IDE extension for suggesting solutions based on a) automated web search results and b) an error/solution repository, which is updated when a web-found solution successfully removed a bug. For this, the IDE's error messages are treated as artifacts which are linked to the respective source code file. The general functionality and support provided by this application resembles those of other tools, e.g. "HelpMeOut" [13].

5   Conclusion

We propose capturing developer-tool interactions in order to enrich the data current traceability methodologies usually focus on. This capturing is achieved by connecting to available interfaces of development tools, e.g. the plugin API of an IDE. As the interactions result in a frequent change of the traced artifacts, a more or less continuous event stream is created. Thus, we call the proposed enrichment *dynamic* tracing data. A goal of this approach is to enable support and assistance throughout development processes. As an example, the dynamic traces could be analyzed in order to offer the developer know-how others already gained in similar processes or situations. Therefore, our approach combines existing research in the fields of software traceability and developer-tool interaction analysis.

The concept and implementation of a framework based on our definition of *dynamic tracing data* has been presented. It builds upon existing applications, methods and experiences. It will not be the final result; it is rather the basis for future research. We plan to integrate more existing work, e.g. for automatically generating additional link candidates, while examining possibilities to simplify and further support the integration. Additionally, we look forward to gather experiences and feedback from using the framework and dynamic tracing data in general. Thus, the procedure presented in Sect. 3.2 is basically understood in an iterative way to refine the results.

Besides examining possible advantages, we are especially interested in systematically detecting limits of the achieved automation. Current vulnerabilities are found in the processes of artifact extraction and link generation. For example, the proposed *generic file adapter* may be overloaded when many file-related

---

[2] https://gource.io/.

events occur close to each other, e.g. when a repository is checked out inside a directory that the adapter is monitoring.

Furthermore, general challenges regarding the integration of heterogeneous software components remain, although we aim at creating a solution which should allow a modular and flexible composition. It is still necessary to write adapters, equalize heterogeneous data, perform model transformations etc. Effort spent on integrating components, applications and methods varies much. Often it depends on the possibilities provided by tools or the availability of implementations and suitable APIs. The *generic file adapter* may be a small step towards a more generally applicable integration of tracing data sources, but implying the limitation of missing detailed interactions.

Our approach does not require modeling or predetermining tracing data. But in fact, the tool adapters implicitly include such models because of their technical limitations. For example, the adapters specify the types of artifacts and links which they are able to extract and generate. Thus, our approach reduces the necessity to predefine traceability on the one hand, but shifts parts of the definition to the actual implementations on the other hand. Finding possible solutions to improve this is part of our ongoing work.

Also, we want to get insights into how our approach is suitable for various domains, for example model-driven development (MDD), rapid prototyping and low code. Existing researches of traceability in MDD tend to feature automation, e.g. the work of Haouam and Meslati [12] and Walderhaug et al. [35]. Thus, using our framework in this domain seems promising. Furthermore, it is planned to apply our approach in manufacturing processes, especially in smart factories and industry 4.0, which aim at highly automated data acquisition and automation [34].

References

1. Aizenbud-Reshef, N., Nolan, B.T., Rubin, J., Shaham-Gafni, Y.: Model traceability. IBM Syst. J. **45**(3), 515–526 (2006). https://doi.org/10.1147/sj.453.0515
2. Anquetil, N., et al.: A model-driven traceability framework for software product lines. Softw. Syst. Model. **9**(4), 427–451 (2010). https://doi.org/10.1007/s10270-009-0120-9
3. Antoniol, G., Canfora, G., Casazza, G., De Lucia, A., Merlo, E.: Recovering traceability links between code and documentation. IEEE Trans. Softw. Eng. **28**(10), 970–983 (2002). https://doi.org/10.1109/TSE.2002.1041053
4. Asuncion, H.U., Asuncion, A.U., Taylor, R.N.: Software traceability with topic modeling. In: 2010 ACM/IEEE 32nd International Conference on Software Engineering, vol. 1, pp. 95–104, May 2010. https://doi.org/10.1145/1806799.1806817
5. Cleland-Huang, J., Gotel, O., Zisman, A. (eds.): Software and Systems Traceability. Springer, London (2012). https://doi.org/10.1007/978-1-4471-2239-5
6. Cleland-Huang, J., Gotel, O.C.Z., Huffman Hayes, J., Mäder, P., Zisman, A.: Software traceability: trends and future directions. In: Proceedings of the on Future of Software Engineering (FOSE 2014), pp. 55–69. ACM, New York (2014). https://doi.org/10.1145/2593882.2593891. http://doi.acm.org/10.1145/2593882.2593891

7. Damevski, K., Shepherd, D., Schneider, J., Pollock, L.: Mining sequences of developer interactions in visual studio for usage smells. IEEE Trans. Softw. Eng. **43**(4), 359–371 (2017). https://doi.org/10.1109/TSE.2016.2592905
8. Egyed, A., Grünbacher, P., Heindl, M., Biffl, S.: Value-based requirements traceability: lessons learned. In: Lyytinen, K., Loucopoulos, P., Mylopoulos, J., Robinson, B. (eds.) Design Requirements Engineering: A Ten-Year Perspective. LNBIP, pp. 240–257. Springer, Heidelberg (2009). https://doi.org/10.1007/978-3-540-92966-6_14
9. Gasparic, M., Murphy, G.C., Ricci, F.: A context model for ide-based recommendation systems. J. Syst. Softw. **128**, 200–219 (2017). https://doi.org/10.1016/j.jss.2016.09.012. http://www.sciencedirect.com/science/article/pii/S0164121216301807
10. Gotel, O., et al.: Traceability Fundamentals. In: Cleland-Huang, J., Gotel, O., Zisman, A. (eds.) Software and Systems Traceability, pp. 3–22. Springer, London (2012). https://doi.org/10.1007/978-1-4471-2239-5_1
11. Gotel, O.C., Finkelstein, C.: An analysis of the requirements traceability problem. In: 1994 Proceedings of the First International Conference on Requirements Engineering, pp. 94–101. IEEE (1994)
12. Haouam, M.Y., Meslati, D.: Towards automated traceability maintenance in model driven engineering. IAENG Int. J. Comput. Sci. **43**(2), 147–155 (2016)
13. Hartmann, B., MacDougall, D., Brandt, J., Klemmer, S.R.: What would other programmers do: suggesting solutions to error messages. In: Proceedings of the SIGCHI Conference on Human Factors in Computing Systems (CHI 2010), pp. 1019–1028. ACM, New York (2010). https://doi.org/10.1145/1753326.1753478, http://doi.acm.org/10.1145/1753326.1753478
14. Li, Y., Maalej, W.: Which traceability visualization is suitable in this context? A comparative study. In: Regnell, B., Damian, D. (eds.) REFSQ 2012. LNCS, vol. 7195, pp. 194–210. Springer, Heidelberg (2012). https://doi.org/10.1007/978-3-642-28714-5_17
15. Maalej, W., Fritz, T., Robbes, R.: Collecting and processing interaction data for recommendation systems. In: Robillard, M.P., Maalej, W., Walker, R.J., Zimmermann, T. (eds.) Recommendation Systems in Software Engineering, pp. 173–197. Springer, Heidelberg (2014). https://doi.org/10.1007/978-3-642-45135-5_7
16. Maalej, W., Sahm, A.: Assisting engineers in switching artifacts by using task semantic and interaction history. In: Proceedings of the 2nd International Workshop on Recommendation Systems for Software Engineering, pp. 59–63. ACM (2010)
17. Mäder, P., Egyed, A.: Do developers benefit from requirements traceability when evolving and maintaining a software system? Empirical Softw. Eng. **20**(2), 413–441 (2015). https://doi.org/10.1007/s10664-014-9314-z
18. Mader, P., Gotel, O., Philippow, I.: Getting back to basics: promoting the use of a traceability information model in practice. In: Proceedings of the 2009 ICSE Workshop on Traceability in Emerging Forms of Software Engineering (TEFSE 2009), pp. 21–25. IEEE Computer Society, Washington, DC (2009). https://doi.org/10.1109/TEFSE.2009.5069578. http://dx.doi.org/10.1109/TEFSE.2009.5069578
19. Mahmoud, A., Niu, N.: Supporting requirements traceability through refactoring. In: 2013 21st IEEE International Requirements Engineering Conference (RE), pp. 32–41, July 2013. https://doi.org/10.1109/RE.2013.6636703
20. Mäder, P., Jones, P.L., Zhang, Y., Cleland-Huang, J.: Strategic traceability for safety-critical projects. IEEE Softw. **30**(3), 58–66 (2013). https://doi.org/10.1109/MS.2013.60

21. Mäder, P., Gotel, O.: Towards automated traceability maintenance. J. Syst. Softw. **85**(10), 2205–2227 (2012). https://doi.org/10.1016/j.jss.2011.10.023. http://www.sciencedirect.com/science/article/pii/S0164121211002779. (Automated Software Evolution)
22. Noyer, A., Iyenghar, P., Engelhardt, J., Pulvermueller, E., Bikker, G.: A model-based framework encompassing a complete workflow from specification until validation of timing requirements in embedded software systems. Softw. Qual. J. **25**(3), 671–701 (2017). https://doi.org/10.1007/s11219-016-9323-9
23. Palihawadana, S., Wijeweera, C.H., Sanjitha, M.G.T.N., Liyanage, V.K., Perera, I., Meedeniya, D.A.: Tool support for traceability management of software artefacts with DevOps practices. In: 2017 Moratuwa Engineering Research Conference (MERCon), pp. 129–134, May 2017. https://doi.org/10.1109/MERCon.2017.7980469
24. Rempel, P., Mäder, P.: Preventing defects: the impact of requirements traceability completeness on software quality. IEEE Trans. Softw. Eng. **43**(8), 777–797 (2017). https://doi.org/10.1109/TSE.2016.2622264
25. Robillard, M.P., Maalej, W., Walker, R.J., Zimmermann, T. (eds.): Recommendation Systems in Software Engineering. Springer, Heidelberg (2014). https://doi.org/10.1007/978-3-642-45135-5
26. Roehm, T., Gurbanova, N., Bruegge, B., Joubert, C., Maalej, W.: Monitoring user interactions for supporting failure reproduction. In: 2013 21st International Conference on Program Comprehension (ICPC), pp. 73–82, May 2013. https://doi.org/10.1109/ICPC.2013.6613835
27. Roehm, T., Maalej, W.: Automatically detecting developer activities and problems in software development work. In: Proceedings of the 34th International Conference on Software Engineering (ICSE 2012), pp. 1261–1264. IEEE Press, Piscataway (2012). http://dl.acm.org/citation.cfm?id=2337223.2337390
28. Sanchez, B.A.: Context-aware traceability across heterogeneous modelling environments. In: Proceedings of the 21st ACM/IEEE International Conference on Model Driven Engineering Languages and Systems: Companion Proceedings (MODELS 2018), pp. 174–179. ACM, New York (2018). https://doi.org/10.1145/3270112.3275332, http://doi.acm.org/10.1145/3270112.3275332
29. Shahid, M., Ibrahim, S., Mahrin, M.N.: An Evaluation of Requirements Management and Traceability Tools. World Academy of Science, Engineering and Technology (WASET), Paris (2011)
30. Singer, J., Elves, R., Storey, M.: NavTracks: supporting navigation in software maintenance. In: 21st IEEE International Conference on Software Maintenance (ICSM 2005), pp. 325–334, September 2005. https://doi.org/10.1109/ICSM.2005.66
31. Snipes, W., et al.: A practical guide to analyzing IDE usage data. In: The Art and Science of Analyzing Software Data (2015)
32. Spanoudakis, G., Zisman, A.: Software traceability: a roadmap, pp. 395–428. World Scientific Publishing (2005)
33. Turban, B.: Tool-Based Requirement Traceability Between Requirement and Design Artifacts. Springer, Wiesbaden (2013). https://doi.org/10.1007/978-3-8348-2474-5
34. Uhlemann, T.H.J., Lehmann, C., Steinhilper, R.: The digital twin: realizing the cyber-physical production system for industry 4.0. Procedia CIRP **61**, 335–340 (2017). https://doi.org/10.1016/j.procir.2016.11.152. http://www.sciencedirect.com/science/article/pii/S2212827116313129. (The 24th CIRP Conference on Life Cycle Engineering)

35. Walderhaug, S., Johansen, U., Stav, E., Aagedal, J.: Towards a generic solution for traceability in MDD. In: ECMDA Traceability Workshop (ECMDA-TW), pp. 41–50 (2006)
36. Wijesinghe, D.B., Kamalabalan, K., Uruththirakodeeswaran, T., Thiyagalingam, G., Perera, I., Meedeniya, D.: Establishing traceability links among software arte-facts. In: 2014 14th International Conference on Advances in ICT for Emerging Regions (ICTer), pp. 55–62, December 2014. https://doi.org/10.1109/ICTER.2014.7083879
37. Ziegenhagen, D., Speck, A., Pulvermüller, E.: Using developer-tool-interactions to expand tracing capabilities. In: Proceedings of the 14th International Conference on Evaluation of Novel Approaches to Software Engineering - Volume 1: ENASE, pp. 518–525. INSTICC, SciTePress (2019). https://doi.org/10.5220/0007762905180525

Automated Software Measurement Strategies Elaboration Using Unsupervised Learning Data Analysis

Sarah A. Dahab$^{(\boxtimes)}$ and Stephane Maag$^{(\boxtimes)}$

Samovar, CNRS, Télécom SudParis, Institut Polytechnique de Paris,
Palaiseau, France
{sarah.dahab,stephane.maag}@telecom-sudparis.eu

Abstract. The software measurement becomes more complex as well as software systems. Indeed, the supervision of such systems needs to manage a lot of data. The measurement plans are heavy and time and resource consuming due to the amount of software properties to analyze. Moreover, the design of measurement processes depends on the software project, the used language, the used computer etc. Thereby, to evaluate a software, it is needed to know the context of the measured object, as well as, to analyze a software evaluation is needed to know the context. That is what makes difficult to automate a software measurement analysis. Formal models and standards have been standardized to facilitate some of these aspects. However, the maintainability of the measurements activities is still constituted of complex activities.

In our previous work, we conducted a research work to fully automate the generation of software measurement plans at runtime in order to have more flexible measurement processes adapted to the software needs. In this paper we aim at improving this latter. The idea is to learn from an historical measurements for generating an analysis model corresponding to the context. For that we propose to use a learning technique, which will learn from a measurements dataset of the evaluated software, as the expert does, and generate the corresponding analysis model.

The purpose is to use an unsupervised learning algorithm to generate automatically an analysis model in order to efficiently manage the efforts, time and resources of the experts.

This approach is well implemented, integrated on an industrial platform and experiments are processed to show the scalability and effectiveness of our approach. Discussions about the results have been provided.

Keywords: Software metrics · Formal measurement · Measurement plan · SVM X-MEANS

1 Introduction

Nowadays, the software systems are more and more complex as well as their issues. Indeed, software systems are integral parts of our lives. From particular

© Springer Nature Switzerland AG 2020
E. Damiani et al. (Eds.): ENASE 2019, CCIS 1172, pp. 341–363, 2020.
https://doi.org/10.1007/978-3-030-40223-5_17

usage to professional one, the systems are more efficient and the expectations are more exacting. They must meet the needs with accuracy and security, which implies the needs to design high standard software systems.

Likewise, the software engineering process becomes more complex due to the complex systems to design. Indeed, in order to design quality software the engineering process must be adapted to meet this need. In order to ensure a quality software engineering process as well as a quality product, it is necessary to have an efficient supervision process. This latter gives crucial information on the developed product over all the development phases, necessary for a suitable engineering process and software product.

However, the rise of software systems and their complexity distributed through diverse development phases and projects lead to a huge amount of data to manage, estimate and evaluate. Considering the quantity of aspects to be measured raising the relevant information to be analyzed and reported become difficult (as concerned by Microsoft Power BI[1]). In this context software measurement becomes then crucial as part of software development projects while the measurement processes become tough. Thus, to ensure a quality and efficient software engineering process, adapted measurement processes are required.

In a previous work [4], we conducted a research work to fully automate the generation of software measurement plans at runtime in order to have more flexible measurement processes adapted to the software needs. Indeed, in most real case studies, that process is fixed in a sense that the expert measures all what he can and not necessarily what he needs. Then a huge amount of data are unnecessarily collected and analyzed. This work has shown that measurement plans can be suggested and adjusted at runtime through a supervised learning-based methodology in reducing the amount of collected data. However, this approach is still dependent to the expert for the initialization step, especially for the elaboration of the training file. This later is manually done and thus, the cost time of this step is high when the samples to classify are highly numerous.

Software measurement is an empirical science which depends on the experience [8]. Currently, it is difficult to define a generic measurement analysis model. It depends on the software project, the used language, the used computer etc. Thereby, to evaluate a software, it is needed to know the context of the measured object, as well as, to analyze a software evaluation is needed to know the context. That is what makes difficult to automate a software measurement analysis.

So as to handle this lack, we proposed, in a more recent work [5], to improve our previous approach by learning from an historical measurements for generating automatically an analysis model corresponding to the context. For that we proposed to use an unsupervised learning technique, which learns from a measurements dataset of the evaluated software, as the expert does, and generates the corresponding analysis model. From an unlabeled software measurements sample, a labeled one is generated. This output is then used as training file to train the classifier used for the analysis and suggestion steps of our previous approach [4]. To do this, we used the clustering algorithm X-MEANS, to

---

[1] https://powerbi.microsoft.com/.

try to discover vector patterns by grouping in clusters the similar vectors of measurements. Then according to the clustering result, the expert associates to each cluster the set of metrics to suggest. Herein, the expert intervention only appears for determining the correlation between classes corresponding to the clusters, and set of metrics, which considerably reduces the expert load and the related time cost.

In this paper, we extend our previous one [5] by explaining in detail the main object of this latter, the analysis model herein called the knowledge basis. Each concept is also formalized. We propose a small survey of unsupervised learning techniques by following our needs and an algorithm describing our hybrid analysis model generation approach.

First, we will introduce some basics definitions and our previous approach, the Metrics Suggester, that we aim to improve by automating the initialization phase. Then we will present our improved approach: first, we will present in more details the composition of an analysis model to better understand the issues and needs to automate its elaboration, then we will introduce the notion of unsupervised learning technique to describe the algorithm X-MEANS [25] used to reach our expectations. Finally, we will present the integration of our approach in an industrial platform and experiments that demonstrate that there is a real interest in integrating an unsupervised learning technique for measuring software.

2   Related Works

Standardization institutes put lots of efforts in defining. They focus on the definition and formalization of software quality models such as the ISO9126 that qualifies and quantifies functional and non-functional properties with software metrics [3]. Besides, two other standardization institutes worked in that way to propose two commonly used norms namely ISO/IEC25010 [18] and OMG SMM [2] in order to guide the measurement plan specification. These two last standards have been reviewed by the research and industrial community, and are adapted, integrated and applied in many domains. In the research literature, several works on software metrics selection for software quality have been provided [9]. Recent techniques based on learning approaches have been proposed. Most of them are dedicated to software defect prediction [19,20,26], metrics selection [1] or even Software testing [17,21]. However, even if these techniques have introduced considerable progress to improve the software quality, they have still some limitations. The measurement plan is still manually fixed by the project manager or the experts in charge of its definition. Furthermore, the implementation of the measures is dependent on the developer and reduce the scalability, maintainability and the interoperability of the measurement process.

While a current study shows the lacks in the use of learning technique for software measurement analysis [11], there are in literature some works which use supervised learning algorithms, especially for software defect prediction [19,26] or for prioritize software metrics [27]. Indeed, there are a lot of software metrics, and currently the measurement processes execute all the metrics continuously. This latter shows that we can prioritize the metrics and thus reduce the number of metrics to be executed.

There are also works which propose to use unsupervised learning technique to estimate the quality of software [29] as "expert-based". They also propose to base on clustering techniques to analyze software quality [28]. Other works propose to combine supervised and unsupervised learning techniques to predict the maintainability of an Oriented Object software [16]. But all of these works focus on the analysis or prediction of one software property. The aim of our approach is to allow the less of expert dependency to evaluate all the software engineering process, and to suggest flexible mp continuously according to the software need.

3   Software Measurement Basics

3.1   Definitions

In this section, we provide some notions of software measurement that we use in our work.

Definition 1. Measure: this is the calculation evaluating a software property (e.g., LoC). Formally, this is a function $f : A \to B | A \in X, B \in \mathbb{B}$ that, from a set of measurable properties A of an object X (also named measurand in software measurement), assigns a value B of a set $\mathbb{B}$.

Definition 2. Measurement: this is a quantification of a measured property [7]. Formally, it refers to the result y of the measure f such as $y = f(A) | A \in X$.

Definition 3. Metric: this is the formal specification of a measurement. It specifies the measurand, the measure(s) and the software property to be measured.

Definition 4. Measurement Plan: is an ordered set of metrics. It is expected to be executed at a specific time t or during a well-defined duration (depending on the measurand(s), the platform, the users, the probes, etc.) and according to an ordered metrics sequence. Besides, they can be run sequentially or in parallel.

3.2   Software Measurement Standard

We try to improve the software measurement process by using learning algorithms to reduce the costs of management and analysis. For that, we try to reduce, on one hand, the expertise charge using unsupervised learning algorithm and on the other hand, to optimize the measurement process performance by reducing its processing load.

In order to reduce the processing load, we proposed a suggestion algorithm. The aim of this latter is to analyze a set of measurements during a period of time and according to the analysis result a suggestion of a new measurement plan is generated. This allows to reduce the processing load by executing at each time the metrics of interest according to the software needed instead of executing all the metrics each time.

To do this, it is necessary to determine the software properties to be analyzed and the corresponding metrics. Therefore, we base our work on the standard ISO/IEC 25000 [13] which defines within 4 divisions the software quality and the measurement of the quality of a software. Especially, the ISO/IEC 25010 [15] division defines the software properties, 8 for quality product, which describe the software quality. And the ISO/IEC 25020 [14] division defines the measures (or metrics), more than 200, which give information on these properties.

4 Automated Software Measurement Analysis and Suggestion

This approach is built into three procedures: the manual elaboration of the analysis model; the automated and dynamic analysis based on the analysis model; and the suggestion of measurement plan based on both latter. And in two main stages: the initialization phase which consists to define the measurement context and the interpretations of the measurements; and the computation phase which includes the measurement analysis and the suggestion of metrics. The first phase is unique and manually fixed at the beginning of the measurement process while the second one is dynamic and in continuous.

4.1 Manual Analysis Model

The manual analysis model, called initial measurement plan, is the basis of our suggestion algorithm. Indeed, the analysis and the suggestion are based on it.

The initial measurement plan MP is elaborated by the expert and it defines the observed set of metrics, the corresponding software properties and the mandatory metrics, the ones that must always be in the suggested measurement plans.

This MP is the definition of the measurement context: what is observed by the software properties, how it is observed by the set of metrics related to the properties and the mandatory ones.

The set of metrics groups all the metrics that could be computed during all the measurement process. Thus, the suggestion is a subset of this set of metrics.

4.2 The Analysis

The analysis consists in classifying a set of measurement data, more precisely a set of vectors $\vec{v}$. Each vector is classified in one class which refers to a software property defined in the initial measurement plan and related to ISO/IEC 25000. To classify the data we use a supervised learning algorithm SVM.

SVM is a linear classifier trained through a training file. This file is elaborated by the expert and it corresponds to a manual classification. Indeed, the expert classifies a set of vectors by labelling each vector by a class. Then, a classifier is trained according to this manual classification. Thereby a specific classifier is then used for a specific analysis. The training file corresponds to the initial measurement plan. The used labels should correspond to the defined class as the set of metrics classified. In fact, the suggestion is based on this specific classification.

It means that each time we want to change the context of the measurement process, a new training file should be done by an expert to generate the corresponding classifier. And this was the main limitation of our approach. Despite an automated and "smart" analysis, our approach is still highly dependent to the expert and quite costly in time.

4.3   The Suggestion

Once all the interesting elements are highlighted by the previous procedure, the new measurement plan can be generated as a subset of metrics which allows to gather more information on these highlighted elements. This makes it possible to orient the next measurement cycle on specific parts of the measured system at runtime and dynamically. In other words, the measurement process is no longer static and fixed on the same elements all the time t but flexible according to the needs at each period of time t_i.

The measurement plan mp_i is so performed by generating a subset composed of the set of metrics associated to the property highlighted as the one of interest by the analysis, the selected metrics by the RFE algorithm and the mandatory metrics defined in the analysis model. If all the vectors are classified in the same class, we thus suggest all the metrics defined in the analysis model.

This procedure is formally described below, by the Algorithm 1. It takes as input the initial measurement plan, herein called mp, the trained classifier f and the set of vectors to be analyzed $\{\vec{v}\}_i$, gathered during the interval $[t_{i-1} - t_i]$. And where mp_i is the suggested measurement plan, mm the defined mandatory metrics and fs the feature selection algorithm (RFE).

To summarize, we propose an analysis of measurements and a suggestion of metrics approach, called the Metrics Suggester, build in three procedures: the configuration phase, manually done, initializes the analysis model and the training file; the analysis phase, composed of the classification and features selection processes; and the suggestion phase that suggests a new measurement plan based on the analysis results and the mapping system of the analysis model.

Through this method, the measurement load is increased only on needs and decreased on less interesting properties. This suggestion approach allows to reach a lighter, complete and relevant measurement during the entire supervision period of the software project. This expert-based automated measurement plan suggestion approach allow to add dynamic flexibility and an automated analysis to the measurement process. The learning technique SVM is used combined with the RFE algorithm to make the automation possible and to manage a huge amount of data with more lightness, flexibility.

However, the training file, necessary to initialize the analysis tool, is elaborated by the expert and it corresponds to a manual classification. The expert

Algorithm 1. Metrics Suggestion.

    Input mp, f, unlabeled $\{\vec{v}\}_i$
1: **Output** mp_i
2: $y \leftarrow \{\}$
3: $mf \leftarrow \{\}$
4: **for each** $\vec{v}^i$ in $\{\vec{v}\}_i$ **do**
5:     $y \leftarrow f(\vec{v}^i)$
6: **end for**
7: **if** $y == 0$ or y without duplicate $== 1$ **then**
8:     **return** mp
9: **else**
10:     $mf \leftarrow fs(f, \{\vec{v}\}_i)$
11:     $mp_i \leftarrow mf + mp \, [most\_common(y) \,] + mp \, [mm \,]$
12:     **return** mp_i
13: **end if**

---

classifies a set of vectors by labelling each vector by a class. Then, a classifier is trained according to this manual work. Moreover, as the analysis is based on a specific context through a specific classifier trained by a file corresponding to the specific analysis model, each time we want to change the context of the measurement process, a new analysis model and training file should be done by an expert to generate the corresponding classifier. This is a major limitation of our approach. Despite an automated and "smart" analysis, our approach is still highly dependent to the experts and quite costly in time.

In order to reduce this load of the experts, we aim at improving this approach by using an unsupervised learning technique to generate automatically the training file. The advantage of using this latter is to reduce the expert cost, but also the dependency of an expert. Indeed, as the software measurement is an empirical science, it depends on the experience on the software or on the property evaluated. There is as many models as there are software projects. Thereby, our purpose is to use learning clustering algorithm X-MEANS as expert to generate automatically the training file according to a measurement dataset of the evaluated project. The expert would only intervene to define the analysis model according to the result of X-MEANS application.

5   The Knowledge Basis

The initialization phase of our metrics suggestion approach, described previously, consists to define the measurement context of a measured software.

This context formally describes what are the software realities to be observed, how to observe them and how to supervise these observations and how to monitor the information. So many information needed to automate the supervision process.

In our previous approach, this context was defined manually by the expert as an analysis model and a training file. The analysis model described what is observed and how to observe it and how to supervise the observation. While the training file describes the way to monitor the information.

Thus, this phase lays the foundation of the entire measurement process. It reunites the knowledge of the expert necessary to delegate to the machine this difficult and repetitive task which is the measurement supervision.

The main objective of this work is to delegate to the maximum the initialization of the knowledge basis to the machine. Up to now, this phase was manually done and the defined knowledge was used as basis to automate the supervision of the measurement. In order to achieve this goal, we describe in details this knowledge basis so that to grasp how to automate their definition.

5.1 Analysis Model

The analysis model defines three fundamental points:

- what is observed: the observed realities,
- how to observe: the means to observe,
- how to supervise: the observation orchestration.

These three points are the basis of all observations and they are interrelated. But mostly, this is the basis necessary to be able to automate the measurement and the supervision.

We associate the first point to the class concept in analysis point of view, and to the property concept in a formal point of view.

The second point, the means to observe, refers to the metrics. Indeed, the means to get the information are the metrics.

Finally, the third point, the orchestration of the observation is defined by the mapping system.

Our analysis model is thus composed of classes, metrics and a mapping system between these latter.

Class. The class concept is herein used as the grouping of different elements that refer to the same thing. Thus, by the notion of class, we refer to one software reality and to the different data that give an information on this software reality.

As these data are different, they give different information but on the same reality. In other word, they give different point of view of one reality.

For example, if we want to observe the ability of a man to be a runner. We have to observe several point: his endurance, his tall, his weight, his tone, his flexibility, etc. All of this information are different but they give an information on the same reality which is the ability to a man to be a runner.

Thereby, a class is a cluster of data on one software property. The property referencing the corresponding reality, such as a class C is a set of atomic reality or sub reality r_i with $i \in 0, ..., n$ and n the number of sub realities necessary to describe the observed reality as formally defined below:

$$C = \{r_1, r_2, ..., r_n\} \tag{1}$$

Thus, to defined a class it is important to know what characterizes the reality in order to well define the informants.

Metric. The metrics are the informants of the observed reality. They are the means to get the information on the reality. More precisely, it gives the state of the observed reality, at the time t.

Knowing that one reality is not totally distinct to another, they can share characteristics. Thus, a single metric can be used as informant for different reality. As shown in the article [12], there are mutual influences between software properties defined by the ISO/IEC 25010 [15]. Herein, we use these metrics as mandatory ones in order to have, through one informant, an information on several properties.

To resume a metric is the function f that gets an information, or a state x on a reality r such as:

$$f(r) = x \tag{2}$$

Finally, it is useful to notice that, according to the value of x, the information does not have the same meaning. And this is on this rule that we will base the automation of the generation of the analysis model.

Mapping. The mapping corresponds to the correlations between what we want to observe and how we want to observe it. This is what we will use to orient the measurement process. This is the basis of the orchestration of the measurement process.

By this mapping, we define how to orient the measurement on a property. The needed information on the property. For that, we associate the property to the means that give the information corresponding to the ones needed.

Thus, the mapping map is the union between class with k parameters to be observed C^k and the set of metrics $\{f_i\}$ with $i \in \{1, ..., k\}$ allowing to gather the information on these k parameters such as:

$$map = \{C^k \cup \{f_i\}\} \tag{3}$$

To sum up, the analysis model gathers the knowledge to orchestrate the measurement process: *what* and *how*. It remains to define how to orchestrate, how to orient the measurement process. And this is the role of the training file.

5.2   Training File

The training file describes how to analyze the information, how to interpret them. This is the analyst of the data about the observed software. According to the value x gathered the interpretation will be different.

The training file groups a set of vectors of metrics values associated to a label. Each field of the vector is a value that corresponds to the state of a reality. Thus, one vector contains information on several realities. And according to the value of each field, the vector is associated to the corresponding reality through labeling.

Measurement Vector. The analyzed data are in the form of a vector $\vec{v}$. This vector is composed of all the metrics defined for the measurement process. So, in one vector we have information on all the observed software properties. And according to the values of the vector fields, this vector will be associated to one property C_i through label y_i referencing the property C_i. As described by the Eq. 4.

$$\vec{v} = y_i \qquad (4)$$

This association is based on the values of the fields. If a field is associated to the ith property C_i, that means the values of the fields corresponding to the metrics that inform on the property C_i are significant while the values of the other fields corresponding to the other properties do not show any interest. Thus, a measurement vector is a set of values x_i^k giving information on the parameter k of the ith property C_i, as defined by the Eq. 5, according to its data pattern.

$$\vec{v} = \{x_i^k\} \qquad (5)$$

Data Pattern. The meaning of the fields is related to their values, that is, depending on whether the value is high or not, their interpretation differs. This different interpretation is based on threshold that the expert knows and who are related to the measured system. But that means, for a given field, if its value is higher or lower than a threshold this field will be interpreted as indicator of interest or not on the corresponding property. By expanding this rule to all the fields of the vector, this leads to types of vectors indicator of interest or not on a property.

Finally, a vector is interpreted as indicator of interest on a property according to its data pattern. If the set of x_i is indicator of interest while the set of x_j is not, then the vector will be related to class C_i. Whereas in the opposite case the vector will be related to class C_j.

To summarize, the training file describes how to analyze all this gathered information. It plays the analyst role. And it will also be our basis for generating automatically the analysis model and the training file.

As our analysis model is a set of clusters (class) corresponding to a set of measurement values (metrics values). And as the measurement vector is associated to a class according to its data pattern, this latter cited, by clustering vectors of historical measurement of a software according to their pattern, we will find the classes, the corresponding metrics and the training file. It will only remain to define the mapping between clusters and metrics for the suggestion.

For that we chosen the clustering algorithm X-MEANS, described in detail below, which aims to discover the different data patterns of a raw dataset.

6   Automated Initialization Phase

In order to improve the initialization phase, we propose to use an unsupervised learning algorithm X-MEANS, for learning from raw measurements data and to initialize automatically the corresponding measurement context.

The purpose is to generate from raw data an analysis model and a training file which define the measurement context, context used as basis by our Metrics Suggester approach.

For that, we propose a hybrid algorithm to generate automatically the measurement context corresponding to the measured software.

In this section, we first describe the unsupervised machine learning in general to detail the chosen algorithm X-MEANS to build our approach. Then, we introduce and formally describe our hybrid analysis model generation algorithm.

6.1   Unsupervised Machine Learning

There are two main types of machine learning [10]:

- Supervised machine learning
- Unsupervised machine learning

The unsupervised machine learning aims to learn in autonomy from samples of data without any prior guidance on the expected prediction. This is the main difference with supervised machine learning which learns from samples of data with the expected predictions through labeling and called training file. Thus, an unsupervised algorithm learns autonomously from experience while searching a structure in the analyzed sample of raw data. This structure is called a structural relation.

Formally that means from a random raw data $x_1, x_2, x_3...$ we try to found the y_i structural relation such as: $x_i \rightarrow y_i$.

Unsupervised machine learning is used for different type of tasks. According to the type of task, the structure relation sought is different. There are 3 main tasks:

- The clustering
- The association rule
- The dimensionality reduction

The Clustering Algorithm. As its name suggests, this algorithm aims to group a set of data according to their similarity into clusters such as each data in one cluster shares common attributes and the data of one given cluster be as distinct as possible with data of the other clusters.

The Association Rule. This algorithm aims to find relation between data of large data samples such as correlation or involvement. For example, to find a relation between a product X and Y such as when x is bought y is too.

The Dimensionality Reduction: This algorithm aims to reduce the dimension of the data. So, it is assumed that the data are vectors with a high number of features. The principle consists to reduce the size of the vectors by finding the corresponding smallest dimension without loss of information. In other words, to remove the features that do not influence the analysis of the data.

The objective of this work is to generate an analysis model that groups measurements vectors of the same type. Thus, the algorithm corresponding to our needs is the clustering one. Thereby, subsequently we focus on the clustering algorithm.

6.2   Clustering Algorithms

The clustering algorithm aims to divide a set of data into cluster by finding similarities between data. The main objective is to minimize the similarity factor intra-clusters and to maximize the one inter-cluster (see Fig. 1).

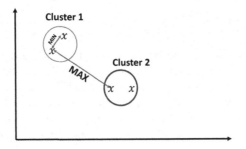

Fig. 1. Clustering aims.

In this case the similarity factor is the distance. But a distance is computed differently according to type of variable: continue, binary, etc... Likewise, there are different methods to compute a distance as the Euclidean, Manhattan ones and so on... Thus, there are several clustering methods whose similarity factor is differently computed according to the used method. The main methods as cited in [22] are:

– Partitioning clustering,
– Hierarchical clustering.

The Hierarchical Method. This method generates a tree of clusters in two different heuristics: by splitting or merging the clusters.

The splitting method starts by one cluster with all the data assigned into then it splits the most dissimilar vector in two clusters. The splitting is repeated until each vector is assigned to its own cluster.

The merging method conversely starts with N clusters, with N the number of data, then it merges the most similar clusters. The merging is repeated until all data are assigned in one unique cluster.

The similarity between cluster is computed in different ways: by assessing the distance of the nearest neighbor, the data in each cluster with the minimum distance; conversely, by assessing the distance between the furthest neighbor, the data in each cluster with the maximum distance; or by assessing the distance between the centroïds of each cluster. The first method is called single linkage, the second complete linkage and the last one average linkage. The Fig. 2 illustrates these methods.

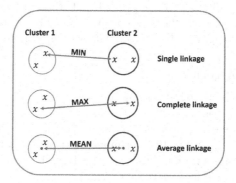

Fig. 2. Similarity assessments for the Hierarchical method.

The Partitioning Method. This method randomly partitions the data in K clusters:

1. it starts by initializing K centroïds,
2. then it assigns to each data the closest centroïds,
3. Then, it updates the centroïd of each cluster by assessing the mean distance of each cluster $i \in \{1, .., K\}$ between the current centroïd and all the data assigned to the cluster i: each mean of each cluster becomes the new centroïd of the cluster.
4. Then, the step 2 and 3 are repeated until the stabilization of the centroïds.

These both methods are complementary, the defaults of one are the advantages of the other [22]. The first method is useful to highlight the embedded structure while the second is useful to discover patterns.

Moreover, for the hierarchical method the number of clusters to be discover does not need to be specified unlike the second. However, the first one is very computationally expensive with a time complexity in $O(N^2 log N)$ and a space complexity in $O(N^2)$, the clustering is static, a data assigned to a cluster could not move to another, and it may fail to separate overlapping. While the second is less expensive with a time complexity in $O(N)$, so it is more adapted to analyze a large data set.

Finally, the method that best fits our needs is the partitioning one. Indeed, we need to discover types of pattern data. The negative point is that it needs to specify the number of clusters and we do not know how many there are. But fortunately, there are algorithms based on this method and free of any prior specification.

To finish, there are several algorithms based on this method but the one that best fits with our expectation is the K-MEANS one[2]. But as K-MEANS needs to specify the number of clusters, we will use the X-MEANS algorithm which is an extension of K-MEANS. It is free from prior initialization and it is more efficient according to the article [24]. There is another algorithm more efficient PG-MEAN [6], but there is not standard library that implements it while X-MEANS is supported by the scikit-learn [23] library.

6.3 X-MEANS Algorithm

X-MEANS [24] is a clustering algorithm, more precisely it is an extension of the K-MEANS algorithm based on the partitioning method.

X-MEANS splits into k clusters a sample of data without initialization of the expected number of clusters k. It determines the best k clusters by minimizing the inter-cluster similarity and satisfying the Bayesian Information Criterion BIC score which is a model selection criterion.

For that, it determines Z initial clusters by defining randomly Z centroïds, then assigns to each data the closest centroïd. Then, it updates the centroïds according to the sum of distances of each cluster. This distance D should be the smallest. Finally, it splits each cluster in two clusters and go to the previous step to have the lowest inter-cluster. A low inter-cluster similarity is ensured by assigning a data to the cluster whose distance to its center is the smallest. Thus, it tends to minimize this following function D.

$$D = \sum_{i=1}^{k} \sum_{j=1}^{n} |c_i, x_j^i| \tag{6}$$

Before each split the BIC score of each cluster model is computed. As example, the initial number of cluster Z is 2. So we have 2 clusters, c and i, with one centroïd each, $k = 1$. For each cluster we compute its BIC score. Then we split each cluster in two sub clusters, that means $k = 2$ for each one. And then we compute the new BIC score of c and i with $k = 2$. If this score is lower than the previous one, we keep the cluster with $k = 1$. Else we split another time each sub cluster in two sub-sub clusters etc. So, if $BIC(c, k = 1) > BIC <_{.}(c, k = 2)$ we keep c with $k = 1$. And if $BIC(i, k = 1) < BIC(i, k = 2)$ we keep i with $k = 2$ and we split each sub cluster of i in two sub clusters while c remains unchanged. After the splitting process this score is used to determine the best model: the one with the higher BIC score.

---

[2] https://scikit-learn.org/stable/modules/clustering.html.

6.4   Hybrid Analysis Model Generation Algorithm

This procedure aims to automate the initialization phase to reduce the dependency to the expert and the involved expensive cost in time. The objective is to dynamically generate an analysis model based on the measured software information.

As reminder, the initialization phase is manually built. Moreover, to initialize the context of the suggestion process of our Metrics Suggester approach, some inputs is needed: the training file and the analysis model. The first one is used to trained the analysis process and the second is used as basis to suggest new measurement plan.

The purpose is then, to learn from historical measurements of the measured software to generate the corresponding analysis model and training file by using the X-MEANS algorithm and to design the correlations between the determined clusters and the sets of metrics correspondingly. Thereby, all needed inputs are well defined.

This last step is manually done by the experts, that is why we call this approach: *hybrid*.

To sum up, our hybrid analysis model generation approach is based on three procedures:

- The clustering of historical raw measurements of the measured software through the unsupervised learning approach X-MEANS. The returned result is used as training file TR.
- The training of the classifier, f, based on this measurement context by using the supervised learning technique SVM.
- And the manual elaboration of the analysis model AM, based on the clustering result.

The Measurement Clustering. This procedure aims to discover the data patterns. From an historical data of the measured software, it will determine the number of vector types by grouping it in clusters.

The historical data are the measurements gathered at the period of time t_0 of our measurement process. And herein called $\{\vec{v}\}_0$. The X-MEANS algorithm is then applied on this unlabeled dataset and it returns a labeled dataset, called $BestAM$, which represents the clustering result. This procedure is formally defined by the Algorithm 2.

The Unsupervised Classifier. Once the clustering process is done, we have a labeled dataset $BestAM$. This dataset is used as training file TR to trained the classifier that will be used for the suggestion.

To train the classifier, we apply the supervised learning technique SVM on the training file generated by the clustering process. This process returns a trained classifier f such as:

$$f = SVM(TR) \tag{7}$$

The Manual Elaboration of Correlations. This procedure manually designs the correlations between the clusters, herein called *Class*, determined by the clustering results and the corresponding set of metrics, $\{Metric\}_i$ with i the cluster i of the set of clusters.

Algorithm 2. Measurements vectors clustering.

Precondition: Function 2-MEANS
    Input Unlabeled $\{\vec{v}\}_0$
    Output *BestAM*
1: BestAM $\leftarrow$ {}
2: *Clusters* $\leftarrow$ 2-MEANS($\{\vec{v}\}_0$)
3: **for each** C in *Clusters* **do**
4:    $C_2 \leftarrow$ 2-MEANS(C)
5:    **if** BIC(C) ¿ BIC(C_2) **then**
6:        *BestAM* $\leftarrow$ *BestAM* $\cup$ C
7:    **else**
8: **go to** step 1 with the cluster C_2
9:    **end if**
10: **end for**
11: **return** *BestAM*

This mapping is then used as analysis model *AM* to suggest new measurement plans corresponding to the analysis results.

Our hybrid approach is formally defined by the Algorithm 3.

Algorithm 3. Hybrid Analysis Model Generation.

    Input unlabeled $\{\vec{v}\}_0$
1: **Output** *AM*
2: $TF \leftarrow$ **Algorithm2**($\{\vec{v}\}_0$)
3: $f \leftarrow$ **SVM**(TR)
4: $AM \leftarrow$ {}
5: **for each** $Class_i$ in TR **do**
6:    $AM \leftarrow AM \cup Class_i \cup \{Metric\}_i$
7: **end for**
8: **return** AM, f

---

7   Experiments

In this section, we present the results of our improved approach for automatically generating a software measurement analysis model based on experience and measurements data history.

First, we present the results of our hybrid analysis model generation through the X-MEANS algorithm and discuss it. Then, we will used this analysis model as input to the metrics suggester tool and present the ensuing suggestion results.

7.1 Automated Analysis Model Generation

Case Study. The case study of this experiment is an in use Oriented Object platform of the European project MEASURE[3]. The measurement data used are the measurement results applied on this platform.

For evaluating our approach, we used a real industrial use case provided by one of the MEASURE partners. This one is based on a modeling tool suite. The analysis of this tool focuses on the developed Java code.

Experimental Setup. The considered set of metrics for the measurement process includes 13 metrics giving information on 3 software properties, as described in Table 1. This MP is defined by the measurement context: the observed metrics during all the processes and the mandatory ones. The properties or classes give information on what is evaluated, but the actual number of classes will be determined by the X-MEANS algorithm. In fact, the initial measurement plan will be defined according to the result of the X-MEANS execution, the expert will define the correlations between subsets of metrics and clusters.

Table 1. Measurement plan.

Index	Metric	Property	Mandatory
1	Code smells	Maintainability	X
2	New Code smells	Maintainability	
3	Technical debt	Maintainability	
4	New Technical debt	Maintainability	
5	Technical debt ratio	Maintainability	
6	Bugs	Reliability	X
7	New Bugs	Reliability	
8	Reliability remediation effort	Reliability	
9	New Reliability remediation effort	Reliability	
10	Vulnerabilities	Security	X
11	New vulnerabilities	Security	
12	Security remediation effort	Security	
13	New Security remediation effort	Security	

The metrics related to the Maintainability property give information on the quality of the code. The ones related to Reliability give information on the reliability of the services and the Security ones are about the vulnerabilities in the code.

In order to execute X-MEANS, we generate a file with a fixed amount of data and a fixed number of groups corresponding to a vector type: the data

---

[3] https://itea3.org/project/measure.html.

are vectors with values which correspond to a property. For example, the fields corresponding to the metrics related to the maintainability property are high and the others are low, herein called vector-type. The objectives are twofold, first to verify if the clustering result matches with the expectation and if the suggestion still provides correct results with the automated labeled data set as input training file.

Clustering Results. As depicted in the Fig. 2, the data are homogeneously distributed in the files 1 and 2: there is the same amount of vector types in each group. A group is a vector-type set. Finally, the data in the files 3 and 4 are heterogeneously distributed. There is a different amount of vectors in each group.

Table 2. Unsupervised clustering results (Source [5]).

File	Raw data	Pattern distribution	Clustering results	Time(s)
1	50	3	2	0.03
2	100	3	6	0.05
3	1000	3	6	0.08
4	10000	3	6	0.15

The column Data gives the amount of vectors per file and the column Distribution gives the number of vector-type (Table 2).

Regarding the clustering result, we can note that when the file is too small, the clustering accuracy is not high. Indeed, the file 1 with 50 vectors and 3 vector-type is grouped in two homogeneous clusters while we expected 3 groups. But with files containing more data, the clustering result is better and promising. The accuracy result is better and they correspond to the expectations and even more, although the number of clusters does not seem to correspond with the one expected, in fact clusters corresponds to those in the groups and the distribution of the vectors in the clusters complies with those in the groups: in fact, in each group there are two types of vectors, the one with values to all fields and the one with values only on the fields referencing the same class and the value 0 for the other fields. The goal was to simulate the case that we gather information only on one property.

Before the experiment, we consider these two types as a same type as both was indicator on the same property. But finally, we conclude by the fact that both are two different types and although they indicate an interest on the same property, they can not be interpreted in the same way. They can lead to different suggestions.

To conclude, X-MEANS shows a good performance to learn as an expert from experiences and to provide a reliable analysis model with considerable time savings. But also, it can be used to validate models, in order to verify the validity of data model.

7.2   Suggestion Results

Finally, the initial measurement plan (MP) is defined by the expert according to the previous step result. In fact, the expert will add to the MP presented in the Fig. 1 the correlation between clusters and a metrics subset.

Once the initial MP is defined, we train the classifier with the file 3. Then, as suggestion experiment, we use as input files to analyze, a dataset of 50000 unclassified vectors divided in 10 subsets of 5000 unclassified vectors. The objective is to see if the suggestion provides correct plans (of metrics).

The Fig. 3 shows the results of suggestions based on the previous analysis model. The results show a dynamic suggestion of measurement plans (mp). Each mp is between 5 and 13 metrics. There is no convergence (e.g., deadlock or undesired fixity in the generated plans) and the suggested mp evolves continuously according to the dataset values.

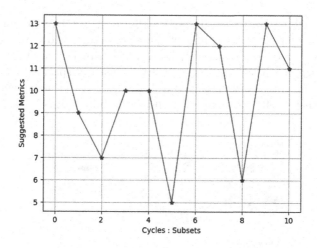

Fig. 3. Suggestions results (Source [5]).

7.3   Industrial Integration

Our analysis and suggestion tool is built as a web application as illustrated in the Fig. 4. The architecture is organized around the machine learning unit (ML tool), which regroups the classification and feature selection algorithms. The library used to develop the learning algorithms is scikit-learn [23].

As our work is taking part of a European project MEASURE, its implementation has been integrated in the related industrial platform as an analysis tool.

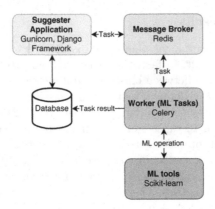

Fig. 4. Our Metrics Suggester tool architecture (Source [5]).

MEASURE Platform. The MEASURE Platform[4] is the research result of the European project ITEA3 MEASURE[5]. This project aims to improve the whole software measurement processes. For that, as described in the Fig. 5, this platform proposes a database as storage of software metrics specified and developed according to the standard language SMM; a storage of measurement results; a cover of the entire software engineering process; and analysis tools.

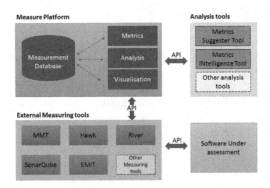

Fig. 5. Overview of the MEASURE platform.

To conclude, our Metrics Suggester tool is integrated in the platform, by using the REST API of the platform. This latter allows to connect our analysis tool to the platform, to gather stored measurements and to generate a dashboard from the platform.

---

[4] https://github.com/ITEA3-Measure.
[5] http://measure.softeam-rd.eu.

8 Conclusion and Perspective

We proposed to improve our previous work by reducing the expert dependency to the management of the analysis process. For that, we propose to use an unsupervised learning algorithm X-MEANS to take the place of the expert and to generate automatically the knowledge basis by learning from an historical database.

We demonstrate the effectiveness of considering unsupervised learning algorithm to reduce further the management cost and improve the performance of such a process. We herein use X-MEANS to automatically generate correlations of a sample of data through clustering by generating an analysis model and a training file as inputs to our previous suggestion approach.

Well implemented and experimented, this approach shows the possibility to generate a reliable model with a low time cost, and also to verify the validity of manual models. The promising results demonstrate us the beneficial contribution of using learning techniques in the software measurement area.

We add this improvement feature to our previous approach the Metric Suggester tool. The integration of this improved tool in the MEASURE platform is planned. The user will be free of the configuration load. Indeed, he will simply have to select the concerned metrics by the measurement process, then the tool will gather automatically from the platform the dataset of measurements corresponding to the selected metrics to generate the clusters to be mapped with the sets of metrics. However, the initialization is not totally automated, the correlations between clusters and set of metrics are still dependent to the expert.

In order to increase the independence to the expert by generating automatically the correlations between clusters and metrics subsets. One possibility is to use a statistic method on the weight of features to found automatically the correlations between clusters and features. This solution could be envisaged in future works.

References

1. Bardsiri, A.K., Hashemi, S.M.: Machine learning methods with feature selection approach to estimate software services development effort. Int. J. Serv. Sci. **6**(1), 26–37 (2017)
2. Bouwers, E., van Deursen, A., Visser, J.: Evaluating usefulness of software metrics: an industrial experience report. In: Notkin, D., Cheng, B.H.C., Pohl, K. (eds.) 35th International Conference on Software Engineering, ICSE 2013, San Francisco, CA, USA, 18–26 May 2013, pp. 921–930. IEEE Computer Society (2013). https://doi.org/10.1109/ICSE.2013.6606641
3. Carvallo, J.P., Franch, X.: Extending the ISO/IEC 9126–1 quality model with non-technical factors for COTS components selection. In: Proceedings of the 2006 International Workshop on Software Quality, WoSQ 2006, pp. 9–14. ACM, New York (2006). https://doi.org/10.1145/1137702.1137706

4. Dahab, S., Porras, J.J.H., Maag, S.: A novel formal approach to automatically suggest metrics in software measurement plans. In: 2018 13th International Conference on Evaluation of Novel Approaches to Software Engineering (ENASE). IEEE (2018)

5. Dahab, S.A., Maag, S.: Suggesting software measurement plans with unsupervised learning data analysis. In: ENASE, pp. 189–197. SciTePress (2019)

6. Feng, Y., Hamerly, G.: PG-means: learning the number of clusters in data. In: Advances in Neural Information Processing Systems, pp. 393–400 (2007)

7. Fenton, N., Bieman, J.: Software Metrics: A Rigorous and Practical Approach. CRC Press, Boca Raton (2014)

8. Fenton, N.E., Neil, M.: Software metrics: roadmap. In: Proceedings of the Conference on the Future of Software Engineering, pp. 357–370. ACM (2000)

9. Gao, K., Khoshgoftaar, T.M., Wang, H., Seliya, N.: Choosing software metrics for defect prediction: an investigation on feature selection techniques. Softw.: Pract. Exp. **41**(5), 579–606 (2011)

10. Goodfellow, I., Bengio, Y., Courville, A.: Deep Learning. MIT Press (2016). http://www.deeplearningbook.org

11. Hentschel, J., Schmietendorf, A., Dumke, R.R.: Big data benefits for the software measurement community. In: 2016 Joint Conference of the International Workshop on Software Measurement and the International Conference on Software Process and Product Measurement (IWSM-MENSURA), pp. 108–114, October 2016. https://doi.org/10.1109/IWSM-Mensura.2016.025

12. Hovorushchenko, T., Pomorova, O.: Evaluation of mutual influences of software quality characteristics based ISO 25010:2011, pp. 80–83, September 2016. https://doi.org/10.1109/STC-CSIT.2016.7589874

13. ISO, I: IEC 25000 software and system engineering-software product quality requirements and evaluation (square)-guide to square. International Organization for Standardization (2005)

14. ISO, I: IEC 25020 software and system engineering-software product quality requirements and evaluation (square)-measurement reference model and guide. International Organization for Standardization (2007)

15. ISO/IEC: ISO/IEC 25010 system and software quality models. Technical report (2010)

16. Jin, C., Liu, J.A.: Applications of support vector mathine and unsupervised learning for predicting maintainability using object-oriented metrics. In: 2010 Second International Conference on Multimedia and Information Technology (MMIT), vol. 1, pp. 24–27. IEEE (2010)

17. Kim, J., Ryu, J.W., Shin, H.J., Song, J.H.: Machine learning frameworks for automated software testing tools: a study. Int. J. Contents **13**(1), 38–44 (2017)

18. Kitchenham, B.A.: What's up with software metrics? - A preliminary mapping study. J. Syst. Softw. **83**(1), 37–51 (2010). https://doi.org/10.1016/j.jss.2009.06.041

19. Laradji, I.H., Alshayeb, M., Ghouti, L.: Software defect prediction using ensemble learning on selected features. Inf. Softw. Technol. **58**, 388–402 (2015). https://doi.org/10.1016/j.infsof.2014.07.005

20. MacDonald, R.: Software defect prediction from code quality measurements via machine learning. In: Bagheri, E., Cheung, J. (eds.) Canadian AI 2018. LNCS, vol. 10832, pp. 331–334. Springer, Cham (2018). https://doi.org/10.1007/978-3-319-89656-4_35

21. Mouttappa, P., Maag, S., Cavalli, A.R.: Using passive testing based on symbolic execution and slicing techniques: application to the validation of communication protocols. Comput. Netw. **57**(15), 2992–3008 (2013). https://doi.org/10.1016/j. comnet.2013.06.019
22. Omran, M., Engelbrecht, A., Salman, A.: An overview of clustering methods. Intell. Data Anal. **11**, 583–605 (2007). https://doi.org/10.3233/IDA-2007-11602
23. Pedregosa, F., et al.: Scikit-learn: machine learning in Python. J. Mach. Learn. Res. **12**, 2825–2830 (2011)
24. Pelleg, D., Moore, A.: X-means: extending k-means with efficient estimation of the number of clusters. In: Machine Learning (2002)
25. Pelleg, D., Moore, A.: X-means: extending k-means with efficient estimation of the number of clusters. In: Proceedings of the 17th International Conference on Machine Learning, pp. 727–734. Morgan Kaufmann (2000)
26. Shepperd, M.J., Bowes, D., Hall, T.: Researcher bias: the use of machine learning in software defect prediction. IEEE Trans. Softw. Eng. **40**(6), 603–616 (2014). https://doi.org/10.1109/TSE.2014.2322358
27. Shin, Y., Meneely, A., Williams, L., Osborne, J.A.: Evaluating complexity, code churn, and developer activity metrics as indicators of software vulnerabilities. IEEE Trans. Softw. Eng. **37**(6), 772–787 (2011). https://doi.org/10.1109/TSE.2010.81
28. Zhong, S., Khoshgoftaar, T., Seliya, N.: Analyzing software measurement data with clustering techniques. IEEE Intell. Syst. **19**(2), 20–27 (2004). https://doi.org/10. 1109/MIS.2004.1274907
29. Zhong, S., Khoshgoftaar, T.M., Seliya, N.: Unsupervised learning for expert-based software quality estimation. In: HASE, pp. 149–155. Citeseer (2004)

Agile Scaled Steps of Doneness: A Standardized Procedure to Conceptualizing and Completing User Stories Across Scrum Teams and Industries

Matthew Ormsby[✉] and Curtis Busby-Earle

Department of Computing, University of the West Indies, Mona Campus,
Kingston, Jamaica
matthew.ormsby@mymona.uwi.edu,
curtis.busbyearle@uwimona.edu.jm

Abstract. Agile software development (ASD) requires a shift in culture when compared to the traditional Waterfall software development. The traditional methods concentrate on project scope, using them to determine cost and time schedule. Agile concentrates on business values, using them to determine quality levels and possible technology constraints. Where waterfall methods are suitable for well-arranged and predictable environment. For an organization, one of the most important differences between agile and waterfall is the return of investment. Organizations are created to generate revenue and moreover profit for its stakeholders. Agile can help to produce earlier return on that investment. This enables an organization to get the maximum returns before their competitors start penetrating their market shares. Agile has scaling frameworks to assist organization transition to ASD. This paper aims to build on the original ENASE paper titled "Scaling A Standardized Procedure To Conceptualizing And Completing User Stories Across Scrum Teams And Industries" by extending the application of the Scaled Steps of Doneness procedure from four teams to six teams and analyze the results.

Keywords: Scaled Steps of Doneness · Agile · Scaling Agile · User story documentation · Definition of done · Steps of Doneness · Scrum · Velocity story points · Estimating · Software development · ENASE

1 Introduction

1.1 Background

For decades, Waterfall software development has been the preferred approach for software development. Organizations across the globe have built their project based on this approach. However, though the approach was widely used, the lack of ability to cope with change frequently resulted in unwanted rework. This would further impact on project timelines and budgeting.

Thanks to the impact of globalization on society, the world is constantly changing and the need to swiftly deliver high quality software products is ever growing. With

© Springer Nature Switzerland AG 2020
E. Damiani et al. (Eds.): ENASE 2019, CCIS 1172, pp. 364–377, 2020.
https://doi.org/10.1007/978-3-030-40223-5_18

these new requirements, Agile software development was born as a reaction. As stated by Collier [1], Agile is a "set of values and principles for software development under which requirements and solutions evolve through the collaborative effort of self-organizing cross-functional teams". Agile embraced frequent collaboration and communication and switched focus of the software to be more customer-centric. Through these core principles Agile has emerged on the international scene as the new way forward for all organizations.

Within Agile there are different methodologies that can be employed to execute on this emerging approach. A few of these methodologies include: Scrum, Kanban, ScrumBan, Extreme Programming and Lean Startup. Interestingly, the 13th Annual State of Agile Report noted Scrum as the most widely operated methodology [2]. 54% of respondents indicated Scrum as the methodology being used. Further, when considering the respondents who have employed a hybrid methodology involving Scrum, the figure grows to 72% of respondents. Scrum is the trendsetter amongst many software teams across the world. It has been emerging as the methodology of choice.

Within a Scrum environment, the ability of the Scrum team to accurately analyze user stories and create estimations is a key tool in understanding the team velocity. Kniberg [3] defines velocity as "a measurement of amount of work done", and each item is weighted in terms of its initial estimate. Velocity serves not only as a statistic for what the team can commit to in the current sprint, but also assists in orchestrating plans for future sprints. Therefore, if a Scrum team's velocity is low in comparison to what was projected, it can result in adjustments to the project roadmap.

This is paramount to the project management triangle (also called the Iron Triangle). The Iron Triangle is a model that encompasses the three constraints of project management: time, cost and scope. It is used to understand the challenges of implementing and executing a project. Historically, many software development teams have experienced difficulties in maintaining a high sprint velocity to successfully deliver a software solution. Difficulties experienced include:

1. User stories not being completed in the current sprint and hence, rolling over to the following sprint.
2. An increase in the number of defects being created. In some instances, team members felt pressured to deliver user stories.
3. And most importantly, unsatisfied clients.

Low sprint velocity would either adversely affect the scheduled release date for the market, project resources or scope. For project success, one of the three areas of the Iron Triangle would have to be negatively impacted to keep the same scope of work for the scheduled timeline with the same size team. Agile software development seeks to continuously deliver project value without affecting the Iron Triangle.

1.2 Motivation

To be accepted by end users, software solutions must comply with and are subject to, sanctions, regulations and legislations. For example, in healthcare, The Health Insurance Portability and Accountability Act of 1996 (HIPAA) is one such legislation, which healthcare solutions must comply with. HIPAA is a United States legislation that speaks to data privacy and security provisions for the protection of individuals' medical information. Additionally, there are many other factors that influence the use of healthcare solutions.

Bin Azhar and Dhillon [4] have identified sixty-eight factors that affect healthcare solutions. In their study they found that the following seven factors appeared most often: perceived usefulness, perceived ease of use, behavioral intention, social-influence, self-efficacy, perceived privacy risk and attitude. Having so many factors to consider, organizations are starting to adopt the stance that solutions should be built in small, iterative and incremental steps. Consequently, there has been a shift whereby organizations are building their consultancy model around Agile Software Development and more specifically, the Scrum methodology.

One of the major motivations in Scrum is to make only the absolute minimum necessary effort to obtain good enough estimates, and then to refine and adjust these during the project as needed. As opposed to other, traditional methods which may put a greater emphasis on detail and accuracy of estimation, while the result in practice hardly justifies the effort spent and gives only a false sense of security to management. Hence, some degree of estimation is always required in any aspect of project planning.

Sithole and Solms [5] posed that to ascertain when a release can be delivered, or an important milestone can be accomplished, one must estimate their team's velocity, that is, how fast they can complete stories on average, or how many stories they can complete in a given time frame (sprint). And for that to be meaningful, the relative size of stories must be known. Therefore, it is recommended for Scrum teams to estimate story points.

During sprint planning, the Scrum team commits to complete a certain number of stories within the upcoming sprint. This is especially hard for inexperienced teams who do not have a feel for their velocity yet, are not good at story point estimation and/or have a fluctuating performance. For a novice team, it may easily occur that the estimated time is significantly more (or less) than the time they have available in the coming sprint, requiring an adjustment (dropping stories from or adding more to the sprint). Majchrzak and Madeyski [6] state that a "proper estimation of time in user stories is a crucial task for both the IT team as well as for the customer, especially in Agile projects. Although Agile practices offer a lot of flexibility and promote a culture of continuous change, there are always clearly defined timeboxed periods where an IT company must commit to delivering working software. Estimating time of user story implementation provides clarity and the opportunity to control the project by the management, yet at the same time, it can increase pressure on software developers. Thus, incorrectly estimated user stories may lead to quality problems including system malfunction, technical debt, and general user experience issues". In their paper, they observe incomplete user story life cycles as a main reason for user story estimation inaccuracy and post-release defects.

1.3 Scaling Agile

The term, "Agile at Scale" was coined by Agile industry professionals. It represents an efficient framework that can be followed when transitioning to Agile. Spotify and Netflix are two organizations which have been highly successful at transitioning to become Agile organizations via the utilization of Agile at Scale. They have been case studied and the steps taken at Spotify to transition to Agile have subsequently been mirrored by thousands of small, medium and large organizations throughout the world.

Challenges When Scaling Agile

Moe and Dingsøyr [7] stated that transitioning an organization to agile is a colossal task as it needs to be scaled out to all aspects of the organization. They prescribed that understanding what to scale and what not to scale are two very important aspects in scaling agile. They suggested the following questions need to be answered by an organization:

1. What need to be in place before scaling?
2. How not to scale?
3. What are the drivers of scaling?
4. How can project and programs be scaled down?
5. How much or how little standardization is needed to be able to scale agile?
6. What extra roles are needed when scaling?
7. What extra practices are needed and how to change current practices?
8. How to scale communities of practice?
9. Are scaling agile different than scaling classical organizations?

Their questions are supported by Nurdiani et al.'s [8] study in which they put forth a baseline checklist for assessing the impact of introducing agile in an organization. The components of their baseline are: workforce, management and organization structure, process and infrastructure. Pries-Heje and Krohn's [9] case study on SimCorp also demonstrates the importance of answering the questions put forth by Moe and Dingsøyr. In their case study, SimCorp, faced three major challenges in their transition to an agile organization.

The first challenge stated that SimCorp had to resolve was the reorganizing of personnel and their skillset as there no direct mapping from old jobs to the new job roles [9]. Additionally, proper training was not in place for staff. Here Moe and Dingsøyr's [7] questions 1, 6 and 7 and Nurdiani et al.'s [8] workforce is highlighted.

Jack Welch submitted "if the rate of change on the outside exceeds the rate of change on the inside, the end is near". Changing the organization mindset to be agile was another challenge experienced by SimCorp as individuals struggled to relinquish their previous method of working [9]. Questions 3 and 7 which were underscored by Moe and Dingsøyr [7] and Nurdiani et al.'s [8] management and organization structure and process are illustrated.

The last reported challenge SimCorp experienced were the effects of isolating the transition to the development team. By isolating the transition to only the development team, going full scale was an issue as supporting functions in the organization were not onboard and it would result in delays of the release and internal friction [9]. This is inconsistent processes and practices. Questions 2, 5 and 8 [7] and Nurdiani et al.'s [8] process and infrastructure are demonstrated.

From Moe and Dingsøyr's [7] questions for organizations wishing to scale, Nurdiani et al.'s [8] checklist for introducing agile and the challenges experienced when scaling in Pries-Heje and Krohn's [9] case study, the following are observed as challenges when scaling:

- Organizational culture failing to align with agile values and principles
- Inconsistent processes and practices
- Organization resistance to change
- Inadequate support, training and education

VersionOne's [2] 13th Annual State of Agile Report further supports this as the report conveyed the following as the top five (5) challenges Agile organizations have experienced in both adopting and scaling Agile:

1. Organizational culture at odds with Agile values
2. General organization resistance to change
3. Inadequate management support and sponsorship
4. Lack of skills/experience with agile methods
5. Inconsistent processes and practices across teams.

1.4 Problem Statement

In response to the procedural problem identified by the organization in Ormsby and Busby-Earle's [10] Evaluation of Novel Approaches to Software Engineering (ENASE) study, we propose an extension of that original paper to further analyze and apply Ormsby and Busby-Earle's [11] procedure and the Scaled Steps of Doneness [10] procedure to six (6) of the scrum teams within this organization.

The objectives of this study were:

1. Verify if the Scaled Steps of Doneness procedure could be successful in scrum teams of different sizes tackling different domain problems;
2. Increase each team's percentage of story points and the net promoter score for the solutions that they were each building.

A limitation of Ormsby and Busby-Earle's [11] study is that it was executed on one scrum team. The next step that arose from the study was to have the procedure incorporated in other technology companies across teams with varying compositions, development tasks and levels of skill.

2   Experimental Approach and Computational Details

Ormsby and Busby-Earle [11] referred to lacunae within the steps of conceptualizing and completing a user story and put forth a generic procedure to address these gaps. This procedure resulted in an average increase in velocity of 2.81%, as well as, morale boosts from all stakeholders as their procedure produced more user-centric user stories and continuous feedback between the scrum team and clients. This helped to address Rothman's [12] concern that teams do not fully understand what done means at different levels in the life cycle of a user story as well as increased the transparency needed for success.

2.1 Experimental Approach

The experimental approach would compromise of applying Ormsby and Busby-Earle's [11] procedure, analyze the results and then apply the Scaled Steps of Doneness.

The following data points on each team were tracked and recorded: number of story points committed to at the beginning of a sprint; number of story points completed at the end of a sprint; and survey completed by customers in which they rated (on a scale of 0–10) how likely they would recommend the product to friends or family.

From these data points, we derived two main statistics:

1. Percentage of story points completed – number of story points completed at the end of a sprint divided by number of story points committed to at the beginning of that corresponding sprint multiplied by 100
2. Net promoter score (NPS) – subtract the percentage of detractors (customers who gave a rating of 0 through 6) from the percentage of promoters (customers who gave a rating of 9 or 10)

Teams used one-week sprints. Each team was also assigned a designated product owner and scrum master and all teams were collocated (Table 1).

Table 1. Team composition and assigned projects for the six teams. Original table taken from 'Scaling a Standardized Procedure to Conceptualizing and Completing User Stories across Scrum Teams and Industries' by M. Ormsby and C. Busby-Earle, 2019, Proceedings of the 14th International Conference on Evaluation of Novel Approaches to Software Engineering, 1, pp. 127–133 [10].

Teams	Solution description	Team size	Core competencies	Age range of team members	Nationality of team members
Team 1	A product to alleviate the account opening process. By alleviating this process, they hoped to increase the number of accounts that were being opened thus increasing the available number of customers that the entire organization can engage in cross selling activities	13	Web & Mobile Development, Banking, Document Management, Testing, User Experience and Marketing	19–51 years old	American, Antiguan, Indian and Jamaican
Team 2	A solution to digitally transform the auto insurance experience for current and prospective customers. This transformation would take the form of both redefining the process to be more efficient and utilize technology to produce a convenient and satisfying experience to customers	9	Mobile Development, Auto Insurance, Payment, Testing, User Experience, Marketing and Legal & Compliance	22–37 years old	Barbadian, British and Jamaican

(*continued*)

Table 1. (*continued*)

Teams	Solution description	Team size	Core competencies	Age range of team members	Nationality of team members
Team 3	A platform to deliver a revamp of the organization digital solutions. This revamp will take the many digital application currently offered to customers and bring them under one platform. This platform will be data driven to give the organization a holistic view of its customers and the products that will better fit their needs	17	Web & Mobile Development, Auto and Life Insurance, Banking, Data Analytics, testing, User Experience, Marketing and Legal & Compliance	21–45 years old	American, Antiguan, Barbadian, Canadian, Indian, Jamaican and Trinidadian
Team 4	A product to drive the investment market in a new direction. This drive will seek to revolutionize investment in the region by empowering existing and prospective customers	8	Web Development, Investment, Data Analytics, Testing, User Experience and Marketing	18–36 years old	American, Indian, and Jamaican
Team 5	A product to engage small-medium companies to take up microloans	7	Web Development, Banking, Data Analytics and Insight, User Experience, Legal, Compliance and Central Reconciliation	23–41 years old	Jamaican
Team 6	A product to digitize all onboarding process across the organization. This product would be a part of Team 2's solution	10	Web & Mobile Development, Data Analytics, testing, User Experience, Marketing and Legal & Compliance	21–28 years old	American, Jamaican, and Trinidadian

2.2   Prior Execution of User Stories

Upon the genesis of an Agile team, one of the necessary action items was that the team was required to create a definition of done for a user story. This is a part of the organizations process in onboarding teams. The definition of done detailed the criteria that would indicate that a user story was completed (a checklist) and was expected to aid each team in understanding, accepting and agreeing the point at which a user story was complete. A team then began sprinting with their newly-formed definition of done.

Table 2. Percentage of story points completed and the NPSs for the last five (5) sprints before introduction of the procedure. Original table taken from 'Scaling a Standardized Procedure to Conceptualizing and Completing User Stories across Scrum Teams and Industries' by M. Ormsby and C. Busby-Earle, 2019, Proceedings of the 14th International Conference on Evaluation of Novel Approaches to Software Engineering, 1, pp. 127–133 [10].

# of sprint before	Team 1		Team 2		Team 3		Team 4		Team 5		Team 6	
	%	NPS	%	NPS	%	NPS	%	NPS	%	NPS	%	NPS
5	27.3	18	72.1	31	72.7	23	68.5	23	15.0	9	65.9	24
4	46.7	18	69.2	31	45.0	27	82.1	19	70.6	21	65.2	35
3	58.8	19	63.6	31	63.3	23	76.2	18	56.3	22	72.8	28
2	67.3	23	76.7	30	65.5	25	60.8	24	63.4	17	57.1	26
1	76.4	24	78.3	31	76.7	25	56.6	22	61.9	24	59.3	25

Table 2 illustrates the percentage of story points completed and the NPS score of the solution following each sprint for the six Agile teams in their last five sprints prior to the implementation of our procedure. Three points can be observed from Table 2:

1. The teams were not stable – the percentage of story points completed and the NPSs never consistently increased;
2. Only one (1) team, in one (1) sprint was able to exceed the 80% mark;
3. Only one (1) team has an average percentage over 70%.

2.3   Introduction of Ormsby and Busby-Earle's [11] Procedure

In the first sprint, following the introduction of the procedure, there was a drop in the percentage of story points completed for all six teams. The teams committed to approximately the same number of points as they did in their previous sprint. In second sprint following the introduction of the procedure, it can be observed that there is a notable increase in efficiency of the teams regarding the percentage of story points completed. In the sprints that followed, the percentage of story points completed steadily and consistently increased. There was a positive impact with the introduction of the procedure as the percentages for the teams were able to surpass the 80% mark. This solved one of the problems that was previously observed when the teams used other procedures. However, this did not solve for the issue of team stabilization. As seen in Table 3, the percentage of story points completed was inconsistent. Our procedure did however aid in customer satisfaction as NPSs improved for all six solutions that were built by the teams.

Table 3. Percentage of story points completed and the NPSs after implementation of our procedure. Original table taken from 'Scaling a Standardized Procedure to Conceptualizing and Completing User Stories across Scrum Teams and Industries' by M. Ormsby and C. Busby-Earle, 2019, Proceedings of the 14th International Conference on Evaluation of Novel Approaches to Software Engineering, 1, pp. 127–133 [10].

# of sprint before	Team 1		Team 2		Team 3		Team 4		Team 5		Team 6	
	%	NPS	%	NPS	%	NPS	%	NPS	%	NPS	%	NPS
1	53.5	24	58.0	30	43.5	28	51.7	23	59.3	23	46.3	25
2	70.7	24	68.5	31	72.7	28	70.1	23	80.3	26	60.6	23
3	80.3	25	84.7	33	79.1	29	82.2	26	78.9	30	76.5	27
4	81.3	28	87.4	38	80.6	29	86.7	31	81.5	31	72.8	30
5	84.1	30	85.4	45	85.7	31	83.3	34	83.2	35	85.3	32
6	86.0	33	88.2	46	85.9	37	84.6	34	76.0	35	81.2	33

2.4   Scaled Steps of Doneness Procedure

To stabilize the percentage of story points completed and the NPS of the teams, adjustments were made to the procedure.

In the first sprint following the adjustment (sprint 1), there was an anticipated drop in the performance of the teams. The drop-in percentage of story points completed was very small as the learning from the other teams and the previous experiment was used by the teams to plan accordingly for the expected drop. In sprint 2, there was a notable increase in percentages of story points completed and the NPSs. This continued and resulted in the desired team stabilization in the subsequent sprints.

Table 4. Percentage of story points completed and the NPSs after adjustment to the procedure. Original table taken from 'Scaling a Standardized Procedure to Conceptualizing and Completing User Stories across Scrum Teams and Industries' by M. Ormsby and C. Busby-Earle, 2019, Proceedings of the 14th International Conference on Evaluation of Novel Approaches to Software Engineering, 1, pp. 127–133 [10].

# of sprint before	Team 1		Team 2		Team 3		Team 4		Team 5		Team 6	
	%	NPS	%	NPS	%	NPS	%	NPS	%	NPS	%	NPS
1	68.1	28	73.2	45	71.1	38	75.6	35	74.1	34	80.9	33
2	88.3	32	87.4	43	87.1	41	87.7	38	85.6	36	82.3	33
3	90.1	35	98.4	61	93.8	43	89.3	39	87.5	38	85.6	34
4	90.1	36	98.9	62	94.6	43	88.9	41	88.0	38	85.2	38
5	91.6	38	97.1	64	93.1	42	87.9	44	90.2	40	87.8	38
6	91.2	38	98.2	64	95.1	44	89.2	46	92.3	43	89.4	41
7	90.9	39	100.0	67	95.2	44	87.1	46	93.8	43	95.6	41
8	92.7	39	98.1	67	98.5	46	90.7	48	93.2	48	96.2	41

3 Analysis of Adjustments

It can be observed in Table 2 that the percentage of story points completed of the six teams was very inconsistent. This was due to the teams learning from their mistakes and applying corrective measures. Teams 1–4 isolated themselves from the rest of the organization and as such, the lessons learned by each team were not shared with the other teams [10]. This engendered within teams a practice of developing solutions for problems that were already solved by another team. Teams 5 and 6 did not isolate themselves like the other teams, as they learned from the other teams mistakes. Teams 5 and 6 were reusing components from the other teams and as such were able to produce more effective functionality.

It is to be noted that the introduction of the Scaled Steps of Doneness procedure came at a cost, as depicted in Table 3. There was an initial drop in the percentage of story points completed. A steady increase was however observed in the subsequent sprints. Further, all the teams were able to surpass the 80% mark and remained above that mark until the completion of their respective development projects.

There was also an increase in the NPS after the introduction of our procedure. Members of the team 1 to 4 indicated that the new procedure helped them to coordinate the opportune times to obtain feedback, i.e. receiving the feedback without distracting the teams [10].

There was insufficient stability in the percentage of story points completed. The organization sought more stability to be able to more efficiently forecast the amount of work the teams could manage. Taking this issue into consideration in addition to the feedback from the respective teams, the Scaled Steps of Doneness procedure was applied.

Each of the Agile teams implemented the Scaled Steps of Doneness and predictably, there was a drop in the percentages of story points completed during the initial sprint for teams 1–4 [10], as seen in Table 4. This was due to team members needing time to become familiar with the new method of working imposed by the Scaled Steps of Doneness. However, teams 5 and 6 anticipated the drop based on the observations from the other teams and planned accordingly. This plan took the form of taking low risk stories (regarding technical competence and customer impact) to commit in the first sprint after the introduction of the procedure. The drop in the story points completed was not considered drastic as all the Agile teams were already familiar with most of the steps of the new procedure. Ormsby and Busby-Earle [10] noted in the proceeding sprints, the percentage of story points continued to increase and quickly stabilized. In the case of teams 1, 2 and 3, they exceeded the 90% mark. Team 4 stabilized in the high 80% but it can be observed that they broke the 90% mark in sprint 14. Additionally, the NPSs increased and showed signs of high success for the teams. This can be observed in Table 4 where all teams increased their net promoter scores, three of the teams surpassed the 40 mark and one of the teams scored a high 67 in the last two sprints of this study. These scores reflect the satisfaction by end-users (Fig. 1).

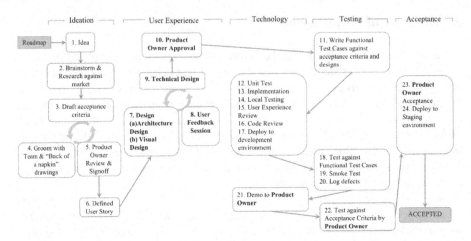

Fig. 1. Scaled Steps of Doneness (SSOD) Procedure. Taken from 'Scaling a Standardized Procedure to Conceptualizing and Completing User Stories across Scrum Teams and Industries' by M. Ormsby and C. Busby-Earle, 2019, Proceedings of the 14th International Conference on Evaluation of Novel Approaches to Software Engineering, 1, pp. 127–133 [10].

A key aspect of the Scaled Steps of Doneness procedure is the immediate contact of the UX team members on a user story, as well as the signoff by the client before the user story goes to the testing and technical team members [10]. This gives each user story a better chance of acceptance. Additionally, it has reduced the number of back and forth interactions between the UX team members and the technical team members.

The Scaled Steps of Doneness procedure also encourages test driven development by ensuring that testing is at the forefront [10]. It gives the testing team members an opportunity to present the developers with test scripts before the technical design is done for the story. This allows the developers to account for edge cases.

4 Conclusion

To summarize, lacunae were identified in the previous processes and analyzed. The Scaled Steps of Doneness procedure was applied and succeeded in stabilizing the teams and achieving high net promoter scores. The results found by Ormsby and Earle's [10] ENASE paper has been extended by the inclusion of two additional scrum teams. The results for these additional teams support the results from the original paper for Teams 1–4.

Empirical evidence has been provided that the Scaled Steps of Doneness procedure helps to solve one of the key problems of working in an Agile environment as stated by the 13th Annual State of Agile [2] report: inconsistent agile practices and processes. This is seen in Table 4, whereby having had the teams understand and implement the procedure, they were able to experience increased percentage of story points completed and net promoter scores. Moreover, it was observed that team morale improved as a result. Further the Scaled Steps of Doneness procedure can adapt to teams of varying skillsets, age and nationality. It should be noted that the majority of the nationalities was represented by North America and The Caribbean. The procedure requires communication among all team members.

Ormsby and Busby-Earle's [11] procedure did not succor in stabilizing the velocities of the teams. This lacuna was due to lack of a clear understanding of the end-users wants as well as the way technology can facilitate the realization of those wants. The designing steps in the User Experience group needed to encompass more feedback steps to truly understand the feasible wants of the end-users. This would have resulted in a clear acceptance of the goal of the user story. Importantly, it enables the organization to determine whether their timelines are on track at an early stage of a project. Earlier feedback ultimately leads to more success.

The results observed in Table 4, indicate the successful impact of the adjustments to the procedure. As the teams continued to settle into the new process, they were able to stabilize their percentage of story points completed and net promoter scores. A product owner was able to produce more accurate forecasts of the amount of work a team could complete when armed with a stabilized percentage of story points completed. This is important as this enables the organization to deduce whether their timelines are on track at an early stage of a project. Earlier feedback leads to more success.

The objective of the Scaled Steps of Doneness procedure is to aid Agile teams by stabilizing their sprint velocity. Jack Welch stated, "when the rate of change outside exceeds the rate of change inside, the end is in sight". In this regard, it can be put forth that if the environment in which solutions is changing is faster than the time it takes to output a solution, then the end is in sight as the solution will fast become outdated and no longer needed. Stabilizing a team's velocity is critical as it helps the team keep pace with constant changes.

Further the procedure assists with this by defining the steps required to meet the Definition of Done (DOD) for teams. Definition of Done is a concept in the Scrum methodology which drives the quality of the work being produced by assessing the completion of a user story. This concept is defined by each Scrum team at the beginning of their Agile journey, however, what is often missing is a strategy to aid teams in reaching this definition. The procedure was able to guide teams in reaching their Definition of Done, regardless of the technological solution being put forth, by standardizing the process of conceptualizing, understanding, defining, implementing, testing and accepting a user story.

Collaboration and communication are key concepts of ASD. The procedure embraces these concepts by encouraging further collaboration and communication. Frequent checkpoints by team members are required throughout the process as this results in an aligned understanding of the user story and an improved chance of producing a quality user story.

Stabilization of user stories and providing a procedure for teams to relate to in adapting to changes greatly benefits Product Owners. Armed with this, Product Owners are better able to forecast the progress of their team and set more accurate expectations with external stakeholders.

An observation from the experiment was that the cost of change is expensive. This was illustrated in both Tables 3 and 4. At introduction of a new procedure, there was a corresponding descent in the percentage of story points completed. Changes are expensive and should be both deliberate and strategic. Moreover, communication of a guiding procedure initially would have also contributed to higher collaboration among team members and overall, stronger team health in the long run. Change management is important in Agile teams, but as seen by teams 5 and 6, plans can be put in place to make the impact minimal.

The research of Silva et al. [13] concluded that there is a need for more and better empirical studies documenting and evaluating the use of the definition of done. These results greatly contribute to further assisting in documenting the definition of done. The goal of the Agile methodology is to create and deliver business value expeditiously. Therefore, if a user story that is done has resulted in bugs within the production environment, that user story can be considered incomplete.

The organization has adopted the SSOD procedure within their culture and have had all subsequent teams incorporate this procedure before they begin sprinting. It should also be noted that the organization has seventeen (17) Agile teams that have integrated our SSOD procedure into their ASD. The SSOD procedure is currently being looked at by another regional organization.

5   Future Work

The Scaled Steps of Doneness procedure was applied to agile teams that were following the Scrum methodology. As observed in VersionOne's 13th Annual State of Agile, Scrum is the primary agile methodology by agile practitioners. The procedure should be applied to other types of agile methodologies for completeness. If it is not applicable to other agile methodologies, then further research work can be done to discover a successful procedure. Large organizations are composed of several divisions and units that sometime function very differently from the next. As such, as these organizations continue to transition to agile, it is probable that they will use multiple methodologies to achieve their goals. This is seen in the 13th Annual State of Agile [2], as the second choice in agile methodologies by agile practitioners is multiple methodologies.

During this research, it was observed, analyzed and concluded that the cost of change for agile teams is expensive. Effective methods to minimize the cost of change in ASD's processes is required.

Finally, this research looked at the composition of agile teams. Further research is required to determine a strategy for team composition based on domain and/or technology stack needed for a solution.

In quoting Albert Einstein, "Learn from yesterday, live for today, hope for tomorrow. The important thing is not to stop questioning".

References

1. Collier, K.: Agile Analytics: A Value-Driven Approach to Business Intelligence and Data Warehousing, p. 121. Pearson Education, New York (2011)
2. 13th Annual State of Agile Report. https://explore.versionone.com/state-of-agile/versionone-13th-annual-state-of-agile-report. Accessed 08 Sep 2019

3. Kniberg, H.: Scrum and XP from the Trenches, 2nd edn. C4 Media Inc, Toronto (2015)
4. Bin Azhar, F., Dhillon, J.: Systematic review of factors influencing the effective use of mhealth apps for self-care. In: 2016 3rd International Conference on Computer and Information Sciences (ICCOINS). IEEE, Malaysia (2016)
5. Sithole, V., Solms, F.: Synchronized Agile. In: SAICSIT 2016 Proceedings of the Annual Conference of the South African Institute of Computer Scientists and Information Technologists. ACM, New York (2016)
6. Majchrzak, M., Madeyski, L.: Factors influencing user story estimations: an industrial interview and a conceptual model, Poland (2016)
7. Moe, N., Dingsøyr, T.: emerging research themes and updated research agenda for large-scale Agile development. A summary of the 5th international workshop at XP2017. In: XP 2017 Proceedings of the XP2017 Scientific Workshops. ACM, Germany (2017)
8. Nurdiani, I., Börstler, J., Fricker, S., Petersen, K.: A preliminary checklist for capturing baseline situations in studying the impacts of Agile practices introduction. In: 2018 ACM/IEEE 6th International Workshop on Conducting Empirical Studies in Industry. IEEE, Gothenburg (2018)
9. Pries-Heje, J., Krohn, M.: The SAFe way to the Agile organization. In: Proceedings of the XP 2017 Scientific Workshops, XP 2017. ACM, Cologne (2017)
10. Ormsby, M., Busby-Earle, C.: Scaling a standardized procedure to conceptualizing and completing user stories across scrum teams and industries. In: Proceedings of the 14th International Conference on Evaluation of Novel Approaches to Software Engineering, vol. 1, pp. 127–133. SciTePress (2019)
11. Ormsby, M., Busby-Earle, C.: A standardized procedure to conceptualizing and completing user stories. In: 2017 International Conference on Computational Science and Computational Intelligence (CSCI). IEEE, Las Vegas (2018)
12. Rothman, J.: Create Your Successful Agile Project: Collaborate, Measure, Estimate, Deliver. The Pragmatic Bookshelf, North Carolina (2017)
13. Silva, A., et al.: A systematic review on the use of definition of done on agile software development projects. In: EASE 2017 Proceedings of the 21st International Conference on Evaluation and Assessment in Software Engineering, pp. 364–373. ACM, New York (2017)

Indoor Localization Techniques Within a Home Monitoring Platform

Iuliana Marin, Maria-Iuliana Bocicor, and Arthur-Jozsef Molnar^(✉)

S.C. Info World S.R.L., Bucharest, Romania
{iuliana.marin,iuliana.bocicor,arthur.molnar}@infoworld.ro
https://www.infoworld.ro/en/

Abstract. This paper details a number of indoor localization techniques developed for real-time monitoring of older adults. These were developed within the framework of the i-Light research project that was funded by the European Union. The project targeted the development and initial evaluation of a configurable and cost-effective cyber-physical system for monitoring the safety of older adults who are living in their own homes. Localization hardware consists of a number of custom-developed devices that replace existing luminaires. In addition to lighting capabilities, they measure the strength of a Bluetooth Low Energy signal emitted by a wearable device on the user. Readings are recorded in real time and sent to a software server for analysis. We present a comparative evaluation of the accuracy achieved by several server-side algorithms, including Kalman filtering, a look-back heuristic as well as a neural network-based approach. It is known that approaches based on measuring signal strength are sensitive to the placement of walls, construction materials used, the presence of doors as well as existing furniture. As such, we evaluate the proposed approaches in two separate locations having distinct building characteristics. We show that the proposed techniques improve the accuracy of localization. As the final step, we evaluate our results against comparable existing approaches.

Keywords: Indoor localization · Received signal strength ·
Trilateration · Kalman filter · Neural network

1 Introduction

The developed world is on the cusp of long-term societal and demographic change heralded by population ageing. The World Health Organisation estimates the number of adults over 60 to double worldwide by 2050 [48]. However, the report finds that advances in healthcare and medicine do not necessarily translate into improved quality of life for older adults. This situation is expected to increase the toll on healthcare system and local government expenditures for care programs. Meijer et al. [27] find that real annual health expenditure increases at 4% per year, with an important part of these funds to be geared towards the older adult population in the future.

© Springer Nature Switzerland AG 2020
E. Damiani et al. (Eds.): ENASE 2019, CCIS 1172, pp. 378–401, 2020.
https://doi.org/10.1007/978-3-030-40223-5_19

However, advancement in the form of diminutive computing platforms, advanced wireless networks and a push towards wearable devices provide an opportunity for technological solutions that supplement healthcare-based measures in older adult care. Special importance is given to systems that enable adults to continue living in their own homes, maintaining good social relations. The European Union identified the increased importance of caring for older adults and created the Active and Assisted Living Programme [1] to help public and private organizations develop and bring solutions to market.

Our presented work is part of the i-Light research project funded by the European Union. Its main objective concerns the development of an extensible and cost-effective cyber-physical platform for home monitoring and assisted living [25]. The main target group are older adults living in their own homes. The hardware side of the platform is represented by a number of intelligent luminaire devices that were developed as part of the project. In addition to lighting, they provide sensing, localization and communication systems using Bluetooth Low Energy and WiFi. The developed luminaires replace existing light bulbs and can communicate between them as well as with a remotely-deployed software server. This approach addresses adoption barriers by reducing deployment costs, simplifying installation and being inconspicuous within the home. Furthermore, a single cloud-based server deployment can service many household deployments, improving cost-effectiveness for additional installations.

The most important innovative aspects as well as platform architecture and main components were already detailed in previous work [4,25,26]. As such, this paper is focused on presenting and evaluating the implemented localization algorithms. The problem of person localization can be partitioned into outdoor and indoor localization. The former is covered by existing and well-known technologies. The first to be made available to the public was the United States' GPS system. Recognising the strategic importance of localization, additional such systems were implemented by the European Union (Galileo), Russia (GLONASS), China (BeiDou-2) and Japan (QZSS). Currently, these latter systems are focused to provide good accuracy within the strategic region of its implementing country. In order to work, all these systems require the device to have direct line of sight toward several satellites in the constellation. Indoors, these systems range between inaccurate at best and completely inoperative. As such, achieving accurate indoor localization required the development of new technologies and algorithms. These include communication via visible light [13], acoustic background fingerprinting [42] and user movements [41]. Given the project requirements detailed in [10], the selected approach was trilateration of the signal strength received from a Bluetooth Low Energy device by at least three intelligent luminaires. This has the advantage of not requiring additional wiring or unsightly devices. System accuracy was evaluated within two locations. The first one was a small home with thick concrete and brick walls [26], and the second one an office building having larger rooms, but fewer and thinner walls. In both cases, the minimum of three devices were deployed.

2   Related Work

Previously described trends have lead to an increase in the number of smart home devices in use, both in homes as well as the workplace and public places. Indoor localization is one of their strong-suits, as it allows monitoring and analysis of visitor behaviour, building customer profiles and understanding patterns of human interaction.

As detailed in the previous section, GPS is the default localization technology used outdoors. Given that satellite signal is easily blocked by buildings [32], several alternative technologies were considered and evaluated for indoor localization. Among them are acoustic and optical signals, radio-frequency identification (RFID), as well as using WiFi and Bluetooth signals for triangulation or trilateration [23,40,49]. When electromagnetic waves are used, the distance between the target of monitoring and a number of beacons is calculated based on the Received Signal Strength Index (RSSI) [15]. In most cases, the beacons are fixed in known locations, and they record the strength of an electromagnetic signal received from the tracked emitter. Due to their ubiquity, a WiFi or Bluetooth signal is usually employed. The received power decreases as the distance the signal must travel increases, using the inverse square law [22,24,31,35]. This allows calculating the distance between the signal emitter and the beacons receiving the signal. Using at least three fixed beacons and applying triangulation or trilateration allows calculating the emitter's physical location.

However, raw RSSI readings can be misleading due to multipath fading, the degree of variance being higher indoors [33]. This is exacerbated by the presence of walls and large items of furniture that affect signal strength. Also, for many use cases, it is desirable to carry out localization without equipping the monitored person with a wearable device, leading to continued research interest in the domain.

One of the proposed solutions to address inherent variance in readings is to apply a filter on the raw RSSI values. The Simultaneous Localization and Configuration algorithm [6] is based on the fast simultaneous localization and mapping problem for RSSI-based localization and can run on a mobile device. Another filter-based approach is the Kalman filter [47], which is generally used to smooth noisy data. The Kalman filter is amenable for smoothing raw RSSI readings and has low computational overhead. It is a recursive filter that evaluates a system's state starting from a series of noisy measurements. Each new measurement is subjected to a weighted mean calculated based on the covariance for reducing uncertainty. After a number of readings, the mean and covariance are recalculated. Kalman filtering can increase the accuracy of indoor localization [34] by lowering accumulated errors [39]. Furthermore, [39] showed that filtering lowered energy consumption and enhanced the stability of the readings.

The beacons used in our paper are intelligent luminaires [25] that have WiFi and Bluetooth communication capabilities and which can replace existing light bulbs. They were designed to ensure that luminaire-related functionality does not impede indoor localization by influencing signal quality or directionality. The luminaires can be mounted into existing wall sockets. In our experiments,

they replaced ceiling-mounted light bulbs, which provided good signal directionality and the advantage that the system looked inconspicuous. Our experiments
were carried out using a smartphone emitting Bluetooth signal recorded and
timestamped by the luminaires. Other Bluetooth compatible devices, such as
smartwatches and emergency buttons can also be used. Our solution's primary
drivers were cost-effectiveness and unobtrusiveness. The proposed setup leads
to low costs associated with deployment and maintenance, and does not look
inconspicuous when installed in a residential building or office.

3   Platform Overview

The i-Light platform was designed to be a home monitoring system for older
adults and relies on energetically efficient, intelligent luminaires, equipped with
an integrated electronic sensor system, indoor localization and communications
that allow continuous, ubiquitous and inexpensive home monitoring. The high-
level system architecture is presented in Fig. 1 [26]. The hardware subsystem is
represented by a wireless network of luminaires, composed of two types of nodes
designated as *smart* and *dummy*. The software subsystem integrates several modules, distributed on different devices: smart and dummy luminaires, software
server and client devices. Both aforementioned subsystems will be expounded in
the following subsections.

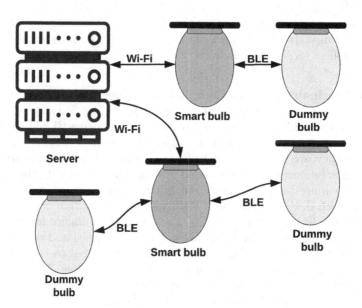

Fig. 1. High-level system architecture [26].

3.1   Wireless Network of Luminaires

The luminaire network is deployed within personal homes to monitor the indoor environment and track the older adult's location. Together, the installed luminaires form a network that completely covers the indoor environment. All location and ambient monitoring data is collected and sent in real time to the software server, which computes the person's indoor location and analyses environmental information continually.

Smart Luminaires. Within the wireless luminaire network smart bulbs represent the resourceful constituents. Using a Raspberry Pi3 board [14] at their core, this type of luminaire offer features such as lighting, ambient sensing and direct communication to the server and with the dummy bulbs. Their design is modular, as this has proved to be the best option to easily isolate manufacturing problems and make changes without rebuilding the entire device. With regard to lighting, the luminaires provide LED intensity management. They also include a sensor module for environment monitoring, which measures temperature, ambient light, humidity, CO_2, dust and volatile organic compound gases. All values measured are sent directly to the software server via WiFi or Ethernet, where they are subsequently analysed. Smart bulbs can also identify Bluetooth-equipped devices and record RSSI values. Furthermore, they can collect RSSI values registered by several dummy luminaires and forward these to the server, where the localization algorithms are run. At system configuration, each of the dummy bulbs must be associated to a smart bulb. This design enables smart luminaires to directly communicate via Bluetooth with their associated dummy bulbs and collect localization data.

Dummy Luminaires. Dummy luminaires are simpler, smaller and lower-cost when compared with smart luminaires. Their limited functionality allows using them for lighting and localization. They rely on a Bluegiga BLE112 Bluetooth Low Energy module [37], which enables them to establish a connection to the smart bulb they are associated with. Dummy bulbs have lighting capabilities, with the light intensity being controlled via the smart luminaire they are connected to. Dummy bulbs also carry out environment scans in order to detect other Bluetooth devices and acquire RSSI values. Localization is carried out on the server according to collected RSSIs. Each dummy luminaire must be associated to a smart one, as the dummies are not WiFi equipped and cannot directly send data to the server. Dummy luminaires stay connected to their associated smart bulb using Bluetooth and transfer the RSSIs in real time. The main advantage of using dummy bulbs is that the system's overall cost is reduced, while sufficient coverage is possible for accurate localization.

Communication Protocol. Communication between smart and dummy light bulbs is achieved via Bluetooth Low Energy. For dummy bulbs, this is provided by the Bluegiga BLE112 module, while the smart bulb employs its onboard Raspberry Pi3. Communication between smart luminaires and the server is accomplished through web services with information transmitted in JSON format.

An important concern in two-way Bluetooth Low Energy connectivity is the master and slave connection roles. Slave devices advertise themselves and wait for connections. Master devices scan the environment and initiate connections to slaves. Smart luminaires act as masters, as after they perform a scan for both Bluetooth devices and dummy luminaires, they initiate connections to both: to Bluetooth devices in order to acquire RSSI values for localization and to dummy bulbs in order to receive the RSSIs collected by them. In order to send data from smart to dummy luminaires, dummy bulbs act as slaves, emitting advertisement packets allowing them to be identified by the smart bulbs. However, in order to detect additional devices in the environment, such as the actual device used for indoor positioning, they must change their role and act as masters. Consequently, dummy luminaires periodically change roles. All data acquired by both luminaire types are sent to the system server and stored in the database, where ambient and RSSI data are processed, localization algorithms executed and real-time alerts are generated, if necessary.

Communication between smart luminaires and the server is accomplished using the MQTT messaging protocol[1]. Bidirectional communication using JSONs is achieved via the publish/subscribe model. This ensures loose coupling between the monitoring system's components. The protocol is characterised by low bandwidth and energy consumption, reliability, and is dedicated to Internet of Things applications. Every smart bulb publishes JSONs using a subject. The subject represents routing information. The server subscribes to several subjects and analyses the received JSONs. The security of sent and received JSON messages is ensured by encryption.

3.2   Software Server Components

The i-Light software system includes a server and a client component. The server component is responsible for the communication with the smart luminaires, collecting and storing environment and location data, data analysis, generating reports and alerts, as well as sending generated alerts to responsible people. The client component is a web application that allows users to configure the system by providing the floor plans of monitored dwellings, registering new luminaires and system users, as well as to generate and view reports.

We briefly depict the main server subsystems. The *indoor localization subsystem* uses RSSI data collected by smart and dummy luminaires and sent to the server. Several times each minute, this component calculates the indoor location of monitored users, and stores this information in the database, where it can be accessed for analysis. The *data acquisition and analysis subsystem* receives data collected by the wireless network's luminaires and sends these to the persistence database. Furthermore, it also performs several types of analyses on the data to

---

[1] http://mqtt.org/.

identify abnormal situations. The *real-time alerts subsystem* is responsible for creating notifications and alerts if a situation that presents risk for the monitored person has been identified. Alerts are persisted in the database, and are sent in real time to both the monitored person and their caregivers via short message service. The *reporting subsystem* is responsible for creating different types of reports, using data collected by the intelligent luminaires and stored in the database. The subsystem exposes a web service for providing statistics and reports. These can be visualised through the web application. The *web application* is a web interface for configuring system preferences, managing intelligent luminaires, users and their associated locations, and viewing different types of reports.

4   Indoor Localization Techniques

In order to increase the accuracy of indoor localization, and achieve a reduction in positioning errors, we evaluate several approaches starting with direct trilateration, which is then improved using several proposed heuristics. An additional technique we evaluate is based on an artificial neural network trained to produce coordinates associated to the person's indoor location.

4.1   Direct Trilateration

The indoor localization algorithm developed for i-Light is based on trilateration. As opposed to triangulation, which employs angles, trilateration computes the position of a target starting from the computed distances between the target and at least three static receivers. In our case, intelligent luminaires are the receivers and a smart device worn by the monitored person is the target. To compute the required distances we start from RSSI measurements and use the RSSI lognormal model described in [9]. Equation 1 describes the manner of calculating the distance, using the RSSI value and 2 other parameters: n, the path-loss exponent and A, the signal strength expressed in dBm, measured at a distance of one meter. The path-loss exponent's value is directly influenced by the physical environment in which the system operates. This includes the surrounding structure, building materials and presence of furniture in the case of indoor environments. Its values range between 1.4 to 5.1, depending on the environment [16].

$$d = 10^{\frac{A-RSSI}{10 \cdot n}} \tag{1}$$

Having three distances computed according to Formula 1, from the target of monitoring to each of the installed luminaires, the position of the target within the environment can be inferred. This is computed as the point of intersection of three circles, each having as centre one luminaire and as radius the computed distance from that luminaire to the target, as shown in Fig. 2.

The target's coordinates, denoted (x, y), are obtained by solving the system of equations in Formula 2, where $(x_i, y_i), i \in \{1, 2, 3\}$ are the luminaires' positions (the circles' centres) and $d_i, i \in \{1, 2, 3\}$ represent the respective computed distances (the circle radii (d_1, d_2, d_3)).

$$\begin{cases} (x - x_1)^2 + (y - y_1)^2 = d_1^2 \\ (x - x_2)^2 + (y - y_2)^2 = d_2^2 \\ (x - x_3)^2 + (y - y_3)^2 = d_3^2 \end{cases} \tag{2}$$

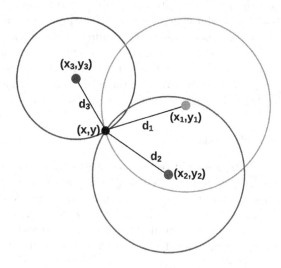

Fig. 2. Illustration for trilateration. The $(x_i, y_i), i \in \{1, 2, 3\}$ dots represent luminaires and the (x, y) dot is the computed position, considering the three circles' radii.

While the above-mentioned positioning method is theoretically sound, in real-world environments, RSSI values are attenuated by various types of obstacles, such as furniture or other indoor objects and walls [5]. Wall type and thickness has a direct influence on signal strength [50], meaning that the equation system cannot be effectively solved. To handle signal noise the following subsections present a number of proposed methods that can be employed on the server side to improve localization accuracy.

4.2 Kalman Filter

The Kalman filter is an algorithm for optimal estimation in linear Gaussian systems [7]. It is suitable for dynamic systems in which the goal is to find the best estimate of a state from indirect or noisy measurements. The technique is well-suited for real-time application, as in order to estimate the current state it only needs information from the previous one. Taking into consideration the technique's purview and advantages, as well as our objectives regarding indoor localization, we decided to select this method for experimentation.

Indoor objects and walls directly influence the received signal strength [5], thus the measurements collected by the intelligent luminaires at discrete points in time are noisy. To obtain the best estimate for the actual RSSI values at one point in time, Kalman filters use a prediction from the best estimate of the previous point in time along with a correction for known external factors, all starting from the assumption that the system variables are random and Gaussian distributed. Starting from some measured values, the algorithm proceeds with two major steps: *prediction* and *update*. First it makes a prediction of the current state, based on the previous state and problem model and then it updates this prediction, based on values measured at that time point and considering potential errors. Another aspect worth mentioning is the *Kalman gain*, which provides more weight to either the estimate or the measurement, according to prediction error. A decrease in estimation error will result in more weight given to estimates. The estimated RSSI values obtained through Kalman filtering will further be used for trilateration, as described in Subsect. 4.1.

4.3   Look-Back-k Heuristic

We propose and evaluate a second technique for error reduction. It is a generalization of the heuristic first presented in [25]. Its name is representative for its main feature: it considers the k previous consecutive measurements for the computation of the current location. The underlying assumption is that a set of several measurements are more accurate than the last one and that by examining several measurements instead of just the current one, the precision can be increased.

In direct trilateration the three distances are computed at each discrete time point when an RSSI measurement is taken, using as input the currently measured RSSI value. If one measurement is faulty, it negatively influences the accuracy of the calculated position. We attempt to alleviate this issue by considering a collection of previous n measurements. For each luminaire l_i, a series of RSSI values (v) are collected at m time points $\{t_1, t_2, \ldots, t_m\}$, as follows: $(v_{l_i}^{t_1}, v_{l_i}^{t_2}, \ldots, v_{l_i}^{t_m})$ where $v_{l_i}^{t_j}$ represents the RSSI value for luminaire l_i, $i \in \{1, 2, 3\}$, at time point t_j, $j \in \{1, \ldots, m\}$. Instead of computing the indoor position p_{t_j} at time point t_j by employing the three values $(v_{l_1}^{t_j}, v_{l_3}^{t_j}, v_{l_3}^{t_j})$, we start from the previous k RSSI measurements, for each luminaire $\{v_{l_i}^{t_j-(k-1)}, \ldots, v_{l_i}^{t_j-2}, v_{l_i}^{t_j-1}, v_{l_i}^{t_j}\}$ and perform the following computations for time point t_j, on this collection:

1. Eliminate outliers. We take into account two procedures for outliers: (1) The minimum and maximum values are outliers; (2) We consider a value to be an outlier if it falls outside of 1.5 times of an interquartile range above the third quartile and below the first quartile.
2. Compute the mean μ_{t_j} and the standard deviation σ_{t_j} for the remaining values.
3. Eliminate all values that are further than one standard deviation from the mean, thus all values outside the interval $[\mu_{t_j} - \sigma_{t_j}, \mu_{t_j} + \sigma_{t_j}]$.
4. Compute the mean of the remaining values μ'_{t_j} and use it in the trilateration process to compute the distance.

4.4 Hybrid Technique

Previously described techniques are intended to reduce localization errors resulting from noisy or erroneous measurements or as a result of interference. A combination of the two could steer towards more accurate indoor positioning results. Hence, this hybrid technique works in two phases: first, RSSI estimates are computed using the Kalman filter after which the look-back-n technique is applied using the estimates as input data.

4.5 Neural Network Based Technique

While the first three techniques rely mainly on trilateration and heuristic methods applied to minimise the impact of noise on input data, this technique stems from machine learning, where it is ubiquitous for both classification and regression. Several recent studies tackling indoor positioning have employed such machine learning models: a four layer deep neural network, combined with a denoising autoencoder and a hidden Markov model is employed in [51] for indoor and outdoor localization; a recurrent neural network which uses WiFi signals for an indoor positioning system is presented in [21]; another recurrent neural network, more specifically a long short-term memory network is used by Urano et al. [43] with BLE signal strength data for indoor localization; Mittal et al. [29] propose a convolutional neural networks based framework for indoor localization, in which the networks use images created from WiFi signatures. Another convolutional deep neural network starting from phase data of channel state information, which is transformed into images based on estimated angles of arrival is presented in [46]. In our model, the neural network input is a triplet that contains the three RSSI values recorded by the intelligent luminaires, while the output is the estimated location, represented as a coordinate pair.

Some of the most important hyper-parameters to fine-tune when working with an artificial neural network are the number of layers, the number of neurons per each hidden layer, type of optimisation algorithm, types of activation functions, learning rate or regularisation. However, there is no universal solution for deciding the optimal parameters' values for a given problem description (and non-linearly separable data) and most network architectures are built based on prior experience, trial and error. Our network starts from a simple architecture, with only one hidden layer. To this we gradually add hidden layers to investigate how this influences the obtained accuracy and to contribute to improved localization. The activation function of choice is rectified linear unit (ReLU) [30] and the optimisation algorithm employed is *adam* [18], an extension to stochastic gradient descent often used in the field of deep learning. Stratified k-fold cross validation is used during training for a more robust model, while the number of training epochs is varied during experimentation.

5   Experimental Evaluation

5.1   Methodology

Given the known impact building layouts and materials have on wireless signal propagation, we carried out our evaluation in two distinct locations. To allow for directly comparing the achieved accuracy, the same three intelligent luminaires were employed in both cases.

The first location was a home, having room dimensions of $2.50\,m \times 3.29\,m$ (bedroom), $2.50\,m \times 1.00\,m$ (study room), $2.34\,m \times 2.21\,m$ (hallway). Additional rooms, such as the kitchen and bathroom were not included in our evaluation. Figure 3a illustrates the layout of the evaluated rooms. One luminaire was ceiling-mounted in each room, replacing existing lighting infrastructure. Luminaire positions in Fig. 3 are marked using yellow circles with black outlines.

The second location was a two-room section of a large multi-storey office building, illustrated in Fig. 3b. Enclosure sizes are $5.60\,m \times 7.80\,m$ for the meeting room and $1.60\,m \times 5.60\,m$ for the hallway. The office covers more than 3 times the home's floor space, as shown in Fig. 3, which is drawn to scale. Two luminaires were deployed in the meeting room, while the third one was installed in the hallway. Both figures include major pieces of furniture, which have a detrimental effect on signal transmission [45]. More importantly, building materials used differ across the considered locations. The home location has both interior and exterior walls of brick and cement, with interior walls being 17 cm thick, while exterior ones are 35 cm [26]. For the office location, exterior walls were made of autoclaved aerated concrete and the indoor ones made of plasterboard. It is known that aerated concrete absorbs electromagnetic waves [19]. The electromagnetic shielding of the plasterboards is proportionally greater as the fiber content increases, while with increasing environment moisture, the shielding effect is decreased [36]. Signal interference was significant within the office location scenario, with 14 WiFi systems and 11 Bluetooth devices enabled around the testing area creating impedance. In both locations, a smartphone located 1 m above the floor was used as signal emitter, while the luminaires acted as signal receivers.

The trilateration formula presented in Sect. 4.1 employs two parameters that need to be calibrated: A - the signal strength at 1 m from the luminaire and n - the path loss exponent. As determined in our experiments the value for A is different for the two scenarios (-87 for the first experiment and -67 for the second). As reported in existing literature [28,44], the value of n varies depending on room shapes and sizes, building materials, wall placement as well as furniture. This value was determined by a grid-search procedure, showing that the most suitable value for both scenarios is $n = 2.5$.

The experimental methodology was similar in both locations. First, the devices were installed and we ensured that a stable link to the remotely-deployed server was working. Then, one person playing the role of *monitored adult* was stationary in several fixed places within the monitored rooms for a duration of around 15 min. A mobile phone was kept on them at a height of 1 m and with

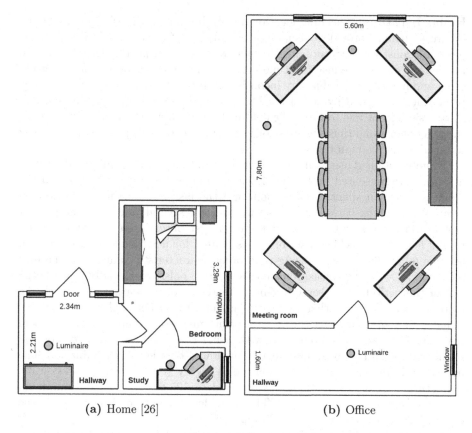

(a) Home [26]   (b) Office

Fig. 3. Partial floor map of dwellings used for evaluation (drawings to scale).

Bluetooth turned on, but not paired to another device. The luminaires recorded RSSI values from the phone at under 10 s intervals each, and sent the raw data to the server for further analysis. The following section details the evaluation carried out on the raw data. Post processing was done exclusively on the software server. The presented methods were implemented server-side and can run in real-time under deployment conditions.

5.2 Results

We present below the results obtained after applying the techniques presented in Sect. 4 for indoor localization, using the two scenarios presented in Sect. 5.1. The *Euclidean distance* was selected as the evaluation measure and the obtained distances were averaged across time points, for each interval. It must be mentioned that RSSI timestamps were not exactly identical for all the rooms in which the measurements were taken. In order to compute the person's location in any given moment t, the closest timestamps to moment t, for each room, were used.

Home Location. The first location for evaluation is the three-room home. Figure 4a, b and c provide a visual representation of the evolution of RSSI values, plotted against the corresponding Kalman estimates. Inspecting these values we notice that during the last two time periods, when the person was in the study room and hallway, the values are inconsistent during the time interval. However, RSSI values recorded by the study bulb while the person was in the bedroom show a significant rise towards the end of the period, which is inconsistent with the other values and thus suggests noisy measurements. This jump is significantly softened using Kalman filtering.

Results obtained using all four direct trilateration-based techniques described in Sect. 4 are presented in Table 1. Each column corresponds to the period the monitored person spent in each room and the last column shows the average error. For the look-back-k technique we consider several values for the parameter k and show results for all of them. A first observation is that the look-back-k heuristic, in which a set of values is used for position computation is on average more efficient than using time point characteristic values. For the first time period, when the measurements seem to be noisier, especially towards the end of the period, we observe a general tendency of decreasing error with the increase of k. For the other two periods, the error either slightly increases or remains the same. However the average positioning error is approximately 10cm lower for $k = 50$, when compared with using raw RSSI values. The reported results correspond to the minimum and maximum-based outlier elimination. The interquartile range-based elimination yields highly similar results: for $k = 50$, the returned error is 126.36 cm (as opposed to 125.80 cm, with the minimum and maximum-based elimination). The same decreasing trend is observed in the case of interquartile range-based elimination.

Kalman filters bring additional improvements. When applying these filters on raw values, and further, using trilateration starting from Kalman estimates, the positioning error is even smaller: more than 21 cm are gained when compared to using raw values and approximately 12 cm when compared to the best result using the look-back technique. Considering the improvements brought by both proposed heuristics, the expectation is that combining them will improve localization even further. This is confirmed by our experiment, as the best result obtained by the hybrid technique leads to the smallest error. The largest difference in error is for the first time interval (column 2:33–2:48), which is expected when considering the noisy values recorded towards the end of the interval, as shown in Fig. 4. Analysing the results of this experiment we conclude that the noise reduction induced by Kalman filtering brings significant enhancement for indoor localization, while the combination of this technique with our proposed look-back-k heuristic can lead to additional improvements.

Raw RSSI values were fed to the neural network described in Sect. 4.5, whose architecture was updated in an iterative manner to investigate the changes in localization accuracy induced by network construction. Table 2 presents the results obtained for different numbers of hidden layers and increasingly more training epochs. All hidden layers have the same number of neurons, which was

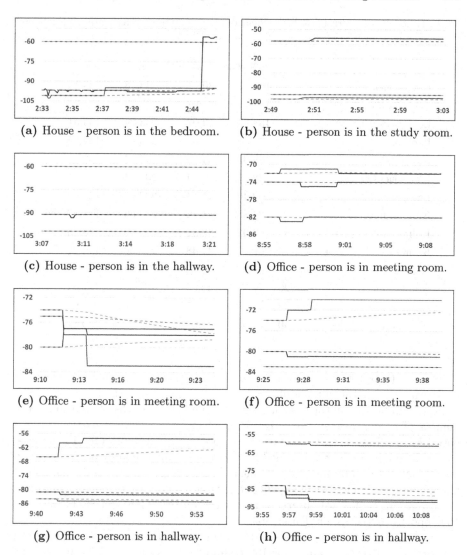

(a) House - person is in the bedroom.

(b) House - person is in the study room.

(c) House - person is in the hallway.

(d) Office - person is in meeting room.

(e) Office - person is in meeting room.

(f) Office - person is in meeting room.

(g) Office - person is in hallway.

(h) Office - person is in hallway.

Fig. 4. Raw RSSIs (continuous lines) and Kalman estimates (dashed lines) for each time interval. Signal strength (dBm) on vertical axis, time on horizontal axis. Luminaires are color coded as follows: magenta (house hallway), black (study room), red (bedroom), orange (meeting room, by the window), blue (meeting room by the wall), green (office hallway). (Color figure online)

determined through experimentation. The network's performance was measured using a stratified 10-fold cross validation technique. Reported results are the averaged errors and standard deviations, based on Euclidean distances, obtained over 10 runs, for all three time periods. More training epochs generally induce lower errors, especially when passing from a lower number (100) to considerably

Table 1. Localization errors for home location. Errors computed as averaged Euclidean distances, reported in centimetres.

	2:33–2:48	2:49–3:04	3:07–3:22	Avg. error
Raw values	141.67	30.71	233.18	135.19
Look-back-5	137.41	31.98	233.23	134.21
Look-back-10	134.22	33.07	233.24	133.51
Look-back-15	131.39	33.82	233.25	132.82
Look-back-20	128.63	34.43	233.24	132.1
Look-back-30	122.51	34.94	233.17	130.21
Look-back-50	109.40	34.94	233.05	125.80
Kalman filter	64.88	43.16	233.56	113.87
Kalman filter + look-back-5	63.92	43.32	233.56	113.60
Kalman filter + look-back-10	62.79	43.48	233.56	113.28
Kalman filter + look-back-15	61.72	43.59	233.55	112.95
Kalman filter + look-back-20	60.72	43.65	233.55	112.64
Kalman filter + look-back-30	58.79	43.67	233.55	112.00
Kalman filter + look-back-50	55.38	43.67	233.55	110.87

higher ones (500, 1000 and so on). However, as soon as convergence is achieved, a further increase in the number of epochs does not bring such significant improvement, as can be seen in the case of 1000, 2000 and 3000 epochs. Alteration of the number of hidden layers causes significant changes in accuracy particularly for networks that have been trained over few epochs, as can be seen for 100 epochs, where the minimum error, obtained for 5 layers is approximately 35 cm less than the maximum one, obtained for just one hidden layer. Again, when the number of training epochs is high, such significant differences no longer appear. Analysing the results in Table 2 we observe that accuracy less than 10 cm is obtained for 1000 epochs and fewer hidden layers.

For the conducted experiments, the highest average error obtained by the network is 48.13 cm, obtained for 100 training epochs and 1 hidden layer. This indicates that the neural network is clearly superior to the methods based on trilateration, where the lowest error obtained after applying the proposed heuristics is 110.87 cm in the case of this experiment. The network obtains almost perfect performance in certain configurations, such as an error of 1.41 cm for 3000 training epochs and 3 hidden layers. On average, the network's performance is altogether efficient, as the average error for the conducted experiments is 10.51 cm and the 95% confidence interval is 10.51 ± 4.02 cm ($[6.49, 14.53]$). While the network is trained for three fixed positions, a network constructed for real time localization should be trained using data collected from multiple positions that cover the entire indoor area and in various settings. Thus, although the artificial neural network seems to be more advantageous than direct trilateration, it also presents some drawbacks, which might make it more difficult to employ during product deployment.

Table 2. Home location. Average error based on Euclidean distance ± standard deviation obtained using the artificial neural network, over 10 runs, with stratified cross-validation. Errors reported in centimetres.

Epochs	Number of hidden layers				
	1	2	3	4	5
100	48.13 ± 37.24	25.98 ± 10.27	21.96 ± 7.88	24.76 ± 21.72	13.02 ± 4.38
500	12.04 ± 3.80	10.92 ± 3.48	9.74 ± 3.23	6.04 ± 2.66	5.81 ± 4.58
1000	9.74 ± 2.56	7.85 ± 4.22	7.35 ± 4.71	7.47 ± 3.39	5.12 ± 3.10
2000	9.59 ± 4.37	6.28 ± 3.57	4.15 ± 3.77	2.94 ± 2.24	2.71 ± 1.67
3000	10.39 ± 3.63	5.20 ± 4.26	1.41 ± 0.87	2.69 ± 2.26	1.57 ± 0.49

The actual and estimated locations obtained using the neural network are illustrated in Fig. 5. Reported locations present the 5 hidden layers network configuration, which performed very accurately, with the computed positions obtained by the network plotted against the actual locations. As seen in Fig. 5a, predicted positions are very close and in many cases overlap the actual location of the monitored person.

Figure 6 illustrates the location of the person during the second time interval, as it is reported by the cyber-physical system's software application. It allows users to map and display the dwelling floor plan together with the estimated real-time location of the monitored person using both 2D and 3D representations.

Office Location. In this section we present the results obtained during the evaluation carried out in the office location. In order to facilitate comparison with results obtained in the previous evaluation, the same methodology was followed. RSSI values were collected from five positions within the location illustrated in Fig. 3b. Recorded RSSI values and their Kalman estimates are illustrated in Fig. 4d–h. For the first three intervals of time (8:55–9:10, 9:10–9:25 and 9:25–9:40) the person was in different spots in the meting room. While for the first and third intervals the RSSIs measured by the three luminaires did not change notably, we noticed that during the second interval values recorded by the window bulb had a larger variance. The last two intervals of time, during which the person stood in the hallway, also presented some more significant changes in the recorded RSSI values. We observe that in all cases Kalman filtering attenuates the differences.

Table 3 shows the localization errors for this experiment, for each interval of time and each technique described in Sect. 4. The obtained results are rather consistent with those obtained during the home scenario: the look-back-n technique and Kalman filtering seem to improve localization on average, but not in

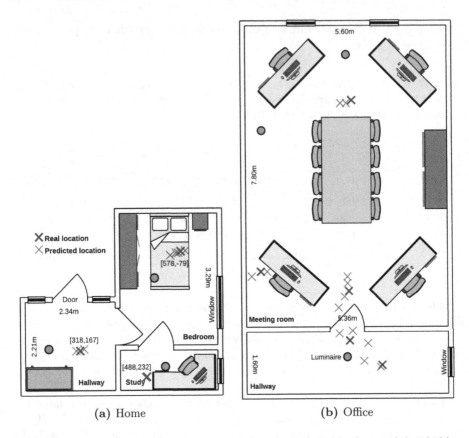

(a) Home   (b) Office

Fig. 5. Indoor positions obtained by the neural networks (3 hidden layers - left, 5 hidden layers - right), after being trained for 3000 epochs, represented on the two-dimensional floor plan of the dwelling (Fig. 3)

all individual cases. For instance, for the second interval of time we notice that the error obtained by processing the Kalman estimates is far greater that the one obtained by processing raw values. We posit this occurs due to Kalman estimates being more similar to the initially recorded RSSI values, which correspond to the person moving from one location to the other. Thus, even though for the best part of the interval the recorded values were lower (−83, for more than 11 out of 15 min), the Kalman estimates are closer to the initial values ([−74, −77]). This type of error can be attenuated by increasing the weight given to measurements recorded for longer periods. Like in the case of the previous evaluation, reported results correspond to the minimum and maximum-based outlier elimination. Again, the interquartile range-based elimination obtained similar results, but slightly higher errors (232.13 cm for look-back-50, as opposed to 222.77 cm and 227.77 cm for Kalman filtering combined with look-back-50).

Using Kalman filters brings additional improvements, similar to the case of the house scenario. When the filter is applied on raw values, and further,

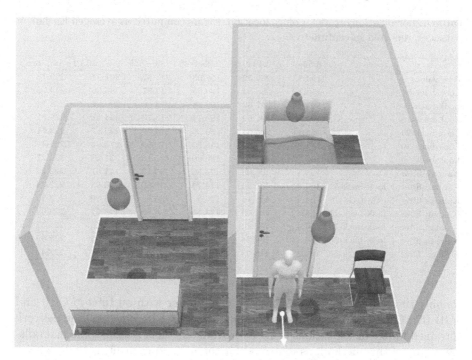

Fig. 6. Illustration of the person's indoor location within the system's interface [26].

when employing trilateration starting from the Kalman estimates, positioning errors are decreased, as shown in Table 3. Analysing the results presented in the table, we conclude that the Kalman filtering noise reduction again improves the accuracy of indoor localization, while its combination with our proposed look-back-k heuristic leads to additional improvements.

One of the differences between the house and office scenarios regards the accuracy of the proposed hybrid technique. While in the first scenario, the hybrid technique produced the smallest errors, in this case we observe different results. The best results with the hybrid technique are obtained when considering Kalman estimates and 5 steps back. All average errors output by Kalman filtering and the look-back-n technique are lower than those generated by using raw values. We observe that the results of this experiment are strongly influenced by the selected positions in the office and the trilateration method used.

The results obtained using the neural network lead to conclusions similar to those obtained within the first location: generally, more layers and more training epochs mean improved accuracy, as illustrated in Table 4. The largest error, obtained by a network with just one hidden layer and after only 100 training epochs is less than half the average error obtained by methods based on trilateration, while the smallest one is less than 8 cm. The average error for the conducted experiments is 35.23 cm and the 95% confidence interval is 35.23 ± 11.86 cm ([23.36, 47.10]). The localization accuracy obtained by the network is good and

Table 3. Localization errors for office location. Errors computed as averaged Euclidean distances, reported in centimetres.

	8:55–9:10	9:10–9:25	9:25–9:40	9:40–9:55	9.55–10:10	Avg. error
Raw values	154.12	280.32	191.03	211.87	311.31	229.73
Look-back-5	154.13	283.61	190.65	212.37	305.06	229.16
Look-back-10	154.14	287.62	190.18	213.06	299.81	228.96
Look-back-15	154.15	291.62	189.71	213.73	294.82	228.81
Look-back-20	154.11	295.64	189.25	214.39	290.17	228.71
Look-back-30	153.87	304.67	188.39	215.52	274.92	227.47
Look-back-50	153.17	325.41	186.89	217.15	231.23	222.77
Kalman filter	154.4	405.09	174.83	235.13	141.67	222.22
Kalman filter + look-back-5	154.4	405.56	174.74	235.36	143.63	222.74
Kalman filter +look-back-10	154.4	406.14	174.62	235.62	145.99	223.35
Kalman filter + look-back-15	154.4	406.69	174.51	235.88	148.27	223.95
Kalman filter + look-back-20	154.4	407.23	174.40	236.12	150.46	224.52
Kalman filter + look-back-30	154.37	408.24	174.2	236.57	154.56	225.59
Kalman filter + look-back-50	154.33	410.02	173.87	237.33	161.57	227.42

training times were lower than 1 min on a computer with an Intel i5 CPU and 8 GB RAM, with all computations running on the CPU. However, the network is trained for 5 exact locations using approximately 2000 records. The main disadvantage of this method, as remarked for the first experiment, is that training it for a larger set of locations in a dwelling would require significantly more time, both for the measurements and for the training process. The results obtained by the best performing network are presented in Fig. 5b. As seen in the figure, the predicted positions are very close to the real ones and many of them overlap.

Table 4. Office location. Average error based on Euclidean distance ± standard deviation obtained using the artificial neural network, over 10 runs, with stratified cross-validation. Errors reported in centimetres.

	Number of hidden layers				
Epochs	1	2	3	4	5
100	106.98 ± 15.11	96.73 ± 23.50	77.57 ± 22.40	70.79 ± 32.97	51.75 ± 9.77
500	84.36 ± 23.08	46.05 ± 18.69	26.42 ± 12.30	19.16 ± 4.55	15.14 ± 3.71
1000	54.45 ± 17.40	30.23 ± 14.54	15.48 ± 8.04	11.16 ± 4.03	10.68 ± 5.18
2000	38.67 ± 13.38	23.44 ± 13.13	10.82 ± 3.56	10.89 ± 3.99	8.48 ± 3.18
3000	27.44 ± 13.13	16.54 ± 11.47	10.20 ± 5.55	9.68 ± 7.40	7.73 ± 4.08

5.3   Comparison with Related Work

Authors of [2] present RADAR, a system that uses the strength of a 2.4 Ghz WiFi signal from the k-nearest neighbour devices to detect location using RSSI. The system was tested in a 980 m^2 floor space of a multi-storey building divided into around 50 rooms. Experimental evaluation showed the system to have a resolution of 3 m, enough for room-level detection.

A similar result was achieved by Battiti et al. [3], who employ WiFi signal and a neural network for person positioning, and achieve similar, room-level resolution. Fariz et al. employ trilateration together with Kalman filters for determining the person's location [11]. The error is between 3.58 and 14.82 m. Deng et al. applied the extended Kalman filter based on fusing WiFi signals [8], lowering the localization error to 2.83 m. Another experiment regarding indoor positioning [20] obtained an error equal to 3.29 m when trilateration was used with Bluetooth and 1.61 m when using a backpropagation neural network.

In Sadowski et al., RSSI-based indoor localization data are collected using WiFi for two scenarios and the reported positioning errors were low [35]. The first scenario consisted of one large room in which a few BLE gadgets and different WiFi systems were placed in order to introduce signal interference. The second scenario involved a smaller room with furniture and no gadgets. In this case, a low degree of commotion was present. The average positioning error for the first scenario was 0.84 m, and for the second scenario it reached 0.48 m. The nodes used for RSSI value estimation were placed on several tables with similar height, restricting the quantity of signal reflections and interference.

In the case of long narrow spaces, Gao et al. [12] used same line dual connection for estimating the person location, because trilateration caused tracking difficulties. This solution considers the loss and gain of RSSI values both for transmitter and receiver. The reported accuracy of this solution was of 1.6 m.

When compared with most relevant existing systems, our solution integrates additional capabilities into a cost-effective device that can be easily deployed and which looks unobtrusive in a typical home or office setting. In our experiments, the luminaires were ceiling-mounted and indoor localization was attempted in five rooms using trilateration combined with filter-based approaches. The complexity of carrying out a controlled evaluation of these technologies means that a detailed comparison with similar approaches cannot be made. Differences in enclosure sizes, room layouts, building materials, presence of large furniture or people, as well as signal interference from nearby devices cannot fully be accounted for outside a laboratory setting.

6   Conclusion

The trend of population ageing started several decades ago and recent data shows that over medium and long term, it is expected to amplify. The more concerning aspect however is that this process is not accompanied by an improved quality of life for older adults [48]. Our research evaluates indoor localization accuracy, an important aspect for an unobtrusive and cost-effective system designed to help older adults live within their own homes. To achieve our goals, the system hardware was implemented in the form of intelligent luminaires that replace existing lighting infrastructure. In addition to environment sensing [25], they provide indoor localization using RSSI from a Bluetooth Low Energy device, such as a standard smartphone or wearable.

We extended our initial evaluation [26] to include two different, but representative locations for an indoor positioning system. We employed direct trilateration-based methods with the minimum number of required beacons and evaluated the accuracy of several post-processing approaches, including Kalman filtering as well as our proposed look-back-k heuristic. We combined the two approaches to verify if an initial noise reduction step improves our heuristic's accuracy. Finally, we trained an artificial neural network to verify whether the expected future location of the monitored person can be accurately determined. While not an actual localization problem, we believe it to represent an important step towards behavioural pattern recognition and profiling, which existing research [17,38] suggests can be important for early detection of several medical conditions related to ageing.

Our evaluation shows that direct trilateration is suitable for achieving room-level localization accuracy in realistic scenarios. However, raw readings presented significant variation. When studying the obtained distance estimations, we observe that in several situations a common intersection could not be identified, resulting in large error margins. This situation arises both because of noisy RSSI readings caused by signal interference, as well as multipath fading and environmental factors. We plan to also experiment with other, more complex algorithms, for instance with non-linear least squares optimisation, to compensate for noisy data. In the undertaken experiments, all post-processing approaches improved the observed accuracy, starting with the Kalman noise reduction filter. In both evaluated scenarios, improved results were obtained when the Kalman filter was combined with our look-back heuristic.

When compared to other indoor positioning systems, our proposed approach does not require the installation of additional devices or wiring, and as shown, can achieve room-level accuracy in realistic scenarios that include signal pollution. Its deployment is straightforward and involves replacing some of the existing light bulbs with intelligent luminaires. A comparative evaluation of localization accuracy is however not feasible, as it would require a controlled but realistic environment where signal pollution can be controlled and where multiple systems could be deployed. As such, we limited ourselves to comparing each system's prerequisites and the obtained results.

With regards to future work, in addition to evaluating more complex algorithms for indoor localization, we aim to carry out an evaluation on the accuracy that can be achieved when tracking multiple targets, as well as moving subjects. In both cases, luminaires will have to increase signal strength polling rate. Accurate indoor localization of moving subjects will better help detect older adult behaviour patterns and identify risky situations, as well as enabling other functionalities in both private and public places.

Acknowledgement. This work was supported by a grant of the Romanian National Authority for Scientific Research and Innovation, CCCDI UEFISCDI, project number 46E/2015, *i-Light - A pervasive home monitoring system based on intelligent luminaires*.

References

1. AAL - Active and Assisted Living Programme: ICT for ageing well (2016). http://www.aal-europe.eu/about/
2. Bahl, P., Padmanabhan, V.N.: RADAR: an in-building RF-based user location and tracking system. In: Proceedings of IEEE INFOCOM 2000, vol. 2, pp. 775–784 (2000)
3. Battiti, R., Thang Le, N., Villani, A.: Location-aware computing: a neural network model for determining location in wireless LANs. In: International Semiconductors Conference, vol. 4 (2002)
4. Bocicor, M.I., et al.: Cyber-physical system for assisted living and home monitoring. In: 13th IEEE International Conference on Intelligent Computer Communication and Processing, pp. 487–493, September 2017. https://doi.org/10.1109/ICCP.2017.8117052
5. Brena, R.F., García-Vázquez, J.P., Galván-Tejada, C.E., Muñoz-Rodriguez, D., Vargas-Rosales, C., Fangmeyer, J.: Evolution of indoor positioning technologies: a survey. J. Sens. **2017**, 21 (2017)
6. Bulten, W., Rossum, A.C.V., Haselager, W.F.G.: Human SLAM, indoor localisation of devices and users. In: IEEE First International Conference on Internet-of-Things Design and Implementation, pp. 211–222 (2016)
7. De Schutter, J., De Geeter, J., Lefebvre, T., Bruyninckx, H.: Kalman filters: a tutorial (1999)
8. Deng, Z.A., Hu, Y., Yu, J., Na, Z.: Extended Kalman filter for real time indoor localization by fusing WiFi and smartphone inertial sensors. Micromachines **6**, 523–543 (2015)
9. Dong, Q., Dargie, W.: Evaluation of the reliability of RSSI for indoor localization. In: Proceedings of the IEEE International Conference on Wireless Communications in Unusual and Confined Areas, pp. 1–6 (2012)
10. Draghici, I.C., et al.: A quantitative research to decide the user requirements for the i-Light system. In: Proceedings of the 21st International Conference on Control Systems and Computer Science (CSCS21), pp. 143–148 (2017)
11. Fariz, N., et al.: An improved indoor location technique using Kalman filter. Int. J. Eng. Technol. **7**(2), 1–4 (2018)
12. Gao, L., et al.: A new approach for wi-fi-based people localization in a long narrow space. Wirel. Commun. Mobile Comput. **2019**, article 9581401 (2019)
13. Haigh, P.A., et al.: Visible light communications: real time 10 mb/s link with a low bandwidth polymer light-emitting diode. Opt. Express **22**(3), 2830–2838 (2014)
14. Halfacree, G., Upton, E.: Raspberry Pi User Guide. Wiley, Hoboken (2012). ISBN:978-1118464465
15. Huang, K., He, K., Du, X.: A hybrid method to improve the BLE-based indoor positioning in a dense Bluetooth environment. Sensors **19**(2) (2019). https://doi.org/10.3390/s19020424. https://www.ncbi.nlm.nih.gov/pmc/articles/PMC6359285/
16. Huang, Y., Zheng, J., Xiao, Y., Peng, M.: Robust localization algorithm based on the RSSI ranging scope. Int. J. Distrib. Sens. Netw. **11**(2), 587318 (2015)
17. Kim, E., Helal, S., Cook, D.: Human activity recognition and pattern discovery. IEEE Pervasive Comput. **9**(1), 48–53 (2010). https://doi.org/10.1109/MPRV.2010.7
18. Kingma, D.P., Ba, J.: Adam: a method for stochastic optimization. CoRR abs/1412.6980 (2014). http://arxiv.org/abs/1412.6980
19. Laukaitis, A., Balevičius, S., Levitas, B.: Investigation of electromagnetic wave absorber based on carbon fiber reinforced aerated concrete, using time-domain method. Acta Phys. Pol. A **113**03 (2008). https://doi.org/10.12693/APhysPolA.113.1047

20. Li, G., et al.: Indoor positioning algorithm based on the improved RSSI distance model. Sensors **18**(9), article number 2820 (2018). https://www.mdpi.com/1424-8220/18/9/2820

21. Lukito, Y., Chrismanto, A.R.: Recurrent neural networks model for WiFi-based indoor positioning system. In: 2017 International Conference on Smart Cities, Automation & Intelligent Computing Systems (ICON-SONICS) (2017)

22. Luo, X., O'Brien, W.J., Julien, C.: Comparative evaluation of received signal strength index (RSSI)-based indoor localization techniques for construction jobsites. Adv. Eng. Inform. **25**, 355–363 (2011)

23. Lymberopoulos, D., et al.: A realistic evaluation and comparison of indoor location technologies: Experiences and lessons learned. In: The 14th ACM/IEEE Conference on Information Processing in Sensor Networks IPSN 2015, pp. 178–189 (2015)

24. Maduskar, D., Tapaswi, S.: RSSI based adaptive indoor location tracker. Sci. Phone Apps Mobile Devices **3**, article number 3 (2017). https://doi.org/10.1186/s41070-017-0015-z

25. Marin, I., et al.: i-Light - intelligent luminaire based platform for home monitoring and assisted living. Electronics **7**, article number 220 (2018). https://www.mdpi.com/2079-9292/7/10/220

26. Marin., I., Bocicor., M.I., Molnar., A.: Indoor localisation with intelligent luminaires for home monitoring. In: Proceedings of the 14th International Conference on Evaluation of Novel Approaches to Software Engineering - Volume 1: ENASE, pp. 464–471. INSTICC, SciTePress (2019). https://doi.org/10.5220/0007751304640471

27. de Meijer, C., Wouterse, B., Polder, J., Koopmanschap, M.: The effect of population aging on health expenditure growth: a critical review. Eur. J. Ageing **10**(4), 353–361 (2013)

28. Miranda, J., Abrishambaf, R., Gomes, T., Cabral, J., Tavares, A., Monteiro, J.: Path loss exponent analysis in wireless sensor networks: experimental evaluation, pp. 54–58, July 2013. https://doi.org/10.1109/INDIN.2013.6622857

29. Mittal, A., Tiku, S., Pasricha, S.: Adapting convolutional neural networks for indoor localization with smart mobile devices. In: Proceedings of the 2018 on Great Lakes Symposium on VLSI, pp. 117–122 (2018)

30. Nair, V., Hinton, G.E.: Rectified linear units improve restricted Boltzmann machines. In: Proceedings of the 27th International Conference on International Conference on Machine Learning, ICML2010, Omnipress, USA, pp. 807–814 (2010). http://dl.acm.org/citation.cfm?id=3104322.3104425

31. Nobles, P., Ali, S., Chivers, H.: Improved estimation of trilateration distances for indoor wireless intrusion detection. J. Wirel. Mobile Netw. Ubiquit. Comput. Dependable Appl. **2**, 93–102 (2011)

32. Ozsoy, K., Bozkurt, A., Tekin, I.: Indoor positioning based on global positioning system signals. Microw. Opt. Technol. Lett. **55**, 1091–1097 (2013)

33. Pu, C.C., Pu, C.H., Lee, H.J.: Indoor location tracking using received signal strength indicator. In: Emerging Communications for Wireless Sensor Networks (2011)

34. Robesaat, J., Zhang, P., Abdelaal, M., Theel, O.: An improved BLE indoor localization with Kalman-based fusion: an experimental study. Sensors **17**(5), article number 951 (2017). https://www.mdpi.com/1424-8220/17/5/951

35. Sadowski, S., Spachos, P.: RSSI-based indoor localization with the Internet of Things. IEEE Access **6**, 30149–30161 (2018)

36. Samkova, A., Kulhavy, P., Tunakova, V., Petru, M.: Improving electromagnetic shielding ability of plaster-based composites by addition of carbon fibers. Adv.

Mater. Sci. Eng. **2018**, article 3758364 (2018). https://doi.org/10.1155/2018/3758364

37. Silicon Labs: Bluegiga BLE112 Bluetooth smart module. http://www.silabs.com/products/wireless/bluetooth/bluetooth-low-energy-modules/ble112-bluetooth-smart-module (2017)

38. Soto-Mendoza, V., Beltrán, J., Chávez, E., Hernández, J., García-Macías, J.A.: Abnormal behavioral patterns detection from activity records of institutionalized older adults. In: Salah, A.A., Kröse, B.J.A., Cook, D.J. (eds.) HBU 2015. LNCS, vol. 9277, pp. 119–131. Springer, Cham (2015). https://doi.org/10.1007/978-3-319-24195-1_9

39. Sung, Y.: RSSI-based distance estimation framework using a Kalman filter for sustainable indoor computing environments. J. Sustain. **8**(11), article 1136 (2016). https://www.mdpi.com/2071-1050/8/11/1136

40. Ta, V.C.: Smartphone-based indoor positioning using Wi-Fi, inertial sensors and Bluetooth. Machine Learning, Université Grenoble Alpes (2017). https://tel.archives-ouvertes.fr/tel-01883828/document

41. Tarrio, P., et al.: An energy-efficient strategy for combined RSS-PDR indoor localization. In: IEEE International Conference on Pervasive Computing and Communications Workshops (PERCOM Workshops), pp. 619–624 (2011)

42. Tarzia, S.P., et al.: Indoor localization without infrastructure using the acoustic background spectrum. In: Proceedings of the 9th International Conference on Mobile Systems, Applications, and Services, p. 155 (2011)

43. Urano, K., Hiroi, K., Yonezawa, T., Kawaguchi, N.: Basic study of BLE indoor localization using LSTM-based neural network. In: Proceedings of the 17th Annual International Conference on Mobile Systems, Applications, and Services, pp. 558–559. ACM (2019)

44. Okorogu, V.N., Onyishi, D.U., Nwalozie, G.C., Utebor, N.N.: Empirical characterization of propagation path loss and performance evaluation for co-site urban environment. Int. J. Comput. Appl. **70**, 34–41 (2013). https://doi.org/10.5120/12001-7888

45. Wang, J.Y., et al.: High-precision RSSI-based indoor localization using a transmission power adjustment strategy for wireless sensor networks. In: 2012 IEEE 14th International Conference on High Performance Computing and Communication, 2012 IEEE 9th International Conference on Embedded Software and Systems (2012)

46. Wang, X., Wang, X., Mao, S.: Deep convolutional neural networks for indoor localization with CSI images. IEEE Trans. Netw. Sci. Eng. (2018). https://doi.org/10.1109/TNSE.2018.2871165

47. Welch, G., Bishop, G.: An introduction to the Kalman filter. Technical report, Department of Computer Science, University of North Carolina at Chapel Hill, Chapel Hill, NC, USA (1995)

48. World Health Organization: World report on ageing and health (2015). https://www.who.int/ageing/events/world-report-2015-launch/en/

49. Xiao, J., Zhou, Z.: A survey on wireless indoor localization from the device perspective. ACM Comput. Surv. **49**, article number 25 (2016). https://doi.org/10.1145/2933232

50. Zargoun, F., Henawy, I.M., Ziedan, N.I.: Effects of walls and floors in indoor localization using tracking algorithm. Int. J. Adv. Comput. Sci. Appl. **7**(3), 34–39 (2016)

51. Zhanga, W., Liua, K., Zhang, W., Zhang, Y., Gu, J.: Deep neural networks for wireless localization in indoor and outdoor environments. Neurocomputing **194**, 279–287 (2016)

Author Index

Printed in the United States
By Bookmasters